EDUCATIONAL ADMINISTRATION

Theory, Research, and Practice

Third Edition

WAYNE K. HOY

Rutgers University

CECIL G. MISKEL

University of Utah

RANDOM HOUSE 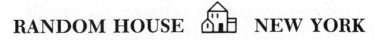 NEW YORK

*This book was developed for
Random House by Lane Akers, Inc.*

Third Edition
987654321
Copyright © 1987, 1982, 1978 by Random House

Library of Congress Cataloging-in-Publication Data

Hoy, Wayne K.
  Educational administration.

  Bibliography: p.
  Includes index.
  1. School management and organization. I. Miskel,
Cecil G. II. Title.
LB2805.H715 1986   371.2   86-10185
ISBN 0-394-34089-2

Manufactured in the United States of America

Preface

Our first and second editions reflected the current state of knowledge in educational administration. The books grew from our beliefs that a substantive body of knowledge about educational organizations was available but neglected by both professors and practitioners and that administrative practice could become less of an art and more of a science. To those ends we used a social-systems perspective to synthesize the structure and recurring processes of educational organizations.

In this revision we have described the relevant new developments in the field, both fresh concepts and recent research findings. Elaboration of concepts and empirical applications should help unravel day-to-day behavior in educational organizations. Our social-systems model of the school continues its evolution. In recognition of the importance of the environmental forces on educational organizations, the framework now more fully incorporates the environment and recognizes the significance of organizational goals as a basic element of the school as a social system. The model is also expanded to deal with irrational and nonrational aspects of organizational behavior. To this end, an analysis of organizational culture, as well as the symbolic and cultural aspects of leadership, has been included. Similarly, new conceptualizations and measures of school climates; new models for coping with stress, involving subordinates in decision making, and avoiding groupthink; and the decision-making strategies of maximizing, satisficing, and incrementally comparing are presented and examined. Finally, new perspectives on careers in education, administrative succession, and bureaucracy have been added to this edition.

Our colleagues and students continue to be important sources of ideas and constructive criticism. We would like to thank Patrick Forsyth, C. J. Tarter, Robert Kottkamp, Jim Giarelli, Adam Scrupski, Hal Robins, Richard Hatley, Betty Malen, Rodney Ogawa, Ann Hart, Michael Murphy, and Donald J. Willower. We also want to express our appreciation to Ellen Blanford, who made extensive contributions to the preparation of the manuscript.

In the first two editions, Bryce Fogarty made extensive and valuable contributions; we are saddened by the loss of a respected and thoughtful colleague.

Finally, we owe a special thanks to all our students who have helped enrich the explanations and ground the theories with their experiences.

WAYNE K. HOY
CECIL G. MISKEL

Contents

Chapter 1

Theoretical and Historical Foundations

Although we set out primarily to study reality, it does not follow that we do not wish to improve it; we should judge our researches to have no worth at all if they were to have only a speculative interest. If we separate carefully the theoretical from the practical problems, it is not to the neglect of the latter; but, on the contrary, to be in a better position to solve them.

EMILE DURKHEIM
The Division of Labor in Society

The science of educational administration is as new as the modern school; the one-room schoolhouse of rural America did not need specialized administrators. Systematic study of administration and development of theories of organization and administration are twentieth-century phenomena. Before exploring the theoretical and historical foundations of educational administration, however, we need a basic understanding of what theory is in the scientific sense. Consequently, we begin the chapter by defining theory and science, delineating the major components of theory, and discussing the interrelationships among theory, research, and practice.

THEORY: A SCIENTIFIC CONCEPT

Much of the skepticism about theory is based on the assumption that educational administration is incapable of becoming a science, a skepticism that has plagued all social sciences. Theory in the natural sciences, on the other hand, has attained respectability not only because it necessarily involves precise description, but also because it describes ideal phenomena that "work" in practical applications.

Most people think that scientists deal with facts, whereas philosophers delve into theory. Indeed, to many individuals, including educational administrators, facts and theories are antonyms; that is, facts are real and their meanings self-evident, whereas theories are speculations or dreams. Theory in educational administration, however, has the same role as theory in physics, chemistry, or biology; that is, providing general explanations and guiding research.

Science and Theory Defined

The purpose of all science is understanding the world in which we live and work. Scientists describe what they see, discover regularities, and formulate theories.[1] Organizational science attempts to describe and explain regularities in behavior of individuals and groups within organizations. Organizational scientists seek basic principles that provide a general understanding of structure and dynamics of organizational life, a task that we are just beginning in educational administration.[2]

Some researchers view science as a static, interconnected set of principles that explains the universe in which we live. We view science as a dynamic process of developing, through experimentation and observation, an interconnected set of principles that in turn produces further experimentation and observation.[3] In this view the basic aim of science is to find general explanations, called "theories." Theory has a central role in science.

As the ultimate aim of science, theory has acquired a variety of definitions. Some agreement is apparent in the field of educational administration that the definition of theory produced by Herbert Feigl is an adequate starting point.[4] Feigl defines theory as a set of assumptions from which a larger set of empirical laws can be derived by purely logicomathematical procedures. Fred N. Kerlinger's more general definition of the term seems more useful for the social sciences. He suggests that, "A theory is a set of interrelated constructs (concepts), definitions, and propositions that present a systematic view of phenomena by specifying relations among variables, with the purpose of explaining and predicting phenomena."[5]

In the study of educational administration, the following definition of theory seems most useful: *Theory is a set of interrelated concepts, assumptions, and generalizations that systematically describes and explains regularities in behavior in educational organizations.* Moreover, hypotheses may be derived from the theory to predict additional relationships among the concepts in the system.

This definition suggests three things. First, theory is logically comprised of concepts, assumptions, and generalizations. Second, its major function is to describe, explain, and predict regularities in behavior. Third, theory is heuristic; that is, it stimulates and guides the further development of knowledge.

Theories are by nature general and abstract; they are not true or false but rather useful or not. Theories are useful to the extent that they are internally consistent and generate accurate predictions about events. Albert Einstein, one of the greatest theorists of all times, captures the essence of theorizing in the following quotation:

> In our endeavor to understand reality we are somewhat like a man trying to understand the mechanism of a closed watch. He sees the face and the moving hands, even hears its ticking, but he has no way of opening the case. If he is ingenious he may form some picture of a mechanism which could be responsible for all the things he observes, but he may never be quite sure his picture is the only one which could explain his observations. He will never be able to compare his picture with the real mechanism, and he cannot even imagine the possibility of the meaning of such a comparison.[6]

COMPONENTS OF THEORY

The nature of the theory can be better understood by looking at the meanings of each of the components of theory and how they are related to one another.

Concepts

A concept is a term that has been given an abstract, generalized meaning. A few examples of concepts in administration are leadership, satisfaction, and informal organization. Scientists invent concepts that help them study and analyze a given phenomenon systematically. In other words, they invent a language to describe behavior in the real world. Two important advantages are derived from defining theoretical concepts.[7] First, theorists, researchers, and practitioners can agree on the meaning of such terms. Second, their abstractness and generality ensures that the concepts are independent of any spatial or temporal setting.

Although concepts are by definition abstract, different levels of abstraction are used.[8] Examples of terms arranged along an abstract to concrete continuum are presented in Table 1.1. Generally speaking, terms that are specific to a particular time or place are concrete and are less useful in developing theories. Most concepts, generalizations, and theories discussed in this book are in the "middle range," that is, they are somewhat limited in scope rather than all-embracing.

A concept can be defined in at least two ways. First, it may be defined in

TABLE 1.1 A Continuum and Examples of the Abstraction Levels of Scientific Concepts

Abstract	Middle Range	Concrete
Social system	School	Crockett Junior High School
Attitudes	Student attitudes	Seventh graders' perceptions of teachers in Crockett Junior High School

terms of other words or concepts. For instance, we might define permissiveness as the degree to which a teacher employs a relaxed mode of pupil control; that is, permissive is defined in terms of "relaxedness." Although this kind of definition may provide one with a slightly better understanding of the term, it is inadequate from a scientific point of view. The researcher must be able to define the concept in measurable terms. A set of operations or behaviors that has been used to measure a concept is its operational definition. For example, an operational definition of permissiveness might be the number of hall passes a teacher issues per day. This definition is limited, clear, and concise. The concept is the specific set of operations measured. IQ is the standard operational definition of intelligence, and dogmatism typically is operationalized in terms of Rokeach's Dogmatism Scale.[9] Operationalism mandates that the procedures involved in the relation between the observer and the measures for observing be explicitly stated so that they can be duplicated by any other equally trained researcher.[10]

A concept that has an operational definition is often referred to as a variable. In fact, many researchers and scientists loosely use the terms "concept" and "variable" to refer to the same thing. Technically, the term "variable" refers to any symbol to which numerical values are assigned. Variables are thus concepts that have operational measures and take on different values.

Assumptions and Generalizations

An assumption is a statement that is taken for granted or accepted as true. Assumptions, accepted without proof, are not necessarily self-evident. In many instances they are definitional in character. For example, Daniel E. Griffiths offers the following two assumptions concerning administration:

1. Administration is a generalized type of behavior found in all human organizations.
2. Administration is the process of directing and controlling life in a social organization.[11]

These two assumptions are taken for granted with little proof. The second is a definition of administration.

A generalization is a statement or proposition that indicates the mutual relationship of two or more concepts. In other words, a generalization links concepts in a meaningful fashion. Many kinds of generalizations are found in theoretical formulation: Assumptions are generalizations if they specify the relationship among two or more concepts; hypotheses are generalizations with limited empirical support (see below); principles are generalizations with substantial empirical support; and laws are generalizations with an overwhelming degree of empirical support (more than principles). Depending on the level of empirical support, the same generalization, at different stages of theory and research development, can be a hypothesis, principle, or law.

RESEARCH AND THEORY

Research is inextricably related to theory; therefore, many of the misconceptions and ambiguities surrounding theory are reflected in the interpretation of the meaning and purpose of research. Kerlinger provides us with the following clear definition: "Scientific research is systematic, controlled, empirical, and critical investigation of hypothetical propositions about the presumed relations among natural phenomena."[12] This definition suggests that research is guided by hypotheses that are empirically checked against observations about reality in a systematic and controlled way. Furthermore, the results of such tests are then open to critical analyses by other researchers.

Haphazard observations followed by the conclusion that the facts speak for themselves do not qualify as scientific research; in fact, such unrefined empiricism can distort reality and does not lead to the systematic development of knowledge. Well-conceived surveys of a broad field for the express purpose of developing hypotheses are at times useful starting points in terms of hypothesis and theory development; ultimately, however, knowledge in any discipline is expanded by research that is guided by hypotheses that are derived from theory.

Hypotheses

A *hypothesis* is a conjectural statement that indicates a relationship between at least two variables. Several examples of different kinds of hypotheses illustrate this point.

> H-1. As group cohesiveness increases, its impact on members increases.
> H-2. Principals who are described as being high on consideration will have faculties with higher morale than principals who are described as being low on consideration.
> H-3. Satisfaction is a function of the congruence between the demands of the organization and the needs of the individual.
> H-4. Teachers with principals who maintain emotional detachment tend to be more loyal than teachers with principals who are excitable.
> H-5. If teacher-administrator relationships are strongly positive, then task-oriented supervision will be more effective than human relations supervision.

Several observations can be made about these hypotheses. First, each hypothesis specifies the relationship between at least two variables. Second, each clearly and concisely describes that relationship. Third, the variables of each hypothesis are such that each could be empirically tested. For example, H-4 expresses the relationship between two variables, emotional detachment of principals and loyalty of teachers. Principals who maintain emotional detachment in their dealings with teachers are predicted to have more loyal teachers than principals who are easily excited. Emotional detachment is measured by the extent to which principals are described by their teachers as being calm and never losing their tempers, whereas loyalty of teachers is determined by testing the degree to which teachers admire, trust, respect, and are willing to follow the principal.

Hypotheses bridge the gaps between theory and research and provide a means to test the theory against observed reality. Hypotheses developed to test theory are deduced directly from the theory. For example, hypothesis H-3 can be deduced from the social systems theory described in Chapter 3. Typically, hypotheses are on a lower level of abstraction than the theoretical generalizations from which they are deduced. Their confirmation in empirical research supports the usefulness of the theory as an explanation. The hypothesis is the researcher's bias; if it is deduced from a theory, the investigator expects that it will be supported by data. If the hypothesis is not supported by data, then the theory is inadequate and must be reformulated or refined. Hypothesis testing as a part of the theory-research process is essential to the development of knowledge in any field of study.

The basic form of knowledge in all disciplines is similar; it consists of concepts, generalizations, and theories, each being dependent on the one preceding it.[13] Figure 1.1 summarizes the basic components of theory that are necessary to the development of knowledge. It shows that concepts are eventually linked together into generalizations that in turn form a logically consistent set of propositions providing generalizations that in turn form a logically consistent set of propositions providing a general explanation of a phenomenon (a theory). The theory is then empirically checked by the development and testing of hypotheses deduced from the theory. The results of the research then provide the data for accepting, rejecting, reformulating, or refining and clarifying the basic generalizations of the theory. Over time, with continued empirical support and evidence, the generalizations develop into principles and laws that explain the phenomenon. In the case of organizational theory, principles and laws are developed to explain the structure and dynamics of organizations. Theory is both the beginning and the end of scientific research. On one hand, theory serves as the basis for generating hypotheses to test verifiable propositions that describe and predict observable empirical phenomena. On the other hand, the ultimate objective of all scientific endeavor is to develop a body of substantive theory.

THEORY AND PRACTICE

Theory is directly related to practice in at least three ways. First, theory forms a frame of reference for the practitioner. Second, the process of theorizing provides a general mode of analysis of practical events. And, third, theory guides practical, rational decision making.

Theory gives practitioners the analytic tools needed to sharpen and focus

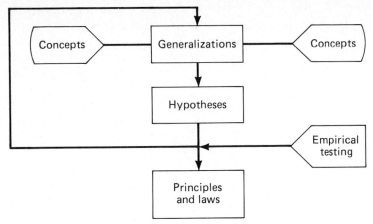

FIGURE 1.1 Theoretical system

their analysis of the problems they face.[14] The administrator so armed can develop alternative solutions to pragmatic problems. Administrators themselves maintain that the most important qualification for their jobs is the ability to use concepts. It is a mistake, however, to assume that the ability to label aspects of a problem by using theoretical constructs from sociology or psychology automatically provides a solution to a problem. Designating a problem as one of role conflict, goal displacement, or anxiety reduction, for instance, does not in itself solve the problem; it may, however, organize the issues so that a reasonable plan of action can emerge.

The theory-practice relationship goes beyond using the concepts and constructs of theorists to label the important aspects of a problem. The scientific approach provides a way of thinking about events for both theorists and practitioners alike. Indeed, the scientific approach is the very embodiment of rational inquiry, whether the focus is theoretical analysis and development, a research investigation, organizational decision making, or problem solving at the personal level. A good general description of this approach is found in John Dewey's analysis, *How We Think*.[15] The process involves identifying a problem, conceptualizing it, proposing generalizations in the form of hypotheses that provide answers to the problems, deducing the consequences and implications of the hypotheses, and testing the hypotheses.

Some differences do exist in the specific ways that theorists, researchers, and practitioners implement and use the scientific approach, but the differences are a matter of degree of rigor and level of abstraction rather than approach. Theorists operate on a higher level of abstraction and generality than researchers, who test hypotheses. Practitioners, in turn, operate on an even lower level of abstraction than researchers because they are primarily concerned with specific problems and events in their organizations.

Similarly, theorists and researchers typically use the scientific approach more rigorously than practitioners and for good reason. Theorists usually preface their propositions with the phrase "other things being equal," and researchers control all other variables except those under study. In contrast, practitioners function in the real world, where other things typically are not equal and all variables are not controllable. Practitioners are constrained by their position, responsibilities, authority, and the immediacy of their problems. Although they do not abandon the scientific approach, practitioners are forced to be more flexible in applying it. For example, educational administrators are probably less concerned than theorists or researchers with generalizability, that is, the extent to which their solutions work for other administrators in other districts. Nonetheless, the approach of theorists, researchers, and thoughtful practitioners is basically the same; it is a systematic and scientific one. One final relationship between theory and practice needs to be mentioned. We can define administration as both the art and the science of applying knowledge to administrative and organizational problems. Such a definition implies that administrators have access to knowledge needed for making decisions. Without theory, however, there is virtually no foundation for knowledge, for the meaningful research that provides information presupposes a theory. Unfortunately, theory and research in educational administration continue to make only modest gains at best. Halpin's biting criticism that books on education, especially those on educational administration, "ooze with verbal slush" points to the lack of substantial knowledge in the field.[16] If educational administration is to become more of a science, then the practical decisions and actions of administrators must be based on knowledge.

Administrative theory does influence practice. Over the last eighty years, the evolution of administrative science can be divided into three general phases: (1) classical organizational thought (1900), (2) human relations approach (1930), and (3) behavioral science approach (1950). These phases, shown in Table 1.2, overlap and continue to develop today.

CLASSICAL ORGANIZATIONAL THOUGHT

Frederick Taylor, the father of the scientific management movement, sought ways to use people effectively in industrial organizations. Taylor's background and experience as laborer, clerk, machinist, foreman, chief draftsman, and finally, chief engineer reinforced his belief that individuals could be programmed to be efficient machines. The key to the scientific management approach is the metaphor of "man as machine."

TABLE 1.2   The Development of Administrative Science, 1900–Present

Beginnings	Developmental Phases of Administrative Science	Pioneers
1900	Classical Organization	Taylor, Fayol, Gulick, Urwick
1930	Human Relations	Follett, Mayo, Roethlisberger
1950	Behavioral Science	Barnard, Simon

Taylor and his associates thought that workers, motivated by economics and limited by physiology, needed constant direction. In 1911, Taylor formalized his ideas in *Principles of Scientific Management,* a few excerpts of which reveal the flavor of his managerial theory.

1. *A Large Daily Task*—Each person in the establishment, high or low, should have a clearly defined daily task. The carefully circumscribed task should require a full day's effort to complete.
2. *Standard Conditions*—The worker should be given standardized conditions and appliances to accomplish the task with certainty.
3. *High Pay for Success*—High pay should be tied to successful completion.
4. *Loss in Case of Failure*—Failure should be personally costly.
5. *Expertise in Large Organizations*—As organizations become increasingly sophisticated, tasks should be made so difficult as to be accomplished only by a first-rate worker.[17]

Taylor and his followers—the human engineers—focused on physical production, and their time and motion studies sought workers' physical limits and described the fastest method for performing a given task.

1. The two hands should begin and end motions simultaneously.
2. Arm movements should be simultaneous and made in opposite and symmetrical directions.
3. Smooth, continuous hand motions are preferable to zigzag or straight-line motions involving sudden or sharp changes in direction.
4. Tools, materials, and controls should be close to and in front of the operator.
5. Tools should be combined whenever possible.[18]

Although Taylor's work had a narrow physiological focus and ignored psychological and sociological variables, he demonstrated that many jobs could be performed more efficiently. He also helped the unskilled worker by improving productivity enough to raise the pay of unskilled labor nearly to that of skilled.[19]

In a similar vein, traditional or classical organizational thought, often called *administrative management theory,* concentrates on the broad problems of departmental division of work and coordination. While Taylor's human engineers worked from the individual worker upward, the administrative managers worked from the managing director downward. Their focuses were different, but their contributions complemented one another.

Henri Fayol, like Taylor, took a scientific approach to administration. Fayol was a French mining engineer and successful executive who later taught administration. According to Fayol, administrative behavior consists of five functions, which he defined as:

To *plan* means to study the future and arrange the plan of operations.

To *organize* means to build up material and human organization of the business, organizing both people and materials.

To *command* means to make the staff do their work.

To *coordinate* means to unite and correlate all activities.

To *control* means to see that everything is done in accordance with the rules that have been laid down and the instructions that have been given.[20]

Lyndall Urwick later amplified these functions in answer to the question, "What is the work of the chief executive?" Gulick responded, "POSDCoRB," an acronym for his seven administrative procedures—planning, organizing, staffing, directing, coordinating, reporting, and budgeting.[21]

To administrative managers, *division of labor* was essential. Accordingly, the more a task could be broken down into its components, the more specialized and, therefore, the more effective the worker would be in performing the task. To complement the division of labor, tasks were grouped into jobs, and these jobs were then integrated into departments. Although the criteria for division could pose conflicting demands, division of labor and the departmentalization it entailed were necessary aspects of management.

Span of control, or the number of workers supervised, was a second principle. In subdividing from the top downward, each work unit had to be supervised and coordinated with other units, and the span of control considered to be most effective was five to ten subordinates. Ths rule of thumb is still widely used in building administrative organizations. The pyramid-shaped structures stemming from this second principle are headed by a single executive, with power and authority flowing uniformly from the top to the bottom.

A third operating tenet of the administrative manager was the *principle of homogeneity* of positions. According to Gulick, a single department could be formed of positions grouped in any of four different ways—major purpose, major process, clientele, or location. Major purpose joined those who shared a common goal. Major process combined those with a similar skill or technology. Clientele or material grouped those who dealt with similar clients or materials. Organization based on location or geographic area brought together those who worked together regardless of function.[22]

Organizing departments in these four ways presents obvious problems. For example, should a school health activity be placed in a department of education or of health? How one answers the question will alter the nature of the service. Homogenizing departments in one of the four ways does not homogenize them in all ways. "The question is not which criterion to use for grouping," James D. Thompson has observed, "but rather in which priority are the several criteria to be exercised."[23]

Both the human engineers and the administrative managers emphasized formal or bureaucratic organization. They were concerned with the division of labor, the allocation of power, and the specifications for each position; they conspicuously neglected individual idiosyncrasies and the social dynamics of people at work. This perspective, aptly termed a "machine model,"[24] implies that an organization can be constructed according to a blueprint, as one would build a bridge or an engine. In summary, the basic features of the traditional or classical administrative models are contained in the following list:

1. *Time and Motion Studies.* The task is carried out in a way that minimizes time and effort.
2. *Division of Labor and Specialization.* Efficiency can be attained by subdividing any operation into its basic components to ensure workers' performance.
3. *Standardization of Tasks.* Breaking tasks into component parts allows for routinized performance.
4. *Unity of Command.* To coordinate the organization, decision making is centralized, with responsibility flowing from top to bottom.
5. *Span of Control.* Unity of command and coordination are possible only if each superior at any level has a limited number of subordinates (five to ten) to direct.
6. *Uniqueness of Function.* One department of an organization should not duplicate the functions performed by another.
7. *Formal Organization.* The focus of analysis is on the official organizational blueprint; semiformal and informal structures created by the dynamic interaction of people within the formal organization are not analyzed.

The greatest shortcoming of machine theory was its rigid conception of organization. As James March and Herbert Simon have observed, the structure and functioning of an organization may be greatly affected both by events outside the organization and by events imperfectly coordinated within it, and neither of these occurrences can be fixed in advance.[25]

HUMAN RELATIONS APPROACH

The human relations movement developed in reaction to the formal tradition of the classic models of administration. Mary Parker Follett, who wrote a series of brilliant papers dealing with the human side of administration,[26] believed that the fundamental problem in all organizations was developing and maintaining dynamic and harmonious relationships. In addition, she thought that conflict was "not necessarily a wasteful outbreak of incompatibilities, but a normal process by which socially valuable differences register themselves for enrichment of all concerned."[27] Despite Follett's work, the development of the human relations approach is usually traced to studies done in the Hawthorne plant of the Western Electric Company in Chicago. These studies are basic to the literature describing informal groups, and the study of informal groups is basic to an analysis of schools.

The Hawthorne studies began with three experiments conducted to study the "relation of quality and quantity of illumination to efficiency in industry."[28] The first illumination experiment was made in three departments. The level of illumination intensity in each department was increased at stated intervals. The results were puzzling. Increased production rates did not correspond with increased lighting, nor did production decline with reduced illumination. In a second experiment, a test group in which illumination intensities were varied was compared to a control group with illumination held constant. Both groups showed increases in production rates that were not only substantial but also nearly identical. Finally, in a third experiment, when the lighting for the test group was decreased and that for the control group held constant, the efficiency of both groups increased. Furthermore, the production rates increased in the test group until the light became so poor that the workers complained they could no longer see what they were doing.

The conclusions were neither as simple nor as clear-cut as the experimenters had originally anticipated. Two conclusions seemed justified: employee output was not primarily related to lighting conditions; and too many variables had not been controlled in the experiments. The startling nature of the findings stimulated more research.

Two Harvard professors—Elton Mayo, an industrial psychologist, and Fritz Roethlisberger, a social psychologist—were retained to continue studying the relationship between physical conditions of work and productivity. The company suspected that psychological as well as physiological factors were involved. From 1927 through 1932, the two researchers conducted a series of experiments that have since become research classics in the social sciences—the Hawthorne studies.[29] The investigators formulated six questions related to the problems of fatigue:

1. Do employees actually get tired out?
2. Are rest pauses desirable?
3. Is a shorter working day desirable?
4. What are the attitudes of employees toward their work and toward the company?
5. What is the effect of changing the type of working equipment?
6. Why does production fall off in the afternoon?[30]

To control intervening variables, six women workers were placed in a separate room for observation. All six performed the standardized task of assembling telephone relays. During the initial phase of work in the Relay Assemble Test Room, physical conditions were held constant and then changed periodically. The frequency and duration of rest pauses, for instance, were systematically manipulated, while both the workday and workweek were varied. During one period, two five-minute rest periods were established, one in the morning and another in the afternoon. These rest pauses were later lengthened to ten minutes. In another period, six five-minute rest breaks replaced two. Change in experimental conditions continued for more than a year. The investigators had not anticipated the findings. Output increased, but the increase was independent of any change in rest pauses or working hours. Production was not related to any specific experimental change.

After a host of experimental manipulations, the researchers reestablished the original conditions of work with no rest periods, no special lunch periods, and the original long workday and workweek. Both the daily and weekly production levels rose to a point much higher than under the nearly identical conditions of the pre-experimental setting. The investigators were further perplexed by the improvement of the workers' attitudes and morale during the long series of experiments. Simple, mechanistic manipulation of working conditions could explain neither the Relay Assembly Test Room experiments nor the similar results of the illumination studies. Obviously, something was happening, but what?

One hypothesis advanced was that the increased output and morale were due to relief from fatigue afforded by rest periods. Subsequent data analysis did not support this explanation. An alternative hypothesis suggested that improved wage incentives were responsible for heightened production and morale. Although the women's pay had been based on group piecework in their regular department, the wage incentive had been slight because the group was so large. In the small experimental group, the women were given an opportunity to earn in more direct proportion to the individual effort expended; hence, production increased. Two separate studies—the Second Relay Assembly Group and the Mica Splitting Test Group—were undertaken to test the wage incentive hypothesis. The studies indicated that the wage incentive factors alone could not have produced the continuous increase in output. Moreover, the power of wage incentives depended on other factors.

Only after further analysis did the researchers examine the experimental situation itself, which had altered the self-images and interpersonal relations of those in the work group. The nature of the supervision also had changed. To maintain cooperative subjects, supervision became informal, nondirective, and personal. Workers were permitted to talk freely in a more relaxed atmosphere, and because they had become objects of considerable attention, they saw their involvement in the experiment as a source of pride. In essence, social relations had been restructured to foster a friendly and cohesive work group. The impact of social conditions became a highly significant finding, and, as the Hawthorne studies continued, increased attention was focused on the social relations within work groups.

The research program's final phase, known as the Bank Wiring Study, analyzed the work group's social structure. Fourteen men—nine wiremen, three soldermen, and two inspectors—assembling terminal banks for use in telephone exchanges, were placed in a Bank Wiring Observation Room. The only other change in working conditions was the presence of a single investigator in the room to observe the workers' behavior. An interviewer remained outside the room and periodically interviewed the men. This phase of the Hawthorne studies lasted seven months and concluded in May 1932.

One generalization became clear almost immediately. The workers' behavior did not conform to the official job specifications. The group developed an informal social structure with norms, values, and sentiments that affected performance.

Patterns of interactions developed as soon as the men were thrown together in the observation room. Friendships formed and two well-defined groups emerged. The informal cliques were evident in interaction patterns both on and off the job. For example, one clique, rather than another, engaged in certain games played during off hours. Even more important than the different interaction patterns were the informal norms that emerged to govern behavior and unify the group. Too much work, and one was a rate buster. Too little work constituted the equally serious, informal offense of chiseling. A no-squealing norm also emerged; no group member should say anything that might injure a fellow member.

The work group enforced respect for informal norms through ostracism, sarcasm, and invective to pressure deviant members. One mechanism to enlist compliance was "binging"—a quick, stiff punch on the upper arm. The bing was not physically damaging, nor was it meant to be; it was a symbolic gesture of group displeasure.

Much activity in the group countered formal role prescriptions. Wiremen and soldermen did not stick to their jobs as prescribed but frequently traded jobs and helped each other. The group also restricted production. Group norms defined a fair day's work below management's expectations, although not so far below as to be unacceptable. Most work was done in the morning. Faster workers simply slowed their pace earlier or reported less work than they had accomplished to save production for slow days. The informal production levels were consistently maintained, even though higher production was possible. Because the group was on a piece rate, higher output would have meant higher wages. Thus, behavior was a function of group norms, not economic incentives.

The experiments at the Hawthorne plant were the first to question many of the basic assumptions made by human engineers and administrative managers. The following propositions summarize the conclusions of the Hawthorne studies:

1. Economic incentive is not the only significant motivator. In fact, noneconomic social sanctions limit the effectiveness of economic incentives.
2. Workers respond to management as members of an informal group, not as individuals.
3. Production levels are limited more by the social norms of the informal organization than by physiological capacities.
4. Specialization does not necessarily create the most efficient organization of the work group.
5. Workers use informal organization to protect themselves against arbitrary management decisions.

6. Informal social organizations interact with management.
7. A narrow span of control is not a prerequisite to effective supervision.
8. Informal leaders are often as important as formal supervisors.
9. Individuals are active human beings, not passive cogs in a machine.

The human relations approach tempered the concentration on organizational structure with an emphasis on employee motivation and satisfaction and group morale. Although these findings date from the 1920s and 1930s, they remain important.

BEHAVIORAL SCIENCE APPROACH

Because the classical and human relations approaches ignored the impact of social relations and formal structure, respectively, the behavioral science approach used both perspectives and added propositions drawn from psychology, sociology, political science, and economics. The focus of the behavioral science approach is work behavior in formal organization.[31]

Chester I. Barnard originated much of the behavioral science approach with his analysis of organizational life in *The Functions of the Executive.*[32] The product of Barnard's years as president of Bell Telephone Company of New Jersey, this book provides a comprehensive theory of cooperative behavior in formal organizations.

Barnard provided the original definitions of formal and informal organizations and cogently demonstrated the inevitable interaction between them. Barnard himself summarized the contributions of his work in terms of structural and dynamic concepts.[33] The structural concepts he considered important were the individual, the cooperative system, the formal organization, the complex formal organization, and the informal organization. His important dynamic concepts were free will, cooperation, communication, authority, the decision process, and dynamic equilibrium.

Herbert Simon, in *Administrative Behavior,* extended Barnard's work and used the concept of organizational equilibrium as a focal point for a formal theory of work motivation.[34] The organization was seen as an exchange system in which inducements are exchanged for work. Employees remain in the organization as long as they perceive the inducements as larger than their work contributions. By integrating economics, psychology, and sociology, the inducements-contributions schema illustrates the interdisciplinary nature of the theory.

Simon criticized classical organization theory because, he maintained, it was based on proverbs "not unlike those used by a Ubangi medicine man to discuss disease."[35] Simon saw administration as a process of rational decision making that influenced the behavior of members of the organization. He succinctly characterized his perspective in the following:

What is a scientifically relevant description of an organization? It is a description that, so far as possible, designates for each person in the organization what decisions that person makes, and the influence to which he is subject in making each of these decisions.[36]

The organization, although providing the framework, information, and values for rational decisions, is limited in its ability to collect and process information, search for alternatives, and predict consequences. Therefore, questions are resolved through *satisficing* rather than through optimizing. In Simon's view, no best solution exists to any given problem, but some solutions are more satisfactory than others.

Other theoretical formulations in behavioral science evolved from the writings of Max Weber (see Chapter 5).[37] Although many of Weber's views are closer to those espoused by the scientific managers than by the behavioral scientists, Weber's discussions of bureaucracy and authority have provided present-day behavioral scientists with a starting point in their conceptions of organizations as social systems that interact with and are dependent upon their environments.

A Systems View

A system is a set of interdependent elements forming an organized whole. Organizations such as schools are systems of social interaction; they are social systems comprised of interacting personalities bound together in mutually interdependent relationships. Early attempts to synthesize the influence of both the formal and informal features of organizational life were cast in the context of closed-systems thought. That is, behavior in formal organizations was explained almost exclusively in terms of forces inside the organization. The organization was isolated from its environment. Little attention was devoted to the impact of environmental or outside forces on internal organizational behavior. In brief, organizations were seen as closed systems.

In the early 1960s, behavioral scientists began shifting their perspectives from a closed-systems to an open-systems perspective. Models of organizational analysis started to stress that organizations not only were influenced by their environments but also dependent upon them. Today, few contemporary organizational theorists and researchers accept the premise that organizations can be completely understood in isolation of events occurring externally; in fact, Marshall Meyer argues "the issue of open versus closed systems is closed, on the side of openness."[38]

Although contemporary organizational thought is anchored in the behavioral sciences, three competing systems perspectives have emerged and continue, each with its share of advocates. W. Richard Scott calls them the rational-systems, natural-systems, and open-systems perspectives.[39] These three popular views of organizations are relatively distinct, yet they are partially overlapping, partially complementary, as well as partially conflicting; and each has its antecedents in earlier thought.

Rational systems.   The rational-systems perspective views organizations as formal instruments designed to achieve specific organizational goals. Rationality is the extent to which a set of actions is organized and implemented to achieve predetermined goals with maximum efficiency.[40] The rational approach has its early roots in the classical organizational thought of the scientific managers. Thus, the behavior of organizations is seen as purposeful, disciplined, and rational. The concerns and concepts of rational-systems theorists are conveyed by such terms as information, efficiency, effectiveness, optimization, implementation, rationality, and design. Furthermore, emphasis is placed upon the limitations of individual decision makers in the context of organizations; hence, the notions of opportunities, constraints, formal authority, rules and regulations, compliance, jurisdiction, objectives, mission, and coordination represent key elements of rationality.

Goal specificity and formalization, however, stand out as the two critical elements in producing rationality in organizations.[41] Goals are the desired ends that guide organizational behavior. Specific goals direct decision making, influence the formal structure, specify the tasks, guide the allocation of resources, and govern design decisions. Ambiguous goals hinder rationality because without clear goals, ordering alternatives and making rational choices are not possible; hence, even when the general organizational goals are vague (as they often are in education), the actual daily operations are guided by specific objectives. Educators may argue endlessly about the merits of progressive and traditional education, but within each school considerable agreement develops around issues such as graduation requirements, discipline policies, and school regulations.

Formalization, or the level of rules and job codification, is another feature that makes organizations rational; formalization produces standardization and regulation of work performance. Rules are developed that precisely and explicitly govern behavior; jobs are carefully defined in terms of acceptable behaviors; role relations are defined independently of personal attributes of incumbents; and sometimes the work flow itself is clearly specified. Formalization is the organization's means to make behavior predictable by standardizing and regulating it. As Simon cogently states, "Organizations and institutions permit stable expectations to be formed by each member of the group as to the behavior of the other members under specific conditions. Such stable expectations are an essential precondition to a rational consideration of the consequences of action in a social group."[42]

Formalization also contributes to the rational functioning of the organization in a number of other important ways.[43] It makes visible the structure of the organizational relationships; thus, formal structures can be modified by managers to improve performance. Management by objectives (MBO), planning, programming, and budgeting systems (PPBS), and performance evaluation and review techniques (PERT) are examples of technical tools used by managers to facilitate rational decision making.[44] Formal structure also promotes discipline and decision making based on facts rather than emotional ties and feelings; in fact, formalization reduces to some extent both positive and negative feelings that members have toward each other. As Merton observes, "Formality facilitates the interaction of the occupants of offices despite their (possibly hostile) private attitudes toward one another."[45] Moreover, formalization renders the organization less dependent on particular individuals. The replacement of individuals is routinized so that appropriately trained individuals can replace with minimal disturbance. Even leadership and innovation needs are addressed by formalization. As Sheldon Wolin notes, "Organization, by simplifying and routinizing procedures, eliminates the need for surpassing talent. It is predicated on 'average human beings.' "[46]

Advocates of the rational-systems perspective focus on the importance of goals and formal structure in determining organizational behavior. Taylor, Fayol, Gulick, and Urwick were early proponents of this perspective. Although Weber and Simon also emphasize the significance of formal structure and rationality in organizations, both were also concerned with the interplay between formal structure and the satisfaction of participants. Simon claims, "No formal organization will operate effectively without an accompanying informal."[47] And Weber's contribution to organizational analyses is noted aptly by Scott, "Although it is clearly possible to criticize and improve upon many specific aspects of Weber's formulation, he remains the acknowledged master of organization theory: the intellectual giant whose conceptions continue to shape definitions of the central elements of administrative systems, and whose historical and comparative vision continues to. challenge and inform our more limited views of organizational forms."[48] (See Chapter 5.)

Natural systems.   The natural-systems perspective provides another view of organization that stands in contrast to rational-system perspective. The natural perspective had its early roots in the human relations approach of the 1930s; it developed in large part as a reaction to the scientific managers and perceived inadequacies of the rational-system model. Although rational-system proponents conceive of organizations as structural arrangements deliberately devised to achieve specific goals, natural-system advocates view organizations as primarily social groups trying to adapt and survive in their particular situation. Natural-system analysts generally agree that goal specificity and formalization are characteristics of organizations, but they argue that other attributes are of much greater significance; in fact, some maintain the formal goals and structure have little to do with what is actually happening in organizations.[49]

The natural-systems view focuses on similarities among social groups. Thus, organizations, like all social groups, are driven primarily by the basic goal of survival, not by specifically devised goals of particular institutions. Gouldner captures the essence of the natural approach when he states, "The organization, according to this model, strives to survive and to maintain its equilibrium, and this striving may persist even after its explicitly held goals have been successfully attained. This strain toward survival may even on occasion lead to the neglect or distortion of the organization's goals."[50] Survival, then, is the overriding goal. Formal organizations are viewed not primarily as means for achieving specific ends, but as ends in themselves.

Just as the natural-systems analysts generally disregard goals as important attributes of organizations, they also view as unimportant the formal structures devised to achieve goals. Although they acknowledge that formal structures do exist, they believe behavior in organizations is regulated primarily by informal structures that emerge to transform the formal system. In this regard, Scott noted the following:

> Individual participants are never merely hired hands but bring along their heads and hearts: they enter into the organization with individually shaped ideas, expectations, and agendas, and they bring them differing values, interests, and abilities. . . . Participants within formal organizations generate informal norms and behavior patterns: status and power systems, communication networks, sociometric structures, and working arrangements. . . . [51]

In sum, goals and structure do not make organizations distinctive; in fact, formal features of organization are overshadowed by more generic attributes such as the desire for the system to survive and the characteristics of the individuals. Whereas the rational-systems perspective stresses the importance of structure over individuals, the natural-systems approach emphasizes individuals over structure. In stark terms, the rational-systems focus is on "structure without people," while the clear reversal of priorities in the natural-systems model produces an orientation of "people without organization."[52]

As we have already noted, the early human-relations pioneers, i.e., Follett, Mayo, Roethlisberger, provided the impetus for the natural-systems model, but their work was much less complete than such later system theorists as Talcott Parsons (see Chapters 2, 3, 12). All natural-systems advocates presume the existence of certain system needs for survival. All are concerned with the mechanisms to achieve these needs. All emphasize the idiosyncratic needs and behaviors of individuals and the spontaneity and overwhelming power of the informal organization. But their views are not consistent on the influence of the environment. In fact, the early human-relations analysts simply did not consider the environment as an important factor; theirs was a closed-system perspective. Later, natural-systems thinkers, however, began to examine the significance of the external environment. In the work of Parsons, for example, the importance of the relationship between the organization and environment is understood. The organization is described as a subsystem embedded within a more comprehensive social system, with the environment viewed as a critical stabilizing element sustaining and legitimating the mission of the organization. Or in the words of Scott, "In many ways, Parsons anticipates the view of open-systems theorists in his treatment of environment."[53]

Open Systems. The open-systems perspective was a reaction to the unrealistic assumption that organizational behavior could be isolated from external forces. Competition, resources, and political pressures of the environment affect the internal workings of organizations. The open-systems model views organizations as not only influenced by environments but also dependent on them. At a general level, organizations are easily pictured as open systems. Organizations take inputs from the environment, transform them, and produce outputs (see Figure 1.2). For example, schools are social systems that take resources such as labor, students, and community direction from the environment; subject these inputs to an educational transformation process to produce literate and educated students and graduates.

Open systems have a number of important characteristics. Here we will briefly mention only a few of the critical system properties of organizations. (In Chapter 3, these and other system attributes will be discussed in more detail.) First, the organization's capacity for feedback (see Figure 1.2) facilitates the repetitive and cyclic pattern of "input—transformation—output." Feedback is information about the system, which enables it to correct itself. Unlike mechanized systems, however, social systems do not always use the information to change. The superintendent of a school system who receives information about falling SAT scores and increased difficulties of graduates to get jobs and enter the colleges of their choice can use this information to identify factors within the system that are contributing to the problem and take corrective action. Yet not all superintendents choose to act. Hence, although feedback provides self-correcting opportunities, the potential is not always realized.

Second, systems that survive tend to move toward a steady state-*equilibrium.* This steady state, however, is not a static. Energy from and to the environment is continuously imported and exported. Although any force that threatens to disrupt the system is countered by forces that seek to maintain the system, systems do exhibit a growth dynamic. Events that throw the system out of balance are addressed by actions that are calculated to move the system toward a new state of balance or equilibrium.

Third, open systems overcome the tendency to run down by demonstrating adaptation. They seek to maintain a favorable position with respect to their environments; they adapt to changing environmental demands. A press from state departments of education for more basic skills programs typically results in accommodation to those demands. Since the principle of equifinality is opera-

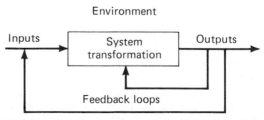

FIGURE 1.2   Basic open-systems model

tive in open systems, organizations can reach the same end from different initial positions and through different paths. Thus, no "one best way" exists to organize, and likely there is no one best way to reach the same end.[54] For instance, schools may select a variety of means to emphasize basic skills.

The open-systems perspective is concerned with both structure and process; it is a dynamic system with both stability and flexibility, with both tight and loose structural relationships. The organization as an arrangement of roles and relationships is not static. To survive, the organization must adapt, and to adapt, it must change. The interdependence of the organization and its environment is critical. Instead of neglecting the environment, as the rational perspective does, or seeing it as hostile, as is the case with the natural-systems perspective, "the open-systems model stresses the reciprocal ties that bind and interrelate the organization with those elements that surround and penetrate it. Indeed, the environment is even seen to be the source of order itself."[55]

Each of the three systems views continues to have its share of contemporary advocates because each highlights a critical set of organizational properties. In our view, however, the open-systems model has the potential to provide a synthesis, a way of combining the perspectives. The open-systems perspective provides a broad framework in which to cast both rational and natural features of organizational life. Organizations are complex and dynamic. They have formal structures to achieve specified goals but are comprised of people who have their own idiosyncratic needs, interests, and beliefs that often conflict with organizational expectations. Thus, organizations have planned and unplanned features, rational and irrational characteristics, and formal and informal structures. In some organizations, rational concerns dominate the relationships, whereas natural, social relationships predominate in others; in fact, over time the relative emphasis on rational and natural concerns may change. But in all organizations, both rational and natural elements exist in a system that is open to its environment. Some scholars will argue that contemporary American schools are open, natural systems; other maintain schools are open, rational systems. Our view is that schools are open systems confronted with both rational and natural constraints that change as the environmental forces change; to neglect either the rational or natural elements is shortsighted. Open-systems theory, then, is the *general framework* for exploring the conceptual foundations of educational administration in this text. Although many theories are discussed in our analyses, the open-systems perspective is the overarching framework.

THEORETICAL DEVELOPMENTS IN EDUCATIONAL ADMINISTRATION

Developments in educational administration parallel those in the broad field of administration. Similar to Taylor's scientific managers, although lacking the rigor of the human engineers, early students of educational administration looked at organizational behavior from the vantage point of job analyses.[56] They observed administrators at work, specifying the component tasks to be performed, determining more effective ways to perform each task, and suggesting an organization to maximize efficiency. Raymond E. Callahan's analysis of schools and of the "cult of efficiency," concentrating on the period from 1910 through 1930, clearly indicates the influence of the scientific managers.[57]

By 1940, however, the impact of the Hawthorne studies was evident in a writing and exhortation on democratic administration. The ill-defined watchword of the period was "democratic"—democratic administration, democratic supervision, democratic decision making, democratic teaching. As Roald Campbell noted, "This emphasis on human relations and democratic practices often meant a series of prescriptions as to how conditions ought to be and how persons in an organization ought to behave. Sometimes these prescriptions took the form of principles."[58]

Supposed principles abounded, but they were usually no more than the observations of successful administrators or the democratic ideologies of college professors. In the 1940s and early 1950s, educational administration was a democratic approach long on rhetoric and woefully short on research and practice.[59]

In the 1950s, however, the behavioral science approach started to make inroads, and by the 1960s a full-scale theory movement emerged to guide the study and teaching of educational administration. Democratic prescription was replaced by analysis, a field orientation and raw observation by theoretical research. In addition, concepts from many disciplines were incorporated into educational administration research.

The theory movement in educational administration, however, was limited by a closed-systems perspective. Like its parent, the general field of organizational theory, the focus of the analyses was on attempts to explain the internal workings of schools without reference to elements in the environment. Thus, it is not surprising that progress toward relevant theory and research in educational administration slowed in the 1970s. The social and political unrest of the late 1960s and the financial and political exigencies of the 1970s—civil rights demonstrations and riots, Vietnam and Watergate, oil crises and other resource shortages—all impinged on the study and practice of educational administration by raising questions about inequality, accountability, and the management of decline. Clearly, environmental factors are important forces affecting life in schools. The tenor of the 1970s not only inspired a renewed press in the field for practice, action, and immediate results but underscored the limitations of closed-systems models. To be sure, research and theory in educational administration advanced during these two decades, but progress was modest. Moreover, criticisms of the behavioral science approach in general and organizational theory in particular were forthcoming from reflective scholars as the extravagant expectations of the theory movement gave way to disillusionment.

By 1979, Griffiths described educational administration as a field in intellectual turmoil.[60] Organizational theory and traditional research were under attack on a number of fronts. The logic of mainstream theory that described organizations as rational instruments of purpose, the focus on the internal operation of organizations with little regard for the influence of the environment, and the universality of organizational theories, all provided bases for criticism. Moreover, Marxist sociologists turned to critiques of traditional organizational theory, interpreting institutional life in terms of power, conflict, contradictions, crisis, and class struggle. For example, Heydebrand maintains that "organizational theory, like other theories in the social sciences, has been dominated by powerful ideological forces which, taken together, have more or less successfully reproduced and legitimized the structure of capitalist society."[61] Finally, contemporary organizational theory was criticized on epistemological grounds. The positivist model of the natural sciences was questioned as the appropriate one for the social and behavioral sciences.

The behavioral science approach will continue to face increased challenges in the future, challenges from practitioners, professors, and the public, who will demand relevance and utility in theory and research.[62] One danger of applying theoretical knowledge from the behavioral sciences is the tendency to overgeneralize it to all situations.[63] Too many behavioral scientists and practitioners assume that their theories apply universally; instead of asking under what conditions ideas and propositions are appropriate, they assume such ideas are always correct. They may think, for example, that participative management is always effective. The quest for universals and simple popular solutions has often led to disillusionment with the behavioral sciences. If the behavioral science approach is to remain productive in the late 1980s and 1990s, theory and research will have to become more refined, useful, and situationally oriented. Rather, what the behavioral science approach can and should offer is a set of conceptual guidelines to aid administrators as they attempt to understand the complexities of organizational life. An open-systems perspective provides such a framework; it calls attention to rational and natural aspects of social life as well as the interdependency of the organization and its environment.

Although problems in the development of theory in educational administration remain, that does not mean that the effort should be abandoned. The road to generalized knowledge can lie only in tough-minded scientific research, not introspection and subjective experience.

PHILOSOPHICAL AND SOCIOLOGICAL FOUNDATIONS OF ORGANIZATIONAL THEORY

Although we have been clear about our view of the nature of theory and research, given the controversy in the field, this chapter concludes with an examination of assumptions about the nature of the social world and the way in which it should be studied. We agree with Gibson Burrell and Gareth Morgan that "all theories of organization are based upon a philosophy of science and a theory of society."[64] Moreover, Burrell and Morgan present one framework for the analysis of the nature of society and social science that is useful in this regard.

First, let us examine some basic assumptions about the nature of social science by examining four questions:

1. Is there a social reality that is external to the individual, or is reality merely a product of one's mind?
2. Is it possible to identify and communicate knowledge in the social sciences that is hard, real, and tangible, or is such knowledge soft, subjective, and transcendental, based on experience and insights that are unique to the individual?
3. Are individuals the product of their environments, or are they masters of the environment? Are their behaviors determined by external conditions, or do individuals have "free will" to control those conditions?
4. Is there an external reality worthy of study? That is, can patterns of regularities and relationships among elements of social life be identified, explained, and generalized? Or are experiences in the social world so subjective and idiosyncratic that the principal concern must focus on how the individual creates and interprets the social world in which he or she lives?

These questions have been framed to identify extreme sets of assumptions; indeed, the polar positions are "reflected in the two major intellectual traditions which have dominated social science over the last two hundred years."[65] The first of these can be described as a social positivism. It is an attempt to apply models and methods from the natural sciences. It examines the social world as if it were the natural world, assuming that an external social reality exists. It also assumes that environment conditions social behavior and that patterns of regularities in social relations can be explained in general terms. In stark contrast stands the second intellectual tradition, German idealism. It is based on the assumption that ultimate reality rests with ideas; hence, social reality is merely a product of the individual's mind. It emphasizes the subjective and transcendental nature of social relations. It refutes the usefulness and relevance of models from the natural sciences. It asserts the individual's ability to make free choices. And it denies that patterns of regularities and relationships among elements of social life can be identified, explained, and generalized. Instead, it stresses how unique individuals create, modify, and interpret the social world in which they live. Thus, social positivism and German idealism define the objective and subjective extremes of the first dimension of the Burrell and Morgan model.

The second dimension of their analytic scheme deals with assumptions about the nature of society. Is order or conflict the basic state of society? Burrell and Morgan argue that two separate sociological perspectives have developed to answer this question—a "sociology of regulation" and a "sociology of radical change." On one hand, a sociology of regulation is concerned with the need to explain why society maintains itself as an entity; hence, it emphasizes stability, order, consensus, social integration, cohesion, solidarity, and actuality. On the other hand, a sociology of radical change focuses on the need to explain why society is characterized by extreme conflict and radical change; therefore, it emphasizes change, structural conflict, modes of domination, contradiction, emancipation, deprivation, and potentiality.[66] These two broad, distinctive sociological perspectives form the extremes for the second dimension of the model—a societal one. When combined, the two dimensions form four distinct perspectives for the analysis of social theory: the functionalist, the radical structuralist, the radical humanist, and the interpretive (see Figure 1.3).

The *functionalist* perspective assumes that the existence of an external social reality is worthy of study. Organizational theorists seek to explain and predict behavior in the social world by searching for regular patterns of social relations and causal relationships among its constituent elements. The development of knowledge is basically a cumulative process in which new knowledge is added to the existing base and false hypotheses are eliminated through systematic empirical research. The overall approach to the functionalist perspective is to provide rational explanations of social affairs, explanations that help us understand order and regularities in social behavior. Using the Burrell and Morgan framework, most contemporary organizational theory falls into the functionalistic cell.

The *radical humanist* perspective accepts a set of assumptions about social reality that is just the opposite of the functionalist view; hence, it is an antiorganizational theory perspective. The radical humanists adopt a subjectivistic

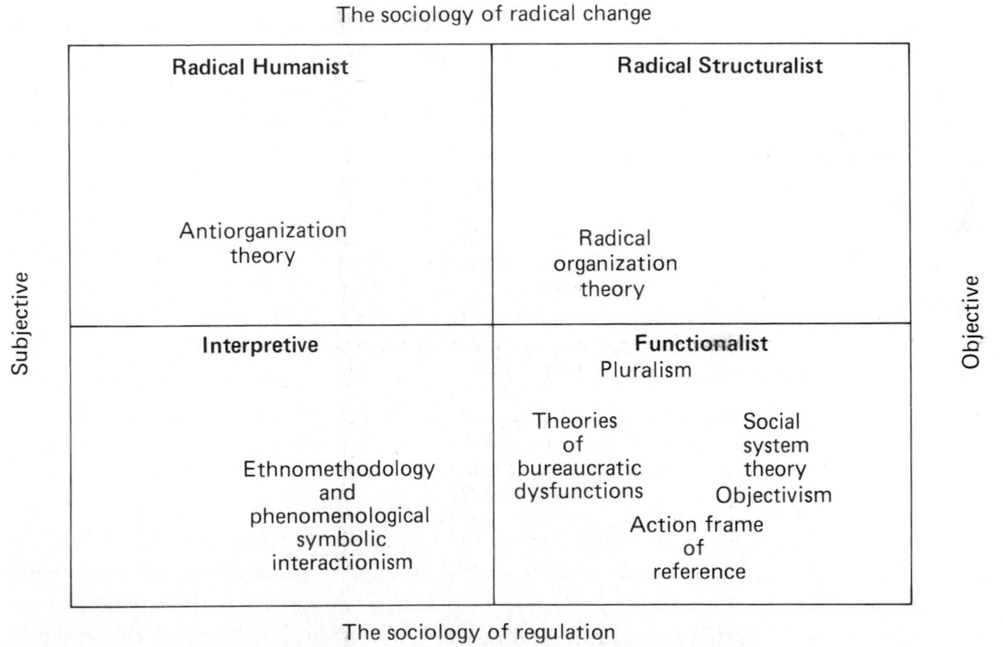

The sociology of radical change

Radical Humanist	**Radical Structuralist**
Antiorganization theory	Radical organization theory
Interpretive	**Functionalist** Pluralism
Ethnomethodology and phenomenological symbolic interactionism	Theories of bureaucratic dysfunctions Social system theory Objectivism Action frame of reference

Subjective — Objective

The sociology of regulation

FIGURE 1.3   The main schools of organizational analysis

SOURCE: G. Burrell and G. Morgan, *Sociological Paradigms and Organizational Analysis.* Copyright 1980 by Heinemann Educational Books Ltd. Reprinted by permission.

viewpoint and embrace a stance that society must be changed; existing social structures must be overthrown so that human development can be released from extant structural constraints. The humanists are not content simply to understand the nature of society; their kind of social theorizing is a critique of the status quo, which emphasizes the alienated state of humanity. Theirs is a critical theory of organizations and society.

Critical theory has its historical roots in the early work of Marx. Marxist critique of the status quo not only highlights the alienated state of workers but argues that it can change practice by illuminating "false consciousness." Jack Culbertson succinctly summarizes the perspective of critical theory as follows:

> It seeks fundamental and major change through direct links with and impact on practice. It seeks to do this through penetrating critiques of the status quo and through the foreshadowing of new and compelling human possibilities for development.[67]

Thus, critical theory is an attractive alternative to those who press for practice, action, and immediate results. The high aspirations of critical theorists, however, have generally not been realized either in education or other fields.[68] Since the assumptions of radical humanism and critical theory are anti-organizational, it is not surprising that contemporary critical theorists in educational administration eschew what they term traditional theory and research in the field.[69]

The *radical structuralist* like the functionalist perspective emphasizes the hard, concrete, and objective nature of social reality. The social world has an independent existence. Further, since the nature of the social and natural worlds are seen as similar, the methods and models of the natural sciences are used to develop a body of social knowledge. Social science, however, is not merely a means to understand society; radical structuralists view it as a means to change the existing social order that alienates mankind. It is the alienation and radical change theme that is common to both the radical humanists and radical structuralists; both aim to release humanity from the pervasive forms of domination that they view as characteristics of contemporary industrial society. But the radical structuralists propose not only a critique of the status quo but a plan to change society using the hard knowledge developed by social science. Karl Marx provided the intellectual foundations for the radical structural perspective, one anchored in a materialistic view of both the natural and social world and one that has served as a basis for many critiques of traditional organizational theory.

Most of the radical structuralist critiques, like those of the radical humanists, are Marxist. They are highly political and accuse organizational theorists of being dupes of the capitalist system, of consciously or unconsciously playing an active role in degrading the worker, of being mindlessly empirical, of neglecting the body of social thought reflected in the mature Marx, of downplaying the significance of class relationships in contemporary society, of neglecting the importance of the state, and of employing analytic models that stress equilibrium and the status quo rather than dynamic change and conflict.[70] Interestingly, in the field of educational administration, most of the Marxist criticism of organizational theory comes from radical humanists, but in the general field it comes from radical structuralists. In both cases, however, political and emancipatory overtones are evident.

The *interpretive* perspective stands in clear contrast to the radical structuralist view; it denies the existence of an external social reality and seeks to explain the social world essentially from the point of view of the individuals directly involved in the social relationship. Thus, the basic nature of social reality is seen as subjective, idiosyncratic, and within the participant's mind, not the observer's. In the tradition of German idealism, interpretive analysis is based on the notion that individuals construct their own social reality; moreover, it is oriented toward understanding the nature of the social world as it exists rather than as it might be. Thus, the concerns are one of order, consensus, and integration rather than change, conflict, and contradiction. Since the interpretive perspective rejects the idea of an independent social reality, its view does not acknowledge the existence of organizations in a concrete way. As Burrell and Morgan note, "From the standpoint of the interpretive paradigm, organizations do not exist."[71] Consequently scholars and researchers in this perspective attempt to demonstrate how the hard, real, and tangible aspects of organizational behavior are dependent upon the subjective interpretations and creations of individuals. Interpretive analysts use two approaches in this quest: ethnomethodology and phenomenological symbolic interactionism. Burrell and Morgan distinguish between the two as follows:

> Whereas the phenomethodological usually focuses upon the way in which individual actors account for and make sense of their world, the phenomenological symbolic interactionist focuses upon social contexts in which interacting individuals employ a variety of practices to create and sustain particular definitions of the world. They demonstrate how "reality" and "facts," as essentially social creations, negotiated through the interaction of various competing themes and definitions of reality.[72]

In educational administration, the interpretive perspective has gained some favor in recent years beginning with the so-called Greenfield-Griffiths debates in which Thomas Greenfield offered a subjectivist perspective as an alternative to the traditional positivistic one used by most theorists and researchers.[73] The goal of interpretive inquiry is not to develop general explanations or to predict aspects of organizational life but rather to achieve—basically through inductive and qualitative modes of inquiry—understandings, interpretations, and meanings of particular contexts. Understanding arrived at through reasoned reflection is the basic objective rather than laws arrived at through the scientific method.[74] Because the interpretive perspective rejects the notion of an independent social reality, knowledge cannot be general; social reality is construed as images in the mind of individuals having no necessary or inevitable forms except as individuals create them and endow them with reality.[75] Thus, the interpretive perspective denies the existence of independent generalizations that explain the structure and dynamics of organizational life.

One of the problems with current philosophic discourse on the nature of knowledge and inquiry in educational administration is the tendency of oversimplification. As Donald J. Willower notes, "In discourses on these issues, it is essential to avoid the naïve misconception that modern philosophical positions boil down to positivism versus phenomenology (or some mixture of it with existentialism or Marxian critical theory or those views alone)."[76] Although the Burrell and Morgan framework is a more refined attempt to describe social and philosophic perspectives, it also suffers from oversimplifiction. It groups together disparate philosophic perspectives and lumps virtually all contemporary organizational theory in a "functionalist" perspective, which can only be accomplished by ignoring the basic tenets of functionalism.[77]

The perspective of this text is open-ended and pragmatic. Knowledge is seen as the product of systematic inquiry, which is guided by theory and subjected to public procedures that are replicable. The fact that our knowledge may be flawed or incomplete should not cause discouragement; it simply underscores the tentative nature of knowledge. New evidence will render many contemporary theories less useful. In this regard, we are like sailors who must repair a rotting ship at sea. We trust all but the weakest timber that we must replace. The knowledge that the timbers we trust today will be replaced tomorrow because they are also rotten in no way suggests that our trust has been misplaced.[78] When systematic methods of inquiry are brought to bear on a range of facts, we are better able to understand and to control them more intelligently and less haphazardly.[79] Consequently, in this text we draw upon whatever research and theories seem useful to administrators in solving organizational problems. Our goal is to provide tentative explanations of social affairs, explanations that help administrators to understand the order and regularities of social behavior in organizations. Administrators who have at their disposal sets of concepts and basic principles of organizational life have powerful tools for observing, interpreting, and changing educational practice.

SUMMARY

Theory is not simply idealistic speculation, nor is it "common sense." Because facts do not speak for themselves, an empirically verifiable framework is needed to give facts meaning. Theory—a set of interrelated concepts, assumptions, or generalizations that systematically describes and explains behavior— provides that framework. Organizational theory functions in the same way theory does in the natural sciences and in the other social sciences: it provides an explanatory system connecting otherwise unrelated information. In addition, theory gives direction to empirical research, it may generate new knowledge, and it serves as a rational guide to action as well. Theory is refined through research, and when theory, in the light of research findings, is applied to individual action, theory is transformed into practice.

There is, then, a symbiosis of theory, research, and practice. In spite of the newness of our field, personal biases, and the sheer complexity of organizational life, all practice is based on some theory. When theory is based on systems that are logical, rational, explicit, and quantitative, practice will be similarly rational. When theory is uniformed, subjective, or anti-rational, practice will reflect those attributes.

The complex organizations of the twentieth century necessitated the study of administration and the development of theory. We can speak of three periods in the evolution of administrative science. First, classical organizational thought, starting with Taylor's scientific analysis of work, focused on the formal organizational structure. Scientific management studies concentrated on work efficiency, particularly the physiological variables, and later dealt with the components of management itself. Fayol listed the components: to plan, to organize, to command, to coordinate, and to control; and Gulick amplified these in his POSDCoRB acronym.

The Hawthorne studies placed the informal organization at the heart of a new philosophy of management, the human relations approach. Whereas scientific management has been criticized for mechanizing employees, human relations has often become an oversimplified solution for all problems.

A third and contemporary phase, the behavioral science approach, balances recognition of both formal and informal organizations. This third perspective, in part a synthesis of the preceding two, uses modern behavioral and social science methods in its analyses.

The behavioral science approach in organizational analysis is primarily a theoretical approach with three competing systems perspectives—rational systems, natural systems, and open systems—each with its share of advocates and each with antecedents in earlier thought. Advocates of the rational-systems perspective focus on the importance of goals and formal structure in determining organizational behavior, whereas natural-systems analysts argue that organizations, like all social groups, are driven primarily by the basic goal of survival. In other words, a rational-systems view stresses the importance of structure over individuals, but the natural-systems perspective emphasizes individuals over structure. The open-systems perspective acknowledges that organizations are not only influenced by but also dependent on their environments. Moreover, organizations are confronted with both rational and natural constraints that change as the environment changes; hence, open-systems theory provides an opportunity for synthesis.

The behavioral science approach of the 1950s and 1960s ushered in a movement toward theory and research in educational administration, but the social and political unrest of the 1970s inspired a renewed press for action and immediate results. The challenge of the 1980s and 1990s is clear. Behavioral science theory must become more refined, useful, and situationally oriented. Organizational theory must explain both rational and natural elements of behavioral as well as environmental constraints on organizational life. Thus, open-systems theory is the general theoretical framework of this text. Finally, our perspective is not only open but it is a pragmatic one. We have assumed that the role of organizational theory and research is to help us understand and explain the order and regularities in organizational behavior. The theories and frameworks discussed throughout the remainder of the text offer administrators a useful set of conceptual guidelines to aid them as they attempt to understand and deal with the complexities of organizational life.

NOTES

1. Earl R. Babbie, *Survey Research Methods* (Belmont, CA: Wadsworth, 1973), p. 10.
2. For a comprehensive discussion of the challenges of developing a science of organizations, see Karlene H. Roberts, Charles L. Hulin, and Denise M. Rousseau, *Developing an Interdisciplinary Science of Organizations* (San Francisco: Jossey-Bass, 1978).
3. James B. Conant, *Science and Common Sense* (New Haven, CT: Yale University Press, 1951), pp. 23–27.
4. Herbert Feigl, "Principles and Problems of Theory Construction in Psychology," in *Current Trends in Psychological Theory* (Pittsburgh: University of Pittsburgh Press, 1951), p. 182. Both Andrew W. Halpin, *Administrative Theory in Education* (Chicago: Midwest Administration Center, University of Chicago Press, 1958), pp. 1–19, and Daniel E. Griffiths, *Administrative Theory,* (New York: Appleton-Century-Crofts, 1959), pp. 27–29, support this definition.
5. Fred N. Kerlinger, *Foundations of Behavioral Research,* 2nd ed. (New York: Holt, Rinehart & Winston, 1973), p. 9. For another general but comprehensive definition of theory in the social sciences, see Jerald Hage, *Techniques and Problems of Theory Construction in Sociology* (New York: Wiley, 1972), pp. 171–177.
6. Albert Einstein and Leopold Infeld, *The Evolution of Physics* (New York: Simon & Schuster, 1938), p. 31.
7. Paul Davidson Reynolds, *A Primer in Theory Construction* (Indianapolis: Bobbs-Merrill, 1971), pp. 45–65.
8. Donald J. Willower, "The Form of Knowledge and the Theory-Practice Relationship," *Educational Theory,* 13 (1963), 47.
9. Milton Rokeach, *The Open and Closed Mind* (New York: Basic Books, 1960), pp. 413–415.
10. Robert Dubin, *Theory Building* (New York: Free Press, 1969), p. 185.
11. Griffiths, *Administrative Theory, op. cit.,* pp. 71–72.
12. Kerlinger, *op. cit.,* p. 11. For an analysis of scientific research in educational administration, see Wayne K. Hoy, "Scientific Research in Educational Administration," *Educational Administration Quarterly,* 14 (1978), 1–12.
13. Willower, *op. cit.,* 47.
14. For an excellent discussion of how the social sciences and the study and practice of educational administration developed, see Jack Culbertson *et al., Social Science Content for Preparing Educational Leaders* (Columbus, OH: Merrill, 1973).

15. John Dewey, *How We Think* (Boston: Heath, 1933).
16. Halpin, *op. cit.,* p. 266.
17. Frederick W. Taylor, "The Principles of Scientific Management," in *Scientific Management* (New York: Harper, 1947), pp. 63–64.
18. R. M. Barnes, *Motion and Time Study* (New York: Wiley, 1949), pp. 556–567.
19. Peter Drucker, *The Age of Discontinuity* (New York: Harper & Row, 1968), p. 272.
20. Lyndall F. Urwick in Luther Gulick and Lyndall F. Urwick (eds.), *Papers on the Science of Administration* (New York: Institute of Public Administration, Columbia University, 1937), p. 119.
21. *Ibid.*
22. *Ibid.,* pp. 15–27.
23. James D. Thompson, *Organizations in Action* (New York: McGraw-Hill, 1968), p. 57.
24. J. C. Worthy, "Factors Influencing Employee Morale," *Harvard Business Review,* 28 (1950), 61–73.
25. James March and Herbert Simon, *Organizations* (New York: Wiley, 1958), p. 27.
26. Mary Parker Follett, *Dynamic Administration: The Collected Papers of Mary Parker Follett,* Henry C. Metcalf and Lyndall F. Urwick (eds.) (New York: Harper, 1941).
27. Mary Parker Follett, *Creative Experience* (London: Longmans and Green, 1924), p. 300.
28. Fritz J. Roethlisberger and William J. Dickson, *Management and the Worker* (Cambridge, MA: Harvard University Press, 1939), pp. 14–17, 28, 87, 128–160, 379–514.
29. An authoritative summary of the studies is found in Roethlisberger and Dickson, *Ibid.*
30. *Ibid.,* p. 28.
31. Herbert Simon, "Administrative Behavior," in David Sills (ed.), *International Encyclopedia of the Social Sciences* (New York: Free Press, 1968), I, 74–79.
32. Chester I. Barnard, *The Functions of the Executive* (Cambridge, MA: Harvard University Press, 1938).
33. Chester I. Barnard, "Comments on the Job of the Executive," *Harvard Business Review,* 18 (1940), 295, 308.
34. Herbert Simon, *Administrative Behavior* (New York: Macmillian, 1947).
35. *Ibid.,* p. xiv.
36. *Ibid.,* p. 36.
37. Max Weber, *The Theory of Social and Economic Organizations,* Talcott Parsons (ed.) (New York: Free Press, 1947).
38. Marshall W. Meyer, "Introduction: Recent Developments in Organizational Research and Theory," in Marshall W. Meyer *et al.* (eds.), *Environments and Organizations* (San Francisco: Jossey-Bass, 1978), p. 18.
39. W. Richard Scott, *Organizations: Rational, Natural, and Open Systems* (Englewood Cliffs, NJ: Prentice-Hall, 1981), pp. 55–132. The discussion of the three perspectives draws heavily from Scott's analyses.
40. *Ibid.,* p. 58.
41. *Ibid.*

42. Simon, *op. cit.,* p. 100.
43. For a more detailed discussion of these contributions see Scott, *op. cit.,* pp. 60–62.
44. *Ibid.,* p. 80.
45. Robert K. Merton, *Social Theory and Social Structure* 2nd ed. (Glencoe, IL: Free Press, 1957), p. 100.
46. Sheldon S. Wolin, *Politics and Vision: Continuity and Innovation in Western Political Thought* (Boston: Little, Brown, 1960), p. 383.
47. Simon, *op. cit.,* p. 148.
48. Scott, *op. cit.,* p. 72.
49. *Ibid,* p. 80. See also Amitai Etzioni, *A Comparative Analysis of Complex Organization* (New York: Free Press, 1961), pp. 71–721, and Charles Perrow, "Demystifying Organization," in Y. Hasenfeld and R. Saari (eds.), *The Management of Human Services* (New York: Columbia University Press, 1978).
50. Alvin Gouldner, "Organizational Analysis," in Robert K. Merton, Leonard Broom, and Leonard S. Cottrell, Jr. (eds.), *Sociology Today* (New York: Basic Books, 1959), pp. 400–428. The quotation appears on p. 405.
51. Scott, *op. cit.,* p. 81.
52. Warren G. Bennis, "Leadership Theory and Administrative Behavior," *Administrative Science Quarterly,* 4 (December 1959), 259–301. The quotation appears on p. 266.
53. Scott, *op. cit.,* p. 100.
54. The open-system properties discussed here are essentially the same as the perspective advanced by David A. Nadler and Michael L. Tushman, "A General Diagnostic Model for Organizational Behavior: Applying a Congruence Perspective," in J. Richard Hackman *et al.* (eds.), *Perspectives on Behavior in Organizations* (New York: McGraw-Hill, 1983), pp. 113–114. See also Daniel Katz and Robert Kahn, *The Social Psychology of Organizations,* 2nd Ed. (New York: Wiley, 1978).
55. Scott, *op. cit.,* p. 120.
56. See, for example, Franklin Bobbit, "Some General Principles of Management Applied to the Problems of City School Systems," in *The Supervision of City Schools,* Twelfth Yearbook of the National Society for the Study of Education, Part I (Chicago: University of Chicago Press, 1913), pp. 137–196.
57. Raymond E. Callahan, *Education and the Cult of Efficiency* (Chicago: University of Chicago Press, 1962).
58. Roald Campbell, "NCPEA—Then and Now," a paper presented at the National Conference of Professors of Educational Administration meeting, University of Utah, August, 1971.
59. *Ibid.*
60. See, for example, Daniel E. Griffiths, "Intellectual Turmoil in Educational Administration," *Educational Administration Quarterly,* 15 (1979), 43–65.
61. W. Heydebrand, "Organizational Contradictions in Public Bureaucracies: Toward a Marxian Theory of Organization," in J. K. Benson (ed.), *Organizational Analysis,* (Beverly Hills: Sage, 1977), pp. 85–109. The quotation is on p. 85.
62. For example, see Donald J. Willower, "Some Issues in Research on School Organizations," in Glenn L. Immegart and William Boyd (eds.), *Currents*

in Administrative Research: Problem Finding in Education (Lexington, MA: Heath, 1979); and Thomas B. Greenfield, "Theory About Organizations: A New Perspective and Its Implications for Schools," in Meredydd Hughes (ed.), *Administering Education: International Challenge* (London: Athlane, 1975).

63. This position is developed more fully by Jay W. Lorsch, "Making Behavioral Science More Useful," *Harvard Business Review,* 57 (1979), 171–180.

64. Gibson Burrell and Gareth Morgan, *Sociological Paradigms and Organizational Analysis* (London: Heinemann, 1980), p. 1.

65. *Ibid.,* p. 7.

66. *Ibid.,* pp. 10–19.

67. Jack A. Culbertson, "Three Epistemologies and the Study of Educational Administration," *UCEA Review,* 22 (1981), 5.

68. *Ibid.*

69. For example, see Richard Bates, "Educational Administration, the Sociology of Science, and the Management of Knowledge," *Educational Administration Quarterly,* 16 (1980), 1–20; and William P. Foster, "Administration and Crisis in Legitimacy: A Review of Habermasean Thought," *Harvard Educational Review,* 50 (1980), 496–505.

70. Burrell and Morgan, *op. cit.,* p. 365.

71. *Ibid.,* p. 260

72. *Ibid.,* p. 271.

73. Thomas B. Greenfield, "Reflections on Organization Theory and the Truths of Irreconcilable Realities," *Educational Administration Quarterly,* 14 (1978), 1–23; Thomas B. Greenfield, "Organization Theory as Ideology," *Curriculum Inquiry* 9 (1979), 97–112; Thomas B. Greenfield, "Ideas Versus Data: How Can the Data Speak for Themselves?" in G. L. Immegart and W. L. Boyd (eds.), *Problem-Finding in Educational Administration: Trends in Research and Practice* (Lexington, MA: D. C. Heath, 1979), pp. 97–112; and Thomas B. Greenfield, "The Man Who Comes Back Through the Door in the Wall: Discovering Truth, Discovering Self, Discovering Organizations," *Educational Administration Quarterly,* 16 (1980), 26–59. See also Daniel E. Griffiths, "Some Thoughts About Theory in Educational Administration–1975," *UCEA Review,* 17 (1975), 11–13; and Daniel E. Griffiths, "The Individual in Organizations: A Theoretical Perspective," *Educational Administrative Quarterly,* 13 (1977), 1–18.

74. Culbertson, *op. cit.,* p. 3.

75. Thomas B. Greenfield, "Reflections on Organizational Theory," *op. cit.,* p. 1.

76. Donald J. Willower, "Evolution in the Professorship: Past, Philosophy, Future," *Educational Administration Quarterly,* 19 (1983), 179–200. Quotation is on p. 187. For a detailed analysis of several other emerging perspectives on the nature of knowledge and practice in educational administration see Gabriele Lakomski, "Theory, Value and Relevance in Educational Administration," in Fazal Rizvi (ed.), *Working Papers in Ethics and Educational Administration 1985* (Australia: Deaken University Printery, 1985), pp. 35–36; and Donald J. Willower, "Educational Administration: Some Philosophical and Other Considerations," *Journal of Educational Administration,* 19 (1981), 115–139.

77. For the basic tenets of functionalism, see Robert K. Merton, *op. cit.,* pp. 19–84.

78. This metaphor is attributed to Quine. See Karlene H. Roberts, Charles L. Hulin, and Denise M. Rosseau, *Developing an Interdisciplinary Science of Organizations* (San Francisco: Jossey-Bass, 1978), p. 15.

79. John Dewey, *The Sources of a Science of Education* (New York: Horace Liveright, 1929), pp. 8–9.

Chapter 2

Organizational Perspectives

The professional need not be a scientist, but he must be sophisticated enough to make competent use of scientific knowledge. . . .

DOUGLAS MCGREGOR
The Human Side of Enterprise

Although we believe that theoretical knowledge can be applied to schools, doubters exist, so the immediate purpose of this chapter is to illustrate the application of such knowledge. To this end, we present various typologies or taxonomies of organizations first. Then, at a higher level of abstraction, we present one theory of formal organization—compliance theory.

THE SCHOOL AS AN ORGANIZATIONAL TYPE

One way to understand how an organization such as a school functions is to develop *typologies*, or classification schemes. These simply group together organizations with similar characteristics. For example, organizations can be publicly or privately owned, voluntary or involuntary, or devoted to production or dispensing service.

Typologies have several characteristics. First, they allow for a comparative study of organizations as diverse as businesses, schools, prisons, and churches. In addition, they are primarily descriptive rather than explanatory; the organizations are described and compared on the basis of one or more characteristics. Finally, good typologies are logical, consistent with theory, and comprehensive. Several well-known typologies with significant implications for educational organizations illustrate this body of knowledge.

Social Functions Typology

Talcott Parsons proposes a typology of organizations based on the social function that they perform for society.[1] Parson's framework for classifying organizations evolves from his general theory of social systems. Thus, he identified four
types of organizations on the basis of four functional imperatives that face all
social systems. In particular, if society is to survive and develop, it must successfully solve four general problems confronting all social systems:

> *Adaptation* involves the problem of acquiring sufficient resources and
> accommodating to the reality demands of the environment.
> *Goal achievement* reflects the problem of defining and implementing
> goals.
> *Integration* incorporates the problem of maintaining solidarity and
> unity among the members of the system.
> *Latency* consists of the problem of maintaining and renewing the
> motivational and cultural patterns of the system.[2]

Parsons argues that it is useful to classify organizations according to their primary societal function; hence, there are four kinds of formal organizations:

Adaptation.   It is the business concerns of society whose primary responsibility
it is to acquire the necessary resources for a prosperous and healthy society.
Economic organizations create wealth, manufacture goods, and provide services.

Goal attainment.   Political organizations have the complex function of setting
and implementing societal goals. Government agencies and other organizations
that allocate power (e.g., banks) are institutions whose chief function is to
achieve basic societal goals. These are organizations oriented to political goals.

Integration.   The problem of maintaining solidarity among the subunits of
society is left to integrative organizations. These are such organizations as the
courts, legal firms, political parties, and social control agencies; their basic
mission is to coordinate and unify the internal operation of society.

Latency.   The problem of creating, preserving, and transmitting the culture of
a society rests with pattern-maintenance organizations. Public schools, universities, churches, and museums are typical of such organizations. Research universities create culture, and like all educational organizations they transmit and
preserve the cultural heritage. Similarly, churches seek to reinforce and build
commitment to certain cultural objects.

Usefulness of the typology.   The Parsonian typology of organizations is especially valuable because of its crucial significance in social system theory. All
social systems, including society, must adapt to their environment, mobilize
resources to obtain their objectives, coordinate and unify their activities, and

motivate their actors. Although each kind of organization specializes in one of the four functions for society, all organizations themselves must meet all four imperatives if they are to survive and develop. It is not surprising, therefore, that our analyses of schools will often focus on these critical functions.

Parsons argues that the important relation between an organization's goals and the broader societal environment has implications for its support and legitimacy.[3] A goal or objective, from the organization's perspective, is its specialized societal function, from the point of view of a larger society. Consequently, organizations may expect support from society that is consistent with the relative value society places on that particular function. If education represents only a modest value for society, then educational institutions can expect to receive a more limited share of resources than other organizations that are more highly valued by society. Moreover, different societies with different values emphasize and support different organizations. Scott, for example, suggests that in America our values are such that we might expect primary support for economic-oriented organizations, whereas in India, the priority of values more likely would emphasize religious and other pattern-maintenance organizations.[4]

Finally, Parsons suggests that his typology can be used to predict differences in the internal structure and operation of organizations.[5] For example, activities in economic-oriented organizations will be governed by the values of economic rationality—maximizing production with minimum cost. Financial return is the basic symbol of success. In contrast, pattern-maintenance organizations such as schools are expected to rise above financial concerns; economic rationality is not the major force. Educational organizations must depend on the recognition that their services are "good in themselves" rather than on their immediate utility. Education is seen as committed to higher interests that involve self-sacrifice.[6] Thus, school administrators must often generate legitimacy and support for schools in an environment that values short-run utility and financial return rather than the intrinsic merit of learning. Even when the rhetoric for excellence in education escalates, one rarely observes a corresponding movement by society to invest the financial resources necessary for major changes in the educational system.

Prime Beneficiary Typology

In contrast to the societal functions, the typology developed by Peter M. Blau and W. Richard Scott classifies organizations on the basis of *cui bono*—who benefits.[7] Blau and Scott propose four groups of prime beneficiaries and corresponding organizational types: (1) the members or rank-and-file participants in mutual-benefit associations (e.g., unions); (2) the owners, managers, and stockholders in business concerns; (3) the public at large or the society in the commonweal organizations (e.g., the army); and (4) the clients or people who technically are outside the organization but who have regular, direct contact with it in service organizations (e.g., students in schools). Blau and Scott emphasize that prime does not mean sole; other groups or individuals who contribute to the organization receive certain rewards in return. In a school, the students are the prime beneficiaries. But teachers and administrators receive salaries, whereas, for its taxes, the public receives contributions to the general welfare.

Mutual-benefit associations.   The prime beneficiary of these organizations is the membership. Besides labor unions, examples of mutual-benefit associations include political parties, professional associations, clubs, and religious sects. The crucial problem facing this group is one of maintaining membership control through internal democracy. One reason for this problem is member apathy. When members are apathetic, they allow an active minority to run the association. An organization can develop a formal administrative structure that emphasizes efficiency at the cost of democratic controls. To win a teachers' strike, for example, democratic procedures that assure teacher control of union leaders may be set aside. Blau and Scott refer to such centralization as the "problem of oligarchy."

Business concerns.   The prime beneficiaries of this group are the owners of organizations such as industrial firms, wholesale and retail stores, and banks. Their primary goal is making profit. In Blau and Scott's terms, the main problem for business concerns is operating efficiently and achieving maximum gains at minimum cost in order to ensure survival and growth in a competitive market.

Commonweal organizations.   The general public is the prime beneficiary of such commonweal groups, which, besides the military services, include the police and fire departments. The problem commonweal organizations face is maintaining external democratic control. The public must control the ends served by these organizations. In commonweal organizations there must be a balance between an efficient administrative apparatus and democratic control by the public.

Service organizations.   Here, the prime beneficiary is the public that has direct contact with the organization; the basic function of the organization is to provide service to clients. In addition to schools, the group includes hospitals, social work agencies, legal aid societies, prisons, and mental health clinics. The central problem is maintaining the client as the prime beneficiary, not the members and employees. In schools, children are the recipients of basic services, not teachers, administrators, or parents. However, because the clients might not know what is best for themselves, Blau and Scott reason, the clients are vulnerable, subject to exploitation, and dependent on the integrity of the professionals.

Applying Blau and Scott's conclusions about service organizations to the schools situation suggests that educators must avoid two apparent dangers. First, teachers and administrators must not lose sight of the students' welfare, either through concern with their own status or through preoccupation with administrative problems. For example, student welfare suffers when discipline becomes a goal in itself rather than a means to an end. Second, educators must not surrender to the students the power to determine the nature of the educational service. What students want is not necessarily what is in their best interests. Teachers and administrators must not sacrifice their professional beliefs and standards for the sake of popularity. Student wishes must be distinguished from their interests.

School administrators also face potential conflicts between mutual-benefit associations and service organizations. Teachers and administrators work in service organizations—the schools. They also belong to ancillary mutual-benefit associations—the various teachers' unions. Thus the school, as a service organization, and the professional groups, as mutual-benefit associations, interact with each other, have different prime beneficiary groups but involve the same individuals. Educators try to improve their own position as beneficiaries of a union, while striving to help the student beneficiaries of the school—conflicting demands, to say the least.

Client Selectivity: A Typology of Service Organizations

Richard O. Carlson has constructed a typology for service organizations based upon client selectivity, that is, the degree to which clients and organizations can choose membership.[8] He argues that client selection methods can affect the internal functioning of service organizations. In some instances, clients choose to participate, whereas in others, they have no choice. The same relationship holds for the organization: it can select clients in some cases, but others must take all clients who are eligible. This two-way selection brings a yes-or-no decision by either the client or the organization. A quadrant structure similar to the one presented in Figure 2.1 is frequently used to synthesize all possible combinations of relationships. The clients' options run across the top (horizontal axis), and the organizations' options run down the side (vertical axis). This yields the four types or quadrants shown in Figure 2.1, comprising Carlson's service-organization typology.

Does the client have control over participation?

	Yes	No
Yes	Type I	Type III
No	Type II	Type IV

Does the organization have control over selection of clients?

FIGURE 2.1 Typology of service organizations based on who controls the selection process

SOURCE: Adapted from Richard O. Carlson, "Environmental Constraints and Organizational Consequences: The Public School and Its Clients," *NSSE Yearbook: Behavioral Science and Educational Administration,* Part II, Volume 63 (Chicago: University of Chicago Press, 1964), p. 265

TYPE I. In this type the organization and the client decide independently on client participation. Carlson claims that this group contains most of the service organizations in the United States and includes private schools and universities, private medical facilities, and public welfare agencies.

Organizations in this group are called "wild" because they must struggle for survival. In other words, enough clients must voluntarily participate or the organization will cease to exist; quality is therefore imperative for survival.

TYPE II. In this service group the organizations do not select clients; the clients select the organizations. State colleges and universities predominate this portion of the typology.

TYPE III. This is an example of a theoretical group rarely found in reality. Service organizations typically do not exist where the organization has a choice and the clients do not. In the past, the military draft did not qualify because the military was not a service organization.

TYPE IV. This group contains public schools, mental hospitals, and prisons, where neither the client nor the organization has a choice about participation. By legal definition the organization must accept and the client must participate. The grouping of schools and prisons together, based on similar characteristics, is enough to cause educators to reflect on the purposes and processes of the public schools. Carlson designates organizations in this group as "domesticated" because their existence is guaranteed by law. As compared to the "wild" organizations, there is no competition for clients, and the funding level is tied not to quality but to quantity.

The most pressing problem in Type IV organizations is the clients' motivational drives. Clients are forced to participate even if they are not interested in the services of the organization. Children have to attend school if they are within a certain age group. Carlson hypothesizes that the result is adaptive behavior by the domesticated organization and by the clients, whether students, patients, or inmates.

The school organization employs two primary adaptive mechanisms to control the unselected students. It may segregate the so-called bad students either by location or by program, obtaining some measure of control while they remain in school. Examples include vocational schools, ability grouping, many so-called alternative schools, and night schools.

The organization may also provide preferential treatment for the good students. Grades, discipline procedures, and enriched curricula favor the middle-class, good student whose values agree with those of the education system.

Students also have adaptive mechanisms. At one extreme is receptive adaption, where students thrive and enjoy school. The opposite extreme is dropping out. Many students, perhaps most, react somewhere between the extremes and gain enough satisfaction to stay in school. One example of moderate adaptation is situational retirement, which describes the attitude of students who are physically but not mentally present. They have good attendance and deportment, are dependable messengers and errand runners, but are academic underachievers. Another student response is rebellious adjustment, the situation in which the student constantly tests behavioral limits to determine how far he or she can depart from accepted norms. Still another response, the side-payment adaption, describes students who attend school for such related activities as athletics, drama, music, and meeting the opposite sex.

Carlson's conclusions about adaptation in Type IV service organizations have practical, empirical, and theoretical implications. Because the school cannot determine who will participate, it may foster discriminatory organizational policies and negative student behaviors. The question is, to what extent do these adaptive mechanisms exist in the public schools and what are the consequences? The organizational mechanism of segregation and preferential treatment seems to make teacher-student relationships more tolerable but often at a high cost to some students. The student mechanism of side-payment adaptation seems to increase the holding power of schools, thereby reducing dropouts.

Compliance Typology

The final organizational typology to be examined is based upon the concept of compliance. Amitai Etzioni refers to compliance as the relationship between the kinds of power applied to subordinates and their resulting involvement in the organization.[9] Based upon the *means* used to make individuals comply with organizational directives, Etzioni identifies three types of power: coercive, remunerative, and normative.

Coercive power depends on either the actual application or threatened application of physical sanctions. In-school detention, suspension, expulsion, and corporal punishment represent typical coercive methods that can be used to gain student compliance.

Remunerative power rests upon the management of material resources and rewards. Salaries, wages, bonuses, and fringe benefits are common applications of remunerative power used to control the behavior of employees.

Normative power derives from the allocation and manipulation of symbolic rewards and sanctions. It can be exercised by influencing esteem, status, or prestige, through the manipulation of positive symbols such as honors, grades, and recommendations.

Corresponding to each type of power are three reactions to power which Etzioni characterizes in terms of the intensity and direction of the subordinates' involvement. Involvement ranges along a continuum from positive through neutral to negative. Intense positive involvement is called *commitment;* intense, negative involvement is termed *alienation;* and mild positive or mild negative involvement is referred to as *calculation.* The continuum is illustrated in Figure 2.2.

The classifications of power and involvement apply to all individuals in a social system; however, the focus is on lower participants, the subordinates at the lowest level of an organization's hierarchy. Students in schools are at the bottom of the structure and are the lower-level participants.

The type of power applied by the organization to the lower participants and the kind of involvement or response they develop form the basis for Etzioni's

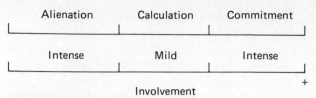

FIGURE 2.2   **Zones of involvement**

compliance typology. Although the three kinds of power and the three kinds of involvement yield a compliance typology with nine categories, three main organizational types are derived (see Figure 2.3). The three diagonal cases shown in the figure which Etzioni calls congruent types, are found most frequently.[10] The compliance relationship is said to be congruent when the nature of participants' involvement in an organization is consistent with the kind of power it applies to them. For instance, coercive power tends to generate alienation; hence, when the match is found, the relationship is congruent.

Each organizational level has its own compliance relationships; however, the predominant compliance pattern of lower-level subordinates is used to classify organizations for two reasons. Compliance is more problematic at that level than at others, and organizations can be more easily distinguished from each other at the lower level. Although the three patterns of compliance exist in virtually all organizations, most organizations rely much more on one pattern than the others; hence, organizations are classified according to their predominant compliance patterns as coercive, utilitarian, or normative. Further within each type, organizations can be ordered in terms of their relative emphasis on the predominant pattern.[11]

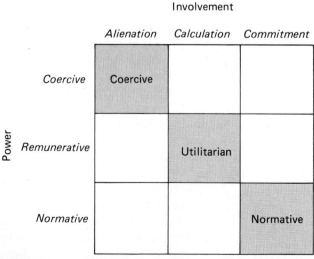

FIGURE 2.3   **Etzioni's compliance types**

Coercive organizations use force or the threat of force as the primary means to control the activities of lower-level subordinates, and the collective response to such power is a high degree of alienation. The two most typical kinds of coercive organizations in contemporary American society are prisons and custodial mental hospitals. Force is the major means of control, and alienation is typical of inmates and patients.

Utilitarian organizations rely mostly on remuneration to gain power over lower-level subordinates, and the response is calculative involvement. Blue-collar industries are typical utilitarian organizations. There are other organizations in this category, however, which may be arranged according to the degree of utilitarianism they exhibit. Following blue-collar industries, which are most strongly utilitarian, are white-collar industries, business unions, farmers' organizations, and peacetime military organizations, each succeedingly less utilitarian.

Normative organizations primarily use normative power to maintain control over lower participants who generally are highly committed to the organization. Typical examples of normative organizations are religious organizations including churches, orders and monasteries, general hospitals, colleges and universities, and social unions. Religious organizations are most "purely" normative because they use normative power more exclusively and receive greater commitment from the rank-and-file participants than others. Public schools, therapeutic mental hospitals and professional organizations, law firms, and newspapers are less purely normative than religious organizations. Although the major means of inducing compliance is still normative in such organizations, secondary means of gaining compliance play important roles. For example, in therapeutic mental hospitals coercion is a significant means of exercising controls, and in professional firms remuneration is important.

Public schools characteristically employ normative power to control students. Typical normative techniques to achieve student compliance include manipulation of grades and honors, sarcasm, reprimands, demerits, teachers' appeals for good behavior, sending students to the office, and modification of peer pressure. Coercion remains a secondary form of control in schools. Although corporal punishment has disappeared in most schools, in-school detention, suspension, and expulsion continue to be used as a last resort. Furthermore, the compulsory nature of public schools virtually guarantees the existence of some uninterested students who resist school. This underlying coercion sets the stage for the development of alienated students and the use of some coercion in schools. Nevertheless, public schools primarily use normative measures to gain student compliance.

Schools can be ordered in terms of their relative emphases on normative and coercive control of students. In those schools where coercion plays a more significant role, students are more alienated.[12] Interestingly, most elementary schools emphasize normative compliance to a greater extent than secondary schools do.[13] But even where student alienation is greatest—for example, in the "P.S. 600s" in New York City, where disciplinary cases are concentrated—coercive actions play less important roles than normative means.[14]

Some Limitations of Typologies

The typologies discussed above as well as those to be presented in subsequent chapters are useful analytic tools. They identify significant features of organizations that are related to the structure and function of organizations. Organizations can vary along many properties. Parsons, Blau-Scott, Carlson, and Etzioni selected the dimensions that they considered most important in explaining organizational behavior. But what organizational behavior? None of the typologies is very effective at explaining goal specificity, interdependency among organizational units, organizational change, or complexity. None was designed to do so. The predictive power of each is limited; in fact, each examines behavior in terms of a different set of dependent or outcome variables.[15]

Parsons' scheme examines the societal functions of each type of organization; his typology is the most abstract and difficult to test. The Blau-Scott formulation, however, is more concrete; it identifies four types of organizations, demonstrates the special problems associated with each, and surveys the research on formal organizations related to each problem. Carlson's typology is most limited. It deals only with service organizations and focuses primarily on schools and other "domesticated organizations." This framework is especially useful for analyzing and generating explanations and research about control in schools (see Chapter 8).

None of the typologies presented in this chapter, or in this book, for that matter, is intended to be a comprehensive and general classification of organizations. Indeed, if these organizational typologies are evaluated by comparing them with typologies in other scientific fields, such as chemistry or biology, they are much less useful. We agree with W. Richard Scott's conclusion that

> one major factor frustrating attempts to classify organizations is that organizations are *open systems*—more open than the systems studied by chemists and biologists. The more open a system, . . . the harder it is to distinguish the system and its environment, the looser the connections among structural elements, and the more autonomous the behavior of the elements—individuals, groups, departments—comprising the system.[16]

It should not be surprising that organizational typologies have less predictive power than biological ones. Nevertheless, some organizational theorists and researchers are turning to biology and ecology for models to develop general organizational typologies.[17]

On balance, however, we believe that a number of extant typologies are useful for both analytic and research purposes. Parsons, Blau-Scott, Carlson, and Etzioni's all provide useful insights for school administrators; however, only Etzioni's compliance typology serves as a basis for the development of a major organizational theory.

COMPLIANCE THEORY

Etzioni uses the concept of compliance—the organizational equivalent of the sociological concept of social order—not only as the basis of an analytical typology, but also as the core variable in the development of a "middle range theory" of organizations.[18] By middle-range theory, he means that comparative statements are made about organizations, but the propositions are not universal; they do not apply to all organizations. Rather, generalizations proposed apply to a certain type of organization—whether normative, utilitarian, or coercive. Further, the propositions that apply to each type of organization also apply, albeit less strongly, to each kind of compliance pattern found within the organization. For instance, generalizations about coerciveness in normative organizations are likely to be found, but they will not apply to the same degree as in coercive organizations. Etzioni uses compliance as the center of his theoretical scheme; all other organizational variables relate to it. To summarize many of the major concepts and generalizations in this scheme, we will explore the relationship between compliance and four organizational variables—goals, elites, communication, and socialization.[19] The theoretical propositions Etzioni derives will be presented and then applied in the school context.

Compliance and Goals

Organizational goals are future states of affairs that the organization is attempting to achieve. Etzioni identifies three types of goals.

Order goals represent the organization's attempts to control the actions of the membership by segregating members or preventing them from engaging in deviant activities. Order-oriented organizations differ in the means that they use to accomplish the goals. As Etzioni notes, "Some merely segregate deviants; others segregate and punish; and still others eliminate deviants altogether."[20]

Economic goals constitute the second type in Etzioni's scheme. These are the dominant goals in an organization when profit is to be made through the production of goods or services.

Culture goals, the third type of goal, project the creation, preservation, application, or reinforcement of symbolic objects collectively known as "culture." Research organizations are primarily devoted to the creation of culture; schools dedicate their efforts to the preservation of culture; professional organizations specialize in the application of culture; and churches reinforce commitment to the symbolic objects the culture accepts.

Etzioni postulates three basic relationships between organizational types and goal types.

1. Organizations with similar compliance structures have similar goals.
2. Organizations with similar goals have similar compliance structures.
3. Three effective combinations of goals and compliance exist.

Coercive organizations tend to have order goals; utilitarian organizations economic goals, and normative organizations culture goals. Theoretically, six other kinds of compliance-goal relationships are possible, but they exist only infrequently because they are less effective. The compliance-goal relationships are summarized in Figure 2.4.

Etzioni's propositions can be applied to schools. If the major goal of the school is to control students and keep them segregated from the general public (i.e., out of the labor market and off the streets), then coercion would be effective. If, however, the school is more concerned with preservation of culture, the transmission of knowledge, and the student social-emotional development, then students must be able to identify with teachers and administrators. Such intense, positive commitment usually develops only through the use of normative power. Coercion makes student identification with the school unlikely. Progressive educational philosophy strongly disapproves of the use of coercive control for precisely this reason.

Classroom order is considered by many teachers a fundamental condition for effective teaching and learning. Indeed, there is a tendency for the means —order or discipline—to become an end in itself. Compliance theory suggests that if the goal is order, then a coercive compliance pattern is most effective in achieving it. For many—teachers and the general public alike—the issue is simple and clear-cut: keep the kids in school, under control, and teach them discipline.

To the professional educator, we argue, the issue is much more complex. Giving and receiving instruction to promote both the cognitive and the social-emotional development of the student are the fundamental purposes of the school. If the purposes could be accomplished without force—if pupils were permitted to learn only what intrigued them in their own way and at their own

Goals

	Order	Economic	Culture
Coercive	Effective		
Utilitarian		Effective	
Normative			Effective

Compliance

FIGURE 2.4 Etzioni's compliance-goal combinations

pace, if good order were not considered a prerequisite to learning, if teachers did not have to be taskmasters, but could simply be helpers and friends—then normative measures would be adequate. But the conditions of compulsory attendance, mass instruction, age grading, state mandates, required courses, and book instruction make it inescapable that some learning will be forced.[21] Nonetheless, teachers who want to intrigue, challenge, and motivate, who want students to identify with school and learning, who are concerned with the total development of the child, and who seek to instill in students that learning is a lifelong process must depend primarily on normative techniques.

Compliance and Elites

Before we analyze the relationship between compliance and elite structures in schools, it is useful to examine the elements of Etzioni's model for the study of elites, that is, leaders and administrators. In particular, attention will be focused upon types of elites, kinds of organizational activity, the nature of relationships among elites and the nature of relationships between elites and subcollectivities (i.e., between elites and various lower-level subgroups within an organization). Table 2.1 summarizes the distinctions Etzioni makes with respect to each of these questions.

Types of elites. Elites are groups of individuals who have power. Etzioni distinguishes elites in terms of the source of their power. Organizational members who derive power exclusively from the office are called *officers;* those who have only personal power are *informal leaders;* and those who have both personal and organizational power are *formal leaders.* Hence, formal organizations contain three types of elites who use different combinations of power to control individual actions.

TABLE 2.1 Etzioni's Model for the Study of Elites

Types of Elites
    Officer—office power only
    Informal leader—personal power only
    Formal leader—office and personal power

Kinds of Organizational Activity
    Instrumental—task oriented
    Expressive—person oriented

Nature of Relations among Elites
    Subordinates versus superordinates
    Cooperation versus antagonism

Nature of Relations between Elites and Subcollectivities
    Subcollectivities—integrated versus segregated
    Elites—amalgamated versus differentiated

Types of activities.   What kind of activities are controlled by organizational elites? Talcott Parsons indicates that all social systems must solve four basic problems: (1) adaptation, (2) goal achievement, (3) integration, and (4) latent pattern maintenance.[22] Within the context of formal organizations, these four basic activities can be collapsed into just two, termed instrumental and expressive activities.[23] *Instrumental activities* are ways of striving for adaptation and goal achievement. Organizations must have structures that enable them to adapt to their environment, mobilize their resources, and continue functioning. Mechanisms are also needed to provide the organization with the means to attain its goals, including structures that specify objectives and allocate, produce, and distribute internal resources. *Expressive activities* deal with the problems of social integration and the maintenance of values. Organizations must find ways to command the loyalties of their members, to motivate them, to coordinate and unify them into a single unit; and to promote consensus on the values that define and legitimize the groups.[24]

Instrumental activity and expressive activity correspond respectively to the goal achievement and group maintenance functions that have been uncovered in the study of groups. Examples of goal achievement activities include initiating action, focusing member attention on goals, clarifying the issues, developing procedural plans, evaluating work quality, and making expert information available. Included among group maintenance activities are keeping interpersonal relations pleasant, giving the minority a chance to be heard, stimulating self-direction, and increasing interdependence among members.[25] As demonstrated in studies of problem-solving groups, there are always some individuals in organizations who press for task accomplishment (instrumental activity) and others who are concerned with the social and emotional needs of the members (expressive activity).[26]

Agreeing with this body of literature, Etzioni concludes that all organizations tend to develop separate elites to control the instrumental and expressive activities. Officers are most likely to control instrumental activities, whereas informal leaders are most likely to control expressive activities.

Relationships among elites.   The elite structure of organizations can also be analyzed in terms of the nature of the relations among elites. Who controls whom? Is interaction among elites antagonistic or cooperative? Etzioni proposes two generalizations. First, in effective organizations those responsible for secondary goals must be subordinate to those responsible for primary goals or means. Second, effective functioning of an organization requires the cooperation of instrumental and expressive elites.

Relationships between elites and subcollectivities.   The relationship between elites and subcollectivities can be examined from several vantage points. To what extent do relationships among lower-level subordinates include members of the elite (i.e., are the two integrated or segregated)? To what degree do subgroups in the organization have a polity, or governing body, of their own (i.e., are the elites differentiated or amalgamated)?

The more coercive the organization, the greater the likelihood that two separate sets of elites will emerge. Officers will tend to control instrumental activities, while informal leaders will direct expressive activities; moreover, the latter group will be subordinate to the former. The two elites may live in open conflict or they may establish an ad hoc spirit of cooperation. For example, in most prisons, members of the elite (officers) are segregated from inmates, and interaction is minimal. The inmates have their own leaders, and generally, correction officers control a rather narrow range of instrumental activities such as work assignments and allocation of some products and services. All expressive activities are directed by informal inmate leaders. Inmates are subordinate to prison officers, who exert overall control, but precarious cooperation, marked by antagonism and conspicuous defiance, exists between the prison officials and inmate leaders. Other organizations such as schools should expect similar relationships if they employ coercive power.

The relationship between the elites and subordinates in normative organizations is the opposite of that of the coercive organization. The more normative the organization, the greater the likelihood that only one highly integrated set of elite members will emerge. Organizational elites will have wide and effective control over both instrumental and expressive activities, and expressive elites will tend to dominate instrumental elites. Cooperation among elites is the norm, and lower-level subordinates and elite members will be integrated, with subordinates accepting organizational control over expressive matters, the major activity of normative organizations.

In utilitarian organizations the relationship between the elite and lower participants lies somewhere in between that which exists in coercive and normative organizations. Employees and the elite are more fully integrated than are inmates and prison officials, but less so than are subordinates and the elite in normative organizations. Most activities in utilitarian organizations are instrumental and are controlled by officers or formal leaders. Expressive activities tend to be informal, limited, and controlled by informal leaders. Relations among elites vary from cooperation to antagonism, but they are rarely as intense as those found in normative and coercive organizations. Instrumental elites typically dominate expressive elites, which assures that the social relations will remain a secondary objective to production.

Elite structure and compliance in schools.   Public schools are normative organizations, but not typical ones; they have many coercive trappings. The theory predicts that variations in power structures and compliance patterns should be reflected in their elite structure of school. The more coercive the school, the more likely that the elite structure will resemble that of a coercive organization. In schools that depend heavily on coercion, sharp cleavages will develop between students and teachers; teachers will act as officers, not leaders; concern will focus on instrumental matters; students will segregate themselves into subcultures with their own leaders controlling expressive activities; the student body may be highly alienated and may display only limited support of school authorities in general and teachers in particular. A caveat is in order, however.

Even in highly coercive schools, normative compliance predominates. Nevertheless, coercion in schools does result in predictable consequences for the elite structure of schools.[27]

If cognitive mastery remains a major objective of the school, then expressive elites (typically students) should be subordinate to instrumental elites (teachers). Even in this instance, however, teachers must gain the student respect, if not admiration, to ensure high student effort. When the goals involve both the cognitive and social-emotional development of students, a more integrated organization is needed, one in which the teachers control both instrumental and expressive activities.

The control of expressive activities by school authorities becomes increasingly difficult as students move from elementary school to middle school to senior high school. Expressive leadership by elementary teachers remains commonplace, but in high schools students usually take over. High schools attempt to establish formal expressive leadership by creating positions to ease the strains produced by instrumental controls; for example, the guidance counselor, band director, and coach represent organizational efforts to formalize expressive leadership.

Schools, then, are not typical normative organizations. Control of instrumental and expressive activities by elites, the nature of relations among elites, and the degree of integration of subcollectivities and elites vary in predictable ways. Although our analysis of the elite structure has focused on students, a similar examination can be made using the teacher as the point of departure. Not surprisingly, the elite structure then begins to resemble that found in utilitarian organizations. For example, as teachers continue to become more militant and as their associations become more unionized, compliance relationships in which they participate are likely to become more like those in a utilitarian organization than like those in a normative one. The theory further predicts that teacher goals will become more economic, the elite structure more segregated, the relationships among teachers and administrators less cooperative, expressive activities less important, and relationships with administrators more instrumental. There will be more emphasis on instrumental communication and socialization, more internal communication blockages, and more limited leadership role for administrators. Administrative leadership will be directed more toward instrumental matters; in fact, expressive leadership attempts by administrators seem increasingly doomed to failure as the compliance relationship between administrators and teachers becomes more utilitarian and less normative.

Compliance and Communication

Etzioni defines organizational communication in terms of two dimensions—substance and direction. With respect to substance, he distinguishes *instrumental communication,* which refers to technical information and knowledge that influences one's cognitive orientation, from *expressive communication,* which deals with attempts to influence attitudes, norms, and values. Preaching, praising, and expressions of rewards are common illustrations of expressive communications to transmit and reinforce proper behavior. With respect to direction, Etzioni distinguishes vertical communication (up or down an organization's hierarchy) from horizontal communication (among members at the same level). Combining the two dimensions results in four communication patterns: vertical instrumental, horizontal instrumental, vertical expressive, and horizontal expressive.

The dominant communication pattern in coercive organizations is vertical instrumental, and it is virtually all downward. Although there is little vertical expressive communication in such organizations, an elaborate system of horizontal expressive communication does develop, often to the detriment of a free flow of information.

Vertical expressive communication is not only common but also essential for the effective performance of normative organizations. In order to achieve their goals, normative organizations must keep the channels of communication open and maintain a steady flow of downward expressive information. Such communication is typically supported by horizontal networks. Although all organizations have upward communication blocks, such impediments are least likely in normative organizations and most likely in coercive ones.

As coercively induced compliance becomes more common in schools, the task of expressive communication becomes more difficult. The successful communication of values in such situations is unlikely. Cognitive mastery may be possible using a system of instrumental communication, but the social-emotional development of the student is impeded by use of coercive means of control. Because some order is requisite for effective group learning, coercion is inescapable, but the need for normative compliance seems clear if teachers are to be successful in the expressive sphere.

Compliance and Socialization

Organizations systematically mold the behavior of personnel and other participants through a variety of procedures and mechanisms that are designed to make goals of individuals correspond with those of the organization. This is the organizational equivalent of socialization. As with communication, Etzioni proposes a two-dimensional scheme for examining socialization in organizations.

Socialization can be viewed first in terms of *substance*. Does the socialization focus on instrumental or expressive activities? The goal *instrumental socialization* is to train individuals to handle technical roles, while *expressive socialization* aims to inculcate norms and values that are necessary for effective role performance. Socialization can also be examined according to the source of the socializing. Socialization can be performed by official agents of the formal organization, or by unofficial members of the organizations. We speak of *formal socialization* when officeholders perform the function, and *informal socialization* when nonofficeholders or subordinates are the source of it. The two aspects of socialization taken together yield four socialization patterns: formal instrumental, informal instrumental, formal expressive, and informal expressive.

Public schools vary in the extent to which expressive or instrumental socialization is used. Generally, schools stress expressive socialization in the primary grades, but as Etzioni cogently observes, "With the movement from grammar school to high school, and high school to college and graduate school, expressive socialization decreases until, in graduate school, instrumental socialization is markedly predominant."[28] In fact, by high school expressive socialization typically becomes chiefly informal and a function of the student peer group, not the teachers.[29] Similarly the use of coercive control over students increases markedly in secondary school.[30] The added use of coercive compliance is predictably associated with much less formal (teacher) and much more informal (student) expressive socialization. Schools that depend on coercive are likely to have little impact on the values, norms, and positive attitudes of students. If public schools are concerned with expressive as well as instrumental socialization, then seeking normative compliance is essential.

As can be seen from our brief review here, compliance theory describes and explains several troublesome issues school administrators face. Organizational power and subordinate involvement combine to influence school goals, leadership patterns, communication processes, and socialization efforts. Reducing the reliance of coercion in schools, for example, may lead educators to many desirable outcomes, including the promotion of high motivation, cognitive and social-emotional learning, positive leadership, and open communications. All are topics that we will discuss throughout the remainder of this book.

SUMMARY

Organizational typologies are useful because they focus attention on important structural and functional similarities between organizations that help explain behavior. Organizations have been distinguished on the basis of societal functions, prime beneficiary, the client-organization selectivity, and compliance pattern. For example, public schools are service organizations in which participation is mandatory and clients are unselected; hence, because some student-clients do not want the services offered, control of students' behavior becomes a central problem.

The concept of compliance is the basis not only of an analytical typology but also of a middle-range theory of organization. Etzioni postulates that normative compliance is consistently related to culture goals, to formal leadership of expressive activities, to cooperation among power holders in organizations, to integration of elites and subgroups, and to expressive communication and socialization. Schools are normative organizations, though they must also use coercion at times. The more prominent coercion is in normative organizations such as schools, the more likely it is that they will adopt order goals. Leadership of expressive activities will then pass from teachers to students, cooperation between students and school officials will be reduced, a separate and antagonistic student subculture will probably develop, and instrumental socialization and communication will dominate expressive processes.

NOTES

1. Talcott Parsons, *Structure and Process in Modern Society* (New York: Free Press, 1960), pp. 16–58. For a similar typology, see Daniel Katz and Robert Kahn, *The Social Psychology of Organizations,* 2nd ed. (New York: Wiley, 1978).
2. Talcott Parsons, Robert F. Bales, and Edward A. Shils, *Working Papers in the Theory of Action* (New York: Free Press, 1953), pp. 183–186.
3. Parsons, *Structure and Process in Modern Societies,* pp. 44–47.
4. W. Richard Scott, *Organizations: Rational, Natural, and Open Systems* (Englewood Cliffs, NJ: Prentice-Hall, 1981), p. 32.
5. Parsons, *Structure and Process in Modern Societies,* pp. 47–56.
6. *Ibid.,* p. 48.
7. Peter M. Blau and W. Richard Scott, *Formal Organizations: A Comparative Approach* (San Francisco: Chandler, 1962), pp. 42–58.
8. Richard O. Carlson, "Environment Constraints and Organizational Consequences: The Public School and Its Clients," *Behavioral Science and Educational Administration,* The Sixty-third Yearbook of the National Society for the Study of Education, Part II (Chicago: University of Chicago Press, 1964), pp. 262–278.
9. See Amitai Etzioni, *A Comparative Analysis of Complex Organizations* (New York: Free Press, 1961).
10. *Ibid.* See also Richard H. Hall, J. E. Hass, and Norman Johnson, "An Examination of the Blau-Scott and Etzioni Typologies," *Administrative Science Quarterly,* 12 (1967), 118–139.
11. Etzioni, *op. cit.,* pp. 23–67.
12. Wayne K. Hoy, "Dimensions of Student Alienation and Characteristics of Public High Schools," *Interchange,* 3 (1972), 38–51.
13. Donald J. Willower, Terry I. Eidell, and Wayne K. Hoy, *The School and Pupil Control Ideology,* Monograph No. 24 (University Park, PA: Penn State Studies, 1967).
14. Etzioni, *op. cit.,* p. 48.
15. For a critical analysis of typologies and taxonomies, see William B. Carper and William E. Snizek, "The Nature and Types of Organizational Taxonomies: An Overview," *Academy of Management Review,* 5 (1980), 65–75. See also Peter K. Mills and Newton Marguilies, "Toward a Core Typology of Service Organizations," *Academy of Management Review,* 5 (1980), 255–256.
16. Scott, *op. cit.,* p. 50.
17. The most ambitious attempt to develop a general organizational classification is Bill McKelvey, *Organizational Systematics: Taxonomy, Evolution, Classification* (Berkeley: University of California Press: 1982). See also Howard E. Aldrich, *Organizations and Environments* (Englewood Cliffs, NJ: Prentice-Hall, 1979); and Michael T. Hannan and John Freeman, "The Population Ecology of Organizations," *American Journal of Sociology,* 82 (1977), 929–964.
18. Etzioni, *op. cit.*
19. Etzioni's theory is much more comprehensive, and the reader is urged to study the entire theory. The theory has generated a large body of empirical work that Etzioni has reviewed and summarized in the revised edition of

his work. See Amitai Etzioni, *A Comprehensive Analysis of Complex Organizations,* Revised and Enlarged (New York: Free Press, 1975).

20. Etzioni, *op. cit.* p. 73.
21. Willard Waller, *The Sociology of Teaching* (New York: Wiley, 1932), p. 355.
22. Talcott Parsons, *Structure and Process in Modern Societies,* pp. 16–96, and Talcott Parsons, Robert F. Bales, and Edward A. Shils, *Working Papers in the Theory of Action,* pp. 183–186.
23. *Ibid.,* and see also Etzioni, 1961, *op. cit.,* pp. 91–93.
24. Blau and Scott, *op. cit.,* p. 39.
25. Dorwin Cartwright and Alvin Zander (eds.), *Group Dynamics* (New York: Harper & Row, 1968), pp. 306–308.
26. Robert Bales and P. Slater, "Role Differentiation in Small Decision-making Groups," in Talcott Parsons *et al.* (eds.), *Family, Socialization, and Interaction Process* (New York: Free Press, 1955). See also Robert Bales, "In Conference," *Harvard Business Review,* 32 (1954), 41–49.
27. James S. Coleman, *The Adolescent Society* (New York: Free Press, 1961).
28. Etzioni, 1961, *op. cit.,* p. 145.
29. Coleman, *op. cit.*
30. Willower, Eidell, and Hoy, *op. cit.*

Chapter 3

The School as a Social System

There is little point in general models if they do not give rise to specific conceptual derivations and empirical applications which illuminate, in however modest a degree, significant day-to-day practices. . . .

JACOB W. GETZELS *et al.*
Educational Administration as a Social Process

The system concept has a rich history in the physical as well as the social sciences. Indeed, as both Alfred N. Whitehead[1] and George C. Homans[2] have observed, the idea of an organized whole, or system, occurring in an environment is fundamental and essential to science. The notion of a social system is a general one. It can be applied to social organizations that are carefully and deliberately planned (formal) or to those that emerge spontaneously (informal).

The school is a system of social interaction; it is an organized whole comprised of interacting personalities bound together in an organic relationship.[3] As a social system, it is characterized by an interdependence of parts, a clearly defined population, differentiation from its environment, a complex network of social relationships, and its own unique culture. As with all formal organizations, analysis of the school as a social system calls attention to both the planned and unplanned—the formal and informal—aspects of organizational life.

SOCIAL SYSTEM

A *social system* is a bounded set of elements (subsystems) and activities that interact and constitute a single social entity.[4] This statement implies that a social system is creative because by definition it has properties and purposes over and above the component parts and relationships. In a school, for example, educated individuals are created. For our purposes, Marvin Olsen defines a social system more specifically.[5] A social system is a model of organization that possesses a distinctive total unity (creativity) beyond its component parts; it is distinguished from its environment by a clearly defined boundary; it is composed of subunits, elements, and subsystems that are at least interrelated within relatively stable patterns (equilibria) of social order. Note this last statement contains several assumptions to be discussed later. Figure 3.1 and the following discussion of each component of the preceding definition-boundaries, equilibria, elements, along with the basic assumptions and synthesis of a basic model, should help increase understanding of the school as a social system.

Boundaries

A given social system such as the school building in Figure 3.1 must be bounded in some manner to separate it from the environment. The school building, as the unit of analysis, coincides with a real unit within the school district. Equally good examples would be the complete school district, a classroom, or the central

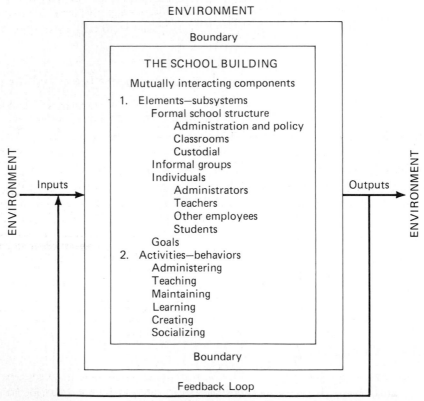

FIGURE 3.1 A graphic illustration of the social systems definition using a school building as the unit of analysis

office. A social-systems model can be a unit of any size that is of analytic value. When using social-systems analysis, it is important to define carefully the boundaries and the unit of analysis.

The environment is anything outside the boundaries of the unit of analysis that (1) affects the attributes of the internal components and (2) is changed by the social system itself (see Chapter 4 for a detailed consideration of external environment). The school district policies and administrators, other school buildings, and the community are some of the objects constituting the environment in Figure 3.1. When the system has no exchange with the environment, it is closed. Normally, however, the boundaries are partially open. The environment contributes students, materials, energy, information, and cultural values; the school returns educated persons, information, and entertainment.

Although organizational environment is typically understood to refer to conditions external to the organization, the clear separation of the organization from its environment is virtually impossible when applied to open systems such as schools. Schools incorporate aspects of environment. Most of the techniques, skills, and knowledge are not invented by the school; they are brought within its boundaries and become part of the system. Likewise, beliefs, norms, rules, and understandings are not only "out there" but also are part of the organization. As Scott cogently concludes, "Participants, clients, constituents all participate in and are carriers of culture. Thus institutional environments are notoriously invasive."[6]

In practice, officials attempt to control the openness of the school. For example, only appropriate clientele is allowed into the school building, and people from the street are locked out. Special efforts, however, such as open houses and athletic events, are held to encourage the district patrons to enter the school building. The result is a partially controlled exchange that modifies both the system's internal and environmental components. This mutual control and exchange mechanism is explained in social system models as homeostasis, feedback, and equilibrium.

Homeostasis, Feedback, and Equilibrium

Homeostasis is a process in which a group of regulators acts to maintain a steady state among the system components. A biological analogy illustrates the concept: when an organism moves from a warm environment to a cold one, homeostatic mechanisms trigger reactions to maintain body temperature. Similarly, in a school building, crucial elements, or subsystems, and activities must be protected so that overall stability is maintained.

The triggering mechanism in the school social system (Figure 3.1) is the *feedback loop*. This mechanism ensures that a portion of the school's behavior and the internal and external environments' reactions to that behavior are filtered back into the system as input. Formal communication structures—PTA and various advisory councils—and informal political contacts are established inside and outside the school building to provide feedback to the school.

Equilibrium exists when the social and biological parts of the system maintain a constant relationship to each other so that no part changes its position or relation with respect to all other parts. As administrators are well aware, disruptive stresses upset this equilibrium and create temporary periods of disequilibrium. A community group may demand that a course such as sex education be deleted. This causes disequilibrium, but the system either changes itself or neutralizes the disruptive forces impinging on it, and restores equilibrium. Because all parts of the social system, a school building in our case, are related, a change in any one part necessarily produces a corresponding change in every other part. Thus, equilibrium is reestablished or maintained. It is easier to understand equilibrium processes if the several implicit assumptions about social systems are made explicit, if elements of the system and its activities are discussed, and if we make some generalizations.

Basic Assumptions for Social-System Models

An assumption is a statement that is taken for granted. In our discussion of social systems, we have made several implicit assumptions. Let us now make these and others explicit. We have gleaned these assumptions from the literature, but the primary sources are Joseph A. Litterer,[7] Jacob W. Getzels and Egon G. Guba,[8] and Charles E. Bidwell.[9]

1. Social systems are comprised of interdependent parts, characteristics, and activities that contribute to and receive from the whole. When one part is affected, a ripple goes through the social system. For example, the principal is confronted by students who want to be included in faculty decision making. The principal is affected and directly or indirectly affects the faculty. The students and principal are using an internal feedback loop.
2. Social systems are goal-oriented, and indeed they may have a multiplicity of goals. In a school building, student learning and control are just two of many goals. The central goal of any school system, according to Bidwell, is the preparation of its students for adult roles.
3. Social systems are peopled. People act in the roles of administrators, teachers, students, custodians, and so forth.
4. Social systems are structural. Different components are needed to carry out specific functions and allocate resources. School systems are to some degree bureaucratic.
5. Social systems are normative. Each person within them is expected to behave in a particular manner. Formal rules and regulations and informal guides prescribe appropriate behavior. In Bidwell's terms, school social systems have role structures that contain a fundamental dichotomy between student and staff roles.
6. Social systems are sanction bearing. The norms for behavior are enforced with reward and punishment. Formal mechanisms include expulsion, suspension, termination, and promotion systems. Informal sanctions include the use of sarcasm and ostracism.
7. Social systems are open systems. The environment typically supplies

inputs to the system; there are exchanges between the system and its environment. Too often organizations are viewed as closed systems, and there is a tendency to disregard the organization's dependency on its broader environment. Schools are affected by the values of the community, by politics, and by history. In brief, they are affected by outside forces.

8. Social systems are conceptual and relative. The concept of social systems is a general one that applies to social organizations regardless of size or purpose. For one purpose, a primary group, such as a family or club, may be considered a social system. For other purposes, a formal organization such as a school system may be taken as a social system, with the various component schools, classrooms, clubs, and teams as subsystems. All formal organizations are social systems, but all social systems are not formal organizations.

These assumptions suggest that a school consists of several subsystems. In Figure 3.1, the formal school structure, informal groups, goals, and individuals comprise these components.

Elements of a Social System

Figure 3.2 is an extraction and elaboration of the elements, or subsystems pictured earlier in Figure 3.1. The basic formulation of a social system presented here comes from Getzels and Guba.[10] According to their model, social behavior is a function of the interaction of role and personality. Two basic elements of social systems model include (1) the institutional, defined in terms of certain roles and expectations, which are organized to fulfill the goals of the system, and (2) the individual, defined in terms of the personalities and needs of the system actors, who provide the energy to achieve the goals. We suggest that behavior in social systems can be understood more clearly by analyzing it in terms of the interaction of these two major elements. With this brief overview and recalling the previous social system's assumptions—that systems are composed of interdependent parts, are goal-oriented, structural, normative, sanction bearing, open, and conceptual—we can now discuss each major element or subsystem.

Institutional element. All social systems have some activities and functions that are accomplished in a fairly stable fashion. For example, if we conceive of society itself as a social system, then the routine and imperative functions of educating, protecting, and governing are performed by the educational, legal, and governmental institutions. Regardless of the nature of the social system, as patterns of behavior become regular and routine, they are said to be institutionalized, and the structures established to perform these institutionalized functions for the social system are called *institutions*.

Roles and expectations are necessary to the functioning of institutions. According to Getzels and Guba, roles are most important and are defined in

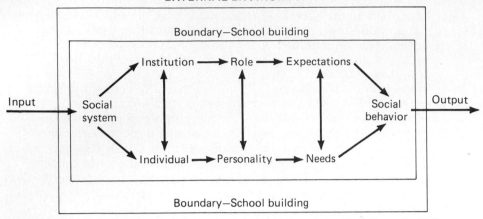

FIGURE 3.2 **Structural elements (subsystems) using the Getzels-Guba systems model**

SOURCE: Adapted from Jacob W. Getzels and Egon G. Guba, "Social Behavior and the Administrative Process," *The School Review,* 65 (1957), 429.

part by expectations. The following characteristics describe the nature of roles:

1. Roles represent positions and statuses within the institution. In a school, these would include the positions of principal, teacher, and student as well as custodial positions.
2. Roles are defined in terms of expectations or normative rights and duties of the position. The expectations specify the appropriate behavior for a specific position. A teacher, for instance, has the right to plan learning experiences for students and has the duty to present them in a pedagogically effective manner. When someone who assumes a role behaves in a manner consistent with the institutional demands of the position, the individual is performing the role. Roles are the institutional blueprints for action, the institutional givens of the office.
3. Roles are variable. Some expectations are critical and mandatory; others are more flexible. Many roles are not precisely prescribed; in fact, the role expectations associated with most positions are wide ranging. It is this range of freedom that makes it feasible for teachers with quite different personalities to perform the same roles without undue tension or conflict.[11]
4. Roles derive their meaning from other roles in the system and in this sense are complementary. It is difficult, if not impossible, to define either the role of student or that of teacher in a school without specifying the relationship of teacher to student.

The institutional element of the social system, then, explains the behavior of individuals in terms of dominant roles and expectations aimed at meeting the goals of the system. The normative approach reflects a distinctly sociological analysis of group behavior. Getzels and Guba have termed the institutional aspects of the system *the nomothetic dimension* (Institution → Roles → Expectations).

Individual element. The other element in the Getzels-Guba model is the individual. The model assumes that social systems are composed of personalities. Although people occupy roles and positions in the school, they are not simply actors devoid of unique needs. It is possible, at a conceptual level, to describe and to predict behavior in a social system solely in terms of positions, roles, and expectations; in fact, that is precisely what we have done thus far in our description of the institutional dimension. However, no two teachers, administrators, or students in the same situation behave exactly the same way. They have different personalities and needs that are reflected in their behavior. Individuals shape the roles that they occupy with their own styles of behavior. For a more complete understanding of behavior in social systems, it is necessary to know about the personalities that occupy the roles, offices, and statuses within the system. What are the underlying need structures that motivate behavior? Such analysis calls attention to the psychological aspects of behavior in the social system.

Just as we analyzed the institution in terms of role and expectations, it is useful at the conceptual level to examine the individual in terms of personality and needs. Getzels and Guba define personality as the dynamic organization within the individual containing need dispositions that govern idiosyncratic reactions to the environment. Personality is defined here in terms of an internal motivational system, not behavior. Yet, it is a motivational system that is dynamic because it is changing, self-regulating, and interacting with its environment. Since no two people have exactly the same motivational system, personalities are unique; hence, variety in behavior is the rule, not the exception.

Needs refer to internal forces that determine the direction and goals of behavior. The needs for achievement, security, acceptance, and expression strongly affect behavior. An individual seeking a given position or membership in an organization often displays such needs. Individuals have a complex set of needs and desires that cause them to behave differently within similar situations. For example, not all students react the same way to open classrooms because they have different needs for structure in performing tasks. Similarly, not all teachers and administrators react the same way to changes in their jobs because of different needs for achievement, domination, security, and so forth.

Needs affect not only the goals an individual will attempt to achieve but also the way an individual perceives the environment. Getzels and his colleagues maintain the following:

A person with a high need for dominance tends to structure the environment in terms of its opportunities for ascendance; a person with a high need for affiliation in terms of its opportunities for sociability; and a person with a high need for cognizance, in terms of its opportunities for under-standing.[12]

For a teacher of the first type, the school is primarily a vehicle to rise in the hierarchy; for the second, it is a social milieu to nurture friendships; and for the third, it is primarily a center of learning.

Finally, just as expectations are patterned and interrelated, so too are needs. Abraham Maslow has identified five basic levels of needs and arranged them in a hierarchy of "prepotency" (see Chapter 7). The more prepotent a need, the earlier it asserts itself in human consciousness and requires responsive behavior. Maslow argues that the higher-level needs of fulfillment, esteem, and belong-ingness become activated as the lower level needs of safety, security, and survival become satisfied.

In brief, the individual element of the social system explains behavior of individuals in psychological terms with reference to the unique personalities and needs of individuals (Individual → Personality → Needs). This personal di-mension of the social system is known as the *idiographic dimension*.

The Basic Model

Thus far, the analysis has focused on two basic elements of social systems—the institutional and the individual. Taken separately, each explains a portion of the behavior in social systems in terms of sociological or psychological concepts. Together, they provide the basis of a sociopsychological theory of group behav-ior in which a dynamic transaction between roles and personality interact. Figure 3.2 provides a summary of the basic model.

Behavior (B) in the system is explained in terms of the interaction be-tween role (R), defined by expectations, and personality (P), the internal need structure of an individual; that is, $B = f(R \times P)$. The proportion of role and personality factors that determine behavior varies with the particular system, role, and personality. In rigid bureaucratic structures, behavior is more likely to be determined by role factors rather than personality characteristics. In less formal social systems, roles are more likely to be secondary considerations while personality attributes are more important. The interplay and blending of role and personality vary widely from system to system; in some systems there is a balance between the two elements; in others, roles submerge per-sonality or vice versa. In virtually all social systems, however, behavior is de-termined by *both* the needs of the institution and the needs of the individ-ual.

The social system operates within and interacts with a larger environment. The inputs from the environment affect both the institution and the individual; consequently, the environment influences behavior within the system, which in turn contributes to system outcomes.

Formal Organization as a Social System: An Expanded and Refined Model

Because of the generality of the social-system model, a wide range of analyses of a variety of social units is possible. It is useful, however, to reformulate the model in order to focus specifically on the determinants of behavior in formal organizations.[13] Although some of the basic elements remain essentially the same, the model can be refined and expanded to fit the distinctive features of formal organizations.

When the accomplishment of an objective requires collective effort, individuals often set up an organization designed to coordinate the activities and to furnish incentives for others to join them in this purpose. Such organizations —explicitly established to achieve certain goals—are formal organizations. It should not be surprising, therefore, that organizational goal is a key element of formal organizations, one that deserves careful attention in attempts to explain organizational behavior.

The fact that a social unit has been formally established does not mean that all activities and interactions of its members conform strictly to the official blueprint. Regardless of the official goals and elaborate bureaucratic expectations, members have their own individual needs and values. Moreover, as individuals interact in a work group, emergent patterns of social life develop— that is, the group develops its own informal practices, values, norms, and social relations.

Thus, behavior in formal organizations is influenced not only by institutional and individual elements but also by goal and work group elements. Further, all the elements and interactions within the system are constrained by important forces from the environment. Finally, formal organizations as social systems must solve the basic problems of adaptation, goal achievement, integration, and latency if they are to survive and prosper. The model of formal organization that we are proposing takes all of these factors into consideration. We begin by examining internal elements of the system—the institution, individual, work group, and goal—and then discuss the impact of the environment on the school and its outcomes.

Institution

The institutional dimension of an organization (Institution→Role→Expectations) refers primarily to bureaucratic expectations of the positions within the organization. From a vast array of vague and contradictory expectations, formal organizations select a few bureaucratic expectations that are reasonably consistent with the organization's goals. As Max G. Abbott notes, "These expectations, which ideally are *functionally specific* and *universalistic,* are generally formalized and codified and adopted as the official rules of the organization."[14] The process of selecting and codifying the *relevant* bureaucratic expectations for a given position mitigates potential conflicts and pressures arising from a role incumbent's other affiliations, both within and outside the organization.

Bureaucratic expectations, therefore, may be better as explanatory concepts than are role expectations. They include rules and regulations or policy, delineate such things as arrival times, building assignments, and job descriptions. Specialization, the expectation that employee behavior will be guided by expertise, complements the rules and regulations. Thus, a teacher is expected to behave in appropriate ways based on the school's rules and the expertise demanded by the instructional job. This institutional element of the school as a formal organization is conceptualized in the following manner.

$$\text{Bureaucracy} \rightarrow \begin{array}{c} \text{Hierarchy of authority} \\ \text{Rules and Regulations} \\ \text{Specialization} \end{array} \rightarrow \text{Expectations} \rightarrow \text{Behavior}$$

Individual

Just as not all expectations are relevant for the analysis of organizational behavior, not all of the need dispositions of an individual's personality are relevant to organizational performance. What are those facets of personality that are most instrumental in determining an individual's role performance? Work motivation constitutes the single most relevant set of needs for employees in formal organizations. We will elaborate extensively on work motivation and needs later, but for our present purposes, the individual element is conceptualized in the following fashion:

$$\text{Individual} \rightarrow \text{Personality and Especially Work Motivation} \rightarrow \text{Needs} \rightarrow \text{Behavior}$$

Behavior (B) is a function (f) of the interaction between bureaucratic role expectations (R) and the relevant personality needs (P) of the organizational member [$B = f (R \times P)$]. For example, the evaluation of the teaching staff is affected by district policy as well as by the principal's own needs. The rules and regulations state that the principal is expected to evaluate each teacher at given intervals with a specified evaluation instrument. The principal acts as a result of this policy. Each principal's behavior differs in the evaluation meetings, perhaps because of motivation needs. One building administrator who has a great personal desire for social acceptance from the teachers may treat these sessions as an opportunity for friendly socializing rather than for evaluating. But another principal lacking such a need for social acceptance, may follow the book and remain analytical in the evaluation. The two principals are affected by both elements, but the first is more influenced by the personality and the second by the bureaucratic role expectations. The ratio of bureaucratic expectations to individual needs, which at least partially determines behavior, will vary with the specific type of organization, the specific job, and the specific person involved. Figure 3.3 presents the general nature of this interaction pictorially. Vertical line A represents a hypothetical situation in which the proportion of behavior controlled by the bureaucratic structure is relatively large, while line B (at the right) represents the situation in which behavior is primarily controlled by individual needs.

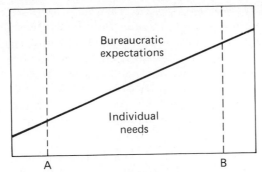

FIGURE 3.3 Interaction of bureaucratic and individual elements affecting social behavior

Military organizations commonly are considered to be represented by line *A*—more bureaucratic control—whereas research and development organizations are better represented by line *B*. Most schools probably fall between these two extremes. Free, open-concept, or Montessori schools would be close to line *B*. Church-related schools are typically thought to be closer to line *A*. Where do administrators and students fall in this regard? Individuals differ; some tend toward line *B*—free spirits—and some toward line *A*—bureaucrats. In our example of the two principals in evaluation sessions, the first with a high need for social acceptance would be near line *B* and the second closer to line *A*.

Work Group

In formal organizations the work group is the mechanism by which bureaucratic expectations and individual needs interact and modify each other. There is a dynamic relationship between bureaucratic role demands, and individual needs emerge as people are brought together in the workplace. The work group develops its own informal status structure and culture, its social organization. This informal organization, with its important group norms becomes another powerful force that affects organizational behavior. That force can be schematically represented as follows.

Work Group → Informal Organization → Norms → Behavior

In a school, peer pressure among teachers has a significant impact on behavior. The group with its informal organization and norms influences behavior for several reasons. Communication of feelings is easy among peers, especially friends. Informal groups maintain cohesiveness and a feeling of personal integrity, self-respect, and independent choice. Since interactions in the informal organization are neither impersonal nor dominated by organizational authority, they furnish opportunities for the individual to maintain his or her personality against the attempts of the bureaucratic organization to submerge, if not destroy it.[15] Members receive important rewards from the group, and group norms are significant in guiding their behavior. For example, accepted informal procedures, not formal rules, may develop among the teachers for disciplining or controlling students; in fact, the custodial informal norms for controlling students become the criteria for judging "effective" teaching in many schools. Good control is equated with good teaching.

Goals

Organizational goals are future states of affairs that the organization is attempting to realize; they are images of desired ends, which organizational members attempt to achieve through the performance of their job.[16] Although relatively easy to define in general terms, the notion of organizational goal is complex. There are status goals and actual goals, official and unofficial goals, abstract and concrete goals, individual and organization goals, and imperative and operational goals. Moreover, goals have different origins and functions; they are used to direct, to motivate, to evaluate, and sometimes to justify behavior.[17]

Rational-systems theorists view organizational goals as essential to understanding and explaining behavior; natural-systems analysts see them as basically irrelevant to organizational behavior. In our view, the concept of goal is a useful analytic tool for the analysis of behavior in schools. In some schools performance will be strongly influenced by organizational goals; in others, the linkage between goals and behavior will be loose. We suspect, for example, that in many elementary schools teacher performance will be more closely related to school goals than in secondary ones. This is in part a function of the greater complexity and professionalization of secondary schools compared with elementary ones.

Herbert Simon has strongly urged the distinction between individual goals, which explain decisions of people to participate and remain in organizations, and organizational goals, which are expected to guide the decisions of participants. Simon prefers to call the former personal motives to distinguish them from organizational goals. In proposing this analytic separation, Simon is well aware of the fact that personal motives at times intrude on organizational goals, but nonetheless, he argues the distinction is valuable. He suggests, for example, that many requirements organizations impose on their members are unaffected by personal motives. Organizational goals, then, are sets of constraints imposed by the organization, which have only an indirect relation with the personal motives of participants.

Occasionally organizational goals are set by one powerful actor at the top of the hierarchy; less frequently, goals are consensually defined by all participants who share in goal setting; most frequently by far, however, goals are set by a process of negotiation that occurs among dominant coalitions.[18] Coalitions are groups of individual who share specific interests. W. Richard Scott describes the negotiation process as follows:

> Each coalition will attempt to impose its preferences (goals) on the larger system, but in the typical case, no single coalition will be able to determine

completely what goals are to be pursued. Coalition members seek out other groups where interests are similar as allies, and then negotiate with those groups whose interests are divergent but whose participation is necessary. One coalition will make a side-payment to another to secure its cooperation. . . . Each coalition whose interests must be taken into account helps to define the goals of the organization. Each negotiated agreement provides guidance to the organization and places constraints on what may be regarded as an acceptable course of action.[19]

All coalitions strong enough to impose constraints on organizational decision making are involved in goal setting; hence, goals are complex sets of constraints. This complexity is one reason why some will argue that organizations have no goals. Simon explains:

> If we use the phrase organizational goals broadly to denote the constraint sets, we will conclude that organizations do, indeed, have goals (widely shared constraint sets). If we use the phrase narrowly to denote the generators (preferences held by individual coalition participants used to propose satisfactory alternatives), we will conclude there is little communality of goals among the several parts of large organization.[20]

The concept of a dominant coalition suggests that individuals and groups with different interests and agendas bargain to form the basis for common action. Moreover, individuals do not have equal power in decision making; the preferences of some are more important than others. Although individuals and groups bring their own preferences and interests into the organization, organizations are more than arenas where existing interests coalesce: they are settings where new interests are created.[21]

Environmental forces have their impact on dominant coalitions. As new and powerful forces emerge, the organization creates offices and mechanisms to deal with them. Scott suggests that as environments become complex and turbulent, the dominant coalition changes to incorporate more and different specialists capable of managing the boundary problems of the system. And as the composition of membership of the dominant coalition changes, the goals of the organization change to reflect these power shifts.[22]

As we proposed earlier, goals have different functions. From a rational perspective, goals provide guidance by supplying criteria to generate and select among alternatives.[23] Moreover, they provide criteria to evaluate the efficacy of decisions and outcomes. From a natural-systems perspective, however, goals serve primarily as bases to motivate and justify behavior. Chester Barnard, for example, argues that goals are a source of identification and motivation for members.[24] And Philip Selznick notes that goals can be used to mobilize support in the environment.[25] Finally, behavior does not always precede goals; consequently, goals may often serve as a basis for justifying rather than guiding behavior. James March cogently observes, "Human choice is at least as much a process for discovering goals as for acting on them.[26]

Scott makes the important point that types of goal statements may not coincide closely not only because they serve different functions but because they have different origins. Abstract, inspirational goals are likely to be set at the institutional level, which seeks to legitimate organizational action to various publics. Administrators are likely to emphasize the cognitive function of goals because it is a basic way for them to shape and direct subordinate performance. Subordinates will be most likely to employ goals statements as justification for their past performance when called upon to explain their behavior. Finally, evaluative goals are most likely to be used by supervisors who are expected to assess subordinate performance and by external groups which depend on the outcomes of the organization.[27]

There are many ways to distinguish among types of organizational goals. For our purposes, the common distinction of official, operative, and operational is most useful.[28] It draws attention to the fact that goals vary in origin, purpose, and specificity.

Official goals are formal statements of purpose formulated by the administration to articulate the mission of the organization. In schools, for example, such statements are developed by the board of education and superintendent and appear in official school publications such as policy manuals and faculty handbooks. Official goals are usually abstract and inspirational—"to educate each student to the best of his or her ability to learn," or "to prepare good citizens for a democratic society." Virtually everyone agrees that these are worthy goals. Thus, they provide the bases for securing support and legitimacy from the public rather than guiding administrative and teacher behavior.

Operative goals reflect the true intentions of the organization. They mirror the actual tasks and activities of the school, irrespective of what officials claim. Official goals, therefore, may be operative or inoperative depending on the extent to which they accurately reflect current educational practices in the school. Some operative goals are widely published (e.g., to improve the reading level of all elementary school children); many are not (e.g., to teach children discipline and order). Less attractive operative goals are typically not publicized; in fact, idealistic, abstract official goals often may be used as a cover for less appealing operative ones.

Operational goals are usually formal statements of expectations that carry with them the specific criteria and evaluation procedures used to measure their achievement. Schools spell out some of their goals in operational terms—for example, "Ninety percent of the students will pass the statewide minimum basic skills test in reading and mathematics."

Behavior in schools is influenced by goals. Official goals serve to justify and legitimate school activities as well as to generate commitment and motivate participants. Operative goals reflect the actual functioning of the school and probably both direct and justify school behavior. Operational goals are formal statements used by the organization to direct and evaluate school activities. Increasingly, as state departments of education try to shape and control education, more emphasis will be placed on operational goals; they provide the criteria and means to evaluate performances, participants, and programs. The goal element of our framework is conceptualized in the following manner:

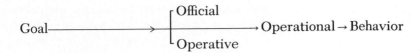

The suggested modifications of the elements originally shown in Figure 3.2 and the new elements are now presented in Figure 3.4. The institutional and individual elements have been recast in less abstract terms, and the elements of work group and goal have been added to the model; hence, the concepts of bureaucracy, informal organization, work motivation, and organizational goals are postulated to be major elements determining the collective and individual behavior in formal organizations such as schools.

Environment

In general, we have defined the environment as everything that is outside the organization, but unlike physical systems, social systems are open; hence, the boundaries are much more ambiguous and the environment more intrusive. There is no doubt that the environment is critical to the organizational functioning of schools. It is the system's source of energy. It provides resources, values, technology, demands, and history—all of which place constraints and opportunities on organizational action.

Which features of the environment are most salient for constraining behavior in schools? There is no quick or simple answer. Both broad and specific environmental factors influence the structure and activities of schools. Larger social, legal, economic, political, demographic, and technological trends have

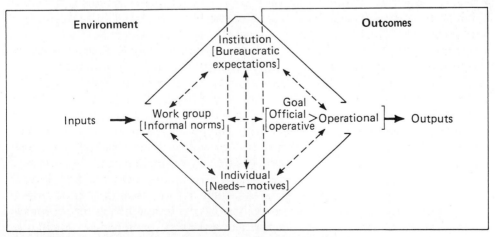

FIGURE 3.4 **Elements of an organizational system**

a potentially powerful impact on schools, but the effects of such general environmental forces are by no means clear. In contrast, interested constituencies and stakeholders such as parents, taxpayers, unions, regulatory agencies, colleges and universities, state legislatures, accrediting agencies, and educational associations have more immediate and direct effects on schools. But again the results are not certain.

The response of the school to environmental factors is conditioned by the degree of uncertainty, the degree of clustering, and the degree of scarcity in the environment. School decision makers monitor the environment for information, and their *perceptions* determine to a large degree the future directions of the organization. Schools, like all organizations, attempt to reduce uncertainty and control their environments; therefore, administrators often resort to strategies to minimize external effects. Moreover, if the groups and organizations of the environment are highly clustered, then the school is faced with a potent set of demands and constraints, and the result will likely be compliance. Finally, schools compete in an environment made up of various resource pools. If resources of a particular kind are scarce, then the internal structure and activities will develop in ways that will facilitate their acquisition.

In brief, schools are open systems that are affected by general and specific external forces. Although there is basic agreement on the importance of the environment, its complexity makes analysis difficult. Nonetheless, we need to consider what factors individually and in relation to others create the basic external demands, constraints, and opportunities to which schools respond. We will return to a detailed analysis of the environment in Chapter 4.

Outcomes

A school, then, can be thought of as a set of elements—goals, individuals, informal and bureaucratic arrangements; however, behavior in organizations is not simply a function of its elements and environmental forces; it is a function of the *interaction* of the elements. Thus, organizational behavior is the result of the dynamic relationship among its elements. More specifically, behavior is a function of the interaction of bureaucratic expectations, individual motives, informal norms, and organizational goals as constrained by environment forces. To understand and predict the behavior in schools, it is useful to examine the six pairs of interactions among the elements in terms of their consistency. We posit a congruence postulate: *Other things being equal, the greater the degree of congruence among the elements of the system, the more effective the system.*[29] For example, the more consistent the informal norms and an organizational goal, the more likely the organization will be to achieve that goal. Likewise, the better the fit between individual motivation and bureaucratic expectations, the more effective the performance. In Table 3.1, critical questions concerning the congruence of each pair of key elements are outlined.

Organizational behavior can be analyzed at the individual, group, or organizational level, but in any case, the critical aspects of behavior are defined by the functional imperatives of all social systems. That is, if an organization is to survive and develop, it must solve the problems of adaptation, goal achieve-

TABLE 3.1 Congruence between Pairs of Key Elements

Congruence Relationships	*Critical Questions*
Individual-institution	To what extent do individual motives coincide with the bureaucratic expectations?
Individual-goal	To what extent do individual motives coincide with the organizational goals? To what extent do individuals have clear or distorted goals?
Individual-work group	To what extent do individual motives coincide with the informal norms of the work group?
Institution-goal	To what extent do bureaucratic expectations coincide with operative and operational goals?
Institution-work group	To what extent do bureaucratic expectations coincide with the informal norms of the work group?
Work group-goals	To what extent do the informal norms of the group coincide with the official, operative, and operational goals?

ment, integration, and latency.[30] Schools must acquire sufficient resources and accommodate to the demands of the environment (adaptation), define and implement their goals (goal achievement), maintain solidarity and unity among students, teachers, and administrators (integration), and maintain and renew the motivational and cultural patterns of the school climate (latency). The model assumes that the effective achievement of these behavioral outcomes is a function of the degree of congruence among the system elements. The key elements, their interactions, the demands and constraints of the environment, and the behavioral outcomes are summarized in Figure 3.5.

Internal Feedback Loops

The social systems model pictured in Figure 3.5 also has both internal and external feedback mechanisms. For example, the formal school structure and the informal groups both attempt to influence individual behavior.[31] Feedback informs individuals how the bureaucratic structure and the informal organization view their behavior. Although the bureaucracy has formal mechanisms and the work group informal ones, both have internal feedback loops.

The formal school organization provides an official definition of the position, its rank in the hierarchy, and a set of expected behaviors that go with it. In fact, the bureaucratic structure has an established incentive pattern for ensuring appropriate behavior. If the school bureaucracy approves of an individual's performance, positive rewards reinforce his or her behavior. If that person's behavior is evaluated as inferior, positive incentives are reduced and negative incentives are increased.

Informal groups similarly influence behavior. As our discussion of the Hawthorne studies in Chapter 1 explained, group norms control behavior. In the

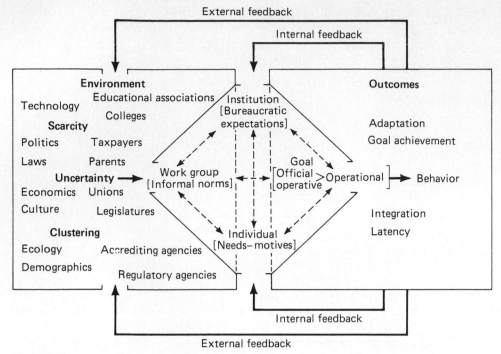

FIGURE 3.5   A social systems model for schools

school building, norms exist within and among all informal peer groups. For example, teachers expect their peers to act appropriately to control students. If a teacher fails to maintain discipline in the classroom, the other teachers apply sanctions: sarcasm and ostracism in the teachers' lounge can have devastating effects on an individual.

External Feedback Loops

Behavior in schools also is monitored through external feedback loops. The culture of the community provides environmental constraints that directly influence bureaucratic expectations, group norms, organizational goal, and indirectly influence individual needs. In spite of attempts by the school to isolate itself, it remains open to community, state, and national forces. The introduction of sex education into the school curriculum, for example, rarely goes unnoticed by the public. In fact, organized community groups provide important inputs about what they consider the goals and outcomes of an acceptable sex education program.

Social behavior in a school is thus affected directly by at least four internal elements, or subsystems—bureaucratic expectations, group norms, organizational goals, and individual needs. Moreover, as Figure 3.5 illustrates, internal and external feedback reinforces appropriate social behavior.

The social-systems model gives a dynamic view of the school, with the feedback mechanisms and elements providing the action components. Good, bad, and neutral events occur constantly, and the dynamic nature of the system becomes even more evident when we consider the ways that students, teachers, and administrators affect one anothers' behavior.

Social-systems analysis also focuses on how the totality—elements and activities—produces a given result. The dynamic result is not predictable with complete accuracy because of the infinite variations that can occur as bureaucracy, subgroups, and individuals modify goals, express values, and exert power through leadership, decision making, and communication activities. Therefore, social-systems analysis must include the concept of equifinality, that is, identical results from different conditions and activities.

CONCEPTUAL DERIVATIONS AND APPLICATIONS

The social-systems model calls attention to a number of important organizational concepts that are useful to the theory and practice of educational administration as well as to research in the field. Many of the administrative problems of formal organizations arise from the fundamental conflict between the needs and motives of the mature individual and the requirements of the bureaucratic organization.[32] Individuals attempt to personalize their roles, that is, to reshape bureaucratic roles so that personal needs can be actualized. Conversely, the organization attempts to mold and fit individuals into the prescribed roles in order to achieve organization goals best. There is a continuing tension between the bureaucratic and individual elements in a formal organization.

Effectiveness, Efficiency, and Satisfaction

Behavior of an individual in a formal organization can be evaluated from the perspectives of the individual and the organization. Chester Barnard was one of the first theorists to make this distinction.[33] An action is *effective* if it accomplishes its specific objective, and *efficient* if it satisfies the motives underlying the immediate objective. Personal behavior can be effective and not efficient, that is, the objective accomplished without satisfying the personal motives behind it. Behavior can also be efficient and not effective, if individual needs are satisfied but the action intended as a means of obtaining that satisfaction is successfully accomplished; or behavior can be simultaneously effective and efficient.

Similar conceptions of effectiveness and efficiency are readily derived from the social-systems model. When behavior is congruent with the bureaucratic expectations for a given role, it is effective. When behavior is consistent with the personal motives of an organizational member, it is efficient. Clearly, personal action can be effective without being efficient or vice versa. However,

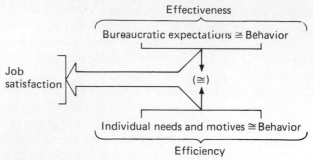

FIGURE 3.6 Effectiveness, efficiency, and job satisfaction

when behavior results in the fulfillment both of bureaucratic expectations and of individual needs and motives, satisfaction with the organization is maximized. *Job satisfaction,* then, depends on the congruence of bureaucratic expectations and individual needs and motives. The relationships are presented schematically in Figure 3.6.

Morale

Another concept that Getzels and Guba derive from the basic model is morale. Although definitions of morale are somewhat arbitrary, many are concerned with group goals. For example, Guba notes that morale is related to the extra expenditure of energy required to accomplish institutional tasks.[34] In this sense high morale can be thought of as the tendency to expend extra effort in the achievement of group goals.

Most definitions of morale include the notions of a communality of goals and a sense of belongingness; however, the systems model also includes an often neglected notion—the extent to which the group goals are rational. *Identification* refers to the communality of goals, that is, the extent to which individual needs are congruent with organizational goals; *belongingness* is the congruence between bureaucratic expectations and personal needs; and *rationality* is the congruence between bureaucratic expectations and organizational goals. The morale of organizational members thus depends upon the extent to which organizational goals and individual needs are one (sense of identification), the extent to which bureaucratic expectations and personal needs are compatible (sense of belongingness), and the extent to which bureaucratic expectations are logical and well-suited for the achievement of organizational goals (sense of rationality). Figure 3.7 suggests that morale in organizations is a function of the interaction of rationality, identification, and belongingness [$M = f(R \times I \times B)$].

Theoretically, morale cannot be high if any one of the three components is low. Administrators attempting to obtain high morale in a school must be concerned with substantial levels of agreement among bureaucratic expectations, personal needs, and organizational goals. In fact, given the notion of job

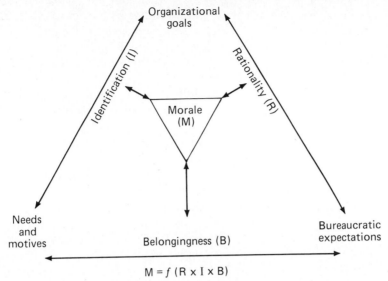

$$M = f\ (R \times I \times B)$$

FIGURE 3.7   Components of morale

satisfaction, it seems likely that satisfaction is a necessary prior condition for the achievement of high morale.

Leadership Style

The model also points to three types of leadership: nomothetic, idiographic, and transactional styles. The styles are abstractions that will not be found in pure form. No individual is a pure "nomothetic leader." Nonetheless, the distinction is a useful one that can be applied in analysis as well as in research.

The *nomothetic style* is characteristic of a leader who goes by the book. Subordinates are expected to conform completely with the bureaucratic expectations. The leader perceives his or her position or office as a center of authority and vigorously applies the same bureaucratic rules and procedures to all subordinates. Above all, the nomothetic administrator strives for close adherence to the organizational expectations, and, typically, seeks conformity and control by the unwavering use of the rewards and penalties designated in the bureaucratic regulations. Such a leader assumes that, if the bureaucratic roles are rationally developed, clearly articulated, and carefully monitored, organizational goals will be attained expeditiously.

In contrast, the *idiographic style* is characteristic of a leader who focuses on individual needs rather than organizational requirements. The idiographic leader expects subordinates to work things out for themselves, to behave in ways which actualize their individual needs, and to be self-directed. Although acknowledging the necessity of some rules and regulations, the idiographic administrator believes that bureaucratic procedures should be tailored to fit the individual needs of subordinates. He or she readily delegates administrative authority, and achieves control of subordinates by depending on the good judgment of the individuals themselves for appropriate behavior. Idiographic leadership is personal and undergirded by the assumption that individuals can and will act in relevant and organizationally meaningful ways without rigid enforcement of carefully defined roles.

The *transactional style* is more difficult to describe because it lacks the distinctiveness and conceptual clarity of the other two. While the idiographic leader in the abstract is concerned only with personal needs and the nomothetic only with bureaucratic demands, the transactional leader is a hybrid concerned with both. Such a leader is interested in the informal organization because he or she derives authority from both the informal and the formal organization. The transactional leader does *not* simply steer a middle course between expectations and needs. On the contrary, he or she attempts to match the appropriate blend of role and need demands with the situation. Thus, whereas a nomothetic leader is bureaucratically oriented and an idiographic leader is personality oriented, the transactional leader is situationally oriented. Notice that the three styles are different ways to achieve the *same* organizational goals; they are not different views of the goals.

One question remains: What style is appropriate in any given situation? That is a question the model does not address, but it is an important issue that we will analyze in detail in Chapter 9.

Bureaucratic Socialization

Organizations attempt to deal with any conflict between bureaucratic requirements and individual needs by establishing the primacy of organizational demands; in fact, bureaucracies systematically mold the behavior of personnel to make individual beliefs and values correspond with those of the organization. This process is referred to as *bureaucratic socialization,* the organization's attempt to induce in members the requisite role orientations for satisfactory performance in an office or position.

Few individuals escape the formative influences of bureaucratic socialization. The values, expectations, incentives, and sanctions of bureaucracies are only some of the socialization mechanisms formal organizations use; the minor interpersonal give-and-take in organizations also helps define a person's organizational identity.[35] Edwin M. Bridges theorizes that socialization in a bureaucracy should produce less behavioral variation among individuals occupying the same role. In his words, "Role performance should be characterized by uniformity rather than diversity with perspectives, outlook, and behavior shaped more and more by institutional position and less and less by personality in the course and service within a bureaucratic role."[36] Robert Merton goes one step further by suggesting that bureaucratic structures, with their patent use of authority and elaborate mechanisms for socialization, have the capacity to modify personality.[37]

Bridges provides some preliminary research data to support his intriguing hypothesis that as principals become socialized—that is, as principals gain experience in the school—their personalities are submerged and they perform the appropriate bureaucratic role behavior with little variation. In a study of twenty-eight elementary principals from a large city school district, Bridges found that open-minded and closed-minded principals with limited experience in the role behaved in predictably *different* fashions; however, there was little difference in the role behavior of experienced principals. Increased experience had a leveling effect on the performance of elementary principals. The dogmatism of some of the principals explained differences in behavior among beginners, but as the principals became socialized, dogmatism had virtually no impact on behavior.[38]

Similarly, Thomas Wiggins found that elementary principals were strongly influenced by the forces of bureaucratic socialization. School bureaucracies mold principals into roles devised to maintain stability.[39] Although the empirical evidence remains limited, there is some support for the notion that in school bureaucracies the part that bureaucratic role and personality factors play in determining behavior vary with the experience the individual has in the role. Figure 3.8 depicts the relationship in terms of the social systems model.

The previous analysis underscores the impact of bureaucratic socialization in the schools and provides another good example of the usefulness of the Getzels and Guba model. The socialization hypothesis clearly builds on the basic model. In addition, a number of other studies demonstrate the influence of bureaucratic socialization on others who occupy roles in schools. According to one such study, beginning teachers become increasingly custodial in their attitudes toward students as they gain experience in the bureaucratic role.[40] Similarly, student teachers have been found to be both more custodial and more bureaucratic after a mere nine weeks in the role of teachers.[41] Apparently, the school bureaucracy quickly begins to impress upon newcomers to a bureaucratic role the value of conformity, impersonality, subordination, and organiza-

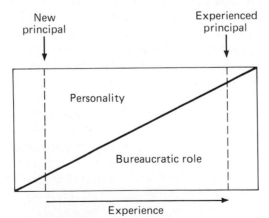

FIGURE 3.8 Hypothesized relationship of role, personality, and experience

tional loyalty. Although the research evidence is somewhat limited, it does suggest that when bureaucratic role expectations and individual needs are in conflict, it is more likely that the school bureaucracy will socialize the individual than that the individual will personalize the role.

Conflict

The model of a formal organization as a social system also suggests that a number of potential conflicts are possible, if not probable, in the organizational life of schools. Theoretically, the opportunity for conflict exists in and among all the major dimensions of the system. Hence, the model focuses attention on role, norm, personality, and goal conflict, and as we have suggested, on conflicts between each pair of elements—namely, role-norm, role-personality, role-goal, norm-personality, norm-goal, and goal-personality conflicts. In addition, conflict between the system components and parts of the environment is likely; for example, conflicts can arise between bureaucratic role expectations and the value structure of the community. Figure 3.9 summarizes the major sources of conflict that are readily derived from the organizational model.

There are a host of *role conflicts* to which an organizational member is susceptible. The numerous bureaucratic expectations associated with one's formal position in the organization often are inconsistent and produce strains. For example, the vice principal of a small school may be expected to serve as both disciplinarian and counselor, or the principal may be expected to be both evaluator and clinical supervisor. In addition, the role of teacher or principal may be subject to a variety of different and incompatible expectations from divergent groups such as the school board, the superintendent, the PTA, and the local teachers' association.

Teachers and administrators face conflicts and pressures not only by virtue of their formal position but also because they occupy several roles in a number of social systems. The roles of parent, church elder, principal, and spouse may all be important roles that produce conflict for a given administrator.

As we have suggested, formal organizations attempt to limit role conflict by elaborating a consistent body of bureaucratic rules, regulations, and procedures. Nevertheless, tension and strains exist within the bureaucratic expectations defining formal positions, and the pressures from many role affiliations outside the formal organization persist.

Personality conflict is another potential source of stress for an organization. We are not using this term to refer to conflicts between people. On the contrary, personality conflict arises from basic incompatibilities in the need structure of the individual. Such conflict is basically a function of personality problems. For example, an administrator may have strong needs for both security and risk taking. As a result the administrator may find it very difficult to display appropriate organizational behavior.

Norm conflict in the informal organization is the functional equivalent of role conflict in the formal; it results when there is inherent conflict and tension between informal norms. An informal organization can produce the same kind

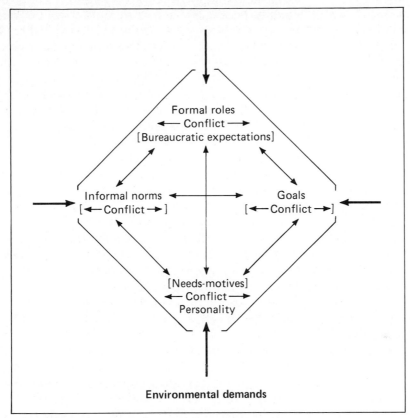

FIGURE 3.9 Sources of organizational conflict

of inconsistencies in its norms as a formal organization does in its bureaucratic expectations.

Goal conflict is still another potential source of difficulty for formal organizations. Most organizations have multiple goals, which are often contradictory. The decision to focus efforts on the teaching of basic minimum skills can detract from the social-emotional development of students. Likewise, order goals conflict with developmental goals, and cost efficiency goals may inhibit innovation initiatives. Moreover, official goals often conflict with operative ones.

Role-norm conflict calls attention to the possible tension between the formal and informal organization. Our discussion in Chapter 1 of the conflict between the official job expectations and the norms of the informal groups of workers in the Bank Wiring Room Study of the Hawthorne Plant provides a classic example. The model depicted in Figure 3.5 underscores the fact that in formal organizations members do not simply respond as isolated individuals; they are members of an informal organization.

Role-goal conflict depicts a situation in which the bureaucratic expectations are inconsistent with organizational goals. The formal requirement that teachers rigorously enforce a dress code may hamper the stated goal of "developing the whole child." Similarly, an expectation for strict teacher control may hinder the teachers' ability to develop "each student to his or her full potential."

Role-personality conflict provides yet another source of organizational tension. Individuals sometimes find themselves in roles for which they are not personally suited. The authoritarian guidance counselor, the disorganized administrator, and the anti-intellectual teacher are examples of personal needs not matching the bureaucratic requirements of the positions.

Norm-personality conflict refers to a similar contradiction in the informal organization. In this case, the personality needs of the individual and the norms of the informal organization are not consistent. For instance, a new group member with a strong need to dominate may be headed for conflict with the established informal group leaders. In most groups, newcomers are expected to conform and respect established patterns initially.

Norm-goal conflict underscores the fact that conflict can occur between the informal organization and goals. In fact, as we saw in the Western Electric Study in Chapter 1, informal norms may undermine the official goals of the organization. When teacher groups are not sympathetic to the official direction of the organization, they resist, ignore, and sometime sabotage it. Attempts to develop a program of individualized instruction, for example, may be met by teacher indifference or hostility.

Goal-personality conflict also highlights the difficulty the formal organization may have in getting individuals to embrace organizational direction. In this case, however, the problem is an individual motivational one rather than a group one. Teachers do not comply with organizational goals for a variety of individual reasons. For example, they may believe it is not in their best interest to comply, or they may not be psychologically equipped to perform as directed by the goals. The source of the problem rests either in unrealistic goals or in the needs and motives of individual teachers.

The school does not exist in a vacuum; it is influenced by its environment, and an important aspect of that environment is the culture consisting in part of societal and community values. The values of the broader social system in which the school is embedded provide yet another source of tension and pressure. Indeed, dominant community values can and do come into conflict with bureaucratic roles, with individual personality, with informal norms, and with organizational goals. The conservative board of education and the liberal principal, the traditional school and the progressive community, and the conservative community and the liberated teacher, all provide examples of this kind of conflict.

Organizational Effectiveness

Just as we defined an individual's effectiveness as the congruence between bureaucratic expectations and individual behavior, we can similarly analyze the collective performance of the school in terms of effectiveness. More specifically, *organizational effectiveness is the degree to which the actual outcomes of the organization are consistent with the expected outcomes.*[42] For example, if a school expects 90 percent of its eighth-grade students to pass the state minimum basic skills test and 95 percent actually pass, then the school is effective on that criterion. Although the proposed definition of effectiveness permits assessment on a host of different criteria, our analysis of schools focuses on the functional needs of adaptation, goal achievement, integration, and latency (see Figure 3.5 and Chapter 12). Moreover, it is hypothesized that the greater the total congruence (lack of conflict) among the basic elements of the system and between the elements and the environmental demands, the greater the effectiveness of the school.

Organizational Problem Analysis in Schools[43]

Administrators can use the system model as a basis for organizational analysis and problem solving. The model serves as a basis for diagnosing difficulties and improving outcomes in schools. Effective school decision makers gather information on the performance levels of their schools, compare the information with the desired performance levels, identify discrepancies and difficulties, search for causes of the problem, develop and select a plan to alleviate the problems, and implement and evaluate the plan (see Chapter 10). The model is particularly useful in diagnosing conflict or lack of congruence among the key elements of the system. The assumption is that overall effectiveness is enhanced by internal and external congruence—that is, a school is more effective when its component pieces fit together. The process of improving congruence is not simply a matter of intuition; in fact, the theory and research in the remainder of this book should be extremely useful in this regard. The implication is that the school administrator who is attempting to diagnose performance in schools needs to become familiar with critical aspects of bureaucracy, informal organization, individual motivation, goals, and environment in order to assess the conflict within the system, improve the congruence, and achieve effectiveness.

In this section, we will simply illustrate how the model coupled with a rational decision-making process yields a powerful and practical set of tools. The process has a number of specific steps; each one will be described briefly.

1. *Identify symptoms.* In many situations there is preliminary information that suggests a problem. Teachers may be apathetic; students may be withdrawn or disruptive; or routine reports from faculty may be consistently late. These events imply the possibility of a problem. It is important to remember, however, that such behavior is usually only symptomatic of the problem rather than the problem itself. Nevertheless, the symptoms should be noted because they signal where to search for problem causes.
2. *Identify problems.* Symptoms merely suggest problems. In the proposed framework, a problem is defined as a difference between expected and actual outcomes. Problems signify a lack of effectiveness at the individual, group, or organizational level. To

verify the existence of a problem, data need to be collected to demonstrate a meaningful difference between the planned and actual outcomes. Although such data identify the problem, they do not specify the causes.

3. *Describe organizational elements.* Information on each of the four elements of the model must also be collected. What are the critical aspects of the bureaucratic structure, informal organization, individual participants, and organizational goals?

4. *Assess the environment demands.* Collect information about relevant aspects of the environment. What are the critical constraints and demands of the environment that may be related to the problem?

5. *Assess congruence.* Using the model and data collected, analyze the congruence among the elements and the fits between each element and the relevant environment demands. Where are the incongruencies?

6. *Predict problem causes.* This step of the process links the congruence analysis with the problem. Having analyzed the data for incongruencies between elements in the system, which conflicts or poor fits are responsible for the outcome problems? The answer is our prediction about the cause(s) of the problem.

7. *Formulate a plan.* The next step is to develop an action plan to reduce the conflict in the system and thereby improve the congruence between key elements. The theories and research associated with each element should be useful in this step. The plan may range from rather obvious changes to collecting more data for a more complex problem.

8. *Evaluate the plan.* Implementation of the plan should be carefully monitored. Evaluation of the actions is necessary to determine if the plan solved the problem. Are the expected results and the actual outcome now the same?

Other steps must also be kept in mind when this problem-solving cycle is used; rational decision analysis also involves generating alternatives, predicting consequences for each alternative, and selecting strategies. The process will be discussed in much more detail later. Our purpose for introducing the process here was to demonstrate the practical utility of the model.

SUMMARY

Social systems are comprised of bounded, purposeful, and mutually interacting elements. Regulated by feedback, such systems continuously attempt to maintain equilibrium. A basic social-systems model was developed by Getzels and Guba. We have drawn upon their work as well as other contemporary organizational theorists to expand and refine the formulation and to apply it to the school as a formal organization. According to the social-systems model for schools, organizational behavior is determined by the interaction of at least four key elements—bureaucratic expectations, informal norms, individual needs and motives, and organizational goals. Moreover, all the elements and interactions within the system are constrained by important demands from the environment as the organization solves the imperative problems of adaptation, goal achievement, integration, and latency. In addition, internal and external feedback mechanisms reinforce appropriate organizational behavior.

Conceptual derivations and application of the model illustrate the usefulness of the perspective in the study and practice of administration. For example, concepts of effectiveness, efficiency, job satisfaction, and morale can be derived. In addition, ten sources of internal conflict emerge from the model as well as the conceptual formulation of three administrative styles. The process of bureaucratic socialization of administrators and teachers demonstrates the significant influences of bureaucratic structures on personalities. Finally, we illustrate how the model coupled with a rational decision-making process yields a powerful and practical set of tools to assess conflict within the system, build congruence among the elements, and improve organizational performance.

The social-systems model also serves as the framework for the rest of the book. Chapters 4 through 12 systematically explicate the relevant elements, theories, research, and processes suggested by this overview. Chapter 13 provides a review, synthesis, and discussion of continuing organizational dilemmas.

NOTES

1. Alfred N. Whitehead, *Science and the Modern World* (New York: Macmillan, 1925), p. 68.
2. George C. Homans, *The Human Group* (New York: Harcourt, Brace & World 1950), p. 87.
3. Willard Waller, *The Sociology of Teaching* (New York: Wiley, 1932), p. 6.
4. A. D. Hall and R. E. Fagen, "Definition of a System," *General Systems: The Yearbook of the Society for General Systems Research,* 1 (1956), 18–28.
5. Marvin E. Olsen, *The Process of Social Organization* (New York: Holt, Rinehart & Winston, 1968), pp. 227–232.
6. W. Richard Scott, "Introduction: From Technology to Environment," in John M. Meyer and W. Richard Scott (eds.), *Organizational Environments: Ritual and Rationality* (Beverly Hills, CA: Sage, 1983), pp. 13–17. Quotation is on p. 16.
7. Joseph A. Litterer, *Organization: Systems, Control, and Adaption,* 2nd ed., Vol. 2 (New York: Wiley, 1969), pp. 1–6, 116–119.
8. The basic Getzels and Guba formulation and the several modifications are found in the following sources: Jacob W. Getzels and Egon G. Guba, "Social Behavior and the Administrative Process," *School Review,* 65 (1957), 423–441; J. W. Getzels and H. A. Thelan, "The Classroom as a Unique Social System," *The Dynamics of Instructional Groups,* Fifty-ninth Yearbook of the National Society for the Study of Education Yearbook, Part II (Chicago: University of Chicago Press, 1960), pp. 53–82; and Jacob W. Getzels, James M. Lipham, and Roald F. Campbell, *Educational Administration as a Social Process: Theory, Research, and Practice* (New York: Harper & Row, 1968), pp. 52–78.
9. Charles E. Bidwell, "The School as a Formal Organization," in James G.

March (ed.), *Handbook of Organization* (Chicago: Rand McNally, 1965), pp. 972–1022.

10. Getzels and Guba, *op. cit.*

11. Talcott Parsons and Edward A. Shils (eds.), *Toward a General Theory of Action* (Cambridge, MA: Harvard University Press, 1951), p. 24.

12. Getzels, Lipham, and Campbell, *op. cit.*, p. 73.

13. This model is primarily a synthesis of the work of Getzel and Guba, *op. cit.;* Harold J. Leavitt, William R. Dill, and Henry B. Eyring, *The Organizational World* (New York: Harcourt Brace Jovanovich, 1973); W. Richard Scott, *Organizations: Rational, Natural, and Open-Systems* (Englewood Cliffs, NJ: Prentice-Hall, 1981); and David A. Nadler and Michael L. Tushman, "A General Diagnostic Model for Organizational Behavior Applying a Congruence Perspective" in J. R. Hackman, E. E. Lawler III, and L. W. Porter (eds.), *Perspectives on Behavior in Organizations* (New York: McGraw-Hill, 1983), pp. 112–124.

14. Max G. Abbott, "Intervening Variables in Organizational Behavior," *Educational Administration Quarterly,* 1 (1965), 1–13.

15. Chester I. Barnard, *Functions of an Executive* (Cambridge, MA: Harvard University Press, 1938), p. 122.

16. Amitai Etzioni, *Modern Organizations* (Englewood Cliffs, NJ: Prentice-Hall, 1964), p. 6, and Scott, *op. cit.* p. 16. Much of our discussion of goals draws upon Scott's analysis in Chapter 12.

17. Scott, *op. cit.*, p. 289.

18. Richard M. Cyert and James G. March, *A Behavioral Theory of the Firm* (Englewood Cliffs, NJ: Prentice-Hall, 1963), pp. 27–32.

19. Scott, *op. cit.*, p. 264.

20. Herbert Simon, "On the Concept of Organizational Goal," *Administrative Science Quarterly,* 9 (1964), 9.

21. Scott, *op. cit.*, p. 266.

22. *Ibid.*, p. 290.

23. Simon, *op. cit.*, 1–22.

24. Barnard, *op. cit.*, pp. 82–95.

25. Philip Selznick, *Leadership in Administration* (New York: Harper & Row, 1957), pp. 14–22.

26. James G. March, "The Technology of Fadishness," in James G. March and John P. Olsen (eds.), *Ambiguity and Choice in Organizations* (Bergen, Norway: Universitetsforlaget, 1976), p. 72.

27. Scott, *op. cit.*, p. 262.

28. Richard M. Steers, *Organizational Effectiveness: A Behavioral View* (Santa Monica, CA: Goodyear, 1977), p. 24.

29. A number of theoretical formulations have proposed such an assumption. For example, see Getzels and Guba, "Social Behavior," pp. 423–441; Nadler and Tushman, *op. cit.*, pp. 119–120; and Amitai Etzioni, *A Comparative Analysis of Complex Organizations* (New York: Free Press, 1961), pp. 12–14.

30. Talcott Parsons, *Structure and Process in Modern Society* (New York: Free Press, 1960), pp. 16–58.

31. Abbott, *op. cit.*

32. Chris Argyris, *Personality and Organizations* (New York: Harper & Row, 1957), p. 66.

33. Barnard, *op. cit.,* pp. 19–20.
34. Egon G. Guba, "Morale and Satisfaction: A Study in Past-Future Time Perspective," *Administrative Science Quarterly,* 3 (1958), 195–209.
35. Edwin M. Bridges, "Bureaucratic Role and Socialization: The Influence of Experience on the Elementary Principal," *Educational Administration Quarterly,* 1 (1965), 19–28.
36. *Ibid.,* p. 20.
37. Robert K. Merton, *Social Theory and Social Structure* (New York: Free Press, 1957), pp. 195–206.
38. Bridges, *op. cit.*
39. Thomas Wiggins, "Why Our Urban Schools Are Leaderless," *Education and Urban Society,* 2 (1970), 169–177.
40. Wayne K. Hoy, "Pupil Control and Organizational Socialization: The Influence of Experience on the Beginning Teacher," *School Review,* 76 (1968), 312–323.
41. Wayne K. Hoy and Richard Rees, "The Bureaucratic Socialization of Student Teachers," *Journal of Teacher Education,* 28 (1977), 23–26.
42. Nadler and Tushman, *op. cit.,* pp. 119–120.
43. This section draws heavily from the organizational analysis of Nadler and Tushman, *op. cit.,* pp. 121–123.

Chapter 4

Schools and Their External Environments

> . . . the characteristics of organizational environments demand consideration for their own sake.
>
> F. E. EMERY and E. L. TRIST
> *"The Causal Texture of Organization Environments"*

In the classical management and human relations perspectives, organizations are viewed as relatively closed systems. The dominant metaphor is that organizations can be understood as simple machines. Efficient internal operations are thought to determine effectiveness. Those early perspectives assume organizational and administrative policies are designed to fulfill a relatively stable set of tasks and goals; therefore, little attention is given to how organizations adapt to their external environments. In contrast, contemporary thought about organizations assumes a much broader view. William L. Boyd and Robert L. Crowson observe that the continuing environmental turbulence of the 1960s showed that a closed-systems model was not adequate for either illuminating or dealing with the pressing problems of educational administrators.[1] As a result of the search for more practically relevant models, organizations such as school systems are now viewed as open systems, which must adapt to changing external conditions to be effective and, in the long term, survive.[2] The open-system concept highlights the vulnerability and interdependence of organizations and their environments. In other words, environment is important because it affects the internal structures and processes of organizations; hence, one is forced to look both inside and outside the organization to explain organizational behavior.

Although the environments of some schools and districts may be relatively simple and stable, most tend to be complex and dynamic. Indeed, the larger social, economic, political, and technological trends all tend to influence the internal operations of schools and districts. Because school organizations are conceptualized as part of a larger universe or environment, an argument can be made that anything that happens in the larger environment may affect the school and vice versa. For example, one only needs to observe the race by school districts to purchase personal computers for instructional purposes to see the effects that recent technology and its projected economic benefits for society have had on the internal processes of schools.

Environment, like a number of other terms in organizational theory, is not a firmly defined concept. Consensus neither exists about what constitutes an organization's environment nor the essential issues to be considered in discussions of organizational environment.[3] Nevertheless, similar definitions, common elements or dimensions, and information and resource dependence perspectives all provide useful descriptions and explanations of school environments.[4]

DEFINING ORGANIZATIONAL ENVIRONMENT

Numerous definitions of organizational environment occur in the literature. Four examples follow:

> Environment is typically seen as everything outside the boundaries of an organization, even though the boundaries are often nebulous and poorly drawn.—Lee G. Bolman and Terrence E. Deal[5]
> Organizational environment is all elements existing outside the boundary of the organization that have the potential to affect all or part of the organization.—Richard L. Daft[6]
> In a general sense, the environment of a system consists of "everything else"—that is everything that is not-system.—W. Richard Scott[7]
> The *external environment* consists of those relevant physical and social factors *outside* the boundaries of the organization . . . that are taken into consideration in the decision-making behavior of individuals in that system.—Gerald Zaltman, Robert Duncan, and Jonny Holbek[8]

A common theme of these definitions is that environment is treated as a residual category of potential and real effects. Defining environment as a residual component of school organizations may be sufficient when the focus of attention is on the internal processes of the school itself, but not when treating the environment as a causal force that is influencing the structure and activities of schools.[9] As a consequence, environment and its effects on the internal aspects of the organization can be understood by defining and analyzing its most salient dimensions.

DIMENSIONS OF ENVIRONMENTS

A distinction between general and specific environments provides an initial clarification of the environment as a residual category.[10] Broad factors, trends, and conditions that can potentially affect organizations comprise the general environment of schools. Examples include technological and informational developments, political structures and patterns of legal norms, social conditions and cultural values, economic factors, and ecological and demographic characteristics. Although the potential exists for general factors to influence a given school or district, their relevance and likelihood of impact are not entirely clear to the organization's members. In other words, ambiguity and uncertainty exist about the effects of the general environment on any specific school.

In contrast, external factors that have immediate and direct effects on organizations are termed the specific environment. As shown in Figure 4.1, specific environmental factors for school districts include constituencies and stakeholders such as individual parents, taxpayer associations, teacher and administrator unions, state and federal government regulatory agencies, colleges and universities, state legislatures, accrediting agencies, and other associations involved in educational policies and practices, (e.g., Parent-Teachers Associations and groups for handicapped or gifted children and athletic and art programs).

The general environment is similar for all organizations. Depending on the particular circumstances, however, specific environments vary from school to school and from district to district. Administrators tend to focus the monitoring and planning processes on specific environmental elements and often fail to recognize that general environmental factors have the potential to influence not only the organization itself, but the specific environments as well. During the 1970s, for instance, the oil pricing policies of the OPEC cartel not only

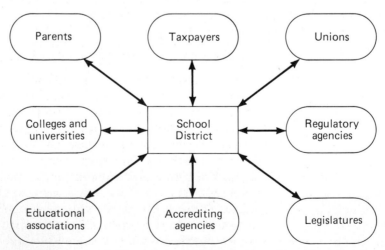

FIGURE 4.1   Selected external constituencies for school districts

tripled or quadrupled the price of utilities for schools but triggered a rapid inflationary cycle that had severe consequences for other school costs. Different aspects of the general environment also interact with each other. For example, political decisions and social attitudes combined to create civil disobedience in educational institutions during the Vietnam War era of the 1960s and early 1970s.

Thus, external environments of schools are complex and difficult to analyze, but an enhanced understanding may be gained by examining general characteristics of the environment. Three dimensions—uncertainty, clustering, and scarcity—are particularly useful.

Uncertainty

Fundamentally, the *degree of uncertainty* involves informational aspects of the environment. The level of uncertainty is determined by the kind and amount of information that organizational decision makers have about trends and changes in environmental conditions. Uncertainty is viewed as a problematic situation confronting organizations. Thus, in conditions of high uncertainty, alternative decisions and their outcomes become increasingly unpredictable and risky.

Stability and complexity affect environmental uncertainty. Stability refers to the extent to which elements in the environment are undergoing change. Stable environments experience little change, while unstable environments experience abrupt and rapid changes. Stability occurs in situations where the set of important elements remains constant and are either unchanging or changing slowly and predictably. Instability arises in situations that are loose and erratic. In conditions of instability, both the value and kinds of environmental elements are changing unpredictably.[11] Instability produces uncertainty.

Complexity refers to the number and similarity of environmental elements to which the organization must relate. A complex environment has a large number of diverse entities that exert significant influence on the organization, while a simple environment is relatively homogeneous and characterized by only a few important external elements. In other words, environments with many diverse and important elements are highly complex. In schools, for example, the number and types of special education populations that must be served would be one indicator of the complexity of a school's environment.

Less complex environments are less uncertain. Fewer important information categories are necessary for decision making; beliefs about cause and effect relations are more certain; and preferences regarding possible outcomes are more clear. Furthermore, when environmental elements are similar, the range of expected behavior, strategies and tactics, and formal goals are relatively easy to understand and handle. In contrast, highly complex environments present memory problems for administrators and organizations.[12] Moreover, causal relationships and preferences for possible outcomes are more uncertain.

The more complex and unstable the environment, the greater the uncertainty for the organization. Schools, like all formal organizations, need determinateness and certainty because they are subject to the criteria of rationality. Hence, schools when confronted with uncertainty will often attempt to cope by creating special parts specifically to deal with it.[13] School districts, for example, develop special units such as offices of public relations to monitor the activities of significant groups in the environment and routinely report their behaviors and attitudes to the administrators.

Clustering

Environments differ in the *degree of clustering* or structuring as compared to anarchy or randomness.[14] At the highly clustered end of this dimension, environments present any organization with a powerful and highly structured set of demands and constraints. The price of survival is compliance; organizations such as schools which deviate too much from the requirements and values of the environment are altered or destroyed. At the other end of the continuum, poorly organized environments lack order, which makes further diversity to be tolerated easily. For example, a school policy might be in conflict with a given aspect of an unclustered community, but the deviance would not be construed as a general or intolerable breach of values. In a clustered community, however, the serious conflict might well produce a strong reaction from highly structured and interconnected community groups.

Scarcity

The *degree of scarcity* is the extent to which the environment has the resources available to support stability and sustained growth of the organization. For example, does the school district have resources to maintain a comprehensive program for the number of students in a school attendance area? Daniel Katz and Robert L. Kahn observe that, as the environment of an organization is examined for available resources, the dimension of scarcity becomes extremely important.[15] The relative abundance of resources in the specific and general environments is the ultimate determinant of sufficient input for any organization. The concept of abundance applies to informational and technical knowledge, economic and human resources, and political and legal support. Under conditions of scarcity, competition for resources among subgroups can take the form of a zero-sum game with each subgroup caring more about its share of finite resources than the overall welfare of the organization. When student enrollments are declining, for instance, administrators may deny student transfers to needed programs in other schools because the action would decrease the human resource base of their schools.

INFORMATION PERSPECTIVE

The information perspective assumes the environment is a source of information that is used by decision makers as a basis for maintaining or changing internal structures and processes.[16] A primary concern of this approach is the degree of uncertainty of information reaching the organization's decision makers. A general assumption is made that decision-making processes are affected both by environmental uncertainty and the equivocal nature of the information generated by unstable and complex environments. An important tenet is that *perception* of information is assumed to be an intervening link between the organization's environment and actions taken by decision makers. Therefore, organizational environment consists of perceived information about the dimensions rather than objective descriptions of the elements themselves. In other words, the information perspective defines environment as the perceptions of external dimensions by organizational decision makers and other participants based on questionable and suspicious communications.

Specific formulations and empirical tests of the information perspective of organizational environments have typically been based on typologies using the dimensions of uncertainty and clustering. We will focus our analysis on four useful typologies that have been the object of considerable attention by organizational theorists.

Typologies of Environments

Emery and Trist developed a now classic four-category typology of organizational environments using uncertainty and clustering.[17] They introduced the concept of "causal texture" to indicate that environmental elements represent threats or opportunities for the organization. Four causal textures or environmental categories were proposed by Emery and Trist: placid, randomized; placid, clustered; disturbed, reactive; and turbulent field. Each type of causal texture represents a different combination of uncertainty and clustering.

Placid, randomized environments are the simplest type. Placid means that the relatively few important specific factors change slowly, and new threats or opportunities are infrequent. The environment is random or unclustered because when change does occur it is not predictable and is not coordinated with other environmental elements. In other words, placid, randomized environments are relatively unchanging, with limited interdependence among specific factors or parts. Thus, the environment poses little threat to the organization.

An example is a small school district in a stable rural community. Years can pass without abrupt changes. Students, teachers, and administrators come from families who have deep roots in the area. Other than an occasional church group and an athletic booster club, few special interest groups make systematic attempts to influence the school. Events that might have a major impact on the district are unlikely. In this kind of environment, the professional staff can concentrate on the day-to-day operations of the school. The environment typically is not a major factor in the administrators' decision making.

Placid, clustered environments are relatively stable, but increased interdependence or growing complexity is evident. Specific elements in the environment are coupled to one another and may act simultaneously to influence the organization. Events in the environment are not random. When threats or

opportunities appear, they come from organized clusters, which may be potentially dangerous to the organization. Because a number of factors may change
simultaneously, planning and forecasting processes are important and day-to-
day operations should allow for possible new events in the environment.

An example is the environment experienced by a moderate to large school
district in a stable community setting. In such a community, the number of
specific elements not only would be large but would be linked together through
a dominant industry, labor union, informal power structure, civic organization,
or religious group. When threats or opportunities appear for the school district,
they will come at the same time from a united or organized set of specific
environmental elements. The dominant industry might decide to introduce a
new product line or expand operations. As a direct request, company officials
themselves would personally ask school officials to introduce new vocational
education programs to assist the economic growth of the firm and community.
As an indirect approach, allied groups such as labor unions and other business
groups would reinforce the need for the new programs.

Disturbed, reactive environments are dynamic and exhibit changes that are
not random. Actions by one organization can disturb the environment and
provoke reactions by others. The disturbed, reactive environment is comprised
of organizations of the same kind that are competing for domination of a
particular segment of the market. Each competing organization attempts to
improve its own conditions by hindering the other, each knowing the others are
playing the same game.

In education, the disturbed, reactive environment is a community with
competing school districts, for example, public and private, each wanting to
dominate. The role of administrators in this type of environment is to plan
decisions and strategic moves to allow for countermoves. If a private school is
claiming high academic achievement and orderly procedures, the planning by
administrators in other schools must consider not only its response but the
reactions of all school organizations in the community. Administrators must
carefully monitor other groups and prepare alternative actions to their moves.
This type of environment may not be widespread today in the United States,
but other countries such as Canada and Australia have well-developed public
and private or separate systems that operate in the same communities. If educational voucher and tuition tax credit plans become popular, the disturbed,
reactive environment could become the predominate atmosphere for school
organizations in the United States.

Turbulent fields are environments characterized by complexity, rapid
change, and clustering. In this type of environment, conditions are so complex
that it is difficult to understand the combination of forces that create the constant change. Multiple factors experience dramatic change and the changes are
linked. The turbulent field can have overwhelmingly negative consequences
for the organization; in fact the environment may change so drastically that the
survival of the organization is threatened. A distinctive feature of the turbulent
field is the interdependence among environmental factors. By shifting together
and influencing each other, the effects are magnified. True turbulent fields are
rare, but when they occur, planning is of little value because the changes are

so dramatic and rapid. Individual organizations cannot adapt successfully through their own actions. Rather, survival depends on the emergence of values that have overriding significance for all members of the field. Social values are coping mechanisms that make it possible to deal with persisting areas of relevant uncertainty. Good illustrations of the turbulent field are difficult to formulate because the environment does not sit still long enough for examination.[18] However, the volatility of the computer industry during the last decade might approximate the uncertainty depicted by the turbulent field environment.

Shirley Terreberry argued that the four types of environments described by Emery and Trist are stages in an evolutionary chain.[19] Extrapolating from Terreberry's work produces the prediction that organizational environments are becoming increasingly turbulent. In today's society placid-randomized environments are probably quite rare. Schools are becoming more and more interconnected with and affected by other organizations, such as state departments of education, legislatures, universities, and businesses.

In addition to Emery and Trist's work, three other typologies of environments based on uncertainty are important to the information perspective. In 1967, Thompson[20] and Lawrence and Lorsch[21] published similar four-celled typologies, both based on the dimensions of stability and complexity. Their work is similar and can be summarized as follows.[22]

	Thompson	*Lawrence and Lorsch*
Cell 1.	Homogeneous—stable	Low diversity—not dynamic
Cell 2.	Homogeneous—shifting	Low diversity—highly dynamic
Cell 3.	Heterogeneous—stable	High diversity—not dynamic
Cell 4.	Heterogeneous—shifting	High diversity—dynamic

To study different conditions of environmental stability, Lawrence and Lorsch investigated the perceptions of organizational decision makers about the environment in three different industries.[23] The researchers were interested in perceived environmental diversity (complexity) and integration (collaboration among the production, sales, and research divisions of the organizations). Their findings and conclusions supported the earlier findings of William R. Dill.[24] When organizations are confronted with increased environmental instability and complexity, they are able to maintain or increase their effectiveness through additional flexibility in their structural configurations.

Duncan[25] elaborated and empirically tested the typologies of Thompson and Lawrence and Lorsch. He used the two primary concepts constituting uncertainty. Stability was defined as static or dynamic while complexity was defined as simple or complex. Combining the aspects of stability and complexity produced the four categories summarized in Figure 4.2.

The four cells shown in Figure 4.2 range from low perceived uncertainty in category one (simple, static), to moderately low uncertainty in category two (static, complex), to moderately high uncertainty in category three (dynamic, simple), to high uncertainty in category four (dynamic, complex). Duncan found

Environmental Complexity

		Simple	Complex
Environmental Change	Stable	Category One: Low Uncertainty 1. Small number of external elements 2. Similar elements 3. Elements remain the same or change slowly	Category Two: Low Moderate Uncertainty 1. Large number of external elements 2. Dissimilar elements 3. Elements remain the same or change slowly
	Unstable	Category Three: High Moderate Uncertainty 1. Small number of external elements 2. Similar elements 3. Elements are in continuous process of change	Category Four: High Uncertainty 1. Large number of external elements 2. Dissimilar elements 3. Elements are in continuous process of change

FIGURE 4.2   Typology of organizational environments based on uncertainty

SOURCE: Adapted and reprinted from Robert B. Duncan, "Characteristics of Perceived Environments and Perceived Environmental Uncertainty," *Administrative Science Quarterly* 17 (1972): 320 by permission of the *Administrative Science Quarterly.* Copyright 1972 by Cornell University.

support for the general hypothesis that the levels of uncertainty for organizations increase significantly across each category from one to two to three to four. The simple, static environment creates the most certainty for organizations, and the dynamic, complex the most uncertainty. Moreover, stability in the environment was a more important contributor to uncertainty than complexity. Both dimensions, however, interact to produce enhanced environmental uncertainty.

In sum, the central characteristics of the information-uncertainty approach are threefold. First, the focus is on the decision makers' perceptions of their environments rather than on the actual characteristics. Second, the fundamental hypothesis is that perceived environmental uncertainty affects the degree of flexibility and bureaucratic nature of organizations. Third, the research approach is based on the subjective perceptions of environmental factors by organizational members.[26]

RESOURCE DEPENDENCY PERSPECTIVE

In contrast to the information perspective that treats environment as the flow of information, resource dependency theory views environment in terms of relative scarcity of resources, and neglects the processes by which information about the environment is gained by the decision makers. Resources are critical in this perspective. Four general types of environmental resources are typically identified—fiscal, personnel (e.g., students, teachers, administrators, school volunteers, and board members)—information and knowledge, and products and services (e.g., instructional materials and test scoring services).[27]

Dependence is the other important concept of the perspective.[28] For educational settings, dependence of a school organization on another organization is directly proportional to the school organization's motivational investment in the resources controlled by a second organization, and inversely proportional to the availability of these resources from other organizations. That is, if the school organization cannot accomplish its goals without the resources controlled by the other organization and is unable to secure them elsewhere, the school organization becomes dependent on the second organization. Conversely, as resources are supplied, the other organization gains power over the school organization. It follows that the greater the resource dependence, the more the organizations will communicate with each other.[29] Notice that dependence is an attribute of the relationship between the organizations and not an attribute of the individual organization in isolation.

A recent set of events illustrates the dependence concept. During the past decade, as fiscal resources from local property taxes and federal grants declined, school districts had an increased motivational investment in securing additional appropriations from state legislatures. As greater percentages of their budgets were supplied by the state, the dependence of school districts on state governments grew dramatically. In a parallel fashion, the power of the state over local school districts expanded; when the reform movement of the mid-1980s began, state legislatures and offices of education were able to dictate educational reforms to school districts.

The fundamental assumption of resource dependency theory is that organizations are unable internally to generate all the resources and functions to maintain themselves.[30] Resources must come from the environment. As a consequence, organizations must enter into exchanges with environmental elements that can supply the needed resources. In exchange for resources, the external groups or organizations may not only consume the organization's outputs but demand certain actions from the organization. For example, individuals who have been educated and trained in the schools contribute their efforts to society, and society demands that schools offer particular types of training.

The fact that all organizations are dependent on their environments makes external control of organizational behavior possible and constraint inevitable. If they are not responsive to the demands of their environments, organizations cannot thrive. But demands often conflict; thus, organizations cannot thrive by simply responding completely to every environmental demand. The challenge for school decision makers is to determine the extent to which the school organization can and must respond to various environmental demands.

An organization's attempts to satisfy the demands of a given group are a function of its dependence on that group relative to other groups and the extent to which the demands of one group conflict with the demands of another. Three factors are critical in determining the dependence of one organization on another. First, the importance of the resource to the organization's continued operation and survival affects the level of dependency. Schools cannot exist without students, but they probably can survive without IBM and Apple computers. Second, organizational dependence is mediated by the amount of discretion the other organization has over the allocation and use of the resource. Legislatures hold immense power over schools because they have the discretion to make rules and appropriate the funds for specific educational programs. Finally, dependence is influenced by the number of alternatives or extent of control that the other organization has over the resource. In other words, the dependence of one organization on the other derives from the concentration of resource control. For example, school district dependence on the federal government lessened during the early 1980s because the reduction of federal funding was replaced by funds from local and state sources.

Organizations strive to avoid becoming dependent on others or to make others dependent on them. Therefore, the resource dependence model also portrays organizations as active and capable of changing and responsive to their environments. Administrators manage their environments as well as their organizations; in fact, Pfeffer maintains that managing the environment may be more important than managing the organization.[31] Members of the organization make active, planned, and conscious responses to environmental contingencies. Organizations attempt to absorb uncertainty and interdependence either completely, as through merger or consolidation, or partially, as through co-optation or the movement of personnel among organizations. Attempts are made to stabilize relations with other organizations, using tactics ranging from tacit collusion to legal contracts. Educational organizations, for example, establish external advisory groups comprised of leading individuals from related organizations or publics to stabilize relationships with other important parties.

In a study based on resource dependency theory, Michael Aiken and Jerald Hage hypothesized that, as interdependence is established between organizations, problems of internal coordination and control increase.[32] Their findings indicate that organizations with more joint programs, and thus a higher degree of dependence on the environment, are more complex themselves, have somewhat less centralized decision-making processes, are more innovative, have greater frequency of internal communication, and tend to be less formalized than organizations with fewer joint programs. Support for the work of Aiken and Hage is provided by the findings of Mindlin and Aldrich[33] that the higher the dependence on other organizations, the lower the formalization and standardization of organizational structure.

In sum, three generalizations capture the essence of resource dependency theory.[34] First, as organizations become increasingly dependent on their environments for securing resources, they require and tend to exhibit a more flexible and adaptive structure, usually associated with less formal and standardized procedures and more decentralized decision making. Second, dependence on external elements for resources can lead to interorganizational relationships such as joint programs and co-optation. Third, research based on this perspective uses archival, observational, and other "objective" methods to gather data.[35]

Toward a Synthesis of the Two Perspectives

An attempt to integrate the information and resource dependency perspectives has been made by Aldrich and Mindlin.[36] They note that discussions of uncertainty and dependence imply that the concepts vary independently of each other. For example, the information perspective maintains that instability and complexity of the environment, as perceived by decision makers, create uncertainty with which the organization must deal. Coping with uncertainty forces the organization to employ less formal and more decentralized decision-making processes. In contrast, the resource dependence holds that similar structural arrangements are necessary when, in the process of obtaining valuable resources, organizations become dependent on other organizations.

The perspectives can be joined in at least two ways. First, the probable joint impact of uncertainty and dependence can be considered. Aldrich and Mindlin argue that an interactive effect exists for uncertainty of information from the environment and dependence on the environment for securing scarce resources. They reason that the effects of either dependence or uncertainty will be felt most strongly when the other factor is also present. Second, the perspectives can be integrated through the study of decision makers' perceptions of the environment. While the information perspective immediately directs attention to the role of perception, perceptions of resource dependence by decision makers also clearly play a large part in determining their reactions to the environment.

CONCEPTUAL DERIVATIONS
AND APPLICATIONS

Because environmental uncertainty and resource dependence threaten organization autonomy and effectiveness, administrators often try to minimize external effects on internal school operations. This strategic response raises questions about the extent to which school organizations control, or even create, their own environments.[37] Within limits, school organizations have the ability to define or enact their own environments.[38] Attempts to reduce uncertainty and dependence can be grouped as internal and interorganizational coping strategies. Both sets of strategies are designed to protect key processes from environmental influences.

Internal Coping Strategies

Buffering, planning, and forecasting.   Organizations try to isolate their technical cores, e.g., instructional activities in schools, from external influences.[39] This strategy of isolation is based on the assumption that efficiency can be maximized only when the technical core is not disturbed by external uncertainties. A process for providing the insulation is to surround instructional activities with buffers that absorb uncertainty from the environment. Therefore, specific departments and roles are created in school organizations to deal with and absorb uncertainty and dependence from a variety of environmental elements. Purchasing, planning, personnel, curriculum, and facilities departments are created to buffer teachers from factors in the school's environment. These departments transfer materials, services, information, money, and other resources between the environment and school district. In addition, a primary role of the principal consists of dealing with parental complaints about teachers. The goal of buffering is to make the technical core as nearly a closed system as possible and, thereby, enhance efficiency.[40]

In unstable environments and high levels of dependency, buffering strategies probably will not adequately protect the instructional program from external influences. Under the conditions of high uncertainty and dependence, school organizations can attempt to control environmental fluctuations by the more aggressive strategies of planning and forecasting. These strategies involve anticipating environmental changes and taking actions to soften their adverse effects. Under these circumstances, a separate planning department is frequently established. In unstable, complex, and dependent situations, planners must identify the important environmental elements, and analyze potential actions and counteractions by other organizations. Planning must be extensive and forecast a variety of scenarios. As conditions continue to change, the plans must be updated.

Adjusting internal operations. Work based on environmental typologies and on innovation and change suggest a contingency approach to organizational design. The way an organization should be designed depends in part on its environment. In other words, no one best way exists to organize schools. Rather, the most effective school structure is one that adjusts to the dimensions of its environment. Several contingency approaches are useful.

The first researchers to indicate that different types of organizational structure might be effective in different situations were Tom Burns and G. M. Stalker.[41] In an early study of twenty English industrial firms, Burns and Stalker demonstrated the relationship between external environment and internal administrative arrangements. Using interviews with managers and their own observations, they found that the type of structure that existed in rapidly changing and dynamic environments was significantly different from the type that existed in stable environments. When the external environment was stable, the internal organization was "mechanistic"—that is, characterized by formal rules and centralized decision making. Relying heavily on programmed behaviors, mechanistic organizations performed routine tasks effectively and efficiently, but responded relatively slowly to unfamiliar events. In highly unstable environments, the internal organization was "organic"—that is informal, flexible, and adaptive. The emphasis was on informal agreements about rules, decentralized decision making, collegial relations, open communication, and influence based on expertise. Burns and Stalker did not conclude that the mechanistic model was inferior to the organic model, but rather, that the most effective structure is one that adjusts to the requirements of the environment—a mechanistic design in a stable environment, and an organic form in an unstable environment.

Organizational arrangements to fit each environmental condition of the typology based on uncertainty (see Figure 4.2) have also been proposed.[42] A synthesis of the proposed configurations is summarized in Figure 4.3.

Taken separately, the two dimensions suggest different organizational configurations. When the environment is simple, internal structures and processes are simple. As complexity increases, however, an organization needs more departments to analyze and relate to the increased elements in its environment. When the environment is stable, internal arrangements tend to be routine, formal, and centralized. As instability increases, the structures and processes tend to become less formal and more decentralized. Moreover, planning assumes added importance because the organization reduces uncertainty by anticipating future changes.

Simple, stable environments yield centralized bureaucratic structures that rely on standardized work processes. In simple, stable environments, for example, school districts would have extensive curricular plans and all teachers would be expected to follow the guides using the same teaching behaviors. In contrast, complex, stable environments lead to somewhat decentralized bureaucratic structures. School districts in complex, stable environments try to coordinate the instructional program through standard skills of teachers. They become bureaucratic because of the standard knowledge and procedures

Environmental Complexity

	Simple	Complex
Stable	Category One: Low Uncertainty 1. Formal, centralized structure 2. Coordination by standardized work processes 3. Few departments, schools or divisions 4. Limited integration	Category Two: Low Moderate Uncertainty 1. Formal, somewhat decentralized structure 2. Coordination by standardized skills 3. Many departments, schools or divisions 4. Some integration
Unstable	Category Three: High Moderate Uncertainty 1. Informal, somewhat decentralized structure 2. Coordination by direct supervision 3. Few departments, schools or divisions 4. Some integration	Category Four: High Uncertainty 1. Informal and decentralized structure 2. Coordination by informal communication 3. Many departments, schools or divisions 4. Extensive integration

Environmental Change (axis label, left side)

FIGURE 4.3 Contingency model for environmental uncertainty and school structure

learned in formal training programs and imposed on the organization by certification and accrediting agencies.[43]

Simple, unstable environments also produce some flexibility in the bureaucratic structure, but decisions tend to remain centralized. Schools in this type of environment use direct supervision to coordinate the instructional program, that is, administrators emphasize classroom observation and evaluation procedures. Complex, unstable environments lead to flexible, informal, and decentralized structures. In complex, unstable environments, school organizations must decentralize decisions to administrators, specialists, and teachers who can comprehend the issues. The school must be responsive to unpredictable changes. Informal communication becomes the prime coordinating mechanism as individuals and groups cope with the uncertain environment.

Just as the information perspective suggests a structural contingency approach, so does the resource dependency model. According to resource dependency theory, the environment does not impose strict requirements for survival. Therefore, a wide range of possible actions and organizational structures are possible; hence, criteria guiding decisions and determining structures become both important and problematic. Internal power differences are important because no single optimal structure or set of actions aligns the organization with its environment. Instead, a range of choices or strategies of alignment is available. The influence of a variety of internal stakeholders may determine, in interaction with the demands of external constituencies, the response of the organization. Resource dependence theory highlights the importance of environmental factors in promoting and restraining organizational decisions and actions, yet at the same time leaves room for the operation of strategic choice on the part of organizational members as they maneuver through known and unknown contexts. In other words, the resource dependence model posits that although environmental influences are important, environmental constraints do not reduce the feasible set of structures to only one form. Rather, a variety of internal structures and actions are consistent with the survival of the organization, which means that although the organization may have the goal of survival, survival does not imply only a single or very limited set of structural forms.[44]

As a note of caution in applying the findings from contingency research, structural and process variations occur across schools as a result of active alternative generation and search procedures to adapt and change the environment. In fact, Boyd argues that schools are neither "mirror images" of the communities they serve nor are they completely insulated bastions dominated by unresponsive and self-serving professional educators.[45] To a considerable extent, school organizations can shape their environments to fit their capabilities.

Spanning organizational boundaries. Creating internal roles that span organizational boundaries to link the school district with elements in the external environment is also an important strategy for coping with uncertainty and dependence. Two classes of functions are typically performed by boundary-spanning roles: to detect information about changes in the external environment and to represent the organization to the environment.

For the detection function, boundary roles concentrate on the transfer of information between the environment and school district. Boundary personnel scan and monitor events in the environment that can create abrupt changes and long-term trends, and communicate the information to decision makers.[46] By identifying new technological developments, curricular innovations, regulations and funding patterns, boundary personnel provide data which enable the school district to make plans and adjust programs. In contrast to buffering personnel, boundary spanners act to keep the school organization an open system in harmony with the environment. A number of individuals in schools, e.g., superintendents and principals, play both buffering and boundary-spanning roles.

For the representation purpose, boundary spanning personnel send information into the environment from the organization. The idea is to influence other people's perceptions of the organization. School districts often have offices of public information whose express purpose is to communicate information to significant stakeholders. Other district offices also can serve this function. For example, community and adult education programs, which primarily attract taxpaying patrons, can exemplify the quality of instruction that is available to the district's students. Business and legal departments can inform legislators about the school district's needs or views on political matters. Similarly, the boards of education and school advisory committees link the school organization to important constituencies in the environment in a highly visible way where they will feel their interests are being represented. Thus, women, minority-group members, and students are appointed in increasing numbers to a variety of advisory committees.[47] Managing the school's image can reduce uncertainty and dependence on the various elements in the environment.

Interorganizational Coping Strategies

Thus far we have described ways in which school organizations can adapt internally to the external environment. Schools also reach out and change their environments. Two types of strategies are used to manage the external environment: establish favorable linkages with key environmental elements and shape the environmental elements. A point to be remembered about attempts to control the environment is that it, too, has some organized character and the ability to fight back.[48]

Establishing favorable linkages. In business organizations a favorite mechanism to reduce competition and dependence is the merger. If a source of raw material is uncertain, buying the supplier removes the dependence on the external element. Although educational organizations cannot rely on mergers, they can enter into joint ventures with other organizations. School districts contract with the private foundations, universities, and federal and state governments to share the risks and costs associated with large-scale innovations and research projects. Current examples of joint ventures include Headstart, Follow Through, Individually Guided Education, special education programs, and vocational education. David M. Boje and David A. Whetten found that, from a variety of organizational linkage strategies, the number of joint ventures was the best predictor of organizational influence on the environment.[49]

Co-optation represents another strategy of developing favorable linkages. Co-opting means bringing leaders from important elements in the environment or the elements themselves into the policy structure of the school organization. Co-optation occurs when influential citizens are appointed to boards of education or to advisory committees. The evidence, however, is mixed for increasing the influence of organizations through advisory councils. The research by Pfeffer[50] was supportive, although findings of Boje and Whetten[51] were not. Another typical example of co-optation is the hiring of militant teachers or other activists to administrative positions. In these roles the co-opted individuals have an interest in the school and are introduced to the needs of the district. As a result they are more likely to include the district's interests in their decision making and less likely to be critical of the decision in which they participated.

Shaping environmental elements.　Politicking is a primary method of shaping environmental elements for school districts. Political activity includes techniques to influence government legislation and regulation. School district officials and paid lobbyists express their views to members of state and federal legislators and other governmental officials. Political strategy can be used to erect barriers against unwanted influences and to establish rules favorable to existing schools and their policies. For example, public schools have engaged in extensive efforts to block state and federal support to private schools. Intense lobbying campaigns have been made against proposals concerning tuition tax credits and educational vouchers.

A related strategy to shape the external environment is forming educational associations that usually have both professional and political missions. Stephen P. Robbins termed this tactic "third party soliciting."[52] A significant portion of the work to influence the environment for education is accomplished jointly with other organizations that have similar interests, e.g., Parent-Teachers Association, National Education Association, American Federation of Teachers, American Association of School Administrators, Council for American Private Education, and National Federation of Urban-Suburban School Districts. The list is long. By pooling resources, individual educators or educational organizations can afford to pay people to carry out activities such as lobbying legislators, influencing new regulations, promoting educational programs, and presenting public relations campaigns. These associations attempt to use state certification boards to restrict entry, regulate competition, and maintain stability in the profession.

A successful attempt to shape educational policy has been detailed by Tim L. Mazzoni and Betty Malen.[53] They analyzed a series of case studies dealing with constituency mobilization to impact state educational policy. In essence, an alliance consisting of the Minnesota Catholic Conference and the Citizens for Educational Freedom wanted the legislature to provide tax concessions for private school parents. Using both electoral and lobbying tactics, the alliance was able to persuade the legislature to endorse a tax concession package. The alliance kept the issue continuously on the legislative agenda, energized sympathetic lawmakers to carry its bills, and, most important, mobilized grassroots constituency pressure to sway votes among legislators. Mazzoni and Malen concluded that the political strategy of constituency mobilization had a significant impact on this policy issue.

The overall implication for practice is that school organizations do not have to be simple passive instruments of the external environment. Both internal and external coping strategies can be used to buffer environmental influences and actually to change the demands. Structures, programs, and processes can be developed by educational administrators to manage the environments of their school organizations.

SUMMARY

The emergence of open-systems theory during the past two decades has highlighted the importance, the external environment on internal school structures and processes. Although it does not have a firm definition, environment can be understood by its most salient dimensions. In this regard, a useful distinction is between broad factors, which are general trends that can *potentially* affect school operations, and specific factors, which are elements or conditions that have immediate and direct effects on schools. Moreover, three general characteristics—uncertainty, clustering, and scarcity—are useful in the analysis of environments of schools.

Two perspectives of the environment have been developed, using the three general factors. The information perspective assumes that the environment is a source of information to be used by organizational decision makers. An important tenet of this approach is that perception is the intervening link between the school's environment and actions taken by decision makers. Research supports the fundamental hypothesis that perceived environmental uncertainty affects the degree of flexibility and bureaucratic configuration of organizations. In contrast, the resource dependency approach assumes that organizations cannot generate internally the needed resources and that resources must come from the environment. As a result, this perspective treats the environment as the degree of scarcity available to maintain stability and growth. School organizations, then, must enter into exchanges with environmental elements that supply the needed resources and can use the products and services of the school. The two perspectives can be joined in two ways. Uncertainty of information and resource dependence interact to enhance the other's effect, and both rely on the environmental perceptions of decision makers.

Because environmental uncertainty and resource dependence threaten organizational autonomy and effectiveness, administrators often try to minimize external effects on the internal school operations. Their responses can be classified as either internal or interorganizational coping strategies. Internal coping strategies include buffering the technical core, planning and forecasting, adjusting internal operations based on contingency theory, and spanning organizational boundaries. Interorganization coping strategies include establishing favorable linkages with important external constituencies and shaping environmental elements through political actions. By using the coping strategies, school administrators can to some degree reduce the environmental uncertainty and dependence of their school organizations.

NOTES

1. William L. Boyd and Robert L. Crowson, "The Changing Conception and Practice of Public School Administration," *Review of Research in Education,* 9 (1981), 311–373.
2. James L. Bowditch and Anthony F. Buono, *A Primer on Organizational Behavior* (New York: Wiley, 1985), p. 158.
3. *Ibid.,* p. 159.
4. Two other perspectives of organizational environments, population ecology and institutionalization will not be considered. Sources presenting the population approach include the following: Glenn R. Carroll, "Organizational Ecology," *Annual Review of Sociology,* 10 (1984), 71–93; Michael T. Hannan and John Freeman, "Structural Inertia and Organizational Change," *American Sociological Review,* 49 (1984), 149–164; Michael T. Hannan and John Freeman, "The Population Ecology of Organizations," *American Journal of Sociology,* 82 (1977), 929–964; and Bill McKelvey, *Organizational Systematics: Taxonomy, Evolution, Classification* (Berkeley, CA: University of California Press, 1982). Sources presenting the institutionalization perspective include the following: Paul DiMaggio and Walter Powell, "The Iron Cage Revisited: Institutional Isomorphism and Collective Rationality in Organizational Fields," *American Sociological Review,* 48 (1983), 147–160; John Meyer and Brian Rowan, "Institutionalized Organizations: Formal Structure as Myth and Ceremony," *American Journal of Sociology,* 83 (1977), 340–363; Brian Rowan, "Organizational Structure and the Institutional Environment: The Case of Public Schools," *Administrative Science Quarterly,* 27 (1982), 259–279; Pamela S. Tolbert, Institutional Environments and Resource Dependence: Sources of Administrative Structure in Institutions of Higher Education," *Administrative Science Quarterly,* 30 (1985), 1–13; and Lynne Zucker, "Organizations as Institutions," *Research in the Sociology of Organizations,* 2 (1983), 1–47.
5. Lee G. Bolman and Terrence E. Deal, *Modern Approaches to Understanding and Managing Organizations* (San Francisco: Jossey-Bass, 1984), p. 44.
6. Richard L. Daft, *Organization Theory and Design* (St. Paul: West, 1983), p. 42.
7. W. Richard Scott, *Organizations: Rational, Natural, and Open Systems* (Englewood Cliffs, NJ: Prentice-Hall, 1981), p. 165.
8. Gerald Zaltman, Robert Duncan, and Jonny Holbek, *Innovations and Organizations* (New York: Wiley, 1973), p. 114.
9. *Ibid.*
10. The discussion of general and specific environments relies on the ideas presented by Bowditch and Buono, *op. cit.,* pp. 159–160.

11. Ray Jurkovich, "A Core Typology of Organizational Environments," *Administrative Science Quarterly,* 19 (1974), 380–394.
12. *Ibid.,* p. 382.
13. James D. Thompson, *Organizations in Action* (New York: McGraw-Hill, 1967), pp. 10–13.
14. Daniel Katz and Robert L. Kahn, *The Social Psychology of Organizations,* 2nd ed. (New York: Wiley, 1978), pp. 126–128.
15. *Ibid.*
16. Howard Aldrich and Sergio Mindlin, "Uncertainty and Dependence: Two Perspectives on Environment," in Lucien Karpik (ed.), *Organization and Environment: Theory, Issues and Reality* (Beverly Hills, CA: Sage, 1978), pp. 149–170.
17. Fred E. Emery and Eric L. Trist, "The Causal Texture of Organization Environments," *Human Relations,* 18 (1965), 21–32. The presentation of the typology relies on the works of Emery and Trist, *ibid.;* and Daft, *op. cit.,* pp. 52–53.
18. Bowditch and Buono, *op. cit.,* p. 164.
19. Shirley Terreberry, "The Evolution of Organizational Environments," *Administrative Science Quarterly,* 12 (1968), 590–613.
20. Thompson, *op. cit.,* pp. 70–73.
21. Paul R. Lawrence and Jay W. Lorsch, *Organization and Environment* (Homewood, IL: Irwin, 1967), pp. 23–53.
22. Jurkovich, *op. cit.*
23. Lawrence and Lorsch, *op. cit.*
24. William R. Dill, "Environment as an Influence on Managerial Autonomy," *Administrative Science Quarterly,* 2 (1958), 409–443.
25. Robert B. Duncan, "Characteristics of Organizational Environments and Perceived Environmental Uncertainty," *Administrative Science Quarterly,* 17 (1972), 313–327.
26. An excellent evaluation is made of the most frequently used perceptual measures of uncertainty by H. Kirk Downey, Don Hellriegel, and John W. Slocum, Jr., "Environmental Uncertainty: The Construct and Its Application," *Administrative Science Quarterly,* 20 (1975), 613–629.
27. Howard Aldrich, "An Organization-Environment Perspective on Cooperation and Conflict between Organizations in the Manpower Training System," in Amant R. Negandi (ed.), *Conflict and Power in Complex Organizations* (Kent, OH: Center for Business and Economic Research, Kent State University, 1972), pp. 11–37; and J. Kenneth Benson, "The Interorganizational Network as a Political Economy," *Administrative Science Quarterly,* 20 (1975), 229–249.
28. Aldrich and Mindlin, *op. cit.,* pp. 156–157, trace the development of the dependency concept through the following works: Richard Emerson, "Power-Dependence Relations," *American Sociological Review,* 27 (1962), 31–41; Peter Blau, *Exchange and Power in Social Life* (New York: Wiley, 1964); David Jacobs, "Dependency and Vulnerability: An Exchange Approach to the Control of Organizations," *Administrative Science Quarterly,* 19 (1974), 45–59; and Sergio E. Mindlin and Howard Aldrich, "Interorganizational Dependence: A Review of the Concept and a Reexamination of the Findings of the Aston Group," *Administrative Science Quarterly,* 20 (1975), 382–392.

29. Andrew H. Van De Ven and Diane L. Ferry, *Measuring and Assessing Organizations* (New York: Wiley, 1980), p. 311.
30. The primary proponent of resource dependency theory probably has been Jeffrey Pfeffer. References to his work include the following: Jeffrey Pfeffer, *Organizations and Organization Theory* (Boston: Pitman, 1982), pp. 192–207; Jeffrey Pfeffer, *Power in Organizations* (Boston: Pitman, 1981), 99–115; Jeffrey Pfeffer, "Size and Composition of Corporate Boards of Directors: The Organization and Its Environment," *Administrative Science Quarterly*, 17 (1972), 218–228; Jeffrey Pfeffer and Gerald Salancik, *The External Control of Organizations: A Resource Dependence Perspective* (New York: Harper & Row, 1978); Jeffrey Pfeffer and Huseyin Leblebici, "The Effect of Competition on Some Dimensions of Organizational Structure," *Social Forces*, 52 (1973), 268–279; and Howard W. Aldrich and Jeffrey Pfeffer, "Environments of Organizations," *Annual Review of Sociology*, 2 (1976), 79–105. The present discussion of resource dependency theory draws heavily from these sources.
31. Jeffrey Pfeffer, "Beyond Management and the Worker: The Institutional Function of Management," *Academy of Management Review*, 1 (1976), 36–46.
32. Michael Aiken and Jerald Hage, "Organizational Interdependence and Intra-Organizational Structure," *American Sociological Review*, 33 (1968), 912–930.
33. Mindlin and Aldrich, *op. cit.*
34. Aldrich and Mindlin, *op. cit.*, p. 161.
35. An excellent example of using the "objective" types of measurement in dependency theory is found in the study by Derek D. Pugh, D. J. Hickson, C. R. Hinings, and C. Turner, "The Context of Organizational Structure," *Administrative Science Quarterly*, 14 (1969), 91–114.
36. Aldrich and Mindlin, *op. cit.*, p. 157.
37. Bowditch and Buono, *op. cit.*, p. 165.
38. Karl E. Weick, *The Social Psychology of Organizing* (Reading, MA: Addison-Wesley, 1969).
39. Thompson, *op. cit.*, pp. 19–24, discusses buffering, smoothing, forecasting, and rationing as internal coping mechanisms. For educational organizations, buffering, planning, and forecasting appear to be widely applicable and, therefore, the present discussion focuses on these strategies.
40. Daft, *op. cit.*, p. 56.
41. Tom Burns and G. M. Stalker, *The Management of Innovation* (London: Tavistock, 1961).
42. Similar recommendations have been made by Robert Duncan, "What Is the Right Organizational Structure? Decision Tree Analysis Provides the Answer," *Organizational Dynamics*, 7 (1979), 59–80; Henry Mintzberg, *The Structuring of Organizations* (Englewood Cliffs, NJ: Prentice-Hall, 1979), pp. 285–287; and Daft, *op. cit.*, pp. 63–64.
43. Mintzberg, *op. cit.*, p. 286.
44. Aldrich and Pfeffer, *op. cit.*, p. 83–84.
45. William L. Boyd, "The Public, the Professional, and Educational Policy Making: Who Governs?", *Teachers College Record*, 77 (1976), 539–577.
46. Daft, *op. cit.*, pp. 56–58.

47. Howard Aldrich and Diane Herker, "Boundary Spanning Roles and Organization Structure," *Academy of Management Review,* 2 (1977), 217–230.
48. Katz and Kahn, *op. cit.,* p. 131.
49. David M. Boje and David A. Whetten, "Effects of Organizational Strategies and Contextual Constraints on Centrality and Attributions of Influence in Interorganizational Networks," *Administrative Science Quarterly,* 26 (1981), 378–395.
50. Pfeffer, *op. cit.,* 1972.
51. Boje and Whetten, *op. cit.*
52. Stephen P. Robbins, *The Structure and Design of Organizations* (Englewood Cliffs, NJ: Prentice-Hall, 1983), p. 163.
53. Tim L. Mazzoni and Betty Malen, "Mobilizing Constituency Pressure to Influence State Education Policy Making," *Educational Administration Quarterly,* 21 (1985), 91–116.

Chapter 5

Bureaucracy and the School

The educational system of a given society reflects that social system, and at the same time it is the main force perpetuating it. It may be perceived as the most powerful means of social control to which individuals must submit, and as one of the most universal models of social relationships to which they will refer later.

MICHAEL CROZIER
The Bureaucratic Phenomenon

The institutional element of a social system is found in the formal organization or, more specifically, as the bureaucratic structure of a school district. Max Weber's general theory of authority structures provides the classic analysis of bureaucratic structures; hence, a good beginning point for our discussion of bureaucracy is the concept of authority. Authority relationships are an integral part of life in formal school organizations. The essence of most student-teacher, teacher-administrator, or subordinate-superior relations is authority. Unfortunately, to many individuals authority and authoritarianism are synonymous. Because this is not the case, authority as a theoretical concept must be clearly defined.

THE CONCEPT OF AUTHORITY

Contrary to some popular beliefs, the exercise of authority in a school typically does *not* involve coercion. Authority must be distinguished from a related concept—power. Power is the ability to get others to do what you want them to do, or as Weber defines it, "the probability that one actor within a social relationship will be in a position to carry out his own will despite resistance."[1] *Power,* for our purposes, is a general and comprehensive term. It includes control that is starkly coercive as well as control that is based on nonthreatening

108

persuasion and suggestion. *Authority* has a narrower scope than power. Weber defines authority as "the probability that certain specific commands (or all commands) from a given source will be obeyed by a given group of persons."[2] Weber is quick to indicate that authority does *not* include every mode of exercising power or influence over other persons. He suggests that a certain degree of voluntary compliance is associated with legitimate commands.[3] Unlike power, authority implies legitimacy; that is, authority is a legitimate kind of power.

Herbert A. Simon proposes that authority is distinguished from other kinds of influence or power in that the subordinate "holds in abeyance his own critical faculties for choosing between alternatives and uses the formal criterion of the receipt of a command or signal as his basis of choice."[4] Therefore, two criteria of authority in schools are crucial in superior-subordinate relationships: (1) voluntary compliance to legitimate commands; and (2) suspension of one's own criteria for decision making and acceptance of the organizational command.

Peter Blau and W. Richard Scott argue that a third criterion must be added to distinguish authority from other forms of social control. They maintain that "a value orientation must arise that defines the exercise of social control as legitimate, and this orientation can arise only in a group context."[5] Authority is legitimized by a value that is held in common by the group. Blau and Scott conclude that a basic characteristic of the authority relation is the subordinates' willingness to suspend their own criteria for making decisions and comply with directives from the superior. This willingness results largely from social constraints exerted by norms of the social collectivity (teachers and students) and not primarily from the power the superior (administrator) brings to bear. Such social constraints are not typical of coercive power and other types of social influence. Authority relations in school organizations, then, have three primary characteristics: (1) a willingness of subordinates to comply; (2) a suspension of the subordinates' criteria for making a decision prior to a directive; and (3) a power relationship legitimized by the norms of a group.

TYPES OF AUTHORITY

Authority exists when a common set of beliefs (norms) in a school legitimizes the use of power as "right and proper." Weber distinguishes three types of authority according to the kind of legitimacy typically claimed by each.[6]

Charismatic authority rests on devotion to an extraordinary individual who is leader by virture of personal trust or exemplary qualities.[7] Charismatic authority tends to be nonrational, affective, or emotional and rests heavily on the leader's personal qualities and characteristics. The authority of the charismatic leader results primarily from the leader's overwhelming personal appeal, and typically a common value orientation emerges within the group to produce an intense normative commitment to and identification with the *person*. Thus, students may obey classroom directives because of a teacher's personal "mystique."

Traditional authority is anchored in an established belief in the sanctity of the status of those exercising authority in the past.[8] Obedience is owed to the traditionally sanctioned *position* of authority, and the person who occupies the position inherits the authority established by custom. In a school, for example, students may accept the authority of the position and the teacher because their parents and grandparents did so before them.

Legal authority is based on enacted laws that can be changed by formally correct procedures. Obedience is not owed to a person or position per se but to the *laws* that specify to whom and to what extent people owe compliance. Legal authority thus extends only within the scope of the authority vested in the office by law.[9] In a school obedience is owed to the impersonal principles that govern the operation of the organization.

Other scholars and organizational theorists have extended these basic concepts of authority. Robert Peabody distinguishes the bases of formal authority —legitimacy and position—from the bases of functional authority—competence and personal or human relations skills (see Table 5.1).[10]

Formal authority is vested in the organization and is legally established in positions, rules, and regulations. In joining the organization, employees accept the authority relation because they agree, within certain limits, to accept the directives of their supervisors; the organization has the right to command and the employees have the duty to obey.[11] The basis of formal authority, then, rests with the legally established agreement between the organization and the employees.

Functional authority has a variety of sources, including authority of competence and authority of person. Although Weber treats authority of competence as part of the legal-rational pattern of bureaucracies, competence is not always limited to position. Technical competence can provide the source for legitimate control and directives in a formal organization regardless of the specific position held. This fact poses a dilemma and conflict for professionals (a subject to which we shall return shortly).

Authority stemming from personal behavior and attributes is another distinct source for legitimate control in the superior-subordinate relationship. In an organizational context, such authority is often informal because the norms of the informal organization often buttress and legitimize the power of the individual.

Weber saw no conflict between formal and functional authority; indeed, his conception of legal-rational authority cuts across the formal-functional distinction and provides for a bureaucratic structure in which the administrative staff becomes legally established and rationally organized.

WEBERIAN MODEL OF BUREAUCRACY

Almost all modern organizations have many of the characteristics enumerated by Weber—a division of labor and specialization, an impersonal orientation, a hierarchy of authority, rules and regulations, and a career orientation.

TABLE 5.1 **Bases of Authority**

	Formal Authority		Functional Authority	
	Legitimacy	*Position*	*Competence*	*Person*
Weber[a]	Legal authority Legal order	Hierarchal office	Rational authority Technical knowledge	Traditional authority Charismatic authority
Urwick[b]		Formal, conferred by the organization	Technical, implicit in special knowledge or skill	Personal, conferred by seniority or popularity
Simon[c]	Authority of legitimacy, social approval	Authority of sanctions	Authority of confidence (technical competence)	Techniques persuasion (as distinct from authority)
Bennis[d]		Role incumbency	Knowledge of performance criteria	Knowledge of the human aspect of administration
Presthus[e]	Generalized deference toward authority	Formal role or position	Technical expertise	Rapport with subordinates, ability to mediate individual needs

[a]Max Weber, *The Theory of Social and Economic Organization*, A. M. Henderson and Talcott Parsons (trans.), Talcott Parsons (ed.) (Glencoe, IL: Free Press, 1947), pp. 328, 339.

[b]L. Urwick, *The Elements of Administration* (London: Sir I. Pitman & Sons, Ltd., 1944), p. 42.

[c]Herbert A. Simon, "Authority," in Conrad M. Arensberg et al. (eds.), *Research in Industrial Administration* (New York: Harper & Row, 1957), pp. 104–106; Herbert A. Simon et al., *Public Administration* (New York: Knopf, 1950), pp. 189–201.

[d]Warren G. Bennis, "Leadership Theory and Administrative Behavior: The Problem of Authority," *Administrative Science Quarterly*, 4 (1959), 288–289.

[e]Robert V. Presthus, "Authority in Organizations," *Public Administration Review*, 20 (1960), 88–91.

Table from Robert Peabody, "Perceptions of Organizational Authority: A Comparative Analysis," *Administrative Science Quarterly*, Volume 6 #4 (1962), 467.

Division of Labor and Specialization

According to Weber, division of labor and specialization mean that "the regular activities required for the purposes of the bureaucratically governed structure are distributed in a fixed way as official duties."[12] Because the tasks in most organizations are too complex to be performed by a single individual, division of labor among positions improves efficiency. In schools, for example, division of labor is primarily for instructional purposes. Within that division, subspecialties are based on level—elementary and secondary—and subject—math, science, and so forth.

Efficiency increases because division of labor produces specialization, which in turn leads to employees who become knowledgeable and expert at performing their prescribed duties. Such division enables the organization to employ personnel on the basis of technical qualifications. Hence, division of labor and specialization produce more expertise in school personnel.

Impersonal Orientation

Weber argued that the working atmosphere of a bureaucracy should provide "the dominance of a spirit of formalistic impersonality, *'sine ira et studio,'* without hatred or passion, and hence without affection or enthusiasm."[13] The bureaucratic employee is expected to make decisions based on facts, not feelings. Impersonality on the part of administrators and teachers assures equality of treatment and facilitates rationality.

Hierarchy of Authority

Offices are arranged hierarchically in bureaucracies; that is, "each lower office is under the control and supervision of a higher one."[14] This bureaucratic trait is made manifest in the organizational chart, with the superintendent at the top and assistants, directors, principals, teachers, and students at successively lower levels.

Hierarchy is perhaps the most pervasive characteristic in modern organizations. Almost without exception, large organizations develop a well-established system of superordination and subordination, which attempts to guarantee the disciplined compliance to directives from superiors that is necessary for implementing the various tasks and functions of an organization.

Rules and Regulations

Weber asserts that every bureaucracy has a "consistent system of abstract rules which have normally been intentionally established. Furthermore, administration of law is held to consist in the application of these rules to particular cases."[15] The system of rules covers the rights and duties inherent in each position and helps to coordinate activities in the hierarchy. It also provides continuity of operations when there are changes in personnel. Rules and regulations thus ensure uniformity and stability of employee action.

Career Orientation

Since employment in a bureaucratic organization is based on technical qualifications, employees think of their work as a career. Whenever there is such a career orientation, Weber maintains, "there is a system of promotion according to seniority, achievement, or both. Promotion is dependent on the judgment of superiors."[16] To foster loyalty to the organization, individuals with special skills must be protected from arbitrary dismissal or denial of promotion. Employees are protected in the sense that superiors are encouraged to make dispassionate decisions. Bureaucracies also institutionalize protection through such devices as civil service and tenure.

Efficiency

To Weber, bureaucracy maximizes rational decision making and administrative efficiency: "Experience tends to universally show that the purely bureaucratic type of administrative organization . . . is, from a purely technical point of view, capable of attaining the highest degree of efficiency."[17] Division of labor and specialization produce experts, and experts with an impersonal orientation make technically correct, rational decisions based on the facts. Once rational decisions have been made, the hierarchy of authority ensures disciplined compliance to directives and, along with rules and regulations, a well-coordinated system of implementation and uniformity and stability in the operation of the organization. Finally, a career orientation provides the incentive for employees to be loyal to the organization and to produce that extra effort. These characteristics function to maximize administrative efficiency because committed experts make rational decisions that are executed and coordinated in a disciplined way.

Ideal Type

Although Weber's conception of bureaucracy is an ideal type that may or may not be found in the real world, it does highlight or emphasize basic tendencies of actual organizations. Hence, as an ideal type, it is quite useful for analytic purposes. As Alvin Gouldner explains, the ideal type may serve as a guide to help us determine how a formal organization is bureaucratized.[18] Some organizations will be more bureaucratically structured than others. A given organization can be more bureaucratized on one characteristic and less on another characteristic. The model, as a conceptual scheme, raises important questions about organizing different kinds of formal bureaucracies. For example, under what conditions are the dimensions of bureaucracy related in order to maximize efficiency? Under what conditions does such an arrangement hinder efficiency?

CRITICISMS OF THE WEBERIAN BUREAUCRATIC MODEL

Functions and Dysfunctions of the Model

Weber's model of bureaucracy is functional in that application of the principles can promote efficiency and goal attainment. There is, however, the possibility of dysfunctional or negative consequences, a possibility to which Weber pays limited attention. Let us consider each of the above bureaucratic characteristics or principles in terms of both possible functions and dysfunctions.

Although division of labor and specialization can produce expertise, they also can produce boredom. The literature is replete with instances where such boredom leads to lower levels of productivity or to a search on the part of employees for ways to make their work life more interesting. The Hawthorne studies discussed in Chapter 1, particularly the Bank Wiring Observation Room studies, provide one example. Indeed, many highly bureaucratized organizations that have experienced the negative consequences of extreme division of labor are enlarging employee responsibility to alleviate boredom.

Impersonality may improve rationally in decision making, but it also may produce a rather sterile atmosphere in which people interact as "nonpersons," resulting in low morale. Low morale, in turn, frequently impairs organizational efficiency.

Hierarchy of authority does enhance coordination, but frequently at the expense of communication. Two of the major dysfunctions of hierarchy are distortion and blockage in communication. Every level in the hierarchy produces a potential communication block, for subordinates are reluctant to communicate anything that might make them look bad in the eyes of their superiors; in fact, there is probably a tendency to communicate only those things that make them look good or those things that they think their superiors want to hear.[19]

Rules and regulations, on one hand, do provide for continuity, coordination, stability, and uniformity. On the other hand, they often produce organizational rigidity and goal displacement. Employees may become so rule-oriented that they forget that the rules and regulations are *means* to achieve goals, not *ends* in themselves. Disciplined compliance with the hierarchy and, particularly, with the regulations frequently produces rigidity and an inability to adjust. Such formalism may be exaggerated until conformity interferes with goal achievement. In such a case, the infamous characteristic of bureaucratic red tape is vividly apparent.[20]

Career orientation is healthy insofar as it produces a sense of employee loyalty and motivates employees to maximize effort. Promotion, however, is based on seniority and achievement, which are not necessarily compatible. For example, rapid promotion of high achievers often produces discontent among the loyal, hard-working, senior employees who are not as creative.

The potential dysfunctional consequences of each bureaucratic characteristic are not adequately addressed in Weber's ideal type. Table 5.2 summarizes some of the dysfunctions as well as the functions of the Weberian model. The question now becomes: Under what conditions does each characteristic lead to functional but not dysfunctional consequences? Whatever the answer to this question, the model remains quite useful as both an analytical tool and a guide to scientific research.

Functions and Dysfunctions of Rules

To illustrate the analytic and research usefulness of the model, we focus on Gouldner's discussion of organizational rules.[21] Almost without exception, large, formal organizations have systems of rules and regulations that guide organizational behavior. For example, most school districts have elaborate policy manuals. Rules are so universally present because they serve important functions.

Organizational rules have an explication function, that is, they explain in rather concise and explicit terms the specific obligations of subordinates. Rules make it unnecessary to repeat a routine order; moreover, they are less ambiguous and more carefully throught out than the hasty verbal command. Rules act as a system of communication to direct role performance.

A second function of rules is to screen, that is, to act as a buffer between the administrator and his or her subordinates. Rules carry a sense of egalitarianism because they can be applied equally to everyone. An administrator's denial of a request from a subordinate can be on the grounds that the rules apply to everyone, superior and subordinate alike, and cannot be broken. Subordinate

TABLE 5.2 Functions and Dysfunctions of the Weberian Model

Dysfunction	Bureaucratic Characteristic	Function
Boredom ⟵	— Division of labor →	Expertise
Lack of morale ⟵	— Impersonal orientation →	Rationality
Communication blocks ⟵	— Hierarchy of authority →	Disciplined compliance and coordination
Rigidity and goal displacement ⟵	— Rules and regulations →	Continuity and uniformity
Conflict between achievement and seniority ⟵	— Career orientation →	Incentive

TABLE 5.3   The Double-Edged Nature of Bureaucratic Rules

Bureaucratic Rules	
Functions	*Dysfunctions*
Explication ⟷	Apathy reinforcement
Screening ⟷	Goal displacement
Punishment-legitimizing ⟷	Legalism
Leeway ⟷	Indulgency

anger is therefore redirected to the impersonal rules and regulations. As Gouldner explains, rules impersonally support a claim to authority without forcing the leader to legitimize personal superiority; conversely, they permit a subordinate to accept directives without betraying his or her sense of being "any man's equal."[22]

Organizational rules may also legitimize punishment. When subordinates are given explicitly prior warning about what behavior will provoke sanctions and about the nature of those sanctions, punishment is legitimate. As Gouldner indicates, there is a deep-rooted feeling in our culture that punishment is permissible only when the offender knows *in advance* that certain behaviors are forbidden; ex post facto judgments are not permissible.[23] In effect, rules not only legitimize but impersonalize the administration of punishment.

Rules also serve a bargaining or "leeway" function. Using formal rules as a bargaining tool, superiors can secure informal cooperation from subordinates. By *not* enforcing certain rules and regulations, one's sphere of authority can be expanded through the development of goodwill among subordinates. Rules are serviceable because they create something that can be given up as well as given use.[24]

For each functional consequence of rules discussed thus far, a corresponding dysfunctional outcome results. Rules reinforce and preserve apathy by explicating the minimum level of acceptable behavior. Some employees remain apathetic because they know how little is required for them to remain secure. When apathy is fused with hostility, the scene is set for "organizational sabotage," which occurs when conforming to the letter of the rule violates the express purpose of the rule.[25]

Although rules screen the superior from subordinates, that protection may become dysfunctional; goal displacement develops and rules become ends in themselves. By using rules to make important decisions, administrators may focus attention on the importance of a rule orientation, often at the expense of more important goals.

Another dysfunctional consequence that emerges from the screening and punishment functions of rules is legalism. When rules and punishments are pervasive, subordinates can adopt an extremely legalistic stance. In effect, they become "Philadelphia lawyers," willing and potentially able to win their case on a technicality. In its extreme form, employees may use legalism as an excuse for inactivity in any area not covered by a rule. When an individual is asked why he or she is not performing a reasonable task, the "pat" answer is, "No rule says I have to." To say the least, such extreme legalism creates an unhealthy climate in schools.

The leeway function of rules—not enforcing them in exchange for informal cooperation—involves the ever-present danger of being too lenient. The classic example of this kind of permissiveness is seen in the indulgency pattern described in Gouldner's study of a factory in which few, if any, rules were enforced; although superior-subordinate relations were friendly, productivity suffered.[26] Table 5.3 summarizes the double-edged nature of bureaucratic rules.

School administrators who are aware can avoid the dysfunctional consequences of rules. The Gouldner model, presented in Figure 5.1, illustrates not only the functional and dysfunctional nature of some rules, but also the unanticipated consequences that create a vicious circle in which rules are perpetuated even though there are new problems and tensions.

As the figure shows, by taking advantage of the screening functions of bureaucratic rules, administrators can gain and maintain some control over

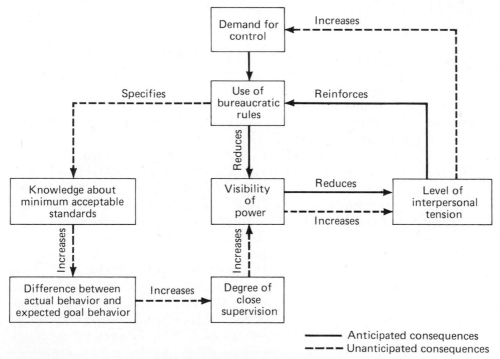

FIGURE 5.1   Anticipated and unanticipated consequences of bureaucratic rules

SOURCE: James G. March and Herbert Simon, *Organizations* (New York: Wiley, 1958), p. 45

organizational activities. They anticipate that general and impersonal rules will be "good" because they provide direction without creating status distinctions. Control is thus maintained by using bureaucratic rules, which in themselves reduce both the visibility of power and the level of interpersonal tension. These anticipated consequences then further reinforce use of bureaucratic rules.

This use of bureaucratic rules, however, may result in unanticipated consequences, as Figure 5.1 also illustrates. For example, because bureaucratic rules provide knowledge about minimum acceptable standards (explication function), an unanticipated consequence may be that minimums become maximums (apathy-preserving and goal-displacement dysfunctions), and the difference between actual behavior and expected behavior for goal achievement becomes visible and creates the need for further action. A frequent administrative response to this may be to increase direct supervision of employees, which in turn increases the visibility of power relations and produces greater interpersonal tension. Because the equilibrium originally sought by instituting the bureaucratic rules is upset, the demand for more control is created.

Thus, although rules are used to mitigate some tensions, they may create others. As a matter of fact, rules may actually perpetuate the tensions that they were meant to dispel. For example, close supervision can produce high visibility of power relations and a high degree of interpersonal tension; yet the use of rules to reduce tension may unintentionally perpetuate the need for additional close supervision; hence, the cycle begins again. The major problems of low motivation and minimal role performance simply are not solved by more rules.

Educational administrators must learn how to anticipate and avoid the negative consequences of bureaucratic rules. They must ask: How can the functional consequences of rules be maximized and the dysfunctional consequences minimized?

Gouldner's research provides some guidelines.[27] He maintains that rules having a punishment-centered pattern are most likely to evoke negative consequences. Punishment-centered rules (1) are initiated by either workers or administrators, but not jointly, to coerce the other group to comply; and (2) result in punishment of one group by the other when they are violated, producing tension and conflict.

On the other hand, representative rules (1) are initiated and supported by both workers and administrators; (2) are enforced by the administration and obeyed by the workers; and (3) result in "educational programs" when rules are violated, since violation is interpreted as a lack of information. Representative rules are least likely to evoke dysfunctional consequences because they have been jointly initiated and are generally supported by the parties concerned. Therefore, representative rules, as contrasted with punishment-centered rules, are more likely to have the desired functional consequences without many of the unintended dysfunctional consequences.

NEGLECT OF THE INFORMAL ORGANIZATION

The Weberian model of organization also has been criticized for its omission of the informal structure.[28] As we indicated in Chapter 3, the dynamics of organizational life can only be understood if, in addition to the formal structure, one is also aware of the rules, groupings, and sanctioning systems that are unofficial in character. These unofficial rules, norms, informal leaders, and groups spontaneously emerge from the interaction of individuals in the organization. This interaction establishes a lasting informal social structure and culture that affect members' behavior.

The impact of the informal on the formal organization can be constructive or destructive. For example, the Bank Wiring Room Study (see Chapter 1) showed that the informal organization restricted production. Evidence also exists, however, that the informal organization can be a constructive force in efficient operation of bureaucratic organizations as well as a mechanism for change.[29]

Charles Page's study of the Navy suggests that the informal structure provides a channel for circumventing formally prescribed rules and procedures that may have positive or negative effects.[30] He proposes that many pressing problems develop for which efficient solutions or communications are not possible within the formal framework; hence, the informal structure assumes added importance. For example, Page observes that official communications must be routed through the "chain of command," which often is a long drawn-out process. Frequently, circumventing the official communications channel through the "grapevine" appears to be precisely what is necessary for solving pressing problems. The knowledgeable and flexible administrator (officer) will use the grapevine, thus avoiding the bureaucratic frustration of those who only play it by the book. As a communication vehicle, the grapevine often provides efficient machinery. Indeed, generally speaking, the informal organization is an important device for implementing crucial organizational objectives.

Laurence Iannaccone's study of schools supports the informal organization's significance. In addition, he suggests that the informal organization can be used as a guide to revising the formal organization.[31] Although such reorganizations may be useful, a thorough knowledge of the informal organization's dynamics can lead to the development of procedures and mechanisms for using the existing informal structure; this generally is more useful than formalization.

The informal organization exists. It is not an enemy to be eliminated or suppressed; on the contrary, it can be a useful vehicle for improving efficiency. It is irrational to administer a formal organization, such as a school, according to the purely technical criteria of rationality and formality because that ignores the nonrational aspects of informal organization.[32] From a theoretical perspective, our position is that administrative practice is enhanced by using both the formal (rational) and informal (nonrational) components of schools.

DUAL NATURE OF THE BUREAUCRATIC MODEL

Another frequent criticism of the Weberian model is the internal contradictions among certain bureaucratic principles of organization. According to Weber, all characteristics of his ideal type are logically consistent and interact for maximum organizational efficiency; however, both theoretical and empirical analyses indicate that things are not so smooth and integrated in the real world of organizational functioning.

Talcott Parsons[33] and Gouldner[34] question whether the guiding principle of bureaucracy is authority based on technical competence and knowledge *or* authority based on legal powers and discipline. Weber maintains that "bureaucratic administration means fundamentally the exercise of control on the basis of knowledge."[35] On the other hand, he writes, "The content of discipline is the consistently rationalized, methodically trained and exact execution of the received order, in which all personal criticism is unconditionally suspended and the actor is unswervingly and exclusively set for carrying out the command."[36] Hence, Weber is proposing the central importance of discipline as well as expertise. Is bureaucratic administration based primarily on expertise, or is it based on disciplined compliance with directives? Unless one assumes that there will be no conflict between authority based on "technical competence and expertise" and that based on "incumbency in a hierarchical position," the seed of contradiction and conflict lies within these two authority bases that are integral to the Weberian model. In fact, Gouldner suggests that Weber may have been implicitly describing not one but two types of bureaucracy.[37]

Do these two sources of authority go together with limited conflict, as Weber suggested, or are they alternate bases of administration as Gouldner and others suggest? A number of studies help us address this question.

Arthur L. Stinchcombe's study of the organization of construction and mass production industries in the United States reveals that the components of Weber's ideal type do *not* form an inherently connected set of variables. Some principles of bureaucracy are relatively uncorrelated with others, while some are highly correlated.[38] Stinchcombe concludes that bureaucracy is but one form of rational administration. For example, construction industries were found to be rationally organized as a "professionalized" labor force that provided direction and control with little hierarchical authority. Control was based primarily on the technical competence and expertise of the craftsmen in the industries. In contrast, hierarchical control and discipline were much more pronounced in the mass production industries. These results support the generalization that there is not one but at least two types of rational administrative structures.

Similarly, in a study of 150 formal organizations in 150 nonindustrialized societies, Stanley H. Udy drew conclusions remarkably close to Stinchcombe's.[39] He found two clusters (groups) of variables, each one composed of bureaucratic and rational elements. Elements within the bureaucratic cluster were positively correlated, and elements within the rational cluster were positively related; however, the two clusters were not positively related. The degree of bureaucratization and the degree of rationality were relatively independent of one another; in fact, there was some tendency for the clusters to be inversely related.

Blau and Scott's analysis of the dual nature of the Weberian model also led them to conclude that Weber failed to distinguish bureaucratic from professional principles.[40] They similarly maintain that bureaucratic discipline and professional expertise are alternative methods for coping with uncertainty. Discipline reduces the scope of uncertainty, while expertise provides the knowledge to handle uncertainty. The crux of the problem seems to be that professionals are often employees of bureaucratic organizations; hence, these alternative modes of rationality are frequently mixed, producing strain and conflict. A typical example is the school principal. Does his or her authority reside in the bureaucratic office or in professional expertise? Obviously, a mixture is present and seems to result in some degree of strife.

BUREAUCRATIC STRUCTURE IN SCHOOLS

Schools are formal organizations with many of the same characteristics as bureaucratic organizations. Max Abbott, for example, using the characteristics of the Weberian model developed earlier in this chapter, has concluded: "The school organization as we know it today, . . . can accurately be described as a highly developed bureaucracy. As such, it exhibits many of the characteristics and employs many of the strategies of the military, industrial, and governmental agencies with which it might be compared."[41] The bureaucratic model is the one that most school administrators adopt, and this may explain why the model can be used to predict accurately certain kinds of behavior in schools.[42]

A basic assumption of bureaucracies is that every subordinate has less technical expertise than his or her superior. This assumption certainly does not apply in schools, nor does it apply in other professional organizations. On the contrary, professionals often have more competence and technical expertise than administrators who occupy a higher level in the organization. Consequently, to find strain and tension in schools between teachers and administrators should not be surprising.

Rather than thinking of schools as being bureaucratic or nonbureaucratic, a more useful approach is to examine the degree of bureaucratization with respect to the important components of the Weberian model. Such an approach differentiates types of organizational structures and also provides a tool to test empirically the extent to which the theoretical components of the model are consistent. Richard H. Hall, D. S. Pugh and his associates at the University of Aston, Jerald Hage, and Henry Mintzberg are among the researchers who have developed and tested variations of this approach with interesting results.

Hall's Approach

One of the most systematic attempts to measure bureaucratization is Richard H. Hall's development of an organizational inventory to measure six central characteristics of bureaucratic structure: (1) hierarchy of authority, (2) specialization, (3) rules for incumbents (i.e., those assuming an organizational role), (4) procedure specifications, (5) impersonality, and (6) technical competence.[43] D. A. MacKay subsequently adapted and modified the organization inventory in his study of bureaucratization of schools.[44] He measured bureaucratic patterns in schools, using the school organizational inventory (SOI), a Likert-type questionnaire that operationalizes the same six dimensions of the organizational inventory. Teachers' perceptions of the bureaucratic structure are elicited by the SOI items. Examples of items for each dimension are provided in Table 5.4.

The SOI has undergone several revisions, and with the exception of the specialization scale, the measures have been found reasonably reliable. After a thorough review of the literature and a factor analysis of the bureaucratic structure of schools, Keith F. Punch concluded that the SOI appears technically adequate for mapping the domain of bureaucratic structure.[45]

The interrelationships of these bureaucratic characteristics of schools also have been explored empirically.[46] Studies indicate that there are *two* relatively distinct patterns of rational organization rather than one completely integrated

TABLE 5.4 Sample Items from the SOI

Hierarchy of Authority Scale

Staff members of this school always get their orders from higher up.
I have to ask the principal before I do almost anything.

Specialization Scale

The instructional program is departmentalized into specific subject areas with specific teachers assigned.

Rules Scale

The teachers are constantly being checked for rule violations.
The school has a manual of rules and regulations for teachers to follow.

Procedural Specifications Scale

We are to follow strict operating procedures at all times.
The same procedures are to be followed in most situations.

Impersonality Scale

No matter how special a pupil's or parent's problem appears to be, the person is treated the same way as anyone else.
We are expected to be courteous, but reserved, at times in our dealings with parents.

Technical Competence Scale

Promotions are based on how well liked you are.
Past teaching experience plays a large part in the assignment of a teacher in this school.

TABLE 5.5 Two Types of Rational Organization in the School Setting

Organizational Characteristics	*Organizational Patterns*
Hierarchy of authority Rules for incumbents Procedural specifications Impersonality	Bureaucratic
Technical competence Specialization	Professional

bureaucratic pattern. Hierarchy of authority, rules for incumbents, procedural specifications, and impersonality tend to vary together, and specialization and technical competence similarly vary together; however, the two groups are found to be independent of or inversely related to each other. In the school, as in other kinds of organizations, the components of Weber's ideal type do *not* necessarily form an inherently connected set of variables; instead, there are likely to be two distinct types of rational organization. These results are summarized in Table 5.5.

In the table we have labeled the first set of characteristics "bureaucratic" and the second set "professional." The distinction once again calls attention both to the potential conflict between authority based on technical competence and expertise and that based on holding an office in a hierarchy and to the potential incompatibility between professionalization and bureaucratization. To lump together the bureaucratic and professional patterns in a single model of bureaucracy seems to obscure important differences among schools. Indeed, separating two patterns of rational organization and administration makes it possible to explore a number of combinations of the two patterns. For example, if each pattern is dichotomized, as shown in Figure 5.2, then four types of organizations are possible.

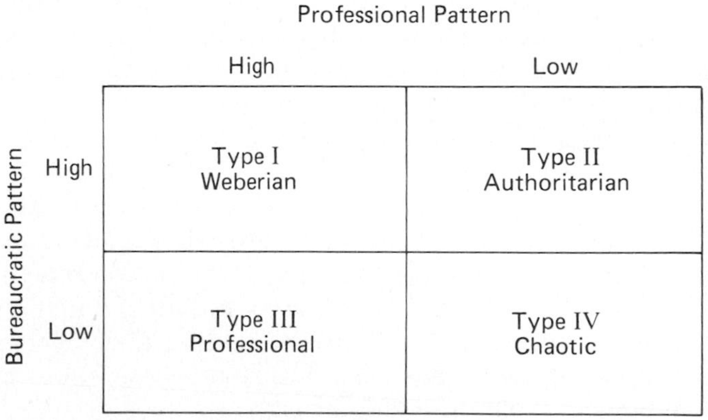

Professional Pattern

	High	Low
High	Type I Weberian	Type II Authoritarian
Low	Type III Professional	Type IV Chaotic

Bureaucratic Pattern

FIGURE 5.2 Typology of school organizational structure

Type I school organization is one in which professionalization and bureaucratization are complementary; both are high. This pattern is similar to the ideal type described by Weber; hence, we call it a "Weberian" structure.

Type II organization rates high on the burcaucratic characteristics and low on the professional ones. Therefore, authority based on position within the hierarchy is stressed. Disciplined compliance with the rules, regulations, and directives is the basic principle of operation. Type II is therefore labeled as "authoritarian." Power is concentrated and flows from top to bottom. Rules and procedures are impersonally applied. The superior always has the last say. Furthermore, promotions to administrative positions typically go to those who have been loyal to the organization and to their superiors. In many respects, this authoritarian structure is similar to the one Gouldner described as a punishment-centered bureaucracy.[47]

Type III (high professional, low bureaucratic) emphasizes shared decision making between the administrators and the professional staff. Members of the staff are viewed as professionals who have the expertise and competence to make important organizational decisions. Rules and procedures serve as guides rather than as strict formats to be applied uniformly. Special cases are likely to be the rule rather than the exception. Teachers have much power in the organizational decision-making process. In brief, decisions are made by those who have the knowledge and expertise to make them. We refer to this type of school structure as "professional."

Finally, Type IV organization has a low degrees of bureaucratization and professionalization. Type IV schools are called "chaotic" structures. Confusion and conflict typify day-to-day operations. Inconsistency, contradiction, and ineffectiveness are likely to pervade the chaotic structure; hence, there will be pressure to move toward one of the other structural types.

This typology presents four potential school structures that are quite different and probably have different consequences for teachers and students alike. Henry Kolesar, for example, found that a sense of student powerlessness was significantly higher in authoritarian than in professional school structures.[48] Geoffrey Isherwood and Wayne K. Hoy uncovered the same finding for teachers in the two types of schools.[49] Overall, the sense of powerlessness among teachers was much greater in authoritarian than in professional structures. But organizationally and socially oriented teachers (those who identify themselves with the values and goals of the organization and of family and friends, respectively) had less of a sense of powerlessness in the authoritarian structure than professionally oriented teachers. The conclusion seems to be that individual work orientation mediates the relationship between organizational structure and alienation. Teachers with an organizational orientation may not be alienated by authoritarian structures and procedures and indeed may be quite content. Gerald H. Moeller and W. W. Charters' finding that teachers in highly bureaucratic systems had more sense of power than those in less bureaucratic systems lends support to this speculation.[50]

It is also true that the type of school organizational structure may influence student achievement. Research by both Barry Anderson[51] and MacKay[52] indicates the possibility that highly bureaucratic structures may have a negative effect on student achievement.

The Aston Team Approach

About the same time Hall developed his questionnaire inventory to measure bureaucratic structure, D. S. Pugh and his associates at the University of Aston in Birmingham, England, constructed an interview inventory to assess the structure of work organizations in what they considered a more objective fashion.[53] The *Aston inventory* is in the Weberian tradition. It recognizes five primary characteristics of organizational structure: (1) specialization of activities, (2) standardization of procedures, (3) formalization of documents, (4) centralization of authority, and (5) configuration of role structure.[54] The original Aston studies were concerned with a large number of diverse work organizations, including manufacturing firms, department stores, and shoe companies.[55] It remained to a group at the University of Alberta to modify the Aston interview inventory in order to make it directly applicable in the study of educational organizations. John Newberry was first to demonstrate that, with some modification, the Aston approach could be used fruitfully to study postsecondary colleges.[56] Expanding on the work of Newberry, Edward A. Holdaway and his colleagues provided evidence that educational organizations may vary widely in bureaucratic structure; they can be highly bureaucratic, strongly professional, both, or neither.[57] This finding is consistent with the typology developed in Figure 5.2 using the Hall approach.

Although the early study of the structure of educational organizations at Alberta centered on postsecondary schools, later work by John Kelsey and Lawrence Sackney adapted the Aston inventory for use in public secondary schools in England and Canada.[58] Table 5.6 illustrates sample interview items for schools. Sackney found that high morale among secondary teachers was related to high specialization, a low degree of centralization and standardization. Moreover, limited participation in organizational decision making (a high degree of centralization) was related negatively to an open organizational atmosphere.[59] The finding was later replicated in a study in New Jersey where John Haymond found that centralization was negatively related to both openness in school climate and loyalty to the principal, but specialization was positively related to both openness and loyalty.[60] Mary Guidette similarly demonstrated a positive relationship between centralization and teacher sense of powerlessness but a negative one between specialization and powerlessness.[61] Consistent with most of the research on bureaucratic structure in schools, the professional element of teacher specialization was highly compatible with openness, loyalty, and sense of control; whereas the bureaucratic dimension of high centralization was associated with closedness, low loyalty, and a sense of powerlessness.

Although conceptual similarities between the Hall and Aston approaches are apparent, they differ in a number of ways. The Hall instrument is a questionnaire requiring subordinates to make subjective assessments of perception

TABLE 5.6 Sample Items from the Modified Aston Interview Schedule for Schools

Characteristic	Performed		Delegated
I. SPECIALIZATION	YES/NO	TO WHOM	FULL-TIME ACTIVITY
A. Producing a school newspaper			
B. Hiring teaching staff			
C. Buying materials and equipment			
D. Development master schedule			

Characteristic	Performed			
II. FORMALIZATION	YES/NO	SCHOOL ONLY	DISTRICT ONLY	DISTRIBUTE TO WHOM
A. Board policy manual				
B. Student handbook				
C. Teacher handbook				
D. Courses of studies				
E. Organizational chart				
F. Faculty minutes				
G. Written maintenance schedule				

III. STANDARDIZATION

A. Tasks of instructors are defined by (1) Intuition and experience, (2) Chair, (3) Administration, (4) Written instruction, (5) All of these

B. Progress reports on students? (1) None, (2) Irregular, (3) Regular

C. Intensity of evaluation? (1) None, (2) Required by tenure, (3) Irregular, (4) Regular

D. Instructional pace determined by (1) Individual teachers; (2) Groups of teachers (3) Chair, committee, administration

TABLE 5.6 (Continued)

Characteristic	Performed	Delegated
IV. CENTRALIZATION Which decision maker—(1) Teacher, (2) Chair, (3) Principal, (4) Superintendent, (5) Board, (6) State—for		
A. Number of teachers in a school		
B. Appointment of a department chair		
C. Allocation of funds to department		
D. Brand of new equipment		
E. Promotion of students		
F. Creation of a new job		
V. CONFIGURATION		
A. Pupil enrollment		
B. Number of teachers		
C. Number of clerical staff members		
D. Number of custodial staff members		

variations in the degree of bureaucracy; the Aston measure is a structured interview with superiors in which feelings and experiences are not probed. The interviewer asks if there are organizational charts, board policy manuals, student handbooks, courses of study, written school rules, written minutes of staff meetings, and regular written administrative bulletins. Documentary evidence exists for many of the interview responses. Clearly, though, the data collected are not completely objective; they do not entirely avoid touching personal feelings. The principal can still hesitate on a query concerning a handbook if he or she feels that not having one suggests poor performance.

The two approaches should be seen as complementary, not competing ones. Both come out of the Weberian tradition, and both use a number of generally recognized characteristics of bureaucracies to conceive and operationalize bureaucratic structure. The differences lie in the research strategy (interview versus questionnaire) and focus (superiors versus subordinates). In the only piece of research on schools to date using both the Hall and Aston methodologies, David A. Sousa and Wayne K. Hoy conclude that the approaches yield similar and complementary views of public secondary schools.[62] Their study of public secondary schools in New Jersey using the two approaches produced a simplified group of the following bureaucratic characteristics:

1. Organizational Control (Aston and Hall)
2. Rational Specialization (Aston and Hall)
3. System Centralization (Aston)
4. Formalization of Routine (Aston).[63]

The study of bureaucratic structure in schools can profit from using both interviews and questionnaires and from questioning both superiors and subordinates. The reliance on a single form of data remains a fundamental weakness of much of our research on educational organizations.

Hage's Axiomatic Theory

Organizations can be described by functions as well as structure. Drawing upon the earlier works of Weber, Barnard, and Thompson, Jerald Hage developed an axiomatic theory of organization by relating structural variables to functional ones.[64] Eight organizational variables, four representing means and four ends, provide not only the conceptual basis for the axioms but also the foundation for defining ideal types of organizations. The four structural variables that comprise the means by which schools are organized to achieve their ends are:

1. *Complexity or specialization.* The number of occupational specialties and the level of training required for the jobs.
2. *Centralization or hierarchy of authority.* The proportion of jobholders involved in decision making and the number of decision areas in which that segment participates.

3. *Formalization or standardization.* The proportion of codified jobs (those in which duties are prescribed by formal job descriptions) and the degree to which employees are free from observing rules.
4. *Stratification or status system.* The differences in rewards and mobility among jobs in the organization.

The four functional variables that constitute the organizational ends with which schools are frequently concerned are:

1. *Adaptiveness or flexibility.* The number of new programs and new techniques implemented in an organization per year.
2. *Production or effectiveness.* The number of units produced per year and the rate of increase in units produced per year. Production is a quantitative variable; it does not necessarily reflect quality.
3. *Efficiency or cost.* Cost required to produce a single unit of production and the amount of idle resources.
4. *Job satisfaction or morale.* Personal contentment with working conditions and the rate of job turnover.

It should be noted that these four organizational ends are similar to the four functional problems that must be solved by all social systems identified by Talcott Parsons and his associates (see Chapter 3).[65] Indeed, Hage equates production with goal achievement, efficiency with integration, adaptiveness with adaptation, and job satisfaction with latent pattern maintenance.[66] Similarly, Hage's four organizational means match Weber's classic characteristics of bureaucracy: centralization corresponds to hierarchy of authority, formalization to rules and regulations, complexity to specialization, and stratification to career orientation. Hence, the theory addresses how four aspects of bureaucratic structure relate to the solution of four basic problems that confront all organizations. The major propositions of the theory may be summarized as follows:

1. The greater the centralization, the higher the production and vice versa.
2. The greater the degree of formalization, the higher the efficiency and vice versa.
3. The greater the centralization, the higher the degree formalization and vice versa.
4. The higher the degree of stratification, the lower the job satisfaction and vice versa.
5. The higher the degree of stratification, the higher the production and vice versa.
6. The higher the degree of stratification, the lower the level of adaptiveness and vice versa.
7. The greater the complexity, the lower the centralization and vice versa.[67]

These seven basic propositions, and the twenty-one corollaries that can be deduced from them, comprise all the possible two-variable relationships. Although it may be constructive to examine each of the propositions, it is even more useful, and perhaps more enlightening, to consider the two extreme types of organizations suggested by the interrelationships among the eight variables. The ideal types that emerge are the organic organization, which emphasizes adaptiveness, and the mechanistic organization, which emphasizes production. Each may be characterized in terms of the eight variables as follows:[68]

Structure and Function	Organic Organization	Mechanistic Organization
Complexity	High	Low
Centralization	Low	High
Formalization	Low	High
Stratification	Low	High
Adaptiveness	High	Low
Production	Low	High
Efficiency	Low	High
Job Satisfaction	High	Low

Schools that follow the mechanistic model define roles, rights and obligations, and status distinctions precisely (i.e., are highly formalized and stratified); have an elaborate system of rules and regulations (i.e., are highly formalized); have a hierarchical structure of control and communication (i.e., are highly centralized); and place little emphasis on the expertise of teachers (i.e., are not very complex). In addition, mechanistic schools stress turning out a large number of graduates and giving many courses at the least possible cost (i.e., have high productivity at low cost). Furthermore, change is avoided; mechanistic schools are unwilling to implement new programs or to experiment with new techniques (i.e., they display a low level of adaptiveness). Finally, it is not surprising that a school in which teachers are denied a strong voice in decisions, and in which teachers are carefully observed and controlled, face widespread teacher job dissatisfaction.

In contrast to the bureaucratic trappings of schools following the mechanistic model, those patterned on the organic model of the school are highly professional in structure. They value the expertise of educators (i.e., are highly complex). Many teachers frequently participate in decision making and policy formulation and are given the freedom to function relatively unimpeded by superiors (i.e., the schools are not highly centralized). Standardized procedures and official rules are limited (i.e., there is a low degree of formalization). Egalitarianism (i.e., a low degree of stratification) is the rule rather than the exception. This structure emphasizes adaptiveness, not production. An atmosphere conducive to innovation develops as well as the functioning of teachers as respected and responsible professionals (i.e., there is a high degree of job satisfaction).

Attention focuses on the improvement of the quality services rather than on expanding production (which results in low production); concerns about quality and change dominate those of costs (producing low efficiency).

Clearly, the sketches of each type of organization are ideals and most schools fall somewhere between the extremes. Yet, no matter which ideal type the school approaches, problems in performance arise. In an adaptive school, low production and excessive costs constitute major problems. In a production-oriented school, the problems of adaptiveness and maintenance of morale surface. Educational administrators thus face an organizational dilemma; the volume of production, efficiency, job satisfaction, and adaptiveness are all valued outcomes, but those organizational characteristics that facilitate production and efficiency are likely to impede satisfaction and adaptiveness and vice versa. Although the dilemma cannot be completely resolved, it requires careful monitoring. We suggest, as a goal for school administrators, the achievement of an *integrated model of organization* with the following characteristics:

Structure and Function	*Integrated Organization*
Complexity	High
Centralization	Moderate
Formalization	Moderate
Stratification	Low
Adaptiveness	High
Production	Moderate
Efficiency	Moderate
Job Satisfaction	High

Research.   The empirical research in schools testing Hage's axiomatic theory is basically supportive.[69] Wayne K. Hoy and his colleagues, found that centralization and formalization were positively correlated and that both of the variables were inversely related to job satisfaction.[70] The findings of Cecil Miskel and his associates found a similar relationship between centralization and job satisfaction.[71] However, their data indicated that formalization and complexity led directly to job satisfaction. Robert W. Hertzel and James E. Walter, in two separate studies, demonstrated that the adaptiveness of schools and school systems was related to the strength of four structural variables.[72] Finally, a study by H. Scott Herrick provides further evidence that adaptiveness is related to the structural variables comprising organizational means of elementary schools.[73]

Desired organizational outcomes vary over time. During the 1960s and early 1970s, considerable attention was directed toward change, innovation, and increased morale; the stress was on adaptiveness and job satisfaction. Beginning in the mid-1970s, however, a shift toward accountability became clear;

schools today are being asked for greater productivity and efficiency. The dilemmas of educational administrators are abundant. There is no single best type of school organization. Each ideal type has advantages and disadvantages. Moreover, as environmental conditions change and as the dominant values in society change, school organizations are also likely to change. Hage's axiomatic theory provides yet another set of tools for administrators to assess their situations and to develop strategies of action.

Mintzberg's Structural Framework

Henry Mintzberg provides another framework for examining bureaucratic structure. He describes structure simply as the ways in which an organization divides its labor into tasks and then achieves coordination among them.[74] Five basic coordinating mechanisms are the fundamental means organizations use to monitor and control work: mutual adjustment, direct supervision, standardization of work processes, standardization of outputs, and standardization of worker skills. These mechanisms glue the organization together.

Mutual adjustment is coordination through the simple process of informal communication. Workers coordinate their efforts by informal discussion and adjustment. Mutual adjustment is direct and basic; it is necessary not only in the simplest organization but also in the most complicated.

Direct supervision is coordination through personal command. One individual has the responsibility for monitoring and controlling the work of others. As the size of an organization increases, the more likely it is that mutual adjustment will become less effective and direct supervision more necessary. As work activities become more and more complicated, however, neither mutual adjustment nor direct supervision is sufficient. Hence, the work is standardized; coordination of parts is achieved by incorporating them in a carefully planned program for the work. There are three basic ways to obtain standardization in organizations—standardize the work processes, the outputs, or the skills.

Standardization of work processes is achieved by specifying or programming the contents of the work. The written directions to assemble a work bench is an example. The process of the work is described carefully in step-by-step directions.

Standardization of outputs is attained by specifying the results of the work; the fundamental dimensions of the product or of the performance are enumerated. Taxicab drivers, for example, are not usually given a route; they are merely told the destination. Similarly, teachers may simply be told that the student should be able to perform at a basic level in a given area; the means to achieve the level may be left to the teacher. The outcomes of the work are described carefully and employees are expected to achieve the standard.

Standardization of skills is a coordination mechanism that provides indirect control of work. Here skills and knowledge are standardized by specifying the kind of training required to do the work. Training supplies workers with patterns of work to be performed as well as the bases of coordination. Mintzberg observes that when an anesthesiologist and a surgeon meet in the operating room, typically little communication occurs; by virtue of their respective training, each knows precisely what to expect. Their standardized skills provide most of the coordination.[75]

Although most organizations of any size use all five means of coordination, each organization specializes in one, a fact that has important consequences for the basic structure of the organization.

Mintzberg also identifies five key parts of the organization (see Figure 5.3). These are the significant aspects of the structure, each with a critical function to perform.

The operating core is comprised of those who perform this basic work, activities directly related to the production of products and services. The core is the heart of the organization; it produces the essential output. In schools, teachers are the operating core, and teaching and learning are the outcomes.

The administrative component of the organization has three parts. First, the *strategic apex* consists of the top administrators (superintendent and assistants) who are charged with the responsibility of ensuring that the organization effectively serves its mission. Those administrators below, who connect the apex with the operating core through the formal authority structure, comprise the *middle line.* In school systems principals are the middle managers. Any organization that relies primarily on direct supervision for control and coordination is bound to have a large middle line. The *technostructure* is the administrative component charged with the responsibility of planning. It is composed of analysts who standardize the work of others and apply their analytic techniques to help the organization adapt to its environment. These analysts design, plan, and train, but they do not directly manage. Curriculum coordinators and instruc-

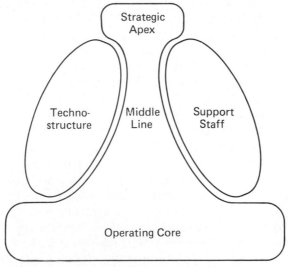

FIGURE 5.3   The five basic parts of organizations

tional supervisors are often members of the school technostructure; their role is to help teachers design and plan instruction and to provide in-service opportunities for professional growth and development.

Finally, a fifth component—the *support staff*—is composed of specialized units that exist to provide support for the organizations outside the operating work flow. In schools, for example, there is a building and grounds department, a maintenance department, a cafeteria, and a payroll department. None of these units is part of the operating core, but each exists to provide indirect support for the school.

These five key parts of the organization and the five coordination mechanisms that hold them together serve as the basis for five configurations:

1. *Simple structure.* The strategic apex is the key part, and direct supervision is the central coordinating device.
2. *Machine bureaucracy.* The technostructure is the key part, and standardization of work processes is the central coordinating device.
3. *Professional bureaucracy.* The operating core is the key part, and standardization of skills is the central coordinating device.
4. *Divisionalized form.* The middle line is the key part, and standardization of outputs is the central coordinating device.
5. *Adhocracy.* The support staff is the key part, and mutual adjustment is the central coordinating device.

Our discussion will focus on the three forms and their variants most likely to be characteristic of schools.

Simple structure.   Organizations that are coordinated by a high degree of direct supervision, that have a small strategic apex with virtually no middle line, and that are highly centralized are simple structures. In such organizations there is little elaboration—little technostructure, little support staff, little division of labor and specialization, and a small administrative hierarchy.

Since power over important decisions tends to be centralized in the hands of the top administrator, the strategic apex is the key part of the organization. Standardization in a simple structure is unnecessary because things are worked out as they arise—there are loose, informal working relations among participants. Thus, communication flows informally, but most of it is between the top administrator and everyone else. The name tells it all, the structure is simple.

New organizations typically begin as simple structures and then elaborate their administrative structures as they grow. Many small organizations, however, retain a simple structure. Informal communications remain effective, and coordination is attended to by a one-person strategic apex. There are variants of the simple structure. For example, the *autocratic organization* is a simple structure in which the top administrator hoards power and rules by fiat; and the *charismatic organization* is a variant in which the leader has the same power not because it is hoarded but because the followers lavish it upon the leader.

The major strength of the simple structure is its flexibility; only one person must act.

The simple structure is of interest because many schools, particularly small elementary school districts, have such a structure. They are administered by autocratic and sometimes charismatic principals who rule with an iron hand. Although some teachers enjoy working in a small, intimate school where its charismatic principal leads the way, others perceive the simple structure as highly restrictive and autocratic. Such structures are highly dependent upon the expertise, imagination, and energy of the chief executive. As the executive goes, so goes the organization. This kind of school faces especially difficult problems in executive succession and as growth renders direct supervision inadequate. Simple structure can be relatively enduring or only a phase in the development and maturing of an organization.

Machine bureaucracy.   Organizations that are fine-tuned and standardized to run as integrated, regulated machines are called machine bureaucracies. The work processes in this kind of structure are routine and standard. Indeed, standardization of work is the prime coordinating mechanism, and the techno-structure is the key part of the structure because it contains the analysts who do the standardizing. In these organizations, a high degree of centralization is supported by considerable formalization: rules and regulations permeate the structure; formal communication *predominates* at all levels; and decision making follows the hierarchical chain of authority.

This is the Weberian structure of bureaucracy—standardized responsibilities, technical qualifications, formal communication channels, rules and regulations, and hierarchy of authority. It is a structure geared for precision, speed, unambiguity, continuity, unity, subordination, and efficiency. Machine bureaucracy is obsessed with control; a control mentality develops from top to bottom. As Mintzberg cogently notes, "The problem in the Machine Bureaucracy is not to develop an open atmosphere where people can talk the conflicts out, but to enforce a closed, tightly controlled one where the work can get done despite them."[76]

Considerable power rests with the administrators of the strategic apex; in fact, the only others to share much power with the top administrators are the analysts of the technostructure, since their role is standardizing the work processes of the organization. Machine structures work best when the work is routine, that is, when an integrated set of simple, repetitive tasks must be performed precisely and consistently by people.[77]

Although many schools have the trappings, most are not machine bureaucracies in the pure sense because typically they lack an elaborate administrative structure, a large middle line, and an elaborate technostructure. In fact, the structure of many public schools is a cross between the simple structure and machine bureaucracy, what Mintzberg calls a *simple bureaucracy.* The simple bureaucracy is centralized and highly bureaucratic, but it has a relatively flat administrative structure. Nonetheless, control remains a major obsession; hence such organizations are confronted by most of the dysfunctional characteristics of bureaucracy already discussed in our analysis of the Weberian model. As long as control, accountability, standardized educational outcomes, and inexpensive services are demanded by society for schools, simple bureaucratic structures will be a configuration for many schools.

Professional bureaucracy. Bureaucratic structure can be defined in terms of "the extent to which behavior is predetermined or predictable, in effect, standardized."[78] Thus, organizations can be bureaucratic without being centralized. Professional bureaucracies are structures that permit both decentralization and standardization at the same time. These organizations use standardization of skills as the prime coordinating mechanism; the operating core is the key organizational part; and professionalization is the crucial process. All such structures rely on the skills and knowledge of their operating professionals to function effectively.

The professional bureaucracy receives its coordination indirectly by relying on the standardization of skills that professionals have acquired in their training; hence, it is not surprising to find relationships in these organizations to be much more loosely coupled than in machine or simple bureaucracies. Professionals are hired and given considerable control over their own work. Many professionals work relatively independently of their colleagues, but closely with their clients. For example, teacher autonomy seems undeniable in some schools. Teachers work alone in their classrooms, are relatively unobserved by colleagues and superiors, and possess broad discretionary authority over their students.[79] This structural looseness of the school supports a professional basis of organizations; however, the demand for uniformity in product, the need for movement of students from grade to grade and school to school in an orderly process, and the long period over which students are schooled required a standardization of activities and, hence, a bureaucratic basis of school organizations.[80]

The administrative structure of the professional bureaucracy is relatively flat. It does not need an elaborate hierarchy to control and coordinate or a technostructure to design work standards. Professionals control themselves and, in a sense, develop their own work standards. The standards of the professional bureaucracy originate largely from outside its structure, in self-governing associations to which the professionals belong. These associations set general standards that are taught by the universities and used by all organizations of the profession. As we have noted before, two sources generate organizational authority. Machine and simple bureaucracies rely on the authority of the position or office, and professional bureaucracies are built on the authority of knowledge and expertise.

Professional bureaucracy is decentralized; a great deal of power rests with the professionals in the operating core. The work is too complex to be supervised directly by managers or standardized by analysts; hence, professionals have a great deal to say about what they do and how they do it. Professionals have close working relations with clients and loose ones with colleagues. It makes more sense to think in terms of a personal strategy for each professional rather than an integrated organizational strategy. Clearly, some schools have the characteristics of the professional bureaucracy—a skilled operating core, standardized work skills, professional norms and autonomy, professional associations, structural looseness, and a flat administrative structure.

One important variant of the professional bureaucracy is the *simple professional bureaucracy.* Such a configuration occurs when highly competent professionals practicing standard skills nevertheless take their direction from a strong leader, as in the simple structure. Consider, for example, the school district with a strong, dynamic superintendent who leads a dedicated and talented group of teacher professionals as a symphony orchestra with a brilliant conductor. Both the direction of the leader *and* the skill of the professionals are critical. Indeed, the leader may even by autocratic, but if he or she can make the professionals perform beyond themselves, the results can be highly efficient and effective.

Schools. The configurations that Mintzberg described are abstract ideals, yet these simplifications of more complex structures do come to life in the analysis of schools. Schools do experience the basic forces that underlie these configurations: the pull to centralize by top management, the pull to formalize by the technostructure, and the pull to professionalize by teachers.[81] Where one pull dominates, then the school will likely be organized close to one of the configurations we have discussed (see Table 5.7). As we have also seen, however, one pull does not always dominate, and two basic processes may have to coexist in balance. Highly professional teachers may have their efforts tightly directed by a dynamic administrator as in a simple professional bureaucracy. Although such an arrangement may work well over the short run, it is bound to produce conflict between the administration and teachers (a topic to be discussed more fully in the next chapter).

TABLE 5.7 **Variants of School Structure Based on Mintzberg**

Structural Form	Key Part	Prime Coordinating Mechanism	Crucial Process
Simple Structure	Apex	Direct Supervision	Centralization
Machine Bureaucracy	Technostructure	Standardization of Work	Formalization
Simple Bureaucracy	Apex	Direct Supervision and Standardization of Work	Centralization *and* Formalization
Professional Bureaucracy	Operating Core	Standardization of Training	Professionalization
Simple Professional Bureaucracy	Apex and Operating Core	Standardization of Training *and* Operating Core	Centralization *and* Professionalization

We have suggested that some small elementary schools are simple structures; they are centralized but informal structures. The chief administrator provides strong (often autocratic) direction in an informal atmosphere unfettered by rules and regulations. A few schools are machine bureaucracies; they are usually found in large districts where an elaborate technostructure attempts to standardized the work or in states with elaborate statewide technostructures. Behavior is formalized by an extensive set of rules, procedures, and job descriptions. Moreover, power tends to be highly centralized in the apex of the structure; authority flows downward. Some schools are also professional bureaucracies. They are staffed by highly competent and well-trained teachers who control their own work and who seek collective control over decisions that affect them. The structure is decentralized and democratic among the professionals; in fact, the professional administrator keeps his or her power only as long as the professionals perceive their interests effectively being served.

Finally, many schools are hybrid variants of the three "ideal types" that have been described. The simple bureaucracy has the basic characteristics of both a simple structure and a machine bureaucracy—it is a highly centralized, formalized, flat administrative structure that uses both direct supervision and standardization for work to coordinate the effort. Schools with strong, aggressive administrators who try to control what is happening in the classroom provide an example. Since administrators cannot be everywhere at once, an elaborate system of formal rules, procedures, and regulations is developed to support the direct supervision. Another hybrid variant, the simple professional bureaucracy, seems quite common in secondary schools. This variant is a combination of the simple structure and the professional bureaucracy. Here highly trained teacher-professionals practicing standard teaching skills take the lead from a strong principal.

A number of elements in the situation influence the particular configuration of schools. The *age* and *size* of a school are likely to influence its structure. As schools age and grow, informal relations and direct supervision are likely to be replaced by formalizations and bureaucratic control. When the technical system is defined as complex (that is, teaching viewed as a complex process requiring individualization and multiple and changing strategies), then a highly professional work force is needed and decentralization of decision making is required. When, on the other hand, the technical system is defined as routine (that is, teaching is viewed as a routine process of providing standard and simple minimum skills), then the technical system can be regulated through bureaucratic procedures. Moreover, the more organizations are controlled externally, the more centralized and bureaucratic they tend to become. Mintzberg argues that the two most effective means to control an organization from the outside are to hold its most powerful decision maker responsible and to impose specific standards, usually in the form of rules and regulations.[82] As school districts are increasingly faced with demands for accountability, minimum basic skills, tests for graduation, and a myriad of other performance targets from state departments of education, the pulls are for more formalization, more centralization, less professionalization, and a more well-developed state technostructure to regulate and control schools; these are the forces of bureaucratization. Bureaucracy is not dead; indeed, it is making a dramatic comeback in the public schools of most states.

A Loosely Coupled System

A recent body of theory and research challenges some of the notions of the school as a bureaucratic structure. Investigators are questioning rationalistic assumptions about the relationship of structure and process to organizational goals. James G. March and Johan P. Olsen refer to educational organizations as "organized anarchies."[83] Karl E. Weick and Howard E. Aldrich propose that elements or subsystems in organizations are often tied together loosely rather than through tight, bureaucratic linkages.[84]

Terrence E. Deal and Lynn D. Celotti argue that the formal organization and the administration of the school do not significantly affect methods of classroom instructions.[85] Similarly, John Meyer and Brian Rowan assert that bureaucratic structure and instruction are disconnected.[86] In brief, schools are seen as organizations with ambiguous goals, unclear technologies, fluid participation, uncoordinated activities, loosely connected structural elements, and a structure that has little effect on outcomes. Analyses such as these are known as *loose coupling theories,* and they are useful additions to bureaucratic theory.[87]

Although loose coupling theories are a relatively new development, more than two decades ago Charles Bidwell analyzed structural looseness in school organizations.[88] He noted that in order to deal with the problem of variability in student abilities on a day-to-day basis, teachers need to have freedom to make professional judgments.

Professional autonomy seems undeniable in schools. Teachers work alone in their classrooms, are relatively unobserved by colleagues and administrators, and possess broad discretionary authority over their students. The result is a structural looseness *within* the school. Similarly, structural looseness exists *among* the school units in the system. Administrators and teachers of each school enjoy broad discretionary powers with respect to curriculum, teaching methods, and teacher selection. For example, even though the system recruits teachers, they typically cannot be assigned to a particular school without the principal's consent.

The structural looseness of the school supports a professional basis of organization; however, the demand for uniformity in product, the need for movement of students from grade to grade and school to school in an orderly process, and the long period of time over which students are schooled required a routinization of activities and, hence, bureaucratic basis of school organization. Bidwell, therefore, depicts the school as a distinctive combination of bureaucracy and structural looseness.[89]

Loose coupling theorists focus on the "disconnectedness of behavior and outcomes" in organizations.[90] Weick develops probably the most thorough analysis of the concept of loose coupling. By loose coupling, he conveys "the image that coupled events are responsive, *but* that each event also preserved its own identity and some evidence of its physical or logical separateness."[91] Loose coupling connotes weak or infrequent ties between any things that are minimally interdependent; hence, the phrase is invoked to refer to a variety of situations.[92]

Most organizations are concerned with who does the work and how well it is performed. Weick suggests that in schools there is loose control over how well the work is done. Inspection of the instructional activities is infrequent, and even when evaluation of teaching does occur, it is usually perfunctory. Under these conditions, tight organizational controls over who does the work—through such activities as hiring, certifying, and scheduling—is exerted.[93]

The Weick thesis is expanded by Meyer and Rowan. They claim that educators typically "decouple" their organizational structure from instructional activities and outcomes and resort to a "logic of confidence."[94] Their argument is that schools are basically personnel-certifying agencies of society. Standardized curricula and certified teachers produce standardized types of graduates, who are then given their appropriate place in the economic and stratification system on the basis of their certified educational backgrounds. Ritual classifications such as elementary teacher, English teacher, principal, fourth-grader, and college prep student provide the basis for tightly structured educational organizations. Schools gain community support and legitimacy by conforming to the legal and normative standards of the wider society. Much less control is exerted over teaching activities because close supervision and rigorous evaluation might uncover basic flaws in the instructional program and produce uncertainties. It is much easier to demonstrate conformity to abstract ritual classifications than to evaluate the effectiveness of the teaching-learning process. Therefore, schools decouple their ritual structure from instructional activities and reinforce the decoupling by embracing an assumption of good faith. The community has confidence in members of the board of education, who in turn have confidence in the teachers. These multiple exchanges of confidences are supported by an abiding faith in the process by which school officials have been certified as professionals.[95]

Empirical evidence to support the existence, extent, and patterns of loose couplings in schools is mixed. On the one hand, a number of studies depict the school as a highly centralized and formalized organization; in fact, one of the most salient features of secondary schools in New Jersey is the apparent rigid hierarchy of authority.[96] High school teachers maintain that they must ask permission and get approval before they do "almost anything;" even small matters have to be referred to a superior for a final answer.[97]

On the other hand, the picture of the schools presented by Meyer and Rowan, and others is quite different.[98] These investigators paint schools as loosely coupled systems where instructional work is basically removed from the control of the organizational structure. Perhaps when teachers claim that they must ask permission and get approval before they do almost anything they are excluding the instructional activity. Although it seems hard to believe that teachers make such a distinction, professional discretion of teachers may be so broad and their autonomy so great concerning classroom instruction that questions of supervision are considered only by teachers with a framework of routine school and classroom management practices.

Two recent studies on the images of school organizations by William Firestone and Robert Herriott specifically examine contrasting school structures.[99] Their work suggests that schools can be grouped into two clusters—rational bureaucracies or loosely coupled systems. Elementary schools were much more likely to be rational bureaucracies characterized by goal consensus, hierarchy of authority, centralization, formalization, and limited teacher autonomy. Secondary schools, in contrast, were more loosely coupled systems with more teacher autonomy but with little goal consensus and much less centralization.[100] Most elementary schools are more tightly structured than secondary schools, but it is a matter of degree. Routine tasks and functions are bureaucratically organized in secondary schools. In fact, a comparative analysis of public secondary schools and social welfare agencies by Hoy and his colleagues found schools to be dramatically more formalized and centralized than the welfare agencies.[101] Not one welfare agency had as much hierarchical control or rule enforcement as the *least* centralized or *least* formalized high school.

Are public schools, then, rigid bureaucracies that need to be loosened, or organizational anarchies that need to be tightened? Our analysis leads us to the conclusions that there are probably two basic organizational domains—a bureaucratic one consisting of the institutional and managerial functions of mediating between the school and community, implementing the law, administering internal affairs, procuring and allocating necessary resources, and mediating between students and teachers; and a professional one involved with the actual technical processes of teaching and learning.[102] The bureaucratic domain is typically a tightly linked and cohesive structure, at times too rigid, preventing adaptation and producing alienation among teachers.[103] The professional sphere is much more loosely structured; teachers have broad discretion to make professional judgments about the teaching-learning process; at times, too much independence produces conflict, confusion, and coordination problems reducing productivity and hindering efficiency.[104] Schools are affected by their environment; they are open systems. As forces in society change, pressures to tighten and loosen organization linkages also vary. Clearly, administrators need to know the organization and be aware of and sensitive to the negative consequences of *both* tight and loose coupling. In general, the public school is a distinctive combination of bureaucratic and professional elements, a theme that we will explore in more detail in the next chapter.

SUMMARY

Authority refers to subordinates' willingness to suspend their own criteria for making decisions and comply with directives from a superior. Legal-rational authority provides the basis for Weber's bureaucratic model. Five distinctive characteristics of bureaucracy—division of labor and specialization, impersonality, hierarchy of authority, rules and regulations, and career orientation—are the chief components of Weber's ideal type. The model has been criticized because it pays insufficient attention to possible dysfunctional consequences of each component, neglects the significance of the formal organization, and ignores the conflict between discipline and expertise.

Schools are bureaucratic structures. The Hall and Aston approaches to the study of bureaucracy are intended to measure the degree of bureaucratization of schools with respect to the important components of the Weberian model. Hall's approach can be used to develop four types of school organizational structures—Weberian, authoritarian, professional, and chaotic—that are quite different and seem to have different consequences for students and teachers. Although Hall's and Aston's approaches differ in research strategy and focus, they can be used as complementary modes of analysis.

Another analysis of bureaucracy in schools, Hage's axiomatic theory, illustrates how bureaucratic structure is related to the solution of the organizational problems of adaptiveness, production, efficiency, and job satisfaction. Three ideal types of organization—organic, mechanistic, and integrated—are presented as alternate ways of addressing these issues. Mintzberg, on the other hand, describes structure simply as the ways in which an organization divides its labor into tasks and achieves coordination among them. His analysis yields five ideal types. Both Hage and Mintzberg view organizations as open systems, which are constrained by their environments.

The final theory we examined, loose coupling theory, offers a useful addition to bureaucratic theory. It depicts the school as a distinctive combination of bureaucracy and structural looseness, one in which the institutional structure is decoupled from instructional activities.

NOTES

1. Max Weber, *The Theory of Social and Economic Organizations,* Talcott Parsons, (ed.), A. M. Henderson and Talcott Parsons (trans.) (New York: Free Press, 1947), p. 152.
2. *Ibid,* p. 324.
3. *Ibid.*
4. Herbert A. Simon, *Administrative Behavior,* 2nd ed. (New York: Free Press, 1957), pp. 126–127.
5. Peter Blau and W. Richard Scott, *Formal Organizations: A Comparative Approach* (San Francisco: Chandler, 1962), pp. 28–29.
6. Weber, *op. cit.,* p. 325.
7. *Ibid,* p. 328.
8. *Ibid.*
9. *Ibid.*
10. Robert L. Peabody, "Perceptions of Organizational Authority: A Comparative Analysis," *Administrative Science Quarterly,* 6 (1962), 463–482.
11. James March and Herbert Simon, *Organizations* (New York: Wiley, 1958), p. 90.

12. H. H. Gerth and C. Wright Mills (eds.), *From Max Weber: Essays in Sociology* (New York: Oxford University Press, 1958), p. 196.
13. Weber, *op. cit.,* p. 341.
14. *Ibid.,* p. 331.
15. *Ibid.,* p. 330.
16. *Ibid.,* p. 334.
17. *Ibid.,* p. 337.
18. Alvin Gouldner, *Studies in Leadership* (New York: Harper, 1950), pp. 53–54.
19. Blau and Scott, *op. cit.,* pp. 121–124.
20. Robert Merton, *Social Theory and Social Structure* (New York: Free Press, 1957), p. 199.
21. The specific functions of rules were systematically analyzed by Alvin Gouldner, *Patterns of Industrial Bureaucracy* (New York: Free Press, 1964), pp. 162–180. The terms applied to the functions of rules discussed here come mainly from Gouldner's analysis.
22. *Ibid.,* p. 166
23. *Ibid.,* pp. 169–170.
24. *Ibid.,* pp. 173–174.
25. *Ibid.,* p. 175.
26. *Ibid.,* pp. 45–56.
27. *Ibid.,* pp. 215–227.
28. Charles H. Page, "Bureaucracy's Other Face," *Social Forces,* 25 (1964), 88–94.
29. Peter M. Blau, *The Dynamics of Bureaucracy* (Chicago: University of Chicago Press, 1955).
30. Page, *op. cit.*
31. Laurence Iannaccone, "Informal Organization of School System," in Daniel Griffiths *et al.* (eds.), *Organizing Schools for Effective Education* (Danville, IL: Interstate, 1962), pp. 227–293.
32. Peter M. Blau, *Bureaucracy in Modern Society* (New York: Random House, 1956), p. 58.
33. See Weber, *op. cit.,* footnote 4, pp. 58–60.
34. Gouldner, *Patterns of Industrial Bureaucracy, op. cit.* pp. 21–24.
35. Weber, *op. cit.,* pp. 339.
36. Gerth and Mills, *op. cit.,* p. 254.
37. Gouldner, *Patterns of Industrial Bureaucracy, op. cit.,* pp. 24. See also Helen Constas, "Max Weber's Two Conceptions of Bureaucracy," *American Journal of Sociology,* 63 (1958), 400–409.
38. Arthur L. Stinchcombe, "Bureaucratic and Craft Administration of Production," *Administrative Science Quarterly,* 4 (1959), 168–187.
39. Stanley H. Udy, " 'Bureaucracy' and 'Rationality' in Weber's Organization Theory," *American Sociological Review,* 24 (1959), 791–795.
40. Blau and Scott, *op. cit.,* pp. 224–247.
41. Max Abbott, "Hierarchical Impediments to Innovation in Educational Organizations," in Max Abbott and John Lovell (eds.), *Changing Perspectives in Educational Administration* (Auburn, AL: Auburn University, 1965), p. 45.
42. *Ibid.* See also Matthew Miles, "Education and Innovation: The Organization in Context," in Abbott and Lovell, *op. cit.,* pp. 54–72.

43. Richard H. Hall, "The Concept of Bureaucracy: An Empirical Assessment," *American Sociological Review,* 27 (1962), 295–308.

44. D. A. MacKay, "An Empirical Study of Bureaucratic Dimensions and Their Relations to Other Characteristics of School Organization" (Ph.D. diss., University of Alberta, 1964).

45. Keith F. Punch, "Bureaucratic Structure in Schools: Towards Redefinition and Measurement," *Educational Administration Quarterly,* 6 (1969), 43–57. This article is excellent for students interested in a critical review of the methodological problems of measuring bureaucratic structure.

46. MacKay, *op. cit.;* Henry Kolesar, "An Empirical Study of Client Alienation in the Bureaucratic Organization" (Ph.D. diss., University of Alberta, 1967); and Geoffrey Isherwood and Wayne K. Hoy, "Bureaucratic Structure Reconsidered," *Journal of Experimental Education,* 41 (1972), 47–50.

47. Gouldner, *Patterns of Industrial Bureaucracy, op. cit.*

48. Kolesar, *op. cit.*

49. Geoffrey Isherwood and Wayne K. Hoy, "Bureaucracy, Powerlessness, and Teacher Work Values," *Journal of Educational Administration,* 9 (1973), 124–138.

50. Gerald H. Moeller and W. W. Charters, Jr., "Relation of Bureaucratization to Sense of Power Among Teachers," *Administrative Science Quarterly,* 10 (1966), 444–465.

51. Barry Anderson, "Socio-Economic Status of Students and School Bureaucratization," *Educational Administration Quarterly,* 7 (1971), 12–24.

52. MacKay, *op. cit.*

53. D. S. Pugh, D. J. Hickson, and C. R. Hinnings, "Dimensions of Organizational Structure," *Administrative Science Quarterly,* 13 (1968), 56–105. See also D. S. Pugh and D. J. Hickson, *Organizational Structure in Its Context* (Westmead, Farnborough, Hants., Eng: Saxon House, D. C. Heath, 1976).

54. Pugh and Hickson, *op. cit.,* p. 2.

55. Pugh, Hickson, and Hinnings, *op. cit.*

56. John. F. Newberry, "A Comparative Analysis of the Organizational Structures of Selected Post-secondary Educational Institutions" (Ph.D. diss., University of Alberta, Edmonton, 1971).

57. Edward A. Holdaway, John F. Newberry, David J. Hickson, and R. Peter Heron, "Dimensions of Organizations in Complex Societies: The Educational Sector," *Administrative Science Quarterly,* 20 (1975), 37–58.

58. John G. T. Kelsey, "Conceptualization and Instrumentation for the Comparative Study of Secondary School Structure and Operation" (Ph.D. diss., University of Alberta, 1973); and Lawrence E. Sackney, "The Relationship Between Organizational Structure and Behavior in Secondary Schools" (Ph.D. diss., University of Alberta, 1976).

59. *Ibid.*

60. John E. Haymond, "Bureaucracy, Climate, and Loyalty: An Aston Study in Education" (Ed.D. diss., Rutgers University, 1982).

61. Mary R. M. Guidette, "The Relationship between Bureaucracy and Staff Sense of Powerlessness in Secondary Schools," (Ed.D. diss., Rutgers University, 1982).

62. David A. Sousa and Wayne K. Hoy, "Bureaucratic Structure in Schools: A

Refinement and Synthesis in Measurement," *Educational Administration Quarterly*, 17 (1981), 21–40.

63. Initially, five dimensions were identified, but further analysis demonstrated that standardization clustered with hierarchy of authority, rules, and procedural specifications to form a strong factor, which Sousa and Hoy named Organizational Control. *Ibid.*, pp. 35–36.

64. Jerald Hage, "An Axiomatic Theory of Organizations," *Administrative Science Quarterly*, 10 (1965), 289–320.

65. Talcott Parsons, Robert F. Bales, and Edward A. Shils, *Working Papers in the Theory of Action* (New York: Free Press, 1953).

66. Hage, *op. cit.*, p. 292.

67. Jerald Hage, *Theories of Organizations* (New York: Wiley, 1980), p. 40.

68. Hage, "An Axiomatic Theory of Organizations," p. 305. The terms organic and mechanistic are originally from Tom Burns and G. M. Stalker, *The Management of Innovation* (London: Tavistock Publications, 1961), pp. 119–125.

69. Several research instruments are available to measure the structural dimensions of Hage's theory. They can be found in the following sources: Michael Aiken and Jerald Hage, "Organizational Alienation: A Comparative Analysis," *American Sociological Review*, 31 (1966), 497–507; and Lloyd K. Bishop and Julius R. George, "Organizational Structure: A Factor Analysis of Structural Characteristics of Public Elementary and Secondary Schools," *Educational Administration Quarterly*, 9 (1973), 66–80.

70. Wayne K. Hoy, Wayne Newland, and Richard Blazovsky, "Subordinate Loyalty to Superior, Esprit, and Aspects of Bureaucratic Structure," *Educational Administration Quarterly*, 13 (1977) 71–85. See also Wayne K. Hoy, Richard Blazovsky, and Wayne Newland, "Organizational Structure and Alienation from Work," paper presented at the American Educational Research Association, Boston, 1980.

71. Cecil Miskel, Robert Fevurly, and John Stewart, "Organizational Structures and Processes, Perceived School Effectiveness, Loyalty, and Job Satisfaction," *Educational Administration Quarterly*, 15 (1979), 97–118.

72. Robert W. Hetzel, "The Relationship Between Organizational Structure and Organizational Adaptability in Departments of Curriculum and Instruction" (Ph.D. diss., University of Wisconsin, 1971); and James E. Walter, "Relationship of Organizational Structure to Adaptiveness in Elementary Schools" (Ph.D. diss., University of Wisconsin, 1973).

73. H. Scott Herrick, "Organizational Structure and Teacher Motivation in Multiunit and Non-Multiunit Elementary Schools" (Ph.D. diss., University of Wisconsin, 1974).

74. Henry Mintzberg, *The Structuring of Organizations* (Englewood Cliffs, NJ: Prentice-Hall, 1979), pp. 3–15. See also Henry Mintzberg, *Structure in Fives* (Englewood Cliffs, NJ: Prentice-Hall, 1983), pp. 1–25; and Henry Mintzberg, "Organizational Structure and Alienation from Work," paper presented at the American Educational Research Association, Boston, 1980.

75. Mintzberg, *The Structuring of Organizations*, pp. 7–8.

76. *Ibid.*, p. 321.

77. *Ibid.*, p. 333.

78. *Ibid.*, p. 86.

79. Charles E. Bidwell, "The School as a Formal Organization," in James G. March (ed.), *Handbook of Organization* (Chicago: Rand McNally, 1965), pp. 975–976.

80. Mintzberg, *The Structuring of Organizations,* p. 351.

81. Mintzberg also identifies the pull to balkanize by the managers of the middle line and the pull to collaborate by the support staff, which are less pronounced in schools and found predominately in divisional structure and adhocracies. *Ibid.*

82. Mintzberg, *Organizational Design,* p. 116.

83. James G. March and Johan P. Olsen, *Ambiguity and Choice in Organization* (Bergen, Norway: Universitetsforlaget, 1976).

84. Karl E. Weick, "Educational Organizations as Loosely Coupled Systems," *Administrative Science Quarterly,* 21 (1976), 1–19; Howard E. Aldrich, *Organizations and Environment* (Englewood Cliffs, NJ: Prentice-Hall, 1979).

85. Terrence E. Deal and Lynn D. Celotti, "How Much Influence Do (and Can) Educational Administrators Have on Classrooms?" *Phi Delta Kappan,* 61 (1980), 471–478.

86. John W. Meyer and Brian Rowan, "The Structure of Educational Organizations," in Marshall W. Meyer *et al.* (eds.), *Environments and Organizations* (San Francisco: Jossey-Bass, 1978), pp. 78–109.

87. For an excellent analysis of the school as a loosely coupled structure, see John W. Meyer and W. Richard Scott, *Organizational Environments: Ritual and Rationality* (Beverly Hills, CA: Sage, 1983).

88. Bidwell, *op. cit.,* pp. 972–1022.

89. *Ibid.*

90. Marshall Meyer *et al.,* p. 15.

91. Weick, *op. cit.,* p. 3, identifies fifteen different usages of the idea of loose coupling.

92. *Ibid.,* p. 5.

93. *Ibid.,* p. 11.

94. Meyer and Rowan, *op. cit.*

95. *Ibid.,* pp. 101–102. See also John W. Meyer and Brian Rowan, "Institutionalized Organizations: Formal Structure as Myth and Ceremony," *American Journal of Sociology,* 83 (1977), 440–463.

96. Hoy, Newland, Blazovsky, *op. cit.,* and Hoy, Blazovsky, Newland, *op. cit.* Data from a new sample of secondary schools in New Jersey also support these generalizations.

97. Hoy, Blazovsky, and Newland, *op. cit.*

98. Meyer and Rowan, "Institutionalized Organizations," *op. cit.,* Deal and Celotti, *op. cit.,* Susan Abramowitz and Ellen Tenenbaum, *High School '77* (Washington, DC: National Institute for Educations, 1978); and John W. Meyer *et al.,* "Instructional Dissensus and Institutional Consensus in Schools" in Marshall W. Meyer *et al.* (eds.), *Environments and Organizations* (San Francisco: Jossey-Bass, 1978), pp. 233–263.

99. William A. Firestone and Robert E. Herriott, "Two Images of Schools as Organizations: An Explication and Illustrative Empirical Test." *Educational Administration Quarterly,* 18 (1982), 39–60; and Robert E. Herriott and William A. Firestone, "Two Images of Schools as Organizations: A Refinement and Elaboration," *Educational Administration Quarterly,* 20

(1984), 41–58. See also William A. Firestone and Bruce L. Wilson, "Using Bureaucratic and Cultural Linkages to Improve Instruction: The Principal's Contribution," *Educational Administration Quarterly,* 21 (1985), 7–31.

100. *Ibid.*

101. Wayne K. Hoy, Richard Blazovsky, and Wayne Newland, "Bureaucracy and Alienation: A Comparative Analysis," *The Journal of Educational Administration,* 21 (1983), 109–121.

102. The institutional, managerial and technical functions are discussed in detail by Talcott Parsons, "Some Ingredients of a General Theory of Formal Organization," in Andrew W. Halpin (ed.), *Administrative Theory in Education* (New York: Macmillan, 1967), pp. 40–72.

103. Hoy, Blazovsky, and Newland, "Organizational Structure and Alienation from Work," and Hoy, Blazovsky, and Newland, "Bureaucracy and Alienation: A Comparative Analysis."

104. For an insightful discussion of the separate zones of control of principals and teachers, see Dan C. Lortie, "The Balance of Control and Autonomy in Elementary School Teaching," in A. Etzioni (ed.), *The Semiprofessions and Their Organization* (New York: Free Press, 1969).

Chapter 6

The Professional in the School Bureaucracy

The weight of evidence . . . suggests . . . a consistent pattern of conflict between teachers and administrators over the control of work, and that professionalization is a militant process.

RONALD G. CORWIN
"Professional Persons in Public Organizations"

The previous chapter developed the concept of bureaucracy as the typical model of organizational structure for schools. We suggested there that conflict between bureaucratic and professional patterns developed as employees became more specialized and expert. This chapter presents the similarities and differences between professional and bureaucratic orientations and career options and problems of professional educators. Particular emphasis is given to teachers and administrators in schools.

CHARACTERISTICS OF A PROFESSIONAL ORIENTATION

Although various definitions of the term "professional" have been advanced, a number of common characteristics emerge. First, professional decisions are based on technical expertise that is acquired through extensive education, training, and practice. Professionals are experts in specific and limited areas who do work that is characterized by complexity and adaptiveness. They diagnose and treat on a case-by-case basis; generalized step-by-step solutions either do not exist or are very complicated. As Peter M. Blau and W. Richard Scott observe, professionals make no claim to generalized wisdom—they are neither sage nor wise.[1] Nonetheless, because of training and expertise, professionals are expected to make technically correct decisions in their areas of specialization. The length of training varies for professionals, but it is usually fairly long. Amitai Etzioni claims that full-fledged professionals are those whose training is five or more years, while semiprofessionals have a shorter prescribed training period.[2]

A second characteristic of a profession is the extent to which practitioners provide service to clients. Indeed, the service ideal is pivotal in legitimizing professional status. Professionals are expected to subordinate their own interests and to act in the best interests of clients. In addition, the clients are particularly vulnerable to the actions of professionals because clients typically need assistance but do not know how to help themselves. They place themselves in the hands of professionals, confident that professionals will act in their best interests. If a professional acts primarily from self-interest, then condemnation and sanctions by colleagues and community members usually damage that self-interest. Hence, the "altruism" of professionals is maintained because failure to conform to the service norm is less rewarding than conformity.

In addition to the service ideal, other norms also govern the professional-client relationship. A professional person is objective, impersonal, and impartial. The relationship with the client is limited to the technical task under consideration; professionals are expected to avoid emotional involvement. Furthermore, they provide impartial treatment in spite of their own personal biases; objectivity and neutrality enable the professional to make reasoned and rational judgments on behalf of clients.

Reference-group orientation is another attribute that plays an important role for professionals. The "significant others" for a professional are colleagues whose knowledge and competence in the field are useful in decision making. The professional's loyalty is to the integrity of the profession and to the service of clients.

A distinctive control structure is another aspect of a profession. In a given field, professionals constitute a group of equals who control themselves. Their expertise is based on theoretical knowledge and skills that are acquired through long training. Professionals expect extensive autonomy in exercising their special competence because they claim that they alone are best suited to make decisions in their specialized area. Patrick B. Forsyth and Thomas J. Danisiewicz elaborate two varieties of autonomy—from the client and from the employing organization.[3] Professionals control their clients as well as being responsive to clients' self-perceived needs. Consequently, as professionals are constrained in the performance of their work by the controls and demands of the organization, their level of professionalism declines. Autonomy of individual practitioners is commonly examined and discussed as an attitude, i.e., their professional orientation.

Finally, professionals have an internalized code of ethics that guides their activities. Performance is controlled primarily by self-imposed standards and peer-group surveillance.[4] Even when professionals err, they will still be defended by their peers as long as they acted responsibly.[5] Indeed, Eliot Freidson maintains that during the past two decades the idea of social control within the professions has been badly eroded.[6] He believes that organized professional associations have flouted the public interest and the informal norms of social control among professionals have not been exercised judiciously and systematically.

Rather than classifying some occupations as "professions" and others not, Edward Gross and Amitai Etzioni believe that a continuum should be used.[7] At one pole of the continuum would be the occupations that have earned the right to call themselves professions. At the opposite pole, the occupations would still be struggling for recognition. The closer an occupation comes to the professional pole, the more independence or autonomy the practitioners claim for themselves.

In summary, a *professional orientation* is characterized by technical competence acquired through long training; adherence to a set of professional norms that includes a service ideal, objectivity, impersonality, and impartiality; a colleague-oriented reference group; autonomy in professional decision making; and self-imposed control based upon knowledge, standards, and peer review.

PROFESSIONAL-BUREAUCRATIC CONFLICT

Professionals and semiprofessionals employed in formal organizations bring into focus a basic conflict between a professional orientation and a bureaucratic orientation. Although many similarities exist between professional and bureaucratic principles, the potential for conflict remains because differences also occur. The major similarities and differences are summarized in Table 6.1.

Both bureaucrats and professionals are expected to have technical expertise in specialized areas, to maintain an objective perspective, and to act impersonally and impartially. Professionals, however, are expected to act in the best interests of their clients, while bureaucrats are expected to act in the best interests of the organization. This apparent conflict between the interests of clients and organization poses a problem for many formal organizations, but for

TABLE 6.1   Basic Characteristics of Professional and Bureaucratic Orientations: Similarities and Differences

Professional Orientation		*Bureaucratic Orientation*
Technical expertise		Technical expertise
Objective perspective		Objective perspective
Impersonal and impartial approach		Impersonal and impartial approach
Service to clients		Service to clients
Colleague-oriented reference group	MAJOR SOURCES OF CONFLICT	Hierarchical orientation
Autonomy in decision making		Disciplined compliance
Self-imposed standards of control		Subordinated to the organization

service organizations such as schools, social work agencies, and hospitals it may not be a major dilemma. Unlike business concerns, the prime beneficiary of service organizations is the client. For service organizations, then, the prime objective of both the bureaucrat and the professional is the same—service to clients.

A fundamental source of conflict does emerge from the system of social control used by bureaucracies and the professions. Professionals attempt to control work decisions. They have been taught to internalize a code of ethics that guides their activities, and this code of behavior is supported by colleagues. Professionals are basically responsible to their profession, and at times they may be censured by their colleagues. On the other hand, control in bureaucratic organizations is not in the hands of the colleague group; discipline stems from one major line of authority. As Blau and Scott explain, "Performance is controlled by directives received from one's superiors rather than by self-imposed standards and peer-group surveillance, as is the case among professionals."[8] Considerable variation exists, however, among various professional groups and in the scope of their professional domains. For example, elementary and secondary school teachers may have a relatively narrow scope, while physicians and scientists typically have broad authority.[9] The ultimate basis for a professional act is professional knowledge; however, the ultimate justification of a bureaucratic act is its consistency with the organizational rules and regulations and approval by a superior. Therein lies the major source of conflict between the organization and the profession, conflict between "professional expertise and autonomy" and "bureaucratic discipline and control."

Nevertheless, Scott argues that, while some conflict exists between professional and bureaucratic principles, the two arrangements are not incompatible in all respects. Both represent alternative paths to the rationalization of a field of action—and at a general level, the two orientations are compatible.[10]

Accommodations to Conflict

The interaction between bureaucrats and professionals can be strained. Teachers resent interference from the administration; professors fight for academic freedom. Of course, different ways are used to resolve the conflict. In some organizations major structural changes have been made. In others, many professionals have developed orientations that are compatible with the demands of their bureaucratic organizations.

One method of accommodation is the development of professional organizations, which are established specifically to produce, apply, preserve, or communicate knowledge. Professional organizations are characterized by the goals they pursue, by the high proportion of professionals (at least 50 percent), and by the authority relations where the professionals have superior authority over the major goal activities. Examples of professional organizations include universities, colleges, many schools, research organizations, therapeutic mental hospitals, larger general hospitals, and social-work agencies. However, full-fledged professional organizations employ professionals whose training is five or more years; semiprofessional organizations, e.g., many elementary and secondary schools, employ individuals whose training is less than five years.[11]

Gross and Etzioni further observe that differences in training produce differences in goals and privileges. Full-fledged professional organizations are primarily devoted to the creation and application of knowledge; their professionals are typically protected by the guarantee of privileged communication. Semiprofessional organizations are primarily concerned with the communication of knowledge, rather than its creation; their professionals generally do not have the guarantee of privileged communication. Elementary schools constitute the most common example of the semiprofessional organization. The differences in training, the type and amount of knowledge, privileged communication, and the use of knowledge apparently are associated with differences in administrative authority. In semiprofessional organizations, professional work has less autonomy, and semiprofessionals often have personality traits and skills more compatible with the administrators than in professional organizations. Hence, semiprofessional organizations are managed more frequently by semiprofessionals themselves than by others. For example, almost all principals and superintendents are former teachers.[12]

Similarly, Henry Mintzberg noted the professional bureaucracies rely on standard skills and knowledge, training and socialization for coordination of organizational activities.[13] Trained and indoctrinated specialists, i.e., professionals, are hired to do the basic work in professional bureaucracies, and they are granted considerable control over their own work. This control means that professionals work in relative independence of their colleagues, but closely with their clients. As suggested in the previous chapter, Bidwell observes that structural looseness in the school organization produces considerable autonomy for teachers.[14] Teachers tend to work alone in their classrooms in relative isolation from colleagues and administrators. Consequently, schools tend to be structured loosely to allow teachers broad discretionary autonomy within their classrooms.

Another method of structural accommodation used to alleviate the bureaucratic-professional conflict is exhibited by hospital organizations. Two authority lines—one professional and one administrative—exist in many hospitals.[15] Oswald Hall describes a hospital's dual authority system as follows:

> . . . the emergence of two chains of command. One of these proceeds from the superintendent of the hospital down through supervisors of nursing, of the kitchen, of the housekeeping staff, of accounts, and so forth, and provides a system of orders, and of accountability, from the top to the bottom of the organization. On the other hand, the hierarchy of the doctors stands completely outside this structure. The doctors have their hierarchy.[16]

Nevertheless, strains still remain in a hospital, especially where professional considerations conflict with bureaucratic ones. Likewise, bifurcation of the professional and bureaucratic domains in some schools reduces the conflict between professional and bureaucratic authority. Yet tensions between them persist. At best, a dual authority structure seems a partial solution.

Even if no changes occur in the organizational structure, professionals may develop role orientations or attitudes that facilitate adjustment to the bureaucratic role demands. Some professionals retain a high commitment to professional skills and develop a strong orientation to reference groups outside the organization; they thus maintain a strong professional orientation. These individuals are dedicated to the profession in general, not to any particular organization. Other professionals may become less committed to professional skills and develop an orientation to a particular organization. They are more interested in approval from administrative superiors within the organization than from professional colleagues outside; a bureaucratic orientation therefore develops. Either of these orientations may be functional: if future personal goals involve securing an administrative position, a bureaucratic orientation may be functional; if advancement within the profession is desired, a professional orientation may be functional.

A number of studies have systematically identified and explored individual accommodations to the conflict between professional and organizational commitment. In this regard Alvin Gouldner's investigation of a small liberal arts college is a well-known study.[17] He identifies two latent organizational types— cosmopolitans and locals—and distinguishes the bases for their accommodation to such conflict. *Cosmopolitans* are those low on loyalty to the employing organization, high on commitment to specialized role skills, and likely to use an outer reference group. *Locals* are those high on loyalty to the employing organization, low on commitment to specialized role skills, and likely to use an inner reference group.

Gouldner's study indicates that the tension and conflict created by an organization's bureaucratic needs for expertise and its social system latency needs for loyalty can be met by adopting either a local or a cosmopolitan orientation. Studies of intellectuals in labor unions,[18] nurses in hospitals,[19] scientists in industrial organizations,[20] and workers in social welfare agencies[21] tend to support Gouldner's findings.

A TYPOLOGY OF COSMOPOLITANS AND LOCALS

In a subsequent, more extensive analysis of the data from the liberal arts college, Gouldner refined and extended his typology of latent organizational identities to include four types of locals and two types of cosmopolitans.[22]

Dedicated locals are "true believers" who identify completely with the goals and objectives of the organization. They are likely to insist that their colleagues possess local value orientations rather than technical expertise. Furthermore, theirs is an inner reference group, which focuses almost exclusively on the values of the bureaucracy.

True bureaucrat locals resist all outside control. They attach much importance to the organization's geographic location. While dedicated locals are concerned with the integrity of organizational values, true bureaucrats are concerned primarily with the security of the organization. They believe that organizational security can be best attained by authoritarian practices and use of formal rules and regulations.

Homeguard locals have limited occupational specialization and commitment. They are administrative-oriented locals, typically in the middle echelon of administration. They seem bound and loyal to the organization because of their local roots. In Gouldner's study, many of the homeguard graduated from the local college, married people who had, or both. In terms of professional contributions and commitments, they make virtually none.

Elder locals are the oldest people in the group and have been involved in the organization the longest. Like all locals, they are highly committed to the organization; in fact, they plan to stay indefinitely. Elders are deeply rooted in the informal organization and evaluate the present in terms of the past. The significant reference group for elders is, of course, other elders.

Outsider cosmopolitans tend to isolate themselves from other organizational participants. In a real sense, they are in, but not of, the organization. They are extremely committed to specialized role skills; their reference group is almost exclusively outside the organization. They do not feel that they get adequate intellectual stimulation from within the organization, have little loyalty to the organization, and do not plan to stay.

Empire-builder cosmopolitans, unlike the outsiders, are integrated into the organizational structure, primarily its formal structure. They have a strong commitment to their departments, and they favor strong departmental autonomy; however, like outsiders, they believe that employment opportunities in other organizations are good, and they are willing to move for the right job.

ANOTHER TYPOLOGY OF LOCALS

Robert V. Presthus provides another conceptual perspective for examining individual accommodations to bureaucratic pressures.[23] His analysis is concerned primarily with locals who tend to adjust successfully in bureaucratic organizations. Presthus postulates that bureaucratic organizations, with their patent status structures and power apparatuses, tend to generate anxiety in organizational members. To most, anxiety is an unpleasant and annoying tension that produces actions to reduce anxiety. Therefore, tension reduction becomes a powerful motivator and reinforcer of organizational behavior. Individuals accommodate themselves to tension by becoming upward mobiles, indifferents, or ambivalents.

Upward mobiles are identified as individuals who embrace the goals of the organization. The organization's values are their values; therefore, in any situation, but especially in conflict situations, organizational values are decisive. Upward mobiles believe in hierarchical authority and accept its demands. Furthermore, upward mobiles are oriented toward ascending the status structure, and they have a genuine, deep, and abiding respect for authority.

Indifferents adopt the most common mode of accommodation. They reject the organizational values of success and power. Their orientation essentially is extravocational and outside the organization. Indifferents separate work from the more meaningful aspects of their lives. To indifferents, work simply is a job that provides economic capital; the job is not a central interest in life.

Ambivalents are usually a small minority who cannot resist the appeals of the organization but still often fail to gain organizational power and success. Ambivalents need security, yet they cannot make the accommodations necessary to achieve it. Ambivalents have an aggressive sense of individuality that frequently does not fit into the bureaucracy's structured way of operating. Moreover, ambivalents are typically unable to accept organizational premises; instead, they make decisions on a particularistic point of view, rejecting authority, adopting permissive views of dissent, and accepting their own impulses rather than their organization's standards. Unlike upward mobiles and indifferents, who represent successful local patterns of accommodation, ambivalents exemplify inappropriate adjustments that typically result in resignation, aggression, or withdrawal.

A DUAL ORIENTATION

Thus far, our analysis has dealt with organizational accommodations to the professional-bureaucratic conflict and with individual accommodations in which the employee has chosen either commitment to the profession or commitment to the organization, not to both. A few studies do suggest that under certain conditions professionals may be committed to both their professions and their organizations. Barney Glaser refers to this as a *dual orientation,* both local and cosmopolitan.[24] Similarly, William Kornhauser labels individuals who hold this dual perspective a mixed type.[25] Whatever the label, it appears that in some organizational contexts, an integration of bureaucratic and professional cultures is reflected in an orientation to both the organization and the profession.

Glaser identifies two conditions that tend to generate a dual orientation among scientists working in organizations. A dual orientation is possible when (1) the organizational goals and the institutional goals (of science) are compatible and (2) the scientists are highly motivated.[26] Russell Thornton's study of junior college teachers also tends to support the development of a dual orientation when organizational practices are consistent with professional objectives.[27] In particular, the more professional the criteria of performance, the more professional the authority relationship and the more professional the supervision. Under this condition the organizational and professional commitments among junior college teachers become compatible. When a high degree of professionalism in organizational involvement exists, individuals can be committed both to the profession and to the organization. Such a dual orientation is especially desirable in service organizations such as schools.

PROFESSIONAL AND BUREAUCRATIC ORIENTATIONS IN SCHOOLS

Whether or not teaching is a full-fledged profession is debatable. However, few would argue either that teachers are closer to the professional end of an occupational continuum than blue-collar and white-collar workers, or that they are further from the professional pole than physicians or lawyers. Nonetheless, the growth of theory and knowledge in teaching, the increased requirements for teacher education, teachers' sense of responsibility for student welfare, strong professional associations, and increased claims for teacher autonomy provide the basis for considering teaching a profession. Behind the drive to professionalize teaching is the desire for increased status and more control over work—in order to gain not only more responsibility but more authority. For many years, teachers believed that they had professional obligations, such as staying after school to help students with their work; now they are demanding professional rights as well, such as selecting their own teaching materials and procedures.[28]

As we have already discussed, the characteristics of bureaucratic organizations are not totally compatible with a professional work group. Findings that many conflicts in schools derive from more general conflict between bureaucratic and professional principles should not be surprising. For example, Ronald G. Corwin studied teacher conflict in schools and found that almost half of the conflict incidents involved teachers in opposition to administrators.[29] The higher the level of professional orientation, the greater the number of conflicts.

Few teachers escape the oral or written exhortations on "professionalism." Consider a few of the following statements made by school administrators: (1) "Teachers who are professional do not meddle in politics"; (2) "All professional people should vigorously exercise their right to participate in the political arena"; (3) "It is your professional duty to teach at least two years in a school system"; (4) "It is your professional duty to vote in public elections"; (5) "It is a teacher's professional duty to attend school activities."

The list could be expanded indefinitely. The inconsistencies and contradictions are obvious. Some administrators use the term "professionalism" as a cry to rally support for the school or for a given decision. For example, a decision to initiate a merit salary program in one school subsequently resulted in a confidential note to all teachers notifying them of their salaries plus the following addendum: "Salary is a confidential and personal matter. It is your professional obligation not to discuss your salary with other teachers." A safe prediction is that many educational administrators have a conception of a "professional" teacher as one who is loyal to the administration and the organization, that is, one who has a bureaucratic orientation.

Given the bureaucratization of schools and the growing professionalization of teachers, continued conflict seems likely. In teaching, the immediate issues of conflict revolve around the amount of control teachers should have over the selection of textbooks, teaching procedures and methods, and curriculum reform and development; however, the underlying issue is neither peculiar to teaching nor school organizations.[30] The conflict is between professional expertise and autonomy and bureaucratic discipline and control.

The conflict probably will continue to exist as long as the teacher's professional authority is not supported by the climate or structure of the organization. As long as the basic bureaucratic structure of the school tends to be authoritarian (i.e., Type II, as defined in the preceding chapter), teacher authority will continue to be a major source of tension. If the organizational structure of the school becomes more professional (i.e., Type III), then the chances for ameliorating the conflict and tension will be greatly improved. In fact, a dual orientation (local-cosmopolitan) of teachers might be the rule rather than the exception. In professional organizational structures, teachers might increasingly have high commitments both to the organization and to the profession. Some research supports the notion that bureaucratic orientation and professional attitudes of teachers need not be in conflict if schools increase the professional autonomy of teachers.[31]

The evidence to date, however, suggests that neither a dual orientation nor a professional organizational structure is common in schools. We have mentioned Corwin's preliminary findings of a predominance of conflicts between teachers and administrators in public schools. In a subsequent, more comprehensive study, Corwin not only confirmed his initial findings but also drew attention to a number of other related findings. According to that study, "rebellious" and "contrary" teachers were both more professional and more militant; in addition, the more professional the orientation of the staff, the greater the amount of conflict in the school; and finally, professional and bureaucratic orientations of teachers were inversely related to each other (i.e., those teachers who were committed to the profession tended not to be loyal to the school organization).[32]

Corwin measured bureaucratic and professional orientations by using two separate Likert-type scales, which have respondents describe the extent of their agreement or disagreement to a series of statements. A bureaucratic orientation contains six aspects: (1) loyalty to the administration, (2) loyalty to the organization, (3) a belief that teaching competence is based on experience, (4) an endorsement of treating personnel interchangeably, (5) an emphasis on standardization and on rules and regulations, and (6) loyalty to the public. Professional orientation includes four aspects: (1) orientation to students, (2) orientation to the profession and professional colleagues, (3) a belief that competence is based on knowledge, and (4) a belief that teachers should have decision-making authority. Items for each scale are given in Table 6.2.

Several other studies of teacher orientations also are relevant. Edward Kuhlman and Wayne K. Hoy studied the bureaucratic socialization of new school teachers.[33] They were interested in the extent to which the professional and bureaucratic orientations of beginning teachers were changed as a result of initial socialization attempts by the school organization. They theorized that a dual role orientation might emerge among new teachers as they were socialized. New teachers, however, did not become both more professional and more bureaucratic in orientation during the first year of teaching. On the contrary, secondary teachers became significantly more bureaucratic and less professional during the first year. The orientations of beginning elementary teachers remained relatively constant, although as a group they were significantly more

TABLE 6.2 Sample Items for the Bureaucratic and Professional Orientation Scales

Bureaucratic Orientation
1. Teachers should be obedient, respectful, and loyal to the principal.
2. What is best for the school is best for education.
3. Pay should be in relation to experience.
4. Teachers of the same subject throughout the system should follow the same kind of lesson plan.
5. Rules stating when the teachers should arrive and depart should be strictly enforced.
6. A good teacher is one who conforms, in general, to accepted standards in the community.

Professional Orientation
1. Unless she is satisfied that it is best for the student, a teacher should not do what she is told to do.
2. Teachers should subscribe to and diligently read the standard professional journals.
3. Teachers should be evaluated primarily on the basis of their knowledge of the subject that is to be taught and their ability to communicate it.
4. The ultimate authority over the major educational decisions should be exercised by professional teachers.

bureaucratic than secondary teachers. The hypothesis was not supported that a dual orientation would evolve during the initial experience of teaching and would enhance the effectiveness of both the professional and the organization. Furthermore, Harold Wilensky's contention regarding an interpenetration of bureaucratic and professional cultures in many organizations was not supported by the findings in secondary schools.[34] The results obtained from the elementary schools, however, indicate that a dual orientation may be possible in less bureaucratic structures like elementary schools, where new personnel already exhibit a highly bureaucratic orientation.

The forces of bureaucratic socialization in a majority of secondary schools seem strong. Most schools begin almost immediately to mold neophytes into roles devised to maintain stability, to encourage subordination, and to promote loyalty to the organization; in fact, the socialization process begins with the student-teaching experience. Student teachers, as a result of their practice teaching experience, appear to become significantly more bureaucratic in orientation.[35]

In sum, research portrays the school as a service organization staffed predominantly with professionals and semiprofessionals. The structure of the school organization is basically bureaucratic, with authoritarian trappings. Teachers as a group are becoming somewhat more professional and more militant; yet the bureaucratic structure, especially at the secondary level, seems quite effective at socializing new members to the appropriate bureaucratic stance, often at the expense of professional considerations. Hence, the school milieu is comprised of a number of countervailing forces. One hopes that administrators and teachers alike will strive to make school organizations more professional and less authoritarian. In such organizations a dual orientation seems likely to become increasingly prevalent, with teachers who are highly committed to both the profession and the organization.

Local and Cosmopolitan Orientations of Administrators

Thus far, the discussion of organizational and professional commitments has been restricted to teachers, but it is also enlightening to use a similar perspective to analyze behavior patterns of school administrators. Richard O. Carlson was the first to identify and study the behavior of two distinct types of school administrators—placebound and careerbound.[36]

Placebound superintendents are insiders who work within a school system until the highest position is achieved. Their careers are basically ascents through the hierarchy in one school system, although they may have changed school systems earlier in their careers. Typically, placebound superintendents complete their careers in the same district in which they were promoted. If they leave the superintendency before retirement age, they often take a lower-level administrative position in the same district. Placebound superintendents are thus insiders with a local orientation.

In contrast, *careerbound superintendents* are outsiders who seek positions wherever they are to be found. Their careers span two or more school systems, and typically, they do not stop with one superintendency. As outsiders, they have never served the district in any other professional capacity. Careerbound superintendents are outsiders whose basic commitments are to the professional career rather than to a particular school or community.

The terms "placebound" and "careerbound" help to distinguish the roles of insiders and outsiders. Insiders are more interested in place than career and, because they have a history in the school system, are an established part of the organization. Outsiders are strangers in the sociological sense and, lacking a history in the school system, are unknown quantities.[37] Carlson's research and analysis of the behavioral patterns of placebound and career bound superintendents led him to the following conclusions.

1. Insiders tend to have a greater commitment to a specific community and school system and a lower commitment to a career of superintendent than do outsiders.
2. School boards tend to elect insiders to the superintendency only when they believe that the schools are being properly administered.
3. Outsiders are in a position to bargain successfully with school boards for higher salaries than insiders; hence, they are better paid.
4. School boards tend to give outsiders, but not insiders, a mandate for organizational change and development.
5. Outsiders usually are more successful than insiders in persuading the school board that changes are needed.

6. Outsiders are more concerned with the development of new rules than insiders. Although insiders are concerned with rules, they focus attention on rules in such a way as to tighten the procedures that exist. Outsiders tend to make rules that alter what exists.

7. The established social system of the school system is temporarily suspended as an outsider takes the helm; however, the established social system remains largely unaltered with the election of an insider. Furthermore, insiders tend to default on the authority relationship with teachers because they do not work to gain teacher support. Outsiders have the advantage in reorganizing and changing the social system of the school district.

8. Outsiders, more than insiders, expand the central office staff of the school system in order to retool the organization and prepare for changes.

9. Tradition within the school system tends to be more of a hindrance to insiders than outsiders in the management of internal group struggles.

10. Outsiders view themselves as expendable in relation to the particular school system, while insiders see themselves as permanent.

11. Insiders do not actively seek a move to another superintendency; hence, insiders have a longer tenure than outsiders.[38]

The profiles that emerge from these findings help explain the different performances of the two types. Insiders are adaptive individuals who change themselves to fit the office. They tend to be stabilizers or maintainers of the status quo. Outsiders are more likely to be innovators and change the office and organization. They tend to be more dedicated to change, reform, and improvement and realize that the price for change will be periodic movement in their own careers. In brief, the data clearly support the conclusion that insiders tend to maintain the school district and outsiders tend to make changes.

Hoy and Fred Aho also have analyzed differences in the behavior of insiders and outsiders, in particular, of secondary school principals.[39] Insiders are principals who were promoted from within, whereas outsiders came to the principalship from outside the organization. Once again, some important distinctions in their behavior patterns were found. Principals who were outsiders had a distinct advantage not only in terms of sound principal-teacher relations but also in their ability to act as agents of change. The following list specifies the details of the outsiders' advantage:

1. Outsiders were less authoritarian in behavior.

2. Outsiders exhibited greater emotional detachment; for example, they were less apt to lose their temper when relationships became difficult.

3. Outsiders had a greater degree of influence with superiors.

4. Outsiders supervised teachers who were more satisfied with their jobs.

5. Outsiders had schools with higher morale.
6. Outsiders commanded a greater degree of loyalty from teachers.
7. Outsiders engaged in more leadership roles in professional groups.
8. Outsiders were more often described by teachers as agents of change.

Comparing the findings for secondary principals with those for superintendents is instructive, although some caution should be exercised because the principals were drawn from one state, New Jersey. A number of differences are apparent, however. Although outsiders who were superintendents tended to be careerbound, whereas insiders were placebound, this was not necessarily the case for secondary principals. The attitudes of insider and outsider principals concerning mobility and occupational goals were not significantly different. In addition, no significant differences appeared in terms of tenure, salary, or age. These findings suggest that for most secondary principals, regardless of whether they were insiders or outsiders, the position may be a steppingstone for higher administrative office rather than a final career goal.

Nonetheless, the results in many respects support Carlson's theoretical analysis of administrative succession and organizational change. In both studies, outsiders tended to be agents of change and insiders did not. Carlson also found that superintendents who were outsiders were more successful in convincing their boards of education that change was needed; however, no difference was found in the ability of principals, regardless of administrative type, to persuade superintendents that change was needed. The data from the two studies suggest the hypothesis that boards of education seek superintendents who are agents of change more frequently than superintendents seek secondary principals who are innovators. Boards of education tend to go to the outside when they want change, and there are twice as many superintendents who are outsiders.[40] The opposite ratio holds for New Jersey secondary principals. Even when a superintendent goes outside for a high school principal, typically a clear mandate for change does not exist. Nevertheless, outsiders are more prone to be perceived by their teachers as agents of change than insiders.

Carlson's analysis of the social system confronting insiders is also relevant for the new principals. Insiders face social systems that are established, well-defined, structured, and relatively unaltered, while outsiders face social systems that have been temporarily suspended because of their arrival. Outsiders, therefore, have an advantage with respect to organizational development and adaptation because they initially have the opportunity to maneuver and to reshape the structure and norms of social systems.[41]

Insiders seem to be trapped in situations that make leadership difficult. Too frequently, they have only the power and authority of the office; hence, they find it difficult to expand the scope of their authority. In order to lead, principals must command informal as well as formal authority. Loyalty, satisfaction, morale, and influence make it much more likely that secondary principals who are outsiders will have informal and formal teacher support, a fact that enhances their effectiveness as leaders.[42]

CONCEPTUAL DERIVATIONS AND APPLICATIONS

Careers of Teachers and Administrators

A career is a sequence of positions occupied by a person during the course of a lifetime.[43] Because almost all careers of educators take place in formal organizational settings, it is important to consider the problems that educators are having in the attainment of professional status, and the career paths of teachers and administrators in school bureaucracies.

Teachers.　A number of serious problems characterize teaching careers that are seriously eroding or even precluding the attainment of true professional status. First, teaching in the elementary and secondary schools has a flat career path or, as Dan C. Lortie maintains, the career is "unstaged."[44] Similarly, Judith Lanier observes that teachers have no opportunity for advancement in their instructional work.[45] Novices have the same role expectations as veterans. Teachers with motivations to excel and achieve generally have two choices—they can remain frustrated in their self-contained classroom or they can leave.

Second, too many of the best teachers leave their instructional careers after a brief foray in the classroom. During the first five years, about 50 percent of a teacher cohort will leave teaching.[46] Moreover, Philip C. Schlechty and Victor Vance found that a disproportionate percentage of those leaving teaching were the most academically talented. These data suggest that teachers lack strong professional career orientations and that schools depend on young, transient college graduates to maintain the teaching force. With additional career opportunities opening for bright women and minority-group members, the traditional talent pool for teaching may be shrinking dramatically.[47]

Third, for most teachers in the United States, the "Three Rs," i.e., their rights, responsibilities and rewards, are designed to attract individuals with modest talent, achievement, and motivation, rather than the most able. Prerogatives and civilities accorded most college graduates are notably absent for most elementary and secondary school teachers. They rarely have an office, telephone, typewriter, or computer terminal—not to mention a secretary or assistant—at their ready disposal. Even common amenities such as coffee breaks, restroom privileges, and lunch hour periods with a respite from their students or clients are seldom readily available.[48] As Mary H. Futrell notes, teachers average forty-six hours of work per week. Although they receive about thirty minutes for lunch, 45 percent of the teachers must supervise students during this period.[49]

Fourth, adequate rewards and compensations are lacking. Following a four- or five-year deferral of income, combined with a costly investment in a college education, the average American teacher works longer hours and receives less pay than most semiskilled workers. Moreover, teachers are not acknowledged to be very academically talented or well educated. Instead, they are too often portrayed as intellectually weak in comparison to members of other professions or semiprofessions.[50]

Fifth, possibly the most discouraging condition of the teaching career is the work load that denies many, if not most teachers the right to excel in teaching without undue hardship and personal sacrifice. If secondary teachers, for example, give only five minutes review and correction to each student's written work per week (assuming a modest 150 students on the average), they have tacked twelve hours onto their work week. Added to the extensiveness of job expectations is the intensity of being in constant contact with the students. Most teachers care deeply about the growth and welfare of their students, but prolonged interaction with large numbers of children at the expense of interaction with other professionals on issues of educational significance dampens both the intellectual and emotional health of teachers. Under current conditions only the most dedicated, self-sacrificing teachers can maintain their inspiration for continued professional growth.[51]

Sixth, more and more organizational directives are coming from state offices of education and central district offices that force teachers to work in increasingly routine ways. Theodore R. Sizer maintains that, in well-intentioned but misguided ways, educational bureaucracies are stampeding toward added top-down control, with standardized mandates for "minutes per day" of instruction to be delivered by all teachers in a way designed by a central authority.[52] Standard, mandated practice threatens professional status and promotes professional-bureaucratic conflict.

To alleviate these problems and to enhance the professional nature of teaching, Schlechty asserts that fundamental changes must be made in the teaching occupation.[53] If educational organizations are to attract, motivate, and retain teachers who are capable of outstanding performance, virtually every vested interest group will be threatened. Moreover, the kinds of reforms that are required go beyond piecemeal efforts. Two areas of proposed reform that have significant potential to alleviate the aversive conditions and to move the teaching career closer to the professional end of the occupational continuum are improved teacher education and career ladders.

TEACHER PREPARATION.[54] In congruence with the characteristic of professional expertise, the preparation of teachers must be considered carefully. A brief historical perspective is needed to understand current practices of preparation. During the mid-nineteenth century, a major reform movement created normal schools to train teachers. Then, as now, the charge was that teachers were inadequately prepared for their jobs. For their time normal schools were successful; they organized and improved the technical aspects of teacher training. At the beginning of the twentieth century, another wave of innovation moved teacher education to universities and changed the normal schools to general purpose state colleges and universities. The second reform movement has not worked very well. A reason for the lack of success is that placing teacher education in the undergraduate university curriculum forced a number of unfortunate and substantive compromises. Both the liberal arts and professional curricula were shortchanged. Important theoretical and practical components had to be deleted. At the same time, the emphasis on "training" that reflects both the normal school and professional traditions has never been easily accepted by other university faculty.

Consequently, the present status of teacher education in the second reform movement is floundering, a condition that is now widely and publicly recognized. Two new waves of reform now seem to be starting. One wave is moving toward deprofessionalizing teaching through narrow apprenticeship programs and minimal competency standards. In contrast, the other move is to upgrade teacher preparation to a graduate-professional level. To help teaching achieve professional status, teacher preparation should exhibit five characteristics. First, teacher education programs must be designed and operated as a cooperative venture with other university faculties and members of the profession. Second, teachers prepared in the programs must be liberally educated people who understand the increasing complexity of society. Third, prospective teachers also must gain the expertise to make complex and subtle judgments and decisions about children, learning, and instruction. For example, recent research-based developments for managing classrooms, cooperative learning, and pacing instruction give teachers powerful technologies to guide their professional practices. Fourth, the programs must be extended to five or more years in length. To define the length of preparation of the professions as five or more years is somewhat arbitrary, and some groups have tried to gain the mantle of "professional" by artificially increasing the length of training programs.[55] In the case of teaching, however, less time means that something must be compromised—liberal education, majors and minors, or professional expertise and practice. Fifth, teacher education programs must prepare teachers for differentiated career paths and long-term commitments to the profession. The current high turnover rate of new recruits represents a huge loss of human capital that schools can ill afford. Teacher education should be the beginning of a gradual induction into the profession and form the initial steps of a legitimate professional career.[56]

CAREER LADDERS FOR TEACHERS.   Probably the most touted and widely mandated reform of teaching is career ladders. Michael J. Murphy defines the concept of career ladders as being a job redesign that provides prospects for promotion, formalizes status ranks for teachers, matches teacher abilities with job tasks, and distributes the responsibilities for school and faculty improvements to the professional staff.[57] Career ladder plans focus on recruitment, retention, performance incentives, and enhanced attractiveness of teaching. At their best this innovation reflects the belief that intelligent and creative teachers can be attracted to teaching and that the overall quality of the teaching force can be improved by a staged career with differential staffing responsibilities and reward allocations.

Murphy and Ann Weaver Hart divide the various approaches to career ladders into two groups—performance recognition models and job enlargement models.[58] Performance recognition models emphasize achievement as a teacher and typically do not carry additional responsibilities or assignments. A merit pay scheme represents this approach. Given the traditional resistance of teachers to merit pay programs, career ladder schemes based on performance recognition will no doubt encounter considerable hostility. A primary problem with this model is the difficulty of maintaining a credible evaluation system. To implement a performance recognition model successfully, Ken Peterson and Anthony Mitchell maintain that teacher evaluation should be based on multiple lines of evidence regarding teacher performance and peer judgments.[59]

Job enlargement models generally include promotions to higher ranks with the assumption of additional duties at each higher step, e.g., mentoring and supervising intern and new teachers, developing curriculum, and program evaluation. Probably the two most highly publicized career programs have been developed by the State of Tennessee and the Charlotte-Mecklenburg School District in North Carolina.[60] A general characteristic of the plans based on the job enlargement model is a hierarchical set of job categories with different role expectations. A typical career path could include the following steps.

1. Teacher candidate stage is for prospective teachers during their college or university preparation.
2. Intern teacher stage includes the period when the beginning teacher is inducted into the profession. Interns would receive close supervision, mentoring, and support as they start work in classroom settings.
3. Novice teacher stage is the time that individuals assume the primary responsibility for teaching various student groups, receive modest levels of supervision, and complete the probationary period of employment and certification.
4. Career teacher stage is for autonomous teachers who are qualified to assume full professional responsibility for teaching the subjects and students for whom they are now properly qualified.
5. Career professional teacher stage is reserved for teachers who accept responsibilities beyond a single classroom, e.g., evaluate curriculum materials, work with probationary teachers in their own schools and across the district, conduct research, develop and deliver in-service projects, and work as curriculum specialists. These teachers would also continue to serve as classroom teachers.

Of course, the categories and responsibilities need to vary for local conditions. Individuals progress as their professional abilities and interests allow.

Albert Shanker maintains that the conditions of teachers and teaching must be improved.[61] Until steps are taken to elevate elementary and secondary teaching to professional careers, in terms of remuneration and respect, expertise, responsibilities, authority and discretion to make educational decisions, and freedom from intrusive direct supervision by administrators, teaching will remain in crisis and the quality of the teaching force suspect. A strong argument can be made that career ladders based on job enlargement can, at least partially, address some of Shanker's concerns. Career ladders can provide teachers with opportunities and incentives to grow professionally, to develop new skills, and to accept new challenges. The innovation also increases teacher involvement in the professional aspects of schooling, i.e., authority over the decision-making process for their clients.

Administrators.   Even though various forms of career ladders are the object of extensive interest, the primary alternative career path open to teachers who want to remain in education requires that they leave classroom teaching and enter the administrative hierarchy. They must move into different organizational strata to achieve new and different responsibilities. In terms of career paths, Karen N. Gaertner describes the administrative hierarchy of schools as being relatively simple.[62] Administrative positions in schools are limited in number, and job titles tend to have the same meaning across school districts and over time. Yet, the structure is neither trivial nor totally regularized as might be the case in a civil service bureaucracy.

Based on her conclusion that little effort had been made to identify and describe the career paths of school administrators and to study administrator mobility, Gaertner grouped twenty-five administrative positions into ten categories shown in Table 6.3. Two regularities in administrator careers emerged from her study. First, public school administrators are relatively immobile. Nearly half of the administrators did not change positions during the five-year period of the study. She estimates that, on the average, administrators change positions every nine or ten years. Second, most moves are into or out of administrative positions, not among administrative jobs. About 30 percent of the moves are from administrative positions either to teaching or to positions outside school systems. Another 48 percent were entrance moves with most coming from teaching.[63]

Gaertner also identified three career paths or patterns for school administrators. One leads to the superintendency through the following linkages: teacher, secondary curriculum specialist, assistant secondary principal, second-

TABLE 6.3   Classification of Administrative Positions in Schools

Superintendent
Assistant, Associate or Deputy Superintendent
Administrative Specialist—Business, Plant and Facilities, Personnel
Administrator of Instruction
Secondary School Principal
Elementary School Principal
Assistant Principal, Secondary
Assistant Principal, Elementary
Curriculum Specialist, Secondary—Consultant, Subject Coordinator, Supervisor
Curriculum Supervisor, Elementary—Consultant, Subject Consultant, Supervisor, Special Education Director

ary principal, superintendent. This path involves direct supervision of the primary work of the school. A second path to the superintendency moves through the following pattern: teacher, secondary curriculum specialist, administrator of instruction, assistant superintendent, superintendent. This is an administrative specialist path. The third pattern is essentially isolated from the top of the hierarchy, peaking at the elementary principal level. This position is fed by the assistant elementary principal position.[64]

In a study of Wisconsin superintendents, James C. March and James G. March found that after they become superintendents their careers tend to be almost random events.[65] However, movement tends to be systematic in two ways. First, localism is profound. About half of the Wisconsin superintendents have a second superintendency; those who have a second superintendency do not travel far. Most moves are less than seventy-seven miles, one-fourth are less than thirty-six miles. Second, superintendents move to better districts, that is, larger and wealthier. In other words, superintendents apparently have a rating hierarchy of districts and attempt to move up the hierarchy. In contrast, March and March note that although superintendents can make distinctions among districts, superintendents are indistinguishable to the districts. The process of evaluating prospective superintendents by school districts does not provide sufficient performance sampling to allow the decisions to be made on a systematic basis. Hence, the careers are almost random sequences of moves.

Sandra Prolman[66] and Judith A. Adkinson[67] assert that the career paths for men and women in school administration not only are different but that women are underrepresented in administrative positions. Prolman notes that career contingencies disadvantage women's careers in school administration. For example, women tend to teach longer than men; women tend to be grouped in elementary schools, and promotions to the upper levels tend to be made from the secondary level; and women hold staff positions in the central office rather than line positions at the school or central office level. For women, early sex role socialization combined with sex stereotyping of occupations contributes to the decision to teach, to the lack of mobility, and to the lack of mobility expectations. The lack of expectations in turn, relates to the longer teaching careers of women and lack of mobility.

Assuming an Administrative Position[68]

A successful career in educational administration means that individuals must progress through a number of bureaucratic positions. Typically, professional educators will assume a series of positions at increasingly higher levels of the school's administrative hierarchy. As a fundamental concept in educational careers, administrator succession is the process of replacing key officials in organizations.[69] This generic phenomenon of changing leaders produces naturally occurring instabilities in the organization and offers challenging opportunities for individuals. The replacement of principals or superintendents is disruptive because it changes the lines of communication, realigns relationships of power, affects decision making, and generally disturbs the equilibrium of normal activities. Based on conventional wisdom, a common expectation is that new administrators will improve the functioning of their schools.

M. Craig Brown proposes three basic hypotheses and explanations for administrator succession and organizational performance.[70] The first is that succession should be a positive influence on effectiveness. Based on the widely held belief about the ability of individuals to control organizational outcomes, Brown reasons that attributions of leader causation of organizational events support the idea that administrative change will have a positive effect on performance. In contrast, the second prediction is that succession creates so much instability that organizational effectiveness suffers, especially from a short-term perspective. The third hypothesis, originally advanced by William A. Gamson and Norman A. Scotch, is that succession plays no causal role in organization functioning.[71] Because success is a function of long-term organizational processes such as recruiting able personnel and acquiring resources, any relationship between succession and performance is spurious. They proposed that succession should be seen as a scapegoating ritual performed during transitory performance slides. A shortcoming of this third position is that it is based on research of managerial changes in athletic teams and may not be generalizable to other organizations such as schools.

Although the available research evidence does not clearly support any of the competing hypotheses, new administrators are expected to maintain or improve existing levels of organizational effectiveness. A number of factors in the succession process are important in affecting the probability of being hired and one's success after being appointed as an administrator. Three factors seem particularly important in school settings—selection process, reason for the succession, and source of the new leader.

Selection process.   Understanding who participates and the methods of recruitment used in the selection process is important for aspiring administrators. In school districts, participants in the selection process for principals typically include the superintendent, senior administrators, e.g., deputy superintendent, personnel directors, long-term principals, and school board members. Superintendents play a primary role in choosing future principals because the management of their school systems depends on principals carrying out the district's decisions and plans. Senior administrators are chosen to participate because their judgments are valued by the superintendent.

Teacher candidates for principalships usually come to the attention of their superintendents through the support of their principals. As teachers volunteer for committees, handle discipline problems, and spend extra time in schools, the principal becomes a mentor, encouraging the teacher to pursue administrative certification and providing opportunities to become visible at the district level.[72] Having obtained a broad reputation, the career path to a principalship is often through being a vice-principal or curriculum coordinator. Then as vacancies occur for school principals, the candidate can apply and, if patient enough, will eventually obtain an appointment. Assessment centers or outside agencies may be used in the recruitment of potential candidates. Their purpose is to provide rigor, structure, and standardization to the evaluation of the candidates' potential as an administrator.[73]

Reason for the succession. A number of reasons account for changing administrators. Succession can be environmentally controlled, as in death, illness, or movement to a better position; or succession can be directly controlled by the organization, as in promotion, demotion, or dismissal.[74] The successor confronts a different set of circumstances, depending on the reason for the vacancy. For instance, death prevents the transfer of accumulated knowledge of the predecessor to the new leader, and consequently, discontinuity may result, accompanied by rapid policy changes. In contrast, if the predecessor remains in the organization, his or her presence acts as a stabilizing influence. In the case of the predecessor advancing to a superior position, the outside recognition of administrator performance is an indicator of successful policies. The successor may feel a reluctance to initiate immediate changes, and because of the apparent inheritance of a well-managed school, may not receive due credit for improvements that are made.

Source of the new leader. As discussed earlier in this chapter, the source of leaders can be divided into two categories—insiders and outsiders. Considerable agreement exists that the source of the successor affects the level of organizational instability that results from changing leaders. Less consensus occurs, however, about the nature of the relationship. Ongoing groups have well-defined informal structures with sets of norms and implied understandings regarding policies and procedures. An outsider, who does not know the exact informal relationships, is often perceived as having a disruptive influence and symbolizes unwelcome change. The result may be isolation from critical sources of information about the inner workings of the organization. However, insiders also have the potential to produce disruption. Even though they have been integrated into the group, they may become isolated from cliques to which they did not belong and may strengthen commitments to previously loyal colleagues. As a result, rivals may raise doubts about the legitimacy of the insider's promotion.[75]

Depending on the circumstances, either an insider or an outsider can be the best choice for an administrative position. When conflict within the organization is high, a candidate from within may better understand and be able to cope than an outsider. An outsider joining a school at a difficult time may unintentionally "step on toes" or be unable to discern the source of problems because he or she lacks the appropriate historical perspective. Inside succession can lead to problems as well. When an educational organization trains several people to fill future vacancies, a surplus often results. The qualified but unchosen individuals often either leave the organization or remain as frustrated and unsupportive employees. Colleges and universities use a selection process that is intended to reduce this type of conflict. In selecting new presidents, vertical promotions are avoided in an attempt to prevent unproductive competition between subunits. Instead, candidates tend to be selected from similar institutions whose characteristics would result in comparable socializing experiences for potential leaders and thus facilitate the smooth assimilation of the new leader in the organization.[76]

During the selection process, new administrators often are given, or perceive that they are given, a mandate either to maintain the existing stability or to initiate change and innovation.[77] They may be told to get rid of "dead wood," "clean house," reorganize the administrative staff, or essentially maintain the status quo. As discussed earlier, the type of mandate depends on whether the successor is an insider or an outsider. Superintendents and to a lesser degree principals, recruited from the outside, often receive a mandate to break established patterns and make structural or personnel changes. For insiders the mandate typically is to continue present operations with only minor changes. In a recent study of principal succession by Dorothy Cosgrove, little evidence was found that the principals in her study received a mandate from the superintendent or other district officials.[78] All of the successors were insiders and perhaps the forces of socialization were strong enough to create an understanding that current policies were to be continued. However, the teachers believed that a mandate for change had been given to the new leaders.

Truly critical phenomena occur for prospective administrators before they arrive on the scene and shortly after arrival. Knowing the workings of the selection process and being aware that instability arising during the succession period makes the new leader particularly visible and can be used to enhance the success in getting and keeping an administrative position.

SUMMARY

The professional form of occupational life and the bureaucratic form of administration are two organizational patterns that are prevalent in modern formal organizations. Often the professional and bureaucratic orientations are in conflict. Strains between the two arise because the need for expertise is frequently incompatible with the need for discipline.

Sometimes, in order to resolve the conflict, structural changes such as establishing professional organizations and allowing dual lines of authority to develop can be made. At other times, individuals must themselves make an accommodation to the conflict between professional and organizational commitment. Some individuals adopt a cosmopolitan orientation, which entails a commitment to one's professional role, while others opt for a local orientation, with primary loyalty to the organization. A dual orientation is also possible.

As teachers have become more professionalized, conflict with the essentially bureaucratic administration has become more marked. To maintain strong and stable cadres of professional teachers and administrators, school organizations must develop career opportunities and assist them as they move into their new positions of leadership.

NOTES

1. Peter M. Blau and W. Richard Scott, *Formal Organizations: A Comparative Approach* (San Francisco: Chandler, 1962), p. 61.
2. Amitai Etzioni, *Modern Organizations* (Englewood Cliffs, NJ: Prentice-Hall, 1964), p. 78.
3. Patrick B. Forsyth and Thomas J. Danisiewicz, "Toward a Theory of Professionalization," *Work and Occupations,* 12 (1985), 59–76.
4. Blau and Scott, *op. cit.,* p. 62.
5. Edward Gross and Amitai Etzioni, *Organizations in Society* (Englewood Cliffs, NJ: Prentice-Hall, 1985), p. 136.
6. Eliot Freidson, "The Changing Nature of Professional Control," *Annual Review of Sociology,* 10 (1984), 1–20.
7. Gross and Etzioni, *op. cit.,* p. 137.
8. *Ibid.,* p. 63.
9. W. Richard Scott, *Organizations: Rational, Natural, and Open Systems* (Englewood Cliffs, NJ: Prentice-Hall, 1981), pp. 154–155.
10. *Ibid.,* p. 156.
11. Gross and Etzioni, *op. cit.,* p. 138. The authors note that the time distinction in training is arbitrary. Moreover, the designation of semiprofessional is not meant to be pejorative.
12. *Ibid.,* pp. 151–154.
13. Henry Mintzberg, *The Structuring of Organizations* (Englewood Cliffs, NJ: Prentice-Hall, 1979), pp. 348–379.
14. Charles E. Bidwell, "The School as a Formal Organization," in James G. March (ed.), *Handbook of Organizations* (Chicago: Rand McNally, 1965), pp. 972–1022. See pp. 975–976.
15. Oswald Hall, "Some Problems in the Provision of Medical Services," *Canadian Journal of Economics and Political Science,* 20 (1954), 459.
16. *Ibid.,* 459.
17. Alvin Gouldner, "Cosmopolitans and Locals: Toward an Analysis of Latent Social Roles—I," *Administrative Science Quarterly,* 2 (1957), 281–306. See p. 290. The terms "local" and "cosmopolitan" were first used somewhat differently by Merton to refer to different types of community influentials. See Robert Merton, *Social Theory and Social Structure* (New York: Free Press, 1957), pp. 387–420.
18. Harold W. Lensky, *Intellectuals in Labor Unions* (New York: Free Press, 1959).
19. Ronald G. Corwin, "The Professional Employee: A Study of Conflict in Nursing Roles," *American Journal of Sociology,* 66 (1961), 604–615.
20. Donald C. Pelz and Frank M. Andrews, *Scientists in Organizations* (New York: Wiley, 1966).
21. Blau and Scott, *op. cit.*
22. Alvin Gouldner, "Cosmopolitans and Locals: Toward an Analysis of Latent Social Roles—II," *Administrative Science Quarterly,* 2 (1958), 444–479.
23. Robert V. Presthus, "Toward a Theory of Organizational Behavior," *Administrative Science Quarterly,* 3 (1958), 48–72. See also Robert V. Presthus, *The Organizational Society* (New York: Random House, 1962).

24. Barney Glaser, "The Local-Cosmopolitan Scientists," *American Journal of Sociology*, 69 (1965), 249–259.
25. William Kornhauser, *Scientists in Industry* (Berkeley: University of California Press, 1962).
26. Glaser, *op. cit.*
27. Russell Thornton, "Organizational Involvement and Commitment to Organization and Profession," *Administrative Science Quarterly*, 15 (1970), 417–426.
28. Ronald G. Corwin, "Professional Persons in Public Organizations," *Educational Administration Quarterly*, 1 (1965), 4.
29. *Ibid.*, 12–15.
30. *Ibid.*, 5.
31. Kevin Marjoribanks, "Bureaucratic Orientation, Autonomy and Professional Attitudes of Teachers," *Journal of Educational Administration*, 15 (1977), 104–113.
32. Ronald G. Corwin, *Staff Conflicts in the Public Schools* (Washington, DC: U. S. Office of Education, Cooperative Research Project No. 2637, 1966), pp. 128, 439–462.
33. Edward Kuhlman and Wayne K. Hoy, "The Socialization of Professionals into Bureaucracies: The Beginning Teacher in the School," *Journal of Educational Administration*, 8 (1974), 18–27.
34. Harold Wilensky, "Professionalization of Everyone?" *American Journal of Sociology*, 70 (1964), 150.
35. Wayne K. Hoy and Richard Rees, "The Bureaucratic Socialization of Student Teachers," *Journal of Teacher Education*, 28 (1977), 23–26.
36. Richard O. Carlson, *Executive Succession and Organizational Change* (Chicago: University of Chicago, Midwest Administration Center, 1962), pp. 69–82.
37. *Ibid.*, pp. 7–8. The terms are not unlike Gouldner's "local" and "cosmopolitan" designations.
38. *Ibid.*, pp. 69–71.
39. Wayne K. Hoy and Fred Aho, "Patterns of Succession of High School Principals and Organizational Change," *Planning and Changing*, 8 (1977), 185–196.
40. Carlson, *op. cit.*
41. Results for elementary principals also support Carlson's analysis. See Harold J. Ganz and Wayne K. Hoy, "Patterns of Succession of Elementary Principals and Organizational Change," *Planning and Changing*, 2 (1973), 185–196.
42. For a discussion of the effects of informal and formal authority on loyalty see Wayne K. Hoy and Leonard B. Williams, "Loyalty to Immediate Superior at Alternate Levels in Public Schools," *Educational Administration Quarterly*, 7 (1971), 1–11; and Wayne K. Hoy and Richard Rees, "Subordinate Loyalty to Immediate Superior: A Neglected Concept in the Study of Educational Administration," *Sociology of Education*, 47 (1974), 268–286.
43. Donald E. Super and Douglas T. Hall, "Career Development: Exploration and Planning," *Annual Review of Psychology*, 29 (1978), 333–372.
44. Dan C. Lortie, *Schoolteacher* (Chicago: University of Chicago Press, 1975), pp. 83–86.

45. Judith Lanier, Goals for Educating Teachers as Professionals, Interim Report #2. (East Lansing: College of Education, Michigan State University, 1985), 6–8.

46. A number of research studies support this finding. See, for example, the following sources: David W. Chapman and Sigrid M. Hutcheson, "Attrition from Teaching Careers: A Discriminant Analysis," *American Educational Research Journal,* 19 (1982), 93–105; Linda Darling-Hammond, *Beyond the Commission Reports: The Coming Crisis in Teaching* (Santa Monica, CA: Rand, 1984), pp. 2–3; and Jonathan H. Mark and Barry D. Anderson, "Teacher Survival Rates in St. Louis, 1969–1982," *American Educational Research Journal,* 22 (1985), 413–421.

47. Darling-Hammond, *op. cit.,* pp. 7–9.

48. Lanier, 1985, *op. cit.*

49. Mary H. Futrell, *The Teaching Profession* (Washington, DC: National Education Association, 1983).

50. Lanier, 1985, *op. cit.*

51. Lanier, 1985, *op. cit.*

52. Theodore R. Sizer, High School Reform and the Reform of Teacher Education, 9th Annual DeGarmo Lecture, Society of Professors of Education meeting, San Antonio, 1984.

53. Philip C. Schlechty, Restructuring the Teaching Occupation: A Proposal (Paper presented at a meeting of the American Educational Research Association, Chicago, 1985).

54. For an excellent review of the research literature on teacher education see Judith E. Lanier, "Research on Teacher Education," in M. C. Wittrock (ed.), *Handbook of Research on Teaching,* 3rd ed. (New York: Macmillan, 1985).

55. Gross and Etzioni, *op. cit.,* Note 3, p. 157.

56. The ideas for reforming teacher education come primarily from the Holmes Group Consortium. The Holmes Group Consortium is comprised of deans of education from a number of research-oriented universities. For additional information see Lanier, Goals for Educating, *op. cit.*

57. Michael J. Murphy, Testimony before the California Commission on the Teaching Profession, Sacramento, 1985.

58. Michael J. Murphy and Ann Weaver Hart, Career Ladder Reforms (Paper prepared for the California Commission on the Teaching Professions, 1985). A copy of the paper can be requested from either author at the Department of Educational Administration, University of Utah, Salt Lake City, UT 84112.

59. Ken Peterson and Anthony Mitchell, "Teacher-Controlled Evaluation in a Career Ladder Program," *Educational Leadership,* 43 (1985), 44–47.

60. Both programs have been described in a number of publications. See, for example, the following sources: Robert C. Hanes and Kay F. Mitchell, "Teacher Career Development in Charlotte-Mecklenburg," *Educational Leadership,* 43 (1985), 11–13; and Tennessee Department of Education, *Administrator/Supervisor Career Ladder Orientation Manual* (Nashville: Tennessee Department of Education, 1985).

61. Albert Shanker, *The Making for a Profession* (Washington, DC: American Federation of Teachers, 1985), p. 6.

62. Karen N. Gaertner, "The Structure of Organizational Careers," *Sociology of Education,* 53 (1980), 7–20.

63. *Ibid.,* pp. 9–11.
64. *Ibid.,* pp. 11–18.
65. James C. March and James G. March, "Almost Random Careers: The Wisconsin School Superintendency, 1940–1972," *Administrative Science Quarterly,* 22 (1977), 377–409; and James C. March and James G. March, "Performance Sampling in Social Matches," *Administrative Science Quarterly,* 23 (1978), 434–453.
66. Sandra Prolman, "Gender, Career Paths, and Administrative Perceptions," *Administrator's Notebook,* 30 (1982), 1–4.
67. Judith A. Adkinson, "Women in School Administration: A Review of the Research," *Review of Educational Research,* 51 (1981), 311–343.
68. For a thorough discussion of administrator succession in educational organizations, see the following work: Cecil Miskel and Dorothy Cosgrove, "Leader Succession in School Settings," *Review of Educational Research,* 55 (1985), 87–105. The narrative on administrator succession draws heavily from this source.
69. Oscar Grusky, "Corporate Size, Bureaucratization, and Managerial Succession," *American Journal of Sociology,* 67 (1961), 261–269. See p. 261.
70. M. Craig Brown, "Administrative Succession and Organizational Performance: The Succession Effect," *Administrative Science Quarterly,* 27 (1982), 1–16.
71. William A. Gamson and Norman A. Scotch, "Scapegoating in Baseball," *American Journal of Sociology,* 70 (1964), 69–72.
72. Daniel E. Griffiths, Samuel Goldman, and Wayne J. McFarland, "Teacher Mobility in New York City," *Educational Administration Quarterly,* 1 (1965), 15–31.
73. D. Catherine Baltzell and Robert A. Dentler, *Selecting American School Principals: A Sourcebook for Educators* (Cambridge, MA: Abt Associates, 1983), pp. 3–17 and 33–34.
74. Oscar Grusky, "Administrative Succession in Formal Organizations," *Social Forces,* 39 (1960), 105–115.
75. *Ibid.*
76. Robert Birnbaum, "Presidential Succession: An Interinstitutional Analysis," *Educational Record,* 52 (1971), 133–145.
77. See the following sources: Grusky, 1960, *op. cit.;* and Gil E. Gordon and Ned Rosen, "Critical Factors in Leadership Succession," *Organizational Behavior and Human Performance,* 27 (1981), 227–254.
78. Dorothy Cosgrove, "The Effects of Principal Succession on Elementary Schools" (Ph. D. diss., University of Utah, 1985).

Chapter 7

Motivation

The distinguishing characteristic of motivated behavior is that it is goal-directed.
EDWARD E. LAWLER III
Motivation in Work Organizations

The most frequently asked questions about human behavior are "why" questions.[1] Why do we initiate effort on a task? Why do individuals persist in working overtime? Why do others avoid intensive work efforts? Why do some programs of motivation raise the levels of effort, and others do not? "Why" questions about behavior are ones of motivation—a fascinating and perplexing area. Responses to the "why" questions are becoming more powerful because the conceptual gains since 1960 are substantial. Motivational models are coming of age; viable and well-articulated theories of motivation now exist.[2]

Administrators who are knowledgeable about why people behave as they do will have an advantage in meeting the challenges and solving the problems that will confront education in the coming decade. A solid understanding of motivation is valuable for explaining causes of behavior in schools, predicting effects of administrative actions, and directing behavior to achieve school goals.[3] To foster a basic knowledge, work motivation will be defined, general and specific formulations will be detailed, and conceptual derivations and applications will be described in the remainder of this chapter.

DEFINITION OF MOTIVATION

The difficulty in defining motivation, as J. W. Atkinson notes, is that the term has no fixed meaning in contemporary psychology.[4] The word is used in a variety of ways. At the most general level, motivation refers to a process governing individual choices among different forms of voluntary activities.[5] John P. Campbell and his associates add specificity to the definition by arguing that motivation involves the direction of behavior, the strength of response, and the persistence of the behavior.[6] The term also includes a number of other concepts, such as drive, need, incentive, reward, reinforcement, goal setting, expectancy, and the like.

According to most definitions, motivation consists of three basic components that activate, direct, and sustain human behavior.[7] Activating forces are assumed to exist within individuals; they lead people to behave in certain ways. Examples of internal forces include memory, affective responses, and pleasure-seeking tendencies. Motivation also directs or channels behavior; that is, it provides a goal orientation. Individual behavior is directed toward something. In order to maintain and sustain behavior, the surrounding environment must reinforce the intensity and direction of individual drives or forces. For our purposes, then, *motivation* is defined as the complex forces, drives, needs, tension states, or other mechanisms that start and maintain voluntary activity toward the achievement of personal goals.

A GENERAL MODEL OF MOTIVATION

An elaboration of the basic definition can yield a generalized model like the one presented in Figure 7.1. Needs, desires, motives, and expectancies are activators or energizers of behavior. Deficiencies in what an individual wants or anticipates create a state of disequilibrium or tension. The individual then attempts to return to a state of equilibrium by adopting certain behaviors that will lead to a reduction of disequilibrium. This is the goal orientation compo-

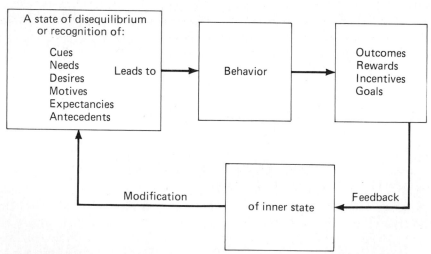

FIGURE 7.1   Generalized cognitive model of human motivation

nent, for the behavior is intended to produce rewards or goal achievements for the individuals. These outcomes then serve as information or feedback that modifies the inner state; that is, decreases or increases the state of disequilibrium. The motivation behavior sequence can begin anew.

An illustration of this phenomenon in a school context follows. A faculty member is asked by an administrator to be chairperson of an important task force. The request creates a disequilibrium for the faculty member. The teacher can anticipate more responsibility, authority, and social interaction, but less free time. The individual has a behavioral decision to make. Acceptance means that action must be initiated to organize and produce for the task force. Refusal means that the time can be used for other professional or personal activities. The outcomes in the first instance include praise, respect, and goal accomplishment. In the second case, they may include administrator disappointment and less time pressures. The outcomes lead to a modification of the inner state and to a reduction of the disequilibrium. Depending on the teacher's desires, greater or lesser satisfaction develops.

As presented and illustrated here, the model in Figure 7.1 represents a cognitive approach to motivation. Cognitive theories view motivation as a sort of "hedonism, of the future."[8] Their basic postulate is that a major determinant of human behavior is the beliefs, expectations, and anticipations individuals have about future events. In other words, individuals have thoughts about events that have happened to them, expectations about what might happen in the future if they pursue a given course of action, and, if asked, will probably indicate what they intend to do about some goal.[9] Hence, people think. And formulations that view behavior as purposeful, goal directed, and based on conscious intentions are labeled cognitive theories.

Theories of motivation that have been used to explain the different aspects of the general model presented in Figure 7.1 can also be classified as content or process approaches.[10] Though the two classes overlap to some degree, enough differences exist to allow us to treat them as distinct. In the remainder of this chapter, we will examine these two sets of approaches, using a variety of cognitive models. Representative theories in each category will be described, compared, and evaluated.

CONTENT APPROACHES TO MOTIVATION

Content, or substantive, theories attempt to specify only what things motivate behavior. In terms of the general model of motivation, content theories delineate either specific needs, motives, or expectancies. The so-called need theories are among the most important content models of motivation. Indeed, one of the most pervasive concepts in the area of work motivation is that of human needs. We continually hear discussions about certain teachers and administrators who have high needs for affiliation, achievement, power, self-actualization, or recognition. Although several content theories can be found in the literature, only two are examined: need hierarchy theory and the motivator-hygiene theory.[11]

Both theories advance the basic argument that human needs constitute the main driving force behind employee behavior in organizational settings.

Need Hierarchy Model

Maslow's *need hierarchy theory* has become a widely discussed perspective in the study of human motivation. The model was derived primarily from Maslow's experience as a clinical psychologist and not from systematic research.[12]

Five basic need levels in the hierarchy (identified and described in Table 7.1) comprise the foundation of Maslow's model.[13] Maslow argues that making a complete list of needs at each level is useless because, depending on how specifically needs are defined, any number can be derived. At the first level of the hierarchy are physiological needs, which consist of the fundamental biological functions of the human organism. Safety and security needs, the second level, derive from the desire for a peaceful, smoothly running, stable society. On the third level, belonging, love, and social needs are extremely important in modern society. Maslow feels that maladjustment stems from frustration of these needs. "My strong impression is also that some proportion of youth rebellion groups—I don't know how many or how much—is motivated by the profound hunger for groupiness, for contact."[14] Esteem needs, at the fourth level, reflect the desire to be highly regarded by others. Achievement, competence, status, and recognition satisfy esteem needs. Finally, Maslow maintains that discontent and restlessness develop unless individuals do what they are best suited to do; that is, unless they meet their need for self-actualization, the fifth level. The meaning of self-actualization is a subject of much discussion. A succinct and simple definition of self-actualization is that it is the need to be what an individual wants to be, to achieve fulfillment of life goals, and to realize the potential of his or her personality.[15]

Maslow's needs are related to one another and are arranged in a hierarchy of prepotency. The more prepotent a need is, the more it precedes other needs in human consciousness and demands to be satisfied. This observation leads to the fundamental postulate of Maslow's theory: higher-level needs become activated as lower-level needs become satisfied. Thus, Maslow points out that a person lives by bread alone—when there is no bread. But when there is plenty of bread, other and higher needs emerge. They, in turn, dominate the person, and, as they become satisfied, are displaced by new needs. The sequence-increased satisfaction, decreased importance, increased importance of next higher need level—repeats itself until the highest level of the hierarchy is reached. Therefore, individual behavior is motivated by an attempt to satisfy the need that is most important at that point.[16]

The successive emergence of higher needs is limited because lower-level needs are never completely satisfied; moreover, if an individual cannot satisfy needs at a given level for any period of time, those needs again become potent motivators. A completely satisfied need is not an effective motivator. Hence, the concept of gratification is as important as that of deprivation. Maslow reasons that gratification releases the person from the domination of one need, allowing

TABLE 7.1   Maslow's Hierarchy of Needs Theory of Human Motivation

Needs	*Physiological and Psychological Indicators*		

Level 5
Self-actualization
  or Self-fulfillment
	Achievement of potential
	Maximum self-development creativity,
	  and self-expression		

Level 4
Esteem
	Self-respect—achievement, competence,
	  and confidence
	Deserved respect of others—status,
	  recognition, dignity, and appreciation		

Level 3
Belonging, love,
  and social activities
	Satisfactory associations with others
	Belonging to groups
	Giving and receiving friendship and
	  affection		

Level 2 Safety and security	Protection against danger and threat Freedom from fear, anxiety, and chaos Need for structure, order, law, limits and stability		
Level 1 Physiological	Hunger Thirst Sex	Taste Smell Touch	Sleep

for the emergence of a higher-level need. Conversely, if a lower-order need is left unsatisfied, it reemerges and dominates behavior. In his later works, Maslow proposed that at the highest level of the hierarchy reversal occurs in the satisfaction-importance relationship.[17] When self-actualization is being realized, increased need strength occurs across the entire hierarchy.

Maslow clearly explains that individual differences affect his theory, yet his model frequently is interpreted too rigidly. Although he maintains that most people have a hierarchy of basic needs, he allows for several general exceptions, including, for instance, people who desire self-esteem more than belonging or those whose level of aspiration is permanently deadened or lowered. A second misconception about Maslow's theory is that one need must be entirely satisfied before the next level of needs emerges. Maslow asserts that normal individuals are usually only partially satisfied in all their basic needs. A more realistic description of the need structure is that the percentage of satisfaction decreases as one goes up the hierarchy of prepotency. Maslow argues that for the majority of people, needs at the first three levels are regularly satisfied and no longer have much motivational effect; however, satisfaction of esteem and self-actualization needs is rarely complete. The higher-level needs continually motivate. The implication for educational organizations is that methods must be developed to satisfy more fully the higher-level needs of students, teachers, and administrators.

Several additional observations about work in educational organizations can be made using Maslow's theory. First, although physiological needs seem reasonably well met for educators, some students are deprived of even the most basic needs and therefore present a potent motivational problem. Moreover, the needs for safety and security, the second hierarchical level, certainly can become motivating factors for school employees and students alike. Administrative actions that arouse uncertainty with respect to continued employment, or discrimination, can affect every individual, from custodian to deputy superintendent. Furthermore, Maslow theorizes that broader aspects of the attempt to seek safety and security are seen in the preference many people have for familiar rather than unfamiliar things, for the known rather than the unknown. In schools, those people who have high safety needs may resist change and desire job security, injury compensation plans, and retirement programs to satisfy those needs.

The need to belong causes an individual to seek relationships with co-workers, peers, superiors, and subordinates. For educators, friendship ties, informal work groups, professional memberships, and school memberships satisfy this need. The need for esteem and status, the fourth hierarchical level, causes an educator to seek control, autonomy, respect from and for others, and professional competence. Finally, the need for self-actualization motivates educators to be the best people they are capable of being. This need is less frequently apparent than others, however, because many individuals are still concerned with lower-level needs. Nevertheless, Maslow clearly advocates that organizations such as schools should provide the highest level of need satisfaction that is possible because self-actualizing teachers and administrators are the best performers.[18] Yet treating people well spoils them for being treated badly. Once a pattern is set to emphasize higher-level needs in administering schools, returning to an emphasis on lower-level needs will be very difficult.

Maslow's need-hierarchy theory, then, is based on two fundamental postulates. First, individuals are "wanting" creatures motivated to satisfy certain needs. Second, the needs they pursue are universal and are arranged in a hierarchy in which lower-level needs must be largely satisfied before higher-level needs can be felt and pursued.

Research Based on Maslow's Theory

Lyman W. Porter has modified Maslow's hierarchy to include autonomy needs, which lie between esteem and self-actualization needs.[19] Porter claims that needs such as those for authority, independent thought and action, and participation are logically distinct from more common esteem items, such as the need for prestige. On the basis of this distinction, and the assumption that physiological needs are adequately satisfied for managerial and professional employees, Porter developed the Need Satisfaction Questionnaire (NSQ).[20] The NSQ has been modified for use in specific organizational settings, including schools.[21] This questionnaire is probably the one most frequently employed in research studies, but other questionnaires based on the need hierarchy are available for use in educational organizations with slight adaptations.[22]

Porter's investigations of managers, using a modified NSQ, indicate that the need for self-actualization is generally the least satisfied. Moreover, esteem, security, and autonomy were more often satisfied for middle-level managers than for lower-level managers.[23] Similarly, higher-ranking officers in the military reported greater need fulfillment and relative satisfaction than lower-ranking officers. In contrast, John B. Miner, after reviewing other studies using the NSQ with business managers, concluded that statistically significant findings were relatively rare, but when significant relationships were obtained, they almost invariably involved the security need.[24]

In educational settings, an early study by Frances M. Trusty and Thomas J. Sergiovanni reports that the largest deficiencies for professional educators were satisfying esteem, autonomy, and self-actualization needs.[25] In a recent investigation, Mary Beth G. Anderson and Edward F. Iwanicki's[26] findings are supportive of Trusty and Sergiovanni. However, the later study indicated a relatively large increase in the deficiency for security needs. Trusty and Sergiovanni also found that administrators, when compared with teachers, have fewer esteem need deficiencies and more self-actualization need deficiencies. The authors conclude that teachers' lack of self-esteem represents the largest source of need deficiency for them. Similarly, a study by Grace B. Chisolm and her colleagues shows that administrators exhibit fewer need deficiencies than teachers on all five subscales—security, social, esteem, autonomy, and self-actualization.[27] The greatest area of deficiency for both administrators and teachers is satisfaction of autonomy needs. Given recent speculations about schools as loosely coupled systems (see Chapter 5), this finding is somewhat surprising.

Evaluation of the Need Hierarchy Theory

Maslow's need hierarchy theory presents an interesting paradox: the theory is widely accepted, but little research evidence exists to support it.[28] In fact, the findings of a number of studies do not support the fundamental assumption of a hierarchy of prepotency; other studies have found modest support.[29] No doubt, the need hierarchy framework needs revision and additional research. Two conclusions appear reasonable. First, the need hierarchy theory is somewhat useful in understanding human motivation, although the debate concerning the number of need levels and their order of gratification is not yet finished. Second, since the data are so scant and based to a considerable extent on questionnaires such as the NSQ, Maslow's theory may be more powerful and robust than the research testing it. Or as Howard S. Schwartz observes, "researchers may have been doing research on something when they sought to test Maslow's theory with self-reports of needs, but it was not Maslow's theory."[30] The need for research is clearly evident.

Motivation-Hygiene Theory

Another popular content theory of motivation is proposed by Frederick Herzberg and his colleagues.[31] Motivation-hygiene theory, which is variously termed the two-factor theory, dual-factor theory, and simply Herzberg's theory, has been widely accepted by administrators. Its basic postulate is that one set of rewards contributes to job satisfaction and a separate set to job dissatisfaction. The two sets of rewards are represented in Table 7.2.

The motivation-hygiene theory is based on Herzberg's findings from his now famous study of industrial employee motivation to work. In interviews with 203 accountants and engineers, Herzberg and his associates used a critical-incidents procedure, which essentially asked each person interviewed to describe events experienced at work that had resulted in either a marked improvement or a significant reduction in job satisfaction.

Analysis of the contents of interview transcripts produced the basic results shown in Table 7.3. The study found that positive events were dominated by references to achievement, recognition (verbal), the work itself (challenging), responsibility, and advancement (promotion). Negative events were dominated by references to interpersonal relations with superiors and peers, technical supervision, company policy and administration, working conditions, and personal life.

TABLE 7.2   Graphic Representation of the Motivation-Hygiene Theory

Job Satisfaction Continuum		
Dissatisfaction (−)	0	*(+) Satisfaction*

	MOTIVATORS OR SATISFIERS
	Achievement
	Recognition
	Work itself
	Responsibility
	Advancement

HYGIENES OR DISSATISFIERS
Interpersonal relations—subordinates
Interpersonal relations—peers
Supervision—technical
Policy and administration
Working conditions
Personal life

Dissatisfaction (−)	0	(+) Satisfaction

TABLE 7.3 Percentage of Good and Bad Critical Incidents in the Herzberg, Mausner, Snyderman Study of Accountants and Engineers

	Percentage	
	Good	*Bad*
MOTIVATORS		
1. Achievement	41*	7
2. Recognition	33*	18
3. Work itself	26*	14
4. Responsibility	23*	6
5. Advancement	20*	11
HYGIENES		
6. Salary	15	17
7. Possibility of Growth	6	8
8. Interpersonal relations—subordinates	6	3
9. Status	4	4
10. Interpersonal relations—superiors	4	15*
11. Interpersonal relations—peers	3	8*
12. Supervision—technical	3	20*
13. Company (school) policy and administration	3	31*
14. Working conditions	1	11*
15. Personal life	1	6*
16. Job Security	1	1

*Significantly different from zero at the 5 percent level.

Based on these findings, the researchers posited that the presence of certain factors acts to increase an individual's job satisfaction, but absence of these factors does not necessarily produce job dissatisfaction. Theoretically, individuals start from a neutral stance; they possess neither positive nor negative attitudes toward a job. Certain factors, called *motivators,* increase job satisfaction beyond the neutral point, but when the motivators are not available, only minimal dissatisfaction results. On the other hand, when factors called *hygienes* are not available, negative attitudes are created, producing job dissatisfaction. Hygienes lead only to minimal job satisfaction. Consequently, motivators combine to contribute more to job satisfaction than to job dissatisfaction. Hygienes combine to contribute more to job dissatisfaction than to job satisfaction.

In brief, the motivation-hygiene theory postulates that one set of factors (motivators) produces satisfaction, while another set (hygienes) produces dissatisfaction. Work satisfaction and dissatisfaction are not opposites; rather they are separate and distinct dimensions of a person's attitude about work. Look again at Table 7.2. Note how each factor starts from a zero point in the middle of the continuum and moves in only one direction—toward dissatisfaction for the hygienes or toward satisfaction for the motivators.

Miner observes further that the five motivator factors are both conceptually and empirically related.[32] When the elements are present in work, the individual's basic needs of personal growth and self-actualization will be satisfied, and positive feelings as well as improved performance will result. The dissatisfier or hygiene factors, when provided appropriately, can serve to remove dissatisfaction and improve performance up to a point. But hygiene elements cannot be relied upon to produce as positive feelings or as high performance levels as are potentially possible.

Comparison of the Two Content Theories

The motivation-hygiene theory, at least on the surface, appears reasonable and appealing. Indeed, this theory has been widely accepted and used as the theoretical rationale for numerous empirical investigations and administrative innovations. A possible explanation for the motivation-hygiene theory's appeal is its close conceptual relationship with Maslow's popular need hierarchy theory. Herzberg established this relationship by asserting that the factors leading to positive job attitudes (motivators) do so because of their potential to satisfy the individual's need for self-actualization. A job represents an important opportunity for self-actualization. By performing the specific tasks, an employee can achieve the rewards—achievement, recognition, responsibility—that reinforce self-actualization. The motivators in the job spur the individual to satisfy his or her need for self-actualization. Conversely, the hygienes can be related to physiological, safety, and social needs. Hygienic factors must meet individual needs for job security, fair treatment, good interpersonal relations, and adequate working conditions. When job surroundings are not conducive to these needs being met, dissatisfaction increases. Both theories emphasize the same set of relationships. Maslow focuses on the general human needs of the psychological person, while Herzberg concentrates on the psychological person in terms of how the job affects basic needs.

Research Based on the Motivation-Hygiene Theory in the Educational Setting

Thomas Sergiovanni[33] replicated the Herzberg study with teachers, and Gene L. Schmidt[34] did likewise with administrators. Both used critical-incidents interviews and then analyzed the content. The results can be found in Table 7.4.

The findings of Sergiovanni and Schmidt support the assertion that satisfiers (motivators) and dissatisfiers (hygienes) tend to be mutually exclusive. For teachers work itself and advancement were not significant motivators. Sergiovanni explains that the job of teacher includes several "maintenance" activities—checking attendance, scheduling, hall duty, lunchroom duty—that lead to dissatisfaction. Because advancement was mentioned only once, teaching is evidently considered a terminal position in the career, with little chance for hierarchical promotion. For administrators work itself and responsibility were mentioned infrequently as motivators. But, contrary to teachers, administrators did view advancement as a motivator.

Several differences between industrial and educational groups should be noted, however. In considering hygienes, teachers differed from business em-

TABLE 7.4 Percentage of Good and Bad Critical Incidents in Replications by Schmidt with Administrators and Sergiovanni with Teachers of the Herzberg, Mausner, and Snyderman Study

| | Administrators | | Teachers | |
| | Percentage | | Percentage | |
	Good	Bad	Good	Bad
MOTIVATORS				
1. Achievement	46*	7	30*	9
2. Recognition	17*	4	28*	2
3. Work itself	1	1	11	8
4. Responsibility	2	5	7*	1
5. Advancement	9*	1	0	1
HYGIENES				
6. Salary	1	2	2	3
7. Possibility of growth	1	0	6	2
8. Interpersonal relations —subordinates	11	34*	7	20*
9. Status	1	0	0	0
10. Interpersonal relations —superiors	5	12*	3	4
11. Interpersonal relations —peers	3	9*	1	15*
12. Supervision—technical	1	5*	1	10*
13. Company (school) policy and administration	3	15*	2	13*
14. Working conditions	0	3	2	6
15. Personal life	0	1	0	5*
16. Job security	1	0	0	1

*Significantly different from zero at the 5 percent level.

ployees in having more problems with subordinate (i.e., students) interpersonal relations than with superordinate (i.e., principal, director, superintendent) relations. The teaching process and social organization themselves tend to explain these findings. Secondary teachers, for the most part, interact with 100 to 200 students a day in the relative privacy of a self-contained classroom. In comparison, teachers interact relatively little with their superiors. In both respects, their situation is unlike that of business employees. Therefore, the difference between industrial employees and teachers is not surprising. With regard to hygiene factors, school administrators are similar to teachers and different from business employees in having more problems involving interpersonal relations with subordinates. Schmidt considers this to be understandable in light of the increased tension between teachers and administrators.

Though these differences were found, the basic Herzberg conclusion was upheld. Employees tend to associate one set of factors with job satisfaction and a different set with job dissatisfaction.

Evaluation of the Motivation-Hygiene Theory

Although Herzberg's theory is the most controversial of any we will consider, it has had profound impact on the field of work motivation. Miner believes that a number of reasons explain the controversy, many of them having little relationship with the scientific or managerial usefulness of the model.[35] The fact remains, however, that scholars other than Herzberg have lost interest in the motivation-hygiene theory and relatively little empirical research has been published based on the theory during the past fifteen years.

Two primary criticisms persist.[36] First, researchers have developed different versions of the motivation-hygiene theory. In fact, five distinct forms of it have emerged.[37] Herzberg himself appears to be responsible for four variations. The different formulations are the result of at least two issues. Should one treat the factors labeled motivators and hygienes as two distinct and cohesive groups, or should each factor be treated as a separate variable with its own unique behavior? When group trends are accepted, the problem of the single exception that frequently occurs when each variable is considered separately does not arise. Second, do the motivator factors contribute only to satisfaction and the hygienes only to dissatisfaction? Table 7.2, which shows the factors starting at zero and contributing only to satisfaction or dissatisfaction, seems to indicate this. But the data presented in Tables 7.3 and 7.4 are not supportive of this contention. For example, in the Herzberg study, recognition was mentioned 33 percent of the time in good critical incidents, but it also was mentioned 18 percent of the time in bad critical incidents. Moreover, possibility for growth, which should be the essence of a self-actualizing motivator, was mentioned in 6 percent and 8 percent of the good and bad incidents, respectively. In the Sergiovanni study, subordinate interpersonal relationships as a hygiene factor were mentioned 7 and 20 percent of the time in good and bad incidents, respectively. Thus, the notion that the factors contribute to both positive and negative job satisfaction is more consistent with the data. Motivators contribute more to satisfaction than to dissatisfaction, while hygienes contribute more to dissatisfaction than satisfaction.

Another criticism of the motivation-hygiene theory is that it is tied to its method. Herzberg's results are thus replicable only when his critical-incidents technique is used. Most studies using the Herzberg technique generally support the motivation-hygiene theory, while most using a different method do not.[38] An explanation of why the critical-incidents interviews produce the two sets of factors is that individuals attribute positive incidents related to achievement or recognition to themselves and negative incidents to the environment. However, when other methods do not designate only a positive or negative situation, the two factors do not emerge.

Some scholars argue that the formulation of the theory is weak.[39] For example, Campbell and his colleagues contend that "the most meaningful conclusion that we can draw is that the two-factor theory has now served its purpose and should be altered or respectively laid aside."[40] Other researchers are somewhat more moderate.[41] They argue that Herzberg deserves a great deal of credit. By calling attention to the need for improved understanding of the role played by motivation in work organizations, he filled a void in the late 1950s. His approach is systematic and his language understandable. Consequently, the most fruitful approach to Herzberg's theory is to use the knowledge to develop better conceptualizations rather than to accept or reject it totally.

COGNITIVE PROCESS MODELS OF MOTIVATION

Instead of trying to reformulate a theory with certain weaknesses, some theorists have taken an entirely different approach to motivation. They are not as concerned as the content theorists with explaining the *things* that motivate behavior. Rather, they focus on behavioral processes—how behavior is started, sustained, and stopped. *Process theories* first attempt to define the major variables that are necessary to explain choice, effort, and the persistence of certain behavior. Then they attempt to specify how the major variables interact to influence outcomes, such as work effort and job satisfaction. In the study of behavior in work organizations, expectancy and goal theories are primary examples of cognitive process approaches to motivation.[42]

Expectancy and goal-setting are concerned with cognitive processes as the major determinants of behavior. Their dominance is illustrated by Terence R. Mitchell's finding that more than 75 percent of the research conducted in the area of work motivation involves expectancy or goal-setting approaches.[43]

Expectancy Theory

During the late 1960s through the early 1980s, the prevalence of *expectancy theory, valence-instrumentality-expectancy, VIE theory* or *value theory* in the literature clearly indicates its centrality to the research on motivation in organizations. While expectancy models have a long history in psychology, the approach was popularized and modified during the 1960s by Victor Vroom and others.[44] In comparison to other formulations of work motivation, expectancy theory presents a complex view of individuals in organizations. The basic assumptions, concepts, and generalizations of expectancy theory, however, are easily identified and portrayed.

Assumptions. Expectancy theory rests on two fundamental premises. First, individuals make decisions about their own behavior in organizations using their abilities to think, reason, and anticipate future events. Motivation is a conscious process governed by laws. People subjectively evaluate the expected value of outcomes or personal payoffs resulting from their actions, and then they choose how to behave.

The second assumption is not unique to expectancy theory, and in fact, it was posed in Chapter 3 as a generalization from social-systems theory; forces in the individual and the environment combine to determine behavior. Individual values and attitudes, for instance, interact with environmental components, such as role expectations and organizational climate, to influence behavior.

Concepts.   Expectancy theory builds on these assumptions with the concepts of valence, instrumentality, and expectancy. As the basic building blocks, each must be defined and discussed. Valence *(V)* refers to the perceived positive or negative value, worth, or attractiveness that an individual ascribes to potential goals, outcomes, rewards, or incentives for working in an organization. It is the strength of a person's desire for a particular reward. Feelings of competence, autonomy, recognition, accomplishment, and creativity, for example, represent valued work outcomes for educators.

Instrumentality *(I)* refers to the perceived probability that an incentive with a valence will be forthcoming after a given level of performance or achievement. Instrumentality is high when individuals perceive a strong association between performance and being rewarded. If teachers think that high student achievement in their classrooms is likely to result in public recognition of their teaching ability, then instrumentality is high.

Expectancy *(E),* refers to the subjective probability or degree of certainty that a given effort will yield a specified performance level. Stated differently, it is the extent to which an individual believes that a given level of activity will result in a specified level of goal accomplishment. Mathematically, the probability can range from zero to one. When expectancy falls to zero, the individual believes that effort is unrelated to performance. However, when expectancy climbs to one, complete certainty exists that performance or goal achievement depends on individual effort. For example, if teachers feel that a high probability exists of improving student achievement by increasing their own efforts, then educators have a high expectancy level. In contrast to instrumentality, which is an outcome-outcome (performance-reward) association, expectancy is an effort-outcome (behavior-performance) relationship.

In general, motivation to behave in a certain way is greatest when the individual believes that (1) the behavior will lead to rewards (high instrumentality), (2) these outcomes have positive personal values (high valence), and (3) the ability exists to perform at the desired level (high expectancy). When faced with choices about behavior, the individual goes through a process of considering questions such as, "Can I perform at that level if I work hard?" "If I perform at that level, what will I receive?" "How do I feel about these outcomes?" The individual then decides to behave in the way that appears to have the best chance of producing the desired rewards.[45]

An expectancy model.   A synthesis of the foregoing assumptions, concepts, and statements produces a general model of behavior. The model is presented with

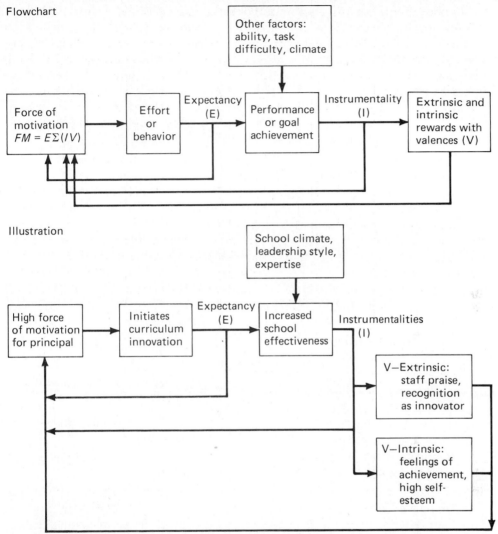

FIGURE 7.2   Expectancy theory in a flowchart format with an illustration for the educational setting

an illustration for the educational setting in Figure 7.2. Moving across the top from left to right, the force of motivation (FM) leads to an observed level of effort by the individual. Effort combines with a number of factors (i.e., ability, task difficulty, favorableness of the situation) to yield a certain level of performance. The probability that a given effort will yield a certain level of performance (expectancy) serves as feedback to modify the force of motivation. The instrumentality of the performance level is assessed by the individual. The probabilities of receiving certain outcomes are assessed and again act as information to change the force of motivation. The outcomes, which can be both intrinsic and extrinsic (these terms are discussed later in this chapter), are evaluated for their desirability. In turn, their subjective values become feedback affecting the force of motivation. The overall formulation of relationships is: force of motivation equals the *product* of expectancy, instrumentality, and valence. More specifically, the basic generalization, stated in equation form, is *FM = EΣ(IV)*.[46] Since this is a multiplicative relationship, when expectancy, instrumentality, or valence falls to zero, effort becomes zero.

The lower portion of Figure 7.2 depicts the expectancy model in a school setting. Essentially, the school principal exhibits a high force of motivation. He or she initiates a new curriculum innovation and perceives the effort as having a good chance of improving the school performance or effectiveness levels. Student achievement or attitudes are likely to improve as a result of the new program. Of course, the supportiveness and expertise of the staff and the principal's leadership style will have an impact on the effectiveness levels as well as the innovation. Given the high force of motivation, the principal thinks that the instrumentalities and valences are high and positive. Both extrinsic and intrinsic rewards will be forthcoming.

Research Based on Expectancy Theory

Measures to test expectancy theory typically take the form of the one summarized in Table 7.5.[47] A few points must be kept in mind. First, questions concerning each of the three components comprise the overall measure. Second, the items for instrumentality and valence contain the same content, but they are presented as probability and importance statements, respectively. In this measure shown, items testing intrinsic and extrinsic domains are included. Third, the responses in this case are scored from one to five. Fourth, the force of motivation is then calculated, using the formula, *FM = EΣ(IV)*. To compute *E,* the values of the responses are summed. To compute *Σ(IV)*, however, the cross-products must be summed, that is, the response value for each instrumentality item must be multiplied by the response value of the parallel valence item and then all are summed. In the present example, *(IV)* for the intrinsic items would be the following: *(a x g) + (b x h)*. To calculate the force of motivation for the intrinsic portion, the value of *E* would be multiplied by the preceding value of *Σ(IV)*.

Several authors have systematically reviewed the literature reporting research based on expectancy motivation theory, and their conclusions are similar.[48] The force of motivation in an expectancy model has been demonstrated to be positively correlated with job satisfaction, effort, and performance in a variety of settings. While the relationships between force of motivation and independent ratings of effort and performance have been significant statistically on a consistent basis, the associations have not been overly strong. In other words, expectancy motivation is an important factor in effort and performance, but other factors in the environment also are important contributors.

TABLE 7.5 Sample Items for Each Component of a Measure for Expectancy Motivation

Instrumentality (I)

Here are some things that could happen to educators if they do their jobs especially well. Write on the line preceding each statement the number from the response category that best describes the likelihood of the event occurring after performing your job especially well.

Response Categories

1. Not at all likely   2. Somewhat unlikely   3. 50–50 chance   4. Quite likely   5. Extremely likely

If you perform your job especially well, how likely is it that each of these things will happen?

INTRINSIC	EXTRINSIC
_____ a. You will feel better about yourself as an educator.	_____ d. Your co-workers will be friendly with you.
_____ b. You will be given a chance to learn new things.	_____ c. Your supervisor will praise you.

Valence (V)

Different people want different things from their work. Here is a list of things that an educator could have on his or her job. How important is each of the following to you?

Response Categories

1. Less important   2. Moderately important   3. Important   4. Quite important   5. Extremely important

How important is . . . ?   *How important is . . . ?*

_____ g. Feeling good about yourself as an educator.   _____ j. The friendliness of your co-workers.

_____ h. The chances you have to learn new things.   _____ k. The praise you receive from your supervisor.

Expectancy (E)

This section is designed to gather information about how educators feel about their jobs. On the line preceding each statement, please write the number of the response category that best describes your feelings.

Response Categories

1. Strongly disagree   2. Disagree   3. Neutral   4. Agree   5. Strongly agree

_____ m. Energetic educators are not particularly successful teachers.

_____ n. Putting forth a high degree of effort leads to a high level of performance.

Investigations conducted in educational organizations based on expectancy theory are beginning to appear in the literature. Richard T. Mowday found that school principals with higher expectancy motivation are more active in attempting to influence district decisions than those with low expectancy motivation.[49] In a study examining the relationship between school structure and teacher motivation, H. Scott Herrick found strong negative correlations between expectancy motivational force and centralization and stratification. Thus, schools that are highly centralized and stratified are staffed with teachers having low forces of motivation.[50]

In a study of teachers in secondary schools and institutes of higher education, Cecil Miskel, JoAnn DeFrain, and Kay Wilcox related the force of motivation to job satisfaction and perceived job performance.[51] The force of motivation was significantly related to job satisfaction and perceived performance for both groups. Similarly, Miskel and his colleagues David McDonald and Susan Bloom found that expectancy motivation of teachers was consistently related to teacher job satisfaction, student attitudes toward school, and perceived school effectiveness.[52]

Linda L. Graham used expectancy theory with a sample of college students.[53] She found moderate to high support for the ability of expectancy theory to predict the satisfaction, participation in activities, and achievement of college students.

The results of investigations in educational settings are similar to those most commonly reported in the literature for other organizational settings. The expectancy model is a good predictor of job satisfaction and a not so good but still statistically significant one for performance. Overall, most research results have supported the theory; people work hard when they think that working hard is likely to lead to desirable rewards from the organization.

Evaluation of Expectancy Theory

Steers and Porter[54] and Miner[55] agree that expectancy theory is a promising approach to understanding work motivation. In regard to its theoretical adequacy, Steers and Porter maintain that expectancy theory provides a comprehensive framework for dealing with complex employee behavior. Even though the theory is being refined, they believe that the thrust is a good one because the cognitive nature of the approach captures the essence of why individuals expend different levels of energy in their jobs. Stated simply, the force of a person to perform depends on the answers to a series of questions that all people ask themselves on a daily basis: Is a reward being offered that I value? If I make the effort, will I be able to improve my performance? If my performance improves, will I actually be rewarded for it? In regard to its empirical evidence, Miner believes that research tests have yielded sufficient theoretical support to conclude that expectancy theory is on the right track. While it cannot explain all motivated behavior in all work organizations, expectancy theory does explain enough about work effort to be pursued further.

In spite of these favorable conclusions, critics describe a number of conceptual and empirical shortcomings of the model.[56] A frequent and strong criticism of expectancy models concerns the process of combining the three components in a multiplicative fashion. The findings from some studies indicate that each separate component shows a moderate relationship with effort or performance. For example, Miskel, DeFrain, and Wilcox found that the component instrumentality has a higher correlation with job performance than the components taken together.[57] However, recent evidence does support the multiplicative model as the most useful predictor of behavior.[58]

Another criticism is that expectancy theory overemphasizes linearity. If any component—expectancy, valence, or instrumentality—increases, then motivation force becomes greater. Behavioral psychologists strongly challenge this notion. Indeed, content theories of motivation posit that when a need reaches a certain level of satisfaction, its potency or force declines. The role of rationality is also overemphasized in expectancy theory. Obviously, individuals neither have the capacity to consider all of the relevant information nor do they always select the best alternative when deciding how to act.

In sum, expectancy theory has generated a large number of investigations. Generally, the results are supportive. Even though questions and criticisms surround the approach, we believe that with carefully designed studies expectancy theory can make valuable contributions to the field of educational administration.

Goal Theory

Although goal theory has early historical origins, Edwin A. Locke and his associates are generally recognized for the development and renewed interest of goal theory or the technique of goal setting in organizations.[59] As a cognitive process approach of work motivation, goal theory became highly popular during the 1970s. Although not fully developed, goal theory appears to be a valuable analytic and practical tool for educational administrators. Goal theory is applied in several important school practices. For instance, many evaluation systems for teachers and administrators are modifications of a management by objectives (MBO) technique. A second example is the widespread use of behavioral objectives to guide decisions on instructional procedures and course content. Therefore, understanding the motivational qualities of goal setting is important to educators.

In comparison to expectancy theory, goal theory is not complex. A goal is defined simply as what an individual consciously is trying to do. Goals have two major characteristics—content and intensity. Content refers to the nature of the activity or desired outcome. Intensity relates to the level of importance a person assigns the goal. Both content and intensity exert directive influence and serve to regulate energy expenditure. Content directs and influences behavior because different goals require varying amounts of effort; intensity acts in the same fashion because important goals are more likely to be accepted, to elicit commitment, and thus foster persistent actions.[60]

The basic postulate of the theory is that intentions to achieve a goal constitute the primary motivating force behind work behavior. Goals direct both mental and physical actions of individuals. Two additional assumptions of the theory are that specific goals are superior to general goals and that difficult goals, when accepted, lead to greater effort than easy goals. To explain the cognitive processes that determine these relationships, Locke proposed the theory illustrated schematically in Figure 7.3. But he cautions that the model outlines only the major processes that lead to goal setting and task performance.

The components describing the goal-setting process are shown in Figure 7.3.[61] The goal-setting process begins with the assumption that the individual knows something about the nature and properties of things that exist in the work environment. This knowledge is gained through perceptions and exercise of reason. Because action or behavior is required to fulfill personal needs, the individual necessarily must judge the elements in the environment (existents) to determine which actions will enhance the individual's well-being. Value judgments are thus the basis for choosing among alternative courses of action. Using a code of values or set of standards, the individual judges which behaviors are good or bad, right or wrong, for or against personal interests. This evaluation is made by estimating the relationship between perceptions of the environment and personal value standards. Emotions are the form in which an individual

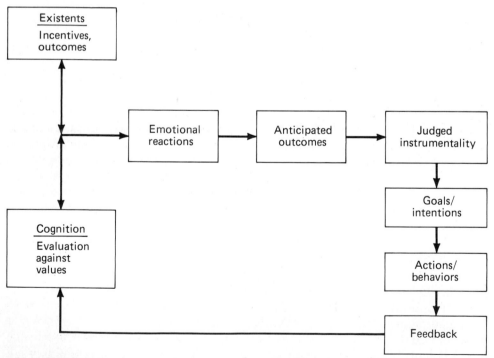

FIGURE 7.3   Schematic illustration of goal theory

experiences value judgments. Based on the alternative that is selected, the individual anticipates new conditions in the work environment and projects instrumentalities for the anticipated behavior and satisfaction. As in expectancy theory, instrumentality refers to a probability that a reward will occur. At this point, the individual is ready to act. With the overall goal in mind, he or she can set subgoals based on a judgment of the probability of achieving the overall goal. If achievement of the goal is judged highly probable, anticipated satisfaction is also high. Feedback is important because knowledge of the results enables an individual to set new goals. Hence, goal theory postulates that values and goals represent two cognitive determinants of behavior.[62]

Locke goes further and notes that most human action is purposive; behavior is regulated and maintained by goals and intentions. The most fundamental effect of goals on mental or physical actions is to direct thoughts and overt behavior to one end rather than another. Since pursuit of some goals requires greater mental concentration and physical effort than others, goals, in the process of directing action, also regulate energy expenditure. For example, if a teacher decides to develop a new set of lesson plans rather than to use existing guides, this action necessarily requires more effort than using the available plans.

Research Based on Goal Theory

Early support for Locke's ideas came primarily from a series of well-controlled laboratory experiments. Most of these studies used college students who performed relatively simple tasks for short periods of time. Since the theory originally relied only on evidence from sheltered and contrived situations, the theory's proponents next attempted to respond to the following question: Can a practice so deceptively simple as setting specific, difficult goals increase the performance of employees in natural organizational settings where experimental effects are absent and goal acceptance is not easily obtained? The evidence from field studies does indicate that goal theory is valid for describing employee behavior in organizations such as schools.[63]

In particular, three generalizations drawn from goal theory enjoy substantial support from findings produced by both laboratory and field research methods.[64] First, specific performance goals elicit a higher level of performance than general goals, such as telling individuals to do their best, or no goals at all. Second, the more difficult the performance goal, the more effort individuals will make if they accept it. Apparently, this generalization holds even when the goal is so difficult that virtually no one can achieve it. However, very difficult goals may not be acceptable and, hence, void the positive relationship between goal and difficulty and performance. Third, subordinate participation in goal-setting activities, as opposed to goal setting by the supervisor alone, leads to employee satisfaction, though it may not increase performance. Available evidence suggests, however, that participation in goal setting may increase the difficulty of the goals that are set and the level of goal acceptance.[65] If difficulty and acceptance increase as some evidence suggests,[66] performance may be higher because of the goal difficulty effect stated in the second generalization listed here. A fourth generalization, which has gained substantial empirical support and is consistent with the goal model presented in Figure 7.3, is that goal setting and feedback combine to enhance employee motivation.[67]

Evaluation of Goal Theory

Research evidence demonstrates that goals are a major source of work motivation. Strong support exists for the basic propositions of goal theory. However, three shortcomings can be pointed out.[68]

First, and perhaps the greatest deficiency, is the failure of the theory to specify what determines goal acceptance and commitment. The processes of how goals are approached need elaboration. For instance, what are the determinants of values and existents? How are emotions translated into goal statements? Expectancy theory provides promising directions for enhancing goal theory. For example, goal acceptance can be correlated with one's expectation that effort will lead to goal attainment. The merger of goal theory and expectancy theory to guide research promises to produce significant results.

A second weakness in the theory concerns the mechanisms that explain how goal acceptance, goal difficulty, and other variables combine to determine effort. Currently, effort and performance can be predicted with some success, but explanations of why goal setting affects employee behavior are just being developed.

A third problem with the perspective, particularly for educational settings, is that the theory is better for predicting outcomes for simple jobs with concrete results, but is less effective when tasks are complex. Since administrative and instructional jobs are complex, it is not surprising that goal-setting programs in educational settings encounter difficulties.

Thus, while goal theory shows promise as an explanation of work motivation and may even enhance other formulations, much remains to be learned about its processes and applications for administrative practice. This is particularly true for educational organizations.

Comparison of Expectancy and Goal Theories

Expectancy and goal theories, as cognitive process models, resemble each other. Both hypothesize that behavior begins with cognitive processes in the individual. They also represent approaches that attempt to specify how a general model of motivation, such as the one presented in Figure 7.1, can be applied to work settings. As shown in Figure 7.4, all three models use similar concepts and practices. The differences are mainly in emphasis and specificity: cognitive disequilibrium in the general model, internal evaluations of values or valences and prospects for rewards are stressed in expectancy theory, and conscious decisions based on values to pursue an intention in goal theory.

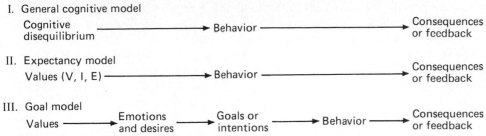

FIGURE 7.4   Comparison of three cognitive process models of motivation

CONCEPTUAL DERIVATIONS
AND APPLICATIONS

School administrators are interested in the question of how they can motivate their staffs. In many cases, they look naïvely at the theories presented as offering relatively simple prescriptions. But theories of work motivation lack the precision to provide simple, unequivocal answers. However, the theories, when used judiciously, offer many suggestions and techniques for improving administrative practice.

In this vein administrators should borrow the best ideas from each theory and apply them to their situations. The content theories of Maslow and Herzberg indicate that administrators must accurately identify and gauge the most important needs of their staffs and use those needs to link job satisfaction with effort or performance. For example, if a need for security has been identified, perhaps the administrator can stress the relationship between high effort and job tenure when communicating with teachers.

Process theories provide additional implications for practice. Expectancy theory indicates that if an employee's level of motivation is deemed inadequate, expectancy, valence, instrumentality can be used as a spur to future efforts. Goal theory suggests that to increase performance the administrators must present clear, difficult goals and make rewards contingent upon meeting them. Moreover, an essential role for the administrator is to help the individual meet his or her need to be competent and self-determining, that is, to become intrinsically motivated.[69] A self-evaluation program is one method that emphasizes intrinsic motivation. Similarly, the professional can be motivated by identifiable opportunities for achievement, constructive and diversified assignments, recognition, advancement in status, and other rewards for achievement.[70]

Although all of these are important, reward systems, work design, and goal setting provide three other practical applications of motivation theory to administration. All three deserve further comment here.

Reward Systems

Incentives, as the organizational counterpart to individual motivation, are rewards, reinforcers, or inducements that employees receive from the organization in return for being productive members. The purpose of incentives offered is to motivate participants to improve their work performance. This fundamental role of incentives in organizations was emphasized about fifty years ago by Chester I. Barnard when he noted that inadequate incentives mean dissolution, change in organizational purpose, or failure of cooperation.[71] More recently, Douglas E. Mitchell, Flora Ida Ortiz, and Tedi K. Mitchell asserted that the incentive system of the school largely determines the strength of teacher motivation to perform work responsibilities.[72]

Organizations develop distributive processes, or incentive systems, to allocate to the working participants a portion of whatever is accomplished by cooperative action. For example, tax monies, prestige, recognition, and achievement are formally distributed to educators. As a basic hypothesis, the incentive system of school organizations is a primary factor affecting educator behavior and is altered largely by the administration in response to changes in the apparent motivations of employees or prospective employees.[73]

Barnard theorized that two classes of incentives—specific and general—are needed. Specific incentives are well defined and include material items (money, things), personal nonmaterial items (distinction, prestige, power), desirable physical work conditions (good lighting, clean classrooms), and ideal benefactions (personal ideals, goals, priorities). Being oriented to individual desires, specific incentives are designed to motivate each person toward cooperative work in a group by providing rewards that have value to each employee. In contrast, general incentives include associational attractiveness (social compatibility), habitual methods and attitudes (standard school routines), opportunities for enlarged participation (shared decision making), and communion (support by the informal organization for what the proper personal attitudes should be). General incentives are nonmaterial, complex because they involve more than a single individual, and created in relation to a social group in the organization. As a consequence, controlling their distribution is a difficult task for administrators.

Interestingly, Barnard observes that organizations such as schools often lack the resources to offer enough specific incentives. Rather than allowing the organization to dissolve or change purposes, administrators use persuasion to change the attitudes of the employees to be satisfied with the incentives offered by the organization. The rhetoric of administrators and public policy makers attempts to persuade teachers to elevate the general incentive of service to children and to reduce their emphasis on specific incentives such as higher salaries and fringe benefits.

Intrinsic and extrinsic incentives.　As noted by Miskel, two terms that are closely related to each other and similar to Barnard's categories, extrinsic and intrinsic, have been used extensively to describe and classify incentives.[74] Extrinsic refers to incentives provided by the organization or other people; intrinsic rewards are those mediated within the individual and that the individual grants himself or herself. Extrinsic outcomes include recognition, money, promotion, harassment, low-ability students, and well-behaved students. Intrinsic outcomes encompass feelings of accomplishment, achievement, and competence.

The distinction differentiates between rewards that are under the direct control of the individual and those that are not. Writers in education have tended to emphasize the importance of intrinsic motivation for teachers. For example, James L. Bess maintained that motivation to high teaching performance depends fundamentally on the strength and quality of satisfaction that can be derived from the task itself.[75] In a study of incentives in schools, Dennis W. Spuck found that perceived levels of intrinsic rewards are more strongly associated with teacher absenteeism, recruitment, and retention than extrinsic inducements.[76] Based on her investigation of reward systems, Ruth Wright concluded that intrinsic incentives hold greater potential for motivating teacher involvement in curriculum tasks than extrinsic rewards.[77] Moreover, intrinsic incentives that promote participation in curriculum tasks are not usually prescribed in school incentive plans. One interpretation of this emphasis on intrinsic motivation and incentives for educators, which is rarely mentioned, is that having severely constrained access to extrinsic rewards, educational organizations must rely on intrinsically motivated behavior of their employees.[78] Because this has been the prevalent condition in education for so long, policy makers have developed extensive mechanisms to convince employees to accept low extrinsic and high intrinsic rewards as being sufficient.

The relationship between intrinsic and extrinsic incentives is a point of controversy. The prevailing generalization has been that both types of rewards combine in an additive fashion. An intensively argued dispute arose when Edward L. Deci postulated that task behavior that allows an individual to feel competent and self-determining is intrinsically motivated.[79] Moreover, external rewards, such as merit pay and feedback about performance, can reduce the task's potential for providing feelings of competence and self-determination. Two explanations of this reduction have been proposed.[80] When external incentives are introduced, they may provide evidence about the person's competence, or the individual may perceive that he or she is performing the task for the reward itself. In either instance, the locus of causality shifts from within the person to the external reward, thereby reducing both the feelings of competence and self-determination.

Nevertheless, the most reasonable implication from current knowledge is that intrinsic and extrinsic rewards have reciprocal effects and both represent effective methods of energizing and maintaining behavior.[81] Therefore, the incentive or distributive system in educational organizations should be elaborate and offer a wide range of intrinsic and extrinsic or specific and general incentives to their employees. Campbell and Pritchard made a much stronger recommendation when they asserted that we should stop talking about need theories and start building lists of reinforcements and how they act as incentives to employees.[82]

Work Redesign and the Job Characteristics Model

Work redesign refers to activities that involve the modification of specific jobs with the intent of increasing both the quality of the employees' work experience and their performance. As a strategy for initiating organizational change, work redesign alters life in organizations in at least four ways: the basic relationship between the individual and what he or she does on the job is changed; behavior is altered directly and tends to stay changed; opportunities for initiating other needed organizational changes arise; and the result in the long term can be organizations that rehumanize rather than dehumanize the people who work in them.[83]

The dominant job design theory during the late 1970s and early 1980s has been the job characteristics model.[84] Primary proponents of the model have been J. Richard Hackman and Greg R. Oldham.[85] The applied approach combines and unifies Maslow's need fulfillment theory of motivation, Herzberg's concern for job redesign and intrinsic motivation, and expectancy theory into a theory of job design.

The concepts and generalizations of the job characteristics model are outlined in Figure 7.5.[86] The theory specifies three psychological states that are critical to attaining desirable work outcomes. First, *feeling of meaningfulness* of the work is the degree to which the individual experiences the job as being valuable and worthwhile. For work to be meaningful, three necessary characteristics are hypothesized: skill variety (work involves a number of activities using different skills and talents), task identity (job requires the completion of an entire segment of work), and task significance (job has a substantial impact on the lives of other people).

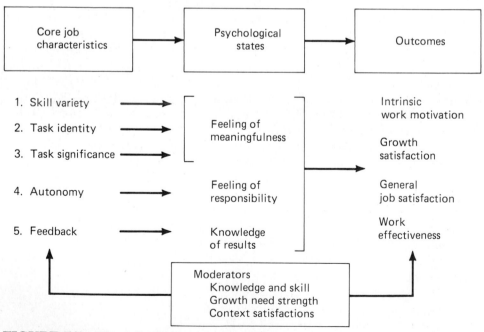

FIGURE 7.5   The job characteristics model

SOURCE: Adapted from J. Richard Hackman and Greg R. Oldham, *Work Redesign* (Reading, MA: Addison-Wesley, 1980), p. 83.

Second, *feeling of responsibility* for work outcomes is the degree to which the individual feels personally accountable for the results of the work he or she performs. Autonomy is postulated to be the primary job characteristic that creates a feeling of responsibility. Autonomy depends on the amount of freedom, independence, and discretion that an individual has to schedule the work and determine the procedures to be used.

Third, *knowledge of results* is the degree to which the individual knows and understands on a continuous basis how effectively he or she is performing the job. The focus is on feedback directly from the job, e.g., when a teacher provides individual instruction to a student and observes the student's learning. In this case the knowledge of results comes from the work activities themselves and not from another person such as an administrator or colleague who collects data or makes a judgment about how well the job is being performed.

The three psychological states are internal to individuals and, therefore, not directly manipulable in designing work. Instead, the five job characteristics, which are reasonably objective, measurable, and changeable properties of the work, foster the psychological states and produce work motivation. Consequently, Hackman and Oldham proposed the generalization that the motivating potential score (MPS) of a job is the product of the sum of the aspects of meaningfulness, autonomy, and feedback. Stated symbolically, the equation is the following:

$$\text{Motivating Potential Score (MPS)} = \left[\frac{\text{Skill Variety} + \text{Task Identity} + \text{Task Significance}}{3} \right] \times \text{Autonomy} \times \text{Feedback}$$

Jobs with high motivating potential create conditions that reinforce employees who have high performance levels.[87] In other words, the characteristics of a job set the stage for the internal motivation or positive psychological states of individuals. Therefore, an additional generalization from the theory is that as the motivating potential scores of employees increase, the outcomes (intrinsic work motivation, growth satisfaction, job satisfaction, and work effectiveness) also increase.

Research. A major strength of the job characteristics model is that the assessment of the core characteristics was relatively easy to accomplish. Consequently, the measurement problems were addressed early in theory's development.[88] To measure the primary variables, Hackman and Oldham developed the job diagnostic survey (JDS) questionnaire.[89] A number of studies employing the JDS have been published. The initial field research by Hackman and Oldham supported the major generalizations of the theory.[90] Other investigations have provided mixed support for the theory.[91]

In the educational setting, Margaret C. Pastor and David A. Erlandson used the JDS with a sample of teachers.[92] While not testing the overall job characteristics model, they did find that the motivational needs of public secondary school teachers are predominately higher order or intrinsic and that job satisfaction is related to teacher needs.

Evaluation. Hackman and Oldham acknowledge several shortcomings in their theory.[93] Individual differences exist among people, and the best ways to define, measure, and include variations among individuals in the model remain open to question. Similarly, the links between job characteristics and psychological states are apparently not as strong as originally suggested. Another problem involves the lack of independence of the job characteristics. The model treats them as though they were independent or uncorrelated, but jobs that are high on one characteristic tend to be high on the others. The concept of feedback as used in the model is not adequately defined. Determining what is and is not job-based feedback is difficult. Finally, the relationships between objective properties of jobs and people's perceptions of those properties are not clear. The model does not consider the inevitable redefinition of the tasks that employees will make to draw more consistent relationships between their jobs and their needs, values, and attitudes. In this regard, Karlene H. Roberts and William Glick strongly criticize the job characteristics model because the approach treats perceptions as "real" data as distinct from objective descriptions of the job characteristics.[94] They maintain that perceptions of task characteristics are just perceptions and do not represent the attributes of tasks. However, convincing arguments have been made that Roberts and Glick's assertion is not true and that perceptions are indeed a useful source of information about jobs.[95] Nevertheless, their sharp criticism may have contributed to a declining scholarly interest in the theory.[96]

Application. While recognizing its limitations, the job characteristics model does provide measures and guidelines that can be used in diagnosing and implementing job redesign for professional employees.[97] In this model work redesign essentially involves improving the five core characteristics of jobs, or increasing the overall motivating potential of the job. Six guidelines are typically given for directing job redesign efforts.[98]

GUIDE 1. Diagnosis of the work system is essential to developing systematic plans to change the core job characteristics. In the diagnostic stage, four questions should be considered. First, does a demonstrated need exist for a work redesign program to improve employee motivation, satisfaction, and performance? The response to this question should be based on sound information. Therefore, the job diagnostic survey (JDS) could be used to provide assessments of the five core job characteristics. Second, do the observed problems have their bases in the motivational properties of the work itself? If the results from the JDS do not indicate low motivating potential scores, job enrichment might not be helpful. If low scores on the JDS are found, however, then specific areas needing change have been identified. Third, are the employees ready for a work redesign program? Only employees who are sufficiently competent to perform the redesigned tasks, desire growth satisfaction in work, and are satisfied with the work context are likely to prosper in new, complex, and challenging jobs. Fourth, will the school organization allow the work redesign to occur? Evidence to date suggests that job redesign programs are most successful in organizations that are organic in nature (see Chapter 5). If the responses to the four questions indicate that a job redesign program is needed and has the potential to be successful, then several strategies are available.

GUIDE 2.   The focus of the redesign should be on the work itself. Change efforts based on diffuse goals or intuition rather than specific, well-conceptualized modifications of the work context frequently have little impact on the work itself. Using a work design theory, such as the job characteristics model, will help administrators maintain an emphasis on the work itself. For example, the central point in redesigning educator work would be the five core job characteristics of skill variety, task identity, task significance, autonomy, and feedback. Given the detailed nature of many teacher contracts and the development of sophisticated management information systems, a reasonable hypothesis is that an erosion has taken place in the value of these job characteristics for teachers during the past several years. Consequently, many schools may need extensive job enrichment programs.

GUIDE 3.   Preparations and contingency plans should be made ahead of time for unanticipated problems and side effects. As hypothesized in social-system theory, when substantial changes are made in the task structure, ripple effects will be felt throughout the organization. If sufficient attention is not given to the side effects, the job redesign program may create problems that will negate the desired outcomes.

GUIDE 4.   The project should be monitored and evaluated continuously to determine whether the anticipated changes are occurring or not. The evaluation should be based on multiple lines of evidence and not solely on anecdotes.

GUIDE 5.   The difficult problems should be confronted as early in the project as possible. Although it is tempting to "sell" the redesign program to the various decision makers, e.g., the administration and teacher or administrator union, before raising the difficult problems, such action is usually not advisable. Even though confronting the issues early may endanger the project, a canceled project may be better than making compromise after compromise to keep the program going after it is started.

GUIDE 6.   The change processes should fit the goals of the job redesign program. The implementation of a job enrichment program needs to use processes that are congruent with the intended result. For instance, if increased autonomy is a goal, then autonomy is to be respected in designing the new jobs. In other words, employees are allowed to do their work with minimal interference, the assumption being that they have the competence and sense of responsibility to seek assistance when they need it.

Miner observes that the developers of the job characteristics model know that many job redesign efforts fail to achieve their objectives and that others die in the pilot project phase. Failures can be explained by shortcomings in all factors of the redesign effort—from diagnosis to inappropriate change processes. In many cases the factors pyramid and ensure failure. In sum, job redesign offers high potential to produce positive results in educational organizations, but the probability of success may not be high.

Goal Setting and Management by Objectives

The major application of goal theory and goal setting is Management by Objectives or simply MBO. The concept of MBO was given prominence by Peter Drucker during the early 1950s.[99] Since its early popularization, MBO has generated widespread appeal in industrial organizations. It is apparently also becoming an important innovation in many educational organizations. In fact, John M. Ivancevich concludes that MBO can no longer be considered a fad because of its long and widespread use in industrial organizations.[100] As a major proponent of the technique, George S. Odiorne observes that MBO has been used extensively in a variety of organizational settings.[101]

Since the concept was first formulated, many definitions have been offered. In an educational context, *management by objectives* refers to the process by which administrators or teachers jointly define their common goals in terms of expected outcomes. These outcomes can then be used to assess each member's contribution.[102] An alternative definition is that MBO is a method of associating objectives with specific positions in a school and linking these objectives with school district plans and goals.[103] As an administrative process, the essential elements appear to be, first, setting goals, second, working toward the goals, and, third, evaluating performance and producing feedback.

As originally conceived by Drucker, MBO is based on Maslow's higher-order needs and Herzberg's motivator factors. Essentially, MBO assumes that if employees are given increased responsibility for developing personal goals in relation to the organization's goals, autonomy in achieving them, and methods for evaluating their achievement, they will work harder and be more effective in their jobs. However, the most extensive theoretical support for MBO obviously comes from goal theory. As a technique, MBO applies the major postulate of goal theory—that behavior is largely the result of intentional actions taken by individuals—to the work setting. In other words, widespread practical applications of MBO preceded a persuasive explanation of why the process can be effective in work settings.

Research. The research that tests the theoretical underpinnings remains scant. For the most part, the investigations have been completed in the industrial sector. For instance, business managers in an MBO program had more favorable attitudes toward their jobs than a control group.[104] However, four problems developed in an MBO program at the Purex Corporation. First, lower-level managers felt that they were not allowed to participate fully in setting objectives. Second, the paperwork required was felt to be a burden. Third, there was felt to be an overemphasis on quantitive measures. Finally, the use of MBO generated extra work for managers.[105] Still, research elsewhere showed that clear statements of objectives produced relatively high levels of subordinate satisfaction with the superior. Moreover, the subordinates believed that the MBO program was important.[106]

In a higher education setting, Y. K. Sketty and Howard M. Carlisle assert that MBO is consistent with the high value that professionals place on involvement, participation, and freedom of action.[107] In addition, they believe that an MBO program provides enough objective data that faculty member performance can be evaluated. In a test of these postulates in a public university, the researchers concluded that the MBO program increased faculty awareness of organizational goals, improved planning, resulted in better performance evaluation data, and improved performance and communication. Success varied with faculty type, however. Lower-ranked, nontenured faculty were more favorable to the program than higher-ranked, tenured members. Moreover, limitations similar to those found in industry (increased paperwork, ambiguous goals, quantitative measures, intangible objectives) were also discovered in the university setting.

Critique.   Research results on the effectiveness of MBO are thus not definitive. The relative benefits versus the costs of introducing an MBO program have not been determined. Until more tightly controlled research is conducted, administrators will have to make assumptions about whether or not an MBO program improves job satisfaction or performance. Table 7.6 concisely states the claims for and against the procedure.

Many districts are positively inclined toward MBO. Because MBO was developed for the industrial sector, differences must be taken into account when the process is used in educational organizations. For example, unlike

TABLE 7.6 Conflicting Claims Regarding MBO

Claims by MBO Proponents	*Counterclaims by MBO Critics*
1. Enhances individual motivation to work by appealing to higher order needs	1. Asserts that all individuals are ready to assume increased responsibility and self-discipline
2. Facilitates communication between superordinates and subordinates	2. Fails to allow lower-level employees full participation in setting objectives
3. Focuses on achieving organizational goals	3. Increases paperwork
4. Evaluates results, not personalities or politics	4. Emphasizes only quantitative evaluations of tangible results
5. Provides job improvement and personal growth	5. Generates extra work for administrators
6. Yields common understandings of organizational goals	6. Yields ambiguous and abstract goals in education

many business goals, which are economic aims that can be readily quantified, educational goals have traditionally been vague. Consequently, asking individual educators to state specific performance objectives may be a violation of their values. Educators may also resist evaluation because many believe that their work is not measurable.

Miner also points out two additional problems with MBO.[108] The needed congruence between getting individuals to strive toward specific, relatively difficult goals and accomplishing the overall organizational goal certainly is not an assured relationship. The basic ideal in a standard MBO program is that goals cascade down the organization level by level until an integrated group of goals emerge.[109] However, goal setting by individuals in schools with relatively ambiguous aims can produce particularly diverse and marginally relevant sets of objectives. Another problem for MBO is that the motivating effects of difficult goals appear to dissipate over time. To counteract the tendency to trivialize the process, goal setting must be reinforced frequently.

Application.   Management by objectives is carried out in four steps, which are summarized in Table 7.7. The first step develops overall educational goals. Although this seems simple, educational goals traditionally have been stated in highly abstract and socially acceptable ways. For use in an MBO program, school district goals must be stated operationally, that is, in such a way that educators will understand the relationship of the goals to their jobs and thus use them as guides to action. The second step establishes for each job—central office (both line and staff positions), building administrators, or teaching positions— what the individual in the position is required to achieve. Usually, the superior and subordinate arrive at these objectives cooperatively. In the third step, objectives of different positions are integrated so that every division of the school district is working to accomplish the same overall goals. For example, if the instructional division's goal is to raise the reading level of elementary children, the staff development and purchasing divisions must have supporting goals. In-service programs and new materials should assist in goal attainment. In the fourth step, measurement and control procedures are established. Quantitative procedures must be developed to measure tangible results. In education, however, qualitative procedures for evaluating less tangible, but exceedingly important, outcomes should not be neglected.

To implement an MBO program, educators must write good objectives— a difficult task. As an aid, Table 7.8 contains suggestions for developing objectives. Two types of criteria are proposed—general and flexible. The general criteria are applicable to all objective statements. For example, objectives

TABLE 7.7   Major Steps in Developing an MBO Program

Step 1. Develop district-wide goals
Step 2. Establish objectives for each position
Step 3. Integrate the objectives with the goals
Step 4. Determine measurement and control procedures

should be clearly stated, acceptable to affected parties, realistic, and attainable. They should comprise tasks that are challenging and contribute directly or indirectly to the organization's overall goals.

Flexible criteria ensure the applicability of performance objectives. Good statements of objectives should concentrate on what and when, not on why and how.[110] As such, four types of objectives—innovative, problem-solving, administrative, and personal—are proposed to help individuals write different types of objectives according to their situations. In some schools or groups, administrators and subordinates may not be concerned with innovation or with a particular problem; they may simply want to ensure that important responsibilities are exercised most effectively. In such a situation, administrative or personal-improvement objectives take priority. Similarly, flexibility and diversity are needed in writing short-range and long-range objectives. Finally, evaluation methods should include quantitative measures of tangible outcomes, such as student achievement, as well as qualitative evaluations of less tangible results, such as satisfaction and improvement in self-concept.

Obviously, implementing an MBO program requires a commitment of school district resources. While the goal-setting process is no panacea, properly applied, it can be an effective administrative technique.

SUMMARY

Motivation consists of complex forces that start and maintain voluntary activity that is undertaken to achieve personal goals. Several competing theories that explain work motivation are consistent with the general model of motivation developed in this chapter. The first of these, Maslow's need hierarchy theory, postulates five hierarchical levels of needs (physiological, security, belongingness, esteem, and self-actualization needs), with higher-level needs activated as lower-level needs are satisfied. The second theory, by Herzberg, recognizes only two factors in work motivation—motivators and hygienes. These consist of

Table 7.8 Criteria for Developing Individual Goals

General Criteria	*Flexible Criteria*
1. Sufficient task	1. Type
2. Clarity	Innovative
Easily communicated	Problem-solving
Simple to understand	Administrative
3. Acceptability	Personal
Personal	2. Time frame
Superordinate	Short-range
Subordinate	Long-range
4. Realistic	3. Evaluation methods
Number	Quantitative
Time	Qualitative
5. Related to organization's goals	

separate sets of components, one set (motivators) contributing to job satisfaction and the other set (hygienes) to job dissatisfaction. Motivator components satisfy higher-level needs for esteem and self-actualization, while hygiene components satisfy the lower-level physiological, security, and belongingness needs.

In addition to the two content theories of work motivation, two process theories were presented. The first, expectancy theory, hypothesizes that motivation is a function of expectancy, valence, and instrumentality. The second, goal theory, postulates that the effort of an individual depends on the difficulty and specificity of the goals that are set.

Several implications for practice can be drawn from motivation theory. The job characteristics model and management by objectives represent two practical approaches that were developed to meet the challenges of new attitudes toward work and changing motivational patterns. Both approaches have strengths and weaknesses that must be carefully analyzed before they are implemented in the educational setting.

NOTES

1. Edward L. Deci, *Intrinsic Motivation* (New York: Plenum, 1975), pp. 3–5.
2. John P. Campbell and Robert D. Pritchard, "Motivation Theory in Industrial and Organizational Psychology," in Marvin D. Dunnette (ed.), *Handbook of Industrial and Organizational Psychology* (Chicago: Rand McNally, 1976), pp. 63–130; Abraham K. Korman, Jeffrey H. Greenhaus, and Irwin J. Badin, "Personnel Attitudes and Motivation," *Annual Review of Psychology*, 28 (1977), 175–196; and Terence R. Mitchell, "Organization Behavior," *Annual Review of Psychology*, 30 (1979), 243–281.
3. David A. Nadler and Edward E. Lawler III, "Motivation: A Diagnostic Approach," in J. Richard Hackman, Edward E. Lawler III, and Lyman W. Porter (eds.), *Perspectives on Behavior in Organizations* (New York: McGraw-Hill, 1977), pp. 26–38.
4. J. W. Atkinson, *An Introduction to Motivation* (New York: Van Nostrand Reinhold, 1964), pp. 273–274.
5. Victor H. Vroom, *Work and Motivation* (New York: Wiley, 1964), p. 6.
6. John P. Campbell, Marvin D. Dunnette, Edward W. Lawler III, and Karl E. Weick, Jr., *Managerial Behavior, Performance, and Effectiveness* (New York: McGraw-Hill, 1970), pp. 340.
7. Richard M. Steers and Lyman W. Porter, *Motivation and Work Behavior*, 2nd ed. (New York: McGraw-Hill, 1979), pp. 3–27.
8. Richard M. Steers and Lyman W. Porter, *Motivation and Work Behavior*, 3rd ed. (New York: McGraw-Hill, 1983), p. 10.
9. Campbell and Pritchard, *op. cit.*, p. 74.
10. Campbell *et al.*, *op. cit.*, pp. 341–356.
11. Two other need theories that will not be considered are ERG Theory and Need Achievement. Excellent sources for ERG Theory include the following: Clayton P. Alderfer, *Existence, Relatedness, and Growth: Human Needs in Organizational Settings* (New York: Free Press, 1972); and Clayton P. Alderfer and Richard A. Guzzo, "Life Experiences and Adults' Enduring Strength of Desires in Organizations," *Administrative Science*

Quarterly, 24 (1979), 247–361. Information about Need Achievement Theory can be found in the following sources: David C. McClelland, *The Achieving Society* (Princeton, NJ: Van Nostrand, 1961); David C. McClelland, "Toward a Theory of Motive Acquisition," *American Psychologist,* 20 (1965), 321–333; and John W. Atkinson and Joel O. Raynor, *Motivation and Achievement* (Washington, DC: Winston, 1974).

12. Campbell and Pritchard, *op. cit.,* p. 97; and Steers and Porter, 1983, *op. cit.,* pp. 27–28.

13. Abraham H. Maslow, *Motivation and Personality,* 2nd ed. (New York: Harper & Row, 1970; 1st ed., 1954), pp. 55–56; and "A Theory of Human Motivation," *Psychological Review,* 50 (1943), 370–396.

14. Maslow, *Motivation and Personality, op. cit.,* p. 44.

15. Campbell and Pritchard, *op. cit.,* p. 97.

16. Edward E. Lawler III, *Motivation in Work Organizations* (Monterey, CA: Brooks/Cole, 1973), p. 28.

17. Maslow, *op. cit.,* 1970, p. 30.

18. Abraham H. Maslow, *Eupsychian Management* (Homewood, IL: Irwin, 1965).

19. Lyman W. Porter, "A Study of Perceived Need Satisfactions in Bottom and Middle Management Jobs," *Journal of Applied Psychology,* 45 (1961), 1–10.

20. Lyman W. Porter, "Job Attitudes in Management: I. Perceived Deficiencies in Need Fulfillment as a Function of Job Level," *Journal of Applied Psychology,* 46 (1962), 375–384.

21. The school form of the NSQ is reproduced in Frances M. Trusty and Thomas J. Sergiovanni, "Perceived Need Deficiencies of Teachers and Administrators: A Proposal for Restructuring Teacher Roles," *Educational Administration Quarterly,* 2 (1966), 168–180.

22. Additional measures of Maslow's need hierarchy can be found in the following sources: Benjamin Schneider and Clayton P. Alderfer, "Three Studies of Measures of Need Satisfaction in Organizations," *Administrative Science Quarterly,* 18 (1973), 489–505; G. Huizinga, *Maslow's Need Hierarchy in the Work Situation* (Groningen, Netherlands: Walters-Noordhoff, 1970); and Vance F. Mitchell and Pravin Moudgill, "Measurement of Maslow's Need Hierarchy," *Organizational Behavior and Human Performance,* 16 (1976), 334–349.

23. Porter, "A Study of Perceived Need Satisfactions in Bottom and Middle Management Jobs," *op. cit.;* and Lyman W. Porter, "Job Attitudes in Management: II. Perceived Importance of Needs as a Function of Job Level," *Journal of Applied Psychology,* 47 (1963), 141–148.

24. John B. Miner, *Theories of Organizational Behavior* (Hinsdale, IL: Dryden, 1980).

25. Trusty and Sergiovanni, *op. cit.*

26. Mary Beth G. Anderson and Edward F. Iwanicki, "Teacher Motivation and Its Relationship to Burnout," *Educational Administration Quarterly,* 20 (1984), 109–132.

27. Grace B. Chisolm, Roosevelt Washington, and Mary Thibodeaux, "Job Motivation and the Need Fulfillment Deficiencies of Educators" (Paper presented at the annual meeting of the American Educational Research Association, Boston, 1980).

28. Mahmoud A. Wahba and Lawrence G. Bridwell, "Maslow Reconsidered:

A Review of Research on the Need Hierarchy Theory," *Proceedings of the 33rd Annual Meeting of the Academy of Management* (Academy of Management, 1973), 514–520; and Mahmoud A. Wahba and Lawrence G. Bridwell, "Maslow Reconsidered: A Review of Research on the Need Hierarchy Theory," *Organizational Behavior and Human Performance,* 15 (1976), 212–240.

29. For a general discussion of the research evidence see the following sources: Miner, *op. cit.;* and Steers and Porter, 1983, *op. cit.* For a recent empirical investigation that casts strong doubt on Maslow's theory see the following: John Rauschenberger, Neal Schmitt, and John E. Hunter, "A Test of the Need Hierarchy Concept by a Markov Model of Change in Need Strength," *Administrative Science Quarterly,* 25 (1980), 654–670. For recent studies showing modest support see the following: Ellen L. Betz, "Two Tests of Maslow's Theory of Need Fulfillment," *Journal of Vocational Behavior,* 24 (1984), 204–220; and Joel Lefkowitz, Mark John Somers, and Karen Weinberg, "The Role of Need Level and/or Need Salience as Moderators of the Relationship between Need Satisfaction and Work Alienation-Involvement," *Journal of Vocational Behavior,* 24 (1984), 142–158.

30. Howard S. Schwartz, "Maslow and the Hierarchical Enactment of Organizational Reality," *Human Relations,* 10 (1983), 933–956. The quotation is found on p. 934.

31. Frederick Herzberg, Bernard Mausner, and Barbara Snyderman, *The Motivation to Work* (New York: Wiley, 1959).

32. Miner, *op. cit.,* p. 78.

33. Thomas Sergiovanni, "Factors Which Affect Satisfaction and Dissatisfaction of Teachers," *Journal of Educational Administration,* 5 (1967), 66–82.

34. Gene L. Schmidt, "Job Satisfaction Among Secondary School Administrators," *Educational Administration Quarterly,* 12 (1976), 68–86.

35. Miner, *op. cit.,* p. 100.

36. For a critical analysis of the two-factor theory see R. J. House and L. A. Wigdor, "Herzberg's Dual-Factor Theory of Job Satisfaction and Motivation: A Review of the Evidence and a Criticism," *Personnel Psychology,* 20 (1967), 369–390; D. A. Whitsett and E. K. Winslow, "An Analysis of Studies Critical of the Motivation-Hygiene Theory," *Personnel Psychology,* 20 (1967), 391–416; and Nathan King, "Clarification and Evaluation of the Two-Factor Theory of Job Satisfaction," *Psychology Bulletin,* 74 (1970), 18–31.

37. *Ibid.*

38. Hanafi M. Soliman, "Motivation-Hygiene Theory of Job Attitudes: An Empirical Investigation and an Attempt to Reconcile Both the One- and the Two-Factor Theories of Job Attitudes," *Journal of Applied Psychology,* 54 (1970), 452–456.

39. Gerald R. Salancik and Jeffery Pfeffer, "An Examination of Need-Satisfaction Models of Job Attitudes," *Administrative Science Quarterly,* 22 (1977), 427–456.

40. Campbell *et al., op. cit.,* p. 381.

41. Steers and Porter, 1979, *op. cit.,* pp. 394–395.

42. Attribution and behavioral theories as two other process approaches will

not be considered. Sources for attribution theory include the following: James M. and Ramona Frasher, "Verification of Administrative Attribution Theory" (Paper presented at the annual meeting of the American Educational Research Association, Boston, 1980); Fritz Heider, "Social Perception and Phenomenal Causality," *Psychological Review,* 51 (1944), 358–374; Fritz Heider, *The Psychology of Interpersonal Relations* (New York: Wiley, 1958); and Bernard Weiner, *Theories of Motivation: From Mechanism to Cognition* (Chicago: Markum, 1972). References to discussions of behaviorism include the following: B. F. Skinner, *Beyond Freedom and Dignity* (New York: Knopf, 1971); B. F. Skinner, *About Behaviorism* (New York: Knopf, 1974); Fred Luthans and Robert Krietner, *Organizational Behavior Modification* (Glenview, IL: Scott, Foresman, 1975); and Lawrence M. Miller, *Behavior Management* (New York: Wiley, 1978).

43. Mitchell, *op. cit.,* p. 252.
44. The roots of expectancy theory can be found in Edward C. Tolman, *Purposive Behavior in Animals and Men* (New York: Appleton, Century, Crofts, 1932). Current versions can be found in the following sources: Vroom, *op. cit.,* Jay Galbraith and L. L. Cummings, "An Empirical Investigation of the Motivational Determinants of Task Performance: Interactive Effects between Instrumentality-Valence and Motivation-Ability," *Organizational Behavior and Human Performance,* 2 (1967), 237–257; George Graen, "Instrumentality Theory of Work Motivation: Some Experimental Results and Suggested Modifications," *Journal of Applied Psychology Monograph,* 53 (1963), 1–25; and Lyman W. Porter and Edward E. Lawler III, *Managerial Attitudes and Performance* (Homewood, IL: Dorsey, 1968).
45. Nadler and Lawler, *op. cit.,* p. 28–48.
46. This specific formula was proposed by Galbraith and Cummings, *op. cit.*
47. Cecil Miskel, Susan Bloom, and David McDonald, "Structural Coupling, Expectancy Climate, and Learning Strategies Intervention Effectiveness: A Pilot Study to Establish the Reliability and Validity Estimates for the Measurement System." Final Report for the Learning Disabilities Institute, University of Kansas, 1980, pp. 70. A copy of the final report and expectancy measure can be requested from Cecil Miskel, University of Utah.
48. Campbell and Pritchard, *op. cit.;* H. G. Heneman III and D. P. Schwab, "An Evaluation of Research on Expectancy Theory Predictions of Employee Performance," *Psychological Bulletin,* 78 (1972), 1–9; and T. R. Mitchell, "Expectancy Models of Job Satisfaction, Occupational Preference, and Effort: A Theoretical, Methodological, and Empirical Appraisal," *Psychological Bulletin,* 81 (1974), 1053–1077.
49. Richard T. Mowday, "The Exercise of Upward Influence in Organizations," *Administrative Science Quarterly,* 23 (1978), 137–156.
50. H. Scott Herrick, "The Relationship of Organizational Structure to Teacher Motivation in Multiunit and Nonmultiunit Elementary Schools." Technical Report No. 322 (Wisconsin Research and Development Centers for Cognitive Learning, the University of Wisconsin, Madison, Wisconsin, ERIC Document ED 101442, 1973).
51. Cecil Miskel, JoAnn DeFrain, and Kay Wilcox, "A Test of Expectancy

Motivation Theory in Educational Organizations," *Educational Administration Quarterly,* 16 (Winter 1980), 70–92.

52. Cecil G. Miskel, David McDonald, and Susan Bloom, "Structural and Expectancy Linkages within Schools and Organizational Effectiveness," *Educational Administration Quarterly,* 19 (1983), 49–82.

53. Linda L. Graham, "Expectancy Theory as a Predictor of College Student Grade Point Average, Satisfaction, and Participation" (Ph. D. diss. University of Kansas, 1980).

54. Steers and Porter, 1983, *op. cit.,* p. 79.

55. Miner, *op. cit.,* p. 161.

56. Mitchell, "Expectancy Models of Job Satisfaction, Occupational Preference, and Effort," *op. cit.;* and Campbell and Pritchard, *op. cit.*

57. Miskel, DeFrain, and Wilcox, *op. cit.*

58. Marcelline R. Fusilier, Daniel C. Ganster, and R. Dennis Middlemist, "A Within-Person Test of the Form of the Expectancy Theory Model in a Choice Context," *Organizational Behavior and Human Performance,* 34 (1984), 323–342.

59. Edwin A. Locke, "Toward a Theory of Task Motivation and Incentives," *Organizational Behavior and Human Performance,* 3 (1968), 157–189; Edwin A. Locke, Norman Cartledge, and Claramae S. Knerr, "Studies of the Relationship between Satisfaction, Goal-Setting, and Performance," *Organizational Behavior and Human Performance,* 5 (1970), 135–139; Anthony J. Mento, Norman D. Cartledge, and Edwin A. Locke, "Maryland vs. Michigan vs. Minnesota: Another Look at the Relationship of Expectancy and Goal Difficulty to Task Performance," *Organizational Behavior and Human Performance,* 25 (1980), 419–440; Edwin A. Locke, Karyll N. Shaw, Lise M. Saari, and Gary P. Latham, "Goal Setting and Task Performance," *Psychological Review,* 90 (1981), 125–152; and Edwin A. Locke, Philip Bobko, and Cynthia Lee, "Effect of Self-Efficacy, Goals, and Task Strategies on Task Performance," *Journal of Applied Psychology,* 69 (1984), 241–251.

60. Miner, *op. cit.,* p. 172.

61. An excellent discussion of goal theory is presented by James C. Naylor and Daniel R. Ilgen, "Goal Setting: A Theoretical Analysis of a Motivational Technology," *Research in Organizational Behavior,* 6 (1984), 95–140.

62. Steers and Porter, 1983, *op. cit.,* p. 58.

63. See Gary P. Latham and Gary A. Yukl, "A Review of Research on the Application of Goal Setting in Organizations," *Academy of Management Journal,* 18 (1975), 824–845.

64. *Ibid.;* Campbell and Pritchard, *op. cit.;* Mitchell, "Organization Behavior," *op. cit.;* and Mento, Cartledge, and Locke, *op. cit.*

65. Terry A. Beehr and Kevin G. Love, "A Meta-Model of the Effects of Goal Characteristics, Feedback, and Role Characteristics in Human Organizations," *Human Relations,* 36 (1983), 151–166; and Gary P. Latham and Timothy P. Steele, "The Motivational Effects of Participation Versus Goal Setting on Performance," *Academy of Management Journal,* 26, (1983), 406–417.

66. Miriam Erez, P. Christopher Earley, and Charles L. Hulin, "The Impact of Participation on Goal Acceptance and Performance: A Two Step Model," *Academy of Management Journal,* 28 (1985), 50–66.

67. Jay S. Kim, "Effect of Behavior Plus Outcome Goal Setting and Feedback on Employee Satisfaction and Performance," *Academy of Management Journal,* 27 (1984), 139–149; John M. Ivancevich and J. Timothy McMahon, "The Effects of Goal Setting, External Feedback, and Self-Generated Feedback on Outcome Variables: A Field Experiment," *Academy of Management Journal,* 25 (1982), 359–372; and Beehr and Love, *op. cit.*

68. See Latham and Yukl, *op. cit.*

69. Deci, *op. cit.*

70. William L. Campfield, "Motivating the Professional Employee," *Personnel Journal,* 44 (1965), 425–428, 442.

71. Chester I. Barnard, *Functions of an Executive* (Cambridge: Harvard University Press, 1938), pp. 32–33, 139–160.

72. Douglas E. Mitchell, Flora Ida Ortiz, and Tedi K. Mitchell, "Executive Summary," *Controlling the Impact of Rewards and Incentives on Teacher Task Performance* (Washington DC: National Institute of Education, U. S. Department of Education, Grant NIE-G-80-0154, 1982).

73. Peter B. Clark and James Q. Wilson, "Incentive Systems: A Theory of Organizations," *Administrative Science Quarterly,* 6 (1961), 129–166.

74. Cecil G. Miskel, "Motivation in Educational Organizations," *Educational Administration Quarterly,* 18 (1982), 65–88.

75. James L. Bess, "The Motivation to Teach," *Journal of Higher Education,* 48 (1977), 243–258.

76. Dennis W. Spuck, "Reward Structures in the Public High School," *Educational Administration Quarterly,* 10 (1974), 18–34.

77. Ruth Wright, "Motivating Teacher Involvement in Professional Growth Activities," *The Canadian Administrator,* 24 (1985), 1–6.

78. J. Daniel Sherman and Howard L. Smith, "The Influence of Organizational Structure on Intrinsic Versus Extrinsic Motivation," *Academy of Management Journal,* 27 (1984), 877–885.

79. Deci, *op. cit.*

80. T. L. Daniel and J. K. Esser, "Intrinsic Motivation as Influenced by Rewards, Task Interest, and Task Structure," *Journal of Applied Psychology,* 65 (1980), 566–573.

81. Richard A. Guzzo, "Types of Rewards, Cognitions, and Work Motivation," *Academy of Management Review,* 4 (1979), 75–86.

82. Campbell and Pritchard, *op. cit.,* p. 73.

83. J. Richard Hackman and J. Lloyd Suttle, *Improving Life at Work* (Santa Monica, CA: Goodyear 1977).

84. Barry M. Staw, "Organizational Behavior: A Review and Reformulation of the Field's Outcome Variables," *Annual Review of Psychology,* 35 (1984), 627–666.

85. J. Richard Hackman and Edward E. Lawler III, "Employee Reactions to Job Characteristics," *Journal of Applied Psychology* Monograph, 55 (1971), 259–286; J. Richard Hackman and Greg R. Oldham, "Development of the Job Diagnostic Survey," *Journal of Applied Psychology,* 60 (1975), 159–170; J. Richard Hackman and Greg R. Oldham, "Motivation Through the Design of Work: A Test of a Theory," *Organizational Behavior and Human Performance* 16 (1976), 250–279; and J. Richard Hackman and Greg R. Oldham, *Work Redesign* (Reading, MA: Addison-Wesley, 1980).

86. In addition to the presentations by Hackman and Oldham cited in the previous note, excellent discussions of the job characteristics model are found in the following sources: Greg R. Oldham and Carol T. Kulik, "Motivation Enhancement Through Work Redesign," in James L. Bess (ed.), *College and University Organization* (New York: New York University Press, 1984), 85–104; and Miner, *op. cit.,* pp. 231–266.

87. Hackman and Oldham, *Work Redesign, op. cit.,* p. 82.

88. Miner, *op. cit.,* p. 239.

89. Hackman and Oldham, "Development of the Job Diagnostic Survey," *op. cit.* The measure can be found in Hackman and Oldham, *Work Redesign, op. cit.*

90. Hackman and Oldham, "Motivation," *op. cit.*

91. Investigations supporting the job characteristics model include the following: Moses N. Kiggundu, "An Empirical Test of the Theory of Job Design Using Multiple Job Ratings," *Human Relations,* 33 (1980), 339–351; Rabi S. Bhagat and Marilyn B. Chassie, "Effects of Changes in Job Characteristics on Some Theory-Specific Attitudinal Outcomes: Results from a Naturally Occurring Quasi-Experiment," *Human Relations,* 33 (1980), 297–313; Christopher Orpen, "The Effects of Job Enrichment on Employee Satisfaction, Motivation, Involvement, and Performance: A Field Experiment," *Human Relations,* 32 (1979), 189–217; and Greg R. Oldham and Howard E. Miller, "The Effect of Significant Other's Job Complexity and Employee Reactions to Work," *Human Relations,* 32 (1979), 247–260. Limited or no support was found for the formulation by Hugh J. Arnold and Robert J. House, "Methodological and Substantive Extensions to the Job Characteristics Model of Motivation," *Organizational Behavior and Human Performance,* 25 (1980), 161–183; and Seymour Adler, Richard B. Skov, and Nat J. Salvemini, "Job Characteristics and Job Satisfaction: When Cause Becomes Consequence," *Organizational Behavior and Human Decision Processes,* 35 (1985), 266–278. Partial support was found by Martin G. Evans, Moses N. Kiggundu, and Robert J. House, "A Partial Test and Extension of the Job Characteristics Model of Motivation," *Organizational Behavior and Human Performance,* 24 (1979), 354–381; and Rodger W. Griffeth, "Moderation of the Effects of Job Enrichment by Participation: A Longitudinal Field Experiment," *Organizational Behavior and Human Decision Processes,* 35 (1985), 73–93.

92. Margaret C. Pastor and David A. Erlandson, "A Study of Higher Order Need Strength and Job Satisfaction in Secondary Public School Teachers," *Journal of Educational Administration,* 20 (1982), 172–183.

93. Hackman and Oldham, *Work Redesign,* pp. 95–97.

94. Karlene H. Roberts and William Glick, "The Job Characteristics Approach to Task Design: A Critical Review," *Journal of Applied Psychology,* 66 (1981), 193–217.

95. Ricky W. Griffin, "Objective and Social Sources of Information in Task Redesign: A Field Experiment," *Administrative Science Quarterly,* 28 (1983), 184–200.

96. Benjamin Schneider, "Organizational Behavior," *Annual Review of Psychology,* 36 (1985), 573–611.

97. Oldham and Kulik, *op. cit.,* provide extensive guidelines for applying of the job characteristics model in college and university settings. Miner, *op.*

cit., gives similar recommendations for a variety of settings. The current discussion relies heavily on these two works.

98. Hackman and Suttle, *op. cit.*

99. Peter Drucker, *The Practice of Management* (New York: Harper, 1954).

100. John M. Ivancevich, "A Longitudinal Assessment of Management by Objectives," *Administrative Science Quarterly,* 17 (1972), 126–136.

101. G. S. Odiorne, *MBO II: A System of Managerial Leadership for the 80s* (Belmont, CA: Fearon Pitman, 1979).

102. Derived from G. S. Odiorne, *Management by Objectives: A System of Managerial Leadership* (New York: Pitman, 1965), and *Management Decisions by Objectives* (Englewood Cliffs, NJ: Prentice-Hall, 1969).

103. Derived from W. J. Reddin, *Effective Management by Objectives: The 3-D Method of MBO* (New York: McGraw-Hill, 1971), pp. 11–19.

104. Herbert Meyer, Emanuel Kay, and John French, "Split-Roles in Performance Appraisal," *Harvard Business Review,* 42 (1965), 123–129.

105. Anthony Raia, "A Second Look at Management Goals and Controls," *California Management Review,* 8 (1966), 49–58.

106. Stephen Carroll and Henry Tosi, "Goal Characteristics and Personality Factors in a Management by Objectives Program," *Administrative Science Quarterly,* 15 (1970), 295–305; and John M. Ivancevich, James Donnelly, and Herbert Lyon, "A Study of the Impact of Management by Objectives in Perceived Need Satisfaction," *Personnel Psychology,* 23 (1970), 139–151.

107. Y. K. Sketty and Howard M. Carlisle, "Application of Management by Objectives in a University Setting: An Exploratory Study of Faculty Reactions," *Educational Administration Quarterly,* 10 (1974), 65–81.

108. Miner, *op. cit.*, p. 196.

109. Edwin A. Locke and Gary P. Latham, *Goal Setting: A Motivational Technique that Works* (Englewood Cliffs, NJ: Prentice-Hall, 1984), p. 143.

110. John B. Lasagna, "Make Your MBO Pragmatic," *Harvard Business Review,* 49 (1971), 64–69.

Chapter 8

The Character of
the Work Group

To administer a social organization according to purely technical criteria of
rationality is irrational, because it ignores the nonrational aspects of social conduct.

PETER BLAU
Bureaucracy in Modern Society

Behavior in organizations is not simply a function of formal expectations, individual needs, and organizational goals. The relationship among these elements
is dynamic. Participants bring with them to the workplace a host of unique
attributes, sentiments, values, needs, and motives. These personal characteristics mediate the rational and planned aspects of organizational life. Moreover,
a collective sense of identity emerges that transforms a simple aggregate of
individuals into a distinctive workplace personality.

This indigenous feel of the workplace has been analyzed and studied under
a variety of labels, including organizational character, milieu, atmosphere, ideology, climate, culture, emergent system, and informal organization. Our analysis of the internal workplace environment will focus on three related concepts
—informal organization, organizational climate, and organizational culture.
Each of these notions suggests a natural, spontaneous, and human side to organization; each suggests that the organizational whole is greater than the sum
of its parts; and each attempts to uncover the shared meanings and unwritten
rules that guide organizational behavior.

INFORMAL ORGANIZATION

Although participants have individually shaped ideas, expectations, and agendas, as well as differing values, interests, and abilities, the social structure of an
organization is not comprised of the formal structure plus the idiosyncratic

beliefs and behavior of individuals but of a formal structure and an informal structure; informal life is also structured and orderly.[1] Informal organization develops in response to the opportunities and constraints created by the formal structure. For example, official rules and regulations must be broad enough to cover a wide variety of situations; consequently, the application of these general procedures often produces problems of judgment, which when successfully addressed, lead to informal practices. Furthermore, since all decisions cannot be anticipated by the official procedures, once again unofficial practices may provide guides for decisions long before formal rules and regulations have been formulated. Moreover, unofficial norms are likely to emerge that regulate performance and productivity.[2]

Groups in organizations develop their own practices, values, norms, and social relations as members interact with each other. Informal leaders and status structures, with their unofficial norms and practices, arise side by side with formal leaders and structures, with their official expectations and practices. The informal organization constrains behavior in schools. We use the term "informal organization" as Blau and Scott do—*not* to refer to all types of emergent patterns of social life but only to those that evolve within the context of formal organizations.[3]

In brief, informal organization is a system of interpersonal relations that forms spontaneously within all formal organizations. It is a system that is not included in the organizational chart or official blueprint. It is the natural ordering and structuring that evolves from the needs of participants as they interact in their workplace. It contains structural, normative, and behavioral dimensions; that is, it includes informal structure, informal norms, and informal patterns of behavior.[4] Teachers, administrators, and students within schools inevitably generate their own informal systems of status and power networks, communication, and working arrangements and structures.

The Dynamics of Informal Organizations[5]

Before continuing our discussion of informal organizations, it is useful to examine the more general notion of social organization. As people interact in social settings, networks of social relations emerge that have important effects on behavior. Suddenly people find themselves behaving in accord with the prevalent social conditions. Roles, norms, values, and leaders all shape individual behavior. The processes that socially organize human behavior emanate from two main sets of social conditions: (1) the structure of the social relations in the group, and (2) the culture of the group; that is, shared beliefs and orientations emerge to unite the members of the group.[6] The major aspects of social organization are summarized in Table 8.1.

Social relations are comprised of patterns of social interactions, for example, communicating, cooperating, and competing. When individuals find themselves together, interaction inevitably occurs. People talk to each other. Some individuals are liked, others disliked. Typically, people seek continued interactions with those they like and avoid interactions with those to whom they are not attracted. These social exchanges produce a differential distribution of

TABLE 8.1   Major Aspects of Social Organization as Defined by Blau and Scott

I. Social Structure: Network of social relations
    A. Social Interactions
        1. Frequency and duration of contacts between individuals
        2. Sentiments toward each other
    B. Status Structure
        1. Differential distribution of social relations in a group
        2. Differential distribution of social relations among groups
II. Culture: Shared orientations
    A. Shared Values
        1. Idealized justifications for behavior
        2. Ideals and ideas of what is desirable
    B. Social Norms
        1. Common expectations of behavior
        2. Socially sanctioned rules of conduct
    C. Roles
        1. Expectations of various social positions
        2. Specific rights and duties

social relations among group members and, importantly, define the status structure of the group.

A member's status in the group, therefore, depends upon frequency, duration, and character of interaction patterns with others, and the extent to which the individual is respected by others in the group. Consequently, some group members are actively sought out while others are avoided; some are admired, others are not; some are leaders, other are followers; and most are integrated as members of a group, although a few are isolated.

The group forms subgroups. Cliques develop within the group structure, some of which have more status, power, significance than others—the "in-group," competing groups, and marginal groups. Membership in such groups provides status in the larger group through the prestige of the subgroup. In brief, the differential patterns of interactions among individuals and groups, and the status structure defined by them, define the social structure of a group.

In addition to the social structure that develops in groups, a culture or a set of shared beliefs, attitudes, and orientations emerges that serves as a normative guide for behavior within the group (see Part II of Table 8.1). As individuals engage in social interaction, common conceptions of desirable and acceptable behavior occur. Common values arise to define ideal states of affairs, and social norms develop that prescribe what individuals should do in different situations and the consequences of deviations from those expectations. Norms contain two important features: a general agreement about appropriate behavior, and mechanisms to enforce expectations. The distinction between norms and values is sometimes a fuzzy one, but generally values define the ends of human behavior, and social norms provide the legitimate and explicit means for pursuing those ends. Finally, and in addition to the general values and norms that are shared and expected to integrate the group, sets of expectations are differentiated according to the role or status position of the individual in the group. The role of "taskmaster" is quite different from the role of "group comedian"; the role of leader is quite different from the role of the follower.

In sum, two main components of social organization include both the social structure of a group with inevitable status distinctions and the culture of a group with its patterns of integration and differentiation. The structure and culture of a group provide powerful forces for molding behavior.

In contrast to social organizations that emerge spontaneously whenever individuals are interacting, the school is a formal organization that has been deliberatively established for the purpose of educating students. Thus, the goals, the rules, the regulations, the formal structure, and the division of labor have all been consciously designed to guide the activities of students, teachers, and administrators. Nonetheless, the spontaneous development and elaboration of social organization occurs. The work group develops its own structure and culture. Informal organization is an intrinsic part of the formal organization.

A Hypothetical Illustration

Imagine the situation of a new school, where the superintendent hires a new principal, who in turn hires an entire new staff of teachers, none of whom know each other. At the beginning of the year, we simply have a collection of individuals bound together by the formal requirements of the school and their jobs. The professional staff, however, will quickly become more than the sum of the individuals composing it. Behavior will not only be determined by the formal expectations of the school but also by the informal structure and culture that spontaneously emerge as the participants interact.

As school begins, faculty members begin to work together, attend meetings, eat together, socialize in the faculty lounge, and plan school activities. Teacher relations will, in part, be determined by the physical features of the school, such as a faculty lounge, a faculty lunchroom, the library, and the arrangement of the classrooms; the technical aspects of the job, for example, departmentalization, team teaching, and extracurricular responsibilities; and social factors such as the leadership styles of the superintendent and principals. The initial relations of teachers in a school can be examined in terms of the formal activities and interactions. Teachers have a need to keep their jobs, and a formal system has been established to achieve school goals.

A number of consequences follow from the establishment of the initial formal relations. New sentiments develop that are different from the work-motivated ones that brought teachers together in the first place. The new sentiments are ones of liking and disliking for other teachers and groups within the school. Some of the teachers will become well liked and respected; their colleagues will frequently ask them for advice and seek them out. Such sentiments and behavior serve as the basis for an informal ranking of individuals and groups. Moreover, new informal activities will develop, some of which are a direct reaction to the formal organization. For example, the inability of faculty to influence policy through the formal structure may result in informal activities, conversations, and initiatives. New patterns of interaction will elaborate themselves in the school, e.g., association in cliques, informal webs of communication, discipline networks centering on informal leadership, and a status structure among groups of teachers. Some informal groups will become more prestigious and powerful than others.

In addition to the informal social structure that develops, a system of informal shared values and beliefs will emerge—the culture of the work group. The faculty will define ideal and appropriate behavior. Their ideal, for example, may be a school characterized by hard work, mastery of the basics, an academic orientation, and positive student-teacher relations. To this end, norms emerge to guide teacher behavior: few hall passes will be issued; substantial and meaningful homework assignments will be made; orderly and industrious classrooms will be maintained; and extra help for students will be readily available. If teachers violate these norms, they lose the respect of their colleagues, and social sanctions will be applied. They may find themselves disparaged and isolated by their colleagues. Teachers will also assume specific informal roles; an unofficial teacher spokesperson may serve as a powerful liaison with the principal; another teacher may provide a strong critical voice of school policy in faculty meetings; still another teacher may organize social activities for the faculty; and there may be the teacher who always offers comic relief, especially when events are tense.

The informal organization, then, arises from the formal organization and then reacts upon it. The development of group norms, the division into cliques, and the ranking of individuals and subgroups are conditioned directly by the formal structure and indirectly by the school environment. Hence, we can begin with the formal system of the school and argue that the informal is continually emerging from the formal and continually influencing the formal. The formal and informal systems go together; after all there is only one organization. Yet the distinction is useful because it calls attention to the dynamic nature of organizational life in schools and to the continuous processes of elaboration, differentiation, and feedback in schools.

The informal system may be favorable and supportive or unfavorable and destructive of the activities of the formal. For example, favorable norms of support for the principal will likely enhance cooperation and produce harmony in the system. Unfavorable norms can make much of the formal operation a meaningless ritual (recall the Western Electric Company studies summarized in Chapter 1). Moreover, if the elaboration of new activities, which is always part of the development of the informal system, is merely "social," then such social activities as games, parties, and similar "country club" activities may impede the serious work of teaching and learning.

Functions of Informal Organization

Informal organizations in schools have at least three important functions. They serve as effective vehicles of communication, as means of cohesion, and as mechanisms for protecting the integrity of the individual.[7]

Formal systems of communication in schools are typically not sufficient and are inevitably supplemented with informal ones. One finding that has been repeatedly demonstrated by researchers is that informal communications exist in all organizations regardless of how elaborate the system of formal communication. Communications flow quickly and freely through the grapevine. These informal patterns of communication in schools are built around social relationships among school members; informal channels arise for such simple reasons as common classroom areas, shared lunch hours, car pools, and friendships. Teachers, like other organizational members, have a need to know what is happening and why; in fact, need for such communications and understanding may be one of the basic reasons for the existence of small, informal groups.[8]

Informal structure provides a channel for circumventing formally prescribed rules and procedures that may have positive or negative effects. Charles Pages' study of informal structure demonstrates that pressing problems develop for which efficient solutions or communications are not possible within the formal framework; hence, the informal structure assumes increased importance.[9] Similarly, Laurence Iannaccone's study also confirmed that when the formal organization of a school does not respond to up-to-line communications from teachers in a satisfactory way, then the informal system is used in an attempt to obtain a satisfactory response.[10] In schools, knowledgeable and flexible administrators can use the informal system to avoid the bureaucratic frustrations and impediments of the formal system. As a communication vehicle, the grapevine provides efficient machinery, provided that administrators recognize its importance, understand its structure and functioning, and are able and willing to use it.

Informal organization in schools also is a means to cohesiveness. Patterns of social relationships typically emphasize friendliness, cooperation, and preservation of the group. Such informal personal relationships provide the social cement that helps hold the faculty together as a whole and makes the school a more pleasant place to work. Norman Boyan's study of the informal organization of a school faculty demonstrates this important function.[11] He observes that the informal system of relationships operated to reduce differentiation among faculty, to assist new and younger teachers make an easier adjustment to the faculty social system, and to develop stronger solidarity. Boyan emphasizes that maintenance of friendly relations and inclusion of all personnel as members of the group was not left to chance; they evolved from an elaborate system of social relations that operated to envelop the entire faculty, such as the faculty Christmas party, the spring picnic, poker and beer sessions to which all the men were invited, the regular teas given by the women teachers, and the regular afternoon pilgrimage to "the Dell." The friendliness and cordiality produced a strong sense of belonging and group solidarity among the teachers.

Finally, the informal organization functions to maintain a sense of personal integrity, of self-respect, and of independent choice among teachers. Unlike the formal organization, the informal system of relations is not dominated by impersonality and formal authority; therefore, individuals can more fully express their personal needs. Although this process sometimes produces conflict with the formal system, the informal system of relationships provides an important means through which teachers can maintain their individual personalities in spite of the organizational demands, ones that invariably attempt to depersonalize individuals. In brief, informal organization in schools is important to administrators because it serves as a means of communication, of solidarity, and of protecting the integrity of the personalities of teachers.

Informal Organization and Administrative Behavior

The authority relation is a basic feature of life in a school because it provides the basis for legitimate organizational control of teachers and students. A primary source of authority in complex organizations is formal authority that is vested in the office or position and not in the particular person who performs the official role.[12] When teachers join a school organization, they accept the formal authority relation. They agree within certain limits to follow directives that administrators issue. In short, they enter into contractual agreements in which they sell their promises to obey commands.[13] Formal authority, anchored and buttressed by formal sanctions, has a somewhat limited scope. The existence of what Chester Barnard refers to as a bureaucratic "zone of indifference"[14]—in which subordinates, including teacher professionals, accept orders without question—may be satisfactory for eliciting certain minimum performance levels, but it seems likely that this does not lead to an efficient operation. In this same vein, Blau and Scott insist:

> Legal authority does not and cannot command the employee's willingness to devote his ingenuity and energy to performing his task to the best of his ability. . . . It [formal authority] promotes compliance with directives and discipline but does not encourage employees to exert effort, to accept responsibilities, or to exercise initiative.[15]

Therefore, a basic challenge facing all administrators, and one especially significant for first-level line supervisors such as school principals, is to find methods to extend their influence over their professional staff beyond the narrow limits of formal positional authority.[16]

Many school administrators have the power and authority of their offices alone. In a sense, they are sterile bureaucrats, not leaders. Barnard suggests that only when the authority of leadership is combined with the authority of position will superiors be effective in inducing subordinates to comply with directives outside the bureaucratic zone of indifference.[17] Indeed, the possession of both formal and informal authority distinguishes formal leaders from officers and informal leaders. Figure 8.1 illustrates these relationships.

How can school administrators broaden the bases of their authority and enhance their leadership position? The informal organization is an important source of authority that frequently remains untapped. Where formal authority is legitimized by legal contracts and cultural ideologies, informal authority is legitimized by the common values and sentiments that emerge in the work

Formal Authority

	Yes	No
Yes	Formal leader	Informal leader
No	Officer	Follower

Informal Authority (vertical axis label)

FIGURE 8.1   Types of authority positions

group. In particular, informal authority arises from the loyalty that the superior commands from group members.[18] The significance of subordinate loyalty to superiors seems clear. Administrators who command subordinate loyalty seem to have a distinct advantage in enlarging their authority base. Hence, we turn to the definition, measurement, and use of an important concept.

Subordinate Loyalty to Superior.   Blau and Scott, in their insightful sociological analysis of formal organizations, first introduced loyalty as an important aspect of hierarchical relationships in formal organizations.[19] Concerning its importance, they write, "Worker productivity was largely associated with factors that were related to loyalty perhaps because supervisors who had won the loyal support of their subordinates were most successful in commanding willing compliance with their directives and in stimulating effort in their work group."[20] Despite the importance of the concept, Blau and Scott did not define it in detail. They simply note that superiors who command loyalty are "liked," "accepted," and "respected."

V. V. Murray and Allan F. Corenblum maintain that at least two other reasonable definitions of the term might be employed—a cognitive or a behavioral definition.[21] The cognitive definition stresses subordinates' unquestioning faith in the person of their supervisor as a leader. The behavioral definition emphasizes the subordinates' willingness to follow the supervisor to a new position as the criterion for determining subordinate loyalty.

In several school studies, the concept of subordinate loyalty to an immediate superior has been conceptually refined and operationally defined.[22] To measure teacher loyalty to a principal, measurement items were adapted to include cognitive, behavioral, and affective aspects of subordinate loyalty. Research indicates that, although subordinate loyalty to a superior may be conceived of in cognitive, behavioral, or affective terms, these dimensions vary concomitantly; hence, the dimensions taken together provide a good index of subordinate loyalty to an immediate superior.

Administrative style and loyalty. Authoritarian principal behavior and teacher loyalty are probably incompatible, a prediction that rests primarily upon the theoretical analysis of Blau and Scott.[23] One strategy for extending the scope of formal authority over subordinates is domination. The authoritarian administrator attempts to increase control by resorting to formal sanctions or to threats of using those sanctions; however, their prolonged use probably tends in the long run to undermine authority. Subordinates, particularly professionals, resent constant reminders of their dependence on the superior, especially in an egalitarian cultural context. Given their strategy of domination and close supervision, authoritarian administrators are unlikely to command loyalty and support from professionals easily. Blau neatly summarized the "dilemma of bureaucratic authority" as follows: "It rests on the power of sanction but is weakened by frequent resort to sanctions in operations."[24] In fact, nonauthoritarian supervisors seem likely to engage in a contrasting strategy—one of leadership in which services and assistance are furnished to subordinates. Using formal authority to perform special favors and services can create social obligations and build goodwill among subordinates. The result should be enhanced development of subordinate loyalty and informal authority.

For a number of reasons, this rationale for predicting a negative relationship between the authoritarian administrator and the teacher is particularly compelling in schools. First, the nature of supervision in schools should focus on helping, not directing, teachers to improve their teaching. Second, because teachers work in closed rooms, they are not easily observed. Moreover, teachers frequently make strong claims for professional autonomy, and close supervision seems likely to be seen as an infringement on that autonomy. Finally, teachers attach great importance to authority based on professional competence, much more so than similar professional groups such as social workers.[25] Therefore, it should not be surprising that consistently the research demonstrates that authoritarian supervisors are not successful at generating teacher loyalty.[26] Close, authoritarian control of teachers does not generate informal authority.

Emotional detachment and hierarchical independence are two other important characteristics of principal-teacher relationships. Emotional detachment is the ability of administrators to remain calm, cool, and collected in difficult situations, and hierarchical independence is the extent to which administrators demonstrate their autonomy from superiors as they interact with teachers. Principals stand in the middle—with the higher administration on one side and professional teaching faculty on the other. Their effectiveness depends on the support they receive from both, yet they are likely to be the objects of conflicting pressures from both groups. Consequently, emotional detachment from subordinates and independence from superiors are important in establishing social support from teachers for principals. Indeed, the research has demonstrated the significance of both, but especially emotional detachment, in generating teacher loyalty to principals.[27]

Similarly, hierarchical influence is another attribute of administrators who are likely to tap into the informal teacher groups for authority to lead. Administrators who are able and willing to exert their influence with their superiors on teachers' behalf are respected and valued by teachers, and they earn the confidence, support, and loyalty of their teachers.[28]

Finally, the authenticity of the principal in dealing with teachers is a critical factor in the administrative process, enabling principals to generate teacher loyalty and informal authority. Leader authenticity is a slippery concept. People glibly talk about genuine, real, and authentic behavior, yet it is another matter clearly to define and measure authenticity.[29] Based on the work of James Henderson and Wayne Hoy, however, three major aspects of leader authenticity—accountability, manipulation, and salience of self over role—have been identified and measured.[30] Thus, principal authenticity is defined as the extent to which teachers describe their principals as accepting responsibility for their actions, as being nonmanipulating, and as demonstrating a salience of self over role. In contrast, inauthentic principals are viewed as those who pass the buck, blame others and circumstances for not being successful, manipulate teachers, and hide behind their formal position. As one would expect, preliminary research has supported the hypothesis that perceived leader authenticity is strongly related to commanding trust and teacher loyalty from teachers.

The implications of these empirical studies seem clear. If administrators are to be successful in developing informal authority, then they need to behave in ways which foster teacher loyalty. In this regard, authoritarian behavior is doomed to failure. Instead, administrators need to demonstrate both their independence from and influence with superiors. Furthermore, even in difficult situations, their behavior needs to be emotionally tempered, calm, and considerate. Perhaps most importantly, their behavior should be authentic; they need to show a willingness to share in the blame, to be nonmanipulative of teachers, and to be unfettered by bureaucratic role demands.

Successful administration is anchored in the informal system of authority. When informal authority is combined with formal authority, administrators become leaders who can motivate teachers to comply with directives that are outside their bureaucratic zones of indifference. The development of informal authority is in large part dependent upon both knowledge of the informal organization and enlightened administrative practice that generates teacher loyalty and trust. Administrators' knowledge of informal norms, sentiments, and patterns of interaction provides them with information to make critical decisions about which unofficial practices are so rooted in the basic teacher work-group norms that they cannot be ignored.[31]

ORGANIZATIONAL CLIMATE

Organizational climate is a broad term that refers to teachers' *perceptions* of the general work environment of the school; it is influenced by the formal organization, informal organization, personalities of participants, and organizational leadership. Put simply, the set of internal characteristics that distinguishes one school from another and influences the behavior of its members is the organizational climate of the school.[32] More specifically, climate is a relatively enduring quality of the school environment that is experienced by teachers, affects their behavior, and is based on their collective perceptions of behavior in schools. The definition of organizational climate as a set of internal characteristics is similar in some respects to early descriptions of personality. Indeed, the climate of a school may roughly be conceived as the personality of a school; that is, personality is to individual as climate is to organization.

Since the atmosphere of a school has a major impact on the organizational behavior and since administrators can have a significant, positive influence on the development of the "personality" of the school, it is important to describe and analyze school climates. Climate can be conceived from a variety of vantage points, but only three perspectives are described in this chapter. Each provides the student and practitioner of administration with a valuable set of conceptual capital and measurement tools to analyze, understand, map, and change the work environment of schools.

(handwritten margin notes:)
① Open to closed continuum
② Organizational Health of Schools
③ Continuum of Control over Students

TEACHER-PRINCIPAL BEHAVIOR: OPEN TO CLOSED

Probably the most well-known conceptualization and measurement of the organizational climate in schools is the pioneering study of elementary schools by Andrew W. Halpin and Don B. Croft.[33] They began mapping the organizational climate of schools when they observed that (1) schools differ markedly in their feel, (2) the concept of morale did not provide an index of this feel, (3) "ideal" principals who are assigned to schools where improvement is needed are immobilized by the faculty, and (4) the topic of organizational climate was generating interest.

The approach they used involved developing a descriptive questionnaire to identify important aspects of teacher-teacher and teacher-principal interactions. Nearly 1,000 items were composed, each of which was designed to answer the basic question: To what extent is this true of your school? From this original bank of items, they developed a final set of sixty-four items called the *organizational climate description questionnaire (OCDQ)*.

The OCDQ is usually administered to the entire professional staff of each school, with each respondent asked to describe the extent to which each statement characterizes his or her school. The responses to each item are scaled along a four-point continuum: rarely occurs, sometimes occurs, often occurs, and very frequently occurs.

The developers administered the final version of the OCDQ to seventy-one elementary schools. Using the statistical technique known as factor-analysis, the sixty-four items were grouped into eight factors, or subtests. Four of the subtests referred to the characteristics of the faculty group, and four described various components of the teacher-principal interactions. These eight clusters of items were named the eight dimensions of school climate. They are presented and defined in Table 8.2.

Halpin and Croft not only mapped profiles for each of the seventy-one elementary schools in their original sample, but also identified, through factor

TABLE 8.2 The OCDQ Subscales

Characteristics of Faculty Behavior

1. Hindrance refers to the teachers' feelings that the principal burdens them with routine duties, committee work, and other requirements that the teachers perceive as unnecessary "busywork."
2. Intimacy refers to the teachers' enjoyment of warm and friendly personal relations with one another.
3. Disengagement refers to the teachers' tendency "to go through the motions" without an actual commitment to the task at hand.
4. Esprit refers to morale growing out of a sense of both task accomplishment and social needs satisfaction.

Characteristics of Principal Behavior

5. Production emphasis refers to close supervisory behavior on the part of the principal. The principal is highly directive and not sensitive to faculty feedback.
6. Aloofness refers to formal and impersonal principal behavior; the principal goes by the "book" and maintains social distance from his or her staff.
7. Consideration refers to warm, friendly behavior by the principal. The principal tries to be helpful and do a little something extra for the faculty when he or she can.
8. Thrust refers to dynamic principal behavior in which an attempt "to move the organization" is made through the example that the principal sets for the teachers.

---

analysis, six basic clusters of profiles, that is, six basic school climates that are arrayed along a rough continuum from open to closed: open, autonomous, controlled, familiar, paternal, closed. Profiles for each of these six climates were developed by using the scores of the eight dimensions of the OCDQ, and it is often possible to place a school into one of the six classifications of climate. A behavioral picture of each climate can be sketched. To illustrate, we will develop briefly composites for the two extremes—the open and closed climates.[34]

The Open Climate

The distinctive feature of the *open climate* is its high degree of thrust and esprit and low disengagement. This combination suggests a climate in which both the principal and faculty are genuine in their behavior. The principal leads through example by providing the proper blend of structure and direction as well as support and consideration—the mix dependent upon the situation. Teachers work well together and are committed to the task at hand. Given the "reality-centered" leadership of the principal and a committed faculty, there is no need for burdensome paperwork (hindrance), close supervision (production emphasis), or impersonality or a plethora of rules and regulations (aloofness). Acts of leadership emerge easily and appropriately as they are needed. The open school is not preoccupied exclusively with either task achievement or social needs satisfaction, but both emerge freely. In brief, the behavior of both the principal and faculty is authentic.

The Closed Climate

The *closed climate* is virtually the antithesis of the open climate. Thrust and esprit are low and disengagement is high. The principal and teachers simply appear to go through the motions, with the principal stressing routine trivia and unnecessary busywork (hindrance), and the teachers responding at minimal and exhibiting little satisfaction. The principal's ineffective leadership is further seen in close supervision (production emphasis), formal declarations and impersonality (aloofness), as well as a lack of consideration for the faculty and an inability or unwillingness to provide a dynamic personal example. These misguided tactics, which are not taken seriously, produce teacher frustration and apathy. The behavior of both principal and teachers in the closed climate is least genuine when inauthenticity pervades the atmosphere of the school.

The Climate Continuum

Some controversy has arisen over the usefulness of the six discrete climates identified by Halpin and Croft. For example, Robert J. Brown's attempt to replicate the original OCDQ findings with a sample of eighty-one elementary schools in Minnesota resulted in the identification of eight, not six, distinct climates along the open-closed continuum.[35] Brown concluded that, although the climate continuum is useful, it may not be advisable to divide the continuum into discrete climates.[36] James F. Watkins also found a general weakness in the "middle" climate types,[37] and John H. M. Andrews, in one of the most comprehensive validity studies of the OCDQ, concluded that the eight dimensions of the OCDQ possess good construct validity but that the designation of discrete climate categories adds nothing to the meaning already present in the subtests and, in fact, detract from the OCDQ.[38] Halpin and Croft, themselves, had some reservations concerning the middle climates:

> We have said that these climates were ranked in respect to openness versus closedness. But we fully recognize how crude this ranking is. As is the case in most methods of ranking or scaling, we are much more confident about the climates described at each end of the listing than we are about those described in between.[39]

One straightforward way to determine the *relative* openness or closedness of a set of school climates is to make use of the following *climate openness index:*

OPENNESS INDEX =
Thrust Score + Esprit Score − Disengagement Score

The higher the index, the more open the climate of the school. Recall that these three OCDQ subtests are the most important characteristics of the open and closed climates, and when used together, they tend to identify open and closed profiles described by Halpin and Croft.[40] When schools with open and closed climates are contrasted, open climates tend to be higher in esprit, thrust, and consideration and lower in disengagement, hindrance, aloofness, and production emphasis.[41]

As defined by the OCDQ, the climate is clearly a description of the perceptions of the faculty. Some may raise the questions of whether the climate is really open. We agree with Halpin that the climate is open (or closed) if the faculty describes it as such. Whether or not it really is cannot be answered and is probably irrelevant. Perceptions of what is "out there" motivate behavior.[42]

Criticisms of the OCDQ

Although the OCDQ is still a widely used measure of school climate, it has a number of other limitations. The instrument has been criticized because it may not be well suited to study large, urban, or secondary schools.[43] At least part of the problem again stems from attempting to designate discrete climate based on Halpin and Croft's "prototypic profile method" of determining climate.[44] Not only do we again have the problem of the middle-climate categories, but the norms used to classify the schools using the prototypic profile method are based on the seventy-one elementary schools in the original study. Not surprisingly, urban and large secondary schools invariably have closed climates.

Paula Silver is critical of the conceptual underpinnings of the OCDQ; she argues that the framework lacks a clear underlying logic, is cumbersome, and lacks parsimony.[45] For example, she notes that although the hindrance subtest is defined by Halpin and Croft as one dimension of teacher behavior, the concept refers to administrative demands rather than interpersonal behavior of teachers. Other conceptual problems also arise. Halpin and Croft themselves question the adequacy of their concept of consideration by suspecting that two or more facets of considerate behavior have been confounded within a single measure.[46] Moreover, the concept measured by the production emphasis subtest seems mislabeled. The measure clearly taps close administration and autocratic behavior, not an emphasis on high production standards. Directive behavior is a more apt description of this aspect of principal behavior.

In a comprehensive empirical attempt to appraise the OCDQ, Andrew Hayes urged revision of the instrument.[47] His analyses strongly suggested that many of the items of the OCDQ were no longer measuring what they were intended to measure, that some of the subtests were no longer valid (e.g., aloofness), that the reliability of some of the subtests was low, and that the instrument needed a major revision.[48] Recent revisions of the OCDQ developed at Rutgers University address many of the criticisms of the original instrument; in fact, two new and simplified versions of the OCDQ were formulated for elementary and secondary schools—the OCDQ–RE and the OCDQ–RS.[49]

The Revised Organizational Climate Descriptive Questionnaire for Elementary Schools (OCDQ–RE)[50]

The revised climate instrument is a forty-two–item measure with six subtests that describe the behavior of elementary teachers and principals. Three dimensions of principal behavior—supportive, directive, and restrictive—are identified. Supportive principal behavior is reflected by genuine concern and support of teachers. In contrast, directive principal behavior is starkly task-oriented with little consideration for the personal needs of the teachers, and restrictive behavior produces impediments for teachers as they try to do their work. Likewise, three critical aspects of teacher behavior are identified—collegial, intimate, and disengaged teacher behavior. Collegial behavior is supportive and professional interaction among teacher colleagues, and intimate behavior involves close personal relations among teachers not only in but also outside school. On the other hand, disengaged behavior depicts a general sense of alienation and separation among teachers in school.[51]

These fundamental features of principal and teacher behavior are elaborated and summarized in Table 8.3. In the tradition of the original OCDQ, the six dimensions of organizational climate are measured by having teachers describe the interactions between and among teachers and the principal. A sample of the format of the OCDQ–RE is presented in Figure 8.2, and sample items for each dimension of the instrument are summarized in Table 8.3.

A factor analysis of the subtests of the OCDQ–RE revealed that the conceptualization and measure of climate rested on two underlying general factors. Disengaged, intimate, and collegial teacher behavior formed the first factor, while restrictive, directive and supportive behavior defined the second factor. Specifically, the first factor was characterized by teachers' interactions that are meaningful and tolerant (low disengagement); that are friendly, close, and supportive (high intimacy); and that are enthusiastic, accepting, and mutually

	Rarely occurs	Sometimes occurs	Often occurs	Very frequently occurs
1. Routine duties interfere with the job of teaching.				
2. Teachers are proud of their school.				
3. The principal monitors everything teachers do.				
4. The principal treats teacher as equals.				

FIGURE 8.2   Sample items from the OCDQ

TABLE 8.3   The Six Dimensions of the OCDQ-RE

Principal's Behavior

1. *Supportive* behavior reflects a basic concern for teachers. The principal listens and is open to teacher suggestions. Praise is given genuinely and frequently, and criticism is handled constructively. Supportive principals respect the professional competence of their staffs and exhibit both a personal and professional interest in each teacher.

SAMPLE ITEMS:

The principal uses constructive criticism.

The principal compliments teachers.

The principal listens to and accepts teachers' suggestions.

2. *Directive* behavior is rigid, close supervision. Principals maintain close and constant control over all teacher and school activities, down to the smallest details.

SAMPLE ITEMS:

The principal monitors everything teachers do.

The principal rules with an iron fist.

The principal checks lesson plans.

3. *Restrictive* behavior hinders rather than facilitates teacher work. The principal burdens teachers with paper work, committee requirements, routine duties, and other demands that interfere with their teaching responsibilities.

SAMPLE ITEMS:

Teachers are burdened with busywork.

Routine duties interfere with the job of teaching.

Teachers have too many committee requirements.

Teachers' Behavior

4. *Collegial* behavior supports open and professional interactions among teachers. Teachers are proud of their school, enjoy working with their colleagues, and are enthusiastic, accepting, and mutually respectful of the professional competence of their colleagues.

SAMPLE ITEMS:

Teachers help and support each other.

Teachers respect the professional competence of their colleagues.

Teachers accomplish their work with vim, vigor, and pleasure.

5. *Intimate* behavior reflects a cohesive and strong network of social support among the faculty. Teachers know each other well, are close personal friends, socialize together regularly, and provide strong support for each other.

SAMPLE ITEMS:

Teachers socialize with each other.

Teachers' closest friends are other faculty members at this school.

Teachers have parties for each other.

6. *Disengaged* behavior refers to a lack of meaning and focus to professional activities. Teachers are simply putting in time and are non-productive in group efforts or team-building; they have no common goal orientation. Their behavior is often negative and critical of their colleagues and the organization.

SAMPLE ITEMS:

Faculty meetings are useless.

There is a minority group to teachers who always oppose the majority.

Teachers ramble when they talk at faculty meetings.

respectful (high collegial relations). In general, this factor denotes an openness and functional flexibility in teacher relationships. Accordingly, it was labeled *openness* in faculty relations.

The second factor is defined by principal behavior that is characterized by the assignment of meaningless routines and burdensome duties to teachers (high restrictiveness); by rigid, close, and constant control over teachers (high directiveness); and by a lack of concern and openness for teachers and their ideas (low supportive). In general, the second factor depicts a functional rigidity and closedness in the principals' leadership behavior; hence, the second general factor was named closedness in principal behavior.

The conceptual underpinnings of the OCDQ–RE are consistent and clear. The instrument has two general factors—one a measure of openness of teacher interactions and the other a measure of openness (or closedness) of teacher-principal relations. Moreover, these two openness factors are independent. That is, it is quite possible to have open faculty interactions and closed principal ones or vice versa. Thus, theoretically, four contrasting types of school climate are possible. First, both factors can be open, producing a congruence between the principal's and teacher's behavior. Second, both factors can be closed, producing a congruence of closedness. Moreover, there are two incongruent patterns. The principal's behavior can be open with the faculty, but teachers may be closed with each other; or the principal may be closed with teachers, while the teachers are open with each other (see Figure 8.3). Table 8.4 provides a summary of the patterns of four climate prototypes. Using this information, a behavioral picture of each climate can be sketched.

Open climate.　The distinctive features of the open climate are the cooperation and respect that exist within the faculty and between the faculty and principal. This combination suggests a climate in which the principal listens and is open to teacher suggestions, gives genuine and frequent praise, and respects the professional competence of the faculty (high supportiveness). Principals also

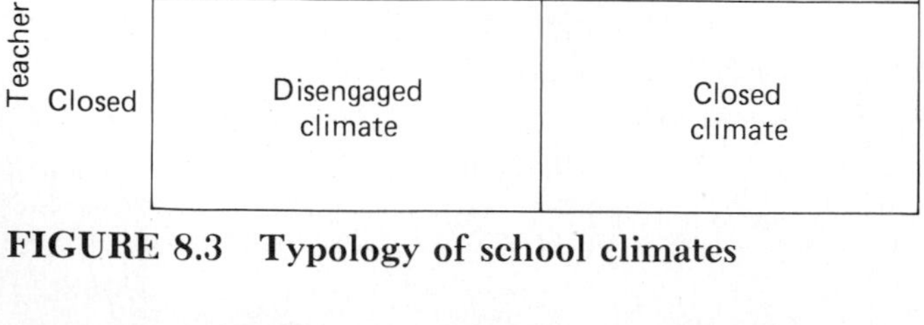

Principal behavior

	Open	Closed
Open	Open climate	Engaged climate
Closed	Disengaged climate	Closed climate

Teacher behavior

FIGURE 8.3　Typology of school climates

TABLE 8.4 Prototypic Profiles of Climate Types

Climate Dimension	Climate Type			
	Open	*Engaged*	*Disengaged*	*Closed*
Supportive	High	Low	High	Low
Directive	Low	High	Low	High
Restrictive	Low	High	Low	High
Collegial	High	High	Low	Low
Intimate	High	High	Low	Low
Disengaged	Low	Low	High	High

give their teachers freedom to perform without close scrutiny (low directiveness) and provide facilitating leadership behavior devoid of bureaucratic trivia (low restrictiveness). Similarly, teacher behavior supports open and professional interactions (high collegial relations) among the faculty. Teachers know each other well and are close personal friends (high intimacy). They cooperate and are committed to their work (low disengagement). In brief, the behavior of both the principal and the faculty is open and authentic.

Engaged climate. The engaged climate is marked, on one hand, by ineffective attempts of the principal to control, and on the other, by high professional performance of the teachers. The principal is rigid and autocratic (high directiveness) and respects neither the professional competence nor the personal needs of the faculty (low supportiveness). Moreover, the principal hinders the teachers with burdensome activities and busywork (high restrictiveness). The teachers, however, ignore the principal's behavior and conduct themselves as professionals. They respect and support each other, are proud of their colleagues, and enjoy their work (highly collegial). Moreover, the teachers not only respect each other's competence but they like each other as people (high intimacy), and they cooperate with each other as they engage in the task at hand (high engagement). In short, the teachers are productive professionals in spite of weak principal leadership; the faculty is cohesive, committed, supportive, and open.

Disengaged climate. The disengaged climate stands in stark contrast to the engaged climate. The principal's behavior is open, concerned, and supportive. The principal listens and is open to teachers (high supportiveness), gives the faculty freedom to act on their professional knowledge (low directiveness), and relieves teachers of most of the burdens of paper work and committee assignments (low restrictiveness). Nonetheless, the faculty is unwilling to accept the principal. At worst, the faculty actively works to immobilize and sabotage the principal's leadership attempts; at best, the faculty simply ignores the principal. Teachers not only do not like the principal but they neither like nor respect each other as friends (low intimacy) or as professionals (low collegial relations). The faculty is simply disengaged from the task. In sum, although the principal is supportive, concerned, flexible, facilitating, and noncontrolling (i.e., open), the faculty is divisive, intolerant, and uncommitted (i.e., closed).

Closed climate.   The closed climate is virtually the antithesis of the open climate. The principal and teachers simply appear to go through the motions, with the principal stressing routine trivia and unnecessary busywork (high restrictiveness), and the teachers responding minimally and exhibiting little commitment (high disengagement). The principal's ineffective leadership is further seen as controlling and rigid (high directiveness) as well as unsympathetic, unconcerned, and unresponsive (low supportiveness). These misguided tactics are accompanied not only by frustration and apathy but also by a general suspicion and lack of respect of teachers for each other as either friends or professionals (low intimacy and noncollegial relations). Closed climates have principals who are nonsupportive, inflexible, hindering, and controlling, and a faculty that is divisive, intolerant, apathetic, and uncommitted.

The Revised Organizational Climate Descriptive Questionnaire for Secondary Schools (OCDQ–RS) [52]

Although the original OCDQ emerged from a sample of elementary schools, the framework also is appropriate for the analysis of secondary schools. Accordingly, a thirty-four–item climate instrument was constructed to describe the behavior of secondary teachers and principals. The instrument is composed of five dimensions—two of the dimensions describe principal behavior and the other three focus on teacher behavior. Supportive behavior is characterized by genuine concern for the personal and professional welfare of the teachers, whereas directive behavior is rigid, domineering management. Although these aspects of secondary school climate are conceptually similar to those at the elementary levels, their measures are not identical. Engaged, frustrated, and intimate behaviors are the critical aspects of teacher behavior in secondary schools. Engaged behavior reflects a faculty that is not only committed to each other but also committed to their students and school. Frustrated teacher behavior describes a general pattern of interference in the school that distracts from the basic task of teaching. Intimate behavior depicts a close network of social relations among the faculty.[53] These basic aspects of administrator and teacher behaviors are elaborated and summarized and sample items for their measurement are illustrated in Table 8.5.

A factor analysis of the subtests of the OCDQ–RS yielded two underlying general factors. Supportive, directive, engaged, and frustrated behaviors defined a major first factor; intimate teacher behavior formed an independent minor factor. The first factor identifies schools that have energetic principals who lead by example, are helpful and supportive, and work toward the satisfaction of both social needs and task achievement of faculty. Teachers find the work environment facilitating—not frustrating—and they energetically engage in their teaching task optimistic about both their colleagues and their students. This first factor is remarkably similar to Halpin and Croft's conception of open-

TABLE 8.5 Dimensions of the OCDQ-RS

Principal's Behavior

Supportive principal behavior is characterized by efforts to motivate teachers by using constructive criticism and setting an example through hard work. At the same time, the principal is helpful and genuinely concerned about the personal and professional welfare of teachers.

SAMPLE ITEMS:

The principal sets an example by working hard himself/herself.

The principal uses constructive criticism.

The principal explains his/her reasons for criticism to teachers.

Directive principal behavior is rigid and domineering supervision. The principal maintains close and constant control over all teachers and school activities down to the smallest details.

SAMPLE ITEMS:

The principal rules with an iron fist.

The principal supervises teachers closely.

The principal monitors everything teachers do.

Teachers' Behavior

Engaged teacher behavior is reflected by high faculty morale. Teachers are proud of their school, enjoy working with each other, and are supportive of their colleagues. Teachers are not only concerned about each other, they are committed to their students. They are friendly with students, trust students, and are optimistic about the ability of students to succeed.

SAMPLE ITEMS:

Teachers help and support each other.

Teachers spend time after school with students who have individual problems.

Teachers are proud of their school.

Frustrated teacher behavior refers to a general pattern of interference from both administrators and colleagues that distracts from the basic task of teaching. Routine duties, administrative paperwork, and assigned non-teaching duties are excessive; moreover, teachers irritate, annoy, and interrupt each other.

SAMPLE ITEMS:

The mannerisms of teachers at this school are annoying.

Administrative paperwork is burdensome at this school.

Assigned non-teaching duties are excessive.

Intimate teacher behavior reflects a strong and cohesive network of social relationships among the faculty. Teachers know each other well, are close personal friends, and regularly socialize together.

SAMPLE ITEMS:

Teachers' closest friends are other faculty members at this school.

Teachers invite other faculty members to visit them at home.

Teachers socialize with each other on a regular basis.

ness; hence it was named openness and conceptualized along a continuum from open to closed. At the secondary school level, however, intimacy was not part of the openness cluster. That is, schools could be either open or closed and still demonstrate a high or low degree of intimacy among the faculty; thus, intimacy stood alone as a second general factor.

Open secondary principal behavior is reflected in genuine relationships with teachers where the principal creates an environment that is supportive and helpful (high supportiveness), encourages teacher initiative (low directiveness), and frees teachers from administrative trivia (low frustration) so they can concentrate on the task of teaching. In contrast, closed principal behavior is rigid, close, and nonsupportive. Open teacher behavior is characterized by sincere, positive, and supportive relationships with students, administrators, and colleagues (high engagement); teachers are committed to their school and the success of their students (high engagement); and the work environment is facilitating rather than frustrating (low frustration). In brief, openness in secondary schools refers to climates where both the teachers' and principal's behaviors are authentic, energetic, goal-directed, and supportive, and in which satisfaction is derived from both task accomplishment and need gratification.

Since the four subtests of the OCDQ–RS all load strongly on the openness factor, it is possible to create an index of the degree of openness of the climate of secondary schools. Scores for each subtest should be standardized and then substituted in the following equation:

$$\text{Openness Index} =$$
$$[\text{supportive} + \text{engaged scores}] - [\text{directive} + \text{frustrated scores}]$$

OCDQ: some research findings.　The revised versions of the OCDQ are recent developments; consequently, there is little empirical study of the relationships between those measures and other school variables. We do know, however, that the openness index from the original OCDQ is highly correlated with the new and refined subtests that measure openness. Thus, it is expected that results from earlier studies will be in large part replicated and refined with the new measures.

Those earlier OCDQ studies demonstrated that the openness of a school's climate was related to the emotional tone of the school in predictable ways. Schools with open climates have less sense of student alienation toward the school and its personnel than those with closed climates.[54] As one might also suspect, studies that examine relationships between characteristics of the principal and the climate of the school often indicate that, in comparison with closed schools, open schools have stronger principals who are more confident, self-secure, cheerful, sociable, and resourceful.[55] Moreover, the teachers who work under principals in open schools express greater confidence in their own and the school's effectiveness.[56] Finally, such principals have more loyal and satisfied teachers.[57]

In conclusion, the OCDQ–RE and OCDQ–RS seem to be useful devices for general charting of school climate in terms of teacher-teacher and teacher-principal relationships. The subtests of each instrument seem to be valid and reliable measures of important aspects of school climate; they can provide climate profiles that can be used for research, evaluation, in-service, or self-analysis. In addition, the openness indices provide means of examining school along an open-closed continuum. Halpin and Croft suggest that openness might be a better criterion of a school's effectiveness than many that have entered the field of educational administration and masquerade as criteria.[58] Although there is much argument about what constitutes school effectiveness (see Chapter 12), there is less doubt that the OCDQ measures provide a useful battery of scales for diagnostic as well as prescriptive purposes.

Organizational Dynamics: Healthy to Unhealthy

The organizational health of a school is another framework for conceptualizing the general atmosphere of a school.[59] The idea of positive health in an organization is not new and calls attention to conditions that facilitate growth and development as well as to those that impede healthy organizational dynamics.[60]

Matthew Miles defines a healthy organization as one that "not only survives in its environment, but continues to cope adequately over the long haul, and continuously develops and extends its surviving and coping abilities."[61] Implicit in this definition is the notion that healthy organizations deal successfully with disruptive outside forces while effectively directing their energies toward the major goals and objectives of the organization. Operations on a given day may be effective or ineffective, but the long-term prognosis is favorable in healthy organizations.

All social systems, if they are to grow and develop, must satisfy the four basic problems of adaptation, goal attainment, integration, and latency.[62] In other words, organizations must successfully solve (1) the problem of acquiring sufficient resources and accommodating to their environments, (2) the problem of setting and implementing goals, (3) the problem of maintaining solidarity within the system, and (4) the problem of creating and preserving the unique values of the system. Thus, the organization must be concerned with the instrumental needs of adaptation and goal achievements as well as the expressive needs of social and normative integration; in fact, it is postulated that healthy organizations effectively meet both sets of needs. As noted earlier in Chapter 2, Talcott Parsons also suggests that formal organizations such as schools exhibit three distinct levels of responsibility and control over these needs—the technical, managerial, and institutional levels.[63]

The technical level produces the product. In schools, the technical function is the teaching-learning process, and teachers are directly responsible. Educated students are the product of schools, and the entire technical subsystem revolves around the problems associated with effective learning and teaching.

The managerial level mediates and controls the internal efforts of the organization. The administrative process is the managerial function, a process that is qualitatively different from teaching. Principals are the prime administrative officers in schools. They must find ways to develop teacher loyalty and trust, motivate teacher effort, and coordinate the work. The administration controls and services the technical subsystem in two important ways: first, it mediates between the teachers and those receiving the services—students and parents; and second, it procures the necessary resources for effective teaching. Thus, teacher needs are a basic concern of the administration.

The institutional level connects the organization with its environment. It is important for schools to have legitimacy and backing in the community. Administrators and teachers need support to perform their respective functions in a harmonious fashion without undue pressure and interference from individuals and groups outside the school.

This Parsonian framework provides an integrative scheme for conceptualizing and measuring the organizational health of a school. Specifically, *a healthy organization is one in which the technical, managerial, and institutional levels are in harmony. The organization is meeting both its instrumental and expressive needs; and is successfully coping with disruptive outside forces as it directs its energies toward its mission.*

Organizational health inventory (OHI). The organizational health of secondary schools is defined by seven specific interaction patterns in schools. These critical components meet both the instrumental and expressive needs of the social system as well as represent the three levels of responsibility and control within the school.

The institutional level is examined in terms of the school's integrity. That is, institutional integrity is the school's ability to adapt to its environment and cope in ways that maintain the soundness of its educational programs. Schools with integrity are protected from unreasonable community and parental demands.

Four key aspects of the managerial level are considered—principal influence, consideration, initiating structure, and resource support. Influence is the ability of the principal to affect the decisions of superiors. Consideration is principal behavior that is open, friendly, and supportive, while initiating structure is behavior in which the principal clearly defines the work expectations, standards of performance, and procedures. Finally, resource support is the extent to which the principal provides teachers with all materials and supplies that are needed and requested.

Morale and academic emphasis are the two key elements of the technical level. Morale is the trust, enthusiasm, confidence, and sense of accomplishment that pervades the faculty. Academic emphasis, on the other hand, is the school's press for student achievement. These seven dimensions of organizational health are summarized by level of responsibility and functional need in Table 8.6. The OHI is a forty-four–item descriptive questionnaire composed of seven subtests to measure each of the basic dimensions of organizational health. Like the OCDQ, the OHI is administered to the professional staff of the school. Teachers are asked to describe the extent to which each item characterizes their school along a four-point scale: rarely occurs, sometimes occurs, often occurs, and very frequently occurs. Sample items of the OHI, grouped by subtest, also are listed in Table 8.6.[64]

Factor analytic techniques were used to develop and refine the OHI. The factor structure of the instrument and the reliability of each of the seven subtests were confirmed by factor analysis in a sample of seventy-eight secondary schools. School scores were standardized with a mean of 50 and a standard

TABLE 8.6 Dimensions of Organizational Health

Institutional Level

Institutional Integrity describes a school that has integrity in its education program. The school is not vulnerable to narrow, vested interests from community and parental demands. The school is able to cope successfully with destructive, outside forces (Instrumental Need).

SAMPLE ITEMS:

Teachers are protected from unreasonable community and parental demands.

The school is vulnerable to outside pressures.*

Select citizen groups are influential with the board.*

Managerial Level

Principal Influence refers to the principal's ability to affect the action of superiors. The influential principal is persuasive, works effectively with the superintendent, but simultaneously demonstrates independence in thought and action (Instrumental Need).

SAMPLE ITEMS:

The principal gets what he/she ask for from superiors.

The principal is able to work well with the superintendent.

The principal is impeded by superiors.*

Consideration refers to behavior by the principal that is friendly, supportive, open, and collegial (Expressive Need).

SAMPLE ITEMS:

The principal is friendly and approachable.

The principal puts suggestions made by the faculty into operation.

The principal looks out for the personal welfare of faculty members.

Initiating Structure refers to behavior by the principal that is task and achievement oriented. The principal makes his/her attitudes and expectations clear to the faculty and maintains definite standards of performance (Instrumental Need).

SAMPLE ITEMS:

The principal lets faculty members know what is expected of them.

The principal maintains definite standards of performance.

The principal schedules the work to be done.

Resource Support refers to a school where adequate classroom supplies and instructional materials are available, and extra materials are easily obtained (Instrumental Need).

SAMPLE ITEMS:

Extra materials are available if requested.

Teachers are provided with adequate materials for their classrooms.

Teachers have access to needed instructional materials.

Technical Level

Morale refers to a sense of trust, confidence, enthusiasm, and friendliness that is exhibited among teachers. Teachers feel good about each other and, at the same time, feel a sense of accomplishment from their jobs (Expressive Need).

SAMPLE ITEMS:

Teachers in this school like each other.

Teachers accomplish their jobs with enthusiasm.

The morale of teachers is high.

Academic Emphasis refers to the school's press for achievement. High but achievable academic goals are set for students; the learning environment is orderly

TABLE 8.6 *(Continued)*

and serious; teachers believe in their student's ability to achieve; and students work hard and respect those who do well academically (Instrumental Need).

  SAMPLE ITEMS:

  The school sets high standards for academic performance.

  Students respect others who get good grades.

  Students try hard to improve on previous work.

*Score is reversed.

deviation of 10. Profiles for three schools are graphed in Figure 8.4. School A represents a school with a relatively healthy climate: all dimensions of health are substantially above the mean. School C, in contrast, is below the mean in all aspects of health; and School B is a typical school—about average on all dimensions.

The subtests of the OHI are modestly correlated with each other, that is, if a school scores high on one subtest, there is some tendency to score higher on some of the other subtests. Furthermore, factor analysis of the subtest demonstrated that one general factor explains most of the variation among the subtests: a factor called school health. The seventy-eight secondary schools in

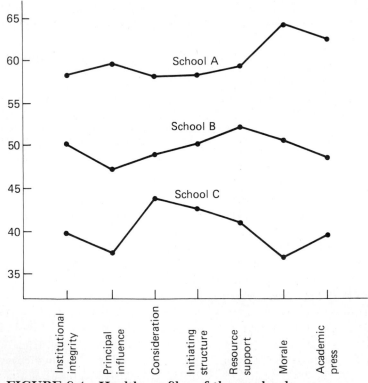

FIGURE 8.4   Health profiles of three schools

the sample arrayed themselves along a continuum with a few schools having profiles of very healthy organizations, a few very unhealthy profiles, and most schools with somewhat mixed profiles in between the extremes. An index of health can be developed simply by summing the standard scores of the seven subtests; the higher the sum, the healthier the school dynamics. It is possible to sketch the behavioral picture for each of the poles of the continuum, that is, the prototypes for very healthy and unhealthy school climates.

Healthy school.   The healthy school is protected from unreasonable community and parental pressures. The board successfully resists all narrow efforts of vested interest groups to influence policy. The principal of a healthy school provides dynamic leadership, leadership that is both task-oriented and relations-oriented. Such behavior is supportive of teachers and yet provides direction and maintains high standards of performance. Moreover, the principal has influence with his or her superiors as well as the ability to exercise independent thought and action. Teachers in a healthy school are committed to teaching and learning. They set high but achievable goals for students; they maintain high standards of performance; and the learning environment is orderly and serious. Furthermore, students work hard on academic matters, are highly motivated, and respect other students who achieve academically. Classroom supplies and instructional materials are accessible. Finally, in a healthy school, teachers like each other, trust each other, are enthusiastic about the work, and are proud of their school.

Unhealthy school.   The unhealthy school is vulnerable to destructive outside forces. Teachers and administrators are bombarded with unreasonable demands from parental and community groups. The school is buffeted by the whims of the public. The principal does not provide leadership: there is little direction, limited consideration and support for teachers, and virtually no influence with superiors. Morale of teachers is low. Teachers feel good neither about each other nor their job. They act aloof, suspicious, and defensive. Finally, the press for academic excellence is limited. Everyone is simply "putting in time."

OHI: some implications.   The OHI is a new instrument, and research using it is limited. Yet, the OHI is a useful tool. It reliably measures seven key dimensions of organizational health of schools. Moreover, its conceptual underpinnings are consistent with many of the characteristics of the effective schools literature: an orderly and serious environment, high and attainable student goals, visible rewards for academic achievement, a cohesive unit based on mutual trust, and dynamic principal leadership, that is, influential principals who blend their behavior to fit the situation.

The preliminary research findings using the OHI are also encouraging. As one would expect, the healthier the organizational dynamics, the greater the degree of faculty trust in the principal, trust in colleagues, and trust in the organization itself. Not surprisingly too, there is a correlation between the openness and health of schools; healthy schools have high thrust, high esprit, and low disengagement. In brief, open schools tend to be healthy and healthy schools tend to be open. Finally, it is hypothesized that a school's health will be significantly related to less student alienation, lower dropout rates, and higher student commitment.

Pupil-Control Orientation: Custodial to Humanistic

Another way to conceptualize the social climate of the school is in terms of dominant control patterns that teachers and principals use to control students. Willard Waller, in one of the first systematic studies of the school as a social system, called attention to the importance of pupil control with regard to both structural and normative aspects of the school culture.[65] In fact, most studies that have focused on the school as a social system have described antagonistic student subculture and attendant conflict and pupil problems.[66] Donald J. Willower and Ronald G. Jones have described pupil control as the "dominant motif" within the school social system, the integrative theme that gives meaning to patterns of teacher-teacher and teacher-principal relations.[67]

Control is a problem that all organizations face.[68] Richard O. Carlson's analysis of the relationship of a client to a service organization indicates that public schools are the type of service organization in which control is likely to be the most acute problem (see Chapter 2). Public schools, along with prisons and public mental hospitals, are service organizations that have no choice in the selection of clients, and the clients must (in the legal sense) participate in the organization.[69] These organizations are confronted with clients who may have little or no desire for the services of the organization, a factor that accentuates the problem of client control.

Both empirical and conceptual considerations lead to the same conclusion —pupil control is a central aspect of school life. Given its saliency, the concept can be used to distinguish among school climates. The conceptualization of pupil control and research initiated by Donald J. Willower, Terry I. Eidell, and Wayne K. Hoy at the Pennsylvania State University provide the basis for such a perspective.[70]

The Penn State researchers postulated pupil-control continuum from custodial to humanistic. These terms refer to contrasting types of individual ideology and the corresponding types of school organizations that they seek to rationalize and justify. The concern here is primarily with the latter, that is, the social beliefs component of climate. Thus, pupil-control ideology is how school officials view the students. Prototypes or composite descriptions of schools with humanistic and custodial pupil-control orientations will now be briefly presented.[71]

The Custodial school.   The model for the *custodial orientation* is the traditional school, which provides a rigid and highly controlled setting in which maintenance of order is primary. Students are stereotyped in terms of their appearance, behavior, and parents' social status. Teachers who hold a custodial orientation conceive of the school as an autocratic organization with a rigid pupil-teacher status hierarchy. The flow of power and communication is unilateral and downward; students must accept the decisions of their teachers without question. Teachers do not attempt to understand student behavior but instead view misbehavior as a personal affront. They perceive students as irresponsible and undisciplined persons who must be controlled through punitive sanctions. Impersonality, cynicism, and watchful mistrust pervade the atmosphere of the custodial school.

The humanistic school. The model for the *humanistic orientation* is the school conceived of as an educational community in which students learn through cooperative interaction and experience. Learning and behavior are viewed in psychological and sociological terms. Self-discipline is substituted for strict teacher control. A humanistic orientation leads to a democratic atmosphere with open channels of two-way communication between pupils and teachers and increased self-determination. The term "humanistic orientation" is used in the sociopsychological sense suggested by Erich Fromm;[72] it stresses both the importance of the individual and the creation of an atmosphere that meets student needs.

The pupil-control ideology form (PCI). In order to operationalize the concept the pupil-control orientation along the custodial-humanistic continuum, the pupil-control ideology form was developed.[73] The PCI form is a twenty-item Likert-type scale with five response categories for each item, ranging from "strongly agree" to "strongly disagree." A sample of specific items of the PCI form are contained in Table 8.7.

Reliability coefficients of the PCI instrument have been consistently high, ranging in the high 0.80s and 0.90s.[74] Similarly, construct validity has been supported in numerous studies.[75] The pupil-control orientation can be measured by pooling the individual ideologies of the professional staff of the school; this represents an estimate of the modal orientation of the school and provides

TABLE 8.7   Selected Items from the Pupil-Control Ideology Questionnaire

Following are some statements about school, teachers, and pupils. Please indicate your personal opinion about statement by writing the appropriate response at the right of each statement.

SA-Strongly agree; A-Agree; U-Undecided; D-Disagree; SD-Strongly disagree

1. It is desirable to require pupils to sit in assigned seats during assemblies.
2. Directing sarcastic remarks toward a defiant pupil is a good disciplinary technique.
3. Teachers should consider revision of their teaching methods if these are criticized by their pupils.
4. Pupils should not be permitted to contradict the statements of a teacher in class.
5. Too much pupil time is spent on guidance and activities and too little on academic preparation.

Source: Donald J. Willower, Terry I. Eidell, and Wayne K. Hoy, *The School and Pupil Control Ideology,* Penn State Studies No. 24. Copyright The Pennsylvania State University Press 1967. By permission of the publisher.

an index of the degree of custodialism (or humanism) in pupil-control orientation of the school.[76]

Pupil-control orientation as a climate measure.   The PCI instrument does not provide the complex measure of either OCDQ or OHI. Yet the concept of pupil control and its measurement allows another view of the school climate, one that focuses on teacher-student relations rather than principal-teacher relations. Perhaps the PCI is a better measure of culture than climate because it deals directly with shared ideologies rather than shared perceptions of behavior. At any rate, the concept of pupil-control ideology has proved to be a powerful predictor of the tone or feeling of the school. Appleberry and Hoy found that humanism in the pupil-control orientation schools and the openness of the organizational climate of the school are strongly correlated ($r = 0.61$).[77]

Furthermore, in order to test the usefulness of the custodial-humanistic framework as an index of school tone or climate, Hoy and Appleberry used the OCDQ variables to compare the most humanistic schools and the most custodial schools in terms of their climate profiles.[78] Schools with a custodial, pupil-control orientation had significantly greater disengagement, less esprit, more aloofness, and less thrust than those with a humanistic, pupil-control orientation. In other words, humanistic schools seem more likely than custodial schools to have: (1) teachers who work well together with respect to the teaching-learning task; (2) teachers who have high morale and are satisfied because of their sense of task accomplishment and fulfillment of social needs; (3) principals who deal with teachers in an informal, face-to-face situation rather than "go by the book"; (4) principals who do not supervise closely but instead motivate through personal example; and (5) a climate marked by openness, acceptance, and authenticity. The concepts of humanism in pupil-control orientation and openness of norms, although different elements of school climate, seem to be highly compatible.

In brief, pupil-control orientation not only provides important information about pupil-teacher relations but also suggests a great deal about the nature of teacher-teacher and teacher-principal relations. Given the importance of pupil control, the custodial-humanistic framework provides a general picture of the school's character, one that can yield a number of general predictions about the nature of the school in a host of important areas. The custodial-humanistic framework also can be used to generate several hypotheses. For example: (1) Custodial schools will have more alienated students than humanistic schools. (2) Custodial schools will have more goal displacement than humanistic schools. (3) Custodial schools will have less open communication both horizontally and vertically than humanistic schools. (4) Formal leadership patterns will be accepted more readily in humanistic than in custodial schools.

Although these propositions are meant to be only illustrations of the usefulness of the framework, the first hypothesis has actual been the basis of a comprehensive study of alienation of 8,600 high school students in 45 schools.[79] Using the PCI, Wayne Hoy examined the relationship between custodial schools and student sense of alienation.[80] The results of the study provided qualified support for the general hypothesis guiding the investigation; namely, the more custodial and closed the school climate, the greater the student sense of alienation. Custodial schools had students who had a greater sense of powerlessness and normlessness than students from humanistic schools; however, such was not the case with student sense of meaninglessness. Meaninglessness is the sensed inability of students to predict future outcomes. Apparently, custodial schools provide structure and direction. The fact that events are predictable, even if they are alienating in other terms, may mitigate against a sense of meaninglessness developing in schools.[81] Alternatively, one might speculate that in response to the threat and general alienation produced by custodialism, the strength and significance of the student subculture may be enhanced, thereby providing social support and cohesion among students and facilitating meaningful activity in the student subculture.

Self-actualization is the other side of the alienation coin. Students are engaged in the ongoing process of growing to their full potential in terms of creative expression, interpersonal effectiveness, and self-fulfillment. Does the school climate influence such development? John Deibert and Wayne Hoy explored this question in a comprehensive study involving more than 4,000 students in forty high schools.[82] As predicted, the humanistic school, not the custodial, provided a healthy social climate for the development of a mature self-image for students; the more humanistic the pupil-control orientation of the school, the greater the chance that high-school seniors were moving toward self-actualization (r = .43). Moreover, Frederick Lunenburg found that student perceptions of a humanistic school climate were positively related to their motivation, task orientation, problem solving, and a seriousness to learn.[83]

Several other studies also have underscored the atmosphere of the school and the student's sense of involvement and identification with the school as important factors in the student's educational growth and development.[84] That evidence suggests a need for public high schools that are less custodial, more humanistic, and more open in climate. Changes in that direction are more easily described than made, and inevitably, they are slow in coming and often unsuccessful; nevertheless, the effort should be made.

ORGANIZATIONAL CULTURE

The notion of organizational culture has resurfaced as a vehicle for understanding the meaning and basic character of organizational life.[85] As we have seen, concern for the culture of the work group is not new. In the 1930s and 1940s, both Elton Mayo and Chester Barnard were stressing the importance of work-group norms, sentiments, values, and emergent interactions in the workplace as they described the nature and functions of informal organization.[86] Likewise Philip Selznick underscored the significance of viewing organizations as institutions rather than merely rational organizations. Institutions, according to Selznick, are "infused with value beyond the technical requirements at hand." This infusion of value produces *a distinctive identity* for the organization. Selznick continues:

> Whenever individuals become attached to an organization or a way of doing things as persons rather than technicians, the result is apprizing of the device for its own sake. From the standpoint of the committed person, the organization is changed from an expendable tool into a valued source of personal satisfaction. . . . Where institutionalization is well advanced, distinctive outlooks, habits, and other commitments are unified, coloring all aspects of organizational life and lending it a social integration that goes well beyond formal co-ordination and command.[87]

Organizational culture is another attempt to get at the feel, sense, atmosphere, character, or image of an organization. It encompasses many of the earlier notions of informal organization, norms, values, ideologies, and emergent systems. What distinguishes the contemporary formulation—as culture—is its anthropological basis.[88] Meryl Reis Louis explains:

> The question is not for strictly psychological or sociological components of the phenomenon, as was the case in the past. Rather, the uniquely integrative and phenomenological core of the subject, in which the interweaving of individuals into a community takes place, has finally become the subject of investigation among social scientists.[89]

The popularity of the term organizational culture is in large part a function of a number of recent popular books on successful business corporations.[90] The basic theme of all these analyses is that effective organizations have strong and distinctive corporate cultures and that a basic function of executive leadership is to shape the culture of the organization.

Definition

The notion of culture brings with it conceptual complexity and confusion. No intact definition for culture from anthropology exists; instead, we find numerous, diverse definitions. It should not be surprising, therefore, that there are many definitions of organizational culture. For example, William Ouchi defines organizational culture as "symbols, ceremonies, and myths that communicate the underlying values and beliefs of that organization to its employees."[91] Jay Lorsch, on the other hand, uses culture to mean "the beliefs top managers in a company share about how they should manage themselves and other employees and how they should conduct their business."[92] Alan Wilkins and Kerry Patterson maintain that, "an organization's culture consists largely of what people believe about what works and what does not,"[93] while Joanne Martin argues that "culture is an expression of people's deepest needs, a means of endowing their experiences with meaning."[94] Howard Schwartz and Stanley

Davis regard culture as "a pattern of beliefs and expectations shared by the organization's members" that produces "norms that powerfully shape the behavior of individuals and groups in organization."[95] But Edgar Schein argues that the culture should be reserved for "the deeper level of *basic assumptions and beliefs* that are shared by members of an organization, that operate unconsciously, and that define in a basic 'taken-for-granted' fashion an organization's view of itself and its environment."[96]

Organizational culture, then, is typically defined in terms of shared orientations that hold the unit together and give it a distinctive identity. But substantial disagreement arises about what is shared—norms, values, philosophies, perspectives, beliefs, expectations, attitudes, myths, or ceremonies. Another problem is determining the intensity of shared orientations of organizational members. Do organizations have a basic culture or many cultures? Moreover, there is disagreement on the extent to which organizational culture is conscious and overt or unconscious and covert.

Although the definitions of climate and culture are blurred, one suggested difference is that culture consists of shared assumptions, values, or norms, while climate is defined by shared perceptions of behavior.[97] To be sure, there is not a large conceptual step from shared assumptions (culture) to shared perceptions (climate), but the difference is real and may be meaningful.

Levels of Culture

One way to begin to untangle some of the problems of definition is to view culture at different levels. As illustrated in Figure 8.5, culture is manifest in norms, shared values, and basic assumptions, each occurring at a different level of depth.[98]

Culture as Tacit Assumptions. [99] At its deepest level, culture is the collective manifestation of tacit assumptions. When members of an organization share a view of the world around them and their place in that world, culture exists. That is, a pattern of basic assumptions has been invented, discovered, or developed by the organization as it learned to cope with its problems of external adaptation and internal integration. This pattern has worked well enough to be considered valid and it is taught to new members as the correct way to perceive, think, and feel in relation to those problems.[100] Since the assumptions have worked repeatedly, they have become so basic that they are taken for granted, tend to be nonconfrontable and nondebatable, and thus, are highly resistant to change. From this perspective, the key to understanding organizational culture is to decipher the tacit assumptions shared by members and to discover how these assumptions fit together into a cultural pattern or paradigm.[101]

Tacit assumptions, as shown in Figure 8.5, are abstract premises about the nature of human relationships, human nature, truth, reality, and environment. For example, is human nature basically good, evil, or neutral? How is truth ultimately determined—is it revealed or discovered? What are the assumed relationships among members of the group—primarily hierarchical, collateral, or individualistic? Five categories of cultural assumptions have emerged from

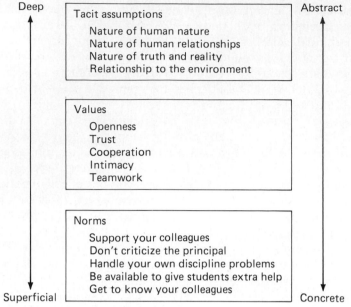

FIGURE 8.5   Levels of culture

the research and provide a framework for analysis (see Table 8.8). The categories are useful because it has been demonstrated that they can be used to build coherent patterns of core organizational beliefs.[102] When organizations develop consistent and articulate patterns of basic assumptions, they have strong cultures.

Schein gives examples of two strong but contrasting cultures. Company *A* has a strong, distinctive culture based on the following assumptions:

1. Truth ultimately comes from individuals.
2. Individuals are responsible, motivated, and capable of governing themselves.
3. Truth is ultimately determined through debate, which necessitates much conflict and testing of ideas in group meetings.
4. Members of an organization are a family; they accept, respect, and take care of each other.

These core assumptions give rise to such shared values as individualism, autonomy, openness, and authority of knowledge. In contrast, Company *B* is guided by the following assumptions:

1. Truth ultimately comes from older, wiser, better-educated, and more experienced participants.
2. Participants are capable and willing to give commitment and loyalty to the organization (to be good "soldiers").

3. Relationships are basically hierarchial.
4. Each member has a niche that is his or her territory that cannot be invaded.
5. Members of the organization are a family who take care of each other.[103]

Here the core assumptions produce such values as respect for authority, respect for territory, and conflict avoidance.

Using this broad perspective of culture, at a minimum, each of the five categories of assumptions described in Table 8.8 should be examined to determine whether there is a consistent pattern of consensus. Then a judgment can be made on whether there is a strong or weak culture, or culture conflict among several groups.

There is no simple way to uncover the basic patterns of assumptions that underlie what people value and do. Schein develops an elaborate set of procedures to decipher the culture of an organization.[104] It is an approach that combines anthropological and clinical techniques and involves a series of encounters and joint explorations between the investigator and various motivated informants who live in the organization and embody its culture. Joint effort usually involves extensive data-gathering activities that explore the history of the organization, critical events, organizational structure, myths, legends, stories, and ceremonies. Questionnaires are eschewed as devices to identify tacit assumptions; at best, it is argued, such instruments produce only some of the espoused values of group members.

Culture as Shared Values.   Values are shared conceptions of what is desirable. They are reflections of the underlying assumptions of culture, and lie at the next

---

TABLE 8.8   Categories of Cultural Assumptions

1. *The Nature of Relationships:* Are relationships between members of the organization assumed to be primarily lineal (i.e., hierarchical), collateral (i.e., group oriented), or individualistic in nature?
2. *Human Nature:* Are human beings considered to be basically good, basically evil, or neither good nor evil?
3. *The Nature of Truth:* Is "truth" (i.e., correct decisions) revealed by external authority figures, or is it determined by a process of personal investigation and testing?
4. *The Environment:* Is there a basic belief that human beings can master the environment, or that they must be subjugated by the environment, or that they should attempt to harmonize with the environment?
5. *Universalism/Particularism:* Should all members of the organization be evaluated by the same standards, or should certain individuals be given preferential treatment?

Source: W. Gibb Dyer, Jr. "The Cycle of Cultural Evolution in Organizations," in Ralph H. Kilmann, Mary J. Saxton, Roy Serpa, and associates, *Gaining Control of the Corporate Culture* (San Francisco: Jossey-Bass, 1985), p. 205.

lower level of analysis. Values often define what members should do to be successful in the organization. When we ask people to explain why they behave the way they do, we may begin to get at the core of values of the organization. Shared values define the basic character of the organization and give the organization a sense of identity. If members know what their organization stands for, if they know what standards they should uphold, then they are more likely to make decisions that will support those standards. They are also more likely to feel part of the organization and to feel that organizational life has important meaning.[105]

William Ouchi's book on the success of Japanese corporations was one of the first of the contemporary analyses of corporate culture.[106] Ouchi argued that the success of effective corporations in both Japan and America was a function of a distinctive corporate culture, one that was internally consistent and characterized by the shared values of intimacy, trust, cooperation, teamwork, and egalitarianism. Success of these organizations was not so much a matter of technology as it was of managing people. He labeled the American organizations with these values Theory Z cultures.

Theory Z organizations have a number of properties that promote this distinctive culture (see Figure 8.6). Long-term employment opportunities create in employees a sense of security and commitment to the organization; participants become invested in the organization. The process of slower rates of promotion creates more opportunities for broadening experiences and diverse career paths as employees perform different functions and occupy different roles. This effectively produces company-specific skills and promotes career development. Participative and consensual decision making demands cooperation and teamwork, values that are openly communicated and reinforced. Individual responsibility for collective decision making demands an atmosphere of trust and mutual support. Finally, concern for the total person is a natural part of the working relationship, which tends to be informal and emphasizes the whole person and not just the individual's work role. This holistic perspective promotes a strong egalitarian atmosphere, a community of equals who work cooperatively on common goals rather than relying on the formal hierarchy. Thus, Theory Z organizations are structured and operate to promote the values of intimacy, trust, cooperation, and egalitarianism. These basic values of the culture influence every aspect of organizational life.

Several other studies of successful corporations also suggest the pivotal importance of strong organizational cultures in fostering effectiveness.[107] Thomas J. Peters and Robert H. Waterman found that excellent companies were brilliant on the basics: "Tools didn't substitute for thinking. Intellect didn't overpower wisdom. Analysis didn't impede action. Rather these companies worked hard to keep things simple in a complex world."[108] Effective companies persisted and thrived because they had strong cultures. The shared values of those cultures included the following:

1. a bias for action (Planning is not a substitute for action.)
2. a client orientation (Serve your customers.)

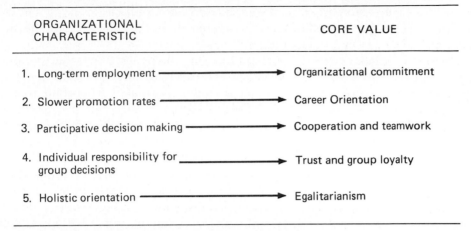

ORGANIZATIONAL CHARACTERISTIC	CORE VALUE
1. Long-term employment	Organizational commitment
2. Slower promotion rates	Career Orientation
3. Participative decision making	Cooperation and teamwork
4. Individual responsibility for group decisions	Trust and group loyalty
5. Holistic orientation	Egalitarianism

FIGURE 8.6 **Theory Z organization and culture**

    3. an innovative orientation (Respect autonomy and entrepreneurship.)
    4. a people orientation (Productivity comes through people.)
    5. an achievement orientation (High-quality products are essential.)

These beliefs and values were held intensely and guided organizational behavior.

What are the values that hold a school together? Schools are for students; experiment with your teaching; teaching and learning are cooperative processes; stay close to your students; strive for academic excellence; demand high but realistic performance; be open in behavior and communication; trust your colleagues; and be professional. Are these core values or empty slogans? If they capture something in which teachers strongly believe, and if they are widely shared, these slogan-like themes define a set of core organizational values.

It is not difficult to use the research findings from corporate cultures and develop an ideal school culture, but the question of effective school cultures is ultimately an empirical one. Unfortunately, little research directly addresses the institutional cultures of effective public schools in terms of basic beliefs and values. William Firestone and Bruce Wilson, however, provide a useful framework for beginning to study the culture of schools.[109] They suggest that the analysis of school culture can be addressed by studying its content, the expressions of culture, and primary communication patterns.

The symbols through which culture is expressed often help identify important cultural themes.[110] Three symbol systems communicate the contents of a school's culture: stories, icons, and rituals. Stories are narratives that are based on true events, but they often combine truth and fiction. Some stories are myths; that is, they communicate an unquestioned belief that can not be demonstrated by the facts. Other stories are legends that are retold and embellished with fictional details. The true event takes on special meaning as they are interpreted and embellished in the school setting. Often stories are about organizational heroes who epitomize the organization; they provide insight into the core values of the organization.[111]

Icons and rituals are also important. Icons are physical artifacts that are used to communicate culture (logos, mottoes, and trophies), and rituals are the routine ceremonies that provide visible examples of what is important in the organization. Much of the culture of a school can be constructed from artifacts, rites, rituals, and ceremonies related to assemblies, faculty meetings, athletic contests, community activities, cafeterias, report cards, awards and trophies, lesson plans, and the general decor of the school.[112]

The examination of the informal communication system is also important in the cultural analysis of the school. The communication system is a cultural network itself. Storytellers, spies, priests, cabals, and whisperers form a hidden hierarchy of power within the school which communicates the basic values of the organization.[113]

Although a framework for examining school culture in terms of the shared values, beliefs, and ideologies is available, the determination of culture at this level of analysis is not easy. The core values of a group or school may be easier to determine than the tacit assumptions, but the analysis remains difficult and time-consuming. Anthropological analyses of the schools are imperative if we are to begin to map the culture of schools.

Culture as Shared Norms.   In stark contrast to the abstract conception of culture as a set of tacit assumptions, or even as shared values, a more concrete perspective on culture emerges when behavioral norms are used as the basic elements of culture (see Figure 8.5). Norms are usually unwritten and informal expectations that occur just below the surface of experience. Norms directly influence behavior. They are much more visible than either values or tacit assumptions; consequently, they provide a more concrete means for helping people understand the cultural aspects of organizational life. Moreover, as the basic building blocks of cultures, if we are concerned with changing organizational behavior, then it is important to know and understand the norms of that culture. As Allen and Kraft cogently note:

> Norms are a universal phenomena. They are necessary, tenacious, but also extremely malleable. Because they can change so quickly and easily, they present a tremendous opportunity to people interested in change. Any group, no matter its size, once it understands itself as a cultural entity, can plan its own norms, creating positive ones that will help it reach its goals and modifying or discarding the negative ones.[114]

Norms are also communicated to participants by stories and ceremonies that provide visible and potent examples of what the organization stands for. Sometimes stories about people are created to reinforce the basic norms of the organization. The principal who stood by the teacher despite overwhelming pressure from parents and superiors becomes a symbol of the cohesiveness and loyalty in a school's culture; it is a story that is retold many times to new teachers. Teachers quickly learn, "don't tell tales out of school," "support your colleagues," and "support your principal." Norms determine the ways people dress and talk; the way participants respond to authority, conflict, and pressure; and the way people balance self-interests with organizational interests. Examples of norms include the following: don't rock the boat; don't criticize fellow teachers to students or parents; all men wear neckties; handle your own discipline problems; don't let students out of class before the bell rings; and change the bulletin boards frequently. Norms are enforced by sanctions; people are rewarded and encouraged when they conform to norms, and confronted, ostracized, or punished when they violate the cultural norms of the group.

Most organizational members can list the norms that operate in their work group and even suggest new norms that would be more effective for improving productivity or morale.[115] A number of ways can be used to surface actual norms, but participants are usually reluctant to specify norms *unless* they are confident that the information will not be used against them or the organization. Thus, anonymity and confidentiality of respondents are crucial in identifying the salient norms in an organization.

Kilmann has successfully used small groups in workshop settings to elicit norms.[116] He suggests that with just a little prodding and a few illustrations to get the group started, members quickly begin to enumerate many norms; in fact, they revel in being able to articulate what beforehand was not formally stated and rarely discussed in conversation.[117]

Prevailing norms map the "way things are" around the organization. Indeed, norm statements often begin with "around here." For example, "Around here, it is all right to admit mistakes, as long as you don't make them again." The key norms of an organization are usually related to such important areas as control, support, innovation, social relations, rewards, conflicts, and standard of excellence. To begin to identify the norms of a school, teachers might be asked to list their views of the school in terms of "around here" statements. For example, they are asked to complete the following statements:

1. At the end of a typical faculty meeting, everyone _____
2. Around here, the real basis for reward _____
3. Around here, control of students _____
4. Around here, decisions are reached through _____
5. Around here, risk-taking _____
6. Around here, differences in opinion are handled by _____
7. Around here, achievement standards _____
8. Around here, we handle problems by _____

Unlike tacit assumptions, norms often can be revealed by carefully constructed survey instruments. The Kilmann-Saxton Culture Gap Survey, for example, has been used to determine not only the actual norms but also the desired norms of organizations. The instrument consists of twenty-eight norm pairs in the areas of task support, task innovation, social relationships, personal freedom. An example of a norm pair from the survey is the following: *"(A)* Share information only when it benefits your own work group, versus *(B)* Share information to help the organization make better decisions."[118] Members are asked to describe both the actual norms and the desired ones. The current normative culture is then determined as well as the gap between the desired and actual norms.

Level of Analysis. The most penetrating definitions of culture emphasize the deepest level of human nature or at least refer to shared ideologies, beliefs, and values.[119] Such definitions are advocated by theorists interested in understanding culture rather than managing it. Organizational participants, however, have difficulty openly identifying their tacit assumptions or discussing their basic assumptions; in fact, they describe such exercises as merely academic.[120] At the other extreme, those definitions of culture that focus on behavioral norms are more useful to consultants and practitioners who are interested in assessing and changing organizational cultures. Organizational members seem more willing and able to identify the prevailing norms of the culture and to discuss them with minimal levels of threat and discomfort. Although the more abstract approaches to defining culture initially seem to be more penetrating, in practice they are less useful; and although the more superficial approaches seem to ignore the more fundamental bases of culture, in practice they offer some specific ways to manage culture, albeit in a very narrow way.[121] Clearly we have much to learn about culture. Therefore, at this point in the development of the concept of organizational culture it is valuable to view and study culture at *all* three levels, that is, in terms of shared norms, core values, and tacit underlying assumptions.

Typologies of Organizational Culture

We conclude our discussion of culture by examining two typologies. Each framework suggests four generic types of organizational cultures. These typologies are analytic abstractions that represent ideal types, and they provide a useful view of cultures.

Nature of transactions. A central aspect of culture involves beliefs about the appropriate nature of social transactions.[122] As people interact in an organization, they exchange such valued things as facts, ideas, permission, and affection. These transactions are governed by rules that are embedded in the implicit values and beliefs of the organization. Robert Quinn and Michael McGrath have identified four cultures based upon the dominant transactional expectations of the organization.[123] In Table 8.9, profiles of the cultures have been sketched in terms of organizational purpose, criteria of performance, the location of authority, legitimate bases of power, decision-making orientations, leadership style, compliance, evaluation, and motivation.

TABLE 8.9 Profile of Four Cultures

	Transactional Expectations or Governing Rules			
	Rational Culture	*Ideological Culture*	*Consensual Culture*	*Hierarchical Culture*
Organizational purpose	Pursuit of objectives	Broad purposes	Group maintenance	Execution of regulations
Criteria of performance	Productivity, efficiency	External support, Resource acquisition	Cohesion Morale	Stability Control
Location of authority	The boss	Charisma	Membership	Rules
Base of power	Competence	Values	Informal status	Technical knowledge
Decision making	Decisive pronouncements	Intuitive insights	Participation	Factual analysis
Leadership style	Directive, Goal oriented	Inventive, Risk orientated	Concerned, Supportive	Conservative, Cautious
Compliance	Contractual agreement	Commitment to values	Commitment from process	Surveillance and control

Source: Robert E. Quinn and Michael R. McGrath, "The Transformations of Organizational Cultures," in Peter J. Frost et. al. (eds.), *Organizational Culture* (Beverly Hills: Sage, 1985), pp. 326–327.

Some implicit beliefs about desirable end states and information processing are reflected in each culture. The *rational culture* is characterized by centralization of power, integrated activities, and an external focus that produces competition with other organizations. Efficiency, productivity, and profit or impact are the central values. Clear goals, individual judgments, and decisiveness are means that push the organization toward maximizing its performance. This culture has many features of the simple structure defined in Chapter 4.

The *developmental culture* is marked by decentralization of power. Moreover, the focus of the organization is on the external concerns of competition and growth. Its broad purposes and charismatic leadership generate commitment to the organization and its values. Insight, invention, and innovation are valued means the organization uses to compete for external support and resources in its quest for expansion and transformation. The developmental culture has many of the features of the strong, effective cultures identified by Peters and Waterman.[124]

The *consensual culture* is characterized by decentralization of power, differentiation of activities, and an internal focus on system maintenance. Transactions are based on discussion, participation, and consensus. Thus, exchanges are typically friendly and cooperative, which foster teamwork, high morale, and trust. This culture is similar to a Theory Z culture.

The *hierarchical culture* is marked by centralization of power and integrated activities as well as an internal focus concerned with maintaining the system. Behavior is driven by formal rules and the execution of regulations. Stability, control, predictability, coordination, and accountability are valued attributes. Accurate measurement, documentation, and computation are central features in an information processing system that strives toward consolidation and equilibrium. This culture typically is associated with machine bureaucracy (see Chapter 4).

These four cultures are pictured in Figure 8.7 in terms of their distribution of power and system orientation.

Human resource orientation.   Another way to classify the cultures of different organizations is by their orientations to human resources.[125] Two basic dimensions of an organization's human resource orientation are concern for people and concern for performance. *Concern for people* reflects the organization's commitment to its people, their well-being and dignity. *Concern for performance* is the organization's expectation that its participants will do the best job they are capable of doing. These two dimensions define four generic types of organizational cultures when they are cross-partitioned. The cultures are depicted in Figure 8.8 as a caring culture, apathetic culture, exacting culture, and integrative culture.

The *caring culture* exhibits high concern for the well-being of its people, but it does not impose very high standards of performance on them. This kind of culture is usually an expression of the paternalistic philosophy of the organization's founders or key leaders. As long as the competitive environment is not threatening, organizations with this culture perform smoothly because of employees' ready compliance with organization's leaders, and they survive and

Distribution of power / Orientation of the system	Internal	External
Decentralization	Consensual culture	Developmental culture
Centralization	Hierarchical culture	Rational culture

FIGURE 8.7 Typology of cultures based on social transactions

Concern for people / Concern for performance	Low	High
High	Caring culture	Integrative culture
Low	Apathetic culture	Exacting culture

FIGURE 8.8 Typology of cultures based on human resource orientation

SOURCE: Adapted from Nirmal K. Sethia and Mary Ann Glinow, "Arriving at Four Cultures by Managing the Reward Systems," in Ralph Kilmann et al. (eds.), *Gaining Control of the Corporate Culture* (San Francisco: Jossey-Bass), p. 104

prosper because of loyalty and steadfastness of their people.[126] Although employees are expected to make reasonable efforts in their daily work, teamwork, cooperation, conformity, and compliance to guidance from supervisors are values that are rewarded; in fact, they are even more important than performance. For example, at J. C. Penney, "a store manager once was severely rebuked by the company's president for making too much profit. That was considered unfair to the customers, whose trust Penney seeks to win."[127]

The *apathetic culture* exhibits an indifference to both people and performance. This culture has problems; in fact, the organization's survival is problematic unless it is protected by an unusual set of circumstances. A general state of demoralization and cynicism permeates the organization, which is often linked to inept or alienated leadership. Cabals, factions, and schisms are rampant, and mistrust, contentiousness, uncertainty, and confusion imbue the apathetic culture. This kind of organization is governed more by vested interests and politics than by the concerns of effectiveness and efficiency. Thus, playing politics, manipulating rules and people, and managing impressions are the ways to get ahead in this culture.

The *exacting culture* demands high performance from employees although it shows little concern for their well-being. Exacting cultures are success driven. People are expendable. Performance counts. Rewards are directly linked to individual performance. Success, competition, risk-taking, innovation, and aggressiveness are basic values. The culture, however, sends out some mixed messages. Although risk-taking and creativity are valued, failure can lead to severe penalties. On the other hand, hoarding resources, withholding information, or being insensitive to fellow workers often are rewarded because they lead to short-term competitive success.[128]

The *integrative culture* exhibits high concern for people as well as high performance demands. The concern for people in this culture is not paternalistic, rather it is a genuine concern for the dignity of the individual. People are assumed to be capable of making significant contributions to the organization and are expected to do so. "Allow people the freedom to be all they can," is a guiding principle. Moreover, status distinctions are downplayed in this culture; hence, a tendency toward informality and egalitarianism. Peter Drucker captures the responsibility of the organization to its people in this culture as follows: "People are weak. People cause problems. . . . And people are a cost and a potential 'threat.' But these are not the reasons why people are employed. The reason is their strength and their capacity to perform. And . . . [t]he purpose of an organization is to make the strengths of people productive and their weaknessess irrelevant."[129] But remember that performance is a core value in this culture and rewards are therefore contingent upon performance. Unlike the exacting culture, however, emphasis is on group, not individual, success. Long-term implications are considered. Cooperation, creativity, risk taking, self-direction, and experimentation are highly valued in an integrative culture.

A comparison of typologies.   The two typologies that have been examined are similar in several ways. Both define four generic categories, but since each category is an ideal type, it is not easy to place any organization exclusively in one category. Most organizations, however, can be classified as being closer to one cultural type than another. Both frameworks dramatically simplify the domain of organizational culture; that is both a strength and weakness. It makes analysis manageable, but at a price. A category does not convey everything about the culture of a given organization.

Although the integrative culture is attractive, neither framework suggests the existence of one best culture. It seems likely that various cultures are more or less effective, depending on situational demands. In fact, George Gordon concludes from his empirical analysis of cultures that contingency factors ". . . such as the characteristics of the industry and the market place and

diversity, size and market positions of the organization define the broad outlines of the appropriate culture."[130] Indeed, Sethia and Von Glinow hypothesize that for protected organizations, "the caring culture, with its emphasis on
security and long-term stability, might be more appropriate, while the dynam-
ic-marketplace companies engaged in a free-wheeling competition, the exacting culture, with its short-term incentives and high-risk compensation, is likely
to be more appropriate."[131] Likewise, Quinn and McGrath suggest that both
the degree of intensity and uncertainty in the environment are related to the
appropriate culture.[132]

Both frameworks imply that leaders with different styles are likely in each
culture; indeed, perhaps different leaders cultivate different cultures. After we
discuss leadership in Chapter 9, the reader will be able to match different
leadership styles with cultural types; in fact, there is a striking resemblance
between Blake and Mouton's Managerial Grid and Sethia and Von Glinow's
culture typology.[133] Although the consensual culture is similar to the caring
culture and the exacting culture similar to the rational culture, the other four
culture types are substantially different. Both typologies seem to have potential
as frames of reference for research and analysis of the cultures of schools, but
clearly much remains to be done in conceptualizing and studying the cultures
of schools.

CONCEPTUAL DERIVATIONS
AND APPLICATIONS: CLINICAL
AND GROWTH-CENTERED STRATEGIES
FOR CHANGING SCHOOLS

We have little information on, let alone answers to, the complex problem of
changing school climates or cultures. Two things are clear, however. There is
no quick and simple way to change the atmosphere of schools. Long-run planning is more likely to produce change than short-run fads.

Alan Brown has presented two general strategies for changing school climate—the clinical strategy and the growth-centered strategy. The two strategies are not alternatives to each other; both can be used simultaneously and,
indeed, both seem necessary for change. The clinical strategy focuses on the
nature of the relationships among the school's subgroups; the growth-center
strategy is concerned with the nature of individual development within the
school. Each of these change strategies offers potential guidelines for the practicing administrator and will be reviewed briefly.

The Clinical Strategy

The manipulation of intergroup and interpersonal interactions can foster
change. Such a strategy for change must proceed through the following steps:

1. *Gaining knowledge of the organization.* The approach begins with
   a thorough knowledge of the dynamics of the school organization.

Such knowledge, of course, comes through careful observation, analysis, and study. The perceptive principal may have acquired much of this knowledge through experience, but, typically, a more systematic analysis is enlightening and valuable. As a prelude to such a study, he or she must understand the salient aspects of organizational life including the basic norms and values of the faculty. The conceptual perspectives provided by such measures as the OCDQ, OHI, and PCI can substantially aid this learning about the school organization.

2. *Diagnosis.* The second step in the process is diagnostic. Here again conceptual capital, from a variety of perspectives, can provide labels for diagnosing potential trouble areas. Poor esprit, high disengagement, custodialism, distorted communication, unilateral decision making, weak motivation, and low academic expectations are examples of such conceptual labels. The extent to which these concepts are clearly defined in the mind of the practitioner and fit together in a broader perspective probably mediate the effectiveness of the diagnosis.

3. *Prognosis.* In the third step, the "clinician" judges the seriousness of the situation and develops a set of operational priorities to improve the situation.

4. *Prescription.* The appropriate course of action is often hidden. Suppose we decided that the school's atmosphere is too custodial in pupil-control orientation. How can the situation be remedied? We might replaced a number of "custodial" teachers with younger "humanistic" teachers. Research suggests, however, that the pupil-control ideology of beginning teachers becomes significantly more custodial as they become socialized by the teacher subculture, which in this case tends to equate tight control with good teaching.[134] Merely replacing a number of custodial teachers without altering basic teacher norms about pupil control will probably have little or no impact. Altering basic teacher norms calls for a more sophisticated strategy. A first step in such a strategy is to eliminate teacher and administrator ignorance about the PCI, that is, to erase the shared misperceptions of educators with respect to pupil-control ideology. Teachers generally think that principals are much more custodial in pupil-control ideology than they themselves are, and conversely, principals typically believe that teachers are more custodial in pupil-control orientation than they report themselves to be.[135] These common misperceptions need to be swept away if a more humanistic perspective is to be achieved. In other words, developing prescriptions at first seems easy enough, but experience shows that solutions to various school problems are usually oversimplified and often irrelevant. If administrators are going to be successful in changing the school climate and culture, then they must change the norms and values of the teacher subculture as well as the basic, shared assumptions of the faculty and administration.

5. *Evaluation.* The last step in the clinical strategy is to evaluate the extent to which prescriptions have been implemented and are

successful. Because planned change in social systems is often slow, continuous monitoring and evaluation are required.

The Growth-Centered Strategy

This approach simply involves the acceptance of a set of assumptions about development of school personnel and the use of these assumptions as to the basis for administrative decision making. The assumptions are the following:

1. *Change is a property of healthy school organizations.* The principal should see organizations, and hence organizational climate, in a constant state of flux.
2. *Change has direction.* Change can be positive or negative, progressive or regressive.
3. *Change should imply progress.* Change should provide movement of the organization toward its goals. Of course not all change represents progress; yet the principal's stance is progress-oriented.
4. *Teachers have high potential for the development and implementation of change.* Principals are always ready to provide teachers with more freedom and responsibility in the operation of the school.[136]

These basic assumptions, if acted on, would allow for a growth policy, which in turn leads to increased opportunities for professional development. From this perspective, administrators would remove obstacles from the path of professional growth and not manipulate people. Finally, the approach should help facilitate a climate of mutual trust and respect among teachers and administrators.

The clinical and growth-centered approaches do not conflict in their assumptions, although they have different focuses—organizational and individual. The astute administrator draws on both strategies to change the climate of the school.

SUMMARY

Three related and overlapping perspectives are used to analyze the character of the workplace. Informal organization, organizational climate, and organizational culture all go beyond the formal and individual aspects of organizational life. Each concept deals with the natural, spontaneous, and human side of organization as attempts are made to uncover shared meanings and unwritten rules that influence behavior.

Informal organization is an emergent system of interpersonal relations that forms spontaneously within all formal organizations as members interact with each other; the work group develops its own unofficial norms, values, structures, and practices. Unlike the formal organization, which is consciously and carefully planned, informal organization is the natural ordering and structuring that evolves in the workplace. Teachers within schools inevitably generate their own informal status and power networks, informal communication systems, and unofficial working arrangements. Moreover, successful administrative practice is rooted in the informal system as well as the formal. To neglect the informal is to ignore the nonrational aspects of organizational behavior; in fact, to neglect either system is shortsighted and counterproductive.

Organizational climate is a broad concept that denotes members' shared *perceptions* of tone or character of the workplace; it is a set of internal characteristics that distinguishes one school from another and influences the behavior of people in school. Three important conceptualizations of school climate were considered. The climate of interaction among teachers can be described along an open to closed continuum, and can be measured by two organizational climate description questionnaires, the OCDQ-RE and OCDQ-RS. Another conceptualization of climate examines the organizational health of schools, that is, the extent to which the school is meeting both its instrumental and expressive needs while simultaneously coping with disruptive outside forces as it directs its energies toward it mission. The health of the school can be mapped using the organizational health inventory (OHI). Still another description views school climate in terms of a continuum of control over students, from humanistic to custodial, and is measured by the pupil-control ideology form (PCI).

Organizational culture is the set of shared orientations that holds a unit together and gives it a distinctive identity. Although climate tends to focus on shared perceptions, culture is defined in terms of shared assumptions, values, and norms. These three levels of culture—shared assumptions, values, and norms—are explored as alternative ways of describing and analyzing the school cultures. The recent popularity of culture is an outgrowth of the business literature, which suggests that effective organizations have strong corporate cultures. Finally, two typologies of cultures are presented to aid in the study and analysis of organizational life in school.

NOTES

1. W. Richard Scott, *Organizations: Rational, Natural, and Open Systems* (Englewood Cliffs, NJ: Prentice-Hall, 1981), p. 83.
2. Peter Blau and W. Richard Scott, *Formal Organizations* (San Francisco: Chandler, 1962), p. 6.
3. *Ibid.,* pp. 6–7.
4. Scott, *op. cit.,* p. 82.
5. Our analysis of informal organizations draws heavily from two sources: Blau and Scott, pp. 2–8, and George C. Homans, *The Human Group* (New York: Harcourt, Brace, and World, 1950), pp. 81–156.
6. Blau and Scott, *op. cit.,* pp. 2–5.
7. Chester I. Barnard, *The Functions of the Executive* (Cambridge, MA: Harvard University Press, 1938), p. 123.
8. Joseph A. Litterer (ed.), *Organizations: Structure and Behavior,* Vol. 1, 2nd ed. (New York: Wiley, 1969), p. 162.

9. Charles H. Page, "Bureaucracy's Other Face," *Social Forces*, 25 (1946), 88–94.
10. Laurence Iannaccone, "The Social System of a School Staff," (Ed. D. diss., Teachers College, Columbia University, 1958). See also Daniel E. Griffiths, David L. Clark, D. Richard Wynn, and Lawrence Iannaccone, *Organizing Schools for Effective Education* (Danville, IL: Interstate Printers & Publishers, 1962), pp. 225–297.
11. Norman J. Boyan, "A Study of the Formal and Informal Organization of a School Faculty: The Identification of the Systems of Interactions and Relationships Among the Staff Members of a School and an Analysis of the Interplay Between These Systems," (Ed.D. thesis, Harvard University, 1951), p. 269.
12. Robert Merton, *Social Theory and Social Structure* (New York: Free Press, 1957), p. 195.
13. John R. Commons, *Legal Foundations of Capitalism* (New York: Macmillian, 1924), p. 284.
14. Barnard, *op. cit.*, pp. 167–170.
15. Blau and Scott, *op. cit.*, p. 140.
16. A good portion of the following analysis is drawn from two studies done in public elementary and secondary schools. See Wayne K. Hoy and Leonard B. Williams, "Loyalty to Immediate Superior at Alternate Levels in Public Schools," *Educational Administration Quarterly*, 7 (1971), 1–11; and Wayne K. Hoy and Richard Rees, "Subordinate Loyalty to Immediate Superior: A Neglected Concept in the Study of Educational Administration," *Sociology of Education*, 47 (1974), 268–286.
17. Barnard, *op. cit.*, pp. 168–171.
18. Blau and Scott, *op. cit.*, p. 144.
19. *Ibid.*
20. Ibid., p. 165.
21. V. V. Murray and Allan F. Corenblum, "Loyalty to Immediate Superior at Alternate Hierarchical Levels in a Bureaucracy," *American Journal of Sociology*, 62 (1966), 77–85.
22. See Hoy and Williams, *op. cit.*, and Hoy and Rees, *op. cit.*
23. Blau and Scott, *op. cit.*, p. 144.
24. Peter M. Blau, *The Dynamics of Bureaucracy* (Chicago: University of Chicago Press, 1955), pp. 76–77.
25. Robert L. Peabody, "Perceptions of Organizational Authority: A Comparative Analysis," *Administrative Science Quarterly*, 6 (1962), 463–482.
26. Hoy and Williams, *op. cit.*, and Hoy and Rees, *op. cit.*
27. Gerald Isaacson, "Leadership Behavior and Loyalty," (Ed.D. diss., Rutgers University, 1983); and Toni Mullins, "Relationships Among Teachers' Perceptions of the Principal's Style, Teachers' Loyalty to the Principal, and Teachers' Zone of Acceptance," (Ed.D. diss., Rutgers University, 1983). Isaacson's study supported the relationship between hierarchical independence and loyalty; the earlier studies did not.
28. *Ibid.*
29. James E. Henderson and Wayne K. Hoy, "Leader Authenticity: The Development and Test of an Operational Measure," *Educational and Psychological Research*, 3 (1983), pp. 63–75.
30. Wayne K. Hoy and James E. Henderson, "Principal Authenticity, School

Climate, and Pupil-Control Orientation," *Alberta Journal of Educational Research,* 2 (1983), pp. 123–130.

31. Blau and Scott, *op. cit.,* p. 143.

32. Renato Taguiri and George H. Litwin (eds.), *Organizational Climate* (Boston: Harvard Graduate School of Business Administration, 1968), pp. 26–27.

33. Andrew W. Halpin and Don B. Croft, *The Organizational Climate of Schools* (Washington, DC: U. S. Office of Education, Research Project, Contract #SAE 543-8639, August 1962), pp. 175–176.

34. Halpin has developed vignettes for all six organizational climates. See pp. 174–181 of the work cited in footnote 33. If one wishes to classify a school into one of the six discrete climates, using the norms developed in Halpin and Croft's regional study of seventy-one elementary schools, a profile-similarity score can be developed and the school "classified." See pp. 174–186 of Halpin.

35. Robert J. Brown, *Organizational Climate of Elementary Schools,* Research Monograph No. 2 (Minneapolis: Educational Research and Development Council, 1965).

36. *Ibid.*

37. James F. Watkins, "The OCDQ—An Application and Some Implications," *Educational Administration Quarterly,* 4 (1968), 52.

38. John H. M. Andrews, "School Organizational Climate: Some Validity Studies," *Canadian Education and Research Digest,* 5 (1965), 333.

39. Halpin and Croft, *op. cit.,* p. 104.

40. *Ibid.,* p. 136.

41. James B. Appleberry and Wayne K. Hoy, "The Pupil Control Ideology of Professional Personnel in 'Open' and 'Closed' Elementary Schools," *Educational Administration Quarterly,* 5 (1969), 74–85.

42. *Ibid.,* p. 147.

43. Fred D. Carver and Thomas J. Sergiovanni, "Notes on the OCDQ," *Journal of Educational Administration,* 7 (1969), 71–81. See also Andrew W. Halpin, "Change and Organizational Climate," *Journal of Educational Administration,* 5 (1967), 5–25.

44. Prototypic profiles for the six organizational climates were developed based on the results of the factor analysis of the school profile in the original sample. Schools can be classified by computation of a profile-similarity score, which indicates numerically the extent to which the school profile is congruent with the prototypic profile that characterizes each of the six climates. In essence, the norms for the climate types were based on a sample of only seventy-one elementary schools. See Halpin, *Theory and Research in Administration, op. cit.,* pp. 174–186.

45. Paula Silver, *Educational Administration: Theoretical Perspectives in Practice and Research* (New York: Harper & Row, 1983), pp. 188–190.

46. Halpin and Croft, *op. cit.*

47. Andrew E. Hayes, "A Reappraisal of the Halpin-Croft Model of the Organizational Climate of Schools" (Paper presented at the Annual Meeting of the American Educational Research Association, New Orleans, 1973).

48. For other technical and psychometric criticisms, see Wayne K. Hoy and Sharon I. R. Clover, "Elementary School Climate: A Revision of the OCDQ," *Educational Administration Quarterly,* 22 (1986), 93–110; and

Kenneth A. Sirotnek, "Psychometric Implications of the Unit-of-Analysis Problem (With Examples from the Measurement of Organizational Climate)," *Journal of Educational Measurement,* 17 (1980), pp. 248–284.

49. The Rutgers research teams were composed of Wayne K. Hoy, Robert Kottkamp, Sharon Clover, John Feldman, and John Mulhern.

50. This section draws heavily from Hoy and Clover, *op. cit.*

51. Reliability coefficients for the subtests are as follows: Supportive (.95), Directive (.89), Restrictive (.80), Collegial (.90), Intimate (.86), and Disengaged (.75). It is interesting to note that the Australian version of the OCDQ for primary schools has only four dimensions, factors similar to our dimensions of supportive, directive, disengaged, and intimate. See A. Ross Thomas and R. C. Slater, "The OCDQ: A Four Factor Solution for Australian Schools?" *Journal of Educational Administration,* 10 (1972), pp. 197–208; and Laurie Brady, "The 'Australian' OCDQ: A Decade Later," *Journal of Educational Administration,* 23 (1985), pp. 53–58.

52. The technical details of the development the OCDQ-RS are provided by Robert Kottkamp, John Mulhern, and Wayne K. Hoy, "Secondary School Climate: A Revision of the OCDQ," (Technical report, Rutgers University, 1985).

53. Reliability coefficients for the subtests are as follows: Supportive (.91), Directive (.87), Engaged (.85), Frustrated (.85), and Intimate (.71).

54. Marvin Hartley and Wayne K. Hoy, "Openness of School Climate and Alienation of High School Students," *California Journal of Educational Research,* 23 (1972), 17–24.

55. Donald P. Anderson, *Organizational Climate of Elementary Schools,* Research Monograph No. 1 (Minneapolis: Educational Research and Development Council, 1964).

56. Andrews, *op. cit.,* pp. 317–334.

57. Lawrence Kanner, "Machiavellianism and the Secondary Schools: Teacher–Principal Relations" (Ed.D. diss. Rutgers University, 1974).

58. Halpin, *Theory and Research in Administration, op. cit.,* pp. 82–83.

59. For greater detail on the Organizational Health Inventory, see Wayne K. Hoy and Patrick B. Forsyth, *Effective Supervision: Theory into Practice* (New York: Random House, 1986).

60. See Matthew B. Miles, "Planned Change and Organizational Health: Figure and Ground," in Fred D. Carver and Thomas J. Sergiovanni (eds.), *Organizations and Human Behavior* (New York: McGraw-Hill, 1969), pp. 375–391.

61. *Ibid.*

62. Talcott Parsons, Robert F. Bales, and Edward A. Shils, *Working Papers in the Theory of Action* (New York: Free Press, 1953), pp. 183–186.

63. Talcott Parsons, "Some Ingredients of a General Theory of Formal Organization," in Andrew W. Halpin (ed.), *Administrative Theory in Education* (New York: Macmillan, 1967), pp. 40–72.

64. The reliability coefficients for the seven subtests are as follows: Institutional Integrity (.91), Principal Influence (.87), Consideration (.90), Initiating Structure (.89), Resource Support (.95), Morale (.92), and Academic Emphasis (.93).

65. Willard Waller, *The Sociology of Teaching* (New York: Wiley, 1932).

66. James S. Coleman, *The Adolescent Society* (New York: Free Press, 1961).

See also Donald J. Willower and Ronald G. Jones, "Control in an Educational Organization," in J. D. Raths *et. al.* (eds.), *Studying Teaching* (Englewood Cliffs, NJ: Prentice-Hall, 1967), pp. 424–428; and C. Wayne Gordon, *The Social System of the High School* (Glencoe, IL: Free Press, 1957).

67. Willower and Jones, *op. cit.*

68. Richard O. Carlson, "Environmental Constraints and Organizational Consequences: The Public School and Its Clients," in Daniel E. Griffiths (ed.), *Behavioral Science and Educational Administration* (Chicago: University of Chicago Press, 1964), pp. 262–276.

69. Some caution should be exercised when comparing public schools with prisons and public mental hospitals. There are important distinctions. For example, prisons and public mental hospitals are "total organizations"; schools are not. In addition, schools are much less coercive in their practices than most prisons and public mental hospitals. Our point is that although control is probably an essential ingredient of all group life, it is especially important in service organizations in which clients are unselected and participation is mandatory. For a discussion of total institutions, see Erving Goffman, "The Characteristics of Total Institutions," in *Symposium of Preventive and Social Psychiatry,* (Washington, DC: Walter Reed Army Institute of Research, 1957), pp. 43–84.

70. Donald J. Willower, Terry L. Eidell, and Wayne K. Hoy, *The School and Pupil Control Ideology* (University Park: Penn State University Studies Monograph No. 24, 1967). See also Donald J. Willower, "Hypotheses on the School as a Social System," *Educational Administration Quarterly,* 1 (1965), 40–51; Donald J. Willower, "Schools as Organizations: Some Illustrated Strategies for Educational Research and Practice," *Journal of Educational Administration,* 7 (1969), 110–127; and Willower and Jones, *op. cit.*

71. For an extended description and discussion of this conceptualization, see Willower, Eidell, and Hoy, *op. cit.*

72. Erich Fromm, *Man for Himself* (New York: Farrar & Rinehart, 1948).

73. The details of the development of the PCI form and its psychometric properties are found in Willower, Eidell, and Hoy, *op. cit.*

74. *Ibid.;* and John S. Packard and Donald J. Willower, "Pluralistic Ignorance and Pupil Control Ideology," *Journal of Educational Administration,* 10 (1972), 82.

75. Willower, Eidell, and Hoy, *op. cit.* See also Wayne K. Hoy, "The Influence of Experience on the Beginning Teacher," *School Review,* 76 (1968), 312–323; and Wayne K. Hoy and James B. Appleberry, "Teacher-Principal Relationships in 'Humanistic' and 'Custodial' Elementary Schools," *Journal of Experimental Education,* 39 (1970), 27–31. Since the publication of the original monograph in 1967 by Willower, Eidell, and Hoy, more than seventy studies have been completed using the PCI. In addition, a new measure, pupil control behavior (PCB), has been developed. See for example, A. Ray Helsel, "Personality and Pupil Control Behavior" (Paper presented at the annual meeting of the American Educational Research Association, Chicago, 1974).

76. Hoy and Appleberry, *op. cit.*

77. Appleberry and Hoy, *op. cit.*

78. Hoy and Appleberry, *op. cit.*

79. Alienation is a complex concept with multiple dimensions. For excellent treatment of the dimensions of alienation, see Melvin Seeman, "On the Meaning of Alienation," *American Sociological Review,* 34 (1959), 783–791.

80. Wayne K. Hoy, "Dimensions of Student Alienation and Characteristics of Public High Schools," *Interchange,* 3 (1972), 38–51.

81. The conceptualization of meaninglessness as a sensed inability to make predictions about future outcomes of behavior may be unduly narrow. Meaninglessness also implies the lack of ability to see some larger purpose or relevance in an activity.

82. John P. Diebert and Wayne K. Hoy, "Custodial High Schools and Self-Actualization of Students," *Educational Research Quarterly,* 2 (1977), 24–31.

83. Frederick C. Lunenburg, "Pupil Control Ideology and Self-Concept as a Learner," *Educational Research Quarterly,* 8 (1983), 33–39.

84. See, for example, J. S. Coleman *et al., Equality of Educational Opportunity* (Washington, DC: U. S. Government Printing Office, 1966); and D. H. Heath, "Student Alienation and School," *The School Review,* 78 (1970), 515–528.

85. For example, see Ralph H. Kilmann, Mary J. Saxton, Roy Serpa and Associates, *Gaining Control of the Corporate Culture* (San Francisco: Jossey-Bass, 1985); and Peter J. Frost, Larry F. Moore, Meryl Reis Louis, Craig C. Lundberg, and Joanne Martin, *Organizational Culture* (Beverly Hills, CA: Sage Publications, 1985).

86. Elton Mayo, *The Social Problems of an Industrial Civilization* (Boston: Graduate School of Business Administration, Harvard University, 1945); Chester I. Barnard, *The Functions of the Executive* (Cambridge, MA: Harvard University Press, 1938). See also F. J. Roethlisberger and William J. Dickson, *Management and the Worker* (Cambridge, MA: Harvard University Press, 1939).

87. Philip Selznick, *Leadership in Administration* (New York: Harper & Row, 1957), p. 17.

88. Meryl Reis Louis, "Perspectives on Organizational Cultures," in Frost *et. al., Organizational Culture,* p. 27.

89. *Ibid.* p. 28.

90. William Ouchi, *Theory Z* (Reading, MA: Addison-Wesley, 1981); Terrence E. Deal and Allan A. Kennedy, *Corporate Cultures* (Reading, MA: Addison-Wesley, 1982); and Thomas J. Peters and Robert H. Waterman, Jr., *In Search of Excellence* (New York: Harper & Row, 1982).

91. Ouchi, *op. cit.,* p. 41.

92. Jay W. Lorsch, "Strategic Myopia: Culture as an Invisible Barrier to Change," in Kilmann *et al., Gaining Control of the Corporate Culture,* p. 84.

93. Alan Wilkins and Kerry Patterson, "You Can't Get There From Here: What Will Make Culture-Change Projects Fail," in Kilmann *et al., Gaining Control of the Corporate Culture,* p. 265.

94. Joanne Martin, "Can Organizational Culture be Managed?" in Frost *et al., Organizational Culture,* p. 95.

95. Howard M. Schwartz and Stanley M. Davis, "Matching Corporate Culture and Business Strategy," *Organizational Dynamics* (Summer 1981), p. 33.

96. Edgar H. Schein, *Organizational Culture and Leadership* (San Francisco: Jossey-Bass, 1985), p. 6.

97. Blake E. Ashforth, "Climate Formations: Issues and Extensions," *The Academy of Management Review,* 10 (1985), 837–847.

98. For similar views, see Schein, *op. cit.,* pp. 1–22, and Kilmann *et al.,* pp. 5–10.

99. This section draws heavily from Schein, *op. cit.*

100. *Ibid.,* p. 9.

101. W. Gibb Dyer, Jr., "The Cycle of Cultural Evolution in Organization," Kilmann *et al., Gaining Control of the Corporate Culture,* p. 204.

102. *Ibid.,* pp. 200–229.

103. Schien, *op. cit.,* p. 110.

104. *Ibid.,* pp. 112–222.

105. Deal and Kennedy, *op. cit.,* p. 2.

106. Ouchi, *op. cit.*

107. Deal and Kennedy, *op. cit.,* and Peters and Waterman, *op. cit.*

108. Peters and Waterman, *op. cit.,* p. 13.

109. William A. Firestone and Bruce L. Wilson, "Using Bureaucratic and Cultural Linkages to Improve Instruction: The Principal's Contribution," *Educational Administration Quarterly,* 21 (1985), 7–30.

110. *Ibid.* See also Stephen R. Barley, "Semiotics and the Study of Occupational Cultures," *Administrative Science Quarterly,* 28 (1983), 393–413; Andrew M. Pettigrew, "On Studying Organizational Cultures," *Administrative Science Quarterly,* 24 (1979), 570–581; and Thomas Danridge, Ian I. Mitroff, and William F. Joyce, "Organizational Analyses," *Academy of Management Review,* 5 (1980), 77–82.

111. Firestone and Wilson, *op. cit.,* pp. 7–30.

112. *Ibid.*

113. Deal and Kennedy, *op. cit.,* p. 15.

114. Robert F. Allen and C. Kraft, *The Organizational Unconscious: How to Create the Corporate Culture You Want and Need* (Englewood Cliffs, NJ: Prentice-Hall, 1982).

115. Kilmann *et al., Gaining Control of the Corporate Culture,* p. 6.

116. *Ibid.,* p. 361.

117. *Ibid.*

118. Ralph Kilmann and M. J. Saxton, *The Kilmann-Saxton Culture Gap Survey* (Pittsburgh, PA: Organizational Design Consultant, 1983).

119. Kilmann *et al., Gaining Control of the Corporate Culture,* p. 7.

120. *Ibid.,* p. 9.

121. *Ibid.*

122. This section draws heavily from Robert E. Quinn and Michael R. McGrath, "The Transformation of Organizational Cultures," in Peter J. Frost *et al., op. cit.,* pp. 315–334.

123. *Ibid.*

124. Peters and Waterman, *op. cit.*

125. This section draws heavily from Nirmal K. Sethia and Mary Ann Von Glinow, "Arriving at Four Cultures by Managing the Reward System," in Kilmann *et al., op cit.,* pp. 400–420.

126. *Ibid.,* pp. 411–412.

127. "Corporate Culture: The Hard-to-Change Values that Spell Success or Failure," *Business Week* (October 27), pp. 148–160.

128. Sethia and Von Glinow, *op. cit.,* p. 413.
129. Peter F. Drucker, *Management: Tasks and Responsibilities* (New York; Harper & Row, 1974), p. 307.
130. George Gordon, "The Relationship of Corporate Culture by Industry Sector and Corporate Performance," in Kilmann *et al., op. cit.,* p. 121.
131. Sethia and Von Glinow, *op. cit.,* p. 412.
132. Quinn and McGrath, *op. cit.,* pp. 329–331.
133. Sethia and Von Glinow, *op. cit.,* pp. 408–418.
134. Alan F. Brown, "Two Strategies for Changing Climate," *CAS Bulletin,* 4 (1965), 64–80. The framework for the following discussion comes from Brown's article.
135. Wayne K. Hoy, "Organizational Socialization: The Student Teacher and Pupil Control Ideology," *Journal of Educational Research,* 61 (1967), 153–155. See also Wayne K. Hoy, "Pupil Control and Organizational Socialization: The Influence of Experience on the Beginning Teacher," *School Review,* 76 (1968), 313–323; and Wayne K. Hoy, "Pupil Control Ideology and Organizational Socialization: A Further Examination of the Influence of Experience on the Beginning Teacher," *School Review,* 77 (1969), 257–265.
136. Packard and Willower, *op. cit.*

Chapter 9

Leadership

The effective functioning of social systems from the local PTA to the United States of America is assumed to be dependent on the quality of their leadership.

VICTOR H. VROOM
Leadership

Leadership is an elusive but fascinating topic of continuing interest to students of administration. Definitions of leadership are almost as numerous as the researchers engaged in its study. The following definitions of leadership are typical examples:

> To lead is to engage in an act that initiates a structure-in-interaction as part of the process of solving a mutual problem.——*John K. Hemphill*[1]

> Leadership is power based predominantly on personal characteristics, usually normative in nature.——*Amitai Etzioni*[2]

> The leader is the individual in the group given the task of directing and coordinating task-relevant group activities.——*Fred E. Fiedler*[3]

> Leadership is a particular type of power relationship characterized by a group member's perception that another group member has the right to prescribe behavior patterns for the former regarding his activity as a group member.——*Kenneth F. Janda*[4]

> The essence of organizational leadership is the influential increment over and above mechanical compliance with the routine directives of the organization.——*Daniel Katz and Robert L. Kahn*[5]

> Leadership is the initiation of a new structure or procedure for accomplishing an organization's goals and objectives or for changing an organization's goals and objectives.——*James Lipham*[6]

Leadership is the process of influencing the activities of an organized group toward goal setting and goal achievement.——*Ralph M. Stog-dill*[7]

Leadership takes place in groups of two or more people and most frequently involves influencing group member behavior as it relates to the pursuit of group goals.——*Robert J. House and Mary L. Baetz*[8]

In addition to these varying definitions of the basic concept, distinctions exist between elected leaders and appointed leaders and formal leaders and informal leaders.

In describing the nature and meaning of leadership, Katz and Kahn identify three major components of the concept: (1) an attribute of an office or position; (2) a characteristic of a person; and (3) a category of actual behavior.[9] A principal occupies a leadership position; a superintendent occupies an even higher leadership position. Obviously, school organizations contain individuals who are not in formal positions of authority, yet who possess and wield influence and power. Conversely, some individuals who occupy leadership positions do not always exercise their power and influence, and others exist in schools who exercise leadership in one position or situation but not in others. Leadership also implies followers; there can be no leader without followers. However, the situations under which different groups and individuals will follow vary considerably. Thus, the concept of leadership remains elusive because it depends not only on the position, behavior, and personal characteristics of the leader but also on the character of the situation. We agree with Gary A. Yukl, however, that research on leadership should be designed to provide information concerning the entire range of definitions, so that it will eventually be possible to compare the utility of different conceptualizations and arrive at some consensus.[10] In the meantime, an abundance of useful conceptual and empirical capital is available for both practitioners and scholars of administration.[11]

THE TRAIT-SITUATION DILEMMA

Traits

Leadership has been an intriguing topic for centuries. Many individuals still believe, as Aristotle did, that "from the hour of birth, some are marked out for subjection, others for rule."[12] This so-called *great man theory of leadership* or the *trait approach* dominated the study of leadership until the 1950s. The approach typically attempts to identify any distinctive physical or psychological characteristics of the individual that relate or explain the behavior of leaders. Psychological researchers using this approach attempt to isolate specific traits that endow leaders with unique qualities that differentiate them from their followers.

The trait approach was all but put to rest with the publication of several literature reviews during the 1940s and 1950s.[13] Ralph M. Stogdill, for example, reviewed about 120 trait studies of leadership that were completed between 1904 and 1947.[14] He classified the personal factors associated with leadership into the following five general categories:

1. Capacity (intelligence, alertness, verbal facility, originality, judgment).
2. Achievement (scholarship, knowledge, athlethic accomplishments).
3. Responsibility (dependability, initiative, persistence, aggressiveness, self-confidence, desire to excel).
4. Participation (activity, sociability, cooperation, adaptability, humor).
5. Status (socioeconomic position, popularity).[15]

Stogdill concluded that the trait approach by itself had yielded negligible and confusing results.

Mann's later review of 125 leadership studies that had generated 750 findings about the personality traits of leaders produced similar conclusions.[16] Many of the traits tentatively isolated as crucial in one study were found to be unimportant in others. Thus, in some groups, effective leaders were assertive and aggressive, in others, mild-mannered and restrained; in some, quick and decisive, in others, reflective and diplomatic. These studies also are limited because the relationships of some of the personality traits differed depending on the type of measuring technique employed. Although Stogdill tentatively identified above-average ability in intelligence, scholarship, dependability, participation and status as qualities enhancing leadership, he hastens to add, "A person does not become a leader by virtue of the possession of some combination of traits, ... The pattern of personal characteristics of the leaders must bear some relevant relationship to the characteristics, activities, and goals of the followers."[17] In brief, the early searches for personality traits to distinguish leaders from followers were remarkably unsuccessful. Leaders with one set of traits are successful in one situation but not in others. Moreover, leaders with different combinations of traits can be successful in the same or similar situations.

Notwithstanding the lack of success in identifying general leadership traits, such studies have persisted. More recent trait studies, however, use a greater variety of measurement procedures, including projective tests, and they focus on managers and administrators rather than other kinds of leaders. Gary Yukl explains:

> One reason for this trend is that the 1948 literature review by Stogdill greatly discouraged many leadership researchers from studying leader traits, whereas industrial psychologists interested in improving managerial selection continued to conduct trait research. *The emphasis on selection focused trait research on the relation of leader traits to leader effectiveness, rather than on the comparison of leaders and nonleaders.*[18]

Yukl's distinction is a significant one. Predicting who will become leaders and predicting who will be more effective are quite different tasks. Hence, the so-called trait studies continue, but they now explore the relationship between traits and leadership effectiveness of administrators.

This second generation of studies has produced a more consistent set of findings; in fact, in 1970, after reviewing another 163 new trait studies, Stogdill concluded:

> The leader is characterized by a strong drive for responsibility and task completion, vigor and persistence in pursuit of goals, venturesomeness and originality in problem solving, drive to exercise initiative in social situations, self-confidence and sense of personal identity, willingness to accept consequences of decision and action, readiness to absorb interpersonal stress, willingness to tolerate frustration and delay, ability to influence other persons' behavior, and capacity to structure interaction systems to the purpose at hand.[19]

The evidence that personality is an important factor in leadership does not represent a return to the original trait assumption that "leaders are born, not made." Rather, it is a more sensible and balanced view, one that acknowledges the influence of both traits and situations.

Situations

Reaction, or perhaps more appropriately overreaction, to the trait approach was so intense during the late 1940s and 1950s that for a time it seemed that both psychologists and sociologists had substituted a strictly situational analysis for the then questionable trait approach. Researchers sought to identify distinctive characteristics of the setting to which the leader's success could be attributed; they attempted to isolate specific properties of the situation that had relevance for leader behavior and performance.[20] The following variables have been postulated as situational determinants of leadership:

1. Structural properties of the organization (size, hierarchical structure, formalization).
2. Organizational climate (openness, participativeness, group atmosphere).
3. Role characteristics (position power, type and difficulty of task, procedural rules).
4. Subordinate characteristics (knowledge and experience, tolerance for ambiguity, responsibility, power).

John P. Campbell and his colleagues came to an interesting conclusion about this phase of leadership study: "Everyone suggests [that] the need for research is great—but actual empirical activity is sparse."[21] Consequently, the jump from "leaders are born, not made" to "leaders are made by the situation, not born," was short-lived. To restrict the study of leadership to either traits or situations is unduly restrictive and counterproductive.

Contingency Approach

The question today is: What traits under what situations are important to leader effectiveness? Most of the prevailing models guiding leadership research involve a *contingency approach.*[22] According to this approach, it is necessary to specify the conditions or situational variables that moderate the relationship between leader traits or behaviors and performance criteria. The evidence indicates that under one set of circumstances, one type of leader is effective; under another set of circumstances, a different type of leader is effective. Yet in order to maximize effectiveness, the intriguing question of what kind of leaders for what kind of situations remains largely unanswered. In the useful words of Robert K. Merton, "Leadership does not, indeed cannot, result merely from the individual traits of leaders; it must also involve attributes of the transactions between those who lead and those who follow. . . . Leadership is, then, some sort of social transaction."[23]

DIMENSIONS OF LEADERSHIP

Theory and research are replete with various frameworks for examining the important aspects of leadership behavior. Most conceptualizations of leadership are multidimensional, that is, supporting at least two distinct types.

In his analysis, Chester I. Barnard distinguishes between the effectiveness and the efficiency of cooperative action.

> The persistence of cooperation depends upon two conditions: (a) its effectiveness; and (b) its efficiency. Effectiveness relates to the accomplishment of the cooperative purpose which is social and nonpersonal in character. Efficiency relates to the satisfaction of individual motives, and is personal in character. The test of effectiveness is the accomplishment of common purpose or purposes; . . . the test of efficiency is the eliciting of sufficient individual will to cooperate.[24]

Similarly, Dorwin Carwright and Alvin Zander, on the basis of findings at the Research Center for Group Dynamics, describe leadership in terms of two sets of group functions.[25] They conclude that most, or perhaps all, group objectives can be subsumed under one of two headings: (1) goal achievement—the achievement of some specific group goal, and (2) group maintenance—the maintenance or strengthening of the group itself. In the same vein, Etzioni, expanding on the work of Talcott Parsons, theorizes that every collectivity must meet two basic sets of needs: (1) instrumental needs—the mobilization of resources to achieve the task—and (2) expressive needs—the social and normative integration of group members.[26]

In one of the more comprehensive delineations of leadership, Stogdill and his associates at Ohio State have proposed twelve dimensions.[27] The dimensions with their descriptions are presented in Table 9.1. As described here, these factors apparently can once again be collapsed to more general components— "system-oriented" and "person-oriented" behaviors.[28] Other theorists and researchers use different labels to refer to similar aspects of leadership behavior; for examples, nomothetic and idiographic,[29] task and social leaders,[30] employee and production orientations,[31] and initiating structure and consideration.[32]

In an attempt to synthesize the theory and research on leadership, David G. Bowers and Stanley E. Seashore have proposed four basic dimensions of the fundamental structure of leadership:

1. Support—behavior that enhances someone else's feelings of personal worth and importance.
2. Interaction facilitation—behavior that encourages members of the group to develop close, mutually satisfying relationships.
3. Goal emphasis—behavior that stimulates an enthusiasm for meeting the group's goal of achieving excellent performance.
4. Work facilitation—behavior that helps achieve goal attainment by activities such as scheduling, coordinating, planning, and by providing resources such as tools, materials, and technical knowledge.[33]

TABLE 9.1 Proposed Leadership Dimensions and Descriptions by Stogdill

System-Oriented	*Person-Oriented*
Production emphasis—applies pressure for productive output.	*Tolerance of freedom*—allows staff members scope for initiative, decision, and action.
Initiation of structure—clearly defines own role and lets followers know what is expected.	*Tolerance of uncertainty*—is able to tolerate uncertainty and postponement without anxiety or upset.
Representation—speaks and acts as the representative of the group.	*Consideration*—regards the comfort, well-being, status, and contributions of followers.
Role assumption—actively exercises the leadership role rather than surrendering leadership to others.	*Demand reconciliation*—reconciles conflicting demands and reduces disorder to system.
Persuasion—uses persuasion and argument effectively; exhibits strong convictions.	*Predictive accuracy*—exhibits foresight and ability to predict outcomes accurately.
Superior orientation—maintains cordial relations with superiors, has influence with them, and strives for higher status.	*Integration*—maintains a close-knit organization and resolves intermember conflicts.

If these four dimensions are collapsed into two, the same dimensions reappear. That is, supportive behavior and interaction facilitation are neatly subsumed under group maintenance functions or expressive activities; goal emphasis and work facilitation tend to be encompassed under goal achievement functions or instrumental activities.

This review is not exhaustive. It must be remembered that the literature, as diverse as it obviously is, generally does support the generalization that there are two distinct categories of leader behavior—one concerned with people and interpersonal relations and the other with production and task achievement. The dichotomy between concern for people and concern for the task effectively differentiates between the human relations movement and the scientific management movement. Table 9.2 summaries and compares some of these basic aspects of leadership behavior. Briefly, the table presents ten well-known sets of respected researchers and theorists whose work on leadership can be reduced to two fundamental concens—organizational tasks and individual relationships.

EARLY LEADERSHIP RESEARCH

The Ohio State Leadership Studies

To students of educational administration, probably the most well-known leader research inquiries are the *leader behavior description questionnaire (LBDQ) studies* started at Ohio State University in the 1940s. Originally devel-

TABLE 9.2 Dimensions of Leadership: Comparisons

Theorist	Concern for Organizational Tasks	Concern for Individual Relationships
Barnard	Effectiveness	Efficiency
Etzioni and Parsons	Instrumental Activities	Expressive activities
Cartwright and Zander	Goal achievement	Group Maintenance
Getzels and Guba	Nomothetic	Idiographic
Halpin	Initiating structure	Consideration
Kahn	Production orientation	Employee orientation
Bales	Task leader	Social leader
Bowers and Seashore	Goal emphasis	Support
	Work facilitation	Interaction facilitation
Brown	System orientation	Person orientation
Stogdill	Production emphasis	Tolerance of freedom
	Initiating structure	Tolerance of uncertainty
	Representation	Consideration
	Role assumption	Demand reconciliation
	Persuasion	Predictive accuracy
	Superior orientation	Integration

oped there by Hemphill and Alvin Coons,[34] the LBDQ was later refined by Halpin and B. J. Winer[35] and Stogdill.[36] It measures two basic dimensions of leader behavior—initiating structure and consideration. Sample items for each factor are contained in Table 9.3.

Initiating Structure includes any leader behavior that delineates the relationship between the leader and the subordinates and, at the same time, establishes defined patterns of organization, channels of communication, and methods of procedure. *Consideration* includes leader behavior that indicates friendship, trust, warmth, interest, and respect in the relationship between the leader and members of the work group.[37] The LBDQ items ask the subjects to describe the behavior of the leader on a five-point scale: always, often, occasionally, seldom, or never. The items are divided into two subscales, one for each of the dimensions of leader behavior the LBDQ measures. Separate scores for these two dimensions, initiating structure and consideration, are determined by summing the item responses relating to each subscale. Subordinates, superiors, or the leader himself or herself can describe the leader's behavior. For example, the LBDQ has been used by students to describe teachers, by teachers to describe principals and superintendents, by principals and superintendents to describe each other, and by board of education members to describe superintendents. In addition, the instrument can be modified to measure how a leader should behave, that is, "ideal" leader behavior.

Early studies using the LBDQ indicated that the consideration and initiating structure factors seemed to be separate and distinct, not opposite ends of the same continuum. Therefore, four quadrants, or leadership styles, can be formed by cross-partitioning on the mean score values of each scale (see Figure 9.1). Each subscale is divided into high and low groups and then combined with one another to yield four groups, or quadrants.

Figure 9.1 is interpreted as follows: Given a set of people who occupy leader positions and their respective LBDQ scores on initiating structure and consid-

TABLE 9.3   Sample LBDQ Items by Subscale*

Initiating Structure Items	*Consideration Items*
He or she makes his/her attitudes clear to the staff.	He or she refuses to explain his/her actions.**
He or she maintains definite standards of performance.	He or she acts without consulting the staff.**
He or she works without a plan.**	He or she treats all staff members as equals.
He or she lets staff members know what is expected of them.	He or she is willing to make changes.
He or she sees to it that staff members are working up to capacity.	He or she is friendly and approachable.
He or she sees to it that the work of staff members is coordinated.	He or she puts suggestions made by the staff into operation.

*Stated for use with male and female leaders.   **Scored negatively.

Consideration

		Low (−)	High (+)
Initiating Structures	High (+)	Quadrant II Low consideration (−) High initiating structure (+) II = (−, +)	Quadrant I High consideration (+) High initiating structure (+) I = (+, +)
	Low (−)	Quadrant III Low consideration (−) Low initiating structure (−) III = (−, −)	Quadrant IV High consideration (+) Low initiating structure (−) IV = (+, −)

FIGURE 9.1   Quadrants formed by using the LBDQ dimensions

eration, those who score above the mean on both dimensions are in quadrant I, the (+,+) quadrant; those below the mean on both dimensions are in quadrant III, the (−,−) quadrant; those who score below the mean in consideration, but above the mean in initiating structure are in quadrant II, the (−,+) quadrant; while those in quadrant IV, the (+,−) quadrant, exhibit the opposite relationship. Consequently, using these two dimensions, four leadership styles are possible.

Halpin sketches the major findings emerging from the Ohio State University LBDQ studies as follows:

1. Initiating structure and consideration as measured by the LBDQ are fundamental dimensions of leader behavior.
2. Effective leader behavior tends most often to be associated with high performance on both dimensions.
3. Superiors and subordinates tend to evaluate the contributions of the leader behavior dimensions oppositely in assessing effectiveness. Superiors tend to emphasize initiating structure, whereas subordinates are more concerned with consideration. Hence, the leader often finds some degree of role conflict.
4. The leadership style characterized by quadrant I, high in both dimensions, is associated with such group characteristics as harmony, intimacy, and procedural clarity, and with favorable changes in group attitude.
5. Only a slight relationship exists between how leaders say they should behave and how subordinates describe that they do behave.
6. Different institutional settings tend to foster different leadership styles.[38]

In brief, school administrators generally are most effective when they score high on both dimensions of leader behavior (quadrant I). After an extensive

LBDQ study, however, Alan F. Brown suggests that, although strength on both dimensions is highly desirable, principals committed to developing effective organizational dynamics may make up for weakness in one dimension with unusual strength in the other.[39] Leaders in quadrant III, weak on both dimensions, tend to be ineffective; indeed, they tend to suffer from a lack of leadership, and general chaos imbues the work situation.

Early studies of superintendents by Halpin suggest that public school norms supported considerate behavior.[40] He speculates that the disinclination to stress initiating structure may reflect the fact that human relations and group dynamics are stressed in education. Apparently, many educators tend to equate initiating structure with an authoritarian leadership style, although this is not the case. Halpin vividly explains:

> An effective leader can Initiate Structure without sacrificing Consideration. Yet we repeatedly encounter superintendents who fear to take a stand, who hesitate to Initiate Structure, lest they be accused of being antidemocratic. This is nonsense, for the superintendents who adopt this attitude can quickly spot the phony who tries to hide his ineptness in the soggy oatmeal of a pseudo group process.[41]

Related LBDQ Research

In two studies of random samples of senior high school principals in New Jersey and elementary and secondary school principals in Kansas, consideration and initiating structure were substantially correlated.[42] The New Jersey study focused on the leadership styles of principals and the "zone of acceptance" of teachers, that is the range of behavior within which subordinates are ready to accept the decisions made by their superiors.[43]

More than four decades ago, Barnard recognized that effective administrative authority involves willing rather than forced compliance.[44] Indeed, a basic characteristic of authority is the willingness of subordinates to comply with directives from superiors. There is a range or continuum of acceptability, which is represented in Figure 9.2.

Applying this concept to administrative decision making, some directives clearly are unacceptable and will not be obeyed. On the other end of the continuum, some decisions are highly acceptable and meet with high interest

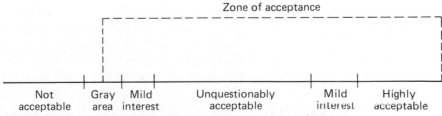

FIGURE 9.2 Continuum for decisive acceptability

and anticipation. In between, four areas are postulated. The first is a gray area, where decisions are either barely acceptable or barely unacceptable. Next are areas toward each end, where only mild interest in the decision exists. In the middle of the range, the decision is accepted without question or interest.[45] This acceptance is explained by the fact that when people join an organization, such as a school, they expect or anticipate that certain demands will be made. For instance, teachers expect to spend a reasonable amount of time completing attendance reports and do not question the validity of such actions. The zone of acceptance, therefore, is the area on the continuum where directives are willingly implemented by subordinates. Moreover, this range can be changed.

School principals are challenged to find ways to extend the scope of authority beyond rather narrow limits of the bureaucratic zone of acceptance. Their basic problem is to gain more authority than the amount formally vested in the office. It is possible that the way principals are perceived as using their formal authority influences the teachers' willingness to comply with their directives.

The LBDQ research suggests that those principals who have high performance on both initiating structure and consideration (quadrant I) should produce a situation that is conducive to a relatively broad zone of acceptance by teachers to their directives.[46] Conversely, principals whose leadership styles place them in quadrant III seem likely to have teachers with the narrowest zone of acceptance. Given the norm in schools that teachers value considerate leaders, a reasonable hypothesis is that those principals high in consideration but low in initiating structure (quadrant IV) would have teachers with a wider zone of acceptance than those principals low in consideration but high in initiating structure (quadrant II).

This hypothesis was tested in a study conducted by Daniel Kunz and Wayne K. Hoy. The index employed to measure the width of the professional zone of acceptance was a thirty-item scale with a Likert-type format. Teachers who were randomly sampled from each school analyzed each item in terms of areas in which their principal might make unilateral decisions. They indicated their probable frequency of compliance in terms of a five-point scale from always to never. Examples of item areas include the following: "the change and modification of existing curricula," "the requirements for student membership in extracurricular activities," and "the degree of student proficiency needed to pass each grade and subject."[47]

The widest professional zone of acceptance appears within schools where the principal was described as strong on both initiating structure and consideration (quadrant I). This finding is consistent with previous research that indicates that administrators high on both dimensions are more effective; in fact, effectiveness may well be related to the leader's ability to obtain willing compliance from subordinates to directives that clearly are outside the bureaucratic zone of indifference. Principals low on initiating structure had teachers with relatively narrow zones of acceptance regardless of whether the principal was high or low in consideration; the mean scores are virtually the same for principals in quadrants III and IV. Moreover, principals with low scores on consideration but high scores on initiating structure (quadrant II) had teachers with nearly as large a professional zone of acceptance as principals strong in both dimensions (quadrant I). These data are summarized in Table 9.4. Differences among the means of the four quadrants were statistically significant.

The hypothesis was thus not supported. Consideration is not more strongly related to the teachers' professional zone of acceptance than initiating structure. Apparently, initiating structure is an overriding factor that is related to the professional zone of acceptance of teachers. Secondary principals who are strong on the dimension of initiating structure also tend to be high on that of consideration; therefore, we speculate that those principals rated high on initiating structure are able to maintain a minimal level of consideration, allowing faculty identification and rapport to develop with the principal. We further theorize that this minimal level of consideration permits the strong emphasis on initiating structure to work in acquiring willing compliance to directives.

Additional statistical analysis to test the hypothesis revealed that this was not necessarily the case. In Table 9.5, the correlation of each LBDQ dimension with the zone of acceptance index is shown first as a zero-order correlation and then as a partial correlation, controlling for the other dimension. The zero-order correlations indicate that both consideration and initiating structure are strongly and significantly related to the zone of acceptance index. When the partial correlation is computed between consideration and zone of acceptance (controlling for initiating structure, that is, statistically removing the effect of initiating structure), the correlation becomes insignificant. On the other hand, the partial correlation between initiating structure and zone of acceptance remains statistically significant even after eliminating the effect of consideration as the table shows. Thus, strength in initiating structure appears to be significantly related to teachers' professional zone of acceptance regardless of the consideration demonstrated by the principal. Those principals who exhibit high initiating structure tend to have teachers with a fairly wide professional zone of acceptance, regardless of the principals' consideration.

The results of a recent study of elementary principals' leadership behavior and the zone of acceptance of teachers reveal a slightly different set of relationships at the elementary level.[48] Similar to the secondary schools, both initiating

TABLE 9.4 Leadership Style of the Principal and Mean Zone of Acceptance Scores of Teachers

		Leadership Style of Principal			
		Quadrant I (+, +)	*Quadrant II* (−, +)	*Quadrant III* (−, −)	*Quadrant IV* (+, −)
Zone of Acceptance	Mean score	80.80	77.76	70.13	69.43
	Number of schools	19	8	18	5

TABLE 9.5 Coefficients of Correlation Between the Dimensions of Leader Behavior and Zone of Acceptance

	Zone of Acceptance	
	r	partial r
Consideration	0.41*	0.05
Initiating Structure	0.57*	0.41*

*p < 0.01, n = 50

structure and consideration were positively related to the zone of acceptance (r = .48 and .36 respectively). But *both* dimensions had significant independent effects on the professional zone of acceptance of teachers. Unlike the secondary schools, the consideration of the elementary principals had a significant independent relationship with the zone of acceptance of teachers.

The findings of Kunz, Hoy, and Leverette support the conclusions made by several scholars who have recently reviewed the research findings on leader behavior.[49] Consideration is typically related to subordinate satisfaction with work and with the leader. While the evidence is somewhat mixed, initiating structure has been identified as a source of subordinate performance. However, situational variables apparently affect the relationship between consideration and initiating structure and affect the criteria of organizational effectiveness as well. Consideration has its most positive effect on the satisfaction of subordinates who work in structured situations or who work on stressful, frustrating, or dissatisfying tasks. In contrast, initiating structure has the greatest impact on group performance when subordinates' tasks are ill defined.

The implications of these findings are fairly clear to us. To neglect initiation of structure limits the effectiveness of the school; to ignore consideration reduces the satisfaction of the subordinates. Certainly, transactional leader behavior—behavior that integrates strength on both initiating structure and consideration into a consistent pattern—is desirable. Nevertheless, the converse also seems likely; there are situations especially favorable to a leadership style that is characterized by strong consideration and limited initiating structure. The matching of leadership style with the appropriate situation in order to maximize effectiveness is a knotty problem to which we will return throughout this chapter. Although attention of most researchers in the field has been focused on the dimensions of leadership emerging from the LBDQ studies at Ohio State University, several other extensive research efforts should be described briefly.

University of Michigan Research Studies

Concurrent with the Ohio State studies, the University of Michigan Survey Research Center conducted a series of studies on leadership behavior.[50] The Michigan research primarily dealt with business and industrial organizations, such as insurance companies, manufacturing concerns, and banks. Some investigations were conducted in hospitals, governmental agencies, and public utilities.

The overall purpose of the Michigan investigations was to locate clusters of leader characteristics that are closely related to each other and to effectiveness criteria. The criteria included job satisfaction, turnover, absenteeism, productivity, and efficiency. Initially, two distinct styles of leadership were identified —production-oriented and employee-centered.[51] Production-oriented leaders emphasize the mission or task to be done and the technical aspects of the job. They stress developing plans and procedures to accomplish the task. Employee-centered leaders believe in delegating decision making and assist followers in satisfying their needs by creating a supportive work environment. Moreover, leaders with an employee orientation are concerned with the subordinates' personal growth, advancement, and achievement. Originally, these two orientations were conceptualized as opposite ends of the same continuum; subsequent research and analyses showed that they were actually independent dimensions, like the dimensions of consideration and initiating structure developed at Ohio State.

Although the many field studies and experiments conducted by the Michigan group are exceedingly difficult to summarize concisely, three generalizations have substantial support.

1. More effective leaders tend to have relationships with their subordinates that are supportive and enhance the followers' sense of self-esteem than less effective ones.
2. More effective leaders use group rather than person-to-person methods of supervision and decision making than less effective ones.
3. More effective leaders tend to set high performance goals than less effective ones.[52]

In sum, the University of Michigan studies complement the Ohio State studies. The findings are limited, however, by the fact that the researchers did not take situational differences systematically into account.

Harvard Studies of Group Leadership

In 1947 a somewhat different line of inquiry was undertaken by the Laboratory of Social Relations at Harvard University under the direction of Robert F. Bales. The purpose of this work was to set up small groups of subjects under laboratory conditions and to study social behavior by direct observation. One of the most startling findings of that laboratory research was that "the concept of 'leader,' if it is taken too literally, can cause the man who thinks he is one to disregard a most important fact—namely, that there is usually another leader in the group whom he can overlook only at his peril."[53]

The findings that emerge from the study also led to the suggestion of a dual leadership model. The individual who was judged by other group members to have the best ideas in contributing to the decision typically was not the best liked. Indeed, Bales posits the existence of two separate leadership roles in small task groups attempting to solve problems—the task leader and the social leader.[54] The task leader keeps the group engaged in the work, whereas the social leader maintains unity in the group and keeps group members aware of their importance as unique individuals and whose special needs and values are respected. Both roles are necessary for the effective operation of the group, yet only a few individuals can hold both roles.

We mention the Harvard studies briefly for several reasons. Unlike the Ohio State and Michigan studies, this research focused on the face-to-face interactions of individuals in small groups studied experimentally. Furthermore, most of the experimental groups were composed of college students rather than of leaders in actual formal organizations. Despite the differences in the unit of analysis, type of research situation, and methodology, the results are remarkably consistent with the Ohio State and Michigan: two leaders appear to develop in social groups and organizations. The findings of these independent investigations support each other.

CONTINGENCY APPROACHES

The behavioral approaches developed at Ohio State University and the University of Michigan and the experimental results from Harvard University are impressive. Yet, the linkage between leadership and important effectiveness indicators such as achievement and satisfaction has not been established conclusively by any of these theories.[55] Therefore, alternative formulations with greater descriptive and explanatory powers have emerged.

The contemporary theory of leadership is referred to as the Contingency Approach. As discussed earlier, contingency theories maintain that leadership effectiveness depends upon the fit between personality characteristics and behavior of the leader and situational variables such as task structure, position power, and subordinate skills and attitudes.[56] Thus, there is no one "best" leadership style. The Contingency Approach attempts to predict which types of leaders will be effective in different types of situations. Currently, the two most widely tested Contingency Theories are Fiedler's Contingency Model and House's Path-Goal Theory.

Fiedler's Contingency Model

Fiedler constructed the first major theory to propose specific contingency relationships in the study of leadership. The basic postulates of Fiedler's model follow:

1. Leadership style is determined by the motivational system of the leader.

2. Group effectiveness is a joint function of the leader's style and the situation's favorableness; that is, group performance is contingent upon the leader's motivations and upon the leader's control and influence in the situation.[57]

The theory departs from previous thinking because it views the leadership situation as an arena in which the leader seeks both to satisfy personal needs and to accomplish organizational goals.[58]

Leadership style. Fiedler carefully and clearly distinguishes between the terms "leadership behavior" and "leadership style." Leadership behavior denotes the specific acts of a leader in directing and coordinating the work of group members. For instance, the leader can commend, make helpful suggestions, and show consideration for the well-being of group members. In contrast, leadership style refers to the underlying need structure of the leader that motivates behavior in various interpersonal situations. In essence, leadership style is a personality characteristic; it does not describe a consistent type of leader behavior. Fiedler underscores this critical distinction between leadership style and leadership behavior for understanding his theory as follows: ". . . important leadership behaviors of the same individual differ from situation to situation, while the need-structure which motivates these behaviors may be seen as constant."[59]

To identify leadership styles, Fiedler developed a simple personality measure called the *least preferred co-worker* (LPC) scale. The LPC scale is a semantic differential consisting of sixteen bipolar items. The respondent is asked to select the person with whom he or she works least well (least preferred co-worker) and then describe that individual on the scale (see Table 9.6). Each item is scored from one to eight, with eight being the most favorable point on the scale. The LPC score is the sum of the item scores of all sixteen items.

A person scoring high on the LPC describes the least preferred co-worker positively. The least preferred co-worker is seen as being pleasant, friendly, efficient, cheerful, and so forth. Thus, even a person with whom it is difficult to work might also be seen as an individual who otherwise has some acceptable, if not admirable, traits. In contrast, the individual scoring low on the LPC describes the least preferred co-worker negatively. The least preferred co-worker is viewed as being unpleasant, unfriendly, inefficient, gloomy, and so forth. The person who rates a least preferred co-worker negatively states a strong rejection of people with whom he or she cannot work. In effect, this person says, "If I cannot work with you, then you're no damn good!"[60]

The meaning of LPC scores is still a matter of some conjecture. The interpretation of what the LPC measures has changed over the years. At first, it was seen simply as a measure of an emotional reaction to individuals with whom the leader found it difficult to work; then, it was thought to differentiate between individuals who had a task orientation as opposed to an interpersonal one, or to measure cognitive complexity; today it is taken as an indicator of the motiva-

TABLE 9.6 A Sample of Items from the Least Preferred Co-worker Questionnaire

Directions. Think of the Person with Whom You Can Work Least Well. The Person May be Someone You Work with Now, or the Person May be Someone You Knew in the Past. The Person Does Not Have to Be the Person You Like Least Well, but Should Be the Person with Whom You Had the Most Difficulty in Getting a Job Done. Describe the Person as He or She Appears to You.

Pleasant	8	7	6	5	4	3	2	1	Unpleasant
Rejecting	1	2	3	4	5	6	7	8	Accepting
Cooperative	8	7	6	5	4	3	2	1	Uncooperative
Quarrelsome	1	2	3	4	5	6	7	8	Harmonious
Helpful	8	7	6	5	4	3	2	1	Frustrating
Distant	1	2	3	4	5	6	7	8	Close
Efficient	8	7	6	5	4	3	2	1	Inefficient
Gloomy	1	2	3	4	5	6	7	8	Cheerful

Adapted from Fred E. Fiedler, *A Theory of Leadership Effectiveness* (New York: McGraw-Hill, 1967), p. 268. Reprinted by permission from McGraw-Hill.

tions of the leader.[61] The LPC is now thought to identify two styles of leadership. Task-oriented leaders score low on the LPC and are motivated by (i.e., derive satisfaction from) successful task accomplishment. Conversely, relationship-oriented leaders score high on the LPC and receive satisfaction from successful interpersonal interactions. In short, leadership style as measured by the LPC represents a cognitive motivational process with the important content being effective task completion (low LPC) or positive interpersonal relationships (high LPC).

If this interpretation of the LPC is correct, then it becomes clear why individuals respond differently on the LPC scale. Those with a low LPC score have negative reactions toward their least preferred co-worker because a co-worker with whom it is difficult to "get the job done" threatens the central motivational orientation of the leader—succeeding at a task. But those with a high LPC score can have neutral or even positive attitudes toward their least preferred co-worker because an ineffective co-worker does not necessarily threaten the leader's orientation of interpersonal success.[62] In elaborating on this interpretation, Fiedler strongly emphasizes that the LPC relates to different goal priorities, not differences in leader behavior. The accomplishment of a task, for example, might well call for considerate and pleasant interpersonal behaviors, while the maintenance of close interpersonal relations might be possible only by driving the group to success. In this latter case the relationship-motivated leader (with a high LPC score) might be quite single-minded about task accomplishment. In general, however, uncertain and stressful situations tend to make the low LPC leaders focus on the task, while leaders with a high score concentrate on their relationships with subordinates. The converse is the case when conditions give the leader security and control.[63]

Situation. An underlying assumption of the Contingency Approach is that different types of situations require different types of leadership; therefore, a second major component of the theory is the situation. To what extent does the situation itself enable the leader to exert influence? Fiedler identifies three major factors that determine the favorableness of the group situation: position power of the leader, task structure, and leader-member relations.

Position power is the degree to which the position itself enables the leader to get subordinates to comply with directives. In organizations, power is formal —authority is vested in the leader's office. Position power determines the extent to which a leader can reward and punish members, whether the group can depose the leader, whether the leader enjoys special or official rank or status that sets him or her apart from group members, and the like.[64] Position power tends to make the job of the leader easier, although it does not inherently guarantee better group performance. To a large extent the power a position carries is determined by the organization.

Task structure is the extent to which the task is clearly specified, verified, and programmed in a step-by-step manner. With highly structured tasks, the leader and group know exactly what to do and how to do it. Unstructured tasks with ambiguous goals, no clear-cut solutions, and a multiplicity of approaches make definitive action by the leader and group difficult. Thus, in terms of directing and controlling groups, the more structured the task, the more favorable the situation for the leader.

Leader-member relations is the extent to which the leader is accepted and respected by the group members. Two factors are important with respect to leader-member relations: the quality of interpersonal relations between the leader and subordinates, and the level of informal authority granted to the leader. In contrast to position power and task structure, which are determined in large part by the organization, the quality of leader-member relations is determined primarily by the leader's personality and behavior. Evidence to date indicates that the quality of leader-member relations is the most important factor in determining the leader's influence over the group members, followed by task structure and position power.[65] Therefore, the leader has more control and influence when (1) the group is supportive, (2) the leader knows exactly what to do and how to do it, and (3) the organization gives the leader means to reward and punish the group members.

Fiedler uses these three factors to form eight situations ordered in terms of their favorableness. Each of the three factors are dichotimized into good or bad leader-member relations, structured or unstructured tasks, and high or low position power. The eight combinations or octants map the range of situations from highly favorable to highly unfavorable. Table 9.7 contains two portrayals of the eight situations. For example, octant I is the most favorable situation with good relations, structured task, and high position power. Octants IV and V are

TABLE 9.7   Two Formulations of Fiedler's Classification of Situational Favorableness

Formulation A

	Degree of Favorableness	Leader-Member Relations	Task Structure	Position Power of the Leader
Octant I	Very Favorable	Good	Structured	High
Octant II		Good	Structured	Low
Octant III		Good	Unstructured	High
Octant IV	Moderate	Good	Unstructured	Low
Octant V	Moderate	Poor	Structured	High
Octant VI		Poor	Structured	Low
Octant VII		Poor	Unstructured	High
Octant VIII	Unfavorable	Poor	Unstructured	Low

Formulation B

Leader-member relations	Good				Poor			
Task Structure	High		Low		High		Low	
Position Power	Strong	Weak	Strong	Weak	Strong	Weak	Strong	Weak
	I	II	III	IV	V	VI	VII	VIII
Octants (situations)	Favorable			Moderate			Unfavorable	

moderate. Good group relations, the most important component, combines with two negative factors to form octant IV, and poor-good relations combines with two positive factors to form octant V. Finally, octant VIII is most unfavorable with all three components being negative.

Leader effectiveness.   The concept of effectiveness is complex and has been defined in numerous ways. Typical indicators of effectiveness include group output, group morale, and satisfaction of group members. Fiedler, however, proposes a simple and straightforward criterion of effectiveness, namely, the extent to which the group accomplishes its primary task. Even though the group's output is not entirely a function of the leader's skills, the leader's effectiveness is judged on how well the group achieves its task. According to Fiedler, turnover rate, job satisfaction, morale, and personal adjustment may contribute to group performance, but they are not in themselves criteria of performance.[66] In many of Fiedler's studies, objective measures of group effectiveness are used—net profit, cost per unit, percentage of wins, number of problems solved. But in all cases, leader effectiveness is determined by the degree to which the task is achieved.

The match: style and situation.   The question still remains: Which style of leadership is most effective in which type of situation? Using data that he collected from a wide variety of group situations (more than 800 groups) over more than ten years, Fiedler categorized the type of situation (one of eight octants), determined the style of the leader, and determined which groups performed their tasks successfully or unsuccessfully. Then for each group, effectiveness of the group performance was correlated with leadership style. Next these correlations were plotted separately for each of the eight situations, presented as octants in Table 9.7. If the median correlations for each situation are plotted and graphed, a curve shaped like that in Figure 9.3 is produced. The shape suggests that the appropriateness of the leadership style for maximizing

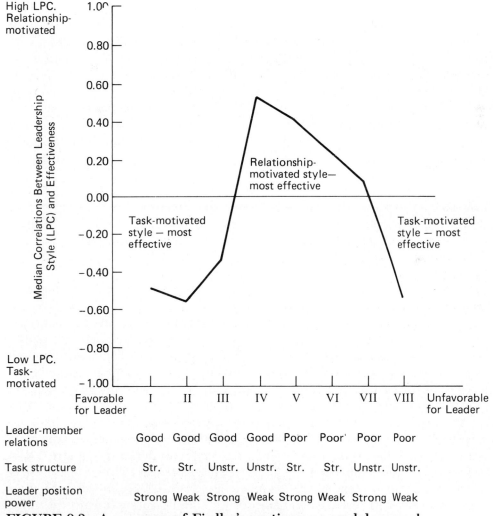

FIGURE 9.3 A summary of Fiedler's contingency model research

SOURCE: Adapted from Fred E. Fiedler, *A Theory of Leadership Effectiveness* (New York: McGraw-Hill, 1967), p. 146. Used with permission of McGraw-Hill Book Company.

group performance is indeed contingent on the favorableness of the situation. From the data, Fiedler develops three major propositions of his Contingency Theory:

1. In favorable situations, task-oriented leaders are more effective than relationship-oriented leaders.
2. In moderately favorable situations, relationship-oriented leaders are more effective than task-oriented leaders.
3. In unfavorable situations, task-oriented leaders are more effective than relationship-oriented leaders.

The basic explanation for effectiveness emerging from Fiedler's research is that favorableness of the situation elicits leader behavior that is consistent with the motivational system of the leader.[67] The primary motivational pattern of leaders appears in situations in which the individual is threatened; leaders pursue their secondary goals in situations in which primary goals are either satisfied or appear secure. Hence, high LPC leaders will concern themselves with relationships in unfavorable situations but with the task in favorable situations. Low LPC leaders will concern themselves with the task in unfavorable situations, but in favorable situations, they will be concerned with having good interpersonal reactions.[68]

According to the theory, leaders with low LPC scores who concentrate on task accomplishment are more effective in the unfavorable situations because the situation triggers directing and controlling behavior that is most likely to get the job done. Anxious concern with interpersonal relations does not produce effectiveness.

In favorable situations, leaders with low LPC are also the more effective but for different reasons. In a highly favorable setting, the leaders can focus on secondary goals because their primary goal is being met. Consequently, the task-oriented leader (with a low LPC score) displays considerate behavior; the relations-oriented leader (with a high LPC score) exhibits task-relevant behaviors. Since task-relevant behaviors are redundant in highly favorable situations (which are characterized by low task ambiguity, high position power, and good leader-member relations), the leader with a low LPC score is more effective than the high LPC scorer in favorable situations.[69]

In situations of medium favorability, research has shown that relations-oriented leaders (with high LPC scores) are more effective, though it is not clear why. One possible explanation is that such leaders experience less stress than task-oriented leaders (with low LPC scores) in response to the same levels of situational unfavorableness. The evidence suggests that the two kinds of leaders respond to stress differently. For example, low LPC scorers in stressful conditions become more assertive, task oriented, directive, and controlling. Such behaviors suggest that they become more rigid and exhibit less variability in behavior than high-scoring leaders, given the same level of unfavorableness. It is possible that under moderate situational favorability behavioral flexibility on the part of leaders is required. If low-scoring leaders experience stress in this type of situation, then it is doubtful that they would be able to exhibit the flexibility needed for group effectiveness. In contrast, leaders with high LPC scores experiencing less stress would be more flexible and adapt as the situation demands. Thus, the differential perception and response to stress provides an explanation for the high performance of leaders with high LPC scores under conditions of medium situational favorability.

Research testing Fiedler's theory. The Contingency Model was inductively developed on the basis of data collected before 1962. Since then, the model has been used to predict group performance in a large variety of social settings.[70] To date only two studies provide rigorous and complete tests of the model; that is, investigations that meet the criteria set by Fiedler and include leaders from all eight situations. One study was supportive; one was not.[71] However, three meta-analyses of research testing the Contingency Model have been performed, and all provide some support. Michael Strube and Joseph Garcia's analysis provides strong statistical support for the model.[72] Similarly, except for octant II, the meta-analysis of Lawrence Peters and his associates is generally supportive, and Ellen Crehan concludes from her meta-analysis that results of studies that adhered to Fiedler's methodology were typically supportive of his model.[73]

Fieldler's model also has been used to predict the leadership effectiveness of principals in the school context. Before one can test the model for principal effectiveness, it is necessary to determine the leadership style of principals, the favorableness of the situations, and the effectiveness of the school. The leadership style of the principal is easily measured. The LPC instrument is simply administered to the principal, and the leadership style is operationalized.

Similarly, a determination of the degree of favorableness of the situation is fairly straightforward. School principals do have position power; they have the formal authority of the office. Thus, the assumption is made that the situation will be either highly favorable or moderately favorable, depending on the leader-member relations.

A variety of ways exist to measure the strength of leader-member relations; Fiedler developed a simple instrument, the *group atmosphere scale (GAS)*. Using a semantic differential format, it is similar to the LPC measure, with the leader being asked to rate the group as a whole. The evidence indicates that leaders apparently are quite perceptive about the degree of support they are receiving from group members. Those who have high support describe the group atmospheres favorably; those with low support describe the group atmospheres unfavorably. Hence, the GAS can be used as an index of the favorableness of the situation.

In applications of the model to school principals, the criterion of effectiveness is the most difficult measurement problem to solve. Because of the disagreement about what constitutes effective educational outcomes, defining and operationalizing effectiveness is at best a perilous task. Interestingly, three attempts to test the Contingency Model in elementary schools employed different criterion measures of effectiveness. Vincent McNamara and Frederick Enns used a rating scheme in which school officials were asked to rate the schools (not the principals) on effectiveness.[74] Leonard B. Williams and Hoy employed a more indirect index of performance based on the perceived level of effective characteristics displayed by elementary teachers.[75] Yvonne M. Martin and her associates measured group effectiveness as the perceived assistance that the group gave to new probationary teachers.[76]

The results of all three studies support Fiedler's Contingency Theory. In schools with principals who are well supported by their teachers (a favorable situation), a task-oriented style is significantly associated with group effectiveness. In schools with principals who are less well supported (a moderately favorable situation), there is some tendency, although not a statistically significant one, for a relationship-oriented style to be associated with school effectiveness.

Three studies, however, do not "prove" a theory. Still, although they were limited to elementary schools and used different criterion measures of effectiveness, their results were remarkably similar and in large part consistent with the Contingency Model. It is likely that, at least in elementary schools, one type of leadership behavior is not appropriate for all conditions. Organizational performance will most likely be improved by matching the leadership style and the school situation.

Fiedler's theory thus represents an ambitious and laudable effort to go beyond the obviously correct but vacuous generalization that "leadership depends on the situation." The model demonstrates some characteristics of situations and individuals that partially explain the leadership phenomenon. Like most pioneering efforts it undoubtedly will be shown to be incorrect in detail if not in substance.[77] Yet, Fiedler's Contingency Model is probably the best attempt at this time to answer the question: What particular style in what special situation?

House's Path-Goal Theory

Path-goal theory is a contingency approach to leadership that was developed by House and refined during the 1970s.[78] Basically, the model integrates concepts that we have considered previously—leader behavior and situation favorableness with a unique definition of effectiveness.

The theory is called path-goal because it explains how leaders influence their subordinates' perceptions of work goals, personal goals, and paths to goal attainment. Accordingly, leaders are effective when they enhance the acceptance, satisfaction, and motivation levels of their subordinates.

Leader Behavior. Unlike Fiedler's theory, path-goal theory focuses on leader behavior, not the motivational basis of action. In particular, the theory includes four basic types of leader behavior.

1. *Directive Leadership:* behavior that clarifies expectations, gives specific direction, asks subordinates to follow rules and procedures.
2. *Achievement-Oriented Leadership:* behavior that sets challenging goals, seeks performance improvements, emphasizes excellence, and shows confidence that subordinates will attain high standards.
3. *Supportive Leadership:* behavior that is considerate, displays concern for the well-being of subordinates, and creates a friendly climate in the work group.
4. *Participative Leadership:* behavior that calls for consultation with subordinates and use of their ideas before decisions are made.[79]

These patterns of leader behavior are based on the Ohio State LBDQ studies. Directive and achievement-oriented behaviors are ways of initiating structure, one of the two basic dimensions of the LBDQ, while supportive and participative leader behaviors represent the other basic dimension, consideration. A fundamental assumption of the path-goal model is that leaders can vary their behavior to match the situation. Thus, leaders can exhibit the type of behavior that is most appropriate to the situation.[80]

Tests of the Path-Goal Theory typically have used the Form XII of the LBDQ, to measure leader behavior. Since the Path-Goal Theory requires specific leader actions to influence subordinate perceptions, critics charge that many of the items comprising the Form XII are too general. Consequently, some investigators have detailed specific acts to form new scales.[81]

Situational Factors. Two types of situational variables are considered in the path-goal theory: (1) personal characteristics of subordinates as they strive to accomplish work goals and derive satisfaction, and (2) environmental pressures and demands.

Specific personal characteristics that are important as contingencies in the situation include personal needs of subordinates (e.g., needs for achievement, understanding, autonomy, change), abilities of subordinates (e.g., knowledge, skills, aptitudes), and personality traits of subordinates (e.g., locus of control). These personal characteristics determine both the potential for motivating subordinates and the manner in which the leader must act. For example, individuals with an internal locus of control believe that events happen in large part because of their own efforts, while those with an external locus of control see little personal control over what happens—it is mostly a matter of luck. Those with an internal locus of control can be expected to respond favorably to participative leadership behavior, and those with an external locus of control will respond more favorably to directive behavior. Similarly, individuals with a high level of perceived ability relative to a task are more apt to resist directive behavior because it will be viewed as unnecessarily restrictive.

The specific environmental variables that are important determinants of the favorableness of the situation include task structure, degree of formalization (i.e., rules and regulations governing subordinate behavior), and supportive norms of the primary work group. Each of these factors can affect subordinate behavior in three ways. First, they may act to motivate and direct subordinates to accomplish the tasks. Second, they may help subordinates clarify their expectations and reinforce the notion that efforts lead to rewards. Of course, they may also restrict initiative and reduce work effort. Third, environmental and task forces may clarify and provide rewards for achieving desired performance. For example, it is possible for the work group itself to supply the needed direction and rewards for subordinates.

Effectiveness. Leader effectiveness in the Path-Goal Theory is defined in terms of the psychological states of subordinates, not in terms of task accomplishment. Leader behavior is effective to the extent that it improves subordinate job satisfaction, increases the acceptance of the leader, and promotes subordinate motivation.

General propositions. Briefly stated, Path-Goal Theory consists of two basic generalizations:

1. Leader behavior is acceptable and satisfying to followers to the extent that they can see it either as an immediate source of satisfaction or as an instrument to future satisfaction.
2. Leader behavior will motivate subordinate performance to the extent that (a) it makes gratification of subordinate needs dependent on effective performance, and (b) it complements the environment of subordinates by providing the coaching, guidance, support, and rewards that are necessary for effective performance of the task but which may be lacking in subordinates or in their environment.[82]

Leaders, then, are effective when their behavior provides subordinates with the guidance and rewards necessary for satisfaction and performance. Their actions are seen as ways to influence subordinates' perceptions of the clarity of the paths to goals and the desirability of the goals themselves. As we have already noted, two classes of situational variables condition leader behavior—personal characteristics of followers and environmental pressures and demands. For example, the degree of task structure moderates the relationship between directive leadership behavior and job satisfaction of subordinates. Figure 9.4 graphically displays this hypothesized relationship. Path-goal theory explains the relationship two ways. Highly directive behavior in ambiguous situations serves to increase satisfaction by clarifying the path to the goal. Moreover, supportive and participative behavior in situations with clear, structured tasks increases subordinates' job satisfaction, while directive behavior is frequently an irritation and tension producer, especially when consideration is low.

In general, directive leadership is appropriate in situations where it is important to reduce role ambiguity or to increase subordinate motivation by making the reward more closely contingent upon subordinate performance. Supportive leadership is desired in situations where boredom or personal anxi-

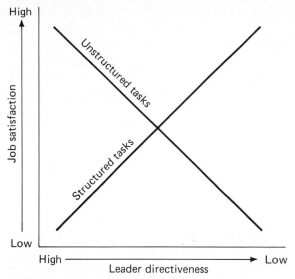

FIGURE 9.4   Hypothesized relationship between directive leadership behavior and subordinate satisfaction with task structure as a contingency factor

ety or lack of self-confidence is low. Achievement leadership is effective behavior in situations where the task is unstructured *and* subordinates need to be challenged by achievable goals. Finally, participative leadership is appropriate in situations where individuals have high needs for autonomy and achievement or in situations with unstructured tasks.[83] The basic concepts and relationships are summarized in Figure 9.5.

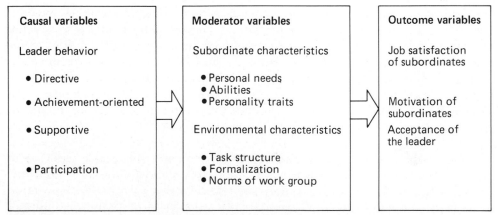

FIGURE 9.5   Summary of the hypothesized relationships in the path-goal theory

Research testing Path-Goal Theory. The Path-Goal model is a relatively recent formulation; hence, it continues to undergo change and refinement. The theory is open in the sense that new variables can be added to increase the power of explanation. As one might expect under these circumstances, the research results have been mixed; some findings support the theory, others do not.[84] The hypotheses relating the effects of leader behavior to subordinate satisfaction have been supported more consistently than those examining the effects of leader behavior on motivational performance. Whether House's Path-Goal Theory will supplement or supplant Fiedler's contingency model awaits further empirical research. We believe, however, that it offers considerable promise for helping to understand the complex process of leadership in schools.

A COMPARISON OF THE CONTINGENCY AND PATH-GOAL MODELS

Three differences between Fiedler's contingency model and House's Path-Goal Theory are readily apparent. First, Path-Goal Theory does not seek to measure the motivational basis of leader behavior, while the contingency theory does not try to measure leader behavior. In fact, Path-Goal Theory in its early versions does not include personality traits of leaders. Second, the models contain contrasting definitions of leader effectiveness. For Fiedler, effectiveness is measured in terms of the extent to which the group accomplishes its task. For House, leader effectiveness is measured in terms of the psychological states of the subordinates. Third, House phrased his theory so that additional variables could be added as new ones became known. Consequently, the opportunities for refining and extending it appear to be greater than for Fiedler's theory.

A Schema of Variables for the Study of Leadership

The leadership models constructed by Fiedler and House are important contributions to a contingency approach of leadership; however, they neglect a number of other concepts and considerations. A good starting point for producing a better understanding of leadership phenomena would be to consider traits, behavior, situations, and effectiveness. In an effort to assist future developments, concepts relating to each of these components are contained in Figure 9.6. The schema there attempts to synthesize the current knowledge about leadership. It does not include every concept, but some of the more important ones are isolated and presented.

Leader traits of educational administrators. Notice that the style variables in Figure 9.6 are divided into two groups—personality and abilities. The concepts of task and interpersonal orientation come from Fiedler's work; the expectation variable is derived from cognitive motivation theory (see Chapter 7); and self-confidence and dominance comprise traits that are consistently associated with leader effectiveness.[85] During the past thirty years, the role of cognitive abilities

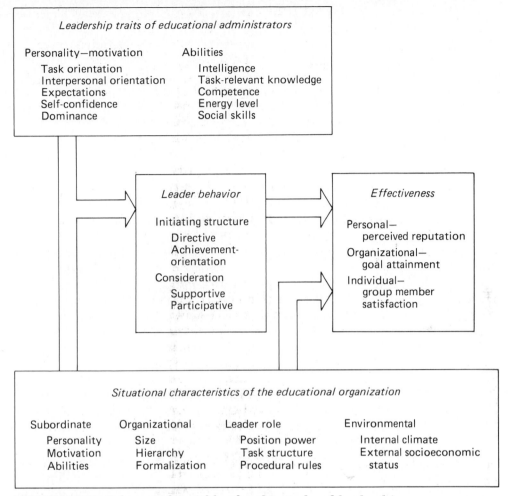

FIGURE 9.6 **Schema of variables for the study of leadership**

may not have received a fair test in leadership research. Recently, evidence produced by two separate groups of scholars demonstrates an overall positive relationship of cognitive abilities with leader performance.[86]

House and Baetz argue that certain properties of all leadership situations are present to a significant degree and are relatively invariant. Therefore, some specific traits are required in most if not all leadership situations. The following hypotheses apply to possible invariant characteristics of the leadership situation in all organizations:

1. Since leadership requires followers, social skills probably will always be needed if acts intended to influence are to be viewed as acceptable by subordinates. Skills such as speech fluency and traits

such as cooperativeness and sociability thus are likely candidates for being general leadership traits.

2. Since leadership requires a predisposition to be influential, traits such as dominance, self-confidence, need for power, and need for influence are hypothesized to be associated with leader effectiveness.

3. Since leadership is most often exercised when specific task objectives or organizational goals must be accomplished, traits such as need for achievement, desire for responsibility, task orientation, energy level, and task-relevant knowledge also are likely to be associated with leadership.[87]

In sum, several traits that for the most part have not been tested in educational organizations appear to be systematically related to leadership.

Situational characteristics of educational organizations. Four categories of situations seem particularly germane to the study of leadership in educational organizations.[88] The basic assumption is that leadership effectiveness cannot be determined adequately without understanding the total situation, including subordinate traits, structural configurations of schools, role definitions, and both internal and external environmental conditions of the school (see Figure 9.6).[89]

Two fundamental generalizations emerge from this set of characteristics. First, the characteristics of the situation combine with the traits of the leader to produce a behavior on the part of the leader which is related to leadership effectiveness. Second, the characteristics of situation have a direct impact on the effectiveness. For example, the motivation and ability levels of teachers and students are related to the goal attainment of schools. Moreover, the socioeconomic status of individuals attending a school is strongly related to student achievement on standardized tests. From a short-range perspective, at least, the situational characteristics of the school may have a greater influence on leader effectiveness than the leader's own behavior. These two generalizations represent tentative hypotheses that should be tested in educational settings.

Leader effectiveness. The outcomes of leadership must be evaluated against effectiveness criteria. Three effectiveness outcomes are listed in Figure 9.6— perception of the leader's reputation, member satisfaction, and organizational goal attainment.

To the practicing administrator, effectiveness is a complicated and subtle topic. Evaluations of performance are important: subjective judgments of the leader by subordinates, peers, and superiors yield measures of effectiveness. In schools, the opinions held by students, teachers, administrators, and patrons are highly significant. A second indicator of leadership effectiveness is the overall satisfaction of organizational participants. Finally, the relative level of achievement of school goals defines the effectiveness of educational leaders. Leadership effectiveness, then, has a more objective dimension—accomplishment of organizational goals—and two subjective dimensions—perceptual evaluations of significant reference groups and overall job satisfaction of subordinates.

A partial test of this schema for school principals was made by Cecil Miskel.[90] The findings are consistent with the contingency approach; a combination of individual and situational variables predicted school effectiveness and perceptual evaluations of principals by teachers and superintendents.

CONCEPTUAL DERIVATIONS AND APPLICATIONS

Managerial Grid®

While developing leadership training seminars, Robert R. Blake and Jane S. Mouton[91] evolved a conceptualization of leadership, which they labeled the Managerial Grid. Like many other models of leadership, the Managerial Grid has two basic dimensions—concern for production and concern for people. Its development paralleled the Ohio State studies, which addressed many of the same issues, and the Grid continues to be used in training programs. Concern for production is not limited to things; instead, it denotes a concern for whatever the organization engages its people to accomplish, that is, the successful accomplishment of the organizational task. Concern for people refers primarily to sound and warm interpersonal relations. Self-esteem and the personal worth of the individual are stressed.

The Managerial Grid, depicted in Figure 9.7, shows these two dimensions and their range of possible combinations. The horizontal axis represents the concern for production dimension, while the vertical axis represents the concern for people dimension. Each axis has been converted to a nine-point scale, with the number 1 representing minimum concern and the number 9 designating maximum concern.

Given the 9×9 grid, it is theoretically possible to map eighty-one leadership styles. Blake and Mouton, however, tend to confine their analysis to the corners and midpoint of the Grid, that is, to the 9, 1 style, the 1, 9 style, the 1, 1 style, the 9, 9 style, and the 5, 5 style. They postulate that the manner in which leaders link these two dimensions defines both how they use the hierarchy and their administrative style. Each style is based on a different set of assumptions about how individuals behave. We turn now to some of the basic assumptions and characteristics of these five styles.

The 9, 1 style—authority-obedience.   The 9, 1 style is a starkly task-oriented style: a high concern for task accomplishment is coupled with a low concern for people. Achievement is the watchword of this approach, and interaction is strictly along authority lines. Quotas and deadlines are commonplace and are used to motivate subordinates. When conflict emerges, it is suppressed by dealing firmly with those involved. Communication is formal, one-way, and downward. In brief, superiors engage in a program of close supervision and tight control, focusing on achievement of the organizational tasks. It is "produce or perish."

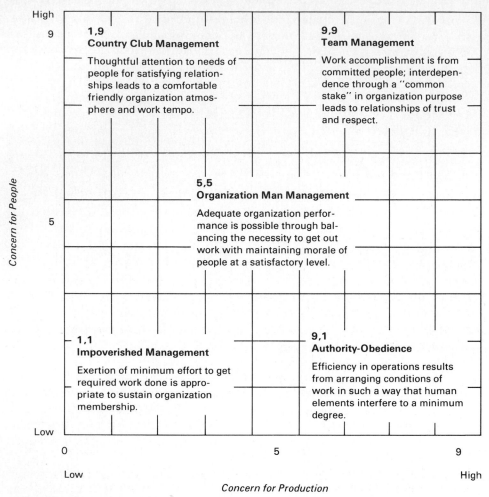

FIGURE 9.7 The Managerial Grid®

SOURCE: The Managerial Grid figure from *The Managerial Grid III*, by Robert R. Blake and Jane Srygley Mouton. Houston: Gulf Publishing Company, Copyright © 1985, page 12. Reproduced with permission.

The 1, 9 style—country club management. The 1, 9 style is characterized by a low concern for tasks coupled with a high concern for people. Sound interpersonal relations are the hallmark of this approach; the dispositions and feelings of people are of overriding importance to the leader. A basic assumption underlying this style is that the needs of task achievement are contrary to the needs of people. Administrators solve this problem by subordinating task requirements to the need-dispositions of subordinates. Goals are kept global, ambiguous, and general; thus, everyone can support them. Communications are informal and concentrate on social and personal topics rather than on task-related matters. Conflict must be avoided if possible; hence, appeasement is the rule rather than the exception. When conflict does erupt, it is smoothed over. In brief, the superior is primarily concerned with winning friends and influencing people.

The 1, 1 style—impoverished management.   The 1, 1 style is characterized by low concern for task achievement and low concern for people. Like the 9, 1 and 1, 9 styles, an incompatibility exists between organizational demands and employee needs; however, because concern is low for both task and people, this style is conspicuous for its lack of leadership activity. The supervisor's approach is to put people on jobs and then leave them alone, hiding behind the rules and regulations in order to remain relatively invisible. In brief, administrators with this leadership style are likely to confine themselves to delivering messages coming down from above.

The 9, 9 style—team management.   The 9, 9 style is characterized by a high concern for both task accomplishment and people. Unlike the other styles, this style assumes no inherent conflict exists between organizational requirements and the needs of people. People who adopt this leadership style want to promote conditions that integrate high productivity and high morale through concerted teamwork. Because it is assumed that, given the opportunities, people are creative, the 9, 9 leadership style emphasizes involving those participants who are responsible for planning and executing the work. Communication is two-way and open. When conflict arises the facts are faced directly and the causes examined so that those involved can resolve the issue. Teamwork, participation, involvement, and group decision making are basic ingredients in the development of such conditions. People tend to support what they have helped to create.

The 5, 5 style—organization man management.   The 5, 5 style is characterized by a conflict between task needs and people needs; but the solution to the conflict is approached through compromise. In other words, equilibrium is achieved in such a way that both organization needs and people needs are accommodated in order not to rock the boat. The posture is one of balancing and satisfying and maintaining the status quo. Extreme positions are naturally avoided. This style assumes that people will work diligently and comply with reasonable directives that are explained. Communication flows through both the formal and informal systems, but formal communication is general rather than specific. The 5, 5 style seems sufficient for getting the job done, but it is probably insufficient for promoting innovation and change.

Implications.   The Managerial Grid is useful from a conceptual point of view for several reasons. It is consistent with the theoretical and research perspectives of the Ohio State, Michigan, and Harvard studies. Furthermore, it introduces a greater range of leadership styles. For example, the balanced leadership of the 5, 5 style was not mentioned in other studies, and other styles can be generated from the Grid that may more fully describe a given leadership pattern. For instance, effective leadership in a military setting might be described as 9, 5—there is high production or mission emphasis with good morale, but decision making is left primarily to the leader, who emphasizes strong concern for people and high morale with moderate, but firm, stress on production. One might hypothesize that, in general, the leadership styles of successful elementary school principals tend more toward 5, 9, while successful secondary school principals tend more toward 9, 5. There are more complex styles that can be conceived by mixing the basic pattern or by looking at shifting or dual patterns.

Blake and Mouton clearly indicate that the integrated style of leadership (9, 9) is the ideal. Their data lead them to conclude that the greater an individual's career accomplishment, the more likely his or her style of approach is 9, 9, or 9, 1, and the less likely his approach is 5, 5 or 1, 9.[92] Although the Managerial Grid has not been used extensively in studying, analyzing, or training leaders of school organizations, it does seem to offer some useful conceptual perspectives that, combined with the Ohio State framework, might provide a heuristic device for studying and analyzing school leadership patterns. For example, most studies using the LBDQ focus their analysis on the four quadrants mapped by initiating structure and consideration. The Grid suggests that it might also be useful to examine leadership that is moderate on both dimensions, (i.e., the 5, 5 style).

Situational Theory

Another theoretical framework that is useful for analyzing and guiding leadership behavior is Situational Theory.[93] Unlike the contingency theories of Fiedler and House, however, Situational Theory has been designed primarily as a vehicle for management training rather than as a guide for research; consequently, there is little systematic, empirical research that tests the theory. Nevertheless, the model provides some valuable insights into leader-follower behavior; it helps leaders diagnose the situation and develop strategies to adapt their leader behavior to meet the demands of the situation. Edgar Schein captures the intent of the theory when he observes that leaders must have the personal flexibility and range of skills necessary to vary their own behavior according to the needs and drives of subordinates. If teachers' needs and motives are different, they must be treated differently.[94]

Situational Theory is an attempt to provide a leader with some understanding of the relationships between effective styles of leadership and the level of maturity of followers. Simply stated, the basic assumption of the theory is that *leader effectiveness depends on the appropriate matching of leader behavior with the maturity of the group or individual.* Although Hersey and Blanchard recognize the importance of many situational variables (e.g., position power, task, time, and so forth), they emphasize maturity of the group or follower as the critical situational variable that moderates the relationship between leader behavior and effectiveness. Two other important characteristics of the theory are noteworthy. First, it applies to both individuals *and* groups. Second, the theory addresses both hierarchical and collegial relationships; therefore, it should have application whether one is attempting to influence the behavior of a subordinate, a superior, or a colleague.

Leader Behavior. Situational Theory deals with the behavior, not the personality, of the leader. In fact, the term "leadership style," unlike Fiedler's definition, refers to one of four patterns of leader behavior; it does not refer to the motivational needs of the individual.

Drawing from the Ohio State Leadership studies and William Reddin's Tri-Dimensional Leadership Effectiveness Model,[95] two dimensions of leadership behavior—task behavior and relationship behavior—are cross-partitioned to define four leadership styles. Leaders are classified as having a style high in task and low in relationship behaviors (Q_1), high in task and high in relationship behaviors (Q_2), high in relationship and low in task behaviors (Q_3) and low in both relationship and task behaviors (Q_4). The typology of styles is depicted in Figure 9.8. Each of these styles can be effective depending on the situation.

Situation. Situational Theory uses only one variable to analyze the nature of the situation—maturity. Maturity is the capacity to set high but attainable goals, the willingness and ability to take responsibility, and the experience of an individual or a group.[96] However, maturity is a relative concept. An individual or a group is not mature or immature in any general sense. Rather, maturity is defined only in relation to a specific task. The question is not, "Is the individual or group mature or immature?" but rather "On this specific job or task, what is the level of maturity of the group or individual?"

Individuals who have a high level of task-relevant maturity not only have the ability, knowledge, experience, and motivation to do the job but also feelings of self-confidence and self-respect about themselves. On the other hand, individuals who have a low level of task-relevant maturity lack the ability,

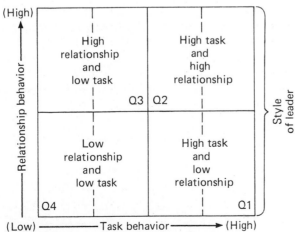

FIGURE 9.8 Hersey and Blanchard's leadership styles

SOURCE: Adapted from Paul Hersey and Kenneth H. Blanchard, *Management of Organizational Behavior: Utilizing Human Resources* (Englewood Cliffs, NJ: Prentice-Hall, 1982). Reproduced with permission.

motivation, and knowledge to do the job, as well as psychological maturity.[97] As shown in Figure 9.9, the situation can be conceived along a maturity-immaturity continuum, which in turn can be used to identify four types of situations (M_4, M_3, M_2, M_1) based on the level of maturity.

In addition to determining the level of maturity of individuals in a group, a leader may also have to determine the maturity level of the group as a whole, especially if the group works together in the same area. Hersey and Blanchard illustrate this situation with a classroom example, explaining that ". . . a teacher may find that a class as a group may be at one level of maturity in a particular area, but a student within that group may be at a different level. When the teacher is one-to-one with that student, he or she may have to behave quite differently than when working with the class as a group."[98] So too with other groups. The maturity of both individuals and the work group determines the appropriate supervisory or leader behavior.

Effectiveness. There is no concise definition of effectiveness in Situational Theory. Success in getting others to do a job in a prescribed way does not guarantee effectiveness. According to Hersey and Blanchard, effectiveness is a complex concept that involves not only objective performance but also human costs and psychological conditions. Thus, the term is defined broadly; it includes the evaluation of how well the group achieves its task as well as the psychological state of individuals and groups. In brief, effectiveness is a function of productivity and performance, the conditions of the human resources, and the extent to which both long and short-term goals are attained.[99]

Matching Style and Situation. According to Situational Theory, effectiveness is promoted by matching leader behavior with the appropriate situation. The match of behavior depends on the level of maturity in the situation. The guid-

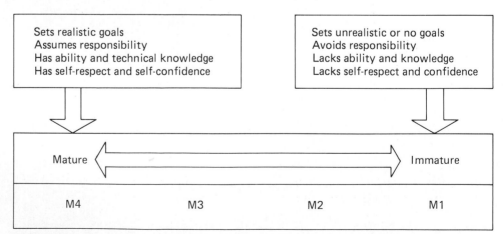

FIGURE 9.9   Maturity–immaturity continuum

ing principal of matching is succinctly stated by Hersey and Blanchard as follows:

> As the level of maturity of their followers continues to increase in terms of accomplishing a specific task, leaders should begin to *reduce* their task behavior and *increase* relationship behavior until the individual or group reaches a moderate level of maturity. As the individual or group begins to move into an above average level of maturity, it becomes appropriate for leaders to decrease not only task behavior but also relationship behavior.[100]

Hersey and Blanchard argue that when the group or individual reaches a high maturity level, little task and relationship behavior from the leader is necessary; leadership emerges from the group. The delegation of leader functions to a mature group is viewed as a positive demonstration of trust and confidence.

The theory is a dynamic one. Leadership behavior changes with the maturity of the group. The leader's goal is to provide the necessary leader behavior while simultaneously helping the group mature and assume more of the leadership itself. This cycle is illustrated by the bell-shaped curve passing through the four leadership quadrants, as shown in Figure 9.10.

The theory, as depicted graphically in Figure 9.10, is a matching of the four leadership patterns (Q_1, Q_2, Q_3, Q_4) with the four situations of maturity (M_1, M_2, M_3, M_4). The appropriate leadership style for each level of follower maturity is portrayed by the curvilinear relationship in each quadrant. The maturity level of followers is expressed below the leadership style along a continuum from immature to mature. The bell-shaped curve means that as the maturity level of one's followers increases along the continuum from immature to mature, the appropriate style of leadership moves according to the curvilinear relationship. Hence, four general guiding propositions can be deduced from the model:

1. When the group is very immature (M_1), a task-oriented (Q_1) leadership style is most effective.
2. When the group is moderately immature (M_2), a dynamic leadership style (Q_2-high task and high relationship behavior) is most effective.
3. When the group is moderately mature (M_3), a relationship-oriented leadership style (Q_3) is most effective.
4. When the group is very mature (M_4), a delegating leadership style (Q_4) is most effective.

The model also denotes that within each leadership quadrant there should be more or less emphasis on task or relationship behavior depending on the level of maturity. Finally, the model suggests that the maturity level of groups or individuals can be improved over time, and task-oriented behavior reduces as the maturity of the group improves.

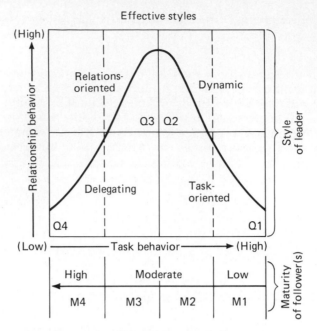

FIGURE 9.10 Effective leader-situation match

SOURCE: Adapted from Paul Hersey and Kenneth H. Blanchard, *Management of Organizational Behavior: Utilizing Human Resources* (Englewood Cliffs, NJ: Prentice-Hall, 1982). Reproduced with permission.

Implications. The leader who can accurately diagnose the maturity of followers has another situational model to guide his or her leadership behavior. Knowing when to be task-oriented and relationship-oriented is a beginning to the improvement of performance. But knowing what to do and doing it are two different things. Some individuals, for example, have a difficult time being task-oriented in their behavior—even when they know it's appropriate. Others have difficulty being relationship-oriented; the task is too important. Finally, some leaders cannot delegate leadership initiatives to a group; they need to lead, even if the group (M_4) can lead itself. Thus, if a leader is to use the model effectively, he or she needs the flexibility in disposition and behavior to be able to change styles. Individuals who have had limited experience using a wide range of styles will probably need a lot of time, practice, and perhaps training before they develop enough flexibility in their behavior to change styles comfortably as the situation demands it.

The model also suggests that simply matching the style with the situation to improve performance is not enough. The leader has another role: to improve the maturity of the group as it engages in a specific task. Ultimately, the leader's goal is to provide the group or individual with the ability, knowledge, skills, responsibility, motivation, and confidence to perform the task without the leader's help. In a sense, the leader's direction and eventually social support will subside as the group or individual grows and develops. Thus, developmental activities are as important as leadership behavior.

A Caution

Both the Managerial Grid and Situational Theory have evolved from the research on leadership as models to help leaders improve their performance. Neither, however, has been subjected to rigorous empirical validation; hence, caution is urged when using either. Moreover, the models employ opposite assumptions about the path to leadership effectiveness. Although most contemporary theorists and researchers reject the notion that there is one best leadership style, Blake and Mouton maintain that the 9, 9 orientation is always the most effective style.[101] Hersey and Blanchard, on the other hand, argue that any one of four styles can be effective under different situations; no one style is best. They suggest that effective leaders are flexible and adaptable. Furthermore, leaders can do more than adapt their behavior to the situation; they can change the situation by developing the skills and confidence of subordinates. Finally, even though a particular style is appropriate in a given situation, it will not necessarily be effective unless the leader has skill in using that style.[102]

Institutional Leadership

Thus far in this chapter our analysis has been descriptive and analytic; however, as we noted in the last chapter, leadership occurs in a cultural context. There is more to leadership than the technical and interpersonal aspects of efficient management. Leadership also has a symbolic side. It rests upon meanings as well as actions. Leaders make meanings. Indeed some would argue that what a leaders stands for is more important than what he or she does.[103]

The term "institutional leadership" comes from Philip Selznick, who argues that a major function of leadership is to infuse the organization with value beyond the technical requirements at hand, that is, to build upon people's need for meaning and create institutional purpose.[104] If successful, participants come to identify with the organization and a sense of community develops. The organization comes to symbolize the group's aspirations and idealism. The institutional leader is responsible for defining the mission of the organization, shaping its culture, and protecting and maintaining institutional integrity. Selznick explains:

> The inbuilding of purpose is a challenge to creativity because it involves transforming men and groups from neutral, technical units into participants who have a peculiar stamp, sensitivity, and commitment. This is ultimately an educational process. It has been said that the effective leader must know the meaning and master the techniques of the educator. . . . The leader as educator requires an ability to interpret the role and character of the enterprise, to perceive and develop models for thought and behavior, and to find modes to communication that will inculcate general rather than merely partial perspectives.[105]

What school leaders stand for and believe about education and schooling, the role of education in our society, how schools should be structured and operated, and how parents, teachers, and students should be treated constitute a basic set of principles that bring meaning and institutional integrity to educational leadership.[106] Successful leaders infuse a common set of values, ideals, and principles in their schools. The task is to build school culture. "Schools are for students;" "Set high, but attainable academic standards;" "Experiment with the content and process of teaching;" "Don't be afraid to make your share of mistakes;" "Teaching and learning are cooperative processes;" "Be open, close, and friendly with students and colleagues;" "Keep the structure and procedures simple and direct;" and "Educate each student to the best of his or her ability." Core values or empty slogans? Such slogan-like themes can be cultivated to define a distinctive set of core values to which teachers are committed, in which teachers take pride, and that make the school much more than a technical vehicle for teaching and learning.

Leaders can help shape the culture of an organization by what they pay attention to and reward. Systematic attention is a powerful way of communicating values and beliefs. Moreover, leader reactions to critical incidents and perceived crises are important in building culture. Crises raise emotional involvement and demonstrate the integrity and values of the organization. Is this organization a community that takes care of its members? Crises give clear answers to such questions. Leaders also provide role models for subordinates through their own deliberate behavior. Actions speak louder than words when it comes to communicating organizational values and beliefs to other members. Finally, the criteria leaders use for recruitment, selection, promotion, and censure communicate both implicitly and explicitly their values.[107]

It is not easy to give daily behavior long-term meaning and value, but that is precisely the goal of institutional leadership. Leaders need to make as well as communicate meanings, a task that is largely symbolic, often intuitive, and frequently involves myths, rituals, and ceremonies. Myths convey unquestioned beliefs that cannot be demonstrated by the facts. Rituals and ceremonies underscore and embellish what is important in the organization. Leaders not only use symbols, ceremonies, and myths; they use the language of uplift and idealism to communicate the distinctiveness of the organization. What is critical is not whether the ideals can be demonstrated but whether they become standards for group striving and identification. It is not the communication of a myth or the performance of ritual that counts; rather, creative institutional leadership depends on the will and insight to see the necessity of myths, rituals, and ceremonies, and above all to create the organizational conditions that will sustain the ideals expressed in them.[108] Myths, rituals, and ceremonies are institution builders; they help to create an integrated social system.

Leadership in schools is a complex process. It involves more than the skill of mastering a style of behavior or a contingency approach. Matching the appropriate leader behavior with a specific situation is important, but so too is the symbolic and cultural side of leadership (see Chapter 8). The issue is not one of choosing between leadership as an instrumental and behavioral activity or leadership as a symbolic and cultural one; it is clearly both.

SUMMARY

Leadership is an important topic in the literature of educational administration. Definitions of leadership vary widely, as do the approaches taken to its study. Originally, research centered on identifying the traits that leaders commonly exhibit, but that emphasis was replaced by concern for the importance of specific properties of the situation to explain leaders' behavior. Today both leader traits and situational variables are recognized as important in explaining leadership.

Studies to determine the basic dimensions of leadership behavior generally identify two distinct categories—concern for the task and concern for individuals and interpersonal relations. Leadership studies of school administrators suggest that the most effective are those that score high on measures of initiating structure (organizational ability) and consideration (ability to relate to subordinates). Leadership studies performed at the Michigan Survey Research Center and at the Laboratory of Social Relations at Harvard, using somewhat different approaches, revealed results remarkably consistent with those at Ohio State.

For a fuller understanding of what makes leaders effective, contingency models that examine the link between personal traits and situational variables must be evaluated. Fiedler's model of leadership effectiveness explores the relationship between leadership style and situational variables such as position power, task structure, and leader-member relations. Research studies in public schools provide evidence to support Fiedler's theory; effectiveness of elementary schools was found to be contingent on the leadership style of the principal and the favorableness of the situation. House's path-goal model focuses not on leadership style, defined in terms of leader traits, but on leader behavior. Like Fiedler, House also looks at situational factors that affect leader effectiveness, but he defines effectiveness not in terms of task accomplishment but in terms of subordinates' psychological states. For the further study of educational leadership, both of these contingency approaches need to be supplemented by consideration of a number of other variables suggested in this chapter.

In addition to formal models of leadership, study of the concept has been advanced by results emerging from management development programs. Blake and Mouton's Managerial Grid and Hersey and Blanchard's Situational Theory offer insights that are consistent with the Ohio State studies, though both need further testing in the school setting.

Finally, leadership is cultural and symbolic as well as instrumental and behavioral. Successful leaders infuse value into organizations, thereby creating institutional meaning and purpose that go beyond the technical requirements of the job. The institutional leader is responsible for articulating the mission of the organization, shaping its culture, and protecting and maintaining its integrity.

NOTES

1. John K. Hemphill, "Administration as Problem Solving," in Andrew W. Halpin (ed.), *Administrative Theory in Education* (New York: Macmillan, 1967), p. 98.
2. Amitai Etzioni, *A Comparative Analysis of Complex Organizations* (New York: Free Press, 1961), p. 116.
3. Fred E. Fiedler, *A Theory of Leadership Effectiveness* (New York: McGraw-Hill, 1967), p. 8.
4. Kenneth F. Janda, "Towards the Explication of the Concept of Leadership in Terms of the Concept of Power," *Human Relations,* 13 (1960), p. 358.
5. Daniel Katz and Robert L. Kahn, *The Social Psychology of Organizations,* 2nd ed. (New York: Wiley, 1978), p. 528.
6. James Lipham, "Leadership and Administration," in Daniel E. Griffiths (ed.), *Behavioral Science and Educational Administration* (Chicago: University of Chicago Press, 1964), p. 122.
7. Ralph M. Stogdill, "Leadership, Membership, and Organization," *Psychological Bulletin,* 47 (1950), 1–14. The quotation appears on page 4.
8. Robert J. House and Mary L. Baetz, "Leadership: Some Empirical Generalizations and New Research Directions," *Research in Organizational Behavior,* 1 (1979), 341–423.
9. Katz and Kahn, *op. cit.,* pp. 527–528.
10. Gary A. Yukl, *Leadership in Organizations* (Englewood Cliffs, NJ: Prentice-Hall, 1981), p. 5.
11. Although a few theorists and researchers have questioned the utility of the concept of leadership, research continues to underscore its importance. For example, see Jonathan E. Smith, Kenneth P. Carson, and Ralph A. Alexander, "Leadership: It Can Make a Difference," *Academy of Management Journal,* 27 (1984), 765–776; and James R. Meindl, Sanford B. Ehrlich, and Janet M. Dukerich, "The Romance of Leadership," *Administrative Science Quarterly,* 30 (1985), 78–102. For a cultural and interpretive perspective of leadership, see Thomas J. Sergiovanni and John E. Corbally (eds.), *Leadership and Organizational Culture* (Urbana: University of Illinois Press, 1984).
12. Aristotle, *Politics,* Book I, Chapter 5.
13. Ralph M. Stogdill, "Personal Factors Associated with Leadership: A Survey of the Literature," *Journal of Psychology,* 25 (1948), 35–71; Cecil A. Gibb, "Leadership," in Gardner Lindzey (ed.), *Handbook of Social Psychology* (Cambridge, MA: Addison-Wesley, 1954), pp. 877–920; and R. D. Mann, "A Review of the Relationships Between Personality and Performance," *Psychological Bulletin,* 56 (1959), 241–270.
14. Stogdill, "Personal Factors Associated with Leadership," *op. cit.*
15. *Ibid.*
16. Mann, *op. cit.*
17. Stogdill, "Personal Factors Associated with Leadership," *op. cit.,* p. 64.
18. Yukl, *op. cit,* p. 15.
19. Ralph M. Stogdill, "Traits of Leadership: A Follow-up to 1970," in Bernard M. Bass (ed.), *Stogdill's Handbook of Leadership* (New York: Free Press, 1981), pp. 73–97; see also Victor H. Vroom, "Leadership," in Marvin D.

Dunnette (ed.), *Handbook of Industrial and Organizational Psychology* (Chicago: Rand McNally, 1976), pp. 1527–1551.

20. John P. Campbell *et al., Managerial Behavior, Performance, and Effectiveness* (New York: McGraw-Hill, 1970), pp. 385–414.
21. *Ibid.*, p. 385.
22. House and Baetz, *op. cit.*, p. 348.
23. Robert Merton, "The Social Nature of Leadership," *American Journal of Nursing,* 69 (1969), 2615.
24. Chester I. Barnard, *The Functions of the Executive* (Cambridge, MA: Harvard University Press, 1938), p. 60.
25. Dorwin Cartwright and Alvin Zander, *Group Dynamics: Research and Theory* (Evanston, IL: Row & Peterson, 1953), p. 549.
26. Etzioni, *op. cit.*, p. 91.
27. Ralph M. Stogdill, *Manual for the Leader Behavior Description Questionnaire—Form XII* (Columbus: Bureau of Business Research, Ohio State University, 1963).
28. Alan F. Brown, "Reactions to Leadership," *Educational Administration Quarterly,* 3 (1967), 62–73.
29. Jacob W. Getzels and Egon G. Guba, "Social Behavior and the Administrative Process," *School Review,* 65 (1957), 423–441.
30. Robert F. Bales, "In Conference," *Harvard Business Review,* 32 (1954), 41–49.
31. Daniel Katz, N. Maccoby, and Nancy C. Morse, *Productivity, Supervision and Morale in an Office Situation* (Detroit: Darel, 1950).
32. Andrew W. Halpin, *The Leader Behavior of School Superintendents* (Columbus: College of Education, Ohio State University, 1956).
33. David G. Bowers and Stanley E. Seashore, "Predicting Organizational Effectiveness with a Four-Factor Theory of Leadership," *Administrative Science Quarterly,* 11 (1966), 238–264.
34. John K. Hemphill and Alvin E. Coons, *Leader Behavior Description* (Columbus: Personnel Research Board, Ohio State University, 1950).
35. Andrew W. Halpin and B. J. Winer, *The Leadership Behavior of the Airplane Commander* (Washington, DC: Human Resource Research Laboratories, Department of the Air Force, 1952).
36. Stogdill, *Manual, op. cit.*
37. Andrew W. Halpin, *Theory and Research in Administration* (New York: Macmillian, 1966), pp. 86–90.
38. *Ibid.*, pp. 97–98.
39. Brown, *op. cit.*
40. Halpin, *Theory and Research in Administration, op. cit.*, pp. 81–130.
41. Andrew W. Halpin, "The Superintendent's Effectiveness as a Leader," *Administrator's Notebook,* 6 (1958), 3.
42. Daniel Kunz and Wayne K. Hoy, "Leader Behavior of Principals and the Professional Zone of Acceptance of Teachers," *Educational Administration Quarterly,* 12 (1976), 49–64; and Cecil Miskel, *Public School Principals' Leader Style, Organizational Situation, and Effectiveness: Final Report* (Washington, DC: National Institute of Education, Department of Health, Education and Welfare, Grant No. NE-G-003-0141, October 1974). The correlation coefficients were 0.67 and 0.50 respectively.

43. Herbert A. Simon, *Administrative Behavior*, 2nd ed. (New York: Free Press, 1957), p. 133.

44. Barnard, *op. cit.*

45. *Ibid.*, pp. 168–169.

46. Zones of acceptance granted to administrators by teachers might be broken down into three basic categories or areas: (1) an organizational maintenance domain dealing with administrative routine, (2) a personal domain relating to issues that are very personal or that have little relevance to the organization, and (3) a professional domain dealing with issues involving professional judgment. It is the area of professional judgment—the one that is most variable and problematic—that is the focus of this analysis. For further discussion, see Delbert K. Clear and Roger C. Seager, "The Legitimacy of Administrative Influence as Perceived by Selected Groups," *Educational Administration Quarterly*, 7 (1971), 46–63; and Kunz and Hoy, *op. cit.*

47. For further information on the same measure, sample, and results, see Kunz and Hoy, *op. cit.*

48. Bonnie B. Leverette, "Professional Zone of Acceptance: Its Relation to the Leader Behavior of Principals and Socio-Psychological Characteristics of Teachers," (Ed.D. diss., Rutgers University, 1984).

49. House and Baetz, *op. cit.*, 360–363; Vroom, *op. cit.*, pp. 1530–1531; Charles N. Greene, "Disenchantment with Leadership Research: Some Causes, Recommendations, and Alterative Directions," in James G. Hunt and Lars L. Larson (eds.), *Leadership: The Cutting Edge* (Carbondale, IL: Southern Illinois University Press, 1977), pp. 57–67; and Terence R. Mitchell, "Organizational Behavior," *Annual Review of Psychology*, 30 (1979), 243–281.

50. For a review of these studies, see Rensis Likert's *New Patterns of Management and Value* (New York: McGraw-Hill, 1961); and *The Human Organization: Its Management and Value* (New York: McGraw-Hill, 1967).

51. Katz, Maccoby, and Morse, *op. cit.*

52. Vroom, *op. cit.*, p. 1532.

53. Robert L. Kahn, "The Prediction of Productivity," *Journal of Social Issues*, 12 (1956), 41–49.

54. Bales, *op. cit.*, pp. 45–66.

55. James L. Gibson, John M. Ivancevich, and James H. Donnelly, Jr., *Organizations: Behavior, Structure, and Processes*, rev. ed. (Dallas, TX: Business Publications, 1976), p. 193.

56. Edwin A. Fleishman, "Twenty Years of Consideration and Structure," in Edwin A. Fleishman and James G. Hunt (eds.), *Current Developments in the Study of Leadership* (Carbondale, IL: Southern Illinois University Press, 1973), pp. 1–37.

57. Fiedler's theory can be found in a number of sources. The most extensive discussion of its development and measurement is contained in Fiedler's 1967 book entitled *A Theory of Leadership Effectiveness, op. cit.* Other sources include Fred E. Fiedler, "Validation and Extension of the Contingency Model of Leadership Effectiveness: A Review of Empirical Findings," *Psychological Bulletin*, 76 (1971), 128–148; Fred E. Fiedler and Martin M. Chemers, *Leadership and Effective Management* (Glenview, IL: Scott, Foresman, 1974); and Fred E. Fiedler, Martin M. Chemers, and

Linda Mahar, *Improving Leadership Effectiveness: The Leader Match Concept* (New York: Wiley, 1976).

58. Fiedler and Chemers, *op. cit.*, p. 73.
59. Fiedler, *A Theory of Leadership Effectiveness, op. cit.*, p. 36.
60. Fred E. Fiedler, "The Leadership Game: Matching the Man to the Situation," *Organizational Dynamics,* 4 (1976), 6–16.
61. Chester A. Shrieshiem and Steven Kerr, "Theories and Measures of Leadership: A Critical Appraisal of Current and Future Directions," in James G. Hunt and Lars L. Larson, *op. cit.*, pp. 9–45. See also Ramadhar Singh, "Leadership Style and Reward Allocation: Does Least Preferred Co-worker Scale Measure Task and Relation Orientation?" *Organization Behavior and Human Performance,* 32 (1983), 178–197.
62. Robert W. Rice, "Psychometric Properties of the Esteem for Least Preferred Co-worker (LPC) Scale," *Academy of Management Review,* 3 (1978), 106–118.
63. Fiedler, "The Leadership Game," *op. cit.*
64. Katz and Kahn, *op. cit.*, pp. 565–566.
65. Fiedler, *A Theory of Leadership Effectiveness, op. cit.*, pp. 32–34. Most of Fiedler's work dealt with interacting task groups.
66. *Ibid.*, p. 9.
67. This interpretation is discussed in greater detail by House and Baetz, *op. cit.*
68. Fred E. Fiedler, *Leadership* (New York: General Learning Press, 1971), p. 15.
69. House and Baetz, *op. cit.*
70. For a review of the early research studies see Fiedler, *A Theory of Leadership Effectiveness, op. cit.*, pp. 154–250. A review of the later research can be found in Fred E. Fiedler, "The Contingency Model and the Dynamics of the Leadership Process," *Advances in Experimental Social Psychology,* 11 (1973), 60–112.
71. The study supporting the model is reported by Martin M. Chemers and G. J. Skrzypek, "Experimental Test of the Contingency Model of Leadership Effectiveness," *Journal of Personality and Social Psychology,* 24 (1972), 172–177. The investigation that failed to support the theory is Robert P. Vecchio, "An Empirical Examination of the Validity of Fiedler's Model of Leadership Effectiveness," *Organizational Behavior and Human Performance,* 19 (1977), 180–206.
72. Michael J. Strube and Joseph E. Garcia, "A Meta-Analytic Investigation of Fiedler's Contingency Model of Leadership Effectiveness," *Psychological Bulletin,* 90 (1981), 307–321.
73. Lawrence H. Peters, Darrell D. Hartke, and John T. Pohlmann, "Fiedler's Contingency Theory of Effectiveness: An Application of the Meta-Analysis Procedures of Schmidt and Hunter," *Psychological Bulletin,* 97 (1985), 274–285; Ellen Patricia Crehan, "A Meta-Analysis of Fiedler's Contingency Model of Leadership Effectiveness," (Ed.D. diss., University of British Columbia, 1985), p. 259. For a critical analysis of the Strube and Garcia meta-analysis, see Robert P. Vecchio, "Assessing the Validity of Fiedler's Contingency Model of Leadership Effectiveness: A Closer Look at Strube and Garcia," *Psychological Bulletin,* 93 (1983), 404–408.
74. Vincent McNamara and Frederick Enns, "Directive Leadership and

Staff Acceptance of the Principal," *Canadian Administrator,* 6 (1966), 5–8.

75. Leonard B. Williams and Wayne K. Hoy, "Principal-Staff Relations: Situational Mediator of Effectiveness," *Journal of Educational Administration,* 9 (1973), 66–73.

76. Yvonne M. Martin, Goeffrey B. Isherwood, and Robert G. Lavery, "Leadership Effectiveness in Teacher Probation Committees," *Educational Administration Quarterly,* 12 (1976), 87–99.

77. Vroom, *op. cit.,* p. 1536.

78. The best early exposition of the theory was made by Robert J. House, "A Path-Goal Theory of Leader Effectiveness," in Fleishman and Hunt, *op. cit.,* pp. 141–177. The theory was derived from earlier work by Martin G. Evans, "The Effects of Supervisory Behavior on the Path-Goal Relationships," *Organizational Behavior and Human Performance,* 5 (1970), 277–298. A report on the theory's early statement and three studies can be found in Robert J. House, "A Path-Goal Theory of Leadership Effectiveness," *Administrative Science Quarterly,* 16 (1971), 321–338. The major revisions of the early model are found in Robert J. House and Terence R. Mitchell, "Path-Goal Theory and Leadership," *Journal of Contemporary Business,* 3 (1974), 81–97; see also J. E. Stinson and T. W. Johnson, "The Path-Goal Theory of Leadership: A Partial Test and Suggested Refinement," *Academy of Management Journal,* 18 (1975), 242–252.

79. House and Mitchell, *op. cit.,* pp. 81–97.

80. Gibson, Ivancevich, and Donnelly, *op. cit.*

81. See, for example, John E. Sheridan, H. Kirk Downey, and John W. Slocum, Jr., "Testing Causal Relationships of House's Path-Goal Theory of Leadership Effectiveness," in James G. Hunt and Lars L. Larson (eds.), *Leadership Frontiers* (Kent, OH: Kent State University Press, 1975), pp. 61–80.

82. Alan Filley, Robert House, and Steven Kerr, *Managerial Process and Organizational Behavior* (Glenview, IL: Scott, Foresman, 1976), p. 254.

83. For extended discussion of the effects of these four kinds of leadership behavior, see Gary A. Yukl, *op. cit.,* pp. 145–151.

84. Extensive reviews of empirical research testing the theory are Filley, House, and Kerr, *op. cit.;* House and Mitchell, *op. cit.;* Chester A. Shriesheim and M. A. Von Glinow, "The Path-Goal Theory of Leadership: A Theoretical and Empirical Analysis," *Academy of Management Journal,* 20 (1977), 398–405; and John B. Miner, *Theories of Organizational Behavior* (Hinsdale, IL: Dryden Press, 1980), pp. 327–351.

85. House and Baetz, *op. cit.;* and Vroom, *op. cit.*

86. House and Baetz, *op. cit.;* and Fred E. Fiedler and Albert F. Leister, "Leader Intelligence and Task Performance: A Test of a Multiple Screen Model," *Organizational Behavior and Human Performance,* 20 (1977), 1–14.

87. House and Baetz, *op. cit.,* p. 352.

88. These characteristics are suggested by Ralph M. Stogdill, *Handbook of Leadership, op. cit.,* p. 411–420; House and Mitchell, *op. cit.;* Fiedler, *A Theory of Leadership Effectiveness, op. cit.;* Richard N. Osborn and James G. Hunt, "Environment and Organizational Effectiveness," *Administra-*

tive Science Quarterly, 19 (1974), 231–246; and George F. Madaus, Peter W. Airasian, and Thomas Kellaghan, *School Effectiveness: A Reassessment of the Evidence* (New York: McGraw-Hill, 1980), pp. 27–110.

89. Descriptive observation shows promise for providing a better understanding of how leaders act in varying situations. An excellent example of this type of research is Robert L. Crowson and Cynthia Porter-Gehrie, "The Discretionary Behavior of Principals in Large City Schools," *Educational Administration Quarterly,* 16 (1980), pp. 27–110.

90. Cecil Miskel, "Principals' Attitudes Toward Work and Co-Workers, Situational Factors, Perceived Effectiveness, and Innovation Effort," *Educational Administration Quarterly,* 13 (1977), 51–70.

91. Robert R. Blake and Jane S. Mouton, *The Managerial Grid III* (Houston, TX: Gulf, 1985), p. 12.

92. *Ibid.,* pp. 31, 96.

93. The most comprehensive description of the theory is presented in Paul Hersey and Kenneth H. Blanchard, *Management of Organizational Behavior: Utilizing Human Resources,* 4th ed. (Englewood Cliffs, NJ: Prentice-Hall, 1982).

94. Edgar H. Schein, *Organizational Psychology* (Englewood Cliffs, NJ: Prentice Hall, 1965), p. 65.

95. William J. Reddin, *Managerial Effectiveness* (New York: McGraw-Hill, 1970); see also William J. Reddin, "The Tri-Dimensional Grid," *Canadian Personnel and Industrial Relations Journal,* 13 (1966), pp. 13–20.

96. Hersey and Blanchard, *op. cit.,* p. 151.

97. *Ibid.,* pp. 150–158.

98. *Ibid.,* p. 151.

99. *Ibid.,* pp. 106–124.

100. Paul Hersey and Kenneth H. Blanchard, *Management of Organizational Behavior: Utilizing Human Resources,* 3rd ed. (Englewood Cliffs, NJ: Prentice-Hall, 1977), p. 163.

101. For their case, see Robert R. Blake and Jane S. Mouton, "A Comparative Analysis of Situationalism and 9, 9 Management by Principle," *Organizational Dynamics,* 10 (Spring 1982), 20–34; and Robert R. Blake and Jane S. Mouton, *The Versatile Manager: A Grid Profile* (Homewood, IL: Dow Jones-Irwin, 1980).

102. Two other popular leadership training models are Leader Match by Fred E. Fiedler and Martin M. Chemers, *Improving Leadership Effectiveness,* 2nd ed. (New York: Wiley, 1984); and 3-D Theory by W. J. Reddin, *Managerial Effectiveness, op. cit.*

103. Thomas J. Sergiovanni, "Leadership as Cultural Expression," in Thomas J. Sergiovanni and John E. Corbally (eds.), *Leadership and Organizational Culture* (Urbana, IL: University of Illinois Press, 1984), p. 106.

104. Philip Selznick, *Leadership in Administration* (New York: Harper & Row, 1957), p. 17.

105. *Ibid.,* pp. 149–150.

106. Sergiovanni, *op. cit.,* p. 108.

107. For a detailed discussion of the primary mechanisms for embedding culture, see Edgar H. Schein, *Organizational Culture and Leadership* (San Francisco: Jossey-Bass, 1985), pp. 223–243.

108. Selznick, *op. cit.,* p. 151.

Chapter 10

Decision Making

The task of "deciding" pervades the entire administrative organization. . . . A general theory of administration must include principles of organization that will insure correct decision making, just as it must include principles that will insure effective action.

HERBERT A. SIMON
Administrative Behavior

Decision making is a major responsibility of all administrators. It is the process by which decisions are not only arrived at but implemented. Until decision making is converted into action, it is only good intention. An understanding of the decision-making process is a *sine qua non* for all school administrators because the school, like all formal organizations, is basically a decision-making structure. Our analysis of decision making begins with an examination of three basic strategies.

The Classical Model: An Optimizing Strategy

Classical decision theory assumes that decisions should be completely rational; it employs an optimizing strategy by seeking the best possible alternative to maximize the achievement of goals and objectives. According to the classical model, the decision-making process is a series of sequential steps:

1. A problem is identified.
2. Goals and objectives are established.
3. *All* the possible alternatives are generated.
4. The consequences of each alternative are considered.
5. All the alternatives are evaluated in terms of the goals and objectives.

6. The *best* alternative is selected; that is, the one that maximizes the goals and objectives.
7. Finally, the decision is implemented and evaluated.

The classical model is an ideal rather than a description of how most decision makers function; in fact, most scholars consider the classical model an unrealistic, if not naïve, ideal. Decision makers virtually never have access to all the relevant information. Moreover, generating all the possible alternatives and their consequences is impossible. Unfortunately, the model assumes intellectual capacities, rationality, and knowledge that decision makers simply don't possess; consequently, it is not very useful to practicing administrators.

THE ADMINISTRATIVE MODEL: A SATISFICING STRATEGY

Given the severe limitations of the classical model, it should not be surprising that a more realistic approach to decision making in organizations has evolved. The complexity of most organizational problems and the limited capacity of the human mind make it virtually impossible to use an optimizing strategy on all but the simplest problems. Herbert Simon was first to introduce the strategy of satisficing in an attempt to provide a more accurate description of the way administrators both do and should make organizational decisions.[1] Before analyzing the satisficing strategy in detail, we examine the basic assumptions upon which it rests.

Basic Assumptions[2]

1. The decision-making process is a cycle of events that includes the identification and diagnosis of a difficulty, the reflective development of a plan to alleviate the difficulty, the initiation of the plan, and the appraisal of its success.

A distinguishing characteristic of this pattern of action is its cyclical nature. This dynamic process solves some problems and creates others. Specific improvements in some situations that foster the achievement of the organization's purposes frequently interfere with other conditions that are also important. The process, however, can result in incremental gains and progress. As Peter M. Blau and W. Richard Scott explain:

> The experience in solving earlier problems is not lost but contributes to the search for solutions to later problems. [This] suggest[s] that the process of organizational development is dialectical—problems appear, and while the process of solving them tends to give rise to new problems, learning has occurred which influences how the new challenges are met.[3]

Consequently, it is quixotic for administrators to believe or even hope that an effective decision-making structure is going to solve all problems. At best, the process employed by thoughtful and skillful executives and their staffs should lead to more rational decisions, but it typically will not result in final decisions. The nature of the process and the nature of formal organizations preclude that possibility.

In the process of decision making, those with the responsibility must go through five sequential steps: (1) recognize and define the problem or issue; (2) analyze the difficulties in the existing situation; (3) establish criteria for resolving of difficulties; (4) develop a plan of or strategy for action, including the specification of possible alternatives, the prediction of probable consequences for each alternative, deliberation, and the selection of an action alternative; and (5) initiate a plan of action. These steps will be developed, elaborated, and discussed in some detail later in this chapter.

Although the process is conceptualized as a sequential pattern because each step serves as a logical basis for the next, the process is also cyclical in nature. Thus, decision making may be entered into at any stage. Moreover, the steps are taken again and again in the process of administering organizations.

2. Administration is the performance of the decision-making process by an individual or group in an organizational context.

The decision-making process is a set of interdependent phases that may be isolated and abstractly described. Administration, charged with the responsibility for decision making, has a number of important attributes: (1) it tends to perpetuate itself; (2) it attempts to protect itself from disruption and destruction from within and is thus concerned with the morale and satisfaction of its employees; (3) it seeks to survive, and it is therefore competitive with other behavior patterns; and (4) it seeks to progress and grow. The impetus for growth is made not only on behalf of the organization but also on behalf of a specifically identifiable administration.

From these characteristics, it follows that administrators are going to perform in a way that will maximize efforts, perpetuate the decision-making process, maintain the administrator's internal integrity, preserve or enhance its position in relation to competing interests, and help it develop and expand.[4]

3. Complete rationality in decision making is virtually impossible; therefore, administrators seek to satisfice because they do not have the knowledge, ability, or capacity to maximize the decision-making process.

Effective administration requires rational decision making. Decisions are rational when they are appropriate for accomplishing specific goals. Administrative decisions, however, are often extremely complex, and their rationality is limited for a number of reasons. First, all the alternatives cannot be considered simply because there are too many options that do not come to mind. In addition, all the probable consequences for each alternative cannot be anticipated because future events are exceedingly difficult to predict accurately and to evaluate realistically. Rationality is limited not only by the extent of administrators' knowledge but also by their unconscious skills, habits, and reflexes as well as their values and conceptions of purpose that may deviate from the organization's goals.[5] Individuals are not capable of making completely rational decisions on complex matters. Hence, most administrative decision making is concerned with the selection and implementation of satisfactory alternatives rather than optimal alternatives. To use Herbert A. Simon's words, administrators "satisfice" rather than "optimize." Nonetheless, they continue to talk about finding the best solutions to problems. What is meant, of course, is the best of the satisfactory alternatives.

Administrators look for solutions that are "good enough." They recognize that their perception of the world is a drastically simplified model of the complex interacting forces that comprise the real world. They are content with this oversimplification because they believe that most real-world facts are not important to the particular problem(s) they face and that most significant chains of causes and effects are short and simple. Consequently, they are satisfied to ignore most aspects of reality because they consider them substantially irrelevant. Administrators make choices, then, using a simplified picture of reality that accounts for only a few of the factors that they consider most relevant and important.[6]

4. The basic function of administration is to provide each subordinate with an internal environment of decision so that each person's behavior is rational from both individual and organizational perspectives.

Because individuals cannot make completely rational decisions, administrators must limit the scope of the decisions so that rationality can be approached. The administrative structure provides organizational members with an environment of goals, objectives, and purposes. This environment narrows and defines the roles, thereby limiting the number of alternatives. According to Simon, rational behavior consists of a means-ends chain.[7] Given certain ends, appropriate means are selected, but once those ends are achieved, they in turn become means for further ends, and so on. After organizational objectives are agreed on, the administrative structure serves as a basis for the means-ends chains. To illustrate, once the ends for organizational members are defined by the directives from a superior, the subordinate's responsibility is primarily to determine the "best" means for attaining those ends. That pattern, along with procedural regulations, narrows the alternatives.

An individual's decision is rational if it is consistent with the values, alternatives, and information that were analyzed in reaching it. An organization's decision is rational if it is consistent with its goals, objectives, and information. Therefore, the organization must be constructed so that a decision that is rational for the individual remains rational for the organization when reassessed from the organizational perspective.[8]

5. The decision-making process is a general pattern of action found in the rational administration of all major functional and task areas.

The specific tasks of school administration can be catalogued in a number of ways. Typically, school administrators are concerned with and responsible for the following areas: (a) curriculum and instruction; (b) negotiations; (c) physical facilities; (d) finance and business; (e) pupil personnel; (f) evaluation and supervision; (g) recruitment, selection, and retention of employees; and (h) public relations.

The decision-making process is essential not only in each of these tasks but also in the broader functional areas of administration. Edward H. Litchfield has identified three broad, functional areas of administration—policy, resources, and execution.[9] A policy is defined as a statement of those objectives that guide the actions of a substantial portion of the total organization. The resources of administration are comprised of people, money, authority, and materials. Execution consists of integration and synthesizing of resources and policy necessary to achieve a purposeful organization.[10]

The policy function is often termed "policy making" or "policy formulation," but it is substantially more.[11] Policies are not only formulated but also programmed, communicated, monitored, and evaluated. Policy making is a special instance of decision making in which the specific issues revolve around policy matters. The decision-making process also is the vehicle for dealing with resource allocation. In determining the need for personnel, supplies, physical facilities, and monies, the administrator is confronted with difficulties and problems that require both deliberate and reflective choice and implementation— the use of the action cycle of the decision-making process. The cycle is repeated in performing the executive function. In order to allocate and integrate the resources consistent with policy mandates and to synthesize conflicting values and tendencies, the executive attempts to administer the system through a continuous series of the cyclical actions that comprise the decision-making process.[12]

Not only is the action cycle the same regardless of functional area, but each of the functions is a requisite of the total process. Furthermore, although policy helps shape the character of the resource and executive functions, resources have an equally important impact on policies, and execution can lead to effective implementation of policy, or can undermine its very existence. Hence, these three functional areas are interdependent.[13]

6. The decision-making process occurs in substantially the same generalized form in most complex organizations.

The cyclical evolution of rational, deliberate, purposeful action, beginning with the development of a decision strategy and moving through implementation and appraisal of results, occurs in all types of organizations.[14] The structure of the process is the same in, for example, military, industrial, educational, or health services organizations. The universality of the decision-making process calls attention to the fact that essentially it is the same regardless of the specific context in which it takes place. Educational organizations are different, however, from industrial organizations in a great many substantive and important ways. For example, the technologies employed by each, as well as the products that result, are quite different. Yet the decision-making process in the areas of policy, resources, and execution are remarkably similar; indeed, it is substantively the same. Therefore, the study of educational administration must concern itself with the general, abstract subject of the decision-making process. Furthermore, much can be learned about educational administration through comparative analyses of the process of administration in a large number of contexts and in different types of organizations.

Decision-Making Process: An Action Cycle

The specific sequence of steps in the decision-making process have already been outlined. The action cycle of that process is illustrated in Figure 10.1. It should be noted that many decision-making action cycles may be occurring simultaneously. One elaborate cycle, regarding fundamental goals and objectives (strategic planning), may be proceeding at the level of the board of education, while smaller and related sequential cycles, regarding curriculum and instruction, pupil personnel services, finance and business management, and facilities planning, may be progressing at the district level. Litchfield describes the complex interaction of events this way:

> "There is . . . a series of wheels within wheels, tangent now at one point, now at another. The totality is administrative action, and the wheels are similar not in size but in the articulate and inarticulate uniformity of their components.[15]

We now turn to a more detailed analysis of each step in the action cycle.

Step 1. Recognize and Define the Problem or Issue

The recognition of a difficulty or disharmony in the system is the first step in the decision-making process. Effective administrators are sensitive to organizational actions and attitudes that do not measure up to the prescribed standards.

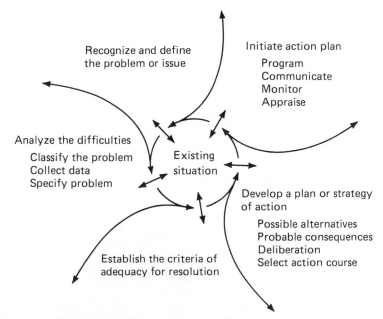

FIGURE 10.1   Decision-making action cycle

The common retort, "We don't have problems; we have answers," often is symptomatic of insensitive administrators who are headed for a great deal of trouble. Although it may be possible for them to maintain equilibrium in the organization over the short run, the likelihood of organizational chaos over the long run seems inevitable.

The recognition and definition of a problem are crucial to the process and frequently do not receive adequate attention. The way a problem is conceptualized is important to subsequent analysis and solution. Not only are sensitivity and perceptual acuteness in the administrator necessary, but a rich conceptual background and a thorough understanding of the formal and informal organizations are desirable in placing the problem in perspective. Too often administrators define problems quickly and narrowly and, in so doing, restrict their options and treat only the symptoms of the problems. For example, the response to a request from a teacher group for more autonomy in selecting curricular materials can be seen by a principal as an attempt to undermine administrative authority. If the problem initially is so conceived, the set of alternatives that the principal considers probably will be unduly narrow and restrictive. Such a teacher request, however, can open up a host of positive creative possibilities for long-range curriculum development. This example, coincidentally, underscores the importance of the security and confidence of the administrator. The secure and confident administrator is unlikely to view such a request as a threat to his or her authority.

During this first stage in the process, it is important to place the problem in realistic perspective. If the problem is complex, its definition likewise will be complicated, perhaps multidimensional. The problem may need to be broken down into subproblems, with each subproblem cycled through the decision-making process. Furthermore, the problem may require several solutions. For instance, the problem of districting in a school system, where large numbers of parents want their children in school X rather than Y, may be settled in the short run by a policy statement indicating that a child will be assigned to a school solely on the basis of geographical location. The long-run solution, however, might well involve equalizing educational opportunities and improving the program of instruction in one or more schools.[16]

In the decision-making process the executive does not necessarily merely react to existing problems. Effective executives are constantly alert to issues that might become problems. In that way they can adopt a course of action that will prevent the problem from developing and promote organizational health and growth.

Step 2. Analyze the Difficulties in the Existing Situation

This stage of the decision-making process is directly related to the first stage; in fact, some writers prefer to combine definition and analysis. However, analysis calls for the classification of the problem. Is the problem unique? Or is it a new manifestation of a typical difficulty for which a pattern of action has already been developed?

Chester I. Barnard distinguished three kinds of decisions, based on where the need for them originates. Intermediary decisions arise from authoritative communications from superiors that relate to the interpretation, application, or distribution of instruction; appellate decisions grow out of cases referred by subordinates; and creative decisions originate in the initiative of the executive concerned.[17]

In contrast, Peter F. Drucker proposed two basic kinds of decisions—generic or unique.[18] Generic decisions arise from established principles, policies, or rules. Indeed, recurring problems are routinely solved by formulaic rules and regulations. A great many of the intermediary or appellate decisions that confront school principals (indeed, all middle-level administrators) are generic. That is, the organization has established mechanisms and procedures for dealing with problems. This does not mean, however, that they are unimportant; it simply means that they belong to a general group of organizational problems that frequently occur and that the organization wants to be prepared to deal with. Such decisions are needed when a principal implements policy mandated by the board, monitors absenteeism among teachers, mediates student-teacher conflicts, and interprets disciplinary procedures. All these generic decisions can be intermediary or appellate decisions (originating from above or below the principal in the hierarchy). In all cases the principal should be able to handle the situation by applying the appropriate rule, principle, or policy to the concrete circumstances of the case.

Unique decisions, however, are probably creative decisions that require going beyond established procedures for a solution; in fact, they may require a modification of the organizational structure. Here the decision maker deals with an exceptional problem that is not adequately answered by a general principle or rule. Creative decisions quite often change the basic thrust or direction of an organization. In order to seek a creative solution, decision makers are free to explore all ideas that are relevant to the problem.

A unique decision might arise when principal and staff work to resolve a curricular issue where there are no established guidelines. The superintendent may specifically request an innovative solution. Completely unique events are rare; nevertheless, the distinction between problems that are routine and those that are unique is an important one in terms of decision making. Two common mistakes administrators need to guard against are (1) treating a routine situation as if it were a series of unique events and (2) treating a new event as if it were just another old problem to which old procedures should be applied.

Once the problem has been classified as generic or unique, the administrator is in a position to address a number of other questions as he or she proceeds with the analysis. How important is the problem? Can the problem be more fully specified? What information is needed to specify the problem further? The original definition of the problem is usually global and general. After classifying and determining the importance of the problem, the decision maker now begins to define more precisely the problem and issues involved. This entails the need for information or data collection. The amount of information that should be collected depends on a number of factors, including the importance of the problem, time constraints, and existing procedures and structure for data collection. The more important the problem, the more information the decision maker gathers. Time, of course, is almost always a constraining factor in data collection. Finally, the existing procedures for data collection may greatly facilitate or entirely prohibit the search for relevant information.

In brief, decision makers need relevant facts. What is involved? Why is it involved? Where is it involved? When? To what extent? Answers to these questions should provide information to map the parameters of the problem. Such information can be collected in formal, sophisticated ways, making use of operations research and computer facilities, as well as in informal ways, through personal contacts, by telephone, or in writing.

Step 3. Establish Criteria for Problem Resolution

After the problem has been analyzed and specified, the decision maker must decide what constitutes an acceptable solution. What are the minimum objectives that are to be achieved? What are the musts compared to the wants? It is not unusual for the perfect solution in terms of outcomes to be unfeasible. What is good enough? In this way, the decision maker establishes his or her aspiration level. That is, what are the criteria for a satisfactory decision? At this point, the decision maker may try to rank possible outcomes along a continuum from minimally satisfying to maximally satisfying; a completely satisfactory outcome usually does not remain after compromise, adaptation, and concession.

Criteria of adequacy need to be specified so that the decision maker knows that a "right" decision is being made and not just one that will be acceptable. In general, the criteria used to judge the decision should be consistent with the organization's mission. What we have referred to as criteria of adequacy, scientists often refer to as "boundary conditions." Any final decision needs to satisfy the boundary conditions that have been specified.

Step 4. Develop a Plan or Strategy for Action

This is the central step of the process. After recognizing the problem, collecting data, and specifying the problem and its boundary conditions, it is necessary for the decision maker to develop a systematic and reflective plan of action. The process involves at least the following steps: specifying alternatives, predicting consequences, and deliberating on and selecting the alternatives for action. Before we proceed to analyze each of these steps, several limitations need to be reiterated. Administrators base their plans of action on simplified pictures of reality; they choose the factors that they regard as most relevant and crucial; and thus are able to come to some general conclusions and take actions without becoming paralyzed by the facts that "could be" indirectly related to the immediate problems. Furthermore, the art of administrative decision making, as Barnard notes, "consists in not deciding questions that are not now pertinent, in not deciding prematurely, in not making decisions that cannot be effective, and in not making decisions that others should make."[19]

The search for alternatives to solve a particular organizational problem frequently is called "problemistic search." It is distinguished from random curiosity and from the search for understanding per se.[20] Problemistic search is straightforward, usually reflecting simplified notions of causality, and it rests on two simple rules: (1) search in the area of the problem symptom(s) and (2) search in the area of the current alternative(s). When these two rules do not produce enough reasonable alternatives, the search is expanded. This type of search probably is the dominant style administrators use in decision making; hence, most decision making is reactive. As we have pointed out, however, this need not be the case. James D. Thompson has suggested that it is possible to develop behavior-monitoring procedures to search the environment for opportunities that are not activated by a problem and therefore continue to be present when a problem solution has been found.[21] He calls this process "opportunistic surveillance" and implies that it is the organizational counterpart of curiosity in the individual. Obviously, a decision-making structure that encourages opportunistic surveillance is more desirable than one that only allows for problemistic search.

Specifying alternatives. A preliminary step in formulating an intention to act is to list all possible alternatives. In actuality, only some of the alternatives are specified because, as we have indicated earlier, people do not have the capacity to think of all alternatives. Nonetheless, advancing a greater number of choices increases the likelihood of finding satisfactory alternatives that meet the already specified conditions.

Creative decision makers are able to develop unique, viable alternatives, an often time-consuming task. Unfortunately, too many administrators do not take the time to develop a comprehensive set of possible alternatives; they see the solution as a simple dichotomy—it is either this or that. Speed in decision making is not something to be overly impressed with; it is often a symptom of sloppy thinking. The impact of a decision is much more important than the technique. Educational organizations need sound decisions, not clever techniques.

Therefore, a modicum of time seems essential in developing as many alternatives as possible. It makes some sense to consider as a first alternative the consequence of "doing nothing." Once in a great while, such an alternative turns out to solve the problem; things work themselves out. Unfortunately, most problems do not just work themselves out, but the decision not to decide should always be reflectively considered.

Another choice available in the decision-making process is the use of temporary alternatives that do not really solve the problem but do provide more time for further deliberation. Temporary alternatives, once refined and more completely thought through, are often the basis for more elaborate proposals. The key in developing preliminary and temporary alternatives is that, if successful, they "buy time" without creating hostility. There is the ever-present danger, however, that this will be seen as stalling; hence, it should be used sparingly and adroitly. Routine decisions often can be handled quickly and effectively. Unique decisions demand more thoughtful and creative decision making. Creative thinking is of particular value in developing of alternatives from which a decision maker must make a deliberate choice. To think creatively, individuals must be able to reduce external inhibitions on the thinking process, to make relativistic and less dogmatic distinctions, to be more willing not only to consider but to express irrational impulses, and to be secure and amenable to brainstorming. Of course, the atmosphere of the organization can either inhibit or facilitate creative thinking.

In brief, the development of effective alternatives typically requires: (1) a willingness to make fewer black-and-white distinctions; (2) the use of divergent and creative thinking patterns; and (3) time to develop as many reasonable alternatives as possible.

Predicting consequences. For each alternative that is developed, probable consequences should be proposed. Although for analytic purposes we have treated specifying alternatives and predicting consequences as separate operations, they usually occur simultaneously. The formulation of alternatives and probable consequences is a good place to use groups—pooling brainpower and experience to make predictions as accurately as possible. By and large, predicting consequences to proposed alternatives is hazardous. On some issues, for example, those involving financial costs, accurate predictions of consequences can be made; however, when trying to anticipate the reactions of individuals or groups, the results typically are much more problematic.

Predicting consequences again underscores the need for a good management information system, and those school structures that have built-in capacities to collect, codify, store, and retrieve information have a distinct advantage in the decision-making process. In addition, consulting with a number of individuals who are in a position to know also improves one's predictive power. For each decision alternative, the consequences can be predicted only in terms of probable rather than certain outcomes.

Deliberating and selecting the course of action. The final phase of developing a strategy for action involves a deliberate analysis of the alternatives and consequences. Sometimes it is helpful to list all the alternatives with their accompanying probable consequences in a probability event chain (see Figure 10.2). The figure is read as follows: Alternative A has three possible consequences (C_1A, C_2A, C_3A), and the probability of each of these consequences occurring is designated $P(C_1A)$, $P(C_2A)$, $P(C_3A)$. Although this procedure may not be completed for each problem-solving issue, every alternative typically has a number of consequences, each with a certain probability of occurring, that must be considered.

In the deliberation, prior to selecting the appropriate alternatives, decision makers carefully weigh the probable consequences of each alternative in light of the criteria for a satisfactory solution. They are then in a position to choose the "best" alternative or to select a series of alternatives that are linked in some

Alternative	Possible consequence	Probability of consequence

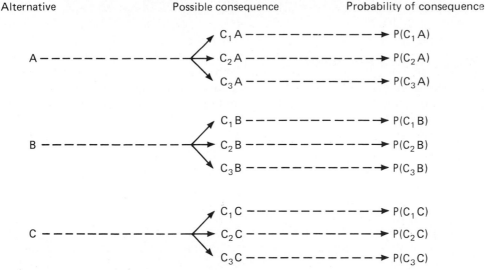

FIGURE 10.2   **Example of a probability event chain**

sequential order, which will provide them with a strategy or plan of action; the more complex or problematic the issue, the more likely the latter course of action.

To illustrate the planning of strategy, let us simplify the procedure. It may be possible to set up a strategy several moves in advance, just as a good chess player does. Alternative *A* may result in a positive and acceptable solution; however, if it does not, the decision maker goes to alternative *B* and, if need be, to alternative *C*, and so on, provided the probable consequences are still satisfactory. Of course, unanticipated consequences may require a rethinking of viable alternatives.

Occasionally decision makers cannot find an acceptable alternative. It is then necessary to reduce the aspiration level; that is, the criteria for a satisfactory solution are reconsidered (return to step 3). A new set of objectives, new alternatives, new data, and a new and more feasible strategy may have to be formulated. In the process of searching for satisfactory alternatives, decision makers seek to keep the activity manageable by using simplified decision rules called heuristics. These are simple rules of thumb that guide the decision making. For example, rules about when to take a "hit" in blackjack or when to bet with the house or when to search for more information in decision making are heuristics.

Obviously, a large number of factors mediate the choice of a preferred alternative or alternatives. The values of the administrator, the cultural context in which the decision is made and implemented, the perceptions of those involved in the process, the importance of the situation, the pressure on the decision maker, and the importance of the goal—all these and other factors intervene in the selection of an alternative. Nonetheless, deliberate, rational, and reflective decisions generally result from following a systematic sequence of steps.

Step 5. Initiate the Plan of Action

Once the decision has been made and a plan of action formulated, the decision needs to be implemented—the final element in the decision-making cycle. The initiation of the plan of action requires at least four steps—programming, communicating, monitoring, and appraising.

Programming.   Decisions must be translated and interpreted into specific programs, that is, the mechanics and specific details for implementing the plan must be specified. For example, the plan to change the system of grading elementary school students contains a specific and detailed set of operations that requires answers to a number of questions. Who has to have information about the plan? What actions need to be taken and by whom? What preparation is needed so that those who have to take action can do so? The action that is to be programmed must be appropriate to the abilities of the people involved. In brief, the program must be realistic and capable of implementation.

What we call "programming" others have called "program planning"—the activity designed to implement decisions. Program planning can be accomplished through a wide range of specific methods and techniques. Which ones are used depends on the sophistication and capabilities of the school organization. Programming may include budgeting, setting behavioral objectives, mapping organizational charts, using network-based management techniques, and specifying other ways of translating a decision into specific programs for allocating authority and physical human resources.

Communicating.   Once the plan has been programmed, it is necessary that each involved individual become aware of his or her responsibilities. Channels of communication among the individuals as well as opportunities for communicating both horizontally and vertically must be given careful attention. For a program to be successful, individuals need to know clearly not only what their own roles are but also the roles of others as they relate to the total plan. Otherwise, efforts may be duplicated, counterproductive, or ineffective. The communication system developed to implement the plan in large part can and should be a crucial mechanism to initiate action and to enhance coordination of the program. Communication is discussed in detail in the next chapter.

Monitoring.   This refers to the process of overseeing the implementation of the plan of action in order to be sure that it is proceeding as scheduled. Information monitoring and reporting must be built into the action cycle of decision making to provide for continuous evaluation of actual events as compared to expectations. The monitoring process is a control process using systematic feedback loops. Standards of performance, once they are set, need to be enforced. Enforcement, however, does not necessarily mean coercive control. There are diverse techniques of control including those that rely on rewards and incentives, punishments, persuasion, and means of inducing identification with organizational goals. Different modes of control and enforcement are more or less effective depending on the situation and the individuals involved, a constant problem for most executives. Continuous feedback reports are necessary to evaluate the progress of implementing a reprogramming of the plan of action, a change in communication procedures, or developing other monitoring techniques.

Appraising.   Once the decision has been programmed, communicated, and monitored, the outcomes still need to be appraised to determine how successful the decision has been. Has the decision been a satisfactory one? What new issues or problems have arisen? Decisions commonly are made in situations where probabilities, not certainties, are weighed. Even the most carefully conceived and executed decisions can fail or become obsolete. Organizational decisions are made in a context of change—facts, values, and circumstances change. Therefore, a fully articulated decision—one that has been reflectively made, programmed, communicated, and monitored—in itself brings about sufficient change to necessitate its own further reevaluation and appraisal.[22] Hence, the appraisal stage is both an end and a new beginning in the action cycle of decision making. As we maintained earlier, there are no ultimate solutions— only satisfactory decisions and solutions for the moment.

THE INCREMENTAL MODEL: A STRATEGY OF SUCCESSIVE LIMITED COMPARISONS

Although the satisficing strategy that we have just described in detail is well-suited to dealing with most problems in educational administration, occasionally some situations require an incremental strategy. If the set of relevant alternatives is undefinable and the consequences of each alternative with respect to a given aspiration level is unpredictable, then even a satisficing strategy has severe limitations.[23] For example, to what new activities should a school administrator allocate more resources? The answer to this question is probably more adequately addressed by considering only alternatives that differ marginally from existing conditions. The underlying assumption of the strategy is that small incremental changes will not produce major unanticipated negative consequences for the organization.

Charles Lindblom first introduced and formalized the incremental strategy.[24] He characterizes this decision-making method as the science of muddling through and argues that it may be the only feasible approach to systematic decision making when the issues are complex and uncertainty and conflict are high. The process is best described as a method of successive limited comparisons. It does not require objectives, exhaustive analysis of alternatives and consequences, or a priori determination of either optimum or satisfactory outcomes. Instead only a very limited set of alternatives, similar to the existing situation, is considered by successively comparing their consequences until decision makers come to some agreement on a course of action.

The incremental process has a number of important features. First, the setting of objectives and the generation of alternatives are not separate activities. Goals and objectives are not established prior to decision analysis. Rather, a feasible course of action emerges as alternatives and consequences of action are explored. Indeed, the more complex the problems, the more likely objectives will change as the decision evolves. Thus, the marginal differences in value between alternative courses of action serve as the basis for decision making rather than any prior objectives.

The incremental model also greatly reduces the number of alternatives. The strategy considers only alternatives that are very similar to the existing situation, analyzes only differences between the current state and proposed outcomes, and ignores all outcomes that are outside the decision maker's narrow range of interest. The complexity of the decision making is dramatically reduced and made manageable.

Lindblom argues that this simplification of analysis, achieved by concentrating on alternatives that differ only slightly, is not a capricious kind of simplification; on the contrary, simplifying by limiting the focus to small variations from existing situations makes the most of available knowledge.[25] Decision makers who limit themselves to a reasonable set of alternatives based on their experience can make predictions of consequences with accuracy and confidence. In addition, by emphasizing only differences among alternatives, time and energy are conserved. The narrow focus on outcomes also avoids the possible paralysis caused by attempts to predict and analyze all possible outcomes of a specific course of action.

Finally, successive comparison is often an alternative to theory. In both the classical and administrative models, theory is viewed as a useful way to bring relevant knowledge to bear on specific problems. As problems become increasingly complex, however, the inadequacies of our theories to guide the decision-making process become more prevalent. The strategy of successive limited comparisons suggests that in such complex situations decision makers will make more progress if they successively compare concrete practical alternatives rather than emphasize more abstract, theoretical analyses.

In brief, the incremental approach has the following distinctive features: (1) setting objectives and generating alternatives occur simultaneously; hence, means-end analysis is inappropriate; (2) good decisions are those decision makers can agree upon regardless of objectives; (3) the number of alternatives and outcomes is drastically reduced by considering only alternatives similar to the current state of affairs; (4) analysis is also restricted to differences between the existing situation and proposed alternatives; and (5) the method eschews theory in favor of successive comparisons of concrete, practical alternatives.

The major differences in the three models of decision making—classical, administrative, and incremental—are compared in Figure 10.3. These three decision strategies can be ordered according to their capacity to deal with complexity and conditions of increasing uncertainty and conflict.[26] When deci-

Classical	Administrative	Incremental
Objectives are set prior to generating alternatives.	Objectives are usually set prior to generating alternatives.	Setting objectives and generating alternatives are intertwined.
Decision making is therefore a means-end analysis: first ends are determined then the means to obtain them are sought.	Decision making is typically a means-end analysis; however, occasionally ends change as a result of analysis.	Since means and ends are not separable, means-end analysis is inappropriate.
The test of a good decision is that it is shown to be the best means to achieve end. (Optimizing)	The test of a good decision is that it can be shown to result in a satisfactory means to achieve the end; it falls within the established boundary conditions. (Satisficing)	The test of a good decision is that decision makers can agree on an alternative without agreeing it is the best means to an agreed objective. (Successive comparing)
Engage in comprehensive analysis; all alternatives and all consequences are considered.	Engage in "problemistic search" until a set of reasonable alternatives is identified.	Drastically limit the search and analysis; focus on alternatives similar to the existing state. Many alternatives and important outcomes are ignored.
There is heavy reliance on theory to guide decision making.	There is reliance on both theory and experience to guide decision making.	Theories are viewed as basically inadequate for complex problems. Successive comparisons reduce or eliminate the need for theory.

FIGURE 10.3 Comparison of the classical, administrative, incremental models of decision making

sions are simple, information complete and certain, and a collective preference (no conflict) exists, then an optimizing strategy is most appropriate. As we have already noted, however, organizational problems are almost never simple, certain, and without conflict in preferences. Even in the case of the traditional application of the classical model—the economic theory of competitive decision —questions abound concerning its suitability.

When uncertainty and conflict are prevalent, as is typically the case in administrative decision making, a satisficing strategy becomes appropriate. The administrative model is flexible and heuristic. Decisions are based on comparisons among consequences of alternatives and the decision maker's aspiration level. Only a partial exploration of the alternatives is performed until a satisfactory course of action is discovered. If satisfactory solutions are not found, then the aspiration level is adjusted downward.

Only when the set of relevant alternatives is undefinable and the consequences of each alternative are unpredictable with respect to a given aspiration level is an incremental strategy a reasonable alternative to the satisficing strategy. In other words, when the situation is exceedingly complex, the incremental strategy is appropriate because it deals with both uncertainty and conflict of interest by assuming that small changes will not produce large negative consequences for the organization.[27]

CONFLICT THEORY OF DECISION MAKING: THE JANIS-MANN MODEL

Regardless of which decision-making strategy is employed, the pressures of the situation and the decision-making process itself often produce stress. Irving Janis and Leon Mann have developed an insightful model of conflict, which answers the following two questions: (1) Under what conditions does stress have unfavorable effects on the quality of decision making? and (2) Under what conditions will individuals use sound decision-making procedures to avoid choices that they would quickly regret?[28]

People handle psychological stress in different ways as they make vital decisions. The main sources of such stress are the fear of suffering from the known losses that will occur once an alternative is selected, worry about unknown consequences when a critical decision is at stake, concern about making a public fool of oneself, and losing self-esteem if the decision is disastrous.[29] Critical decisions usually involve conflicting values; therefore, decision makers face the unsettling dilemma that any choice they make will require sacrificing ideals or other valued objectives. Thus, the decision makers' anxiety, shame, and guilt rise, which increases the level of stress.[30]

There is no question that errors in decision making are a result of many causes, including poor analysis, ignorance, bias, impulsiveness, time constraints, and organizational policies. But another major reason for many poorly conceived and implemented decisions is related to the motivational consequences of conflict—in particular, attempts to overcome stress produced by extremely difficult choices of vital decisions. As a result, a variety of defensive mechanisms are employed by people as they try to cope with the stress of the decision-making situation, most of which impede the efficiency of the process.

Janis identified five basic patterns of coping with psychological stress:

1. *Unconflicted adherence.* The decision maker ignores information about risks and continues what has begun.
2. *Unconflicted change.* The decision maker uncritically accepts whatever course of action is most salient or popular, without concern for costs or risks.
3. *Defensive avoidance.* The decision maker evades the conflict by procrastinating, shifting the responsibility elsewhere, constructing wishful rationalizations, minimizing expected unfavorable consequences, and remaining selectively inattentive to corrective feedback.
4. *Hypervigilance.* The decision maker panics and searches frantically for a solution, rapidly vacillating back and forth between alternatives, and then impulsively siezes upon a hastily contrived solution that promises immediate relief. The full range of

alternatives and consequences is neglected because of emotional excitement, repetitive thinking, and a cognitive constriction that produces simplistic ideas and a reduction in immediate memory span.
5. *Vigilance.* The decision maker searches carefully for relevant information, assimilates the information in an unbiased manner, and then evaluates the alternatives reflectively before making a choice.[31]

The first four patterns are typically dysfunctional and lead to defective decisions. Although vigilance is no panacea, it is most likely to lead to effective decisions.

Even when decision makers are vigilant, however, they sometimes make mistakes by taking cognitive shortcuts to deal with the multiplicity of judgments that are essential. All kinds of people, including scientists and statisticians, make cognitive errors such as overestimating the likelihood that events can be easily imagined, giving too much weight to information about representativeness, relying too much on small samples, and failing to discount biased information.[32] Moreover, all these kinds of errors probably increase when decision makers are under psychological stress.

The coping strategies of unconflicted adherence or unconflicted change promote sloppy and uncritical thinking because of a lack of motivation to engage in careful decision analysis. Defensive avoidance is used to elude the work required for vigilant decision making. If the decision maker cannot pass the buck or postpone the decision, the defensively avoidant person usually makes a quick choice to "get it over with" and then engages in wishful thinking and rationalization—playing up the positive reasons and down-playing the negative ones. Hypervigilance produces a panic-like state in which the decision maker temporarily is overwhelmed by information as a result of being overly attentive to both relevant and trivial data. The informational overload and sense of imminent catastrophe contribute to the hypervigilant decision maker's tendency to use such simple-minded decision rules as "do whatever the first expert advises."[33]

The vigilant decision maker is most effective because he or she not only avoids many of the traps of the other four patterns, but also because vigilance requires (1) a careful survey of a wide range of alternatives, (2) an analysis of the full range of objectives to be fulfilled and the values implicated by the choice, (3) an analysis of the risks and drawbacks of the choice, (4) intensive search for new information relevant to further evaluation of alternatives, (5) conscientious evaluation of new information or expert judgment, even when such information does not support the initial preferred course of action, (6) reexamination of both positive and negative consequences of alternatives, including those originally regarded as unacceptable, and (7) detailed plans for implementing the selected course of action with special attention to contingency plans that might be required if various anticipated risks were to develop.[34] Notice the similarity of these seven criteria for vigilant information processing and the satisficing strategy that we have already discussed.

What are the conditions that make for vigilance? Janis and Mann propose a conflict-model of decision making by specifying the psychological conditions that mediate the five coping patterns and their accompanying levels of stress. The model is summarized in Figure 10.4. The basic idea of the model is that when confronted with a decision-making situation, reflective decision makers either consciously or unconsciously consider four issues. Their responses to four questions determine whether they engage in vigilant information processing or whether they use a less effective method of solving the problem.

Something has to trigger the process. Challenging negative feedback in which the decision maker perceives that things are going badly or that a situation is out of control most often initiates the decision-making process. But it is also possible that the process will begin as a result of a significant opportunity, which is perceived by the decision maker.

ISSUE ONE.   Once the process begins, the decision maker's first question to him- or herself is: "Are the risks serious if I don't change?" If it is determined that the risks of not changing anything are not serious, then the result is a state of unconflicted adherence. The decision maker simply adheres to the current situation and avoids stress and conflict.

ISSUE TWO.   If the answer to the first question is affirmative, however, then the level of stress increases slightly, and the decision maker is likely to ask a second question: "Are the risks serious if I do change?" Here the emphasis is on losses associated with changing. If the anticipated losses of changing are minimal, then the risks are not serious and the decision maker is predicted to accept uncritically the first reasonable alternative, that is, to opt for a state of unconflicted change. Again stress is limited.

ISSUE THREE.   If the answer to the second question is yes, then stress builds because there are serious risks in both changing and not changing. The anxiety typically produces the next question: "Is it realistic to hope to find a better solution?" If the decision maker believes there is no realistic hope of finding a better solution, then the result is a state of defensive avoidance. In order to escape from the conflict and reduce the stress, the individual avoids making the decision by either passing the buck or by rationalizing the current situation.

ISSUE FOUR.   If, however, there is some perceived hope for a better solution, then the decision maker inquires: "Is there sufficient time to search and deliberate?" If the decision maker perceives insufficient time, then a state of hypervigilance may occur. Panic sets in and the individual seizes upon a hastily contrived solution that promises immediate relief. If time is ample, then the decision maker is much more likely to engage in vigilant information processing, a process that enhances the effectiveness of the decision making through careful search, appraisal, and contingency planning. Clearly, administrators should avoid unconflicted adherence, unconflicted change, defensive avoidance, and hypervigilance; however, the forces of labor, time, and stress are operating

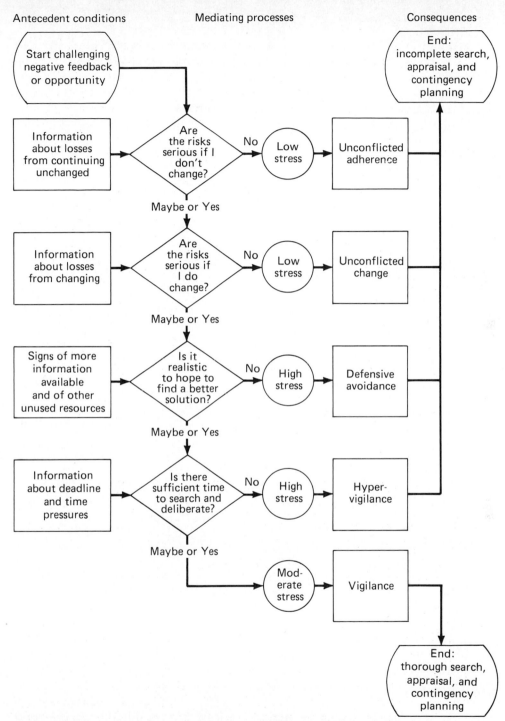

FIGURE 10.4 The conflict-theory model of decision making

SOURCE: Irving L. Janis and Leon Mann, *Decision Making: A Psychological Analysis of Conflict, Choice, and Commitment* (New York: Free Press, 1977).

against vigilance. Nevertheless, knowing the dangers of defective decision making and when they are most likely to occur should help avoid them.

DECISION MAKING IN EDUCATIONAL ADMINISTRATION

Probably the most comprehensive study of decision making in education was a three-year study of 232 elementary school principals completed by Educational Testing Service and Teachers College, Columbia University.[35] The principals who participated gathered for one week in twenty locations throughout the country. In order to compare the decision making and performance of different principals, researchers developed a simulated school situation based on a carefully selected real school, and many of the administrative problems were drawn from actual situations in this school. Participants were asked to perform and make decisions concerning a wide variety of tasks. They wrote articles for the local paper, observed (via kinescope) and rated beginning teachers, taped a speech for the PTA, participated in conferences and committee meetings, and made decisions on a large assortment of problems presented as items in their in-baskets. In addition, researchers collected demographic information and personality data on the participants through an extensive series of tests.

The results of the data analysis revealed two overall differences in handling the decision-making items. First, some principals tended to stress preparing for action, while others emphasized the actual taking of action. Second, some principals did more work on solving the problem than others, at all phases of the decision-making process. The more effective principals stressed preparation for decision making and did the most work in the process (the most industrious did about four times as much work as the least industrious). The results of the study are succinctly summarized by a single quote describing the effective principal, "He works at organizing preparation for his decisions."[36]

The study revealed that principals who are effective decision makers engage in a large amount of preliminary work: they seek more information; they differentiate between fact and opinion; and they frequently obtain the views of others. On the other hand, principals who make quick yes or no decisions without preparation tend to be less effective.

The results of this study support using the administrative decision-making cycle. There also are a substantial number of educational decision-making studies that deal with subordinate participation in the process.

PARTICIPATION IN DECISION MAKING

We have described the decision-making process as a complete cycle of events by which an organization makes and implements decisions. But other authors frequently conceive of decision making simply in terms of a conscious selection of choice among alternatives. In reaching a decision, an individual typically (1) defines the problem, (2) specifies alternatives, (3) predicts consequences for each alternative, and (4) selects from among the alternatives.[37] This procedure might be referred to as the "short version" of the decision-making process. It is concerned with the formulation of an intention to act, not with the implementation of the decision in terms of programming, communicating, monitoring, or appraising. Nonetheless, it is instructive to focus attention on the shortened version, especially when analyzing participation in the decision-making process. L. Coch and John R. P. French conducted an early study on the effects of participation in decision making, using a series of field experiments at the Harwood Manufacturing Corporation.[38] Harwood provided employees with health studies, background music while they worked, recreation programs, and, in general, good working conditions. Despite these progressive managerial practices, the workers were resistant to changes in their jobs and work procedures even when they realized that competitive conditions required changes. In an effort to improve the situation, Coch and French (with management's approval) experimented with ways to overcome the resistance while simultaneously increasing productivity and reducing turnover. Three carefully matched groups of employees were studied:

1. In Group A, the workers were given only short, routine announcements concerning the need for change and the changes to be made. There was no opportunity to participate in the decision.
2. In Group B, the employees were notified of a proposed change, the necessity of the change was explained, and the specifics were elaborated. This group of workers, however, was allowed some representation in designing those changes.
3. In Group C, the individuals were treated much the same as Group B, except that there was total representation (everyone was involved) in planning the new jobs.

About one month after the experimental procedures were implemented, the differences among the groups were clear. In the no-participation group (Group A), production did not improve, and absenteeism, employee turnover, and the number of grievances increased. In the two groups with some participation (B and C), production rose to impressively high levels, and employee turnover, absenteeism, and grievances were quite limited. Two and one half months after the completion of the initial experiment, Group A was transformed to a total representative group (Group C), and in spite of their poor initial performance, they relearned the new jobs and attained a much higher level of productivity. The results of the experiment demonstrated the positive outcomes of participation.

Other studies also have supported the desirability of participation in decision making in business as well as educational organizations.[39] The following generalizations summarize much of the research and theoretical literature on teacher participation in decision making:

1. The opportunity to share in formulating policies is an important factor in the morale of teachers and in their enthusiasm for the school organization.
2. Participation in decision making is positively related to the individual teacher's satisfaction with the profession of teaching.
3. Teachers prefer principals who involve them in decision making (regardless of whether the teachers have high or low dependency needs).
4. Teachers neither expect nor want to be involved in every decision; in fact, too much involvement can be as detrimental as too little.
5. Participation in decision making has consequences that vary from situation to situation.
6. The roles and functions of both teachers and administrators in decision making need to be varied according to the nature of the problem.
7. Both internal and external factors affect the degree of participation in decision making by teachers.
8. Typical administrators are likely to prove ineffective due to deficiencies of acceptance by subordinates as well as due to limitations on the quality of the decision.
9. In order to maximize the positive contributions of shared decision making and to minimize the negative consequences, the administrator needs to answer the following questions: (a) Under what conditions should teachers be involved? (b) To what extent and how should teachers be involved? (c) How should the decision-making group be constituted? (d) What role is most effective for the principal?[40]

CONCEPTUAL DERIVATIONS AND APPLICATIONS

Should teachers be involved in decision making and policy formulation? As we have already implied, this is the wrong question because teachers should and should not be involved. Involvement can produce either positive or negative consequences. The appropriate question is, "Under what conditions should subordinates be involved in decision making?"

The concept of zone of acceptance, explained in Chapter 9, is useful as we seek to answer this question. As we indicated there, subordinates are willing to comply with some administrative directives without question, and the range of actions they are willing to take at the administrator's request is their zone of acceptance.[41]

A Model for Shared Decision Making in Schools: Zone of Acceptance

Edwin M. Bridges postulates that (1) as the administrator involves teachers in making decisions located in their zone of acceptance, participation will be less effective and (2) as the administrator involves teachers in making decisions clearly located outside their zone of acceptance, participation will be more effective.[42] The problem for the administrator, therefore, is to determine which decisions fall inside and which outside the zone. An operational definition of zone of acceptance is useful here. Bridges proposed two tests to identify issues that clearly fall within the subordinates' zone of acceptance: (1) the test of relevance and (2) the test of expertise. We have elaborated on the criteria he developed.

The test of relevance is embodied in the question: "Do the subordinates have a high personal stake in the decision?" If they have a personal stake, interest in participation usually will be high. If there is no personal stake, subordinates typically will be receptive to the superior's directive.

The test of expertise deals with the extent to which teachers are qualified to make useful contributions to the identification or solution of the problem. Are the teachers capable of making a meaningful contribution? Do they have the expertise? To involve subordinates in decisions that are outside their scope of experience and sphere of competence is likely to cause them unnecessary frustration.

Keeping the model simple, if subordinates have a personal stake (high relevance) in the decision and have the knowledge to make a useful contribution (high expertise), then the decision clearly falls outside the zone of acceptance, and subordinates should be involved in the decision-making process. If the issue is not relevant and it falls outside their sphere of competence, however, then the decision clearly falls within the zone of acceptance and involvement should be avoided. Indeed, involvement in the latter case is likely to produce resentment because subordinates typically will not want to be involved.

The tests proposed for identification of issues with respect to the zone of acceptance do not cover two other marginal situations in which the answers are less clear. First, it is possible for subordinates to have a personal stake in the issue while having little expertise. Should they be involved in this case? Not often! To do so frequently asks for trouble. If they really have nothing substantive to contribute, the decision ultimately will be made by those with the expertise (not subordinates), and a sense of frustration and hostility may be generated by attempts to involve them. Subordinates, in fact, may perceive the experience as an empty exercise in which the decisions have "already been made." Indeed, Daniel L. Duke, Beverly K. Showers, and Michael Imber conclude from their research that shared decision making is often viewed by teachers as a formality or attempt to create the illusion of teacher influence.[43] On the other hand, occasionally it may be useful to involve teachers in a limited way. When involvement is sought under these circumstances, it must be done skillfully. Its major objectives should be open communication with subordinates and, hopefully, the lowering of potential resistance to the decision.

A second marginal situation results when subordinates have no personal stake in the situation but do have the knowledge to make a useful contribution. Should they be involved? Only occasionally! To involve subordinates indiscriminately in decisions of this type is to increase the likelihood of alienation. Although their involvement under these circumstances increases the administrator's chances of reaching a higher quality decision, subordinates too often are likely to wonder "what the administrator gets paid for." These conditions and responses are summarized in Figure 10.5.

In addition to determining when teachers should be involved in decision making, the administrator also must decide the role and extent of that involvement. For explanatory purposes, we will focus on the four-step, short version of decision making: define the problem, list alternatives, predict consequences for alternatives, and make the choice.

In Type I situations (see Figure 10.5), where the issue is clearly outside the subordinates' zone of acceptance, the subordinates' role in decision making should be maximum. That is, subordinates should be involved as early as possible, and they should be given as much freedom as possible in defining the problem and specifying the objectives. Subordinates have less and less actual involvement as they are engaged in the second, third, and fourth steps of the process. If the problem has been defined and the alternatives and consequences specified by the administrator (Steps 1, 2, and 3), participation by subordinates would have to be limited to the final phase of decision making. But subordinate involvement in Steps 2 and 3 can be and often is useful to the administrator as he or she tries to generate alternatives and to predict accurately the consequences of the various alternatives. The general rule for Type I situations, then, is to involve subordinates as early as possible.

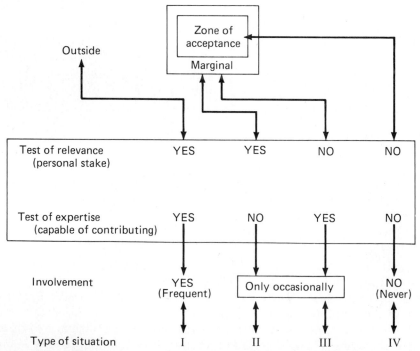

FIGURE 10.5   Situations and involvement in decision making

Type II situations are marginal; they are neither clearly outside nor inside the zone of acceptance. On those relatively infrequent occasions when subordinates are involved, the involvement should be limited. Involvement at Step 4 in the process may be appropriate here because the main purpose of involvement is to communicate the rationale for and lower resistance to the decision. Further, it should be made clear that the administrators, not subordinates, will make the final decision.

Type III situations also are marginal. Again, only occasionally should teachers be involved in decision making. The purpose for involving teachers here is primarily to improve the decision. Hence, if possible, it is wise to involve teachers at Step 2 or 3 (sometimes Step 1). Groups are often more likely to generate a wide variety of alternatives and more accurately predict consequences than an individual. It is important for the administrator to indicate clearly to the subordinates the boundaries within which they operate. The administrator must not, indeed cannot, appear to grant a tabula rasa for action when in reality they all are bound by organizational restrictions or higher authority. For example, if the superintendent has already defined the problem and specified the alternatives he or she considers viable, it is unwise for principals to act as though their teachers had complete freedom to define and solve the problem.

Type IV situations clearly fall inside the zone of acceptance. These are administrative decisions that should not involve subordinates.

Once the administrator has determined that subordinates will be involved, the next decision is to select the constitutional arrangement of the decision-making group. Guy E. Swanson has identified three major types of constitutional arrangements that are classified in terms of how the group is to arrive at a decision:

1. The democratic-centralist arrangement is probably the most frequently used mode. The leader presents a problem to subordinates and asks for comments, suggestions, reactions, and ideas. The decision is clearly the administrator's, but he or she tries to reflect the subordinates' participation and feelings in the final decision.
2. The parliamentarian arrangement binds group members to whatever a majority agrees is a given course of action. All members of the group, including the leader, have an equal vote.
3. The participant-determining arrangement requires a total consensus of the group on the appropriate action to be taken. Like the parliamentarian mode, all members of the group have an equal vote.[44]

For each decision-making situation, there is a corresponding and appropriate constitutional arrangement.[45] When the decision issue falls clearly outside the zone of acceptance (i.e., is a Type I situation), administrators should maximize participation in the decision-making process. But what kind of group arrangement is most helpful? The participant-determining mode is a powerful decision-making procedure when it is used successfully; however, because it requires total consensus, this arrangement is usually unrealistic, and it is used only if complete agreement is essential. Even in such cases, however, the costs are high in terms of time, energy, and frustration. The democratic-centralist arrangement also might be used in Type I situations, but such an arrangement seems less likely than others to maximize participation and involvement. It seems most likely, therefore, that the parliamentarian arrangement will be used most often in situations where teachers have both a personal stake and a high degree of expertise (Type I).

The administrator in the parliamentarian group plays a crucial role in ensuring that the majority does not alienate the minority, whose cooperation is often necessary for the implementation of the decision. The administrator must give the minority the opportunity to have a fair hearing before any decision is reached, thereby providing them with a chance to alter or temper the majority view. If the administrator uses the participant-determining style, the major goal will be to build consensus. His or her role here is one of guiding the discussion in such a way that the similarities of opposing viewpoints can be used as a base for building consensus. The administrator seeks to delineate advantages of various proposals in order to integrate all views and develop compromise alternatives. The role of the administrator in both parliamentarian and participant-determining groups is a neutral one, geared to facilitating the flow of communication so that the subordinates make their decisions based on the relevant facts.

In Type II and Type III situations, subordinates are involved less often and in a more limited way. They usually are involved because the administrator, who clearly has the responsibility for making the decision, wishes either (1) to communicate openly in order to lower staff resistance and gain support or (2) to improve the quality of the decision by using ideas and information that can be gained from the teachers. Given either of these objectives, the democratic-centralist mode seems most useful. Under this constitutional arrangement, the leader presents the problem to the staff and asks for their reactions and thinking before reaching a conclusion. All should be aware that in the final analysis the decision is the administrator's. If the objective of participation is to improve the quality of the decision, then more involvement at an earlier stage seems desirable. The leader should try to focus on the problem-solving process rather than on specifying a solution; in fact, research indicates that a better-quality decision is more likely to arise from the group if the leader exercises neutrality by withholding evaluation and criticism of ideas and avoiding a show of surprise at unusual ideas.[46] Free and open communication needs to be encouraged.

On the other hand, if the objective of the participation is to lower resistance to a decision by gaining acceptance, the administrator's role probably will be to communicate openly the rationale for the proposed action. Bridges has suggested that a risk technique might be used.[47] This strategy involves the staff in considering risks or dangers likely to develop if a specific alternative is implemented; hence, teachers can express their fears, anxieties, and opposition before the action is taken. Such an approach not only gives the administrator an idea of potential staff resistance but also provides an opportunity to supply additional information, which hopefully allays anxieties and opposition and creates a climate of acceptance.

This model for shared decision making is not a panacea. It is not a substitute for sensitive and reflective administrative thought and action; it simply provides some rough guidelines for determining when and how teachers and principals should be involved in joint decision making. The effectiveness of decisions is determined by both the quality of the decision and the acceptance and commitment of subordinates to implement the decision.

The model for shared teacher-principal decision making is summarized in Figure 10.6. The central concept is the zone of acceptance of teachers, which

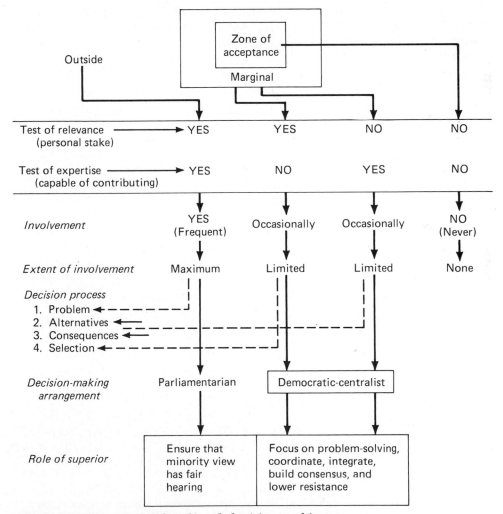

FIGURE 10.6 Model for shared decision making

is determined by two criteria—the test of relevance and the test of expertise. If an issue is highly relevant to participants, who are highly expert, then it clearly falls outside the zone of acceptance, and teachers frequently should be involved in decision making. The involvement should be as early as possible in the process in order to maximize participation. Typically, there will be a parliamentarian decision-making arrangement in which the group decides and the principal facilitates the process by ensuring that the minority receives a fair hearing. If, however, an issue is of low relevance and participant expertise is also low, then the issue clearly falls inside the zone of acceptance, and the model suggests teacher involvement in the decision-making process is neither desirable nor effective.

There also are two marginal cases, where issues do not fall clearly within the zone of acceptance. When teachers have a high personal stake in the decision but a low potential for contributing significantly, they should be involved only occasionally. Under those circumstances when they are involved, the objective is to communicate the mechanics of the decision-making process openly in order to lower resistance; hence, involvement is usually late in the process, with the principal informing teachers of the facts in a systematic fashion. Indeed, using a democratic-centralistic arrangement, the principal may solicit advice from teachers concerning the final selection of alternatives for action (step 4). The second marginal case occurs when teachers have no personal stake in the decision but have a high potential for contributing important knowledge. Again, involvement should take place only occasionally, with the objective to improve the quality of the decision. Participation should be fairly early in the decision-making process (typically, step two or three), but the democratic-centralist mode should be used because the principal will ultimately make the final decision. The teachers are aids in the process, and the role of the principal should be one of focusing on problem solving and idea generation in order to develop a better decision.

A Model for Shared Decision Making: Decision Rules

Another set of guidelines for determining when and to what extent subordinates should be involved in decision making has been proposed by Victor Vroom and Phillip Yetton.[48] Their model is more complicated than the one just presented, but it is a useful complement. It is also a contingency approach that suggests that participation in decision making should depend on the nature of the problem and the situation. Based upon the existing empirical evidence, two sets of rules were developed that should be used to determine the form and amount of subordinate participation in decision making in different situation.[49]

The first set contains three rules designed to enhance the *quality* of the decisions.

1. *The information rule.* If the quality of the decision is important and if the superior does not possess sufficient information and

expertise to solve the problem alone, then a unilateral decision is inappropriate; in fact, its use risks a low-quality decision.

2. *The trust rule.* If the quality of the decision is important and if the subordinates cannot be trusted to decide on the basis of the organizational goals, then decision through group consensus is inappropriate. Indeed, the superior's lack of control over the decision may jeopardize its quality.

3. *The unstructured problem rule.* Given an important decision, if the superior lacks information or expertise and if the problem is unstructured, then the method chosen to solve the problem should include sufficient procedures for collecting information. Participation of knowledgeable subordinates should improve the quality of the decision.

The second set of rules is designed to enhance the *acceptance* of decisions by subordinates.

1. *The acceptance rule.* If subordinate acceptance of the decision is critical for effective implementation and if it is not certain that an autocratic decision would be accepted, then some sharing of the situation and participation of others are necessary. To deny any participation in the decision making risks the necessary acceptance.

2. *The conflict rule.* If acceptance of the decision is critical and if an autocratic decision is not certain to be accepted, then the decision-making process should be structured to enable those in disagreement to resolve their differences with full knowledge of the problem. Thus, group participation is necessary; all subordinates should have an opportunity to resolve any differences.

3. *The fairness rule.* If the quality of the decision is not important, but its acceptance is critical and problematic, then a group decision should be made. A group decision will likely generate more acceptance and commitment than a hierarchical one.

4. *The acceptance priority rule.* If acceptance is critical, not assured by an autocratic decision, and if subordinates can be trusted, only group decision making is appropriate. Any other method provides the unnecessary risk that the decision will not be fully accepted or receive the necessary subordinate commitment.

Five alternate methods of making decisions are offered by Vroom and Yetton, which can be ordered along a continuum from unilateral to shared.[50] Beginning with unilateral, each of these decision-making options is briefly described as follows.

1. *Unilateral.* The administrator uses existing information to make the decision alone.

2. The administrator seeks information from subordinates, then makes the decision alone.
3. The administrator consults with relevant subordinates *individually*, soliciting their ideas and suggestions, then makes the decision, which may or may not reflect the subordinates' influence.
4. The administrator consults with the group to obtain their collective ideas through discussion, then makes the decision, which may or may not reflect the subordinates' influence.
5. *Shared.* The administrator shares the situation and problem with the group, then the group decides. All group members share equally as they generate, evaluate, and attempt to reach consensus in a decision.

The decision rules (contingency factors) and the alternate ways of making decisions can be linked; in fact, seven questions are presented that the administrator can ask himself or herself to determine the most appropriate decision-making option. The questions and the paths to the most appropriate action are presented in Figure 10.7. The administrator can analyze the situation by answering yes or no to each question and then follow the path to the most favorable action.

There is no question that the Vroom-Yetton model is relatively complex and time-consuming. Nonetheless, it provides another useful framework for determining when, how, and to what extent subordinates should be involved in decision making. Moreover, research does show that if administrators follow the directives of the model, they are more likely to be successful.[51]

The two models of shared decision making just presented are complementary. The first uses the notion of zone of acceptance to guide participation in decision making. It is a simple but powerful model that can be used quickly and efficiently. The second model, the Vroom-Yetton model, is much more time-consuming; it involves a series of seven sequential questions. Our advice is to use the first model routinely and, when time permits, use the second model to validate and refine actions derived from the first.

A Caution on Group Decision Making: Groupthink

There is little question that group decision making can be an effective process, but there are some dangers even when the conditions call for a group decision. Time is always a potential constraint on participation in decision making, and group decisions typically require more time than individual decisions. Participation involves discussion, debate, and often conflict; in fact, as the number of actors increases in the process, coordination becomes more important and difficult. Speed and efficiency are not basic advantages of group decision making.

Although participation in decision making can produce rampant conflict in the group, success in group problem solving often produces a strong cohesiveness, especially among members of smaller "in" groups. Too much cohesiveness

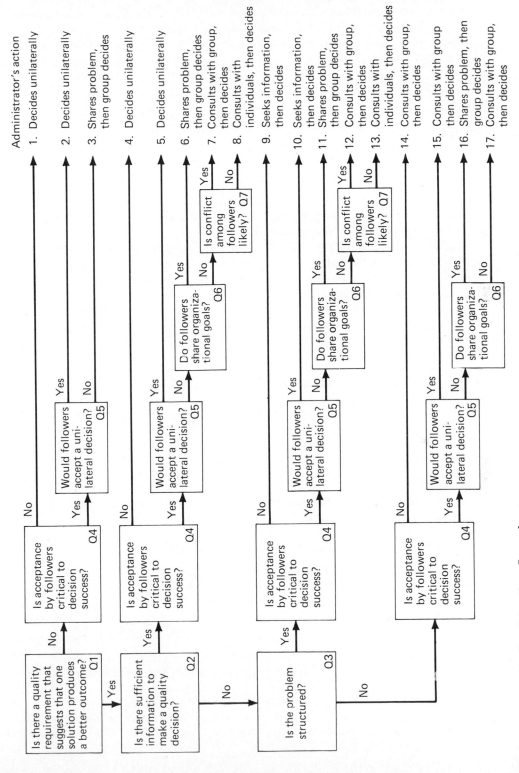

FIGURE 10.7 Participation flow chart

can be as dangerous as conflict. Conflict prevents action; strong cohesiveness promotes uniformity within the group. The problem with uniformity is that it can produce a likemindedness that is uncritical. Janis highlights this concurrence-seeking tendency among moderately or highly cohesive groups. When the tendency is dominant, the members use their collective cognitive resources to develop rationalizations consistent with shared illusion about the invulnerability of their organization; that is, they display the *groupthink syndrome.*[52]

The following eight main symptoms of groupthink characterize historic decision-making fiascoes.

1. *Illusion of invulnerability.* Members ignore obvious danger, take extreme risks, and are overly optimistic.
2. *Collective rationalization.* Members discredit and explain away warnings contrary to group thinking.
3. *Illusion of morality.* Members believe their decisions are morally correct, ignoring the ethical consequences of their decisions.
4. *Excessive stereotyping.* The group constructs negative stereotypes of rivals outside the group.
5. *Pressure for conformity.* Members pressure any in the group who express arguments against the group's stereotypes, illusions, or commitments, viewing such opposition as disloyalty.
6. *Self-censorship.* Members withhold their dissenting views and counterarguments.
7. *Illusion of unanimity.* Members perceive falsely that everyone agrees with the group's decision; silence is seen as consent.
8. *Mindguards.* Some members appoint themselves to the role of protecting the group from adverse information that might threaten group complacency.[53]

Conditions that foster groupthink.　Janis provides a comprehensive analysis of the conditions that encourage groupthink.[54] In addition to group cohesiveness, structural faults of the organization and provocative situational contexts contribute to groupthink (see Figure 10.8).

The likelihood that groupthink will occur in cohesive groups depends on how many of the antecedent conditions listed in Figure 10.8 exist. One of the most potent conditions is insulation from direct contact with others in the same organization who are not members of the in-group of policy makers. As Janis explains:

For example, an insulated group of executives is likely to receive only brief and unimpressive summaries of warning about the insurmountable difficulties of implementing a strategic reorganization or a new method of production that is under consideration. The top commanders of the organization may end up concurring on a course of action that many middle-

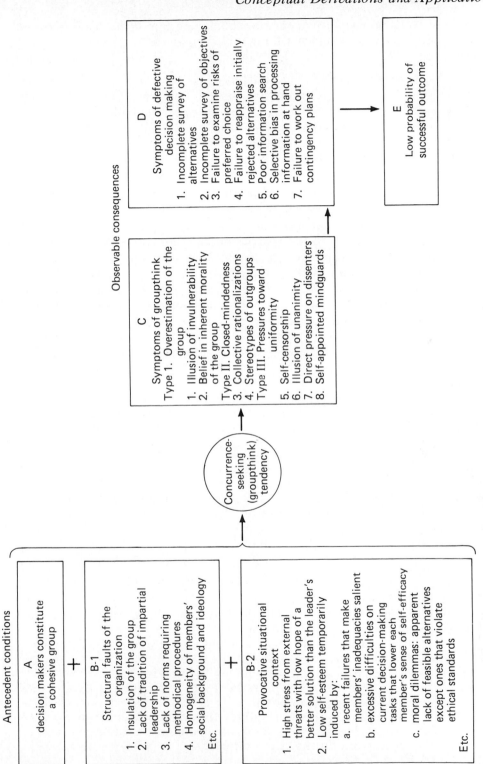

FIGURE 10.8 Theoretical analysis of groupthink

SOURCE: Irving L. Janis, "Sources of Error in Strategic Decision Making," in Johannes M. Pennings and Associates (eds.), *Organizational Strategy and Change* (San Francisco: Jossey-Bass, 1985), p. 172.

level and lower-level personnel on the firing line could have informed them in advance would not be feasible.[55]

Lack of impartial leadership also will encourage concurrence-seeking, especially when the leader is strong and charismatic. Followers seek to please such leaders, and knowing a leader's initial preferences channels their thinking. Moreover, lack of norms requiring systematic analysis as well as homogeniety of members' social background and ideology contribute to likemindedness.

Similarly, the situational context may nurture groupthink. We have already discussed the negative consequences produced by stress. High stress from external threats combined with little hope that the leader will advance a better solution pushes the group toward uncritical consensus. Furthermore, low self-esteem of the group, temporarily induced by recent failures, excessive difficulties, and moral dilemmas, foster groupthink. All these antecedent conditions promote a tendency toward concurrence seeking, which in turn produces the consequences of groupthink—overestimation of the group, closed-mindedness, and pressure of unanimity. Such behavior makes for low vigilance in decision making, which ultimately results in defective decision making with a low probability of a successful outcome (see Figure 10.8).

Avoiding Groupthink.   There are a number of ways to prevent groupthink. The following ten recommendations is a tentative set of prescriptions for counteracting the conditions that foster groupthink.

1. The group should be made aware of the causes and consequences of groupthink.
2. The leader should be neutral when assigning a decision-making task to a group, initially withholding all preferences and expectations. This practice will be especially effective if the leader consistently encourages an atmosphere of open inquiry.
3. The leader should give high priority to airing objections and doubts, and be accepting of criticism.
4. Groups should always consider unpopular alternatives, assigning the role of devil's advocate to several strong members of the group.
5. Sometimes it is useful to divide the group into two separate deliberative bodies as feasibilities are evaluated.
6. Spend a sizable amount of time surveying all warning signals from rival groups and organizations.
7. After reaching a preliminary consensus on a decision, all residual doubts should be expressed and the matter reconsidered.
8. Outside experts should be included in vital decision making.
9. Tentative decisions should be discussed with trusted colleagues not in the decision-making group.
10. The organization should routinely follow the administrative practice of establishing several independent decision-making groups to work on the same critical issue or policy.[56]

SUMMARY

An understanding of the decision-making process is vital to successful administration. Three basic strategies of decision making are identified and described. The optimizing strategy of the classical model is found not to be useful to administrators because it assumes perfect information, rationality, and human capacity not found in the actual world of administration.

Although completely rational decision making is impossible, administrators need a systematic process to enhance the selection of satisfactory solutions. Thus, a strategy of satisficing is central to decision making in the administrative model. Here decision making is a cycle of activity that includes recognition and definition of the problem, analysis of difficulties, establishment of criteria for an adequate resolution, development of a plan of action, and the initiation of the plan. Because of its cyclical nature, the decision-making action cycle may be entered at different stages and the stages are gone through again and again in the process of administration. Recognition and definition of the problems are important phases of the cycle. How the administrator conceptualizes a problem has tremendous impact on its eventual solution. Analysis of the difficulties in the existing situation places the problem in the context of a particular organization and provides answers to what, where, why, when, and how. In establishing criteria of adequacy for resolution of difficulties, decision makers compare their "musts" and "wants." The central step of the process is developing a plan for action that necessarily involves specifying alternatives, predicting consequences of alternatives, deliberating, and selecting alternatives for action. The final step of the action cycle, initiating the plan of action, includes programming, communicating, monitoring, and appraising.

The satisficing strategy is well-suited for dealing with most problems in educational administration; however, when the set of alternatives is undefinable and the consequences of each alternative are unpredictable with respect to a given aspiration level, then an incremental strategy is more appropriate. This process is a method of successive limited comparisons; only a limited set of alternatives, similar to the existing situation, is considered by successively comparing their consequences until agreement is reached on a course of action. It is assumed that small changes are not likely to produce large negative consequences for the organization.

Regardless of the strategy, decision making often causes stress. The conditions under which stress has unfavorable effects on the quality of decision making are discussed, and five coping mechanisms that decision makers are most likely to use in stressful situations are analyzed.

Studies show that it is not always beneficial for administrators to involve subordinates in decision making. Two models are proposed to help administrators determine under what conditions subordinates should share in the decision-making process. The first uses the tests of relevance and expertise as a guide for participation, while the second uses two sets of rules concerning the quality and acceptance of decisions to determine the form and amount of subordinate participation in decision making in different situations. Finally, the conditions that foster groupthink are analyzed, and suggestions are proposed for avoiding them.

NOTES

1. Herbert A. Simon, *Administrative Behavior* (New York: Macmillan, 1974). Recent research, however, suggests that many administrators ignore normative methods prescribed by scholars for effective decision making and persist in questionable decision tactics. See Paul C. Nutt, "Types of Organizational Decision Process," *Administrative Science Quarterly*, 29 (1984), 414–450.
2. The basic assumptions in the following section come primarily from Edward H. Litchfield, "Notes on a General Theory of Administration," *Administrative Science Quarterly*, 1 (1956), 3–29; Simon, *op. cit.;* and Herbert A. Simon, *Models of Man* (New York: Wiley, 1957).
3. Peter M. Blau and W. Richard Scott, *Formal Organizations: A Comparative Approach* (San Francisco: Chandler, 1962), pp. 250–251.
4. Litchfield, *op. cit.,* 27–28.
5. Simon, *Administrative Behavior,* p. 241.
6. *Ibid.,* pp. xxv–xxvi.
7. *Ibid.,* pp. 1–78.
8. *Ibid.,* p. 243.
9. Litchfield, *op. cit.,* 20–21.
10. *Ibid.,* 21.
11. What has been termed policy making in the public sector has recently been discussed under the title of strategic formulation in the private sector. See Henry Mintzberg, "Patterns in Strategy Formulation," *Management Science*, 24 (1978), 934–948. See also Johannes M. Pennings and Associates, *Organizational Strategy and Change* (San Francisco: Jossey-Bass, 1985).
12. Litchfield, *op. cit.,* p. 21.
13. *Ibid.,* 22.
14. *Ibid.,* 28.
15. *Ibid.,* 13.
16. The problem is much more complex, however, if it also involves the integration of minority students into segregated schools.
17. Chester I. Barnard, *The Functions of the Executive* (Cambridge, MA: Harvard University Press, 1938), pp. 190–191.
18. Peter F. Drucker, *The Effective Executive* (New York: Harper & Row, 1966), pp. 113–142.
19. Barnard, *op. cit.,* p. 194.
20. Richard M. Cyert and James G. March, *A Behavioral Theory of the Firm* (Englewood Cliffs, NJ: Prentice-Hall, 1963). See also Bernard M. Bass, *Organizational Decision Making* (Homewood, IL: Irwin, 1985), pp. 54–56.
21. James D. Thompson, *Organizations in Action* (New York: McGraw-Hill, 1968), pp. 151–153, 158.
22. Litchfield, *op. cit.,* 19.
23. See Anna Grandori, "A Prescriptive Contingency View of Organizational Decision Making," *Administrative Science Quarterly*, 29 (1984), 192–208.

24. Charles E. Lindblom, "The Science of Muddling Through," *Public Administrative Review,* 19 (1959), 79–99. See also Charles E. Lindblom, *The Policy-Making Process* (Englewood Cliffs, NJ: Prentice-Hall, 1968); and David Braybrook and Charles E. Lindblom, *The Strategy of Decision* (New York: Free Press, 1963).

25. Lindblom, "The Science of Muddling Through," p. 201.

26. Gradori, *op. cit.,* pp. 192–208.

27. *Ibid.*

28. This section draws heavily on two sources: Irving L. Janis and Leon Mann, *Decision Making: A Psychological Analysis of Conflict, Choice, and Commitment* (New York: Free Press, 1977); and Irving L. Janis, "Sources of Error in Strategic Decision Making," in Johannes M. Pennings and Associates (eds.), *op. cit.,* pp. 157–197.

29. Janis, "Sources of Error," p. 183.

30. *Ibid.*

31. *Ibid.,* pp. 183–184.

32. *Ibid.,* p. 185; R. E. Nisbett and L. Ross, *Human Interferences: Strategies and Shortcomings in Social Judgments* (Englewood Cliffs, NJ: Prentice-Hall, 1980); and Amos Tversky and Daniel Kahneman, "Availability: Heuristic for Judging Frequency and Probability," *Cognitive Psychology,* 5 (1973), 207–232.

33. Janis, "Sources of Error," p. 185–186.

34. Janis and Mann, *Decision Making.*

35. John K. Hemphill, Daniel E. Griffiths, and Norman Frederiksen, *Administrative Performance and Personality* (New York: Teachers College, Columbia University, 1962).

36. John K. Hemphill, "Personal Variables and Administrative Styles," *Behavioral Science and Educational Administration,* Sixty-third Yearbook of the National Society for the Study of Education, Part II (Chicago: University of Chicago Press, 1964), p. 194.

37. Robert Tannenbaum, "Managerial Decision-Making," (Reprint No. 9) (Los Angeles: Institute of Industrial Relations, University of California, 1950), pp. 23–24.

38. L. Coch and John R. P. French, Jr., "Overcoming Resistance to Change," *Human Relations,* 1 (1948), 512–532.

39. See, for example, Robert H. Guest, *Organizational Change: The Effect of Successful Leadership* (Homewood, IL: Dorsey, 1960); Victor H. Vroom, *Some Personality Determinants of the Effects of Participation* (Englewood Cliffs, NJ: Prentice-Hall, 1960); Frederick R. Wickert, "Turnover and Employees' Feelings of Ego-Involvement in the Day-to-Day Operations of a Company," *Personnel Psychology,* 4 (1951), 185–197; Edwin M. Bridges, "Teacher Participation in Decision-Making," *Administrator's Notebook,* 1 (1952), 1–4; Chiranji La Sharma, "Who Should Make What Decisions?" *Administrator's Notebook,* 3 (1955), 1–4; Joseph A. Allutto and James A. Belasco, "Patterns of Teacher Participation in School System Decision-Making," *Educational Administration Quarterly,* 9 (1973), 27–41; James A. Belasco and Joseph A. Allutto, "Decisional Participation and Teacher Satisfaction," *Educational Administration Quarterly,* 8 (1972), 117–125; James A. Conway, "Test of Linearity Between Teachers' Participation in Decision Making and Their Perceptions of Schools as Organizations," *Administra-*

tive Science Quarterly, 21 (1976), 130–139; Victor H. Vroom, "Leadership," in Marvin D. Dunnette (ed.), *Handbook of Industrial and Organizational Psychology* (Chicago: Rand McNally, 1976), pp. 80–96; and Allan M. Mohrman, Jr., Robert A. Cooke, and Susan Albers Mohrman, "Participation in Decision Making: A Multidimensional Perspective," *Educational Administration Quarterly,* 14 (1978), 13–29. For a comprehensive and somewhat critical review of participation in decision making, see Edwin A. Locke and David M. Schweiger, "Participation in Decision-Making: One More Look," *Research in Organizational Behavior,* 1 (1979), 265–339. Similarly, for a recent review of participative decision making in education, see James A. Conway, "The Myth, Mystery, and Mastery of Participative Decision Making in Education," *Educational Administration Quarterly,* 3 (1984), 11–40. See also Nak Jin Moon, "The Construction of a Conceptual Framework for Teacher Participation in School Decision Making," (Ed.D diss., University of Kentucky, 1983).

40. These last four questions provide Edwin Bridges with the basis for developing a model of shared decision making in the school principalship. The model for shared decision making in the following section draws heavily from Bridges' pioneering article. See Edwin M. Bridges, "A Model for Shared Decision-Making in the School Principalship," *Educational Administration Quarterly,* 3 (1967), 49–61. For a useful distinction between shared decision making and delegation see Wayne K. Hoy and David Sousa, "Delegation: The Neglected Aspect of Participation in Decision Making," *Alberta Journal of Educational Research,* 30 (1984), 320–331.

41. Simon, *op. cit.,* p. 133. The concept of zone of acceptance is essentially what Barnard, *op. cit.,* refers to as the "zone of indifference." We prefer Simon's label, which avoids the negative connotations that might be associated with indifference.

42. Bridges, "A Model for Shared Decision-Making," *op. cit.,* 51.

43. Daniel L. Duke, Beverly K. Showers, and Michael Imber, "Teachers and Shared Decision Making: The Costs and Benefits of Involvement," *Educational Administration Quarterly,* 16 (1980), 93–106.

44. Guy E. Swanson, "The Effectiveness of Decision-Making Groups," *Adult Leadership,* 8 (1959), 48–52.

45. Little systematic research has been done in terms of matching constitutional arrangements with situations; hence, the matchings proposed to maximize effectiveness are somewhat speculative in nature.

46. Edwin M. Bridges and Wayne J. Doyle, "The Effects of Hierarchical Differentiation on Group Productivity, Efficiency, and Risk-Taking," *Administrative Science Quarterly,* 13 (1968), 305–319; and Chris Argyris, "Interpersonal Barriers to Decision-Making," *Harvard Business Review,* 44 (1966), 84–97.

47. Bridges, "Model for Shared Decision-Making," *op. cit.*

48. Victor H. Vroom and Phillip W. Yetton, *Leadership and Decision Making* (Pittsburgh: University of Pittsburgh Press, 1973), pp. 11–58.

49. *Ibid.,* pp. 33–35.

50. *Ibid.,* p. 134.

51. Victor H. Vroom and Arthur G. Jago, "On the Validity of the Vroom-Yetton Model," *Journal of Applied Psychology,* (1978), 151–162. For a critical analysis of the model, see George R. H. Field, "A Critique of the Vroom-

Yetton Contingency Model of Leadership Behavior," *Academy of Management Review,* 4 (1979), 249–257.

52. Janis, "Sources of Error," p. 169.
53. Janis and Mann, *Decision Making;* see also Irving I. Janis, *Groupthink: Psychological Studies of Policy Decisions and Fiascoes* (Boston: Houghton Mifflin, 1982).
54. Janis, "Sources of Error," pp. 171–182.
55. *Ibid.,* p. 174.
56. *Ibid.,* pp. 180–181.

Chapter 11

Communication

The essential executive functions . . . are, first, to provide the system of communication. . . .

CHESTER I. BARNARD
The Functions of the Executive

Communication permeates every aspect of school life. Teachers instruct, using oral, written, and other media such as videotapes, computers, and art forms. Students demonstrate their learning through similar media. Superintendents and principals spend 70 percent or more of their time communicating.[1] In a sense, students, teachers, and administrators earn their living in schools by communicating.[2] An understanding of communication, therefore, is central to the study of educational administration because it offers an additional conceptual viewpoint for examining the school as a social system. Pervasiveness of the process alone makes communication a useful object of study.[3]

Moreover, Chester I. Barnard observed that commonly held goals are necessary for cooperative effort.[4] Goals become known and useful—that is, dynamic—only when they are communicated. In complex organizations, the translation of goals into units of concrete action and subsequent goal accomplishment depend on communication. Establishing a communication network and process, therefore, becomes the first task of the organizer and the continuous task of the administrator. As Herbert A. Simon succinctly stated, "Without communication there can be no organization."[5]

Communication and Problems of Administration

As a basic, dynamic process, communication underlies the organizational and administrative variables of bureaucracy, informal organization, motivation, leadership, and decision making. Before concluding, however, that communication provides all the answers to the problems confronting educational administrators, four caveats must be observed. First, because process is everywhere in organizations, communication is difficult to isolate as a separate phenomenon for investigation.[6] The concept merges too easily with leadership, decision making, and other variables.

Second, the conclusion should not be drawn that all school problems involve communication. Open information flow generally is a healthy condition, but considering communication a universal solution to all problems oversimplifies administrative practice. More often than not, difficulties in communicating are not, strictly speaking, communication problems.[7] Instead, the problems commonly attributed to communication failure only reflect breakdowns in other fundamental components of school life. Overly mechanistic structures, administrative disorganization, or closed interpersonal climates in schools may be the root problem rather than failed communication.

Third, communication reveals as well as eliminates problems.[8] For example, a conflict in values among teachers, students, and administrators may go unnoticed until communication is attempted. Conversely, communication may obscure existing problems. The popularity enjoyed by the word "image" reflects in part an unattractive preoccupation with communication as a method of changing how the school is perceived without changing the school itself. For instance, the demise of public relations departments and the emergence of public information departments in school districts may suggest more concern for image than substance.

Fourth, communication is a process that evokes action and is far from being the substance of good administration. The best communication cannot compensate for poor educational plans, programs, or ideas. In fact, the administrator who is a good communicator but who has faulty ideas about instruction merely leads the school more quickly toward failure.

Even though these caveats represent limitations, communication does serve several pervasive and integrative functions in the school organization. To claim that communication is the universal problem solver, however, is naïve. In this chapter, we will define and discuss communication while attempting to keep both the important functions and the cautionary guides in proper perspective.

DEFINITIONS OF COMMUNICATION

Attempts to define communication in terms that are universally applicable have been frustrated by the multifaceted nature of the process, which is characterized by subtlety, variety, and ubiquity. In reviewing the literature, Frank E. X. Dance, for instance, discovered ninety-five definitions, containing at least fifteen themes, that suggest different and sometimes contradictory approaches to understanding communication.[9] For our purposes, however, the definition provided by Philip V. Lewis is useful.[10] Communication means sharing messages, ideas, or attitudes that produce a degree of understanding between a sender and receiver. In everyday usage, communication implies an attempt to share meaning by transmitting messages among people.[11] Since our focus is on the school organization, we will assume that the sharing of messages, ideas, or attitudes occurs in schools among administrators, teachers, students, parents, and other interested constituencies. From this perspective Simon's definition of communication provides the basic organizational formulation: Communication is ". . . any process whereby decisional premises are transmitted from one member of an organization to another."[12]

Implicit in all the definitions is the notion that communication involves at least two people—a sender and a receiver. An administrator does not communicate in a vacuum, but with the public, students, teachers, and other employees. The definition also implies that communication must be meaningful. Communication does not take place unless the receiver correctly or accurately interprets the information being transmitted. Understanding, however, is a highly relative matter. Low levels of understanding can develop between people who do not speak the same language. Body motions, facial expressions, voice intonations, and speech rapidity convey meaningful information. In an administrative context, communication requires a high level of understanding.

Human action is needed to accomplish goals in schools. Goal-directed behavior is elicited through communication. Therefore, the greater the clarity of the message, the more likely administrator, teacher, and student actions will proceed in fruitful directions. Administrators want receivers such as teachers and students to understand and accept their ideas and to act on them. For example, a principal conveys to the staff the school's goals and provides guidelines for their accomplishment. One goal might be to individualize instruction, and the guidelines would include the development of learning packages. As the educational leader, the principal emphasizes the validity of the goal, stresses the usefulness of the new procedures, and encourages teacher action to implement the program. The extent of action depends in large measure on how effectively the principal has communicated the goal and accompanying procedures.

Communication in schools is thus successful or accurate when the sender of a message and the receiver have a very similar comprehension of the message's content.[13] Two frameworks for analyzing and understanding communication processes are sociopsychological and formal-informal organizational theories. The two approaches focus on individual attributes and organizational factors, respectively.

SOCIOPSYCHOLOGICAL THEORY OF COMMUNICATION

Because communication plays such central roles in schools, the key issue is not whether administrators engage in communication or not, but whether administrators communicate effectively or poorly. Communication is unavoidable to an organization's functioning; only effective communication is avoidable.[14] In other words, people must exchange information in schools, but to develop shared meanings requires positive efforts by educators and other participants.

Communication among people depends on a combination of personal and environmental factors. As such, a basic generalization is that the meaning of a message is to be found in what people take to be the meaning and not necessarily in the intended content. So-called semantics problems arise because the same word means different things to different people. Strictly speaking, an administrator cannot convey meaning, only words. The same word may have a wide variety of meanings because people have different communication abilities, knowledge levels, and backgrounds.

When school administrators speak of management prerogatives, for instance, they typically are referring to the planning and allocating of resources better to accomplish educational goals. Management prerogatives to teachers, however, often mean autocratic and paternalistic decision making by administrators who do not consult with them. Conversely, binding arbitration to teacher negotiators means a procedure that assures good-faith bargaining by both sides during the negotiation process; to administrators, however, binding arbitration frequently means a power-grabbing ploy. The words assume alternative meanings because individuals have personally experienced different environmental or social forces. The sociopsychological theory of communication considers an individual's personal and social context basic to the communication process.

A commonly used model of the communication process that incorporates this perspective is illustrated in Figure 11.1.[15] The process is conceptualized as a communication loop. On the left portion of the figure, individual *A* initiates a message; it is received by individual *B*, who in turn considers possible courses of action. If individual *B* responds or provides feedback, the roles of *A* and *B* are reversed. As pictured at the right of Figure 11.1, individual *B* now becomes the source of a message and individual *A* the receiver. Exchange in the loop continues as two-way communication. This process is accomplished in a social situation where an organization's bureaucratic structure and its informal structure produce noise or static that interferes with understanding. To explicate the model further, each portion will be described separately.

Source

The source, or sender, is the originator of a message (see Figure 11.1). The communicator need not be a person; a newspaper, professional journal, or organizational position, such as the office of the assistant superintendent for finance, may be the source.

The effectiveness of a message depends in part on the level of credibility that the receiver attributes to the sender.[16] Source, or sender, credibility consists of the trust and confidence that the receiver has in the words and actions of the communicator. The level of credibility, in turn, influences the reactions of the receiver to the words and actions of the sender.[17] In some cases the identity and reputation of the source, far from authenticating the message, lead

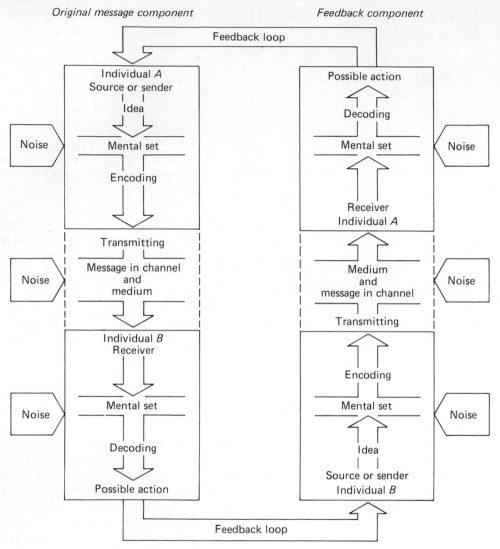

Original message component   *Feedback component*

FIGURE 11.1   A sociopsychological model of two-way communication

instead to the receiver's distorting the information or ignoring the message completely.[18] For example, faculty members who view the principal as dishonest and manipulative probably will distort all communications from that source.

Idea.   The sender must create an idea or choose a fact to communicate. The idea or fact is the content of the message. In other words, the source must have something to say before the content can be "said." This first step is crucial because the succeeding steps are nonsensical without a message.

Encoding and mental sets. The source initiates a message by encoding a thought, that is, organizing the idea into a series of symbols such as words or pictures that he or she feels will communicate the correct meaning to the intended receiver. These symbols are arranged for rationality, coherence, and compatibility with the method of delivery, or medium. The sender selects a particular medium because the encoding must be done in relation to the transmitting medium as well as the receiver's characteristics. A telegram, for instance, usually is worded differently from an office memo, and both are different from face-to-face conversation. We will have more to say about the medium in our discussion of transmitting.

The mental set of the sender, that is, the person's particular psychological characteristics, also limits the encoding process. Communication skills, knowledge of the subject, and personality factors such as attitudes, values, interests, and motivational needs are traits or mental conditions that combine to limit, screen, or filter what is encoded and the quality of the message.[19] For example, the assistant superintendent for instruction when communicating with principals screens out information that he or she thinks is not pertinent to building administration; principals filter information to the assistant superintendent that might reflect negatively on their performance.

Transmitting

Transmitting transforms the encoded message into a signal and places it into a channel. The symbols that have been ordered inside a person's mind are placed into physical movement. Transmitting, therefore, involves the message, channel, and medium.

Message. The result of the encoding process is the message or the content to be conveyed. The message is the idea that an individual—be it an administrator, teacher, student, parent—hopes to communicate to the intended receiver. The exact form of the message depends to a large extent on the channel and medium that are used to carry it.

Channel. The channel is the routing pattern that the message is to follow. One channel is vertical (up and down the hierarchy of authority), and another is horizontal (across the same level of hierarchy). The channel also can be formal or informal. In any case, the idea becomes a physical reality in the channel as opposed to a psychological reality in the sender's mind.

Medium. The medium is the carrier of the message. The content can be transmitted in a verbal-oral medium as in direct face-to-face speech, or electronically via telephone, radio, or television. Similarly, the medium can be verbal-written as in memos, letters, and newspapers. The transmission also can be made through a nonverbal medium as in body language or gestures and symbolically with things that surround us.

The most familiar form of human communication is speech, which uses the best-known type of human signals, the sounds that constitute words. Primary oral communication consists of making sounds that are transmitted directly in face-to-face situations, or that are transmitted indirectly through such electronic devices as telephones and audio or video recorders. Secondary verbal communication consists of written word signals transmitted through devices such as letters and memos.

Richard L. Daft and Robert H. Lengel hypothesize that the communication media used in organizations determine the richness of information processed by the receiver.[20] Moreover, communication media and richness can be placed on the parallel five-step continua, as follows:

	Step 1	Step 2	Step 3	Step 4	Step 5
MEDIUM	Face-to-Face	Telephone	Written Personal	Written Formal	Numeric Formal
RICHNESS	Highest	High	Moderate	Low	Lowest

Rich media combine multiple cues, rapid feedback, and a variety of language. The face-to-face medium is the richest form because it provides immediate feedback through verbal and visual cues. While verbal feedback is rapid, the telephone medium is less rich than face-to-face because the visual cues are absent. Written communication is described as being moderate or low in richness because feedback is slow and only written information is conveyed. Addressed correspondence is personal in character and somewhat richer than general memos and bulletins, which are anonymous and impersonal. Formal numeric documents, e.g., computer print-outs containing quantitative data, convey the least rich information because numbers do not have the information-carrying capacity of natural language.

As might be expected from the discussion of richness, when the effects of written and oral media are compared, a problem faces the communicator.[21] Comprehension is higher when information is presented in written form. However, opinion change is greater in face-to-face interactions. The appropriate medium thus depends on the purpose, that is, understanding or persuading.

Redundancy in media increases both the richness of the information and the accuracy of message transmission.[22] Generally, the most effective (i.e., accurate) communication efforts use a combination of written and oral media; the next most effective is oral alone; and written is least powerful.[23] The combination of written and oral media is seldom inappropriate. Written communication alone can be effective in two situations—where information requires future action or where it is general. The oral medium by itself also can be effective in two situations demanding immediate feedback—for administering reprimands and settling disputes.

While redundancy in media usually leads to better communication, vocal and written messages carry only a small part of the information that administrators convey when they interact with others. At least as important as verbal signals are the less fully understood nonverbal signals. The raised eyebrow, the firm handshake, and the impatient tapping of the fingers are well-known actions or nonverbal media that communicate meaning (semantics). Nonverbal communication is all behavior of communicative value except speech done in the presence of another. Even silence and rigid inactivity may tell the other person that the communicator is angry, annoyed, depressed, or fearful. Although this definition of nonverbal communication suggests a rather all-inclusive domain, a gray area still exists between verbal and nonverbal communication. This area, called "paralanguage," is vocal but not strictly oral. Paralanguage includes stress, inflection, and speed of speech, as well as non-word vocalizations such as grunts, laughter, sighs, and coughs.[24]

People also surround themselves with various symbols that can communicate information to others.[25] An arrangement of the administrator's office with a center for informal conversations, a display of personal memorabilia and decorations, and a relatively close distance between the chairs and desk, for instance, represents a nonverbal symbolic mode of communication that transmits powerful messages to visitors.

Problems of semantics arise for the educational administrator who sends contrasting messages in verbal and nonverbal media. The verbal and nonverbal messages must be congruent for effective understanding. An illustration of this generalization usually occurs when a new administrator meets with the staff. A typical verbal statement is, "If you have any questions or problems, please come by my office, and we'll discuss the situation. My door is always open." When a staff member interprets the words literally and does visit the principal, the nonverbal messages probably will determine the meaning of the verbal message. If the person is met at the door, ushered to a chair, and a productive conference results, the verbal message is reinforced, and the meaning is understood. If, however, the administrator remains in the chair behind the desk, leaves the staff member standing or seats him or her across the room, and continues to write, the verbal message is contradicted. A semantics problem results; the meanings of the messages conflict.

Receiver

Internal processes similar to those in the source also occur in the receiver. The physical stimulus is taken from the channel by the receiver's sensory organs, ordinarily the eyes and ears, and is sent to the mental decoder, where the receiver gives meaning to the message. If the listener is effective and cooperative, he or she attempts to interpret the message as intended by the sender. However, "meanings" can never be literally transferred from one individual to another.[26] All that passes between the message sender and message receiver is a pattern of physical stimuli. If the light and sound waves form a recognizable symbol, the receiver can then translate the symbol and mentally create some kind of meaning.

As is the case with the sender, no receiver can totally ignore the psychological characteristics or mental sets. The receiver also has communication ability, knowledge of the subject, interests, values, and motivational needs that combine to limit qualitatively what is decoded. Consequently, the meaning the receiver applies is not exactly what the sender intended. Meanings may, of course, be relatively comparable, but they are never identical.

The receiver's psychological characteristics also constitute a mental set that limits the range of response alternatives. Based on experience, the receiver selects how to act or respond to the message. The actions serve as feedback to the sender.

Feedback

As illustrated in Figure 11.1, the action of the receiver of the message is designated feedback. In the broadest sense, this concept refers to any response from someone who has received a message. Similar to feedback in social systems (see Chapter 4) and process models of motivation (see Chapter 7), this process provides two benefits. First, feedback supplies a clue to how successful the communication process was, and second, the knowledge of results forms a basis for correcting or modifying future or additional communications.[27] The response may be either conscious or unconscious. For example, a student who falls asleep during a class lecture provides as much feedback to the teacher as the student who responds to examination questions.

The feedback loop provides two-way communication. Two-way communication is a reciprocal process; each participant initiates and receives messages. Each is a source or receiver only temporarily, with the roles shifting as messages are passed. Unlike one-way communication, two-way communication requires channels that form a continuous loop in two-way exchanges, or mutual feedback. This means that each participant initiates messages and that each message affects the next one.

The use of feedback improves the communication process by reducing the chance of major disparities between the information or idea received and the one intended. Teachers use examinations for feedback. Administrators can use paraphrasing, perception checking, and surveys to ensure that the messages received are the ones originally sent. The literature verifies the generalization that feedback processes do increase the accuracy of communication.[28] Moreover, recent research suggests that the feedback process can influence the level of effort expended and the types of strategies used in task performance.[29] Therefore, communication has a direct impact on the performance of the school. Feedback will be discussed in greater detail later in this chapter.

Noise

In Figure 11.1 each phase of the communication process is clouded by situational noise. Noise is any distraction that interferes with sending or receiving the message. The electronic analogy is static on the radio. A physical analogy is trying to talk, at some distance, when the wind is so high that the sound waves are dissipated.

Successful message transmission presumes that whatever situational noise exists is not great enough to obscure the signal or divert the receiver's attention from it. The noise that we commonly associate with poor transmission is physical: the temperature of the room is uncomfortable; a noisy fan is running; the room is too large and the sound does not carry to the back; or the waiters are clearing the tables just as the after-dinner speaker begins to talk.

Personal traits also cause noise in the channel. Prejudices of the sender and receiver toward sexual, racial, social class, and ethnic groups constitute noise in the communication process and distorts the message.

Situational noise resulting from social factors interacting with the personal factors also produces more troublesome problems for school communication than physical interference. For example, closed organizational climates, punishment-centered bureaucratic structures, and authoritarian leaders create distracting noise in the communication processes of a school. In such cases, group membership becomes important. Militant teachers cannot hear arbitrary administrators.

In sum, the sociopsychological model of two-way communication (see Figure 11.1) posits that the meaning of a message depends on both the content itself and the organizational context. Charles A. O'Reilly and Louis R. Pondy succinctly state the relationship with the following formula: Meaning = Information + Context.[30] The essence of the formula and approach can be understood by considering a series of questions:

1. Who is speaking to whom and what roles do they occupy? Administrator and teacher? Teacher and student? Administrator and parent?
2. Is the language or set of symbols able to convey the information and be understood by both the sender and receiver?
3. What is the channel or medium being used?
4. What is the content of the communication? Positive or negative? Relevant or irrelevant?
5. What is the context in which the communication is taking place? What factors are creating noise that blocks or distorts the message?

Research Methods and Findings Based on Sociopsychological Communication Theory

In terms of the sociopsychological model, nonverbal meanings and perceptions of the communication process have significant research foundations. Both areas seem to be fruitful areas for future exploration.

Nonverbal meaning. Nonverbal communication research is concerned with the meanings of paralanguage, body motion, and spatial cues. Two nonverbal modes of communication probably are of greatest interest to researchers in educational administration: the use of the face (particularly when the cues are not congruent with verbal cues), and the way people at work use space to convey meaning. The typical measurement system in this type of qualitative research consists of a set of observation categories that define the items of interest.[31]

One of the few research studies of nonverbal meaning in educational administration was completed by James M. Lipham and Donald C. Francke.[32] They developed a three-category typology of nonverbal behavior and used it to study promotable and nonpromotable principals. Their first category, structuring of self, includes self-maintenance, clothing, physical movement, and posture. The second category, structuring of interaction, includes greeting others, placement of others, interaction distance, and interaction termination. The third category, structuring of environment, includes environment decor, spatial arrangements, neatness, environmental noise, and the use of status symbols.

Significant differences were found between promotable and nonpromotable principals in their structuring of both interaction and the environment. For example, promotables tended to walk from behind their desks to greet visitors and take care of their coats and hats. Moreover, the promotable principals tended to seat visitors either alongside the desk or at the administrator's side of the desk at a distance of three to four feet. The nonpromotables, on the other hand, tended to position visitors in front and at the center of their desks at distances ranging from five to twelve feet. In structuring the environment, only the evidence of personal items distinguished between the groups. The offices of promotable principals, as compared to nonpromotables, contained numerous personal items—photographs, paintings, citations, and assorted knickknacks. In addition, environmental noise and interruptions tended to be higher in the offices of the nonpromotables. Lipham and Francke noted that in some schools as many as a dozen students were sent to the office for misbehavior or errands. Finally, promotable principals differed from nonpromotables in the use of nameplates as status symbols. Although nameplates usually were in evidence in all offices, promotables used them in functional ways (e.g., as paperweights) rather than as status symbols.

Perceptions of the communication process.   Unlike many other areas of organizational research, the attitude questionnaire has not been the primary technique for data collection in studies of communication.[33] One group of attitudes that has emerged as an important topic of research, however, is satisfaction with the communication process. Communication satisfaction is the personal satisfaction that results from successfully communicating with someone.[34] According to Cal W. Downs and Michael D. Hazen, an employee's perception of the organization's communication system is comprised of several dimensions.[35] They proposed the following indicators of communication satisfaction: explanation of policies; advance notice of changes; freedom to make suggestions; recognition and expression of appreciation for good performance; and adequacy of information on matters regarded as relevant by the employee. Using these indicators, Downs and Hazen developed the communication satisfaction survey (CSS) to measure employee perceptions of an organization's communication system. The questionnaire essentially asks a person, "How satisfied are you with the amount and quality of information in your organization?"

Jean Hagewood Nicholson adapted the CSS for use in schools.[36] She examined the perceptions of secondary teachers in an urban school system. Overall, Nicholson found that the educators were satisfied with the quantity and quality of communication in the district and that satisfaction with communication is positively related to overall job satisfaction. However, the teachers were least satisfied with the personal feedback that they were receiving and the general climate for communication. Similar relationships also apparently exist in university settings. Using the CSS, Hedy H. Gordon found that university administrators were least satisfied with personal feedback, media quality, and communication climate.[37]

From the perspective of social-psychological theory, the communication satisfaction findings suggest that the lack of two-way communication and the existence of situational noise constitute the most serious problems for understanding what is communicated in educational organizations. Indeed, interpersonal communication always has an enormous advantage over organizational communication in achieving accuracy, because in a face-to-face situation individuals can easily ask each other whether the message is clear and the meaning accurate. The feedback mechanisms in organizations are not as efficient and effective as those in the more informal personal communication context.[38]

FORMAL-INFORMAL ORGANIZATIONAL THEORY OF COMMUNICATION

Formal Organization and Communication

In the traditional bureaucratic model (see Chapter 5), *formal communication channels* traverse the organization through the hierarchy of authority. Barnard calls these channels "the communication system."[39] According to Barnard, several factors must be considered when developing and using the formal communication system: (1) the channels of communication must be known; (2) the channels link every member of the organization; (3) the line of communication must be as direct and as short as possible; (4) the complete line of communication typically is used; and (5) every communication is authenticated as being from the correct person occupying the position and within his or her authority to issue the message. Accuracy is supposed to be insured by the emphasis placed on formal, written communication. The implicit assumption of this model is that by adhering strictly to the assigned duties, and because the superiors have been selected on the basis of competence, the context is the same for all organizational members.[40]

Figure 11.2 illustrates a school district's formal communication system using Barnard's descriptive statements. Note that the chart delineates the communication channels and that every member reports to someone. The directors report to the assistant superintendent for instruction, who, with the assistant superintendent for finance, reports to the superintendent. The line of commu-

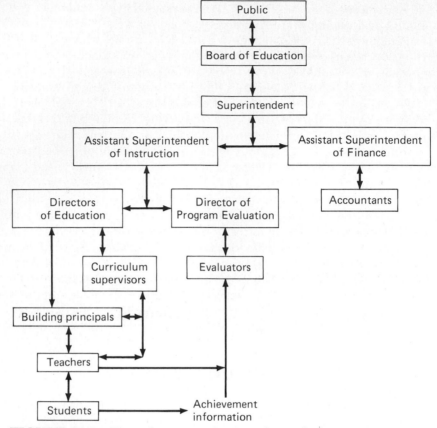

**FIGURE 11.2   Formal communication channels for program
implementation in a school district**

nication from the superintendent to the teachers goes through five hierarchical
levels. This is reasonably short and direct for a large school district. Adding
specific names and the bureaucratic rules and regulations that define the jobs
places this system in compliance with Barnard's suggestions.

Purposes of formal communication.   Barnard viewed the objective of communication as being one of coordinating the organization's parts.[41] Similarly, James
G. March and Herbert A. Simon postulate that the capacity of an organization,
such as a school, to maintain a complex, highly interdependent pattern of
activity is limited by its ability to handle the communication required for
coordination.[42] The greater the efficiency of communication within a school,
the greater the ability to coordinate interdependent activities such as the scope
and sequence of curriculum content and instructional procedures.

Lee G. Bolman and Terrence E. Deal postulated four purposes for organizational communication: transmitting facts and information; exchanging information, needs, and feelings; influencing or manipulating others; and telling stories

about the organization.[43] Similarly, Lee O. Thayer proposed that organizational communication has four primary functions: informing someone; instructing or directing someone; evaluating someone or something; and influencing another's thought or behavior.[44] The administrator, for instance, initiates messages to accomplish one or more of these functions in the school. Given the essential purposes, school organizations require formal communication to survive, and to map patterns that typically follow the hierarchy of authority (see Figure 11.2). The organizational structure facilitates or inhibits the flow of information in the school.

Effects of school structure on communication.   Three characteristics of school bureaucracies seem particularly critical to the formal system of communication. They are the degree of centralization in the hierarchy, the organization's shape, and the level of information technology.

The degree of *centralization* is critical to the effectiveness of communication systems.[45] In centralized schools, a few positions in the structure have most of the information-obtaining ability. For example, the superintendent and two assistant superintendents pictured in Figure 11.2 would gather most of the information for the formal system of communication. If the district is decentralized, however, the information-obtaining potential is more or less spread evenly among all of the positions. Research examining the different information-obtaining abilities supports the finding that centralized structures are more efficient communicators when the problems and tasks are relatively simple and straightforward. When the problems and tasks become more complex, however, decentralized hierarchies appear to be more efficient.

The number of hierarchical levels or tallness versus flatness of the school organization—its *shape*—also affects the communication processes. For example, a school district with five levels, such as the one depicted in Figure 11.2, differs in its ability to communicate across levels and from top to bottom from systems with more or fewer levels. While noting that no explicit research has been conducted that relates shape and communication effects, Porter and Roberts propose the following hypothesis.[46] Tall organizations maximize communication difficulties across more than two levels and minimize difficulties between two levels of the organization because in tall organizations a relatively small number of subordinates report to a given superior and a relatively high homogeneity exists between any two levels.

Finally, *technology* also appears to have a significant effect on organizational communication, though that effect remains somewhat speculative. As we noted in Chapter 5, writers subscribing to the position that schools are loosely coupled maintain that educational organizations have a relatively low level of technology. However, Peter F. Drucker postulates that the 1980s will be a period when communication systems will become more technologically sophisticated.[47] We are living in a creative and dynamic era that is producing fundamental changes, as is apparent in such advances as computer networks, communication satellites, and data handling devices. Until recently, electronic information exchange has largely been adapted to convey voice, vision, and graphics as distinct and separate types of communication. During the next few years, simultaneous and instantaneous transmission of voice, vision, and graphics to many locations will be possible. The potential influence of such technology on all aspects of communication in schools, e.g., administrative and instructional, is tremendous. Since we lack theoretical models that explain traditional communication effects, the new technology may well create both new problems and new opportunities for educational administrators. Clearly, information processing represents an area in which theory development and research efforts could yield highly significant results for better understanding educational organizations and their administration.

Effects of the external environment on communication. In Chapter 4, the effects of uncertainty and complexity on school structures and processes were considered. O'Reilly and Pondy believe that the effects can be explained using a communication perspective.[48] As uncertainty and complexity increase, two factors emerge that require heightened information processing by individuals, groups, and the organization itself. First, in situations of high uncertainty, strategies must be developed to obtain some degree of predictability. Hence, additional information processing is necessary. Second, in conditions of high complexity, elevated levels of communication are received and must be processed. From this perspective, organizations such as schools must accurately monitor critical factors in their external environments, process information to make decisions, and coordinate and control subunits and members. The ability to receive, process, and communicate information in a timely and accurate fashion, therefore, becomes crucial to organizational performance of schools.

Informal Organization and Communication

Messages that pass through the organizational structure of schools, but are not shown on the hierarchical chart, are called informal communications.[49] Informal channels, commonly called "grapevines," exist in all organizations regardless of how elaborate the formal communication system happens to be. One fact that has been observed repeatedly by researchers and by participants in organizations is that people who are in groups, cliques, or gangs tend to reach an understanding on things or issues very quickly. They communicate easily and well among themselves. This need for communication and understanding may be one of the basic reasons for the existence of small groups.[50]

Facts, opinion, attitudes, suspicions, gossip, rumors, and even directives flow freely through the grapevine. Built around social relationships among the school members, informal channels develop for such simple reasons as common office areas, similar duties, shared coffee breaks and carpools, and friendships. Social relationships and communication channels arise at all organizational levels of the school. Returning to Figure 11.2, informal communication patterns exist at the central office. One central office group might include some of the directors, an assistant superintendent, some supervisors, an evaluator, and an

accountant. Certainly, informal communication channels thrive among building principals and within teacher groups and the student body.

Complementary Networks: Formal and Informal Communication

As we have noted, formal and informal communication channels exist in all
educational organizations. Both the substance and direction of communication
can make the two systems complementary.

Substance.   In terms of content, communication can be thought of as instrumental or expressive.[51] Instrumental communication distributes information
and knowledge that affect cognitive orientations. Administrative directives,
policies, curricular objectives and materials, and attendance data are typical
examples. The purpose of instrumental communication is to develop consensus
about methods and procedures. Expressive communication, on the other hand,
attempts to change or reinforce attitudes, norms, and values. Appropriate affective orientations toward students, militancy, discipline, and organizational rewards are typical examples of the substance of expressive communication.

Formal communication channels carry both instrumental and expressive
content. The informal network can enhance both. For example, the grapevine
serves as a barometer of opinion and sentiment. School administrators can often
tap the informal flow for information about morale of students, teachers, and
other administrators. They also can float trial balloons to test the receptivity of
a new procedure or program. For instance, an administrator may want to
introduce a new in-service program for teacher preparation. Before making a
final decision, the hypothetical possibilities are discussed informally with some
staff members. As the information flows through the grapevine, the sentiment
can be monitored. Depending on the reaction, the administrator uses the formal communication system to announce the plans for the new program, allows
the program to remain hypothetical, or formally quashes the rumor. Barnard
has suggested that this type of test communication flows without interruption
in the informal channels, but would be either inconvenient or raise issues
calling for premature decisions in the formal channels.[52] In addition to serving
as a testing ground, the informal network can be a positive vehicle for achieving
satisfaction and personal expression by meeting the need to communicate or
socially interact. Informal channels reward school members with little financial
cost to the district; they therefore provide gratification of the social needs of
many organizational members.

Direction.   The direction of information flow also demonstrates the possible
complementary nature of formal and informal communication networks. Information flows vertically and horizontally in both networks.

Vertical flow refers to the upward and downward direction of communication through the different levels of the school's hierarchy. Information is passed
down or up the line of authority through memos, directions, policies, and
programs of action. In formal downward communication, information passes

through the chain-of-command, that is, through the superordinate-subordinate status structure. Robert Katz and Daniel L. Kahn identified five types of communications from superior to subordinate: (1) instructions about specific tasks, (2) a rationale about why the task needs to be done and how it relates to other tasks, (3) information about organizational procedures and practices, (4) feedback about the individual's performance level, and (5) information about the need for individual commitment to the organization's goals.[53] Downward vertical communication is relatively easy to send, but subordinates often may misunderstand the message.

Upward communication is a means by which subordinates are made accountable to superiors. Such communication is often viewed as an instrument of administrative control; subordinates have a tendency to emphasize positive information, withhold negative data, and communicate what they think the "boss wants to hear." Both the accuracy and frequency of upward communication are impacted by the combined characteristics of subordinates, superordinates, the messages themselves, and the organization.[54] The informal channel can assist administrators to assess the accuracy of formal upward communication.

Most communication activity among administrators in formal settings is vertical.[55] Accuracy is important in such communications. In general, research indicates that the more tangible and the more objective the information, the more likely that subordinates will communicate accurately with their superiors. The frequency of communication between them also affects the accuracy of the exchange.

Horizontal flow indicates that communication flows not only upward and downward but horizontally among organizational members at the same hierarchical level of the school. A principal, for instance, may provide information to another principal, who, in turn, passes it to still other principals. Such communication is the strongest and most easily understood.[56] Horizontal communication can be either formal or informal. In Figure 11.2, the lateral communication link between the two assistant superintendents would be formal, but the exchanges among the teachers would be informal.

The major purpose of horizontal communication is coordinating educational activities on the same level. For example, principals communicate so that their activities or curriculum emphases will be similar in different schools. But coordination through the transfer of written information often fails.[57] Consequently, written messages frequently are supplemented by conferences of peers in hopes that a more personal informal interchange of ideas will facilitate efforts at coordination.

The direction of communication affects the ease, the content, and the accuracy of organizational communication, and informal communication can either complement or undermine the formal flow. Given the present state of knowledge with respect to communication, the prospects for extensive technological change during the 1980s, the time seems ripe to pursue a program of vigorous research on formal and informal communication networks.

Research Testing Models of Formal and Informal Communication

The paucity of empirical data regarding communication in educational organizations may be related to the characteristics of the empirical methods currently used to conduct communication research. Content analysis (which deals with what is communicated), sociometry (which reveals to whom it is communicated), and interaction analysis (which focuses on the frequency with which it is communicated) are time-consuming and difficult to use; however, the methods have become less arduous with computers and portable audiotaping and videotaping equipment.

In addition to these research methods, other means for investigating organizational communication include participant observation, continuous observation, communication sampling, general communication surveys, and network surveys (a class of techniques that includes sociometry).[58] The last two procedures have been used in educational organizations. Specifically, general surveys have been used to describe communication frequency, openness, and accuracy as well.

General communication surveys. Three questionnaires designed to assess communication accuracy, openness, and frequency comprise Table 11.1. The first two instruments—testing information accuracy and communication openness—were constructed by Charles A. O'Reilly III and Karlene H. Roberts.[59] Although the instruments were developed in military and medical settings, the content and wording of the items make them suitable for use in educational organizations. The last instrument, measure of communication frequency, was developed by John Meyer and Elizabeth Cohen[60] and W. W. Charters, Jr.[61] The first five items test task-relevant topics, and the last two involve task-irrelevant subjects. All three instruments exhibit excellent measurement characteristics.

Using the accuracy and openness surveys, O'Reilly and Roberts found support for the postulate that the task structures of work groups act to improve or detract from the accuracy and openness of the transmitted communication.[62] High levels of group cohesion and two-way communication among employees produce greater accuracy. Groups with specialized skills and high status were more open in information exchanges than other groups. Similarly, Edwin M. Bridges and Maureen T. Hallinan found a positive correlation between the frequency of communication among teachers and faculty group cohesion and the level of work interdependence of the teachers.[63] Further, accuracy and openness had a positive impact on performance. However, the frequency of communication among educators may not be high. In a study conducted by Cecil Miskel, David McDonald, and Susan Bloom, teachers reported that they communicated with other teachers several times a week, with the principal about once a month, and with a learning disabilities specialist about once a month.[64]

Network surveys. Network surveys provide information about informal communication patterns. With the advent of large capacity computers, scholars

TABLE 11.1 Survey Measures to Describe the Accuracy, Openness, and Frequency of Organizational Communication

Response Format and Items for the Information Accuracy Measure
Response Format: Seven-point extent of agreement or disagreement scale
1. The information I receive is often inaccurate.
2. I can think of a number of times when I received inaccurate information from others in this group.
3. It is often necessary for me to go back and check the accuracy of information I have received.
4. I sometimes feel that others do not understand the information they have received.
5. The accuracy of information passed among members of the group could be improved.

Response Format and Items for the Communication Openness Measure
Response Format: Seven-point extent of agreement or disagreement scale
1. It is easy to talk openly to all members of this group.
2. Communication in this group is very open.
3. I find it enjoyable to talk to other members of this group.
4. When people talk to each other in this group, there is a great deal of understanding.
5. It is easy to ask advice from any member of this group.

Response Format and Items for the Frequency of Communication Measure
Response Format: How often do you talk with teachers (the principal, the superintendent) about the following topics? (Five-point scale from daily to never)
1. General curriculum plans for a class
2. Student reactions to a specific lesson
3. The schedule of teaching activities
4. Getting teaching resources or supplies
5. Learning the needs of a particular student
6. Personal gripes or concerns about work
7. Matters unrelated to school and teaching

have increasingly used sociometric surveys to describe communication structures.

Sociometry represents one means of assessing the attractions, or attractions and repulsions, of members of a group to one another.[65] Sociometric data are usually collected using a brief questionnaire or short interview. Respondents such as teachers and administrators are asked to indicate the frequency and importance of interactions with other staff members in the school with whom they discuss educational and social subjects. Two-way communication exists between individuals when the sender and receiver choose each other. Individuals who are not chosen by other respondents are designated "isolates." The informal channels and groups can be mapped by methods ranging from simple sociograms to highly sophisticated computer analyses.[66]

The results from research using a sociometric technique across a variety of settings indicate that communication patterns in organizations are extraordinarily complex. A large majority of all participants interact consistently with many other individuals and in far greater numbers than is suggested by formal organization charts. Generally, communication groups form along task-focused lines rather than around formal authority. Moreover, if the authority network is taken as the formal organization and the social network represents the informal one, the amount of overlap between the two is not great. While the task network is larger and better developed than the social network, both are closely related to each other and critical to the organization.[67] Based on findings from the medical setting, the location of educators in the network will influence the adoption and use of new technology.[68] Peer influence is important in communicating information about the availability and validity of new practices and procedures.

In research designed to study communication isolates, Patrick B. Forsyth and Wayne K. Hoy employed a sociometric procedure in five educational organizations.[69] They examined isolation from friends, from perceived actual control, from respected co-workers, and from formal organizational control. The results, without exception, indicate that being isolated in one instance carries over to other instances.[70] In other words, communication isolates in educational organizations tend to be separated from perceived control, respected co-workers, the school's control structure, and sometimes friends. The potentially destructive aspect of this isolation for schools is that it can lead to alienation and perhaps to detrimental behaviors. To counteract this negative effect, administrators must devise extremely powerful alternative communication processes because the isolates are not reachable by existing formal and informal channels of communication.

Bruce G. Barnett examined teacher influence and network structure in three high schools.[71] He found that administrators are likely to be dependent on teachers who have access to certain resources, especially information. In exchange for these resources, teachers can influence administrator behavior. Some teachers gain influence and power because they have information about how to get things accomplished or who can resolve specific problems. Similarly, department chairs, committee members, and teachers with specialized skills also possess important information. As a result of their knowledge and positions in the communication network, they can exert considerable power in the decision-making processes of school organizations.

Joseph W. Licata and Walter G. Hack used a sociometric interview procedure to describe the informal communication structure of the grapevine linking principals in a medium-sized suburban school district.[72] The researchers found that secondary-level school principals formed informal groups which are characterized as being somewhat "guildlike." That is, the communication patterns were based on common professional interests and the need for mutual aid and protection. In contrast, the elementary-level principals seemed to cluster into two "clanlike" groups. One clan of the elementary principals communicated informally with others who either (1) had earlier worked with or for the same school, (2) had shared a common ancestor or mentor, or (3) had close social ties as friends, neighbors, or relatives. In sum, the principals at the secondary-level structured the grapevine around professional survival and development while the principals at the elementary level tended to communicate informally with those who had traceable lineages and distinct familial ties.

An excellent study executed by Charters combined the sociometric and frequency surveys of communication.[73] In a high school and five elementary schools, a sociometric procedure was used to chart the communication networks. Charters asked the subjects for the names of other staff members with whom they talked regularly. In addition, the teachers indicated the frequency of their contacts (several times daily, daily, weekly) and their nature (work, friendship, or mixed).

Charters found a gross difference between the high school and the elementary schools in the amount of communication. Elementary schools exhibited a much larger volume, with most teachers in direct contact with one another. In contrast, only 15 percent of the high school staff pairs interacted regularly.

This difference in communication volume is partially explained by staff size. The average number of contacts per staff member declined with increasing faculty size. Larger facilities and physical dispersion along with specialized personnel (guidance counselors or special teachers) who are not in the main flow of classroom instruction, help explain the impact of size on communication volume. Charters did note, however, that size alone does not account for the entire difference. Elementary school staffs communicate more than high school staffs.

Finally, Charters found that stability in the communication patterns is related to the division of labor and physical proximity. Teachers in the same subject specialty and, to a lesser extent, those closer together form enduring communication networks. Thus, three factors—level and size of school, specialization, and proximity—affect the horizontal communication patterns in schools.

A variation of sociometry, the episodic communication channels in organization (ECCO) survey, was designed in the early 1950s by Keith Davis.[74] The survey consists of a simple one-page or two-page questionnaire that asks the respondent to indicate (1) how much, if any, of a particular message was received; (2) when it was received; (3) the location at which it was received; (4) from whom it was received; (5) through what channels and what media it was received; and (6) in some cases, what was done with it. The ECCO survey requires the serial administration of two or more questionnaires, each of which traces a different message through the same organization. This approach allows a researcher to describe, compare, and contrast longitudinally both informal and formal communication.

The ECCO survey method has been used in business and industry,[75] government,[76] and higher education.[77] For present purposes one of the more relevant investigations was made in a university setting by Janet Snyder Sanders.[78] She studied message transmission among five administrative areas (executive office, academic affairs, business affairs, research and graduate studies, and student affairs) and across four levels of hierarchy (executive group level, vice-president level, dean and director level, and assistant dean and director level).

Three messages were traced through these areas and levels over a period of one month. In the administrative areas, the content of the message affected the pattern of information flow. Student affairs, however, received less information than any other administrative area, and more of the information it did receive was inaccurate. A similar trend was found by hierarchical level, the lower levels receiving less volume and the messages received becoming increasingly distorted as they moved downward. Person-to-person conversations and mass media (especially newspapers) were the most widely used media, higher-level administrators using the face-to-face method more frequently than others. Finally, for all levels and areas, the office was the usual place where the message was received. Contrary to expectations, the coffee break was not used frequently for message transmission.

Additional research studies using network methods have high potential for providing elaborate and insightful descriptions of organizational communication patterns and how schools accommodate to different messages. For example, during contract negotiations, a study of information flow (networks) and sources of distortion could add to our theoretical and practical understandings of both the negotiation and communication processes.

CONCEPTUAL DERIVATIONS AND APPLICATIONS

Totally accurate personal and organizational communication in schools obviously is impossible. Planning the communication and using the knowledge from communication theory, however, can improve the efficiency and effectiveness of administrative communication. At a general level, suggestions can be drawn for enhancing personal and organizational communication.

To improve personal communication ability, guidelines can be drawn from the steps of the sociopsychological communication process described in Figure 11.1. Seven general guides are suggested:

1. determine the objective for placing the information into the communication flow;
2. identify the audience and their characteristics that might produce distortions in the message;
3. encode the message to fit the relationship between the sender and receiver to diminish the amount of distortion by the receiver;
4. determine the medium (media) and transmission channels; establish a mutual interest with the receiver;
5. release the message at the most opportune time to maximize its psychological impact;
6. consider the volume and do not overload the communication channels;
7. and measure the results with feedback (the single most important method for improving communication).[79]

Improving school communication requires a planned program of organizational development. Suggestions for this approach to improving school communications include the following:

1. assess the organizational design of the communication system against criteria suggested earlier in this chapter by Barnard;[80]
2. develop mechanisms to facilitate the communication process, e.g., close proximity of personnel, convenient sites for formal and informal interaction, mechanical linkers such as telephones and computers, and a committee system to accomplish tasks and make decisions;
3. establish information storage and retrieval systems;
4. select personnel with good communication skills;
5. and develop an in-service training program to improve communication skills for the existing staff.

At a more specific level, three sets of conceptual derivations and applications are useful in analyzing and improving communication in schools. These are the following: communication skills, feedback, and organizational roles.

Individual communication skills. Despite the many barriers to interpersonal communication, a number of methods can be used to minimize inaccuracies in the process.[81] Two sets of skills stand out: sending skills, i.e., the ability to make oneself understood; and listening skills, i.e., the ability to understand others.

As a key to effective communication, *sending skills* of educators need to be developed. Five methods can improve sending skills of individuals. First, appropriate and direct language should be used. Educational jargon and complex concepts should be avoided when simpler words will do. Second, clear and complete information should be provided to the listener. Third, noise from the physical and psychological environments should be minimized. During parent conferences, for example, steps need to be taken to eliminate telephone interruptions and to reduce stereotypes held by either the professional educator or parent. Fourth, multiple channels should be employed to stimulate a number of the receivers' senses (sight and sound). Fifth, face-to-face communication and redundancy should be used whenever possible.

As a second primary factor in effective communication, *active listening* is required for relatively accurate, two-way exchanges between the sender and receiver. Active listening requires both a willingness and ability to listen to a complete message, and to respond appropriately to the message's content and intent, i.e., feelings, values, and emotions. Accepting another individual's feelings and trying to understand his or her message in the context of those feelings can improve the accuracy of communication in school organizations. An important component of administrator behavior, therefore, is to create conditions that allow people to say what they really mean and to be heard.

Feedback. As a process in which one person tells another person how he or she feels about what has been said or done, feedback is a special case of two-way communication. A sustaining force for the interest in feedback is the long-accepted generalization that feedback has a positive effect on both individual motivation and performance.[82] Consequently, feedback is an important resource for the organization. Feedback also is a valuable resource for individuals throughout their tenure in schools. Educators often want to perform well and pursue many personal goals beyond what is expected by school organization. To the extent that performance and other personally held goals are important to the individual, feedback on their behavior directed at achieving these goals becomes a valuable informational resource. For example, feedback reduces uncertainty about roles and tasks, signals the relative importance of various goals, and creates conditions that allow displays of competence for individuals.

Unfortunately, feedback is not always useful. In this regard, Downs makes three important points.[83] First, feedback must be pursued vigorously because people do not always give it voluntarily. In many situations, administrators, teachers or students would rather risk doing the task incorrectly than ask for clarification. Second, feedback consists of nonverbal as well as verbal messages; people sometimes speak loudest with their feet (i.e., they walk away to avoid contact). Third, bogus feedback is rather common. Neutral or positive feedback is easier to give than negative assessments, even when holding negative reactions. Most of us are fairly adept at sending back messages that do not really represent our true reactions. Unfortunately, some people rationalize such behavior as tact, human relations, or survival.

Consequently, both personal skill and preparation or planning are essential to give and receive helpful feedback.[84] Too often educators assume that, because they have written or said something, the message has been received. This assumption causes innumerable communication breakdowns. Therefore, steps to insure adequate feedback are essential to maintaining an effective communication system.

John Anderson provides insightful observations about giving and receiving feedback.[85] He suggests four criteria as guides. The first, most general, and most significant criterion is to insure that the feedback is *intended* to be helpful to the recipient. In other words, the sender of the message must ask himself or herself beforehand, "Do I really believe that the information is likely to be helpful to the other person?" If the answer to the question is yes, the second step or criterion is the level understanding of the feedback. To enhance the likelihood of accurate communication, feedback should be specific rather than general and, other things being equal, recent examples of behavior are better than old ones. The third criterion is the level of acceptance of the feedback. While circumstances always exist that make the acceptance of critical feedback difficult, Anderson proposes that acceptance is particularly dependent on trust within the group, expression of wanting to help, use of descriptive rather than evaluative information, and appropriate timing of the meeting. The final criterion is level of ability of the recipient to use the feedback.

Several methods can be used to collect information for giving feedback, such as formal surveys, observations of nonverbal behavior, sensitivity to unsolicited data, and systematic conversations with other individuals. For example, the communication satisfaction survey is a practical tool for balancing two somewhat contradictory demands on a communication system: the needs to promote bureaucratic efficiency and to cultivate professional employee job satisfaction. The CSS can be used to monitor the satisfaction of employees with the communication system and make appropriate adjustments. The complexity of the process suggests that careful planning and use of the theory are essential for improving individual communication.

Organizational roles.   As observed in Chapter 4, organizations develop boundary-spanning roles to establish communication links with their environments. Similarly, O'Reilly and Pondy note the importance of the communication role or function that a person may serve within a network or organization.[86] One's place in the communication network can determine employee attitudes and behaviors. In this regard, three communication roles—gatekeepers, liaisons, and isolates—appear to be particularly important.

Gatekeepers are individuals who in the course of their jobs must pass or control the flow of information to others. Some jobs provide more opportunities for gatekeeping than others. For example, the administrative assistant to the superintendent decides what information will be brought to the superintendent's attention. As a result of controlling the channels of communication, gatekeepers many times gain considerable power. O'Reilly and Pondy observe that the potential power associated with gatekeepers creates an interesting paradox for managers. The level of specialization and size of most school districts ensure that no administrator is independent of other employees' expertise and that the volume of communication is too great to allow a complete and open flow of all available communication. Consequently, information is always edited as it passes through successive levels of the hierarchy. Upper-level administrators, therefore, rely on the accuracy of gatekeepers. To insure accuracy and timely information flows, and to reduce dependence on individual gatekeepers, schools support redundant and overlapping information systems.

Liaisons hold memberships in different groups and serve to link groups. Having contracts in different divisions, departments, or schools, liaisons disseminate information across group boundaries. In other words, liaisons perform the vital function of keeping groups informed about each other's activities. O'Reilly and Pondy believe that the interactions among liaisons and group members do not occur with great frequency or formality, but, when communication occurs regularly, the members usually know what the others are doing. As described in Chapter 5, these important linkages are weak ties or loose couplings. Liaisons many times are formally assigned by the organization to link different departments or committees and ensure accurate communication among them. In other situations, liaisons emerge informally and serve the same purpose as their formally appointed colleagues.

Isolates were defined earlier in this chapter as individuals who have very few or no communication contacts with other organizational members. Employee isolation is a concern because a lack of communication activity is typically accompanied by feelings of alienation, low job satisfaction, little commitment to the work organization, and low performance. Therefore, active participation in communication networks seems to produce positive outcomes, while isolation appears to be associated with disaffection.

SUMMARY

Communication is so pervasive in schools that it is a fundamental and integrative process in educational administration. Communication means to share messages, ideas, or attitudes that produce understanding between the sender and receiver. From the study of communication processes, four major conclusions seem clear. First, communication is purposive for both the initiator and the receiver. Second, communication is a sociopsychological phenomenon that is explained by information theory. According to this theory, individuals exchange ideas or facts with other persons when interacting in social situations; the meanings of those messages are determined by the people who interpret them. Third, messages traverse formal and informal channels, using a variety of verbal and nonverbal media. Fourth, to ensure a high level of understanding, feedback mechanisms are essential.

Although perfection is impossible, several techniques are available to measure and to improve the communication process at both the individual and the organizational levels. Further research in the area of communication should aid in understanding and improving the process. As Porter and Roberts have noted, "Communication represents such an under-theorized and under-researched area that it offers excellent opportunities for future contributions to the growing body of knowledge about behavior in organizations."[87]

NOTES

1. This generalization is supported by the findings from a number of studies using a structured observation technique. See, for example, Nancy J. Pitner and Rodney T. Ogawa, "Organizational Leadership: The Case of the Superintendent," *Educational Administration Quarterly*, 17 (1981), 45–65; William J. Martin and Donald J. Willower, "The Managerial Behavior of High School Principals," *Educational Administration Quarterly*, 17 (1981), 69–90; and John T. Kmetz and Donald J. Willower, "Elementary School Principals' Work Behavior," *Educational Administration Quarterly*, 18 (1982), 62–78.
2. Alfred Goud Smith, *Communication and Culture* (New York: Holt, Rinehart & Winston, 1966), p. 1.
3. Ithiel de Sola Pool and Wilbur Schramm, *Handbook of Communication* (Chicago: Rand McNally, 1973), p. v.
4. Chester I. Barnard, *The Functions of the Executive* (Cambridge, MA: Harvard University Press, 1938), pp. 89, 106.
5. Herbert A. Simon, *Administrative Behavior*, 2nd ed. (New York: Free Press, 1957), p. 154.

6. Lyman W. Porter and Karlene H. Roberts, "Communication in Organizations," in Marvin D. Dunnette (ed.), *Handbook of Industrial and Organizational Psychology* (Chicago: Rand McNally, 1976), pp. 1533–1559.

7. Jay Hall, "Communication Revisited," *California Management Review,* 15 (1973), 56–67.

8. Daniel Katz and Robert L. Kahn, *The Social Psychology of Organizations,* 2nd ed. (New York: Wiley, 1978), p. 429.

9. Frank E. X. Dance, "The 'Concept' of Communication," *Journal of Communication,* 20 (1970), 201–210.

10. Philip V. Lewis, *Organizational Communications: The Essence of Effective Management* (Columbus, OH: Grid, 1975), p. 5.

11. Porter and Roberts, *op. cit,* p. 1554.

12. Simon, *op. cit.,* p. 154.

13. Lewis, *op. cit.,* p. 6.

14. James L. Gibson, John M. Ivancevich, and James H. Donnelly, Jr., *Organization: Behavior, Structure, Processes,* rev. ed. (Dallas, TX: Business Publications, 1976), p. 318.

15. Similar models can be found in a variety of sources. See, for example, Keith Davis, *Human Relations at Work* (New York: McGraw-Hill, 1967), pp. 316–320; Kenneth E. Andersen, "Variant Views of the Communicative Act," in Howard H. Martin and Kenneth E. Andersen (eds.), *Speech Communication: Analysis and Readings* (Boston: Allyn & Bacon, 1968), pp. 2–23; M. L. DeFleur and O. N. Larson, *The Flow of Information* (New York: Harper, 1958), p. 8; and Wilbur Schramm, "How Communication Works," in Wilbur Schramm (ed.), *The Process and Effects of Mass Communication* (Urbana, IL: University of Illinois Press, 1955), pp. 3–26. An early formulation of using a similar perspective is the following: Claude E. Shannon and Warren Weaver, *The Mathematical Theory of Communication* (Urbana, IL: University of Illinois Press, 1949).

16. Willard R. Lane, Ronald G. Corwin, and William G. Monahan, *Foundations of Educational Administration* (New York: Macmillan, 1966), p. 72.

17. Gibson, Ivancevich, and Donnelly, *op. cit.,* p. 325.

18. David G. Bowers, *Systems of Organizations: Management of the Human Resources* (Ann Arbor, MI: University of Michigan Press, 1976), p. 40.

19. David K. Berlo, *The Process of Communication* (New York: Holt, Rinehart & Winston, 1970), pp. 30–32.

20. Richard L. Daft and Robert H. Lengel, "Information Richness: A New Approach to Managerial Behavior and Organizational Design," *Research in Organizational Behavior,* 6 (1984), 191–233. See pp. 195–198.

21. Porter and Roberts, *op. cit.,* p. 1563.

22. W. Charles Redding, *Communication Within the Organization* (West Lafayette, IN: Purdue Research Council, 1972), pp. 68–87.

23. Dale A. Level, Jr., "Communication Effectiveness: Method and Situation," *Journal of Business Communication,* 9 (1972), 19–25.

24. Suggested sources for further information on nonverbal communication include Shirley Wietz, *Nonverbal Communication* (New York: Oxford University Press, 1974); and M. L. Knapp, *Nonverbal Communication in Human Interaction* (New York: Holt, Rinehart & Winston, 1972).

25. James L. Bowditch and Anthony F. Buono, *A Primer on Organizational Behavior* (New York: Wiley, 1985), p. 85–86.

26. Redding, *op. cit.,* pp. 27–28.
27. *Ibid.*
28. Harold Guetzkow, "Communication in Organizations," in James G. March (ed.), *Handbook of Organizations* (Chicago: Rand McNally, 1965), pp. 534–573; and Lewis, *op. cit.,* pp. 95–96.
29. David A. Nadler, "The Effects of Feedback on Task Group Behavior: A Review of the Experimental Research," *Organizational Behavior and Human Performance,* 23 (1979), 309–338.
30. Charles A. O'Reilly and Louis R. Pondy, "Organizational Communication," in Steven Kerr (ed.), *Organizational Behavior* (Columbus, OH: Grid, 1979), 119–150. The formula appears on page 137.
31. This methodology usually takes the form of participant observation or ethnographic research and has been recently popularized. An excellent introduction to the approach is James P. Spradley, *Participant Observation* (New York: Holt, Rinehart & Winston, 1980).
32. James M. Lipham and Donald C. Francke, "Nonverbal Behavior of Administrators," *Educational Administration Quarterly,* 2 (1966), 101–109.
33. Porter and Roberts, *op. cit.,* p. 1582.
34. Lee O. Thayer, *Communication and Communication Systems* (Homewood, IL: Irwin, 1968).
35. Cal W. Downs and Michael D. Hazen, "A Factor Analytic Study of Communication Satisfaction," *Journal of Business Communication,* 14 (1977), 63–73.
36. Jean Hagewood Nicholson, "Analysis of Communication Satisfaction in an Urban School System" (Ph.D. diss., George Peabody College for Teachers of Vanderbilt University, 1980).
37. Hedy H. Gordon, "Communication Analysis of Administrators in an Academic Organization" (M. A. thesis, University of Kansas, 1979), pp. 59–62.
38. Katz and Kahn, *op. cit.,* p. 432.
39. Barnard, *op. cit.,* pp. 175–176.
40. O'Reilly and Pondy, *op. cit.,* pp. 123–124.
41. *Ibid.*
42. James G. March and Herbert A. Simon, *Organizations* (New York: Wiley, 1958), p. 162.
43. Lee G. Bolman and Terrence E. Deal, *Modern Approaches to Understanding and Managing Organizations* (San Francisco: Jossey-Bass, 1984), p. 247.
44. Lee O. Thayer, *Administrative Communication* (Homewood, IL: Irwin, 1961), pp. 133–205.
45. Porter and Roberts, *op. cit.,* pp. 1568–1571.
46. *Ibid.*
47. Peter F. Drucker, *Managing in Turbulent Times* (New York: Harper & Row, 1980), pp. 51–53.
48. O'Reilly and Pondy, *op. cit.,* pp. 125–127.
49. Lewis, *op. cit.,* p. 41.
50. Joseph A. Litterer (ed.), *Organizations: Structure and Behavior,* 2nd ed., Vol. 1 (New York: Wiley, 1969), p. 162.
51. Amitai Etzioni, *A Comparative Analysis of Complex Organizations* (New York: Free Press, 1961), pp. 137–141.
52. Barnard, *op. cit.,* p. 225.

53. Katz and Kahn, *op. cit.,* pp. 440–443.
54. An excellent discussion of upward communication is presented in the following source: Michael J. Glauser, "Upward Information Flow in Organizations: Review and Conceptual Analysis," *Human Relations,* 8 (1984), 613–643.
55. Porter and Roberts, *op. cit.,* pp. 1574–1576.
56. Lewis, *op. cit.,* p. 40.
57. William G. Scott, *Human Relations in Management* (Homewood, IL: Irwin, 1962), pp. 185–191.
58. Keith Davis, "Methods for Studying Informal Communication," *Journal of Communication,* 28 (1978), 112–116.
59. Charles A. O'Reilly III and Karlene H. Roberts, "Task Group Structure, Communication, and Effectiveness in Three Organizations," *Journal of Applied Psychology,* 62 (1977), 674–681.
60. John W. Meyer and Elizabeth Cohen, *The Impact of the Open-Space School upon Teacher Influence and Autonomy: The Effects of an Organizational Innovation,* Technical Report No. 21 (Palo Alto, CA: Stanford Center for Research and Development in Teaching, 1971, ERIC No. ed 062 291).
61. W. W. Charters, Jr., *Measuring the Implementation of Differentiated Staffing* (Eugene, OR: Center for the Advanced Study of Educational Administration, 1973).
62. O'Reilly and Roberts, *op. cit.*
63. Edwin M. Bridges and Maureen T. Hallinan, "Subunit Size, Work System Interdependence, and Employee Absenteeism," *Educational Administration Quarterly,* 14 (1978), 24–42.
64. Cecil Miskel, David McDonald, and Susan Bloom, "Structural and Expectancy Linkages within Schools and Organizational Effectiveness," *Educational Administration Quarterly,* 19 (1983), 49–82.
65. Gardner Lindzey and Donn Byrne, "Measurement of Social Choice and Interpersonal Attractiveness," in Gardner Lindzey and Elliot Aronson (eds.), *The Handbook of Social Psychology,* 2nd ed., Vol. 2 (Reading, MA: Addison-Wesley, 1968), pp. 452–525.
66. Noel Tichy and Charles Fombrun, "Network Analysis in Organizational Settings," *Human Relations,* 32 (1979), 923–965; James R. Lincoln, "Intra- (and Inter) Organizational Networks," *Research in the Sociology of Organizations,* 1 (1982), 1–38; and Ronald S. Burt, "Models of Network Structure," *Annual Review of Sociology,* 6 (1980), 79–141. A source to consult for specific methodological information is the following: Ronald S. Burt and Michael J. Minor (eds.), *Applied Network Analysis* (Beverly Hills, CA: Sage, 1984). A collection of articles based on the use of network procedures can be found in the following work: Peter V. Marsden and Nan Lin (eds.), *Social Structure and Network Analysis* (Beverly Hills, CA: Sage, 1982).
67. O'Reilly and Pondy, *op. cit.,* p. 131.
68. James G. Anderson and Stephen J. Jay, "The Diffusion of Medical Technology: Social Network Analysis and Policy Research," *Sociological Quarterly,* 26 (1985), 49–64.
69. Patrick B. Forsyth and Wayne K. Hoy, "Isolation and Alienation in Educational Organizations," *Educational Administration Quarterly,* 14 (1978), 80–96.
70. The results of a subsequent study of elementary schools were similar, ex-

cept that isolation from friends was not related to isolation from formal authority. See Arlene E. Zielinski and Wayne K. Hoy, "Isolation and Alienation in Elementary Schools," *Educational Administration Quarterly,* 19 (1983), 27–45.

71. Bruce G. Barnett, "Subordinate Teacher Power in School Organizations," *Sociology of Education,* 57 (1984), 43–55.

72. Joseph W. Licata and Walter G. Hack, "School Administrator Grapevine Structure," *Educational Administration Quarterly,* 16 (1980), 82–99.

73. W. W. Charters, Jr., "Stability and Change in the Communication Structure of School Facilities," *Educational Administration Quarterly,* 3 (1967), 15–38.

74. Keith Davis, "Methods of Studying Communication Patterns in Organizations," *Personnel Psychology,* 6 (1953), 301–312.

75. See two works by Keith Davis: "Management Communication and the Grapevine," *Harvard Business Review,* 31 (1953), 43–49; and "Success of Chain-of-Command Oral Communication in a Manufacturing Management Group," *Academy of Management Journal,* 11 (1968), 379–387.

76. See Harold Sutton and Lyman W. Porter, "A Study of the Grapevine in Governmental Organization," *Personnel Psychology,* 21 (1968), 223–230.

77. See Janet Snyder Sanders, "Utilization of Lines of Communication Within the Administration of the University of Kansas Described by ECCO Analysis" (Ph.D. diss, University of Kansas, 1976).

78. *Ibid.*

79. Leonard R. Sayles and George Strauss, *Human Behavior in Organizations* (Englewood Cliffs, NJ: Prentice-Hall, 1966), pp. 246–249.

80. Barnard, *op. cit.,* pp. 175–181.

81. The discussion in this section relies on the ideas found in Bowditch and Buono, *op. cit.,* pp. 88–90.

82. Susan J. Ashford and L. L. Cummins, "Feedback as an Individual Resource: Personal Strategies for Creating Information," *Organizational Behavior and Human Performance,* 32 (1983), 370–398.

83. Cal W. Downs, *Organizational Communicator* (New York: Harper & Row, 1977).

84. Edward H. Rockey, *Communicating in Organizations* (Lanham, MD: University Press of America, 1984), p. 107; and John Anderson, "Giving and Receiving Feedback," in Paul R. Lawrence, Louis B. Barnes, and Jay W. Lorsch (eds.), *Organizational Behavior and Administration* (Homewood, IL: Irwin, 1976), pp. 103–111.

85. *Ibid.*

86. O'Reilly and Pondy, *op. cit.,* pp. 132–134.

87. Porter and Roberts, *op. cit.,* p. 1585.

Chapter 12

Organizational Effectiveness

Effectiveness is one of the most pervasive yet least delineated organizational constructs relevant to all participants in organizational life.

PAUL S. GOODMAN AND JOHANNES M. PENNINGS
New Perspectives on Organizational Effectiveness

When professional educators, school district patrons, or legislative members gather, a frequent topic of conversation is school effectiveness. The people discussing this topic generally employ terms such as "accountability," "student achievement," "competency tests," "dropout rates," "teacher job satisfaction," and "faculty morale." The acute interest in organizational effectiveness is neither a new phenomenon nor unique to education. For the past one hundred years, writers representing both the private and public sectors have expressed concern about the effective and efficient operation of virtually all types of organizations.

The controversy surrounding organizational effectiveness of schools shows no signs of abating. In fact, the plethora of recent reports calling for educational reform suggests that the level of public and political interest and fascination will continue to grow. However, many of the arguments or discussions conclude with the generalization that effectiveness cannot be defined and measured. Our position is that organizational effectiveness represents such a central theme in the theory and practice of educational administration that the difficult questions regarding the concept cannot be avoided. The issue will not go away, nor should it.

Education is not devoid of effectiveness indicators. Educators and members of the public acknowledge that different schools achieve different levels of success, even with similar student populations. Based on real or imagined information, parents may decide, for example, to locate in a given attendance area because they know that Horace Mann Elementary maintains excellent academic standards while John Dewey Elementary lacks strong discipline procedures. Moreover, schools report results to the public that the officials believe represent their accomplishments. Patrons are invited to art shows, music performances, and athletic events because these activities illustrate school productivity. At the level of practice, effectiveness indicators are known and used.

At the level of theory, however, controversy about organizational effectiveness still becomes intense when specific questions are raised. Which criteria and how many define school effectiveness? Who determines the criteria? Is effectiveness a short-term or long-term phenomenon? For years arguments over the correct replies have raged, but few answers have emerged. We will now look at recent theoretical approaches to organizational effectiveness that offer some promise of integrating and focusing future efforts to supply these answers.

THEORETICAL APPROACHES TO ORGANIZATION EFFECTIVENESS

To ask a global question about whether a school is effective or ineffective is a virtually useless exercise. Effectiveness is not one thing; hence, a one-dimensional definition is not adequate. Rather, a school or any organization can be effective and ineffective depending on the criteria used, which may be independent of one another. Without a theoretical model as a guide, it is impossible to state that one school is more effective than another, or to say that a given indicator is a measure of effectiveness, or to plan ways to change the school. Two theoretical models in particular—the goal model and the system resource model—provide a basis for making these judgments and for taking the action necessary to work toward school effectiveness.[1]

Goal Model of Organizational Effectiveness

Definitions and goal types. Traditionally organizational effectiveness has been defined in terms of the degree of goal attainment. Amitai Etzioni's widely held definition is that "an organizational goal is a desired state of affairs which the organization attempts to realize."[2] An organization is effective if the observable outcomes of its activities meet or exceed organizational goals. Although they acknowledge several weaknesses in the *goal model,* a number of scholars maintain that goals and their relative accomplishment are essential in defining organizational effectiveness.[3] Goals provide direction and reduce uncertainty for organizational participants and a standard for assessment of the organization.

In a goal model of organizational effectiveness, a distinction must be made between official and operative goals.[4] Official goals are formal statements of purpose by the board of education concerning the nature of the school's mission. These statements usually appear in board of education publications and faculty and staff handbooks. Typically, official goals can be characterized as abstract and aspirational in nature (e.g., the students will achieve their full potential). They are usually timeless, and serve the purpose of securing support and legitimacy from the public rather than for guiding administrator and teacher behaviors.

In contrast, operative goals reflect the true intentions of a school organization. That is, operative goals mirror the actual tasks and activities performed in the organization, irrespective of what it claims to be doing. Hence, official goals in schools may be operative or inoperative depending on the extent to which they accurately represent actual educational practices. Some operative goals are widely published (e.g., recent efforts to place students with handicaps in regular classrooms), while others are not (e.g., efforts to provide custodial care of students for six to eight hours per day). In fact, attractive official goals in some districts act as expedient covers to less attractive operative goals such as racism and sexism.

Assumptions and generalizations.   Two assumptions underlie the goal model.[5] First, a rational group of decision makers in the organization have in mind a set of goals that they wish to pursue. Second, the goals are few enough in number to be administered and are defined concretely enough to be understood by the participants. If the assumptions are accepted, it follows that the decision makers should be able to assess organizational effectiveness and to develop measures to determine how well the goals are being achieved. Although decision makers obviously are not completely rational, the two assumptions and the generalization that flow from them should not be rejected without careful consideration. In fact, administrative practices have been developed to enhance goal specification and goal achievement. For example, management by objectives (see Chapter 7), cost-benefit analysis, and behavioral objectives for instruction are used to specify goals in schools. Administrators also use levels of centralization and formalization of the school's bureaucratic structure and guidelines for the scope and sequence of curriculum to plan for goal attainment. However, several shortcomings of the goal concept and the goal model should be noted.

Criticisms of the goal approach.   Among the criticisms of using goals to assess organization effectiveness are the following:

1. Too often the focus is on the administrator's goals rather than those set by teachers, students, and the school's patrons. Researchers tend to ask only the administrators about the content of school goals rather than other constituencies. They fail to account for the diverse expectations that are expressed by the operative goals of a school.
2. In many instances the researchers overlook the multiplicity of goals, and the contradictory nature of organizational goals is neglected.

The goal model tends to be logical and internally consistent, but in reality the school's goals often conflict. In Chapter 2, for instance, we observed that compliance theory postulates that order and culture goals frequently co-exist in schools.

3. Organizational goals are retrospective. They serve to justify school and educator action, not to direct it.
4. Organizational goals are dynamic, while the goal model is static. Goals change as contextual factors and behavior vary, but the model remains the same.
5. The official goals of the organization may not be its operative goals. Because the analysis of actual operations is complex and difficult, a researcher may be unable to identify accurately the operative goals, and therefore must rely on personal judgments about what ends are implied by the operational practices. As a result official goals may be given greater emphasis than the important operative goals.[6]

Given these strong criticisms, Ephraim Yuchtman and Stanley E. Seashore argue that the goal model of organizational effectiveness is inadequate.[7] Instead, they propose a system resource model.

System Resource Model of Organizational Effectiveness

Definition.   Similar to the resource dependence view of external environments discussed in Chapter 4, the *system resource model* defines effectiveness as the organization's ability to secure an advantageous bargaining position in its environment and to capitalize on that position to acquire scarce and valued resources. The concept of bargaining position implies the exclusion of specific goals as ultimate effectiveness criteria. Rather the system resource model directs attention toward the more general capacity of the organization to procure assets. Consequently, this definition of effectiveness focuses on the continuous, never-ending behavioral process of exchange of and competition over scarce and valued resources. Each time a state legislature meets to appropriate tax monies for schools, this process is visible. Educational organizations compete in an environment of state politics with transportation, social welfare, correctional, and other agencies and organizations to acquire the valued commodity of state aid. At a somewhat more subtle level, competition between public and private schools is increasing. As the number of school-age youngsters and as the prospects of educators for continued employment in the public schools decline, competition for students will intensify. According to the system resource model, effective schools will sustain growth or minimize decline by advantageous bargaining with parents and students or legislators. Hence, the criterion for effectiveness becomes the organization's ability to acquire resources.

Assumptions and generalizations.   The literature dealing with the system resource model contains several implicit assumptions.[8] First, the organization is assumed to be an open system that exploits its external environment. In other words, a social-systems model, such as the one presented earlier in Chapter 3, with organizational, individual, and group dimensions and feedback loops, forms the basis for evaluating organizational effectiveness. Second, before an organization attains any size at all, the demands it faces become so complex that defining a small number of meaningful organizational goals may be impossible.

A generalization emerging from the assumptions is that in more effective organizations bureaucratic expectations, informal groups, and individual needs work together better to produce an impact on the environment than they do in less effective organizations. All organizations emphasize the need for adequate resources and avoidance of undue strain. Educational administrators, for instance, place great importance on maintaining harmony because harmonious actions enhance organizational effectiveness.

The strong dependence on the environment forces the organization to concentrate on adaptive functions to compete successfully for resources. From the system resource perspective, effective organizations are those with sensitive monitoring mechanisms that provide information about new behavior that can lead to the acquisition of more assets. Currently, many colleges, universities, and school districts are assessing the demand for educational services by the nontraditional student. They are attempting to mine the rich resources of this underserved student population by offering a plethora of adult, easy access, and outreach programs. The final criterion the researcher must use to assess organizational effectiveness according to the system resource model is internal consistency. The model predicts that an effective organization will distribute resources judiciously over a wide variety of coping and monitoring mechanisms.

Criticisms of the system resource approach.   The system resource model of organizational effectiveness has several alleged defects, especially when applied to educational organizations.[9] For one thing, placing too much emphasis on inputs may have damaging effects on outcomes. When an educational organization becomes consumed by the acquisition of resources, other functions may be neglected. For example, in order to stem declining enrollments, many colleges and universities are engaging in intense and expensive competition for students, thus compromising program rigor and quality.

Critics also allege that since increasing inputs or acquiring resources is an operative goal for the organization, the system resource model is actually a goal model. Thus, the differences between the goal and the system resource approaches may represent an argument over semantics. As Richard H. Hall has observed, "The acquisition of resources does not just happen. It is based on what the organization is trying to achieve—its goal—but is accomplished through the operative goals."[10] In other words, the system resource model actually verifies the operative goal concept; in fact, Richard M. Steers has argued that the two approaches are complementary. Indeed, a possible, even highly desirable, approach is to conceptualize organizational effectiveness by combining the two perspectives.[11]

Integration and Expansion of the Goal and System Resource Models

Both the goal and system resource models share one crucial assumption, namely, "that it is possible, and desirable, to arrive at the single set of evaluative criteria, and thus at a single statement of organizational effectiveness."[12] In the goal model, effectiveness is defined in terms of the relative attainment of feasible objectives having to do with physical facilities and equipment, the human energy of students and employees, curricular technologies, and some commodity, such as money, that can be exchanged for other resources. The resource model, based on the open system concept, places great value on the harmonious operations of the organization's components, the ability to adapt, and the optimization of the leadership, decision making, and communication processes.

Several theorists have attempted to integrate the two approaches, and although their ideas differ slightly, they agree that the use of goals cannot be avoided.[13] Behavior is explicitly or implicitly goal directed, and organizational behavior is no exception. However, from a system resource framework, goals become more diverse and dynamic; they are not static, ultimate states, but are subject to change over time. Moreover, the attainment of some short-term goals can represent new resources to achieve subsequent goals. Thus, a cyclic nature characterizes goals in organizations when a systems framework is used.

In order to convey an understanding of the subtle nuances of organizational effectiveness, the integrated model must be expanded to include four additional characteristics—a time dimension, different organizational levels, multiple constituencies, and multiple criteria.

Time dimension. One factor producing divergence in the assessment of effectiveness criteria is time. Time is a neglected dimension of educational administration. Martin Burlingame speaks of the rhythm of seasons; that is, clear cycles characterize the school calendar—the year begins in fall, breaks for a holiday in the winter, and ends in the spring. Educators know that certain times of the school year hold greater potential for crises, disruption of the system, and reduced goal attainment.[14] The last few days of the school year, for example, provide conditions for chaos. Knowing this, educators develop coping mechanisms to handle these short-term performance problems. On the other hand, declining enrollments and consolidating small schools represent long-term problems of survival.

The influence of time on organizational effectiveness can be conceptualized with a continuum of success ranging from short-term, through intermediate, to long-term.[15] For schools, representative indicators of short-term effectiveness include student achievement, morale, job satisfaction, and loyalty. Criteria for intermediate success encompass adaptiveness and development of the school organization and instructional programs, career advancement of the educators, and success of the former students. From the system resource framework, the ultimate long-term criterion is survival of the organization.

Another influence of time is that the criteria for organizational effectiveness do not remain constant. As constituencies change their preferences, new constraints and expectations evolve to define school effectiveness. During the 1970s, for example, schools emphasized socio-emotional growth of students, but with the reform reports of the early 1980s, the public started to demand that cognitive growth be preeminent. As a consequence, performance that is effective today is likely to be ineffective tomorrow as preferences and constraints change.[16] Robert E. Quinn and Kim Cameron hypothesize that the specific criteria of effectiveness shift as organizations move through their life cycles. In the early entrepreneurial stage, flexibility and resource acquisition are prime criteria. As organizations mature, however, the primary criteria become communication, stability, productivity, efficiency, and goal setting.[17] The goal of the effective school is, continually, to *become* effective rather than *be* effective.[18] Hence, when discussing school effectiveness, the dimension of time is an essential component.

Different organizational levels.   Criteria for organizational effectiveness can be chosen for different levels: the individual educator or student, work group, school building, and school district. Because our present focus is on organizational effectiveness, the unit of analysis should be carefully defined in terms of the organization rather than the individual. For educational settings, appropriate levels at which to assess effectiveness include the school, the school district, or a school district division such as instruction, business and finance, or facilities operations.

Multiple constituencies.   Effectiveness criteria always reflect the values and biases of constituencies or stakeholders, that is, interested individuals and groups within or outside the school who have a stake in organizational effectiveness.[19] For schools or other organizations with multiple constituencies or interest groups, the effectiveness criteria typically are drawn from a number of perspectives. This means that multiple stakeholders play critical roles that define the goals and also provide information for their assessment.[20] For the educational setting, the debate regarding the definitions of a good school has been joined by scholars, parents, students, teachers, politicians, governmental officials, taxpayers, and employers.[21] To say the least, this list depicts a diverse set of interest groups.

As a further complicating factor, constituent groups prefer different criteria. For example, administrators and board of education members emphasize structural or bureaucratic measures of effectiveness such as facilities usage, budgetary procedures, or personnel practices, in part because these represent factors under their control.[22] In contrast, the teachers emphasize process indicators of effectiveness. They maintain that effectiveness must be measured in terms of the various instructional methods and processes. Students, taxpayers, and politicians, however, focus primarily on product or outcome measures. They evaluate schools in terms of academic achievement and the values of graduates.

Therefore, a combination of the goal and system resource models requires the inclusion of multiple constituencies that define and evaluate school effectiveness using a variety of criteria. This perspective has been termed a "relativistic multiple-contingency" approach to organizational effectiveness.[23] The relativistic approach assumes that no single statement about organizational effectiveness is possible or desirable. In other words, various stakeholders in and around the school organization require different kinds of effectiveness measures. No single effectiveness indicator, or a simple, general list, will suffice.[24]

Multiple criteria.   A basic assumption throughout this discussion has been that organizational effectiveness is a multidimensional concept. No single ultimate criterion such as student achievement or overall performance can capture the complex nature of organizational effectiveness. In the combined goal-system resource approach, effectiveness indicators must be derived for each phase of the open-system cycle—input, transformation, and output. Virtually every phase, process, or outcome variable can be and has been used as an indicator of effectiveness. The development of a multidimensional index or composite measure of organizational effectiveness requires the selection of key concepts. Choosing the most appropriate and representative effectiveness variables can be an overwhelming task, however. For instance, John P. Campbell used thirty categories to classify a comprehensive list of organizational effectiveness indicators.[25] Similarly, Steers found fifteen different criteria in a sample of only seventeen studies of effectiveness.[26]

To bring some order and direction to the study of organizational effectiveness, a theoretical model is needed to guide the choice of effectiveness indicators.[27] Raymond F. Zammuto believes that a useful approach is to remember that organizations are social inventions to satisfy human needs.[28] People participate in exchange relationships with organizations to receive valued outcomes. Continued participation or support of the organization is dependent on the continued creation of valued outcomes by the organization as perceived by the participants. In other words, schools gain licenses to exist by creating valued outcomes. In the context of valued outcomes, an excellent model to guide the selection of specific criteria is provided by Talcott Parsons.[29] He has postulated that a social system's survival depends on the exercise of four critical functions. These functions are fundamental to resource acquisition and can be considered organizational goals. As discussed earlier (see Chapters 3 and 5), all social systems must solve the four functional problems of adaptation, goal achievement, integration, and latency.

Adaptation is concerned with the system's need to control its environment. Schools accommodate themselves to the basic demands of the environment and their constituencies by attempting to transform the external situation by changing their internal programs to meet new conditions. Goal achievement is the gratification of system goals. The system defines its objectives and mobilizes its resources to achieve these desired ends. Typical indicators of goal attainment for educational organizations are academic achievement, resource acquisition, and quality of students and services. Integration refers to a social solidarity within the system, i.e., the process of organizing, coordinating, and unifying social relations into a single unity. Among the primary social concerns of the school are employee job satisfaction, interpersonal conflict, student absentee-ism, and morale. Finally, latency is the maintenance of the integrity of value system, (i.e., the system's motivational and cultural patterns). Effective schools require a high commitment and appropriate behavior on the part of educators and students to reinforce the organization's norms and values. Typical indica-tors that a school is effectively performing for the latency function include loyalty, a central life interest in school work, a sense of identity with the institu-tion, individual motivation to work, and role-norm congruence.

An integrated model. Specific criteria to measure each of these can be drawn from Campbell[30] and Steers.[31] The results of merging the general dimensions, specific criteria or indicators, and other perspectives of effectiveness are sum-marized in Table 12.1. Consequently, an integrated goal-system resource model of organizational effectiveness can be derived by having the four neces-sary functions of social systems act as operative goals. By adding specific indica-tors of achievement of the four goals and by considering the time frame, organi-zational level, and constituencies applicable to each indicator, we can complete the model.

The result is a more comprehensive theoretical formulation for guiding future research efforts. Researchers who use this model to study the organiza-tional effectiveness of schools would proceed in three steps. First, they would determine the constituencies that would define the important operative goals. The researchers themselves may do the defining or it may be some other school group. Second, they would specify a time dimension, focusing on short-term, medium-term, or long-term goals. Third, they would identify several criterion variables. To make a comprehensive evaluation of school effectiveness, they would have to include indicators from each of the four critical goals. For exam-ple, a comprehensive study of short-term and intermediate-term school effec-tiveness from the perspective of the students could use innovativeness of the curriculum, academic achievement, student satisfaction with instruction, and students' sense of identity with the school.

RESEARCH BASED ON SELECTED EFFECTIVENESS CRITERIA

Several of the concepts that have been suggested as indicators of organizational effectiveness have been given detailed attention in earlier chapters. Others such as productivity and efficiency, in the classic, private economic sense, seem less important to educational organizations. A few indicators, however, that are highly relevant to schools have been the subject of research but have not yet been discussed. Those concepts, which will be analyzed as indicators of effec-tiveness, include: adaptability (flexibility and innovation), achievement, job sat-isfaction, and central life interests. Note that they are indicators, respectively, of adaptation, goal achievement, integration, and latency.

TABLE 12.1   Dimension, Indicators and Added Perspectives of Organizational Effectiveness

Dimensions of Effectiveness—Critical Functions of Social Systems	Multiple Indicators for *EACH* Dimension of Effectiveness	Added Perspectives for *EACH* Indicator of Effectiveness
Adaptation	Adaptability-flexibility Innovation Growth Development Control over equipment	*Time:* Short-term Intermediate Long-term *Level:* Individual Classroom School District division District *Constituencies:* Students Teachers Administrators Public
Goal Attainment	Achievement Productivity Resource acquisition Efficiency Quality	*Time:* Short-term Intermediate Long-term *Level:* Individual Classroom School District division District *Constituencies:* Students Teachers Administrators Public
Integration	Satisfaction Employee turnover Student absenteeism Conflict-cohesion Climate Open communication	*Time:* Short-term Intermediate Long-term *Level:* Individual Classroom School District division District *Constituencies:* Students Teachers Administrators Public
Latency	Loyalty Central life interests Sense of identity Motivation Role and norm congruency	*Time:* Short-term Intermediate Long-term *Level:* Individual Classroom School District division District *Constituencies:* Students Teachers Administrators Public

Adaptability

Of all the criteria for organizational effectiveness, Steers found that adaptability and the closely related concepts of flexibility and innovation are used most frequently by researchers as effectiveness measures.[32] This set of criteria links the ability of organizations to modify their operating procedures with the internal and external forces that induce change. In schools, adaptability can be defined in terms of the abilities of the professional educators to sense forces of change and to initiate new policies and practices for the emergent demands.

Measurement. Contrary to Steer's findings, Campbell found that although many people write about this criterion, relatively few attempt to measure it.[33] When adaptiveness is measured, the questionnaire is the most common measurement instrument. However, questionnaires with adequate psychometric properties for assessing flexibility in educational organizations are limited. Moreover, many studies assess the readiness to adapt rather than the actual adaptive response. The reason is that although administrators and teachers can and do plan and implement policies to encourage a sense of readiness for innovation, when the time comes for an adaptive response, the school either adapts or it does not.

Research. Two investigations in educational settings represent fairly typical studies of adaptability. Eugene W. Ratsoy and his associates used a questionnaire procedure to study adaptability of schools to changes in a university-based teacher education program.[34] They found that the schools demonstrated a readiness to increase the length of the program, to add more student teachers, and to change the role of the cooperating teachers. In short, the criterion was a readiness to adapt.

Cecil Miskel related principal leadership traits and situation factors to the level of innovation effort in schools.[35] Innovation effort was defined as the number of new programs initiated or maintained to improve the organizational functioning of the school. A questionnaire measure asked the teachers and principal to identify recent modifications and innovations in school programs or procedures during the school year. Schools with low levels of technology and experienced, security-oriented principals were not very innovative. While this study measured not just readiness to change, it did not specify the external forces that helped bring about the adaptations.

Thus, although adaptability is an important indicator of organizational effectiveness, the sparseness of sound measures and research studies suggests that more intensive investigation of the area is needed.

Achievement

When speaking of school performance, many parents, government policy makers, and scholars define organizational effectiveness narrowly. Usually they mean student scores on standardized tests measuring cognitive skills.

While most would acknowledge other criteria, they typically ignore the school's role in developing motivation, creativity, self-confidence, and aspirations—all of which are needed for future success in school and adult life. For example, although researchers George F. Madaus and his colleagues noted the importance of attitudes, values, and interests as student outcomes from schooling, they confined their discussion of effectiveness almost totally to cognitive skills.[36]

Two apparent reasons explain the over-reliance on standardized test scores. The first is political and the second practical. Eric A. Hanushek argues that several important constituencies of education see test scores as having intrinsic value.[37] Although many educators disagree, parents, students, and government policy makers often agree that the tests are essential for measuring accountability. Furthermore, standardized test scores are commonly available to the public; hence, measuring cognitive outcomes is easier than measuring noncognitive ones.[38] In the words of Charles E. Bidwell and John D. Kasarda, "While the goals of schooling are many and vague, the academic attainment of students is clearly among them. Moreover, it is the only output of schools and school districts that is widely and publicly measured."[39]

Even though expediency, rather than theory, has too often guided research programs on school effectiveness, student achievement is an important indicator of goal attainment. Moreover, so many influential constituencies believe in the intrinsic value of student achievement as measured by a standardized achievement tests that administrators and teachers must address questions about what factors in schooling lead to higher test scores.

Measurement.　　Essentially, all schools and school districts, and many states as well, have testing programs. In the late 1970s, twenty-nine states had or were considering competency-based testing programs.[40]

The most frequently used testing instruments come in batteries of subscales that purport to measure a variety of skills. The most widely used standardized achievement tests include the Iowa Test of Basic Skills and the Metropolitan Achievement Test. Virtually all the test batteries measure knowledge of English and mathematics. Science, social studies, and other subject areas form additional achievement subscales.

Ready access to achievement data eases the data collection tasks of the researcher; however, some scholars argue that a major liability of standardized tests is their relative insensitivity to school-specific pupil achievements.[41] The content of a subject area such as language arts is so vast, and the emphasis on content between school districts so diverse, that standardized tests cannot adequately measure the achievements, skills, processes, and learning that are specific to school instruction.

In theoretically guided studies, research using standardized test scores is badly needed in educational administration. Still, these devices must be used reasonably and knowledgeably. A researcher must have an in-depth grasp of the technical knowledge of measurement and standardized achievement tests.

Research.   Two approaches to studies of cognitive achievement as an indicator of organizational effectiveness appear in the literature. The first is designated "production function research," and it became popular in the mid-1960s. Also termed "input-output analysis," the technique was developed by microeconomists to predict the output of a system using sets of input or independent variables. In a school setting, the input groups usually are classified as home resources, school resources, community characteristics, student resources, and peer group characteristics, while the outputs are scores on achievement tests.[42] The purpose is primarily to predict an outcome, rather than explaining how the outcome was produced. Standardized test scores became important when the popular educational production function research created a demand for reliable instruments to measure outcomes.

The most influential educational study reflecting this approach, *Equality of Educational Opportunity*, was conducted by James S. Coleman and his associates.[43] Popularly known as the Coleman Report, it remains the largest survey of American public education ever taken. Nationally, 645,000 students completed standardized ability and achievement tests as well as forms to describe their family backgrounds. Approximately 60,000 teachers responded to questionnaires about their educational experiences, teaching tenure, attitudes, and verbal ability. Finally, data on a variety of organizational variables, including class size, school organization, libraries, and laboratory facilities, were collected from over 4,000 schools.

The most surprising finding concerned the role the school had in pupil achievement. When home background variables were controlled, school factors appeared to explain little variance in the test scores. What mattered most was not the material quality of the school, but the students' home backgrounds before entering the school.

Doubts that school facilities contributed to student achievement were reinforced by the results of the early evaluations of Head Start and Title I compensatory education programs.[44] Few lasting educational effects were found. A large number of production function studies conducted primarily by economists followed in the late 1960s and early 1970s.[45]

Many of the early researchers concluded pessimistically that schools have little impact on the development of their students. If this view is accepted, building a case for additional education expenditures to provide more teachers, better facilities and new curriculum resources becomes exceedingly difficult. However, recent interpretations of earlier studies and new findings yield a more optimistic picture.[46] The recent studies leave little doubt that learning in the home is extremely important. No matter how they are measured, differences in socioeconomic background of the family lead to significant differences in student achievement. The most reasonable interpretation is that measures of socioeconomic status are simply proxies for the quality of learning environment in the home—nutrition, physical surroundings, parental attitudes, education, and so forth. Still, little room for doubt exists that differences among schools and teachers are important to achievement. Schools are not homogeneous in their effects on students; schools differ in effectiveness. Though this is the case, the measurement of those specific attributes of teachers and schools that are important to achievement remains somewhat uncertain, especially using production function methods. In fact, Madaus and his colleagues stated unequivocally that "empirical researchers have not clearly identified any variable related to instruction, policy, or resources which consistently affects output."[47]

The lack of adequate measures will continue to be a problem with production function research because researchers are interested primarily in prediction. Without such measures it will be impossible to pinpoint processes that induce and explain the cognitive development of students.

Within the last decade, scholars and effective schools advocates have claimed that, by focusing on process characteristics such as instructional methods and school climate, variables can be found that consistently relate to student achievement on standardized tests.[48] These researchers take an alternate approach to the study of cognitive achievement that can be termed "organizational research."

A well-known investigation relating organizational climate to student achievement was conducted by Wilbur B. Brookover and his associates.[49] Their study of elementary schools described various expectancies of students, teachers, and principals. The expectancy of learning and commitment to learning as climate indicators explained as much as 80 percent of the variance in student achievement. In other words, the achievement levels in schools are high when the students, teachers, and principals expect, and are committed to, learning. Neither the socioeconomic nor the racial composition variables added much to the explanation.

Similarly, John Stewart related teacher perceptions of climate as measured by Likert's profile of a school to student achievement scores as measured by the Iowa Test of Basic Skills.[50] He found a positive relationship between climate and student achievement: Schools with more participative climates had students who scored higher on the standardized achievement tests.

Cross-cultural studies suggest that the processes and atmosphere of schools contribute more to student achievement than the physical presence of particular resources and facilities or the status traits (education, experience) of teachers.[51] Seemingly, what the students and educators do in schools and classrooms —how they reward each other, interact, spend their time, and pursue common objectives—influences performance on achievement tests.

After reviewing the literature, Steven T. Bossert, David C. Dwyer, Brian Rowen, and Ginny V. Lee concluded that the administrative behavior of principals is important to school effectiveness.[52] Similar to the leadership studies cited in Chapter 9, no single style of management appears appropriate for all schools. Rather the findings reported in the research literature reaffirm the usefulness of contingency approaches to organizational effectiveness and leadership. In other words, effectiveness depends on the appropriate matching of situational variables, e.g., shape of the administrative hierarchy, organization of the curricular program, type of classroom instructional procedures and school climate, and the leadership style of the principal.

Similarly, David L. Clark, Linda S. Lotto, and Terry A. Astuto summarized the literature on effective schools. They contend that effective schools focus on academic achievement of students, maintain high expectations for student achievement, allocate and use academic learning time effectively and efficiently, maintain an orderly and supportive school climate, provide learning opportunities for teachers and students, and employ regular programs of evaluation and feedback to students. But the key, they believe, lies in the people who inhabit schools at particular times and their interactions within the educational organization. The search for effectiveness in schools is the search for excellence in people.

To knowledgeable educators, these findings and assertions may not be too surprising, but they do represent a start in verifying the ways that schools influence cognitive development. If government policy makers and the public are to be convinced of the need for additional resources, this line of research must be pursued and expanded vigorously. In addition to climate variables, bureaucratic, motivational, leadership, and communication processes should be studied in schools and in classrooms to explain further how schools impart academic achievement.

In sum, although standardized achievement tests contain conceptual, empirical, and political traps for educators seeking an indicator of school effectiveness, they are essential in measuring performance. A third indicator of performance, job satisfaction, is less controversial than student achievement, though it too is little understood.

Job Satisfaction

The formal study of job satisfaction did not start until the Hawthorne studies in the early 1930s (see Chapter 1). However, prior to those studies scientific managers had implicitly recognized the concept in conjunction with worker fatigue. Since the 1930s, job satisfaction has been studied extensively. Edwin A. Locke, for example, estimates that a minimum of 3,350 articles were published on the subject by early 1972.[53] Moreover, the number was growing by over 100 new publications each year.

Why does job satisfaction attract so much interest? Originally, job satisfaction became important because the early proponents of a human relations approach convinced both theorists and administrators that a happy worker is a productive worker. More recently, the study of job satisfaction has intensified with a general concern for the quality of working life, epitomized during the 1970s by the publication of *Work in America*.[54] Yet even with the new emphasis on the concept, our understanding of job satisfaction remains limited. However, some agreement on the appropriate definition of job satisfaction does exist.

The classic attempt to define job satisfaction was made in 1935 by Robert Hoppock.[55] He cautioned about the difficulty of formulating an adequate definition because of the limited amount of knowledge then available on the subject.[56] Nevertheless, he defined job satisfaction as any combination of psychological, physiological, and environmental circumstances that cause a person to say, "I am satisfied with my job."

Other definitions of the concept have been formulated. Job satisfaction has been conceived as the affective orientations of individuals toward work roles that they are presently occupying.[57] Similarly, satisfaction has been thought to refer to an affective response of an individual to the job; it results when on-the-job experiences relate to the individual's values and needs.[58] Finally, one researcher has defined job satisfaction as the "pleasurable or positive emotional state resulting from the appraisal of one's job or job experiences."[59] In educational settings job satisfaction can be said to be present and past-oriented affective state that results when the educator evaluates her or his work role. Though several acceptable definitions of the concept exist, measurement remains a problem.

Measurement.   The typical methods of measuring job satisfaction employ questionnaires that vary primarily in their directness in assessing the concept. The most direct method is a single question such as, How satisfied are you with your present job? Usually responses follow from very satisfied to very dissatisfied. This procedure is not entirely adequate because the reliability of a single item cannot be assessed. A slightly less direct approach uses a series of items that probe various components or indicators of job satisfaction. Table 12.2 presents an example of such a scale. Developed by Cecil Miskel, the seven-item measure displays adequate reliability (0.81) and high face validity. The overall job satisfaction questionnaire, with slight variations, has served to measure the criterion variable in several studies.[60]

Edward Holdaway constructed a more extensive measure to assess the job satisfaction of teachers on particular facets of their work.[61] Based on extensive interviews with teachers, items in teacher contracts, a literature review, and pilot tests, he selected fifty-two items to measure seven job satisfaction factors. The factors and example items comprise Table 12.3. As the table shows, several important dimensions of teacher work are scrutinized. This diverse content combined with the fact that the instrument was carefully developed, indicate that the questionnaire can serve as an excellent measure in future studies.

A widely used indirect measure of overall satisfaction is the *job descriptive*

TABLE 12.2 Overall Job Satisfaction Questionnaire

Response categories: Strongly Disagree, Disagree, Neutral, Agree, Strongly Agree
  1. As I evaluate my future as an educator, I feel my level of satisfaction will increase.
 *2. I am somewhat dissatisfied with my job.
 *3. If I came into enough money so that I could live comfortably without working, I would quit my job.
 *4. I often think of changing jobs.
 *5. My job as an educator gives me a great deal of personal satisfaction.
  6. I am satisfied with my job.
 *7. Most other educators are more satisfied with their jobs than I am.

*Reverse score

TABLE 12.3 Factors and Example Items for Questionnaire Testing Job Satisfaction with Facets of Work

Response categories: Not Relevant/Not Applicable, Highly Dissatisfied, Moderately Dissatisfied, Slightly Dissatisfied, Slightly Satisfied, Moderately Satisfied, Highly Satisfied, Neutral

Factor 1. Recognition and Status
   Status of teachers in society
Factor 2. Students
   Attitudes of students to learning
Factor 3. Resources
   Availability of library resources
Factor 4. Teaching Assignment
   Freedom to select teaching methods
Factor 5. Involvement with Administrators
   Involvement in school decision making
Factor 6. Work Load
   Number of hours taught each week
Factor 7. Salary and Benefits
   Salary

index (JDI). Patricia Cain Smith and her associates developed this instrument during the mid-1960s, and it has been tested extensively.[62] Sample items from the JDI are contained in Table 12.4. The instrument contains five subscales—work on present job, supervision, present pay, people on your present job, and opportunities for promotion. Each subscale contains nine or eighteen items. This is a carefully developed instrument that has been demonstrated repeatedly to give high reliability and validity estimates across a great many work settings.[63]

Research. During the 1960s and early 1970s, strikes, sanctions, and professional negotiations gave evidence of a general state of dissatisfaction among teachers. Research studies indicated, however, that teachers traditionally have not been discontent. In 1935, Hoppock found to his surprise that less than 10 percent of the teachers he sampled were dissatisfied.[64] In 1951, Francis S. Chase found less than 8 percent of the teachers were dissatisfied with their jobs.[65] Rex Fuller and Miskel, in 1972, also found that less than 8 percent of their educator sample were dissatisfied; in fact, 88.6 percent stated that they were satisfied or very satisfied with their jobs.[66] A reasonable conclusion is that, during the past forty or so years, the percentage of dissatisfied teachers has remained at relatively stable, low levels—below 10 percent.

One possible factor contributing to the relatively low level of discontent is a socially biased response set of teachers, who have always been told that they should derive satisfaction from serving children. Consequently, to voice low job

TABLE 12.4   Sample Item from the Job Descriptive Index

Instructions: Place a "Y" beside each item that describes a particular aspect of your present job—work, pay, promotion, supervision, and people. Place an "N" if the item did not describe that aspect or "?" if you cannot decide. (NOTE: The response shown beside each item is the one scored in the "satisfied" direction for each scale.)

Work on Present Job		*Supervision*	
___Y___	Fascinating	___Y___	Asks my advice
___Y___	Good	___Y___	Influential
___N___	Tiresome	___N___	Bad
___N___	Frustrating		
Present Pay		*People on Your Present Job*	
___N___	Barely live on income	___Y___	Stimulating
___N___	Insecure	___Y___	Responsible
___N___	Less than I deserve	___N___	Talk too much
Opportunities for Promotion			
___N___	Opportunity somewhat limited		
___Y___	Promotion on ability		
___Y___	Fairly good chance for promotion		

satisfaction may be socially unacceptable for a professional educator. Support for this contention is found when the data from direct and indirect measures of job satisfaction are compared. Fuller and Miskel measured the satisfaction level directly with the question, Overall, how do you feel about your job—the things you actually do at school? Teachers had to choose from five categories, ranging from very satisfied to very dissatisfied, that were scaled arbitrarily from five to one. The mean value was 4.15. In contrast, Miskel, Douglas Glasnapp, and Richard Hatley used an indirect measure (See Table 12.2) and found the average to be substantially lower.[67]

Several more formal theories have been proposed to explain the level of the job satisfaction. One of them, the discrepancy hypothesis, was proposed by Smith and her associates. They posited that job satisfaction is best explained by a discrepancy between the work motivation of jobholders and the incentives offered them by the organization.[68] Similar conceptualizations are found in inducements-contributions theory[69] and cognitive dissonance theory.[70] These positions postulate that job satisfaction levels are related to the perceived difference between what is expected or desired as fair and reasonable return (individual motivation) and what is actually experienced in the job situation (organizational incentives).

Elaborating on these concepts for the educational organization, Max Abbott hypothesized that as long as educators remain in a school system, they perform according to the way the positions are defined.[71] In doing so, the educators anticipate a relationship between the expected performance and the school district's rewards. If they perform and the anticipated rewards are not forthcoming, or if they perceive the rewards as negative, dissonance results. In seeking an explanation for such dissonance, the educators question the accuracy of their perceptions. Any shift in perceptions makes them alter their beliefs in order to accommodate the perceived inequities. Such a modification also involves a concomitant change in the affective responses to the job, that is, a shift in the job satisfaction levels.

The discrepancy hypothesis of job satisfaction developed out of this analysis. The hypothesis, presented pictorially in Table 12.5., proposes a direct positive relationship between workers' job satisfaction levels and the degree of congruence between ideal work conditions and perceived work conditions. If the needs that motivate an individual to work are satisfied exactly by the organization's incentives, no dissonance exists and job satisfaction is high. If an individual's needs are greater than the rewards received for work, a discrepancy exists that leads to dissatisfaction. But if the rewards exceed needs, the discrepancy yields positive job satisfaction. Findings by Miskel and his colleagues support the discrepancy hypothesis in the educational setting.[72]

Another theory that attempts to explain the level of job satisfaction conceptualizes in terms of combinations of variables such as job, personality and motivation, situation, and personal characteristics (age, sex) to indicators of job satisfaction. The general relationship hypothesis, as it is called, seeks to correlate job satisfaction with virtually all of the variables suggested in the social systems model (see Chapter 3). Several excellent reviews of the research testing the general relationship hypothesis are available.[73]

After reviewing the literature, Ratsoy concluded that teacher job satisfaction, in general, is lower in schools where the teachers perceive a high degree of bureaucracy.[74] Later evidence, however, suggests that this statement is too general. When specific bureaucratic dimensions of schools are related to job satisfaction, a complex picture emerges. Bureaucratic factors that enhance status differences among the professionals, such as the hierarchy of authority and centralization, produce low satisfaction levels. But factors that clarify the job and yield equal applications of school policy promote high levels of satisfaction.[75] For example, fair application of the rules that help delineate job responsibilities enhance the job satisfaction of employees.

Work motivation is also consistently correlated with job satisfaction. Motivator and hygiene needs (see Chapter 7) contribute to teacher and administrator satisfaction. Expectancy motivation also has been found to be significantly

TABLE 12.5   Discrepancy Hypothesis of Job Satisfaction

Individual Work Motivation Factors
(Valued Outcomes of Work)
Minus
Organizational Incentives
Yields
Job Satisfaction

If the subtraction yields a positive value, motivational desires are greater than the incentives received, dissatisfaction results. Conversely, if the subtraction produces a negative value, rewards exceed desires and satisfaction results.

related to teacher job satisfaction.[76] Similarly, as the organizational climates of schools become more open or participative (see Chapter 8), the level of teacher satisfaction increases.[77]

Leadership, decision-making, and communication processes also influence educator job satisfaction. The effects of the leadership styles of school administrators have long been recognized.[78] The nature of the relationships between teachers and administrators and the quality of leadership correlates highly with teacher morale: the better the relationship and the better the quality of leadership, the higher teacher morale tends to be. More recent findings affirm the earlier assertions to this effect. Greater participation in decision making, especially concerning instructional methods, yields enhanced teacher job satisfaction.[79] Moreover, the lack of opportunities to participate in decision making is the greatest source of teacher dissatisfaction.[80] Finally, the quality of the communication processes relates to overall teacher job satisfaction.[81] Communicating clearly to employees the scope of the job, how their contributions are related to the school's goals, and how they are being judged, for instance, are positively correlated with job satisfaction.

One final topic of research on job satisfaction is the relationship between job satisfaction and work performance. Intuitively, more satisfied educators perform at higher levels than dissatisfied educators. This belief remained relatively unchallenged until 1955, when a critical analysis of the literature revealed that the relationship is not a simple direct one.[82] Similarly, another comprehensive review of the literature found that satisfaction and performance have a low but positive correlation.[83] Even with this modest relationship, a controversy rages over which variable causes the other.[84] We agree with Locke that performance and satisfaction are best viewed as separate indicators of organizational effectiveness.[85] Only in special circumstances should we expect causal relationships between them.

We may conclude from this brief survey with the observation that although knowledge about job satisfaction, as an indicator of school effectiveness, tends to be somewhat fragmented, it is a topic of great interest to educators. A reason for the fragmentation is that many investigations lack theoretical foundations and the results remain isolated facts. Work is needed to provide a coherent theory in the area.

Central Life Interests

As an indicator of the critical latency function of social systems (see Table 12.1.), central life interests can be defined as a set of attitudes that defines the preferences of individuals for doing favored activities in chosen settings. Given the wide range of activities in daily life, each person selects only a few for primary attention. Strong attachments to and involvements in crucial interest areas develop. Having school activities as a central life interest means that a disproportionate share of time, emotion, commitment, and energy is invested in the organization in relation to other life activities. Consequently, the performance of the school increases as the employees' central life interests focus on the work setting.

Measurement. Two instruments suitable for use in schools are available to assess the central life interests of teachers. An early version of the *central life instrument questionnaire* has been refined to produce one with thirty-two items.[86] Each question poses a type of behavior and asks the individual to indicate in which setting (work, some other, or no particular setting) she or he prefers to act. An illustrative item is: "I am most interested in (a) things about my job, (b) things I usually do around the house or in the community, and (c) just about everything I do."

Miskel, Glasnapp, and Hatley developed a shorter and somewhat more general measure of central life interests specifically for the educational setting.[87] Reproduced in Table 12.6, the measure is comprised of seven items. Its estimated reliability is 0.73.

Research. Evidence suggests that structural and personal variables in the school strongly influence the central life interests of teachers.[88] For example, schools perceived as having high status differences between teachers and administrators, less shared decision making, and more rules and regulations tend to be staffed by teachers who have low central life interests in work. Moreover, the findings of Dan C. Lortie suggest that the career structure and work rewards of schools mitigate against teachers exhibiting high central life interests in teaching.[89] In teaching, few districts have promotion systems to provide teachers with opportunities to move upward in a hierarchy and to gain higher and higher rewards. Becoming an administrator or specialist blurs one's identity as a teacher and leads to discontinuance of tasks one is used to performing. Consequently, many teachers report that their central life interests are not in the job. One result is that almost every male teacher in Lortie's study had either a strong avocational interest or an additional source of employment income. The strongest commitments came from older, single teachers.

While these findings paint a somewhat negative picture, they also provide ideas about methods to increase the work-related interests of teachers. For

TABLE 12.6 **A Short Measure of Central Life Interests**

Response categories: Strongly Disagree, Disagree, Neutral, Agree, Strongly Agree

*1. My central life interests lie *outside* of my job at school.
 2. My main interests in life are closely related to my job in the school.
*3. When I am worried, it is usually about things related to my job.
*4. I believe that other things are more important than my job at school.
 5. Most of my energy is directed toward my job.
 6. In talking to friends, I most like to talk about events related to my job.
 7. My central concerns are job related.

*Reverse score.

educators to have central life interests within the work setting, the situation must yield extensive unimpeded opportunities for rewards. To use the tenets of expectancy motivation theory as an explanation, the school must clearly delineate a relationship between educator performance and receiving desired incentives.

Overall Organizational Effectiveness

Not unlike the use of the four necessary functions of a social system as criteria, Paul E. Mott combined several important outcomes to formulate a model of organizational effectiveness.[90] He integrated the following components: quantity and quality of the product, efficiency, adaptability, and flexibility. Mott reasoned that these five criteria define the ability of an organization to mobilize its centers of power for action to achieve goals and to adapt. Effective schools produce higher student achievement, generate more positive student attitudes, adapt better to environmental constraints, and deal more potently with internal problems. Clearly, Mott's perspective is consistent with the integrated goal-system resource model of organizational effectiveness developed in this chapter.

Measurement. Although we have cautioned against single indicators, a short global measure based strongly in a theoretical model and used with other instruments can begin to improve our understanding of organizational effectiveness. Mott developed an eight-item measure for use in a variety of organizational settings. The questionnaire has been modified for studies in schools.[91] The resultant *index of perceived organizational effectiveness* is shown on Table 12.7. Its careful development and high estimated reliability in schools make it a strong candidate for use as an overall measure in future studies; in fact, Mott concludes that the evidence suggests, with appropriate safeguards, that the subjective evaluations of employees provide a fairly valid measure of organizational effectiveness. Recent support for this conclusion has been provided by Wayne K. Hoy and Judith Ferguson.[92] Using the index of perceived organizational effectiveness and the theoretical framework developed in this chapter, they found that perceived overall effectiveness of secondary schools was significantly related to indicators of all four of Parsons' systems imperatives, e.g., adaptation, goal attainment, integration, and latency, for growth and survival.

Research. Mott has made extensive use of the index of perceived organizational effectiveness. He found few significant relationships between the centralization of decision making and effectiveness.[93] In highly centralized organizations, effectiveness tended to be lower. Moreover, effectiveness was greater when the leaders provided more structure for the tasks to be done and when the climate was open. Findings in the school setting support Mott's conclusions.[94] Formalization and complexity of the school structure and participative climates are conducive to organizational effectiveness. Similarly, Miskel, McDonald, and Bloom found that high organizational effectiveness as perceived

TABLE 12.7 The Index of Perceived Organizational Effectiveness

Every educator produces something during work. It may be a "product" or a "service." The following list of products and services are just a few of the things that result from schools:

Lesson plans	Student learning	Athletic achievements
Community projects	Instruction	Art and music programs
New curricula	Teacher-parent meetings	

Please indicate your responses by checking the appropriate line for each item.

a. Of the various things produced by the people you know *in your school,* how *much* are they producing?

____Low production   ____Moderate   ____High
____Fairly Low   ____Very high production

b. How good is the *quality* of the products or services produced by the people you know in your school?

____Poor quality   ____Fair quality   ____Good quality
____Low quality   ____Excellent quality

c. Do the people in your school get maximum output form the available resources (money, people, equipment, etc.)? That is, how *efficiently* do they do their work?

____Not efficiently   ____Fairly efficiently
____Very efficiently   ____Not too efficiently
____Extremely efficiently

d. How good a job is done by the people in your school in *anticipating* problems and preventing them from occurring or minimizing their effect?

____A poor job   ____A fair job   ____A very good job
____An adequate job   ____An excellent job

e. How *informed* are the people in your school about innovations that could affect the way they do their work?

____Uninformed   ____Moderately informed   ____Informed
____Somewhat informed   ____Very informed

f. When changes are made in the methods, routines, or equipment, how *quickly* do the people in your school accept and adjust to the changes?

____Very slowly   ____Fairly rapidly   ____Rapidly
____Rather slowly   ____Immediately

g. How *many* of the people in your school readily accept and adjust to the changes?

____Many less than half   ____The majority
____Many more than half   ____Less than half
____Nearly everyone

h. How good a job do the people in your school do in *coping* with emergencies and disruptions?

____A poor job   ____A fair job   ____A good job
____An adequate job   ____An excellent job

by teachers is associated with strong linkages to the principal in the area of student discipline, support from special education experts, time for classroom activities, and high expectancy motivation.[95]

It is clear from what has been said thus far that many variables are needed to assess adequately the complex effects of organizational and administrative processes on school effectiveness. Although the knowledge in this area is still somewhat limited, we can draw several practical implications from the research that has been done.

CONCEPTUAL DERIVATIONS AND APPLICATIONS

Most efforts to change a school represent attempts to improve its effectiveness.[96] Given the large number of approaches to planned organizational change, how does an administrator know which to use? The answer, in general, is that a variety of strategies should be used simultaneously rather than one at a time. Harvey A. Hornstein and his colleagues have proposed several strategies for improving organizational effectiveness that we shall consider next.[97]

Individual Strategies of Planned Change

Individual strategies of change assume that individual change, at least to some extent, must precede organizational change. The typical strategies for changing individuals involve training, counseling, selection and placement, and termination. In schools, training probably receives the greatest emphasis. School districts frequently pay for graduate education of teachers and administrators, and, increasingly, educator contracts contain provisions for in-service training. Moreover, only a small percentage of schools begin a new academic year without a few days of skill development and attitude enhancement.

Changing the individual has long been regarded as a major, though indirect, approach to organizational improvement. However, as Daniel Katz and Robert L. Kahn warn, "Attempts to change organizations by changing individuals have a long history of theoretical inadequacy and practical failure."[98] Past programs to improve effectiveness have too often disregarded organizational outcomes and oversimplified the process of change. Therefore, programs directed toward the individual must be considered in conjunction with the characteristics and effectiveness criteria of the school. Placing the emphasis on training, as many schools do, to improve the school is not sufficient; in fact, little evidence exists that the usual forms of training improve the functioning of organizations.[99] Clearly, additional strategies are needed.

Technostructural Strategies of Planned Change

Technostructural intervention strategies are of two types.[100] One type seeks to change structural variables of the school organization, e.g., hierarchical shape, reward policies, centralized or decentralized decision-making processes, and communication frequency.[101] The goal of structural modifications usually is integration—joining and coordinating parts or functions of the school organization, e.g., instruction and administration, for overall task achievement.[102] Typical examples of this approach include either centralizing or decentralizing decision making, changing the patterns and forms of communication, and developing operative goals through group processes.

The second type of strategy is to alter the technology or the way the school organization provides programs of education to change students. In schools technology includes instructional and administrative methods, work flow, e.g., scope and sequence of the curriculum, and equipment. Common examples of technology changes include introducing new instructional procedures and curriculum programs, moving to an open-space classroom arrangement or schools within a school, and instituting an evaluation plan for teachers.

Survey Feedback Strategies of Planned Change

Survey feedback constitutes a highly popular strategy to bring about change. Feedback procedures consist of systematically collecting and analyzing information about the school and reporting the data to the appropriate individuals or groups. The participants in the change program can use the information for assessment of needs, problem solving, and planning.

Four conditions enhance the impact of survey feedback change programs.[103] First, if school members participate in the collection, analysis, and interpretation of the data, they gain a feeling they have a stake in the proposed solutions. Second, if the participants discuss concrete information germane to their functioning, change is more likely to be accomplished. Third, if members can gain knowledge of the relative success of their actions and acts, they may be motivated to make additional efforts. Fourth, if group norms develop in support of change, they may encourage individual initiatives.

The power of survey feedback to improve organizational processes was demonstrated in the long-term, large-scale Michigan ICL study of change methods in business organizations.[104] This strategy produced the most consistent long-term improvements of any that were used. Moreover, the changes entrenched and remained after the change program ended. In a slightly more conservative interpretation, Edgar F. House and Thomas G. Cummings assert that the impact of survey feedback is on attitudes and perceptions of the situation.[105] They believe that survey feedback is best viewed as a bridge between diagnosis of organizational problems and the implementation of active problem-solving methods.

Organization Development Strategies of Planned Change

Born as a loosely defined set of techniques during the mid-1950s, first applied in school settings during the mid-1960s, used as a "buzz word" during the early 1970s, sold as a panacea by would-be consultants during the mid-1970s, organization development (OD) shows promise as a useful approach to planned change of schools during the next decade.[106] The approaches to OD matured as the expectations of proponents became more realistic and healthy. Criticism and evaluation became acceptable. For example, C. Brooklyn Derr, as an early advocate, later questioned its appropriateness for schools.[107] More recently, however, Michael Fullan, Matthew B. Miles, and Gib Taylor critically reviewed the literature and concluded that OD is a useful approach for school improvement.[108]

Several definitions of organization development have been proposed over the past twenty-five years. For our present purposes, we will synthesize several and define it as the process of changing the cultural or climate of a school organization by applying knowledge from behavioral science during a period of planned and sustained effort for improving organizational effectiveness.[109] Four points of elaboration need to be made.

First, the process is meant to change the system, not the individual. This makes OD different from the traditional laboratory (sensitivity) training and management development programs which stress individual changes. The emphasis is on organizational phenomena such as problem solving, communication, and leadership.

Second, the organization's culture or climate includes a set of learned and shared assumptions that regulate member behavior. By definition, OD attempts to improve the levels of collaboration, participation, and trust, and to reduce the level of conflict. In other words, a primary goal is to enhance the general quality of life in schools.

Third, OD involves deliberately planned change rather than organization drift. Some portion of the school's resources—time, energy, money—must be linked to outside consultants in a continuous maintenance and rebuilding program. Because school organizations are not easily or quickly transformed, a two- or three-year effort is needed for serious and self-sustained change.

Fourth, the theories, research findings, and research methodologies from sociology and social psychology serve as the knowledge foundation for OD. As Hornstein and his associates have observed, the different phases of an OD intervention require different techniques of change.[110] They postulate two phases—a period of diagnosis followed by a period of intervention. These two phases, however, are not rigidly sequential because the process of diagnosis is in itself an intervention.

The diagnostic phase of OD consists of gathering data, identifying problem areas, and then determining the causes of the problem. Following this phase, participants must make decisions about which OD intervention technologies should be used. Possibilities include team development, intergroup problem-solving sessions, training interventions, task-process consultations, laboratory training, and interpersonal process consultation. Obviously, different combinations of these methods should be used for arriving at the most appropriate change program.

As a process of cultural change, OD promises to alleviate problems associated with educational administration. Combined with other planned change strategies, e.g., individual, survey feedback, and technostructural, significant improvements in the organizational effectiveness of schools can become a reality.[111] As evidence for this assertion, a description of such a program for change using different strategies is offered below.

An Example of a Planned Change Program that Improved an Urban High School

George J. Crawford, Cecil Miskel, and M. Claradine Johnson developed and guided a planned change program for a period of three years.[112] Located near the center of the city, the high school population consisted of about 2,000 students and 100 professional staff members.

The program's primary objective was to improve the school's organizational effectiveness. Statistics for student suspension, withdrawal (dropout), and failure rates showed that the school was not operating effectively. For example, 8.2 percent of the students were suspended; 30 percent of the sophomore class withdrew from school; and 33 percent of the sophomores failed at least one subject. Moreover, the disproportionately high rate of withdrawal among minority students clearly demanded attention. The school could be characterized as having traditional curricular offerings and being custodial in its approach to controlling students.

The program of change used the four approaches to social intervention discussed earlier. The strategy of changing individuals was based upon a sociopsychological model, especially the early ideas of Kurt Lewin.[113] Lewin conceived change as a modification of the forces that maintain stable behavior patterns of individuals in the organization. He believed that behavior at any given time is the result of two sets of forces—those attempting to maintain current behaviors in a state of equilibrium, and those promoting change. When the forces are about equal, the status quo tends to be maintained. To induce change in behavior displayed in organizations, therefore, either the forces promoting change must be increased, the forces holding the behavior constant must be decreased, or some combination of both. Consequently, the faculty and staff formed groups to enhance their interpersonal skills and to use a three-stage process of "unfreezing," changing (acquiring), and "refreezing" attitudes, values, norms, skills, and behaviors.

The technostructural strategies started with the development of twenty goal statements, ranked in order of importance by participants. During the last half of the first year and the beginning of the second year, several new programs were then introduced. Peer counseling, a career education curriculum, and an independent study center were instituted as modifications of the instructional program. Other closely related changes included a new teacher-as-adviser program, revised enrollment procedures for greater student choice in classes, and the publication of a course description catalog.

Survey feedback was used during the entire program of change. Two sets of data were collected regularly and shared systematically with the staff in discussion sessions. Failure, withdrawal, and suspension levels were tabulated annually. In addition, on four occasions—before the program started and at the end of each school year—all staff members and a selected group of students completed the profile of a school questionnaire testing climate.

Organizational development techniques were used in the program of change as well. The program lasted three years and involved the faculty, staff, and students in the systematic assessment, diagnosis, and transformation of the school. The OD activities were aimed simultaneously at both the organization and individual. Emphasis was placed on skill and attitude development to improve school communications and to increase the level of participation in the decisions involving students. The values, attitudes, and skills of those involved were thought to be of fundamental importance to the quality of life in the high school.

What effect did the combined program have on the organizational effectiveness of the school? Clearly, the school's ability to adapt was enhanced. The school lost its tradition-bound character and became flexible and innovative. The results for goal achievement are somewhat less clear, however. For the white students, the failure and suspension rates increased slightly. For the black students, the failure, withdrawal, and suspension levels declined somewhat. In terms of performing its function of integration (the question of climate), overall the school became slightly more open and participative. Greater participation in the decision processes, team cooperation, and team building, for example, represent valuable gains. Finally, some evidence of improvement in performance on the latency criterion was provided on Likert's profile of a school questionnaire. Perceived commitment to organizational goals increased in the early stages of the program and was maintained until the program ended.

Dramatic increases in the school's effectiveness levels are not apparent. But the gains with respect to the four criteria support the contention that planned change efforts using a variety of strategies can improve the functioning of educational organizations. Moreover, where positive change is achieved, it appears to be durable and lasting.[114] A cautionary note must be added, however. Such efforts are not panaceas for administrative problems. Instead, they are resource-consuming activities that may gradually improve school effectiveness over an extended period of time.

SUMMARY

Organizational effectiveness plays so central a role in the theory and practice of education that a better understanding of the concept is essential to the field. Two general approaches, a goal perspective and a system resource model, dominate the study. The differences between the two, however, seem more a matter of semantics than substance; therefore, the approaches can be merged to form a single, integrated goal-system resources model for the analysis of organizational effectiveness in schools. The synthesis can be made by using the four functions of a social system identified by Parsons as multiple operative goals for organizations. Specifically, adaptation, goal achievement, integration, and latency guide the selection of indicators of effectiveness. These indicators are the several constituencies of schools over the short and long term. For a school, effectiveness of a school is clearly not one thing; it is a complex, multidimensional phenomenon defined in terms of both goals and system resources. Unfortunately most research of school effectiveness is piecemeal and has not been guided by a theoretical model.

Administrators attempting to improve the effectiveness of schools must engage in planned organizational change. Such change can be brought about by individual, technostructural, survey feedback and organizational development strategies. For maximum effectiveness the techniques should be employed in concert.

NOTES

1. Three other models of organizational effectiveness appear with some frequency in the literature. The internal processes model is presented by David A. Nadler and Michael L. Tushman, "A Congruence Model for Organizational Assessment," in Edward E. Lawler, David A. Nadler, and Cortlandt Cammann (eds.), *Organizational Assessment: Perspectives on the Measurement of Organizational Behavior and the Quality of Working Life* (New York: Wiley, 1980), pp. 261–278. The strategic constituencies model is described by Terry Connolly, Edward M. Conlon, and Stuart Jay Deutsch, "Organizational Effectiveness: A Multiple Constituency Approach," *Academy of Management Review,* 5 (1980), 211–217; and Jeffrey Pfeffer and Gerald R. Salancik, *The Organizational Control of Organizations: A Resource Dependence Perspective* (New York: Harper & Row, 1978). The legitimacy model is detailed by R. H. Miles and Kim S. Cameron, *Coffin Nails and Corporate Strategies* (Englewood Cliffs, NJ: Prentice-Hall, 1982); and Raymond F. Zammuto, *Assessing Organizational Effectiveness* (Albany: State University of New York Press, 1982). The approaches are not mutually exclusive, and essential elements of the internal processes model and multiple or strategic constituencies model are incorporated into the integrated framework presented later in this chapter. An excellent source that presents and evaluates the different perspectives is the following: Kim S. Cameron and David A. Whetten, *Organizational Effectiveness: A Comparison of Multiple Models* (New York: Academic, 1983).
2. Amitai Etzioni, *Modern Organizations* (Englewood Cliffs, NJ: Prentice-Hall, 1964), p. 6.
3. Michael T. Hannan and John Freeman, "Obstacles to Comparative Studies," in Paul S. Goodman and Johannes M. Pennings (eds.), *New Perspectives on Organizational Effectiveness* (San Francisco: Jossey-Bass, 1977), pp. 106–131; John P. Campbell, "On the Nature of Organizational Effectiveness," in Goodman and Pennings, *op. cit.,* pp. 13–55; Richard M. Steers, *Organizational Effectiveness: A Behavioral View* (Santa Monica, CA: Goodyear, 1977); James L. Price, "The Study of Organizational Effectiveness," *Sociological Quarterly,* 13 (1972), 3–15; Richard H. Hall, *Organizations: Structure and Process* (Englewood Cliffs, NJ: Prentice-Hall,

1972); W. Richard Scott, "Effectiveness of Organizational Effectiveness Studies," in Goodman and Pennings, *op. cit.,* pp. 63–95; and Richard L. Daft, *Organization Theory and Design* (St. Paul: West, 1983), pp. 82–92.

4. Steers, *op. cit.,* pp. 23–25.
5. Campbell, *op. cit.,* pp. 19, 22–29.
6. Kim Cameron, "Measuring Organizational Effectiveness in Institutions of Higher Education," *Administrative Science Quarterly,* 23 (1978), 604–632.
7. Ephraim Yuchtman and Stanley E. Seashore, "A System Resource Approach to Organizational Effectiveness," *American Sociological Review,* 32 (1967), 891–903. In building the system resource model, Yuchtman and Seashore relied heavily on Amitai Etzioni, "Two Approaches to Organizational Analysis: A Critique and Suggestion," *Administrative Science Quarterly,* 5 (1960), 257–278; and Daniel Katz and Robert L. Kahn, *The Social Psychology of Organizations* (New York: Wiley, 1966), pp. 149–170.
8. Yuchtman and Seashore, *op. cit.;* Campbell, *op. cit.;* and Paul S. Goodman and Johannes M. Pennings, "Toward a Workable Framework," in Goodman and Pennings, *op. cit.,* pp. 147–184.
9. Cameron, *op. cit.,* 605; Scott, *op. cit.,* pp. 75–89; Steers, *op. cit.,* p. 48; and Bruce A. Kirchhoff, "Organization Effectiveness Measurement and Policy Research," *Academy of Management Review,* 2 (1977), 347–355.
10. Hall, *op. cit.,* p. 100.
11. Steers, *op. cit.,* p. 48.
12. Connolly, Conlon, and Deutsch, *op. cit.,* p. 212.
13. Goodman and Pennings, "Toward a Workable Framework," *op. cit.;* Steers, *op. cit.,* pp. 4–6, 48; and Campbell, *op. cit.,* p. 50.
14. Martin Burlingame, "Some Neglected Dimensions in the Study of Educational Administration," *Educational Administration Quarterly,* 15 (1979), 1–18.
15. James L. Gibson, John M. Ivancevich, and James H. Donnelly, Jr., *Organizations: Behavior, Structure and Processes,* rev. ed. (Dallas, TX, Business Publications, 1976), p. 64.
16. Kim S. Cameron, "The Effectiveness of Ineffectiveness," *Research in Organizational Behavior,* 6 (1984), 235–285. See pp. 239–240.
17. Robert E. Quinn and Kim Cameron, "Organizational Life Cycles and Shifting Criteria of Effectiveness: Some Preliminary Evidence," *Management Science,* 29 (1983), 33–51.
18. Zammuto, *op. cit.,* p. 161.
19. Cameron, *op. cit.,* 606.
20. Connolly, Conlon, and Deutsch, *op. cit.*
21. James H. Balderson, "Who Likes the 'Good' School?" *Canadian Administrator,* 16 (1977), 1–4.
22. Scott, *op. cit.,* pp. 87–89.
23. Michael Keeley, "Impartiality and Participant-Interest Theories of Organizational Effectiveness," *Administrative Science Quarterly,* 29 (1984), 1–25.
24. Rosabeth Kanter and Derick Brinkerhoff, "Organizational Performance: Recent Developments in Measurement," *Annual Review of Sociology,* 7 (1981), 321–349.

25. Campbell, *op. cit.,* pp. 36–39.
26. Richard M. Steers, "Problems in the Measurement of Organizational Effectiveness," *Administrative Science Quarterly,* 20 (1975), 546–558.
27. James H. Stewart, "Factors Accounting for Goal Effectiveness: A Longitudinal Study," in S. Lee Spray (ed.), *Organizational Effectiveness: Theory, Research, Utilization* (Kent, OH: Kent State University Press, 1976), pp. 109–121; and Douglas T. Hall and Cynthia V. Fukami, "Organizational Design and Adult Learning," in Barry M. Staw (ed.), *Research in Organizational Behavior,* 1 (1979), 125–167.
28. Zammuto, *Assessing Organizational Effectiveness, op. cit.,* p. 4.
29. Talcott Parsons, *Structure and Process in Modern Societies* (New York: Free Press, 1960). The work of Parsons has been used by other scholars to guide the analysis of organizational effectiveness and educational policy. See, for example, the following: Hall and Fukami, *op. cit.;* and William Lowe Boyd and Robert L. Crowson, "The Changing Conception and Practice of Public School Administration," *Review of Research in Education,* 9 (1981), 311–373.
30. Campbell, *op. cit.,* pp. 13–55.
31. Steers, "Problems in the Measurement of Organizational Effectiveness," *op. cit.*
32. *Ibid.,* 547.
33. Campbell, *op. cit.,* p. 38.
34. Eugene W. Ratsoy, Gail R. Babcock, and Brian J. Caldwell, *Organizational Effectiveness in the Educational Practicum Program—1977–1978* (Edmonton, Canada: University of Alberta, 1978).
35. Cecil Miskel, "Principals' Attitudes Toward Work and Co-workers, Situational Factors, Perceived Effectiveness, and Innovation Effort," *Educational Administration Quarterly,* 13 (1977), 51–70.
36. George F. Madaus, Peter W. Airasian, and Thomas Kellaghan, *School Effectiveness: A Reassessment of the Evidence* (New York: McGraw-Hill, 1980), pp. 111–171.
37. Eric A. Hanushek, "A Reader's Guide to Educational Production Functions" (Paper presented at the Conference on School Organization and Effects, National Institute of Education, San Diego, CA: 1978).
38. *Ibid.,* p. 10; and Madaus, Airasian, and Kellaghan, *op. cit.,* pp. 112–113.
39. Charles E. Bidwell and John D. Kasarda, "School District Organization and Student Achievement," *American Sociological Review,* 40 (1975), 57.
40. Madaus, Airasian, and Kellaghan, *op. cit.,* p. 166.
41. *Ibid.*
42. Lawrence J. Lau, "Education Production Functions" (Paper presented at the Conference on School Organization and Effects, National Institute of Education, San Diego, CA: 1978).
43. James S. Coleman *et al., Equality of Educational Opportunity* (Washington, DC: U. S. Government Printing Office, 1966).
44. Madaus, Airasian, and Kellaghan, *op. cit.,* pp. 29–33.
45. Several excellent reviews of this literature are available, including Lau, *op. cit.;* Hanushek, *op. cit.,* Dean Jamison, Patrick Suppes, and Stuart Wells, "The Effectiveness of Alternative Instructional Media: A Survey," *Review of Educational Research,* 44 (1974), 1–67; H. A. Averich *et al., How Effective Is Schooling: A Critical Review and Synthesis of Research Findings* (Santa Monica, CA: Rand, 1972); Richard J. Murnane, "Interpreting

the Evidence on School Effectiveness," *Teachers College Record,* 83 (1981), 19–35; Donald E. MacKenzic, "Research for School Improvement: An Appraisal and Some Recent Trends," *Educational Researcher,* 12 (1983), 5–17; Brian Rowen, Steven T. Bossert, and David C. Dwyer, "Research on Effective Schools: A Cautionary Note," *Educational Researcher,* 12 (1983), 24–31; and David L. Clark, Linda S. Lotto, and Terry A. Astuto, "Effective Schools and School Improvement: A Comparative Analysis of Two Lines of Inquiry," *Educational Administration Quarterly,* 20 (1984), 41–68.

46. Hanushek, *op. cit.,* pp. 46–51.
47. Madaus, Airasian, and Kellaghan, *op. cit.,* p. 9.
48. See, for example, the following sources: Benjamin S. Bloom, *Human Characteristics and School Learning* (New York: McGraw-Hill, 1976); and Ronald Edmonds, "Some Schools Work and More Can," *Social Policy,* 9 (1979), 28–32.
49. Wilbur B. Brookover *et al.,* "Elementary School Social Climate and School Achievement," *American Educational Research Journal,* 15 (1978), 301–318.
50. John W. Stewart, "Bureaucratic Structure, Interpersonal Climate, and Student Achievement" (Ph.D. diss., University of Kansas, 1978).
51. Madaus, Airasian, and Kellaghan, *op. cit.,* pp. 105–108.
52. Steven T. Bossert, David C. Dwyer, Brian Rowen, and Ginny V. Lee, "The Instructional Management Role of the Principal," *Educational Administration Quarterly,* 18 (1982), 34–64.
53. Edwin A. Locke, "The Nature and Causes of Job Satisfaction," in Marvin D. Dunnette (ed.), *Handbook of Industrial and Organizational Psychology* (Chicago: Rand McNally, 1976), pp. 1297–1349.
54. U. S. Department of Health, Education, and Welfare, *Work in America,* Report of a Special Task Force (Cambridge, MA: MIT Press, 1973).
55. Robert Hoppock, *Job Satisfaction* (New York: Harper, 1935).
56. *Ibid.,* p. 47.
57. Victor Vroom, *Work and Motivation* (New York: Wiley, 1964), p. 99.
58. Patricia Cain Smith, "The Development of a Method of Measuring Satisfaction: The Cornell Studies," in Edwin A. Fleishman, (ed.), *Studies in Personnel and Industrial Psychology* (Homewood, IL: Dorsey, 1967), pp. 343–350.
59. Locke, *op. cit.,* p. 1300.
60. Cecil Miskel and Ed Gerhardt, "Perceived Bureaucracy, Teacher Conflict, Central Life Interests, Voluntarism, and Job Satisfaction," *Journal of Educational Administration,* 12 (1974), 84–97; Cecil Miskel, Douglas Glasnapp, and Richard Hatley, "A Test of the Inequity Theory for Job Satisfaction Using Educators' Attitudes Toward Work Motivation and Work Incentives," *Educational Administration Quarterly,* 11 (1975), 38–54; and Cecil Miskel, JoAnn DeFrain, and Kay Wilcox, "A Test of Expectancy Work Motivation Theory in Educational Organizations," *Educational Administration Quarterly,* 16 (1980), 70–92.
61. Edward A. Holdaway, *Job Satisfaction: An Alberta Report* (Edmonton, Canada: University of Alberta, 1978); and Edward A. Holdaway, "Facet and Overall Satisfaction of Teachers," *Educational Administration Quarterly,* 14 (1978), 30–47.

62. Patricia Cain Smith, L. M. Kendall, and C. L. Hulin, *The Measurement of Satisfaction in Work and Retirement* (Chicago: Rand McNally, 1969). This book is out of print and the copyright for the JDI is held by Bowling Green State University, 1975. Information concerning the scales and norms can be obtained from Dr. Patricia C. Smith, Department of Psychology, Bowling Green State University, Bowling Green, OH 43403.

63. Robert T. Golembiewski and Samuel Yeager, "Testing the Applicability of the JDI to Various Demographic Groupings," *Academy of Management Journal,* 21 (1978), 514–519.

64. Hoppock, *op. cit.,* p. 155–156.

65. Francis S. Chase, "Factors for Satisfaction in Teaching," *Phi Delta Kappan,* 33 (1951), 127–132.

66. Rex Fuller and Cecil Miskel, "Work Attachments and Job Satisfaction Among Public School Educators" (Paper presented at the annual meeting of the American Educational Research Association, Chicago, 1972), p. 8. A similar level of job satisfaction appears to exist in the general population of the United States. In the *IRS Newsletter,* 2 (1974), 7, it was reported that over the last fifteen years 80 to 95 percent of the workers say that they are satisfied with their jobs.

67. Cecil Miskel, Douglas Glasnapp, and Richard Hatley, *Public School Teachers' Work Motivation, Organizational Incentives, Job Satisfaction, and Primary Life Interests: Final Report* (Washington, DC: Office of Education, Department of Health, Education and Welfare, 1972), pp. 69–79.

68. Smith, Kendall, and Hulin, *op. cit.*

69. James G. March and Herbert A. Simon, *Organizations* (New York: Wiley, 1958).

70. Leon Festinger, *A Theory of Cognitive Dissonance* (Evanston, IL: Row, Peterson, 1957).

71. Max Abbott, "Intervening Variables in Organizational Behavior," *Educational Administration Quarterly,* 1 (1965), 1–13.

72. Miskel, Glasnapp, and Hatley, "A Test of the Inequity Theory for Job Satisfaction, Using Educators' Attitudes toward Work Motivation and Work Incentives," *op. cit.*

73. See Locke, *op. cit.;* Holdaway, *Job Satisfaction: An Alberta Report, op. cit.;* and Alan William Rice, "Individual and Work Variables Associated with Principal Job Satisfaction" (Ph.D. diss., Edmonton, Canada: University of Alberta, 1978).

74. Eugene W. Ratsoy, "Participative and Hierarchical Management of Schools: Some Emerging Generalizations," *Journal of Educational Administration,* 11 (1973), 161–170.

75. Cecil Miskel, Robert Fevurly, and John W. Stewart, "Organizational Structures and Processes, Perceived School Effectiveness, Loyalty, and Job Satisfaction," *Educational Administration Quarterly,* 15 (1979), 97–118; McGrae C. Grassie and Brian W. Carss, "School Structure, Leadership Quality, Teacher Satisfaction," *Educational Administration Quarterly,* 9 (1973), 15–26; Ed Gerhardt, "Staff Conflict, Organizational Bureaucracy, and Individual Satisfaction in Selected Kansas School Districts" (Ph.D. diss., University of Kansas, 1971); and Harrell H. Carpenter, "Formal Organizational Structural Factors and Perceived Job Satisfaction of Classroom Teachers," *Administrative Science Quarterly,* 16 (1971), 460–465.

76. Cecil Miskel, JoAnn Defrain, and Kay Wilcox, "A Test of Expectancy Work Motivation Theory in Educational Organizations," *Educational Administration Quarterly,* 16 (1980), 70–92; and Cecil Miskel, David McDonald, and Susan Bloom, "Structural and Expectancy Linkages within Schools and Organizational Effectiveness," *Educational Administration Quarterly,* 19 (1983), 49–82.

77. Miskel, Fevurly, and Stewart, *op. cit.;* and Grassie and Carss, *op. cit.*

78. C. E. Blocker and R. C. Richardson, "Twenty-five Years of Morale Research—A Critical Review," *Journal of Educational Sociology,* 36 (1963), 200–210.

79. Studies supporting this conclusion include James A. Belasco and Joseph A. Allutto, "Decisional Participation and Teacher Satisfaction," *Educational Administration Quarterly,* 8 (1972), 44–58; and Allen M. Mohrman, Jr., Robert A. Cooke, and Susan Albers Mohrman, "Participation in Decision Making: A Multidimensional Perspective," *Educational Administration Quarterly,* 14 (1978), 13–29.

80. Holdaway, *Job Satisfaction: An Alberta Report, op. cit.*

81. Jean Hagewood Nicholson, "An Analysis of Communication Satisfaction in an Urban School System" (Ph.D. diss., George Peabody College for Teachers, Vanderbilt University, 1980).

82. Arthur H. Brayfield and Walter H. Crockett, "Employee Attitudes and Employee Performance," *Psychological Bulletin,* 52 (1955), 396–424.

83. Frederick Herzberg *et al., Job Attitudes: A Review of Research and Opinion* (Pittsburgh: Psychological Service of Pittsburgh, 1957).

84. Charles N. Greene and Robert E. Craft, Jr., "The Satisfaction-Performance Controversy—Revisited," in Richard M. Steers and Lyman W. Porter (eds.), *Motivation and Work,* 2nd ed. (New York: McGraw-Hill, 1979), pp. 270–287.

85. Locke, *op. cit.,* p. 1333.

86. Robert Dubin and Daniel R. Goldman, "Central Life Interests of American Middle Managers and Specialists," *Journal of Vocational Behavior,* 2 (1972), 133–141.

87. Miskel, Glasnapp, and Hatley, "A Test of the Inequity Theory for Job Satisfaction Using Educators' Attitudes toward Work Motivation and Work Incentives," *op. cit.*

88. Miskel and Gerhardt, *op. cit.;* Miskel, Glasnapp, and Hatley, "A Test of the Inequity Theory for Job Satisfaction Using Educators' Attitudes toward Work Motivation and Work Incentives," *op. cit.;* Miskel, Defrain, and Wilcox, *op. cit.;* and Robert Dubin and Joseph E. Champous, "Central Life Interests and Job Satisfaction," *Organizational Behavior and Human Performance,* 18 (1977), 366–377.

89. Dan C. Lortie, *Schoolteacher: A Sociological Study* (Chicago: University of Chicago Press, 1975), pp. 89–100.

90. Paul E. Mott, *The Characteristics of Effective Organizations* (New York: Harper & Row, 1972).

91. Miskel, Fevurly, and Stewart, *op. cit.;* and Miskel, McDonald, and Bloom, *op. cit.*

92. Wayne K. Hoy and Judith Ferguson, "A Theoretical Framework and Exploration of Organizational Effectiveness in Schools," *Educational Administration Quarterly,* 21 (1985), 117–134.

93. Mott, *op. cit.*, pp. 179–185.

94. Miskel, Fevurly, and Stewart, *op. cit.*

95. Miskel, McDonald, and Bloom, *op. cit.*, p. 70.

96. An excellent discussion of change in schools is found in the following source: Michael Fullan, *The Meaning of Educational Change* (New York: Teachers College Press, 1982).

97. Harvey A. Hornstein *et al.*, *Social Interventions* (New York: Free Press, 1971).

98. Daniel Katz and Robert L. Kahn, *The Social Psychology of Organization,* 2nd ed. (New York: Wiley, 1978), p. 658.

99. *Ibid.*, p. 660.

100. Hornstein *et al.*, *op. cit.*, pp. 143–156.

101. Excellent discussions of changing organizational components can be found in the following sources: John Child, *Organization: A Guide to Problems and Practice,* 2nd ed. (London: Harper & Row, 1984); and Jay R. Galbraith, *Organizational Design* (Reading, MA: Addison-Wesley, 1977).

102. Edgar F. Huse and Thomas G. Cummings, *Organizational Development and Change,* 3rd. ed. (St. Paul, MN: West, 1985), p. 41.

103. Floyd C. Mann, "Studying and Creating Change: A Means to Understanding Social Organization," in Hornstein *et al.*, *op. cit.*, pp. 294–309.

104. David G. Bowers, "OD Techniques and Their Results in 23 Organizations: The Michigan ICL Study," *Journal of Applied Behavior Science,* 9 (1973), 21–43.

105. Huse and Cummings, *op. cit.*, p. 135.

106. A somewhat detailed discussion of the history of OD can be found in the following source: W. Warner Burke and Leonard D. Goodstein, *Trends and Issues in OD: Current Theory and Practice* (San Diego: University Associates, 1980).

107. C. Brooklyn Derr, " 'O. D.' Won't Work in Schools," *Education and Urban Society,* 8 (1976), 227–241.

108. Michael Fullan, Matthew B. Miles, and Gib Taylor, "Organization Development in Schools: The State of the Art," *Review of Educational Research,* 50 (1980), 121–183.

109. Hornstein *et al.*, *op. cit.*; Richard A. Schmuch and Matthew B. Miles, *Organization Development in Schools* (Palo Alto, CA: National Press Books, 1971), pp. 2–3; and Huse and Cummings, *op. cit.*, pp. 1–3.

110. Hornstein *et al.*, *op. cit.*

111. Not all scholars agree with Hornstein and his associates that these approaches represent separate sets of strategies. Huse and Cummings conceptualize organizational development as the overarching framework, with individual, survey feedback and technostructural techniques being specific approaches within the overall change strategy.

112. George J. Crawford, Cecil Miskel, and M. Claradine Johnson, "A Case Analysis of an Urban High School Renewal Program," *Urban Review,* 12 (1980), 175–199.

113. Kurt Lewin, *Field Theory in Social Science* (New York: Harper, 1951).

114. Stanley E. Seashore and David G. Bowers, "Durability of Organizational Change," *American Psychologist,* 25 (1969), 227–233.

Chapter 13

Synthesis

Management will make full use of the potential capacities of its human resources only when each person in the organization is a member of one or more effectively functioning work groups that have a high degree of group loyalty, effective skills of interaction, and high performance goals.

RENSIS LIKERT
New Patterns of Management

The preceding chapters present a substantial body of knowledge that constitutes, we hope, a strong argument for a behavioral systems approach to educational administration. In this chapter, we review the social-systems model that will serve as a theoretical synthesis of ideas developed in the text. Intrinsic dilemmas of the model will then be considered.

A MODEL OF SYNTHESIS

Systems theory (see Chapter 3) is biological rather than mechanical in origin. As a conceptual language, it is useful in describing the recurring, dynamic processes in educational organizations. According to the social-systems model for schools, organizational behavior is determined by at least four sets of key elements—bureaucratic expectations, informal norms and values, individual needs and motives, and organizational goals. These elements make up a mechanism that takes inputs from the environment and transforms them. The elements and interactions within the system are constrained by important demands from the environment as the organization solves the imperative problems of adaptation, goal achievement, integration, and latency. In addition, internal and external feedback mechanisms reinforce appropriate organizational behavior.

In brief, the model in Figure 13.1 summarizes the major external and internal features of organizations conceived as open social systems. Of course the figure cannot capture the dynamic movement of a system as it responds to its environment through internal processes and as it produces such products as student learning or employee satisfaction. Although we must dissect an organization if we are to understand its elements, we should not lose sight of the working whole.

Environment

School organizations are open systems, which must adapt to changing environmental conditions to be effective and, in the long term, to survive. The environments of schools (see Chapter 4) affect their internal structures and processes. General social, economic, political, and technological trends influence the internal operations of schools as do more specific aspects of the environment such as unions, taxpayer associations, state legislatures, state and federal regulatory agencies, and accrediting agencies. Although the general environment is similar for all organizations, specific environmental factors are more likely to vary from district to district.

Environments are complex and difficult to analyze, but three general dimensions are useful in this regard—the degree of uncertainty, clustering, and

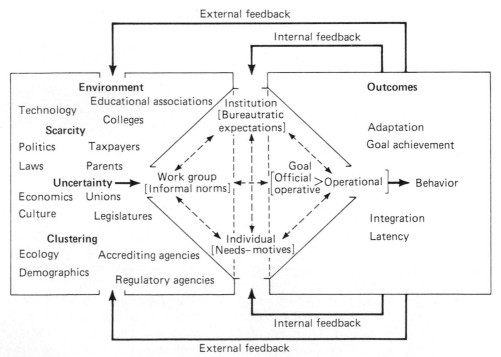

FIGURE 13.1   A social system model for schools

scarcity. The more complex and unstable the environment, the greater the uncertainty for the organization. Like all organizations, schools strive for determinateness and certainty because they are under pressure to demonstrate rationality. Clustering is the degree to which environments are organized and structured. Clustered environments produce strong constraints; in fact, the price for survival may be compliance. Finally, the degree of scarcity is the extent to which resources are available in the environment. Scarcity produces competition with other organizations for resources.

Two perspectives of the environment have been developed using these three general factors. An information perspective assumes that the environment is a source of information that will be used by organizational decision makers. Perceived organizational uncertainty affects the flexibility and bureaucratic configuration of organizations. On the other hand, the resource dependency approach assumes that organizations cannot generate internally the needed resources and that resources must come from the environment. Thus, schools must enter into exchanges and competition with environmental units to obtain the requisite products and services.

Since environmental uncertainty, scarcity of resources, and strong clustering threaten organizational autonomy and effectiveness, administrators often attempt to develop strategies to gain more control over the environment. Internal coping strategies include buffering the technical core, planning or forecasting, adjusting internal operations based on contingency theory, and spanning organizational boundaries. Interorganizational coping strategies include establishing favorable linkages with important external constituencies and shaping environmental elements through political actions.

Bureaucratic Structure

Bureaucratic structure (see Chapter 5) is the formal organization specifically established to achieve explicit goals and carry out administrative tasks. Whatever the organizational goals, such structural properties as rules, regulations, hierarchy, and division of labor are consciously designed to attain those goals effectively.

Max Weber's concept of authority is fundamental to understanding the influence of bureaucracy on social behavior. Even before joining an organization, individuals grant the use of formal authority to the organization when they voluntarily agree to comply with legitimate commands and suspend judgment in advance of the commands. These agreements are sanctioned by group norms. The beneficial result is that the formal administrative structure then has the right, within limits, to define the role expectations that influence social behavior and resulting goal attainment.

Bureaucratic authority is characteristically realized in specialization, rules and regulations, and hierarchy of authority. In Weber's analysis, bureaucracy employs authority through these means to achieve rational decision making and maximize efficiency. Division of labor and specialization produce impersonal experts who make technically correct, rational decisions based on fact. Once these decisions have been made, the hierarchy of authority implements a disciplined, coordinated compliance to directives through rules and regulations. Career-oriented employees have an incentive to be loyal and productive.

Although probably the best known, Weber's is not the only theory of organizational structure. Jerald Hage, for instance, developed an axiomatic theory that is gaining in scientific acceptance. Hage's model incorporates eight characteristics of formal organizations, four representing means and four representing ends. The means variables are centralization, formalization, complexity, and stratification; the ends variables are adaptiveness, production, efficiency, and job satisfaction. The means concepts proposed by Hage are similar to Weber's concept of bureaucracy, and the ends are derived from Talcott Parsons' analysis of the necessary functions of social systems. Of interest to us are the structural properties of the school organization and functional problems that must be solved to improve effectiveness (see Chapters 5 and 12).

Henry Mintzberg provides still another framework for examining bureaucratic structure. He describes structure simply as the ways in which an organization divides its labor into tasks and then achieves coordination among them. Mutual adjustment, direct supervision, and standardization are basic coordinating mechanisms, the glue that holds the organization together. His analysis yields five ideal types. Both Hage and Mintzberg describe organizations as structures that are influenced by their environments, that is, open systems.

A recent body of theory and research challenges some of the traditional notions of the school as a bureaucratic structure. The concept of loose coupling in schools calls attention to ambiguity in goals, unclear educational technologies, fluid participation, coordination problems, and a structure disconnected from educational outcomes. The distinctive combination of bureaucracy and structural looseness has important consequences for organizational behavior (see Chapter 5).

Individual Needs and Motives

As motivation initiates and maintains goal-directed activity, it affects outcomes. An aspect of personality, motivation is a complex of forces, drives, tensions, and expectations. Content approaches to motivation (see Chapter 7) specify only what things motivate behavior; they tend to focus on needs, motives, or expectancies. Cognitive process theories of motivations, however, are less concerned with things that motivate and more interested in behavioral processes—how behavior is started, sustained, and stopped. We discussed four theoretical formulations to describe motivation in a social system. Note the interplay of this individual element with structure, informal organization, and organizational goals.

Abraham H. Maslow's theory views individual needs rising in five hierarchical levels. These include physiological, security, belongingness, esteem, and self-actualization. Significantly, higher-level needs do not become active until lower-level needs are met. Maslow hypothesizes that motivational needs at the higher levels promote behavior that is more important to the organization and vice versa. Another popular content approach to motivation is Frederick Herzberg's motivation-hygiene theory. Motivators and hygienes are separate sets of components that contribute, respectively, to job satisfaction and job dissatisfaction. Like Maslow, Herzberg posited that expectations drawn from motivator factors result in behavior leading to higher personal as well as organizational goals.

Expectancy theory, formulated for work settings by Victor Vroom, is the most widely accepted cognitive process approach to motivation. The model assumes fundamentally that individual choice is predictively related to psychological events manifested in behavior. Hypothetically, motivation, in the strict sense of the word, is the product of expectancy, valence, and instrumentality. When employees perceive a high level of performance as personally satisfying, they will try to perform better.

Edwin Locke originally proposed goal theory as a cognitive process. He defined a goal as what an individual is consciously trying to do. Intentions to achieve a goal constitute the primary motivating forces of work behavior. Two postulates undergird the formulation: specific goals are superior to general goals, and difficult goals, when accepted, lead to greater effort than easy goals.

Organizational Goals

Organizational goals are distinct from personal motives. Although personal motives at times intrude on organizational goals, many of the requirements that organizations impose on their members are unaffected by personal motives. Organizational goals are sets of constraints imposed by the organization, which have only an indirect relation with the personal motives of members. Sometimes organizational goals are set by one powerful actor at the top of the hierarchy; less frequently goals are consensually defined by all participants who share in goal setting; however, most frequently goals are set by a process of negotiations that occurs among dominant coalitions in the organization.

Goals have different functions. Boards of education typically focus on abstract, inspirational goals as they seek to legitimate organizational action to various publics. Administrators are most likely to emphasize the cognitive function of goals since it is a basic way for them to shape and direct subordinate behavior. Subordinates will likely use goals as justification for past performance when called upon to explain their behaviors. And supervisors and external groups often stress the evaluation function of goals as they assess the performance outcomes of the organization.

Three different kinds of goals were defined in our analysis of behavior in social systems—official, operative, and operational goals. Official goals serve to justify and legitimate school activities as well as to motivate and generate commitment. Operative goals reflect the actual functioning of the school and probably both direct and justify school behavior. Operational goals are formal statements used by the organization to direct and evaluate performance.

The Work-Group Atmosphere

Our analysis of the internal atmosphere of schools focused on three related and overlapping concepts—informal organization, climate, and culture (see Chapter 8). Each of these notions goes beyond the formal and individual aspects of organizational life. Each suggests a natural, spontaneous, and human side to organization; each suggests that the whole is greater than the sum of its parts; and each deals with shared meanings and unwritten rules that guide organizational behavior.

Informal organization is a system of interpersonal relations that forms spontaneously within all formal organizations as members interact in their workplace. Teachers within schools inevitably generate their own informal system: informal norms, unofficial status and power networks; informal communication systems, and informal working arrangements and behaviors. This natural ordering and structuring of organizational life is a critical ingredient for explaining organizational behavior.

Organizational climate is a relatively enduring quality of the school environment that is experienced by members, affects their behavior, and is based on their collective perceptions of behavior in schools. A climate emerges through the interaction of members and exchange of sentiments among them. The climate of a school is its "personality." Three different conceptualizations of climate were described and analyzed.

When schools have an open climate, we find that principals and faculty are acting authentically, but when the climate is closed, everyone simply goes through the motions of education without dedication and commitment. As might be expected, research has shown that such affective characteristics as positive student and faculty attitudes are related to openness of climate.

The climate of schools can also be examined in terms of organizational health. A healthy school is one that is meeting both its instrumental and expressive needs, while successfully coping with disruptive outside forces as it directs its energies toward its mission. The healthier the organizational dynamics of a school, the greater are the trust and openness in member relations.

Finally, the social climate of schools was conceived along a continuum of pupil control orientation ranging from custodial to humanistic. This formulation is based on the dominant expectations teacher and principals have of how their methods would control student behavior. Schools with custodial expectations are rigidly controlled settings in which the primary concern is order. In contrast, humanistic schools are characterized by an emphasis on student self-discipline and cooperative student-teacher actions and experiences. A humanistic climate is associated with less student alienation and goal displacement than a custodial climate.

Organizational culture is the set of shared orientations that holds a unit together and gives it a distinctive identity. Although climate tends to focus on shared perceptions, culture is defined in terms of shared assumptions, values, and norms. These three levels of culture—assumptions, values, and norms—are explored as alternative ways of describing and analyzing schools. Recent research on business organizations suggests that effective organizations have strong corporate cultures: cultures characterized by intimacy, trust, cooperation, egalitarianism, a bias for action, and orientations that stress quality, innovation, and people.

Outcomes and Products

Expectations defined by the bureaucracy, group, and individual combine to determine whether organizational and personal goals will be attained (see Chapter 12). When goals are achieved, the school organization is effective, an assertion compatible with Parsons' system variables of adaptation, goal attainment, integration, and latency. These four functions act as multiple operative goals for organizations; that is, they guide in the selection of effectiveness measures as defined by multiple constituencies for schools over the short and long term. Effectiveness of educational organizations is not one thing; it is a complex multidimensional phenomenon.

Feedback Loops

The knowledge of the outcomes enters two different types of feedback loops. Internally, the relative level of goal achievement serves as an indicator of the need to adjust to one or more of the organizational dimensions. Externally, the school's products are evaluated by the community. The evaluation provides informational input and influences the bureaucratic structure, goals, work group, and individual personalities.

Put bluntly, administrators are responsible for school effectiveness. On one hand, they must respond to the expectations and information carried in the feedback loops, and on the other hand, they must maintain or increase goal-directed behavior of teachers, students, and other employees. One of the major administrative problems—control of outcomes—requires not only the allocation of resources but also the integration of the four organizational dimensions (structure, goals, work group, and individual personality). Fulfillment of administrative functions requires the exercise of leadership, decision making, and communication.

Leadership

Leadership is behavior that demonstrates a concern for the task, for individuals, and for interpersonal or group relations. Stated differently, it is a sequence of activities by a leader (e.g., administrator, teacher, or student) that sets the tone of their interactions with one another and for their performance behavior. The literature generally supports a dual leadership model (see Chapter 9). That is, it recognizes two general and distinct categories of leader behavior—one concerned with people and interpersonal relations, and the other with organizational structure and task achievement.

The Ohio State leadership studies, using the leader behavior description questionnaire (LBDQ), isolated two dimensions of leader behavior with this measure—initiating structure and consideration. Initiating structure is that dimension of behavior that delineates the relationship between the leader and subordinates while establishing defined patterns of organization, channels of communication, and methods of procedure. Consideration is that dimension of behavior that indicates friendship, trust, warmth, interest, and respect between the leader and individuals in the work group. Administrative behavior derived from initiating structure probably focuses on bureaucratic structure and formal goals to modify outcomes. In contrast, behavior derived from consideration is more likely to emphasize individual needs and the informal aspects of the work group to change organizational outcomes.

Research indicates that school administrators generally are more effective when they are high on both consideration and initiating structure. Based on the above assertions, this is expected because such administrators could work effectively on all the social systems elements to influence work behavior. Although a strong showing on both dimensions is highly desirable, administrators seemingly can compensate for weakness in one with unusual strength in the other. In some situations, high initiating structure may be more important than consideration in affecting educational outcomes (see Chapter 9). The early Michigan survey research studies and the Harvard studies of group leadership basically supported the Ohio State findings.

Fred Fiedler's Contingency Model was an important contribution to leadership theory because it combined style, situation, and effectiveness variables. The style variable, having to do with whether individuals are relationship-oriented or task-oriented individuals, is conceptually similar to the LBDQ subscales of consideration and initiating structure. Again, the theory postulates that the leader emphasizes a particular dimension of the social systems model in order to modify outcomes. Fiedler recognized that the variables to be changed must be considered in conjunction with the leader's style and the organization's situational components. He argued that the variables comprising the style and situation must be matched to maximize effectiveness. The research findings support two generalizations: (1) task-oriented leaders are more effective in situations that are highly favorable or in situations that are relatively unfavorable, and (2) relationship-oriented leaders tend to be more effective in situations that are moderate in terms of favorableness.

Robert House's Path-Goal Theory of leadership postulated that leadership behavior is acceptable and satisfying to followers when it is a source of either immediate or future satisfaction. Directive behavior in unstructured situations increases satisfaction by clarifying the path to goal achievement. Conversely, considerate behavior in structured situations enhances effectiveness by reducing tensions likely to be created by an unnecessary and more direct approach.

Leadership in schools is a complex process. It involves more than the mastering of a set of leadership skills or the matching of the appropriate leader behavior with a specific situation. Leadership is an instrumental and behavioral activity, but it is also a symbolic and cultural one. Successful leaders infuse value, affect informal norms, and create institutional meaning and purpose that go beyond the technical demands of the job. In brief, school leaders must be able to influence and work through all of the key elements of the school social system—bureaucratic structure, formal goals, individuals, and the work group. Administrators are aided in this regard through two other processes—decision making and communication.

Decision Making

Decision making is behavior that is exhibited in selecting and implementing a course of action from among alternatives (see Chapter 10). This behavior affects the different dimensions of school organization and their outcomes. Therefore, an understanding of the decision-making process is vital to successful administration.

Although completely rational decision making is impossible, administrators need a systematic process to enhance the selection of satisfactory solutions; hence, a strategy of satisficing is central to administrative decision making. The process is conceptualized as being cyclical with distinct phases: recognition and definition of a problem, analysis of difficulties, establishment of criteria of success, development of an action plan, and the initiation and appraisal of the plan. Due to its cyclical nature, administrators go through the stages repeatedly. This administrative strategy is well-suited for dealing with most problems. Occasionally, however, the set of alternatives is undefinable or the consequences of each alternative are unpredictable with respect of a given aspiration level; here an incremental strategy is more appropriate. This process is a method of successive limited comparisons; only a limited set of alternatives, similar to the existing situation, is considered by successively comparing their consequences until agreement is reached on a course of action.

Research suggests the quality of administrative action can be judged by the amount of preparation for implementing a course of action, and by the amount of work done in making the decision. Effective decision makers engage in substantial preliminary work; they seek more information; differentiate between fact and opinion; and frequently encourage subordinate participation in the process. In complex organizations communication is necessary to translate the decisions into concrete action.

Communication

Communication is behavior that conveys the desired meaning of a message between two or more parties (see Chapter 11). The initiation of structure, the development of considerate relationships, and the implementation of decisions become reality through this administrative behavior. Communication is dynamic because it is a method of acting that continually affects the different elements of social organization.

The sociopsychological model of communication postulates that individuals stimulate psychological processes of other persons when interacting in social situations. The messages, transmitted through a variety of verbal and nonverbal media traverse the formal hierarchical channels or informal group channels. In the context of communication, the feedback loops are mechanisms to ensure high levels of understanding.

Administrative Behavior, Interdependent Elements, and Equifinality

We have been arguing that administrative behavior must be considered in relation to the primary dimensions or elements of a social organization. Bureaucratic structure, goals, work group, and individual motivation represent "leverage points" that can be used to influence the performance of organizational members.[1] Two major generalizations are apparent. First leadership, decision making, and communication modify outcomes. If one dimension is consciously manipulated by a leader, a ripple effect is created, the other dimensions are affected, and a new combination of expectations and behaviors results. Second, a variety of means is available to reach desired goals (the principle of equifinality).

Table 13.1 contains three examples of the first generalization. Assume leadership behavior is changed (through training or replacement) so that the principal recognizes and rewards outstanding teacher performance. As a result, such higher levels of motivation as recognition and achievement are emphasized. But when this input occurs, role expectations and incentives must also be raised, achievement goals will be specified, and the group may increase the normative expectations regarding what constitutes appropriate standards. Therefore, all four dimensions are modified, thus increasing the quality outcome, as the result of a change directed primarily at a single dimension or leverage point.

Similarly, decentralizing the decision-making process delegates formal authority to individuals lower in the organization's structure. This represents a change in the system's bureaucratic dimension. The decrease in the hierarchy of authority results in modified role expectations and perhaps a change in goal. Consequently, more people will be interacting, and the climate should become more open and participative. Decentralization also alters the individual dimension by increasing the emphasis on responsibility and risk. Thus, changing one part modifies the other dimensions with the behavioral outcome being an increase in group work activity.

A final example occurs when the levels of informal communication increase between superordinates and subordinates (see Table 13.1). This represents a change in the group dimension. As the climate changes, information exchange and behavior that is mutually supportive increase. Indirectly, the bureaucratic expectation of impersonalization will decrease, formal goals may change, and the individual expectations for personal integrity, self-respect, and independent choice will increase. An effect on behavior is an increase in subordinate and superordinate interaction, which should result in better decisions, higher loyalty, and greater individual satisfaction.

Thus, administrative behavior works through leverage on each dimension of a social system to affect the school's outcomes. A given administrator may rely

TABLE 13.1 **Anticipated Effects of Administrative Behavior on the Elements of the Social System and Observed Behavior**

Administrative Behavior	*Anticipated Effects on Social System Elements*	*Anticipated Behavioral Effects*
LEADERSHIP Recognize and reward excellent performance	Bureaucracy—more differentiated role expectations Goal—set performance standards Group—raised normative standards Individual—more emphasis on higher levels of motivation	Increase in outcome quality—higher job satisfaction and effectiveness
DECISION MAKING Place the decision-making authority close to the problem's origin (decentralization)	Bureaucracy—decrease in the hierarchy of authority Goal—more participation Group—more open or participative climate Individual—increased emphasis on responsibility and risk factors of motivation	Increase in group work activity
COMMUNICATION Maintain informal information exchanges	Bureaucracy—decrease impersonalization Goal—reduce formal communication Group—increase in normative support Individual—increase in identity and emphasis on social needs	Increase in superordinate-subordinate interaction

primarily on a single leverage point (e.g., improving the work group climate), but the resulting interaction will influence the bureaucratic, goal, and individual dimensions as well.

The preceding conclusion leads to the second major generalization regarding the concept of equifinality. If a particular outcome is desired, a number of different administrative actions can be used on any leverage point to attain similar results. In other words, different patterns of administrative behavior and organizational expectations can lead to the same outcome. The implication from this statement is that a variety of alternatives exists to improve the effectiveness of educational organizations; there is no one best way. The challenge is to match the strengths of the administrators or leaders with appropriate leverage points.

CONTINUING DILEMMAS

Although both change and dilemmas will, apparently, always be with us, dilemmas, unlike change, need not accelerate. Peter M. Blau and W. Richard Scott maintain that the concept of dilemma contributes to our understanding internal pressures for change.[2] A dilemma arises when one is confronted by decision alternatives in which any choice sacrifices some valued objectives in the interest of others. Daniel Katz and Robert L. Kahn have elaborated on this definition by distinguishing between problems and dilemmas.[3] Problems are difficulties that can be solved by past precedents or by the application of existing policy. Dilemmas are not soluble within the existing framework. Solutions and perfect adjustments are impossible. Because dilemmas are endemic to social organizations, they serve as perpetual sources of change.

The fundamental dilemma facing formal organizations is order versus freedom. Both order and freedom are desirable and necessary conditions for high levels of effectiveness, but increasing one decreases the other. The tension between order and freedom is manifest in three operational dilemmas: coordination and communication, bureaucratic discipline and professional expertise, and managerial planning and individual initiative. These elements or dimensions have been discussed throughout the book.[4]

Coordination and Communication

Two-way communication with unrestricted exchange of ideas, criticism, and advice contributes to effective problem solving in at least three ways: it furnishes social support to individual participants; it provides an error-correcting mechanism; and it fosters a healthy competition for respect.

Problem-solving situations often produce stress and anxiety for individual participants and lead to mental blocks that interfere with effective development of their thinking. However, when individuals communicate openly, good ideas are likely to receive the approval of others (thus reducing anxiety) and to promote further participation, development, and refinement of ideas; hence, social support derived from an unrestricted exchange of ideas aids in problem solving.

It is not easy for a person to detect mistakes in his or her own thinking. An individual takes a set framework to the problem-solving situation that makes it difficult to see the problem from a different perspective. Open and free-flowing communication brings a variety of perspectives, experiences, and information to bear on the common task; hence, the chances of identifying an error in thinking are increased. Other members of the group are more prone to spot inconsistencies and blind spots than the individual; therefore, two-way communication facilitates error correction. Finally, open, two-way communication motivates members of a group to make expert suggestions in order to win the respect and esteem of fellow participants.

While the free flow of information improves problem solving, it also impedes coordination. Unrestricted communication may drown effective action in a sea of conflicting ideas. True, information helps in selecting good ideas, but too many ideas hinder agreement, and coordination requires agreeing on a single master plan.

Coordination in organizations is accomplished primarily through hierarchical differentiation, but such structure impedes decision making because it interferes with the free flow of information (see Chapter 5). In fact, differentiation, centralized direction, and restricted communication appear essential for effective coordination. In brief, those very things that enhance the coordination process also hinder the free flow of communication. Organizations require both effective coordination and effective problem solving. But the hierarchical structure in organizations that facilitates efficient coordination also impedes communication and problem solving. The dilemma seems inherent in the conflicting requirements of coordination and problem solving because there is the simultaneous need for restricted and unrestricted communication. The conflict, which causes adaptation and change, cannot be readily resolved and needs continuing attention.

Bureaucratic Discipline and Professional Expertise

The similarities and differences between the characteristics of professional and bureaucratic orientation (see Chapter 6) lead to a second dilemma. While both orientations stress technical competence, objectivity, impersonality, and service, the unique structure of the professions is a basic source of conflict. Professionals attempt to control themselves through self-imposed standards and group surveillance. In contrast, bureaucratic employees are expected to adhere to rules and regulations and to subordinate themselves to the hierarchy. The ultimate basis for a professional act is the professional's knowledge; the ultimate justification of a bureaucratic act is its consistency with organizational rules and regulations and approval by a superior. The conflict is between professional expertise and autonomy, and bureaucratic discipline and control. The significance of the discord is brought into sharp focus when we examine employees who are subject to both forms of social control: professionals working in bureaucracies.

There are different ways to resolve the strain created by the merger of these two institutional means of control. In some organizations, major structural changes have been instituted through the development of two separate authority lines—one professional and one administrative. Nonetheless, when professional considerations conflict with bureaucratic ones, dividing authority seems to be a partial solution at best. Without organizational change some individuals (called locals, upwardly mobiles, indifferents, ambivalents, and cosmopolitans) attempt to accommodate themselves to the conflict by developing role orientations that are compatible to the bureaucracy or the profession, and some adopt orientations that are compatible with both. Although accommodation is made, the conflict remains a continuing dilemma and thus a fundamental issue.

Professional expertise and bureaucratic discipline are alternative modes of coping with uncertainty. Discipline restricts its scope, while expertise provides knowledge and social support to cope with uncertainty. Blau and Scott held that the struggle will remain as long as professionals are employed in bureaucratic organizations. It seems likely that the professional-bureaucratic dilemma will become an even more significant internal one in schools as teachers and administrators become more professionalized and continue to function in school organizations that are essentially bureaucratic in nature.

Managerial Planning and Individual Initiative

According to Blau and Scott, a third manifestation of the tension between order and freedom is the need for both managerial planning and individual initiative. The disharmony between them poses a major difficulty in the administrative process, which includes not only the development of plans to solve problems but their subsequent implementation and appraisal. The setting of organizational decision making is the organization as a collectivity. The exercise of any independent judgment must be compatible with the thrust of the formal organization. There is continuous pressure from the formal organization through its elaborate bureaucratic machinery to subordinate individual initiative to organizational directives. The organization is, of course, interested in creative, individual efforts, but only when they do not conflict with formal plans.

How can the organization encourage individual initiative without confounding administrative planning? We have suggested a number of organizational responses. Two models for shared decision making have been introduced that delineate under what conditions the individual should be involved in the decision-making process (see Chapter 10). The arrangement calls for harnessing the creative initiative of individuals in a constructive way that is beneficial to both the organization and the person. We have sketched the characteristics of a professional organizational structure in which emphasis would be placed on shared decision making rather than on autocratic bureaucracy (see Chapter 6). Further, we described a number of organizational climates—the open climate, the healthy school climate, and the humanistic school—that would tend to lessen the conflict between compliance and initiative (see Chapter 8).

In brief, organizations can be structured and organizational climates and cultures can be developed that minimize the conflict between administrative planning and individual initiative. This is not to suggest that the dilemma can be resolved. The best that we can probably hope for is a healthy balance between compliance and initiative, a balance continually disrupted by the conflicting need for order and freedom.

CONCLUSION

The position that we have held throughout this book embodies what Peter F. Drucker calls "reality."[5] Knowledge has become the central resource. The systematic acquisition of knowledge—that is, organized formal education—must supplement experience as the foundation for increasing productive capacity and improving performance. Increasingly, performance will depend on the ability to use concepts, ideas, and theories as well as skills acquired through experience.

The dilemmas we have explored demand basic changes in administrators. They require new training, knowledge, and policies and a sloughing off of deeply entrenched practices of today's society. The practice of administration can become one of deepened dilemmas or of heightened achievements. We hold that a path to the latter is through further theory and research in educational organizations.

NOTES

1. This discussion and Table 13.1 were strongly influenced by the writings of George H. Litwin and Robert A. Stringer, Jr., *Motivation and Organizational Climate* (Cambridge, MA: Harvard University Press, 1968), pp. 168–170, 178–186.
2. Peter M. Blau and W. Richard Scott, *Formal Organizations: A Comparative Approach* (San Francisco: Chandler, 1962), pp. 223–224, 242–250.
3. Daniel Katz and Robert L. Kahn, *The Social Psychology of Organizations,* 2nd ed. (New York: Wiley, 1978), pp. 760–773.
4. The discussion that follows is based on the narrative of Blau and Scott, *op. cit.*
5. Peter F. Drucker, *The Age of Discontinuity* (New York: Harper & Row, 1968), pp. 38–41.

Bibliography

Abbott, Max. "Hierarchical Impediments to Innovation in Educational Organizations," in Max Abbott and John Lovell (eds.), *Change Perspectives in Educational Administration* (Auburn, AL: Auburn University, 1965), pp. 40–53.

———. "Intervening Variables in Organizational Behavior," *Educational Administration Quarterly,* 1 (1965), 113.

Abramowitz, Susan, and Ellen Tenenbaum. *High School '77.* Washington, DC: National Institute for Education, 1978.

Adkinson, Judith A. "Women in School Administration: A Review of the Research," *Review of Educational Research,* 51 (1981), 311–343.

Adler, Seymour, Richard B. Skov, and Nat J. Salvemini. "Job Characteristics and Job Satisfaction: When Cause Becomes Consequence," *Organizational Behavior and Human Decision Processes,* 35 (1985), 266–278.

Aiken, Michael, and Jerald Hage. "Organizational Alienation: A Comparative Analysis," *American Sociological Review,* 31 (1966), 497–507.

———, and Jerald Hage. "Organizational Interdependence and Intra-Organizational Structure," *American Sociological Review,* 33 (1968), 912–930.

Alderfer, Clayton P. *Existence, Relatedness, and Growth: Human Needs in Organizational Settings* (New York: Free Press, 1972).

———, and Richard A. Guzzo. "Life Experiences and Adults' Enduring

Strength of Desires in Organizations," *Administrative Science Quarterly,* 24 (1979), 347–361.

Aldrich, Howard E. *Organizations and Environment* (Englewood Cliffs, NJ: Prentice-Hall, 1979).

————, and Sergio Mindlin. "Uncertainty and Dependence: Two Perspectives on Environment," in Lucien Karpik (ed.), *Organization and Environment: Theory, Issues and Reality* (Beverly Hills, CA: Sage, 1978), pp. 149–170.

————. "An Organization-Environment Perspective on Cooperation and Conflict between Organizations in the Manpower Training System," in Amant R. Negandi (ed.), *Conflict and Power in Complex Organizations* (Kent, OH: Center for Business and Economic Research, Kent State University, 1972), pp. 11–37.

————, and Jeffrey Pfeffer. "Environments of Organizations," *Annual Review of Sociology,* 2 (1976), 79–105.

————, and Diane Herker. "Boundary Spanning Roles and Organization Structure," *Academy of Management Review,* 2 (1977), 217–230.

Allen, Robert F., and C. Kraft. *The Organizational Unconscious: How to Create the Corporate Culture You Want and Need* (Englewood Cliffs, NJ: Prentice-Hall, 1982).

Allutto, Joseph A., and James A. Belasco. "Patterns of Teacher Participation in School System Decision Making," *Educational Administration Quarterly,* 9 (1973), 27–41.

Andersen, Kenneth E. "Variant Views of the Communicative Act," in Howard H. Martin and Kenneth E. Andersen (eds.), *Speech Communication: Analysis and Readings* (Boston: Allyn and Bacon, 1968), pp. 2–23.

Anderson, Barry. "Socio-Economic Status of Students and Schools Bureaucratization," *Educational Administration Quarterly,* 7 (1971), 1224.

Andersen, Donald P. *Organizational Climate of Elementary Schools,* Research Monograph No. 1. Minneapolis: Educational Research and Development Council, 1964.

Anderson, James G., and Stephen J. Jay. "The Diffusion of Medical Technology: Social Network Analysis and Policy Research," *Sociological Quarterly,* 26 (1985), 49–64.

Anderson, John. "Giving and Receiving Feedback," in Paul R. Lawrence, Louis B. Barnes, and Jay W. Lorsch (eds.), *Organizational Behavior and Administration* (Homewood, IL: Irwin, 1976), pp. 103–111.

Anderson, Mary Beth G., and Edward F. Iwanicki. "Teacher Motivation and Its Relationship to Burnout," *Educational Administration Quarterly,* 20 (1984), 109–132.

Andrews, John H. M. "School Organizational Climate: Some Validity Studies," *Canadian Education and Research Digest,* 5 (1965), 317–334.

Appleberry, James B., and Wayne K. Hoy. "The Pupil Control Ideology of Professional Personnel in 'Open' and 'Closed' Elementary Schools," *Educational Administration Quarterly,* 5 (1969), 74–85.

Argyris, Chris. "Interpersonal Barriers to Decision Making," *Harvard Business Review,* 44 (1966), 84–97.

————. *Personality and Organizations* (New York: Harper, 1957).

Aristotle. *Politics,* Book I, Chapter 5.

Arnold, Hugh J., and Robert J. House. "Methodological and Substantive Extensions to the Job Characteristics Model of Motivation," *Organizational Behavior and Human Performances,* 25 (1980), 161–183.

Ashford, Susan J., and L. L. Cummings. "Feedback as an Individual Resource: Personal Strategies for Creating Information," *Organizational Behavior and Human Performance,* 32 (1983), 370–398.

Ashforth, Blake E. "Climate Formations: Issues and Extensions," *Academy of Management Review,* 10 (1985), 837–847.

Atkinson, J. W. *An Introduction to Motivation* (Princeton, N.J.: Van Nostrand, 1964).

———, and Joel O. Raynor. *Motivation and Achievement* (Washington, DC: Winston, 1974).

Averich, H. A., S. J. Carroll, T. S. Donaldson, H. J. Kiesling, J. Pincus. *How Effective Is Schooling: A Critical Review and Synthesis of Research Findings* (Santa Monica, CA: Rand, 1972).

Babbie, Earl R. *Survey Research Methods* (Belmont, CA: Wadsworth, 1973).

Balderson, James H. "Who Likes the 'Good' School?" *The Canadian Administrator,* 16 (1977), 1–4.

Bales, Robert F. "In Conference," *Harvard Business Review,* 32 (1954), 41–49.

———, and P. Slater. "Role Differentiation in Small Decision-making Groups," in Talcott Parsons *et al. Family, Socialization, and Interaction Process* (New York: Free Press, 1955), 259–306.

Baltzell, D. Catherine, and Robert A. Dentler. *Selecting American School Principals: A Sourcebook for Educators* (Cambridge, MA: Abt Associates, 1983), pp. 3–17 and 33–34.

Barley, Stephen R. "Semiotics and the Study of Occupational Cultures," *Administrative Science Quarterly,* 28 (1983), 393–413.

Barnard, Chester I. "Comments on the Job of the Executive," *Harvard Business Review,* 18 (1940), 295–308.

———. *Functions of an Executive* (Cambridge, MA: Harvard University Press, 1938).

Barnes, R. M. *Motion and Time Study* (New York: Wiley, 1949).

Barnett, Bruce G. "Subordinate Teacher Power in School Organizations," *Sociology of Education,* 57 (1984), 43–55.

Bass, Bernard M. *Organizational Decision Making* (Homewood, IL: Irwin, 1985), pp. 54–56.

Bates, Richard. "Educational Administration, The Sociology of Science, and the Management of Knowledge," *Educational Administration Quarterly,* 16 (1980).

Beehr, Terry A., and Kevin G. Love. "A Meta-Model of the Effects of Goal Characteristics, Feedback, and Role Characteristics in Human Organizations," *Human Relations,* 36 (1983), 151–166.

Belasco, James A., and Joseph A. Allutto. "Decisional Participation and Teacher Satisfaction," *Educational Administration Quarterly,* 8 (1972), 44–58.

Bennis, Warren G. "Leadership Theory and Administrative Behavior," *Administrative Science Quarterly,* 4 (December 1959), 259–301.

Benson, J. Kenneth. "The Interorganizational Network as a Political Economy," *Administrative Science Quarterly,* 20 (1975), 229–249.

Berlo, David K. *The Process of Communication.* (New York: Holt, Rinehart & Winston, 1970).

Bess, James L. "The Motivation to Teach," *Journal of Higher Education,* 48 (1977), 243–258.

Betz, Ellen L. "Two Tests of Maslow's Theory of Need Fulfillment," *Journal of Vocational Behavior,* 24 (1984), 204–220.

Bhagat, Rabi S., and Marilyn B. Chassie. "Effects of Changes in Job Characteristics on Some Theory-Specific Attitudinal Outcomes: Results from a Naturally Occurring Quasi-Experiment," *Human Relations,* 33 (1980), 297–313.

Bidwell, Charles E. "The School as a Formal Organization," in James G. March (ed.), *Handbook of Organization* (Chicago: Rand McNally, 1965), pp. 972–1022.

———, and John D. Kasarda. "School District Organization and Student Achievement," *American Sociological Review,* 40 (1975), 55–70.

Bierstedt, Robert. *Emile Durkheim* (Great Britain: Dell, 1966).

Birnbaum, Robert. "Presidential Succession: An Interinstitutional Analysis," *Educational Record,* 52 (1971), 133–145.

Bishop, Lloyd, and Julius R. George. "Organizational Structure: A Factor Analysis of Structural Characteristics of Public Elementary and Secondary Schools," *Educational Administration Quarterly,* 9 (1973), 66–80.

Blake, Robert R., and Jane S. Mouton. *The Managerial Grid III* (Houston, TX: Gulf, 1985).

———, and Jane S. Mouton. "A Comparative Analysis of Situationalism and 9, 9 Management by Principle," *Organizational Dynamics,* 10 (Spring 1982), 20–34.

———, and Jane S. Mouton. *The Versatile Manager: A Grid Profile* (Homewood, IL: Irwin, 1980).

Blau, Peter M. *Bureaucracy in Modern Society* (New York: Random House, 1956).

———. *Exchange and Power in Social Life* (New York: Wiley, 1964).

———. *The Dynamics of Bureaucracy* (Chicago: University of Chicago Press, 1955).

———, and W. Richard Scott. *Formal Organizations: A Comparative Approach* (San Francisco: Chandler, 1962).

Blocker, C. E., and R. C. Richardson. "Twenty-five Years of Morale Research —A Critical Review," *Journal of Educational Sociology,* 36 (1963), 200–210.

Bloom, Benjamin S. *Human Characteristics and School Learning* (New York: McGraw-Hill, 1976).

Bobbitt, Franklin. "Some General Principles of Management Applied to the Problems of City School Systems," in *The Supervision of City Schools,* Twelfth Yearbook of the National Society for the Study of Education, Part I (Chicago: University of Chicago Press, 1913) 137–196.

Boje, David M., and David A. Whetten. "Effects of Organizational Strategies and Contextual Constraints on Centrality and Attributions of Influence in Interorganizational Networks," *Administrative Science Quarterly,* 26 (1981), 378–395.

Bolman, Lee G., and Terrence E. Deal. *Modern Approaches to Understanding and Managing Organizations* (San Francisco: Jossey-Bass, 1984).

Bossert, Steven T., David C. Dwyer, Brian Rowen, and Ginny V. Lee. "The Instructional Management Role of the Principal," *Educational Administration Quarterly,* 18 (1982), 34–64.

Bowditch, James L., and Anthony F. Buono. *A Primer on Organizational Behavior* (New York: Wiley, 1985), p. 158.

Bowers, David G. "OD Techniques and Their Results in 23 Organizations: The Michigan ICL Study," *Journal of Applied Behavioral Science,* 9 (1973), 21–43.

———. *Systems of Organizations: Management of the Human Resource* (Ann Arbor, MI: University of Michigan Press, 1976).

———, and Stanley E. Seashore. "Predicting Organizational Effectiveness with a Four-Factor Theory of Leadership," *Administrative Science Quarterly,* 11 (1966), 238–264.

Boyan, Norman J. "A Study of the Formal and Informal Organization of a School Faculty: The Identification of the Systems of Interactions and Relationships Among the Staff Members of a School and an Analysis of the Interplay Between These Systems" (Ed.D. thesis, Harvard University, 1951), p. 269.

Boyd, William L., and Robert L. Crowson. "The Changing Conception and Practice of Public School Administration," *Review of Research in Education,* 9 (1981), 311–373.

———. "The Public, the Professional, and Educational Policy Making: Who Governs?" *Teachers College Record,* 77 (1976), 539–577.

Brady, Laurie. "The 'Australian' OCDQ: A Decade Later," *Journal of Educational Administration,* 23 (1985), 53–58.

Braybrook, David, and Charles E. Lindblom. *The Strategy of Decision* (New York: Free Press, 1963).

Brayfield, Arthur H., and Walter H. Crockett. "Employee Attitudes and Employee Performance," *Psychological Bulletin,* 52 (1955), 396–424.

Bridges, Edwin M. "Bureaucratic Role and Socialization: The Influence of Experience on the Elementary Principal," *Educational Administration Quarterly,* 1 (1965), 19–28.

———. "A Model for Shared Decision Making in the School Principalship," *Educational Administration Quarterly,* 3 (1967), 49–61.

———. "Teacher Participation in Decision Making," *Administrator's Notebook,* 12 (1964), 1–4.

———, and Maureen T. Hallinan. "Subunit Size, Work System Interdependence, and Employee Absenteeism," *Educational Administration Quarterly,* 14 (1978), 24–42.

———, and Wayne J. Doyle. "The Effects of Hierarchial Differentiation on Group Productivity, Efficiency, and Risk Taking," *Administrative Science Quarterly,* 13 (1968), 305–319.

Brookover, Wilbur B., John H. Schweitzer, Jeffrey M. Schneider, Charles H. Beady, Patricia K. Flood, and Joseph M. Wisenbaker. "Elementary School Social Climate and School Achievement," *American Educational Research Journal,* 15 (1978), 301–318.

Brown, Alan F. "Reactions to Leadership," *Educational Administration Quarterly,* 3 (1967), 62–73.

———. "Research in Organizational Dynamics: Implications for School Administrators," *Journal of Educational Administration,* 5 (1967), 43–44.

———. "Two Strategies for Changing Climate," *CAS Bulletin,* 4 (1965), 64–80.

Brown, M. Craig. "Administrative Succession and Organizational Performance: The Succession Effect," *Administrative Science Quarterly,* 27 (1982), 1–16.

Brown, Robert J. *Organizational Climate of Elementary Schools,* Research Monograph No. 2 (Minneapolis: Educational Research and Development Council, 1965).

Burke, W. Warner, and Leonard D. Goodstein. *Trends and Issues in OD: Current Theory and Practice* (San Diego: University Associates, 1980).

Burlingame, Martin. "Some Neglected Dimensions in the Study of Educational Administration," *Educational Administration Quarterly,* 15 (1979), 1–18.

Burns, Tom, and G. M. Stalker. *The Management of Innovation* (London: Travistock, 1961).

Burrell, Gibson, and Gareth Morgan. *Sociological Paradigms and Organizational Analysis* (London: Heinemann, 1980).

Burt, Ronald S. "Models of Network Structure," *Annual Review of Sociology,* 6 (1980), 79–141.

————, and Michael J. Minor (eds.). *Applied Network Analysis* (Beverly Hills, CA: Sage, 1984).

Callahan, Raymond E. *Education and the Cult of Efficiency* (Chicago: University of Chicago Press, 1962).

Cameron, Kim. "Measuring Organizational Effectiveness in Institutions of Higher Education," *Administrative Science Quarterly,* 23 (1978), 604–632.

————, and David A. Whetten. *Organizational Effectiveness: A Comparison of Multiple Models* (New York: Academic, 1983).

————. "The Effectiveness of Ineffectiveness," *Research in Organizational Behavior,* 6 (1984), 235–285.

Campbell, John P. "On the Nature of Organizational Effectiveness," in Paul S. Goodman and Johannes M. Pennings (eds.), *New Perspectives on Organizational Effectiveness* (San Francisco: Jossey-Bass, 1977), pp. 13–55.

————, Marvin D. Dunnette, Edward E. Lawler III, and Karl E. Weick, Jr. *Managerial Behavior, Performance, and Effectiveness* (New York: McGraw Hill, 1970).

————, and Robert D. Pritchard. "Motivation Theory in Industrial and Organizational Psychology," in Marvin D. Dunnette (ed.), *Handbook of Industrial and Organizational Psychology* (Chicago: Rand McNally, 1976), pp. 63–130.

Campbell, Roald. "NCPEA—Then and Now" (Paper presented at the National Conference of Professors of Educational Administration meeting, University of Utah, August 1971).

Campfield, William L. "Motivating the Professional Employee," *Personnel Journal,* 44 (1965), 425–428, 442.

Carlson, Richard O. "Environmental Constraints and Organizational Consequences: The Public School and Its Clients," in Daniel E. Griffiths (ed.), *Behavioral Science and Educational Administration* (Chicago: University of Chicago Press, 1964), pp. 262–276.

————. *Executive Succession and Organizational Change* (Chicago: University of Chicago, Midwest Administration Center, 1962).

Carpenter, Harrell H. "Formal Organizational Structural Factors and Perceived Job Satisfaction of Classroom Teachers," *Administrative Science Quarterly,* 16 (1971), 460–465.

Carper, William B., and William E. Snizek. "The Nature and Types of Organizational Taxonomies: An Overview," *Academy of Management Review*, 5 (1980), 65–75.

Carroll, Stephen, and Henry Tosi. "Goal Characteristics and Personality Factors in a Management by Objective Program," *Administrative Science Quarterly*, 15 (1970), 295–305.

Cartwright, Dorwin, and Alvin Zander. *Group Dynamics: Research and Theory.* 3rd ed. (Evanston, IL: Row, Peterson, 1968).

Carver, Fred D., and Thomas J. Sergiovanni. "Notes on the OCDQ," *Journal of Educational Administration*, 7 (1969), 71–81.

Chapman, David W., and Sigrid M. Hutcheson. "Attrition from Teaching Careers: A Discriminant Analysis," *American Educational Research Journal*, 19 (1982), 93–105.

Charters, W. W., Jr. *Measuring the Implementation of Differentiated Staffing* (Eugene, Ore.: Center for the Advanced Study of Educational Administration, 1973).

————. "Stability and Change in the Communication Structure of School Faculties," *Educational Administration Quarterly*, 3 (1967), 15–38.

Chase, Francis S. "Factors for Satisfaction in Teaching," *Phi Delta Kappan*, 33 (1951), 127–132.

Chemers, Martin M., and G. J. Skrzypek. "Experimental Test of Contingency Model of Leadership Effectiveness," *Journal of Personality and Social Psychology*, 24 (1972), 172–177.

Child, John. *Organization: A Guide to Problems and Practices*, 2nd ed. (London: Harper & Row, 1984).

Chisolm, Grace B., Roosevelt Washington, and Mary Thibodeaux. "Job Motivation and the Need Fulfillment Deficiencies of Educators" (Paper presented at the Annual Meeting of the American Educational Research Association, Boston, 1980).

Clark, David L., Linda S. Lotto, and Terry A. Astuto. "Effective Schools and School Improvement: A Comparative Analysis of Two Lines of Inquiry," *Educational Administration Quarterly*, 20 (1984), 41–68.

Clark, Peter B., and James Q. Wilson. "Incentive Systems: A Theory of Organizations," *Administrative Science Quarterly*, 6 (1961), 129–166.

Clear, Delbert K., and Roger C. Seager. "The Legitimacy of Administrative Influence as Perceived by Selected Groups," *Educational Administration Quarterly*, 7 (1971), 46–63.

Coch, Lester, and John R. P. French, Jr. "Overcoming Resistance to Change," *Human Relations*, 1 (1948), 512–532.

Coleman, James S. *The Adolescent Society* (New York: Free Press, 1961).

————, E. Q. Campbell, C. J. Hobson, J. McPartland, A. M. Mood, F. D. Weinfeld, and R. L. York. *Equality of Educational Opportunity* (Washington, DC: U.S. Government Printing Office, 1966).

Commons, John R. *Legal Foundations of Capitalism* (New York: Macmillan, 1924).

Conant, James B. *Science and Common Sense* (New Haven: Yale University Press, 1951).

Connolly, Terry, Edward J. Conlon, and Stuart Jay Deutsch. "Organizational Effectiveness: A Multiple-Constituency Approach," *Academy of Management Review*, 5 (1980), 211–217.

Constas, Helen. "Max Weber's Two Conceptions of Bureaucracy," *American Journal of Sociology*, 63 (1958), 400–409.

Conway, James A. "Test of Linearity Between Teachers' Participation in Decision Making and Their Perceptions of Schools as Organizations," *Administrative Science Quarterly*, 21 (1976), 130–139.

———. "The Myth, Mystery, and Mastery of Participative Decision Making in Education," *Educational Administration Quarterly*, 3 (1984), 11–40.

"Corporate Culture: The Hard-to-Change Values that Spell Success or Failure," *Business Week* (October 27), 148–160.

Corwin, Ronald G. "The Professional Employee: A Study of Conflict in Nursing Roles," *American Journal of Sociology*, 66 (1961), 604–615.

———. "Professional Persons in Public Organizations," *Educational Administration Quarterly*, 1 (1965), 1–22.

———. *Staff Conflicts in the Public Schools* (Washington, DC: U.S. Office of Education, Cooperative Research Project No. 2637, 1966).

Cosgrove, Dorothy. The Effects of Principal Succession on Elementary Schools (Ph.D. diss., University of Utah, 1985).

Crawford, George J., Cecil Miskel, and M. Claradine Johnson. "A Case Analysis of an Urban High School Renewal Program," *Urban Review*, 12 (1980), 175–199.

Crehan, Ellen Patricia. "A Meta-Analysis of Fiedler's Contingency Model of Leadership Effectiveness" (Ed.D. diss., University of British Columbia, 1985).

Crowson, Robert L., and Cynthia Porter-Gehrie. "The Discretionary Behavior of Principals in Large City Schools," *Educational Administration Quarterly*, 16 (1980), 45–69.

Culbertson, Jack A. "Three Epistemologies and the Study of Educational Administration," *UCEA Review*, 22 (1981).

———, Robin Farquar, Bryce M. Fogarty, and Mark R. Shibles. *Social Science Content for Preparing Educational Leaders* (Columbus, OH: Merrill, 1973).

Cyert, Richard M., and James G. March. *A Behavioral Theory of the Firm* (Englewood Cliffs, NJ: Prentice-Hall, 1963).

Daft, Richard L. *Organization Theory and Design* (St. Paul: West, 1983).

———, and Robert H. Lengel. "Information Richness: A New Approach to Managerial Behavior and Organizational Design," *Research in Organizational Behavior*, 6 (1984), 191–233.

Dance, Frank E. X. "The 'Concept' of Communication," *Journal of Communication*, 20 (1970), 201–210.

Daniel, T. L., and J. K. Esser. "Intrinsic Motivation as Influenced by Rewards Task Interest, and Task Structure," *Journal of Applied Psychology*, 65 (1980), 566–573.

Danridge, Thomas, Ian I. Mitroff, and William F. Joyce. "Organizational Analyses," *Academy of Management Review*, 5 (1980), 77–82.

Davis, Keith. *Human Relations at Work* (New York: McGraw-Hill, 1967).

———. "Management Communication and the Grapevine," *Harvard Business Review*, 31 (1953), 43–49.

———. "Methods for Studying Informal Communication," *Journal of Communication*, 28 (1978), 112–116.

————. "Methods of Studying Communication Patterns in Organization," *Personnel Psychology,* 6, 1953, 301–312.

————. "Success of Chain-of Command Oral Communication in a Manufacturing Management Group," *Academy of Management Journal,* 11 (1968), 379–387.

Deal, Terrence E., and Lynn D. Celotti. "How Much Influence Do (And Can) Educational Administrators Have on Classrooms?" *Phi Delta Kappan,* 61 (1980), 471–473.

————, and Allen A. Kennedy. *Corporate Cultures* (Reading, MA: Addison-Wesley, 1982).

Deci, Edward L. *Intrinsic Motivation* (New York: Plenum, 1975).

DeFleur, M. L., and O. N. Larson. *The Flow of Information* (New York: Harper, 1958).

Derr, C. Brooklyn. " 'O.D.' Won't Work in Schools," *Education and Urban Society,* 8 (1976), 227.

Dewey, John. *How We Think* (Boston: Heath, 1933).

————. *The Sources of a Science of Education* (New York: Horace Liveright, 1929).

Diebert, John P., and Wayne K. Hoy. "Custodial High Schools and Self-Actualization of Students," *Educational Research Quarterly,* 2 (1977), 24–31.

Dill, R. William. "Environment as an Influence on Managerial Autonomy," *Administrative Science Quarterly,* 2 (1958), 409–443.

DiMaggio, Paul, and Walter Powell. "The Iron Cage Revisited: Institutional Isomorphism and Collective Rationality in Organizational Fields," *American Sociological Review,* 48 (1983), 147–160.

Downey, H. Kirk, Don Hellriegel, and John W. Slocum, Jr. "Environmental Uncertainty: The Construct and Its Application," *Administrative Science Quarterly,* 20 (1975), 613–629.

Downs, Cal W. *Organizational Communicator* (New York: Harper & Row, 1977).

————, and Michael D. Hazen. "A Factor Analytic Study of Communication Satisfaction," *Journal of Business Communication,* 14 (1977), 63–73.

Drucker, Peter F. *The Age of Discontinuity* (New York: Harper & Row, 1968).

————. *The Effective Executive* (New York: Harper & Row, 1966).

————. *Managing in Turbulent Times* (New York: Harper & Row, 1980).

————. *The Practice of Management* (New York: Harper & Row, 1954).

————. *Management: Tasks and Responsibilities* (New York: Harper and Row, 1974).

Dubin, Robert. *Theory Building* (New York: Free Press, 1969).

————, and Daniel R. Goldman. "Central Life Interests of American Middle Managers and Specialists," *Journal of Vocational Behavior,* 2 (1972), 133–141.

————, and Joseph E. Champous. "Central Life Interests and Job Satisfaction," *Organizational Behavior and Human Performance,* 18 (1977), 366–377.

Duncan, Robert B. "Characteristics of Organizational Environments and Perceived Environmental Uncertainty," *Administrative Science Quarterly,* 17 (1972), 313–327.

————. "What is the Right Organizational Structure? Decision Free Analysis Provides the Answer," *Organizational Dynamics,* 7 (1979), 59–80.

Duke, Daniel L., Beverly K. Showers, and Michael Imber. "Teachers and

Shared Decision Making: The Costs and Benefits of Involvement," *Educational Administration Quarterly,* 16 (1980), 93–106.

Dyer, W. Gibb, Jr., "The Cycle of Cultural Evolution in Organization," Ralph H. Kilmann *et al. Gaining Control of the Corporate Culture* (San Francisco: Jossey-Bass, 1985), pp. 200–230.

Edmonds, Ronald. "Some Schools Work and More Can," *Social Policy,* 9 (1979), 28–32.

Einstein, Albert, and Leopold Infeld. *The Evolution of Physics* (New York: Simon & Schuster, 1938).

Emerson, Richard. "Power-Dependence Relations," *American Sociological Review,* 27 (1962), 31–41.

Emery, Fred E., and Eric L. Trist. "The Causal Texture of Organization Environments," *Human Relations,* 18 (1965), 21–23.

Erez, Miriam P., Christopher Earley, and Charles L. Hulin. "The Impact of Participation on Goal Acceptance and Performance: A Two Step Model," *Academy of Management Journal,* 28 (1985), 50–66.

Etzioni, Amitai. *A Comparative Analysis of Complex Organizations* (New York: Free Press, 1961).

———. *Modern Organizations* (Englewood Cliffs, NJ: Prentice-Hall, 1964).

———. "Two Approaches to Organizational Analysis: A Critique and Suggestion," *Administrative Science Quarterly,* 5 (1960), 257–278.

Evans, Martin G. "The Effects of Supervisory Behavior on the Path-Goal Relationships," *Organizational Behavior and Human Performance,* 5 (1970), 277–298.

———, Moses N. Kiggundu, and Robert J. House. "A Partial Test and Extension of the Job Characteristics Model of Motivation," *Organizational Behavior and Human Performance,* 24 (1979), 354–381.

Feigl, Herbert. "Principles and Problems of Theory Construction in Psychology," in *Current Trends in Psychological Theory* (Pittsburgh: University of Pittsburgh Press, 1951).

Festinger, Leon. *A Theory of Cognitive Dissonance* (Evanston, IL: Row, Peterson, 1957).

Fiedler, Fred. "The Contingency Model and the Dynamics of the Leadership Process," *Advances in Experimental Social Psychology,* 11 (1973), 60–112.

———. "The Leadership Game: Matching the Man to the Situation," *Organizational Dynamics,* 7 (1976), 6–16.

———. *A Theory of Leadership Effectiveness* (New York: McGraw-Hill, 1967).

———. "Validation and Extension of the Contingency Model of Leadership Effectiveness: A Review of Empirical Findings," *Psychological Bulletin,* 76 (1971), 128–148.

———, and Albert F. Leister. "Leader Intelligence and Task Performance: A Test of a Multiple Screen Model," *Organizational Behavior and Human Performance,* 20 (1977), 1–14.

———, and Martin M. Chemers. *Leadership and Effective Management.* (Glenview, IL: Scott, Foresman, 1974).

———, Martin M. Chemers, and Linda Mahar. *Improving Leadership Effectiveness: The Leader Match Concept* (New York: Wiley, 1976).

———. *Leadership* (New York: General Learning Press, 1971).

———, and Martin M. Chemers. *Improving Leadership Effectiveness,* 2nd ed. (New York: Wiley, 1984).

Field, George R. H. "A Critique of the Vroom-Yetton Contingency Model of Leadership Behavior," *The Academy of Management Review*, 4 (1979), 249–257.

Filley, Alan, Robert House, and Steven Kerr. *Managerial Process and Organizational Behavior* (Glenview, IL: Scott, Foresman, 1976).

Firestone, William A., and Robert E. Herriott. "Two Images of Schools as Organizations: An Explication and Illustrative Empirical Test," *Educational Administration Quarterly*, 18 (1982), 39–60.

——, and Bruce L. Wilson. "Using Bureaucratic and Cultural Linkages to Improve Instruction: The Principal's Contribution," *Educational Administration Quarterly*, 21 (1985), 7–31.

Fleishman, Edwin A. "Twenty Years of Consideration and Structure," in Edwin A. Fleishman and James G. Hunt (eds.), *Current Developments in the Study of Leadership* (Carbondale, IL: Southern Illinois University Press, 1973), pp. 1–37.

Follett, Mary Parker. *Creative Experience* (London: Longmans and Green, 1924).

——. *Dynamic Administration: The Collected Papers of Mary Parker Follett*, Henry C. Metcalf and Luther Urwick (eds.) (New York: Harper, 1941).

Forsyth, Patrick B., and Wayne K. Hoy. "Isolation and Alienation in Educational Organizations," *Educational Administration Quarterly*, 14 (1978), 80–96.

——, and Thomas J. Danisiewicz. "Toward a Theory of Professionalization," *Work and Occupations*, 12 (1985), 59–76.

Foster, William P. "Administration and Crisis in Legitimacy: A Review of Habermasean Thought," *Harvard Educational Review*, 50 (1980).

Frasher, James M., and Ramona S. Frasher. "Verification of Administrative Attribution Theory" (Paper presented at the Annual Meeting of the American Educational Research Association, Boston, 1980).

Freidson, Eliot. "The Changing Nature of Professional Control," *Annual Review of Sociology*, 10 (1984), 1–20.

Fromm, Erich. *Man for Himself* (New York: Farrar & Rinehart, 1948).

Frost, Peter J., Larry F. Moore, Meryl Reis Louis, Craig C. Lundberg, and Joanne Martin. *Organizational Culture* (Beverly Hills, CA: Sage, 1985).

Fullan, Michael, Matthew B. Miles, and Gib Taylor. "Organization Development in Schools: The State of the Art," *Review of Educational Research*, 50 (1980), 121–183.

——. *The Meaning of Educational Change* (New York: Teachers College Press, 1982).

Fuller, Rex, and Cecil Miskel. "Work Attachments and Job Satisfaction Among Public School Educators" (Paper presented at the Annual Meeting, American Educational Research Association, Chicago, 1972).

Fusilier, Marcelline R., Daniel C. Ganster, and R. Dennis Middlemist. "A Within-Person Test of the Form of the Expectancy Theory Model in a Choice Context," *Organizational Behavior and Human Performance*, 34 (1984), 323–342.

Futrell, Mary H. *The Teaching Profession* (Washington, DC: National Education Association, 1983).

Gaertner, Karen N. "The Structure of Organizational Career," *Sociology of Education*, 53 (1980), 7–20.

Galbraith, Jay, and L. L. Cummings. "An Empirical Investigation of the Motivational Determinants of Task Performance: Interactive Effects Between Instrumentality-Valence and Motivation-Ability," *Organization Behavior and Human Performance,* 2 (1967), 237–257.

————. *Organizational Design* (Reading, MA: Addison-Wesley, 1977).

Gamson, William A., and Norman A. Scotch. "Scapegoating in Baseball," *American Journal of Sociology,* 70 (1964), 69–72.

Ganz, Harold J., and Wayne K. Hoy. "Patterns of Succession of Elementary Principals and Organizational Change," *Planning and Changing,* 8 (1977), 185–196.

Gerhardt, Ed. "Staff Conflict, Organizational Bureaucracy, and Individual Satisfaction in Selected Kansas School Districts" (Ph.D. diss., University of Kansas, 1971).

Gerth, H. H., and C. Wright Mills (eds.). *From Max Weber: Essays in Sociology* (New York: Oxford University Press, 1946).

Getzels, Jacob W., and Egon G. Guba. "Social Behavior and the Administrative Process," *School Review,* 65 (1957), 423–441.

————, and H. A. Thelen. "The Classroom Group as a Unique Social System," *The Dynamics of Instructional Groups,* The Fifty-ninth Yearbook of the National Society for the Study of Education, Part II (Chicago: University of Chicago Press, 1960), pp. 52–83.

————, James M. Lipham, and Roald F. Campbell. *Educational Administration as a Social Process: Theory, Research, and Practice* (New York: Harper and Row, 1968).

Gibb, Cecil A. "Leadership," in Gardner Lindzey (ed.). *Handbook of Social Psychology* (Cambridge, MA: Addison-Wesley, 1954), pp. 877–920.

Gibson, James L., John M. Ivancevich, and James H. Donnelly, Jr. *Organizations: Behavior, Structure, and Processes,* rev. ed. (Dallas, TX: Business Publications, 1976).

Glaser, Barney. "The Local-Cosmopolitan Scientist," *American Journal of Sociology,* 69 (1965), 249–259.

Glauser, Michael J. "Upward Information Flow in Organizations: Review and Conceptual Analysis," *Human Relations,* 8 (1984), 613–643.

Goffman, Erving. "The Characteristics of Total Institutions," in *Symposium on Prevention and Social Psychiatry* (Washington, DC: Walter Reed Army Institute of Research, 1957), pp. 43–84.

Golembiewski, Robert T., and Samuel Yeager. "Testing the Applicability of the JDI to Various Demographic Groupings," *Academy of Management Journal,* 21 (1978), 514–519.

Goodman, Paul S., and Johannes M. Pennings. "Toward a Workable Framework," in Paul S. Goodman and Johnnes M. Pennings (eds.), *New Perspectives on Organizational Effectiveness* (San Francisco: Jossey-Bass, 1977), pp. 147–184.

Gordon, C. Wayne. *The Social System of the High School* (New York: Free Press, 1957).

Gordon, Hedy H. "Communication Analysis of Administrators in an Academic Organization" (Master's thesis, University of Kansas, 1979).

Gordon, Gil E., and Ned Rosen. "Critical Factors in Leadership Succession," *Organizational Behavior and Human Performance,* 27 (1981), 227–254.

Gouldner, Alvin. "Cosmopolitans and Locals: Toward an Analysis of Latent Social Roles—I," *Administrative Science Quarterly,* 2 (1957), 291–306.

————. "Organizational Analysis," in Robert K. Merton, Leonard Broom, and Leonard S. Cottrell, Jr. (eds.), *Sociology Today* (New York: Basic Books, 1959), pp. 400–428.

————. "Cosmopolitans and Locals: Toward an Analysis of Latent Social Roles —II," *Administrative Science Quarterly,* 2 (1958), 444–479.

————. *Patterns of Industrial Bureaucracy* (New York: Free Press, 1964).

————. *Studies in Leadership* (New York: Harper, 1950).

Graen, George. "Instrumentality Theory of Work Motivation: Some Experimental Results and Suggested Modifications," *Journal of Applied Psychology* Monograph, 53 (1963), 1–25.

Graham, Linda L. "Expectancy Theory as a Predictor of College Student Grade Point Average, Satisfaction, and Participation" (Ph.D. diss., University of Kansas, 1980).

Grandori, Anne. "A Prescriptive Contingency View of Organizational Decision Making," *Administration Science Quarterly,* 29 (1984), 192–208.

Grassie, McGrae C., and Brian W. Carss. "School Structure, Leadership Quality, Teacher Satisfaction," *Educational Administration Quarterly,* 9 (1973), 15–26.

Greene, Charles N. "Disenchantment with Leadership Research: Some Causes, Recommendations, and Alternative Directions," in James G. Hunt and Lars J. Larson (eds.), *Leadership: The Cutting Edge* (Carbondale, IL: Southern Illinois University Press, 1977).

————, and Robert E. Craft, Jr. "The Satisfaction-Performance Controversy—Revisited," in Richard M. Steers and Lyman W. Porter (eds.), *Motivation and Work,* 2nd ed. (New York: McGraw-Hill, 1979), pp. 270–287.

Greenfield, Thomas B. "The Man Who Comes Back Through the Door in the Wall: Discovering Truth, Discovering Self, Discovering Organizations," *Educational Administration Quarterly,* 16 (1980), 26–59.

————. "Theory About Organizations: A New Perspective and Its Implications for Schools," in Meredydd Hughes (ed.), *Administering Education: International Challenge* (London: Athlane, 1975).

————. "Ideas Versus Data: How Can the Data Speak for Themselves?" in G. L. Immegart and W. W. Boyd (eds.), *Problem-Finding in Educational Administration: Trends in Research and Practice* (Lexington, MA: Heath, 1979), pp. 97–112.

————. "Reflections on Organization Theory and the Truths of Irreconcilable Realities," *Educational Administration Quarterly,* 14 (1978), 1–23.

————. "Organization Theory as Ideology," *Curriculum Inquire* 9 (1979).

Griffeth, Rodger W. "Moderation of the Effects of Job Enrichment by Participation: A Longitudinal Field Experiment," *Organizational Behavior and Human Decision Processes,* 35 (1985), 73–93.

Griffin, Ricky W. "Objective and Social Sources of Information in Task Redesign: A Field Experiment," *Administrative Science Quarterly,* 28 (1983), 184–200.

Griffiths, Daniel E. *Administrative Theory* (New York: Appleton-Century-Crofts, 1959).

————. "Intellectual Turmoil in Educational Administration," *Educational Administration Quarterly,* 15 (1979), 43–65.

————. "Some Thoughts About Theory in Educational Administration—1975," *UCEA Review,* 17 (1975).

————. "The Individual in Organizations: A Theoretical Perspective," *Educational Administrative Quarterly,* 13 (1977), 1–18.

————, David L. Clark, D. Richard Wynn, and Laurence Iannaccone (eds.). *Organizing Schools for Effective Education* (Danville, IL: Interstate, 1962).

Gross, Edward, and Amitai Etzioni. *Organizations in Society* (Englewood Cliffs, NJ: Prentice Hall, 1985).

Grusky, Oscar. "Corporate Size, Bureaucratization, and Managerial Succession," *American Journal of Sociology,* 67 (1961), 261–269.

————. "Administrative Succession in Formal Organizations," *Social Forces,* 39 (1960), 105–115.

Guba, Egon G. "Morale and Satisfaction: A Study in Past-Future Time Perspective," *Administrative Science Quarterly,* 3 (1958), 195–209.

Guest, Robert H. *Organizational Change: The Effect of Successful Leadership* (Homewood, IL: Dorsey, 1960).

Guetzkow, Harold. "Communication in Organizations," in James G. March (ed.), *Handbook of Organizations* (Chicago: Rand McNally, 1965), pp. 534–573.

Guidette, Mary R. M. "The Relationship between Bureaucracy and Staff Sense of Powerlessness in Secondary Schools" (Ed.D. diss., Rutgers University, 1982).

Guzzo, J. Richard. "Types of Rewards, Cognitions, and Work Motivation," *Academy of Management Review,* 4 (1979), 75–86.

Hackman, J. Richard, and J. Lloyd Suttle. *Improving Life at Work* (Santa Monica, CA: Goodyear, 1977).

————, and Edward E. Lawler III. "Employee Reactions to Job Characteristics," *Journal of Applied Psychology* Monograph 55 (1971).

————, and Greg R. Oldham, "Development of the Job Diagnostic Survey," *Journal of Applied Psychology,* 60 (1975), 159–170.

————, and Greg R. Oldham, "Motivation through the Design of Work: A Test of a Theory," *Organizational Behavior and Human Performance,* 16 (1976), 250–279.

————, and Greg R. Oldham, *Work Redesign* (Reading, MA: Addison-Wesley, 1980).

Hage, Jerald. "An Axiomatic Theory of Organizations," *Administrative Science Quarterly,* 10 (1965), 289–320.

————. *Techniques and Problems of Theory Construction in Sociology* (New York: Wiley, 1972).

————. *Theories of Organizations* (New York: Wiley, 1980), p. 40.

Hall, A. D., and R. E. Fagen. "Definition of a System," *General Systems: The Yearbook of the Society for General Systems Research,* 1 (1956), pp. 18–28.

Hall, Douglas T., and Cynthia V. Fukami. "Organizational Design and Adult Learning," *Research in Organizational Behavior,* 1, (1979), 125–167.

Hall, Jay. "Communication Revisited," *California Management Review,* 15 (1973), 56–67.

Hall, Oswald. "Some Problems in the Provision of Medical Services," *Canadian Journal of Economics and Political Science,* 20 (1954), 456–466.

Hall, Richard H. "The Concept of Bureaucracy: An Empirical Assessment," *American Sociological Review,* 27 (1962), 295–308.

————. *Organizations: Structure and Process* (Englewood Cliffs, NJ: Prentice-Hall, 1972).

———, J. E. Haas, and Norman Johnson. "An Examination of the Blau-Scott and Etzioni Typologies," *Administrative Science Quarterly* 12 (1967), 118–139.

Halpin, Andrew W. (ed.). *Administrative Theory in Education* (Chicago: Midwest Administration Center, University of Chicago, 1958).

———. "Change and Organizational Climate," *Journal of Educational Administration,* 5 (1967), 5–25.

———. *The Leader Behavior of School Superintendents* (Columbus, OH: College of Education, Ohio State University, 1956).

———. "The Superintendent's Effectiveness as a Leader," *Administrator's Notebook,* 6 (1958), 1–4.

———. *Theory and Research in Administration* (New York: Macmillan, 1966).

———, and B. J. Winer. *The Leadership Behavior of the Airplane Commander* (Washington, DC: Human Resources Research Laboratories, Department of the Air Force, 1952).

———, and Don B. Croft. *The Organizational Climate of Schools* (U.S. Office of Education, Research Project (Contract #SAE 543-8639, August 1962).

Hammond-Darling, Linda. *Beyond the Commission Reports: The Coming Crisis in Teaching* (Santa Monica, CA: Rand, 1984).

Hannan, Michael T., and John Freeman. "Obstacles to Comparative Studies," in Paul S. Goodman and Johannes M. Pennings (eds.), *New Perspectives on Organizational Effectiveness* (San Francisco: Jossey-Bass, 1977), pp. 106–131.

———, and John Freeman. "Structural Inertia and Organizational Change," *American Sociological Review,* 49 (1984), 149–164.

———, and John Freeman. "The Population Ecology of Organizations," *American Journal of Sociology,* 82 (1977), 929–964.

Hanes, Robert C., and Kay F. Mitchell. "Teacher Career Development in Charlotte-Mecklenburg," *Educational Leadership,* 43 (1985), 11–13.

Hanushek, Eric A. "A Reader's Guide to Educational Production Functions" (Paper presented at the Conference on School Organization and Effects, National Institute of Education, 1978).

Hartley, Marvin, and Wayne K. Hoy. "Openness of School Climate and Alienation of High School Students," *California Journal of Educational Research,* 23 (1972), 17–24.

Hayes, Andrew E. "A Reappraisal of the Halpin-Croft Model of the Organizational Climate of Schools" (Paper presented at the Annual Meeting of the American Educational Research Association, New Orleans, 1973).

Haymond, John E. "Bureaucracy, Climate, and Loyalty: An Aston Study in Education" (Ed.D. diss., Rutgers University, 1982).

Heath, D. H. "Student Alienation and Schools," *School Review,* 78 (1970), 515–528.

Heider, Fritz. *The Psychology of Interpersonal Relations* (New York: Wiley, 1958).

———. "Social Perception and Phenomenal Causality," *Psychological Review,* 51 (1944), 358–374.

Helsel, A. Ray. "Personality and the Pupil Control Behavior" (Paper presented at the Annual Meeting of the American Educational Research Association, Chicago, 1974).

Hemphill, John K. "Administration as Problem Solving," in Andrew W. Halpin (ed.), *Administrative Theory in Education* (New York: Macmillan, 1958), pp. 89–118.

———. "Personal Variables and Administrative Styles," *Behavioral Science and Educational Administration,* Sixty-third Yearbook of the National Society for the Study of Education, Part II (Chicago: University of Chicago Press, 1964), pp. 178–198.

———, and Alvin E. Coons. *Leader Behavior Description.* (Columbus, OH: Personnel Research Board, Ohio State University, 1950).

———, Daniel E. Griffiths, and Norman Frederiksen. *Administrative Performance and Personality* (New York: Teachers College, Columbia University, 1962).

Henderson, James E., and Wayne K. Hoy. "Leader Authenticity: The Development and Test of an Operational Measure," *Educational and Psychological Research,* 2 (1983), 123–130.

Heneman, H. G. III, and D. P. Schwab. "An Evaluation of Research on Expectancy Theory Predictions of Employee Performance," *Psychological Bulletin,* 78 (1972), 1–9.

Herrick, H. Scott. "Organizational Structure and Teacher Motivation in Multiunit and Non-multiunit Elementary Schools" (Unpublished doctoral dissertation, University of Wisconsin, 1974).

———. "The Relationship of Organizational Structure to Teacher Motivation in Multiunit and Non-multiunit Elementary Schools," Technical Report No. 322. (Madison, WI: Wisconsin Research and Development Center for Cognitive Learning, The University of Wisconsin, Madison, Wisconsin, ERIC Document ED 101442, 1973.)

Hersey, Paul, and Kenneth H. Blanchard. *Management of Organizational Behavior: Utilizing Human Resources,* 3rd ed. (Englewood Cliffs, NJ: Prentice-Hall, 1977).

———, and Kenneth H. Blanchard. *Management of Organizational Behavior: Utilizing Human Resources,* 4th ed. (Englewood Cliffs, NJ: Prentice-Hall, 1982).

Herriot, Robert E., and William A. Firestone. "Two Images of Schools as Organizations: A Refinement and Elaboration," *Educational Administration Quarterly,* 20 (1984), 41–58.

Herzberg, Frederick, Bernard Mausner, R. O. Peterson, and Dora F. Capwell. *Job Attitudes: Review of Research and Opinion* (Pittsburgh: Psychological Service of Pittsburgh, 1957).

———, Bernard Mausner, and Barbara Snyderman. *The Motivation to Work* (New York: Wiley, 1959).

Hetzel, Robert W. "The Relationship Between Organizational Structure and Organizational Adaptability in Departments of Curriculum and Instruction" (Ph.D. diss., University of Wisconsin, 1971).

Heydebrand, W. "Organizational Contradictions in Public Bureaucracies: Toward a Marxian Theory of Organization," in J. K. Benson, *Organizational Analysis,* (Beverly Hills, CA: Sage, 1977).

Holdaway, Edward A. "Facet and Overall Satisfaction of Teachers," *Educational Administration Quarterly,* 14 (1978), 30–47.

———. *Job Satisfaction: An Alberta Report* (Edmonton, Alberta: University of Alberta, 1978).

———, John F. Newberry, David J. Hickson, and R. Peter Heron. "Dimensions of Organizations in Complex Societies: The Educational Sector," *Administrative Science Quarterly,* 20 (1975), 37–58.

Homans, George C. *The Human Group* (New York: Harcourt, Brace and World, 1950).

Hoppock, Robert. *Job Satisfaction* (New York: Harper, 1935).

Hornstein, Harvey A., Barbara B. Bunker, Warner W. Burke, Marion Gindes, and Roy J. Lewicki. *Social Intervention* (New York: Free Press, 1971).

House, Robert J. "A Path-Goal Theory of Leadership Effectiveness," *Administrative Science Quarterly,* 16 (1971), 321–338.

———. "A Path-Goal Theory of Leader Effectiveness," in Edwin A. Fleishman and James G. Hunt (eds.), *Current Developments in the Study of Leadership* (Carbondale, IL: Southern Illinois University Press, 1973), pp. 141–177.

———, and L. A. Wigdor. "Herzberg's Dual-Factor Theory of Job Satisfaction and Motivation: A Review of the Evidence and a Criticism," *Personnel Psychology,* 20 (1967), 369–390.

———, and Mary L. Baetz. "Leadership: Some Empirical Generalizations and New Research Directions," *Research in Organizational Behavior,* 1 (1979), 341–423.

———, and Terence R. Mitchell. "Path-Goal Theory and Leadership," *Journal of Contemporary Business,* 3 (1974), 81–97.

Hoy, Wayne K. "Dimensions of Student Alienation and Characteristics of Public High Schools," *Interchange,* 3 (1972), 38–51.

———. "Pupil Control and Organizational Socialization: The Influence of Experience on the Beginning Teacher," *School Review,* 76 (1968), 312–323.

———. "Organizational Socialization: The Student Teacher and Pupil Control Ideology," *Journal of Educational Research,* 61 (1967), 153–155.

———. "Pupil Control Ideology and Organizational Socialization: A Further Examination of the Influence of Experience on the Beginning Teacher," *School Review,* 77 (1969), 257–265.

———. "Scientific Research in Educational Administration," *Educational Administration Quarterly,* 14 (1978), 1–12.

———, and Fred Aho. "Patterns of Succession of High School Principals and Organizational Change," *Planning and Changing,* 2 (1973), 82–88.

———, and James B. Appleberry. "Teacher Principal Relationships in 'Humanistic' and 'Custodial' Elementary Schools," *Journal of Experimental Education,* 39 (1970), 27–31.

———, and Leonard B. Williams. "Loyalty to Immediate Superior at Alternate Levels in Public Schools," *Educational Administration Quarterly,* 7 (1971), 1–11.

———, Richard Blazovsky, and Wayne Newland. "Organizational Structure and Alienation from Work" (Paper presented at the American Educational Research Association, Boston, 1980).

———, Richard Blazovsky and Wayne Newland. "Bureaucracy and Alienation: A Comparative Analysis," *The Journal of Educational Administration,* 21 (1983), 109–121.

———, and Richard Rees. "The Bureaucratic Socialization of Student Teachers," *Journal of Teacher Education,* 28 (1977), 23–26.

———, and Richard Rees. "Subordinate Loyalty to Immediate Superior: A Neglected Concept in the Study of Educational Administration," *Sociology of Education,* 47 (1974), 268–286.

————, Wayne Newland, and Richard Blazovsky. "Subordinate Loyalty to Superior, Esprit, and Aspects Bureaucratic Structure," *Educational Administration Quarterly,* 13 (1977) 71–85.

————, and Leonard B. Williams, "Loyalty to Immediate Superior at Alternate Levels in Public Schools," *Educational Administration Quarterly,* 7 (1971), 1–11.

————, and David Sousa. "Delegation: The Neglected Aspect of Participation in Decision Making," *Alberta Journal of Educational Research,* 30 (1984), 320–331.

————, and Judith Ferguson. "A Theoretical Framework and Exploration of Organizational Effectiveness in Schools," *Educational Administration Quarterly,* 21 (1985), 117–134.

————, and Sharon I. R. Clover. "Elementary School Climate: A Revision of the OCDQ," *Educational Administration Quarterly,* 22 (1986).

————, and Patrick B. Forsyth. *Effective Supervision: Theory into Practice* (New York: Random House, 1986).

————, and James E. Henderson. "Principal Authenticity, School Climate, and Pupil-Control Orientation," *Alberta Journal of Educational Research,* 2 (1983), 123–130.

Huizinga, G. *Maslow's Need Hierarchy in the Work Situation* (Netherlands: Wolters-Noordhoff nv Groninger, 1970).

Hunt, James G., and Lars L. Larson (eds.), *Leadership Frontiers* (Kent, OH: Kent State University Press, 1975), pp. 61–80.

Huse, Edgar F., and Thomas G. Cummings. *Organizational Development and Change,* 3rd ed. (St. Paul, MN: West, 1985).

Iannaccone, Laurence. "Informal Organization of School Systems," in Daniel Griffiths *et al.* (eds.), *Organizing Schools for Effective Education* (Danville, IL: Interstate, 1962, pp. 227–293.

————. "The Social System of a School Staff" (Ed.D. diss., Teachers College, Columbia University, 1958).

Immegart, G. L., and W. L. Boyd (eds.). *Problem-Finding in Educational Administration: Trends in Research and Practice* (Washington, DC: Heath, 1979).

Isaacson, Gerald. "Leadership Behavior and Loyalty" (Ed.D. diss., Rutgers University, 1983).

Isherwood, Geoffrey, and Wayne K. Hoy. "Bureaucracy, Powerlessness, and Teacher Work Values," *Journal of Educational Administration,* 9 (1973), 124–138.

Ivancevich, John. "A Longitudinal Assessment of Management by Objectives," *Administrative Science Quarterly,* 17 (1972), 126–136.

————, James Donnelly, and Herbert Lyon. "A Study of the Impact of Management by Objectives in Perceived Need Satisfaction," *Personnel Psychology,* 23 (1970), 139–151.

————, and J. Timothy McMahon. "The Effects of Goal Setting, External Feedback, and Self-Generated Feedback on Outcome Variables: A Field Experiment," *Academy of Management Journal,* 25 (1982), 359–372.

Jacobs, David. "Dependency and Vulnerability: An Exchange Approach to the Control of Organizations," *Administrative Science Quarterly,* 19 (1974), 45–59.

Jamison, Dean, Patrick Suppes, and Stuart Wells. "The Effectiveness of Alternative Instructional Media: A Survey," *Review of Educational Research,* 44 (1974), 1–67.

Janda, Kenneth F. "Towards the Explication of the Concept of Leadership in Terms of the Concept of Power," *Human Relations,* 13 (1960).

Janis, Irving L., and Leon Mann. *Decision Making: A Psychological Analysis of Conflict, Choice, and Commitment* (New York: Free Press, 1977).

———. "Sources of Error in Strategic Decision Making," in Johannes M. Pennings and associates, *Organizational Strategy and Change* (San Francisco: Jossey-Bass 1985), pp. 157–197.

———. *Groupthink: Psychological Studies of Policy Decisions and Fiascoes* (Boston: Houghton Mifflin, 1982).

Jurkovich, Ray. "A Core Typology of Organizational Environments," *Administrative Science Quarterly,* 19 (1974), 380–394.

Kahn, Robert L. "The Prediction of Productivity," *Journal of Social Issues,* 12 (1956), 41–49.

Kanner, Lawrence. "Machiavellianism and the Secondary Schools: Teacher-Principal Relations" (Ph.D. diss., Rutgers University, 1974).

Kanter, Rosabeth, and Derick Brinkerhoff. "Organizational Performance: Recent Developments in Measurement," *Annual Review of Sociology,* 7 (1981), 321–349.

Katz, Daniel, N. Maccoby, and Nancy Morse. *Productivity, Supervision, and Morale in an Office Situation* (Detroit: Darel, 1950).

———, and Robert L. Kahn. *The Social Psychology of Organizations,* 2nd ed. (New York: Wiley, 1978).

Keeley, Michael. "Impartiality and Participant-Interest Theories of Organizational Effectiveness," *Administrative Science Quarterly,* 29 (1984), 1–25.

Kelsey, John G. T. "Conceptualization and Instrumentation for the Comparative Study of Secondary School Structure and Operation" (Ph.D. diss., University of Alberta, 1973).

Kerlinger, Fred N. *Foundations of Behavioral Research,* 2nd ed. (New York: Holt Rinehart & Winston, 1973).

Kiggundu, Moses N. "An Empirical Test of the Theory of Job Design Using Multiple Job Ratings," *Human Relations,* 33 (1980), 339–351.

Kilmann, Ralph H., Mary J. Saxton, Roy Serpa, and associates. *Gaining Control of the Corporate Culture* (San Francisco: Jossey-Bass, 1985).

———, and M. J. Saxton. *The Kilmann-Saxton Culture Gap Survey* (Pittsburgh, PA: Organizational Design Consultant, 1983).

Kim, Jay S. "Effect of Behavior Plus Outcome Goal Setting and Feedback on Employee Satisfaction and Performance," *Academy of Management Journal,* 27 (1984), 139–149.

King, Nathan. "Clarification and Evaluation of the Two-Factor Theory of Job Satisfaction," *Psychological Bulletin,* 74 (1970), 18–31.

Kirchhoff, Bruce A. "Organization Effectiveness Measurement and Policy Research," *Academy of Management Review,* 2 (1977), 347–355.

Knapp, M. L. *Nonverbal Communication in Human Interaction* (New York: Holt, Rinehart, & Winston, 1972).

Kmetz, John T., and Donald J. Willower. "Elementary School Principals' Work Behavior," *Educational Administration Quarterly,* 18 (1982), 62–78.

Kolesar, Henry. "An Empirical Study of Client Alienation in the Bureaucratic Organization" (Ph.D. diss., University of Alberta, 1967).

Korman, Abraham K., Jeffrey H. Greenhaus, and Irwin J. Badin. "Personnel Attitudes and Motivation," *Annual Review of Psychology,* 28 (1977), 175–196.

Kornhauser, William. *Scientists in Industry* (Berkeley: University of California Press, 1962).

Kottkamp, Robert, John Mulhern, and Wayne K. Hoy. "Secondary School Climate: A Revision of the OCDQ" (Technical report, Rutgers University, 1985).

Kuhlman, Edward, and Wayne K. Hoy. "The Socialization of Professionals into Bureaucracies: The Beginning Teacher in the School," *Journal of Educational Administration,* 8 (1974), 18–27.

Kunz, Daniel, and Wayne K. Hoy. "Leader Behavior of Principals and the Professional Zone of Acceptance of Teachers," *Educational Administration Quarterly,* 12 (1976), 49–64.

Lakomski, Gabriele. "Theory, Value and Relevance in Education Administration," in Fazal Rizvi (ed.). *Working Papers in Ethics and Educational Administration 1985* (Australia: Deaken University Printery, 1985), pp. 35–36.

Lane, Willard R., Ronald G. Corwin, and William G. Monahan. *Foundations of Educational Administration* (New York: Macmillan, 1966).

Lanier, Judith. *Goals for Educating Teachers as Professionals, Interim Report #2* (East Lansing, MI: College of Education, Michigan State University, 1985).

———. "Research on Teacher Education," in M. C. Wittrock (ed.), *Handbook of Research on Teaching,* 3rd ed. (New York: Macmillan, 1985), pp. 527–569.

Lasagna, John B. "Make Your MBO Pragmatic," *Harvard Business Review,* 49 (1971), 64–69.

Latham, Gary P., and Gary A. Yukl. "A Review of Research on the Application of Goal Setting in Organizations," *Academy of Management Journal,* 18 (1975), 824–845.

———, and Timothy P. Steele. "The Motivational Effects of Participation Versus Goal Setting on Performance," *Academy of Management Journal,* 26 (1983), 406–417.

Lau, Lawrence J. "Education Production Functions" (Paper presented at the Conference on School Organization and Effects, National Institute of Education, 1978).

Lawler, Edward E. III. *Motivation in Work Organizations* (Monterey, CA: Brooks/Cole, 1973).

Lawrence, Paul R., and Jay W. Lorsch. *Organization and Environment* (Homewood, IL: Irwin, 1967).

Leavitt, Harold J., William R. Dill, and Henry B. Eyring. *The Organizational World* (New York: Harcourt Brace Jovanovich, 1973).

Lefkowitz, Joel, Mark John Somers, and Karen Weinberg. "The Role of Need Level and/or Need Salience as Moderators of the Relationship between Need Satisfaction and Work Alienation-Involvement," *Journal of Vocational Behavior,* 24 (1984), 142–158.

Lensky, Harold W. *Intellectuals in Labor Unions* (New York: Free Press, 1959).

Level, Dale A., Jr. "Communication Effectiveness: Method and Situation," *Journal of Business Communication,* 9 (1972), 19–25.

Leverette, Bonnie B. "Professional Zone of Acceptance: Its Relation to the

Leader Behavior of Principals and Socio-Psychological Characteristics of Teaching" (Ed.D. diss., Rutgers University, 1984).

Lewin, Kurt. *Field Theory in Social Science* (New York: Harper, 1951).

Lewis, Philip V. *Organizational Communications: The Essence of Effective Management* (Columbus, OH: Grid, 1975).

Licata, Joseph W., and Walter G. Hack. "School Administrator Grapevine Structure," *Educational Administration Quarterly* 16 (1980), 82–99.

Likert, Rensis. *The Human Organization: Its Management and Value* (New York: McGraw-Hill, 1967).

———. *New Patterns of Management* (New York: McGraw-Hill, 1961).

Lincoln, James R. "Intra-(and Inter) Organizational Networks," *Research in the Sociology of Organizations,* 1 (1982), 1–38.

Lindblom, Charles E. "The Science of Muddling Through," *Public Administrative Review,* 19 (1959), 79–99.

———. *The Policy-Making Process* (Englewood Cliffs, NJ: Prentice-Hall, 1968).

Lindzey, Gardner, and Donn Byrne. "Measurement of Social Choice and Interpersonal Attractiveness," in Gardner Lindzey and Elliot Aronson (eds.), *The Handbook of Social Psychology,* 2nd ed., Vol. 2. (Reading, MA: Addison-Wesley, 1968), pp. 452–525.

Lipham, James. "Leadership and Administration," in Daniel Griffiths (ed.), *Behavioral Science and Educational Administration, Sixty-third Yearbook of the National Society for the Study of Education* (Chicago: University of Chicago Press, 1964), pp. 119–141.

———, and Donald C. Francke. "Nonverbal Behavior of Administrators," *Educational Administration Quarterly,* 2 (1966), 101–109.

Litchfield, Edward H. "Notes on a General Theory of Administration," *Administrative Science Quarterly,* 1 (1956), 3–29.

Litterer, Joseph A. *Organizations: Systems, Control, and Adaptation.* Vol. 2, 2nd ed. (New York: Wiley, 1969).

——— (ed.). *Organizations: Structure and Behavior,* Vol. 1, 2nd ed. (New York: Wiley, 1969), p. 162.

Litwin, George H., and Robert A. Stringer, Jr. *Motivation and Organizational Climate* (Boston: Harvard University Press, 1968).

Locke, Edwin A. "The Nature and Causes of Job Satisfaction," in Marvin D. Dunnette (ed.), *Handbook of Industrial and Organizational Psychology* (Chicago: Rand McNally, 1976), pp. 1297–1349.

———. "Toward a Theory of Task Motivation and Incentives," *Organizational Behavior and Human Performance,* 3 (1968), 157–189.

———, and David M. Schneiger. "Participation in Decision Making: One More Look," *Research in Organizational Behavior,* 1 (1979), 265–339.

———, Norman Cartledge, and Claramae S. Knerr. "Studies of the Relationship between Satisfaction, Goal-Setting, and Performance," *Organizational Behavior and Human Performance,* 5 (1970), 135–139.

———, Karyll N. Shaw, Lise M. Saari, and Gary P. Latham. "Goal Setting and Task Performance," *Psychological Review,* 90 (1981), 125–152.

———, Philip Bobko, and Cynthia Lee. "Effect of Self-Efficacy, Goals, and Task Strategies on Task Performance," *Journal of Applied Psychology,* 69 (1984), 241–251.

———, and Gary P. Latham. *Goal Setting: A Motivational Technique That Works* (Englewood Cliffs, NJ: Prentice-Hall, 1984), p. 143.

Lorsch, Jay W. "Making Behavioral Science More Useful," *Harvard Business Review,* 57 (1979) 171–180.

———. "Strategic Myopia: Culture as an Invisible Barrier to Change," in Ralph H. Kilmann *et al., Gaining Control of the Corporate Culture* (San Francisco: Jossey-Bass, 1985), pp. 84–103.

Lortie, Dan C. *Schoolteacher: A Sociological Study* (Chicago: University of Chicago Press, 1975).

———. "The Balance of Control and Autonomy in Elementary School Teaching," in A. Etzioni (ed.), *The Semiprofessions and Their Organization* (New York: Free Press, 1969).

Louis, Meryl Reis. "Perspectives on Organizational Cultures," in Peter J. Frost *et al., Organizational Culture* (Beverly Hills: Sage, 1985), pp. 73–95.

Lunenburg, Frederick C. "Pupil Control Ideology and Self-Concept as a Learner," *Educational Research Quarterly,* 8 (1983), 33–39.

Luthans, Fred, and Robert Kreitner. *Organizational Behavior Modification* (Glenview, IL: Scott, Foresman, 1975).

MacKay, D. A. "An Empirical Study of Bureaucratic Dimensions and Their Relations to Other Characteristics of School Organization" (Ph.D. diss., University of Alberta, 1964).

MacKensie, Donald E. "Research for School Improvement: An Appraisal and Some Recent Trends," *Educational Research,* 12 (1983), 5–17.

McClelland, David C. *The Achieving Society* (Princeton, NJ: Van Nostrand, 1961).

———. "Toward a Theory of Motive Acquisition," *American Psychologist,* 20 (1965), 321–333.

McKelvey, Bill. *Organizational Systematics: Taxonomy, Evolutions, Classification* (Berkley: University of California Press, 1982).

McNamara, Vincent, and Frederick Enns. "Directive Leadership and Staff Acceptance of the Principal," *Canadian Administrator,* 6 (1966), 5–8.

Madaus, George F., Peter W. Airasian, and Thomas Kellaghan. *School Effectiveness: A Reassessment of the Evidence* (New York: McGraw-Hill, 1980).

Mann, Floyd C. "Studying and Creating Change: A Means to Understanding Social Organization," in Harvey Hornstein *et al.* (eds.), *Social Intervention* (New York: Free Press, 1971), pp. 294–309.

Mann, R. D. "A Review of the Relationships between Personality and Performance," *Psychological Bulletin,* 56 (1959), 241–270.

March, James C., and Herbert Simon. *Organizations* (New York: Wiley, 1958).

———, and Johan P. Olsen. *Ambiguity and Choice in Organization* (Bergen, Norway: Universitetsforlaget, 1976).

———, and James G. March. "Almost Random Careers: The Wisconsin School Superintendency, 1940–1974," *Administrative Science Quarterly,* 22 (1977), 377–409.

———. "The Technology of Fadishness," in James G. March and Johan P. Olsen (eds.), *Ambiguity and Choice in Organizations* (Bergen, Norway: Universitetsforlaget, 1976), p. 72.

———, and James G. March. "Performance Sampling in School Matches," *Administrative Science Quarterly,* 23 (1978), 434–453.

Marjoribanks, Kevin. "Bureaucratic Orientation, Autonomy and Professional Attitudes of Teachers," *Journal of Educational Administration,* 15 (1977), 104–113.

Mark, Jonathan H., and Barry D. Anderson. "Teacher Survival Rates in St.

Louis, 1969–1982," *American Educational Research Journal,* 22 (1985), 413–421.

Marsden, Peter V., and Nan Lin (eds.). *Social Structure and Network Analysis* (Beverly Hills, CA: Sage, 1982).

Martin, Joanne. "Can Organizational Culture Be Managed?" in Frost *et al., Organizational Culture,* p. 95.

Martin, William J., and Donald J. Willower. "The Managerial Behavior of High School Principals," *Educational Administration Quarterly,* 17 (1981), 69–90.

Martin, Yvonne M., Geoffrey B. Isherwood, and Robert G. Lavery. "Leadership Effectiveness in Teacher Probation Committees," *Educational Administration Quarterly,* 12 (1976), 87–99.

Maslow, Abraham H. *Eupsychian Management* (Homewood, IL: Irwin, 1965).

————. *Motivation and Personality,* 2nd ed. (New York: Harper & Row, 1970).

Mayo, Elton. *The Social Problems of an Industrial Civilization* (Boston: Graduate School of Business Administration, Harvard University, 1945).

Mazzoni, Tim L., and Betty Malen. "Mobilizing Constituency Pressure to Influence State Education Policy Making," *Educational Administration Quarterly,* 21 (1985), 91–116.

Meidl, James R., Sanford B. Ehrlich, and Janet M. Dukerich. "The Romance of Leadership," *Administrative Science Quarterly,* 30 (1985), 78–102.

Mento, Anthony J., Norman D. Cartledge, and Edwin A. Locke. "Maryland vs. Michigan vs. Minnesota: Another Look at the Relationship of Expectancy and Goal Difficulty to Task Performance," *Organizational Behavior and Human Performance,* 25 (1980), 419–440.

Merton, Robert. "The Social Nature of Leadership," *American Journal of Nursing,* 69 (1969), 2614–2618.

————. *Social Theory and Social Structure* (New York: Free Press, 1957).

Meyer, Herbert, Emanuel Kay, and John French. "Split-roles in Performance Appraisal," *Harvard Business Review,* 42 (1965), 123–129.

Meyer, John W., and Elizabeth Cohen. *The Impact of the Open-Space School Upon Teacher Influence and Autonomy: The Effects of an Organizational Innovation, Technical Report No. 21* (Palo Alto, CA: Stanford Center for Research and Development in Teaching, 1971, ERIC No. Ed 062 291).

————, and Brian Rowan. "Institutionalized Organizations: Formal Structure as Myth and Ceremony," *American Journal of Sociology,* 83 (1977), 440–463.

————, and Brian Rowan. "The Structure of Educational Organizations," in Marshall W. Meyer *et al.* (eds.), *Environments and Organizations* (San Francisco: Jossey-Bass, 1978), pp. 78–109.

———— *et al.* "Instructional Dissensus and Institutional Consensus in Schools," in Marshall W. Meyer *et al., Environments and Organizations* (San Francisco: Jossey-Bass, 1978).

————, and W. Richard Scott. *Organizational Environments: Ritual and Rationality* (Beverly Hills, CA: Sage, 1983).

Meyer, Marshall W. "Introduction: Recent Developments in Organizational Research and Theory," in Marshall W. Meyer *et al.* (eds.), *Environments and Organizations* (San Francisco: Jossey-Bass, 1978).

Miles, Matthew. "Education and Innovation: The Organization in Context," in Max Abbott and John Lovell (eds.), *Changing Perspectives in Educational Administration* (Auburn, AL: Auburn University, 1965), pp. 54–72.

Miles, Matthew B. "Planned Change and Organizational Health: Figure and Ground," in Fred D. Carver and Thomas J. Sergiovanni (eds.), *Organizations and Human Behavior* (New York: McGraw-Hill, 1969), pp. 375–391.

Miles, R. H., and Kim S. Cameron. *Coffin Nails and Corporate Strategies* (Englewood Cliffs, NJ: Prentice-Hall, 1982).

Miller, Lawrence M. *Behavior Management* (New York: Wiley, 1978).

Mills, Peter K., and Newton Marguilies. "Toward a Core Typology of Service Organizations," *Academy of Management Review*, 5 (1980), 255–265.

Mindlin, Sergio E., and Howard Aldrich. "Interorganizational Dependence: A Review of the Concept and a Reexamination of the Findings of the Aston Group," *Administrative Science Quarterly*, 20 (1975), 382–392.

Miner, John B. *Theories of Organizational Behavior* (Hinsdale, IL: Dryden, 1980), pp. 327–351.

Mintzberg, Henry. *The Structuring of Organizations*. (Englewood Cliffs, NJ: Prentice-Hall, 1979).

———. *Structure in Fives* (Englewood Cliffs, NJ: Prentice-Hall, 1983).

———. "Organizational Structure and Alienation from Work" (Paper presented at the American Educational Research Association, Boston, 1980).

———. "Patterns in Strategy Formulation," *Management Science*, 24 (1978), 934–948

Miskel, Cecil. "Principals' Attitude Toward Work and Co-workers, Situational Factors, Perceived Effectiveness, and Innovation Effort," *Educational Administration Quarterly*, 13 (1977), 51–70.

———. *Public School Principals' Leader Style, Organizational Situation, and Effectiveness: Final Report* (Washington, DC: National Institute of Education, Department of Health, Education and Welfare, Grant No. NE-G-00-3-0141, October 1974).

———, Douglas Glasnapp, and Richard Hatley. *Public School Teachers Work Motivation, Organizational Incentives, Job Satisfaction, and Primary Life Interests, Final Report* (Washington, DC: Office of Education, Department of Health, Education and Welfare, 1972).

———, Douglas Glasnapp, and Richard Hatley. "A Test of the Inequity Theory for Job Satisfaction Using Educators' Attitudes toward Work Motivation and Work Incentives," *Educational Administration Quarterly*, 11 (1975), 38–54.

———, and Ed Gerhardt. "Perceived Bureaucracy, Teacher Conflict, Central Life Interests, Voluntarism, and Job Satisfaction," *Journal of Educational Administration*, 12 (1974), 84–97.

———, JoAnn DeFrain, and Kay Wilcox. "A Test of Expectancy Work Motivation Theory in Educational Organizations," *Educational Administration Quarterly*, 16 (1980), 70–92.

———, Robert Fevurly, and John Stewart. "Organizational Structures and Processes, Perceived School Effectiveness, Loyalty, and Job Satisfaction," *Educational Administration Quarterly*, 15 (1979), 97–118.

———, Susan Bloom, and David McDonald. "Structural Coupling, Expectancy Climate, and Learning Strategies Intervention Effectiveness: A Pilot Study to Establish the Reliability and Validity Estimates for the Measurement System" (Unpublished final report for the Learning Disabilities Institute, University of Kansas, 1980).

———, David McDonald and Susan Bloom. "Structural and Expectancy Linkages within Schools and Organizational Effectiveness," *Educational Administration Quarterly,* 19 (1983), 49–82.

————. "Motivation in Educational Organizations," *Educational Administration Quarterly,* 18 (1982), 65–88.

————, and Dorothy Cosgrove. "Leader Succession in School Settings," *Review of Educational Research,* 55 (1985), 87–105.

Mitchell, Douglas E., Flora Ida Ortiz, and Tedi K. Mitchell. "Executive Summary," *Controlling the Impact of Rewards and Incentives on Teacher Task Performance* (Washington, DC: National Institute of Education, U. S. Department of Education, Grant NIE-G-80-0154: 1982).

Mitchell, Terence R. "Expectancy Models of Job Satisfaction, Occupational Preference, and Effort: A Theoretical, Methodological and Empirical Appraisal," *Psychological Bulletin,* 81, (1974), 1053–1077.

————. "Organization Behavior," *Annual Review of Psychology,* 30 (1979), 243–281.

Mitchell, Vance F., and Pravin Moudgill. "Measurement of Maslow's Need Hierarchy," *Organization Behavior and Human Performance,* 16 (1976), 334–349.

Moeller, Gerald H., and W. W. Charters, Jr. "Relation of Bureaucratization to Sense of Power Among Teachers," *Administrative Science Quarterly,* 10 (1966), 444–465.

Mohrman, Allan M., Jr., Robert A. Cooke, and Susan Albers Mohrman. "Participation in Decision Making: A Multidimensional Perspective," *Educational Administration Quarterly,* 14 (1978), 13–29.

Moon, Nak Jin. "The Construction of a Conceptual Framework for Teacher Participation in School Decision Making" (Ed.D. diss., University of Kentucky, 1983).

Mott, Paul E. *The Characteristics of Effective Organizations* (New York: Harper & Row, 1972).

Mowday, Richard T. "The Exercise of Upward Influence in Organizations," *Administrative Science Quarterly,* 23 (1978), 137–156.

————, and Michael L. Tushman. "A Congruence Model for Organizational Assessment," in Edward E. Lawler, David A. Nadler, and Cortlandt Cammann (eds.), *Organizational Assessment: Perspectives on the Measurement of Organizational Behavior and the Quality of Working Life* (New York: Wiley, 1980), pp. 261–278.

Mullins, Toni. "Relationships Among Teachers' Perception of the Principal's Style, Teachers' Loyalty to the Principal, and Teachers' Zone of Acceptance" (Ed.D. diss., Rutgers University, 1983).

Murnane, Richard J. "Interpreting the Evidence on School Effectiveness," *Teachers College Record,* 83 (1981), 19–35.

Murphy, Michael J. Testimony before the California Commission on the Teaching Profession, Sacramento, 1985.

————, and Ann Weaver Hart. Career Ladder Reforms (Paper prepared for the California Commission on the Teaching Professions, 1985).

Murray, V. V., and Allan F. Corenblum. "Loyalty to Immediate Superior at Alternate Hierarchical Levels in a Bureaucracy," *American Journal of Sociology,* 62 (1966), 77–85.

Nadler, David A. "The Effects of Feedback on Task Group Behavior: A Review of the Experimental Research," *Organizational Behavior and Human Performance,* 23 (1979), 309–338.

———, and Edward E. Lawler III. "Motivation: A Diagnostic Approach," in J. Richard Hackman, Edward E. Lawler III, and Lyman W. Porter (eds.), *Perspectives on Behavior in Organizations* (New York: McGraw-Hill, 1977), pp. 26–38.

———, and Michael L. Tushman. "A General Diagnostic Model for Organizational Behavior Applying a Congruence Perspective" in J. R. Hackman, E. E. Lawler III, and L. W. Porter (eds.), *Perspectives on Behavior in Organizations* (New York: McGraw-Hill, 1983), pp. 112–124.

Naylor, James C., and Daniel R. Ilgen. "Goal Setting: A Theoretical Analysis of a Motivational Technology," *Research in Organizational Behavior,* 6 (1984), 95–140.

Newberry, John F. "A Comparative Analysis of the Organizational Structures of Selected Post-secondary Educational Institutions" (Unpublished doctoral diss., University of Alberta, Edmonton, 1971).

Nicholson, Jean Hagewood. "Analysis of Communication Satisfaction in an Urban School System" (Ph.D. diss., George Peabody College for Teachers of Vanderbilt University, 1980).

Nisbett, R. E., and L. Ross. *Human Interferences: Strategies and Shortcomings in Social Judgments* (Englewood Cliffs, NJ: Prentice-Hall, 1980).

Nutt, Paul C. "Types of Organizational Decision Process," *Administrative Science Quarterly,* 29 (1984), 414–450.

Odiorne, G. S. *Management by Objectives: A System of Managerial Leadership* (New York: Pitman, 1965).

———. *Management Decisions by Objectives* (Englewood Cliffs, NJ: Prentice-Hall, 1969).

———. *MBO II: A System of Managerial Leadership for the 80s.* Belmont, CA: Pitman, 1979.

Oldham, Greg R., and Howard E. Miller. "The Effect of Significant Other's Job Complexity and Employee Reactions to Work," *Human Relations,* 32 (1979), 247–260.

———, and Carol T. Kulik. "Motivation Enhancement Through Work Redesign," in James L. Bess (ed.), *College and University Organization* (New York: New York University Press, 1984), 85–104.

Olsen, Marvin E. *The Process of Social Organization* (New York: Holt, Rinehart & Winston, 1968).

O'Reilly, Charles A. III, and Karlene H. Roberts. "Task Group Structure, Communication, and Effectiveness in Three Organizations," *Journal of Applied Psychology,* 62 (1977), 674–681.

———, and Louis R. Pondy. "Organizational Communication," in Steven Kerr (ed.), *Organizational Behavior* (Columbus, OH: Grid, 1979), 119–150.

Orpen, Christopher. "The Effects of Job Enrichment on Employee Satisfaction, Motivation, Involvement, and Performance: A Field Experiment," *Human Relations,* 32 (1979), 189–217.

Osborn, Richard N., and James G. Hunt. "Environment and Organizational Effectiveness," *Administrative Science Quarterly,* 19 (1974), 231–246.

Ouchi, William. *Theory Z* (Reading, MA: Addison-Wesley, 1981).

Packard, John S., and Donald J. Willower. "Pluralistic Ignorance and Pupil

Control Ideology," *Journal of Educational Administration,* 10 (1972), 78–87.

Page, Charles H. "Bureaucracy's Other Face," *Social Forces,* 25 (1946), 88–94.

Parsons, Talcott. "Some Ingredients of a General Theory of Formal Organization," in Andrew W. Halpin (ed.), *Administrative Theory in Education* (New York: Macmillan, 1958).

———. *Structure and Process in Modern Societies* (New York: Free Press, 1960).

———, and Edward A. Shils (eds.). *Toward a General Theory of Action* (Cambridge, MA: Harvard University Press, 1951).

———, Robert F. Bales, and Edward A. Shils. *Working Papers in the Theory of Action* (New York: Free Press, 1953).

Pastor, Margaret C., and David A. Erlandson. "A Study of Higher Order Need Strength and Job Satisfaction in Secondary Public School Teachers," *Journal of Educational Administration,* 20 (1982), 172–183.

Peabody, Robert L. "Perceptions of Organizational Authority: A Comparative Analysis," *Administrative Science Quarterly,* 6 (1962), 463–482.

Pelz, Donald C., and Frank M. Andrews. *Scientists in Organizations* (New York: Wiley, 1966).

Pennings, Johannes M., and associates. *Organizational Strategy and Change* (San Francisco: Jossey-Bass, 1985).

Perrow, Charles. "Demystifying Organization," in Y. Hasenfeld and R. Saari (eds.), *The Management of Human Services* (New York: Columbia University Press, 1978).

Peters, Lawrence H., Darrell D. Hartke, and John T. Pohlmann. "Fiedler's Contingency Theory of Effectiveness: An Application of the Meta-Analysis Procedures of Schmidt and Hunter," *Psychological Bulletin,* 97 (1985), 274–285.

Peters, Thomas J., and Robert H. Waterman, Jr. *In Search of Excellence* (New York: Harper & Row, 1982).

Peterson, Ken, and Anthony Mitchell. "Teacher-Controlled Evaluation in a Career Ladder Program," *Educational Leadership,* 43 (1985), 44–47.

Pettigrew, Andrew M. "On Studying Organizational Cultures," *Administrative Science Quarterly,* 24 (1979), 570–581.

Pfeffer, Jeffrey. *Organizations and Organization Theory* (Boston: Pitman, 1982), pp. 192–207.

———, and Gerald R. Salancik. *The Organizational Control of Organizations: A Resource Dependence Perspective* (Englewood Cliffs, NJ: Prentice-Hall, 1982).

———. *Power in Organizations* (Boston: Pitman, 1981), pp. 99–115.

———. "Size and Composition of Corporate Boards of Directors: The Organization and Its Environment," *Administrative Science Quarterly,* 17 (1972), 218–228.

———, and Gerald Salancik. *The External Control of Organizations: A Resource Dependence Perspective* (New York: Harper & Row, 1978).

———, and Huseyin Leblebici. "The Effect of Competition on Some Dimensions of Organizational Structure," *Social Forces,* 52 (1973), 268–279.

———. "Beyond Management and the Worker: The Institutional Function of Management," *Academy of Management Review,* 1 (1976).

Pitner, Nancy, and Rodney T. Ogawa. "Organizational Leadership: The Case of the Superintendent," *Educational Administration Quarterly*, 17 (1981), 45–65.

Pool, Ithiel de Sola, and Wilbur Schramm. *Handbook of Communication* (Chicago: Rand McNally, 1973).

Porter, Lyman W. "A Study of Perceived Need Satisfactions in Bottom and Middle Management Jobs," *Journal of Applied Psychology*, 45 (1961), 1–10.

———. "Job Attitudes in Management: I. Perceived Deficiencies In Need Fulfillment as a Function of Job Level," *Journal of Applied Psychology*, 46 (1962), 375–384.

———. "Job Attitudes in Management: II. Perceived Importance of Needs as a Function of Job Level," *Journal of Applied Psychology*, 47 (1963), 141–148.

———, and Edward E. Lawler III. *Managerial Attitudes and Performance* (Homewood, IL: Dorsey, 1968).

———, and Karlene H. Roberts. "Communication in Organizations," in Marvin D. Dunnette (ed.), *Handbook of Industrial and Organizational Psychology* (Chicago: Rand McNally, 1976), pp. 1533–1589.

Presthus, Robert V. "Toward a Theory of Organizational Behavior," *Administrative Science Quarterly*, 3 (1958), 48–72.

———. *The Organizational Society* (New York: Random House, 1962).

Price, James L. "The Study of Organizational Effectiveness," *Sociological Quarterly*, 13 (1972), 3–15.

Prolman, Sandra. "Gender, Career Paths, and Administrative Perceptions," *Administrator's Notebook*, 30 (1982), 1–4.

Pugh, D. S., D. J. Hickson, C. R. Hinnings. "Dimensions of Organizational Structure," *Administrative Science Quarterly*, 13 (1968), 56–105.

———, and D. J. Hickson. *Organizational Structure in its Context* (Westmead, Farnborough, Hants., England: Saxon House, D. C. Heath, 1976).

———, D. J. Hickson, C. R. Hinings, and C. Turner. "The Context of Organizational Structure," *Administration Science Quarterly*, 14 (1969), 91–114.

Punch, Keith F. "Bureaucratic Structure in Schools: Towards Redefinition and Measurement," *Educational Administration Quarterly*, 6 (1969), 43–57.

Quinn, Robert E., and Kim Cameron. "Organizational Life Cycles and Shifting Criteria of Effectiveness: Some Preliminary Evidence," *Management Science*, 29 (1983), 33–51.

———, and Michael R. McGrath. "The Transformation of Organizational Cultures," in Peter J. Frost *et al. Organizational Culture* (Beverly Hills, CA: Sage Publications, 1985), pp. 315–334.

Raia, Anthony. "A Second Look at Management Goals and Controls," *California Management Review*, 8 (1966), 49–58.

Ratsoy, Eugene W., Gail R. Babcock, and Brian J. Caldwell. *Organizational Effectiveness in the Educational Practicum Program—1977–1978* (Edmonton, Alberta: University of Alberta, 1978).

Rauschenberger, John, Neal Schmitt, and John E. Hunter. "A Test of the Need Hierarchy Concept by a Markov Model of Change in Need Strength," *Administrative Science Quarterly*, 25 (1980), 654–670.

Reddin, W. J. *Effective Management by Objectives: The 3-D Method* (New York: McGraw-Hill, 1971).

———. "The Tri-Dimensional Grid," *The Canadian Personnel and Industrial Relations Journal*, 13 (1966), 13–20.

————. *Managerial Effectiveness* (New York: McGraw-Hill, 1970).

Redding, W. Charles. *Communication Within the Organization* (West Lafayette, IN: Purdue Research Council, 1972).

Reynolds, Paul Davidson. *A Primer in Theory Construction* (Indianapolis: Bobbs-Merrill, 1971).

Rice, Alan William. "Individual and Work Variables Associated with Principal Job Satisfaction" (Ph.D. diss., University of Alberta, 1978).

Rice, Robert W. "Psychometric Properties of the Esteem for Least Preferred Co-worker (LPC Scale)," *Academy of Management Review,* 3 (1978), 106–118.

Robbins, Stephen P. *The Structure and Design of Organizations* (Englewood Cliffs, NJ: Prentice-Hall, 1983).

Roberts, Karlene H., Charles L. Hulin, and Denise M. Rousseau. *Developing an Interdisciplinary Science of Organizations* (San Francisco: Jossey-Bass, 1978).

————, and William Glick, "The Job Characteristics Approach to Task Design: A Critical Review," *Journal of Applied Psychology,* 66 (1981), 193–217.

Rockey, Edward H. *Communication in Organizations* (Lanham, MD: University Press of America, 1984).

Roethlisberger, F. J., and William J. Dickson. *Management and the Worker* (Cambridge, MA: Harvard University Press, 1939).

Rokeach, Milton. *The Open and Closed Mind* (New York: Basic Books, 1960).

Rowan, Brian. "Organizational Structure and the Institutional Environment: The Case of Public Schools," *Administrative Science Quarterly,* 27 (1982), 259–279.

————, Steven T. Bossert, and David C. Dwyer. "Research on Effective Schools: A Cautionary Note," *Educational Researcher,* 12 (1983), 24–31.

Sackney, Lawrence E. "The Relationship Between Organizational Structure and Behavior in Secondary Schools" (Ph.D. diss., University of Alberta, 1976).

Salancik, Gerald R., and Jeffrey Pfeffer. "An Examination of Need-Satisfaction Models of Job Attitudes," *Administrative Science Quarterly,* 22 (1977), 427–456.

Sanders, Janet Snyder. "Utilization of Lines of Communication within the Administration of the University of Kansas Described by ECCO Analysis" (Ph.D. diss., University of Kansas, 1976).

Sayles, Leonard R., and George Strauss. *Human Behavior in Organizations* (Englewood Cliffs, NJ: Prentice-Hall, 1966).

Schein, Edgar H. *Organizational Psychology* (Englewood Cliffs, NJ: Prentice-Hall, 1965).

————. *Organizational Culture and Leadership* (San Francisco: Jossey-Bass, 1985).

Schlechty, Philip C. *Restructuring the Teaching Occupation: A Proposal* (Paper presented at a meeting of the American Educational Research Association, Chicago, 1985).

Schmidt, Gene L. "Job Satisfaction Among Secondary Administrators," *Educational Administration Quarterly,* 12 (1976).

Schmuck, Richard A., and Matthew B. Miles. *Organization Development in Schools* (Palo Alto, CA: National Press Books, 1971), pp. 2–3.

Schneider, Benjamin, and Clayton P. Alderfer. "Three Studies of Measures of Need Satisfaction in Organizations," *Administrative Science Quarterly,* 18 (1973), 489–505.

――――. "Organizational Behavior," *Annual Review of Psychology,* 36 (1985), 573–611.

Schramm, Wilbur. "How Communication Works," in Wilbur Schramm (ed.), *The Process and Effects of Mass Communication* (Urbana, IL: University of Illinois Press, 1955), pp. 3–26.

Schwartz, Howard M., and Stanley M. Davis. "Matching Corporate Culture and Business Strategy," *Organizational Dynamics* (Summer 1981), p. 33.

Schwartz, Howard S. "Maslow and the Hierarchical Enactment of Organizational Reality," *Human Relations,* 10 (1983), 933–956.

Scott, William G. *Human Relations in Management* (Homewood, IL: Irwin, 1962).

Scott, W. Richard. "Effectiveness of Organizational Effectiveness Studies," in Paul S. Goodman and Johannes M. Pennings (eds.), *New Perspectives on Organizational Effectiveness* (San Francisco: Jossey-Bass, 1977), pp. 63–95.

――――. "Introduction: From Technology to Environment," in John M. Meyer and W. Richard Scott (eds.), *Organizational Environments: Ritual and Rationality* (Beverly Hills, CA: Sage, 1983), pp. 13–17.

――――. *Organizations: Rational, Natural, and Open System* (Englewood Cliffs, NJ: Prentice-Hall, 1981).

Seashore, Stanley E., and David G. Bowers. "Durability of Organizational Change," *American Psychologist,* 25 (1969), 227–233.

Seeman, Melvin. "On the Meaning of Alienation," *American Sociological Review,* 34 (1959), 783–791.

Selznick, Philip. *Leadership in Administration* (New York: Harper & Row, 1957).

Sergiovanni, Thomas. "Factors Which Affect Satisfaction and Dissatisfaction of Teachers," *Journal of Educational Administration,* 5 (1967), 66–82.

――――, and John E. Corbally (eds.). *Leadership and Organizational Culture* (Urbana, IL: University of Illinois Press, 1984).

――――. "Leadership as Cultural Expression," in Thomas J. Sergiovanni and John E. Corbally (eds.), *Leadership and Organizational Culture* (Urbana, IL: University of Illinois Press, 1984).

Sethia, Nirmal K., and Mary Ann Von Glinow. "Arriving at Four Cultures by Managing the Reward System," in Kilmann *et al., Gaining Control of the Corporate Culture* (San Francisco: Jossey-Bass, 1985), pp. 400–420.

Shanker, Albert. *The Making of a Profession* (Washington, DC: American Federation of Teachers, 1985).

Shannon, Claude E., and Warren Weaver. *The Mathematical Theory of Communication* (Urbana, IL: University of Illinois Press, 1949).

Sharma, Chiranji La. "Who Should Make What Decisions?" *Administrator's Notebook,* 3 (1955), 1–4.

Sheridan, John E., H. Kirk Downey, and John W. Slocum, Jr. "Testing Causal Relationships of House's Path-Goal Theory of Leadership Effectiveness," in James G. Hunt and Lars L. Larson (eds.), *Leadership Frontiers* (Kent, OH: Kent State University Press, 1975), pp. 61–80.

Sherman, J. Daniel, and Howard L. Smith. "The Influences of Organizational

Structure on Intrinsic Versus Extrinsic Motivation," *Academy of Management Journal,* 27 (1984), 877–885.

Shrieshiem, Chester A., and Steven Kerr. "Theories and Measures of Leadership: A Critical Appraisal of Current and Future Directions," in James G. Hunt and Lars L. Larson (eds.), *Leadership: The Cutting Edge* (Carbondale, IL: IO Southern Illinois University Press, 1979), pp. 9–45.

———, and M. A. Von Glinow. "The Path-Goal Theory of Leadership: A Theoretical and Empirical Analysis," *Academy of Management Journal,* 20 (1977), 398–405.

Silver, Paula. *Educational Administration: Theoretical Perspectives in Practice and Research* (New York: Harper & Row, 1983).

Simon, Herbert A. *Administrative Behavior,* 2nd ed. (New York: Macmillan, 1957).

———. *Administrative Behavior,* 2nd ed. (New York: Macmillan, 1974).

———. *Models of Man* (New York: John Wiley, 1957).

———. "Administrative Behavior," in David Sills (ed.), *International Encyclopedia of the Social Sciences* (New York: Macmillan, 1968).

———. "On the Concept of Organizational Goal," *Administrative Science Quarterly,* 9 (1964), 1–22.

Singh, Ramadhar. "Leadership Style and Reward Allocation: Does Least Preferred Co-worker Scale Measure Task and Relation Orientation," *Organization Behavior and Human Performance,* 32 (1983), 178–197.

Sirotnek, Kenneth A. "Psychometric Implications of the Unit-of-Analysis Problem (With Examples from the Measurement of Organizational Climate)," *Journal of Educational Measurement,* 17 (1980), 248–284.

Sizer, Theodore R. "High School Reform and the Reform of Teacher Education," 9th Annual DeGarmo Lecture, Society of Professors of Education meeting, San Antonio, 1984.

Sketty, Y. K., and Howard M. Carlisle. "Application of Management by Objectives in the University Setting: An Exploratory Study of Faculty Reactions," *Educational Administration Quarterly,* 10 (1974), 65–81.

Skinner, B. F. *About Behaviorism* (New York: Knopf, 1974).

———. *Beyond Freedom and Dignity* (New York: Knopf, 1971).

Smith, Alfred Goud. *Communication and Culture* (New York: Holt, Rinehart & Winston, 1966).

Smith, Jonathan E., Kenneth P. Carson, and Ralph A. Alexander. "Leadership: It Can Make a Difference," *Academy of Management Journal,* 27 (1984), 765–776.

Smith, Patricia Cain. "The Development of a Method of Measuring Satisfaction: The Cornell Studies," in Edwin A. Fleishman (ed.), *Studies in Personnel and Industrial Psychology* (Homewood, IL: Dorsey, 1967), pp. 343–350.

———, L. M. Kendall, and C. L. Hulin. *The Measurement of Satisfaction in Work and Retirement* (Chicago: Rand McNally, 1969).

Soliman, Hanafi M. "Motivation-Hygiene Theory of Job Attitudes: An Empirical Investigation and an Attempt to Reconcile Both the One- and Two-Factor Theories of Job Attitudes," *Journal of Applied Psychology,* 54 (1970), 452–461.

Sousa, David A., and Wayne K. Hoy. "Bureaucratic Structure in Schools: A Refinement and Synthesis in Measurement," *Educational Administration Quarterly,* 17 (1981), 21–40.

Spradley, James P. *Participant Observation* (New York: Holt, Rinehart & Winston, 1980).

Spuck, Dennis W. "Reward Structures in the Public High School," *Educational Administration Quarterly,* 10 (1974), 18–34.

Staw, Barry M. "Organizational Behavior: A Review and Reformulation of the Field's Outcome Variables," *Annual Review of Psychology,* 35 (1984), 627–666.

Steers, Richard M. *Organizational Effectiveness: A Behavioral View* (Santa Monica, CA: Goodyear, 1977).

———. "Problems in the Measurement of Organizational Effectiveness," *Administrative Science Quarterly,* 20 (1975), 546–558.

———, and Lyman W. Porter. *Motivation and Work Behavior,* 2nd ed. (New York: McGraw-Hill, 1979).

———, and Lyman W. Porter. *Motivation and Work Behavior,* 3rd ed. (New York: McGraw-Hill, 1983).

Stewart, James H. "Factors Accounting for Goal Effectiveness: A Longitudinal Study," in S. Lee Spray (ed.), *Organizational Effectiveness: Theory, Research, Utilization* (Kent, OH: Kent State University Press), pp. 109–121.

Stewart, John W. "Bureaucratic Structure, Interpersonal Climate, and Student Achievement" (Ph.D. diss., University of Kansas, 1978).

Stinchcombe, Arthur L. "Bureaucratic and Craft Administration of Production," *Administration Science Quarterly,* 4 (1959), 168–187.

Stinson, J. E., and T. W. Johnson. "The Path-Goal Theory of Leadership: A Partial Test and Suggested Refinement," *Academy of Management Journal,* 18 (1975), 242–252.

Stogdill, Ralph M. "Leadership, Membership, and Organization," *Psychological Bulletin,* 47 (1950), 1–14.

———. *Manual for the Leader Behavior Description Questionnaire—Form XII* (Columbus, OH: Bureau of Business Research, Ohio State University, 1963).

———. "Personal Factors Associated with Leadership: A Survey of the Literature," *Journal of Psychology,* 25 (1948), 35–71.

———. "Traits of Leadership: A Follow-up to 1970," in Bernard M. Bass (ed.), *Stogdill's Handbook of Leadership* (New York: Free Press, 1981), pp. 73–97.

Strube, Michael J., and Joseph E. Garcia. "A Meta-Analytic Investigation of Fiedler's Contingency Model of Leadership Effectiveness," *Psychological Bulletin,* 90 (1981), 307–321.

Super, Donald E., and Douglas T. Hall. "Career Development: Exploration and Planning," *Annual Review of Psychology,* 29 (1978), 333–372.

Sutton, Harold, and Lyman W. Porter. "A Study of the Grapevine in a Governmental Organization," *Personnel Psychology,* 21 (1968), 223–230.

Swanson, Guy E. "The Effectiveness of Decision-Making Groups," *Adult Leadership,* 8 (1959), 48–52.

Tagiuri, Renato, and George H. Litwin (eds.). *Organizational Climate* (Boston: Harvard Graduate School of Business Administration, 1968).

Tannenbaum, Robert. "Managerial Decision-Making" (Reprint No. 9) (Los Angeles: Institute of Industrial Relations, University of California, 1950).

Taylor, Frederick W. *Scientific Management* (New York: Harper, 1947).

Tennessee Department of Education. *Administrator/Supervisor Career Ladder*

Orientation Manual (Nashville: Tennessee Department of Education, 1985).

Terreberry, Shirley. "The Evolution of Organizational Environments," *Administrative Science Quarterly*, 12 (1968), 590–613.

Thayer, Lee O. *Administrative Communication* (Homewood, IL: Irwin, 1961).

———. *Communication and Communication Systems* (Homewood, IL: Irwin, 1968).

Thomas, A. Ross, and R. C. Slater. "The OCDQ: A Four Factor Solution for Australian School?" *Journal of Educational Administration*, 10 (1972), 197–208.

Thompson, James D. *Organizations in Action* (New York: McGraw-Hill, 1968).

Thornton, Russell. "Organizational Involvement and Commitment to Organization and Profession," *Administrative Science Quarterly*, 15 (1970), 417–426.

Tichy, Noel, and Charles Fombrun. "Network Analysis in Organizational Settings," *Human Relations*, 32 (1979), 923–965.

Tolbert, Pamela S. "Institutional Environments and Resource Dependence: Sources of Administrative Structure in Institutions of Higher Education," *Administrative Science Quarterly*, 30 (1985), 1–13.

Tolman, Edward C. *Purposive Behavior in Animals and Men* (New York: Appleton-Century-Crofts, 1932).

Trusty, Francis M., and Thomas J. Sergiovanni. "Perceived Need Deficiencies of Teachers and Administrators: A Proposal for Restructuring Teacher Roles," *Educational Administration Quarterly*, 2 (1966), 168–180.

Tversky, Amos, and Daniel Kahneman. "Availability: Heuristic for Judging Frequency and Probability," *Cognitive Psychology*, 5 (1973), 207–232.

Udy, Stanley H. " 'Bureaucracy' and 'Rationality' in Weber's Organization Theory," *American Sociological Review*, 24 (1959), 791–795.

Urwick, Lyndall F. *Papers on the Science of Administration*, in Luther Gulick and Lyndall F. Urwick (eds.) (New York: Institute of Public Administration, Columbia University, 1937).

U.S. Department of Health, Education and Welfare. *Work in America*, Report of a Special Task Force (Cambridge, MA: MIT Press, 1973).

Van De Ven, Andrew H., and Diane L. Ferry. *Measuring and Assessing Organizations* (New York: Wiley, 1980).

Vecchio, Robert P. "An Empirical Examination of the Validity of Fiedler's Model of Leadership Effectiveness," *Organizational Behavior and Human Performance*, 19 (1977), 180–206.

———. "Assessing the Validity of Fiedler's Contingency Model of Leadership Effectiveness: A Closer Look at Strube and Garcia," *Psychological Bulletin*, 93 (1983), 404–408.

Vroom, Victor H. "Leadership," in Marvin D. Dunnette (ed.), *Handbook of Industrial and Organizational Psychology* (Chicago: Rand McNally, 1976), pp. 1527–1551.

———. *Some Personality Determinants of the Effects of Participation* (Englewood Cliffs, NJ: Prentice-Hall, 1960).

———. *Work and Motivation* (New York: Wiley, 1964).

———, and P. W. Yetton. *Leadership and Decision Making* (Pittsburgh: University of Pittsburgh Press, 1973).

———, and Arthur G. Jago. "On the Validity of the Vroom-Yetton Model," *Journal of Applied Psychology* (1978), 151–162.

Wahba, Mahmoud A., and Lawrence G. Bridwell. "Maslow Reconsidered: A Review of Research on Need Hierarchy Theory," *Organizational Behavior and Human Performance*, 15 (1976), 211–240.

———, and Lawrence G. Bridwell. "Maslow Reconsidered: A Review of Research on the Need Hierarchy Theory," *Proceedings of the 33rd Annual Meeting of the Academy of Management*, 1973, 514–520.

Waller, Willard. *The Sociology of Teaching* (New York: Wiley, 1932).

Walter, James E. "Relationship of Organizational Structure to Adaptiveness in Elementary Schools" (Ph.D. diss., University of Wisconsin, 1973).

Watkins, James F. "The OCDQ—An Application and Some Implications," *Educational Administration Quarterly*, 4 (1968), 46–60.

Weber, Max. *The Theory of Social and Economic Organizations*, Talcott Parsons (ed.), A. M. Henderson and Talcott Parsons (trans.) (New York: Free Press, 1947).

Weick, Karl E. "Educational Organizations as Loosely Coupled Systems," *Administrative Science Quarterly*, 21 (1976), 1–19.

———. *The Social Psychology of Organizing* (Reading, MA: Addison-Wesley, 1969).

Weiner, Bernard. *Theories of Motivation: From Mechanism to Cognition* (Chicago: Markham, 1972).

Whitehead, Alfred N. *Science and the Modern World* (New York: Macmillan, 1925).

Whitsett, D. A., and E. K. Winslow. "An Analysis of Studies Critical of the Motivator-Hygiene Theory," *Personnel Psychology*, 20 (1967), 391–416.

Wickert, Frederic R. "Turnover and Employees' Feelings of Ego-Involvement in the Day-to-Day Operations of a Company," *Personnel Psychology*, 4 (1951), 185–197.

Wietz, Shirley. *Non-Verbal Communication* (New York: Oxford, 1974).

Wiggins, Thomas. "Why Our Urban Schools Are Leaderless," *Education and Urban Society*, 2 (1970), 169–177.

Wilensky, Harold. "Professionalization of Everyone?" *American Journal of Sociology*, 70 (1964), 137–158.

Wilkins, Alan, and Kerry Patterson. "You Can't Get There From Here: What Will Make Culture-Change Projects Fail," in Ralph H. Kilmann *et al.*, *Gaining Control of the Corporate Culture* (San Francisco: Jossey-Bass, 1985), pp. 262–292.

Williams, Leonard B., and Wayne K. Hoy. "Principal-Staff Relations: Situational Mediator of Effectiveness," *Journal of Educational Administration*, 9 (1973), 66–73.

Willower, Donald J. "The Form of Knowledge and the Theory-Practice Relationship," *Educational Theory*, 13 (1963), 47–52.

———. "Hypotheses on the School as a Social System," *Educational Administration Quarterly*, 1 (1965), 40–51.

———. "Schools as Organizations: Some Illustrated Strategies for Educational Research and Practice," *Journal of Educational Administration*, 7 (1969), 110–127.

———. "Some Issues in Research on School Organization," in Glenn L. Immegart and William Boyd (eds.), *Currents in Administrative Research:*

Problem Finding in Education (Lexington, MA: Heath, 1979), pp. 63–86.

———. "Evolution in the Professorship: Past, Philosophy, Future," *Educational Administrational Quarterly,* 19 (1983), 179–200.

———. "Educational Administration: Some Philosophical and Other Considerations," *Journal of Educational Administration,* 19 (1981), 115–139.

———, and Ronald G. Jones. "Control in an Educational Organization," in J. D. Raths, J. R. Pancella, and J. S. Van Ness (eds.), *Studying Teaching* (Englewood Cliffs, NJ: Prentice-Hall, 1967).

———, Terry L. Eidell, and Wayne K. Hoy. *The School and Pupil Control Ideology,* Monograph No. 24, University Park: Pennsylvania State University, 1967.

Worthy, J. C. "Factors Influencing Employee Morale," *Harvard Business Review,* 28 (1950), 61–73.

Wright, Ruth. "Motivating Teacher Involvement in Professional Growth Activities," *The Canadian Administrator,* 24 (1985), 1–6.

Yuchtman, Ephraim, and Stanley E. Seashore. "A System Resource Approach to Organizational Effectiveness," *American Sociological Review,* 32 (1967), 891–903.

Yukl, Gary A. *Leadership in Organizations* (Englewood Cliffs, NJ: Prentice-Hall, 1981).

Zaltman, Gerald, Robert Duncan, and Johnny Holbek. *Innovations and Organizations* (New York: Wiley, 1973).

Zammuto, Raymond F. *Assessing Organizational Effectiveness* (Albany, NY: State University of New York Press, 1982).

Zielinski, Arlene E., and Wayne K. Hoy. "Isolation and Alienation in Elementary Schools," *Educational Administration Quarterly,* 19 (1983), 27–45.

Zucker, Lynne. "Organizations as Institutions," *Research in the Sociology of Organizations,* 2 (1983), 1–47.

Index